JUAN CARLOS

JUAN CARLOS

A People's King

PAUL PRESTON

HarperCollins*Publishers*

HarperCollins*Publishers*
77–85 Fulham Palace Road,
Hammersmith, London W6 8JB

www.harpercollins.co.uk

Published by HarperCollins*Publishers* 2004

1   3   5   7   9   8   6   4   2

A catalogue record for this book
is available from the British Library

ISBN 0 00 255632 4

Set in Postscript Linotype Sabon by
Rowland Phototypesetting Ltd,
Bury St Edmunds, Suffolk

Printed and bound in Great Britain by
Clays Ltd, St Ives plc

In Memory of
José María Coll Comín

ACKNOWLEDGEMENTS

This book has been a very long time in preparation. Over the many years of thinking about, researching and writing this book, I have benefited from the readiness of numerous figures to speak to me about their experiences. I would therefore like to express my thanks to the following who, in different ways, have illuminated various aspects of the book:

Alfonso Armada Comyn
Alberto Aza Arias
Anna Balletbó
Carlos Blanco Escolá
Rafael Calvo Serer
Santiago Carrillo
HM King Constantine of the Hellenes
Antonio Elorza
Fabián Estapé
Sabino Fernández Campo
Antonio Fontán
Felipe González
Nicholas Gordon-Lennox
Joe Haines
Laureano López Rodó
Rodolfo Martín Villa
Francisco José Mayans
Gregorio Peces-Barba
Miguel Primo de Rivera y Urquijo
José Joaquín Puig de la Bellacasa
Miquel Roca
Ana Romero
Jorge Semprún

Narcís Serra
Herbert Spencer
José Utrera Molina
Eugenio Vegas Latapie

I would also like to acknowledge my considerable debt to three friends who gave me crucial help in the location of essential documentation – Gerald Howson, Mariano Sanz González and Chon Tejedor Palau.

I derived enormous benefit from conversations with many friends who kindly let me discuss ideas and interpretations with them. In this regard, I thank Luis Aznar, Nicolás Belmonte, Rafael Borràs, Fernando Coca Vañó, Miguel Dols, Sheelagh Ellwood, Francisco Espinosa Maestre, Helen Graham, Angela Jackson, Fernando Serrano Suñer y Polo. I owe an enormous amount to Lala Isla, for encouragement and detailed reading of draft chapters, to Jonathan Gathorne-Hardy for his comments on style and structure, to Gabriel Cardona, for the humour and generosity with which he answered my endless questions about military matters, and to my wife Gabrielle, for help with psychological issues and for her constant moral and intellectual support.

I would also like to thank three friends for their input into the production of the final manuscript of this book, Cristóbal Pera in Barcelona and Philip Gwyn Jones in London for their sensitive editing and Margaret Stead for her hawk-eyed and perceptive copy-editing.

The book is dedicated to the memory of my friend José María Coll Comín. Pepe was there at the beginning. I wish he could have been there at the end.

CONTENTS

ONE

In Search of a Lost Crown
1931–1948

There are two central mysteries in the life of Juan Carlos, one personal, the other political. The key to both lies in his own definition of his role: 'For a politician, because he likes power, the job of King seems to be a vocation. For the son of a King, like me, it's something altogether different. It's not a question of whether I like it or not. I was born to it. Ever since I was a child, my teachers have taught me to do things that I didn't like. In the house of the Borbóns, being King is a profession.'[1] In those words lies the explanation for what is essentially a life of considerable sacrifice. How else is it possible to explain the apparent equanimity with which Juan Carlos accepted the fact that his father, Don Juan, to all intents and purposes sold him into slavery? In 1948, in order to keep the possibility of a Borbón restoration in Spain on Franco's agenda, Don Juan permitted his son to be taken to Spain to be educated at the will of the Caudillo. In a normal family, this act would be considered to be one of cruelty, or at best, of callous irresponsibility. But the Borbón family was not 'normal' and the decision to send Juan Carlos away responded to a 'higher' dynastic logic. Nevertheless, the tension between the needs of the human being and the needs of the dynasty lies at the heart of the story of the distance between the fun-loving boy, Juanito de Borbón, and the rather stiff prince Juan Carlos with his perpetually sad look. The other, rather more difficult puzzle, is how a prince emanating from a family with considerable authoritarian traditions, obliged to function within 'rules' invented by General Franco, and brought up to be the keystone of a complex plan for the continuity of the dictatorship should have committed himself to democracy.

I

The mission to which Juan Carlos was born, and which would take precedence over any personal life, was to make good the disaster that had struck his family in 1931. On 12 April 1931, nationwide municipal elections had seen sweeping victories for the anti-monarchical coalition of Republicans and Socialists. King Alfonso XIII, an affable and irresponsible rake, had earned considerable unpopularity for his part in the great military disaster at Annual in Spain's Moroccan colony in 1921. Even more, his collusion in the establishment of a military dictatorship in 1923 had sealed his fate. When he learned that his generals were not inclined to risk civil war in order to overturn the election results, he gave a note to his Prime Minister, Admiral Aznar. 'The elections celebrated on Sunday show me clearly that today I do not have the love of my people. My conscience tells me that this wrong turn will not last forever, because I always tried to serve Spain, my every concern being the public interest even in the most difficult moments.' He went on to say, 'I do not renounce any of my rights.' In that statement can be distantly discerned the process whereby Spain lost a monarchy, suffered a dictatorship and regained a monarchy. The hidden message to his supporters was that they should create a situation in which the Spanish people would beg him to return. This would be the seed from which the military uprising of 1936 would grow. However, its leader, General Franco, despite being a self-proclaimed monarchist and one-time favourite of Alfonso XIII, would not call him back to be King. One reason perhaps was that Alfonso XIII also said, 'I am King of all Spaniards, and also a Spaniard.' Those words would often be used by Alfonso's son and heir, Don Juan, and would occasion the sarcastic mirth of the dictator. They would be used again on the day of the coronation of King Juan Carlos.[2]

On 14 April 1931, on his painful journey from Madrid, via Cartagena, into exile in France, the King was accompanied by his cousin, Alfonso de Orleáns Borbón. The Queen, Victoria Eugenia of Battenburg, a granddaughter of Queen Victoria, was escorted into exile by her cousin, Princess Beatrice of Saxe-Coburg, the wife of Alfonso de Orleáns Borbón.[3] The government of the Republic quickly published a decree depriving the exiled King of his Spanish citizenship and the royal family of its possessions in Spain. After a short sojourn in the Hôtel Meurice on the rue de Rivoli in Paris, the royal family moved to a house in Fontainebleau. There, Alfonso XIII received delegations of conspirators against the Second Republic and gave them his approval and encouragement.[4]

In addition to the blow of exile, Alfonso XIII suffered considerable personal sadness. Without the scenery of the palace and the supporting cast of courtiers, the emptiness of his relationship with Victoria Eugenia was increasingly exposed. Not long after their arrival at Fontainebleau, the King remonstrated with the Queen about her closeness to the Duke and Duchess de Lécera who had accompanied her into exile. The marriage of the Duke, Jaime de Silva Mitjans, and the lesbian Duchess, Rosario Agrelo de Silva, was a sham but they stayed together because both were in love with the Queen. Despite persistent rumours, which niggled at Alfonso XIII, the Queen always vehemently denied that she and the Duke had been lovers. Nevertheless, when the bored Alfonso XIII took a new lover in Paris and the Queen in turn remonstrated with him, he tried to divert the onslaught by throwing in her face the alleged relationship with Lécera. She denied it but, as tempers rose, he demanded that she choose between himself and Lécera. Fearful of losing their support, on which she had come to rely, she replied, by her own account, with the fateful words, 'I choose them and never want to see your ugly face again.'[5] There would be no going back.

Another reason for Alfonso's long-deteriorating relationship with Victoria Eugenia was the fact that she had brought haemophilia into the family. The couple's eldest son, Alfonso, was of dangerously delicate health. He was haemophilic and, according to his sister, the Infanta Doña Cristina, 'the slightest knock caused him terrible pain and would paralyse part of his body.' He often could not walk unaided and lived in constant fear of a fatal blow. When the recently appointed Director General of Security, Emilio Mola, made his courtesy visit to the palace in February 1930, he was shocked: 'I also visited the Príncipe de Asturias [the Spanish equivalent of the Prince of Wales] and only then did I fully understand the intimate tragedy of the royal family and comprehend the pain in the Queen's face. He received me standing up and had the kindness to ask me to sit. Then he tried to get up to see me out and it was impossible: a flash, of anguish and of resignation, passed across his face.'[6] Alfonso formally renounced his right to the throne on 11 June 1933 in return for his father's permission to contract a morganatic marriage with an attractive but frivolous girl he had met at the Lausanne clinic where he was receiving treatment. Edelmira Sampedro y Robato was the 26-year-old daughter of a rich Cuban landowner.

Immediately following his eldest son's renunciation of his dynastic rights, Alfonso XIII arranged for a number of prominent monarchists to put pressure on his second son, Don Jaime, to follow his brother's example. Don Jaime was deaf and dumb – the result of a botched operation when he was four. Cut off from the world, both by dint of his royal status and his deafness, he had grown into a singularly immature young man. The monarchist leader José Calvo Sotelo persuaded him that his inability to use the telephone would significantly diminish his capacity to take part in anti-Republican conspiracies.[7] Alfonso married Edelmira in Lausanne, in the presence of his mother and two sisters. Neither his father nor three brothers deigned to attend. On the same day, in Fontainebleau, 21 June 1933, Don Jaime, who was single at the time, finally agreed to renounce his rights to the throne, as well as those of his future heirs. The renunciation was irrevocable and would be ratified on 23 July 1945. In spite of this, he would later contest its validity, thereby complicating Juan Carlos's rise to power.[8]

In his 1933 letter to his father, Don Jaime wrote: 'Sire. The decision of my brother to renounce, for himself and his descendants, his rights to the succession of the crown has led me to weigh the obligations that thus fall on me . . . I have decided on a formal and explicit renunciation, for me and for any descendants that I might have, of my rights to the throne of our fatherland.'[9] Don Jaime would, in any case, have lost his rights when, in 1935, he also made a morganatic marriage, to an Italian, Emmanuela Dampierre Ruspoli, who although a minor aristocrat was not of royal blood. It was not a love match and would end unhappily.[10]

In the summer of 1933, during a royal skiing holiday in Istria, Alfonso's fourth son, Don Gonzalo – who also suffered from haemophilia – was involved in a car crash and died as a result of an internal haemorrhage.[11] His first son fared little better. After his allowance was slashed by the exiled King, Alfonso's marriage to Edelmira did not survive. They divorced in May 1937. Two months later, he married another Cuban, Marta Rocafort y Altuzarra, a beautiful model. The marriage lasted barely six months and they were also divorced, in January 1938. Having fallen in love with Mildred Gaydon, a cigarette girl in a Miami nightclub, Alfonso was on the point of marrying for a third time when tragedy once more struck the Borbón family. On the night of 6 September 1938, after leaving the club where Mildred worked, he too was involved in a car crash and, like his brother Gonzalo, died of internal bleeding.[12]

As a result of the successive renunciations of Alfonso and Jaime, the title of Príncipe de Asturias fell upon Alfonso XIII's third son, the 20-year-old Don Juan. When he received his father's telegram informing him of this, Don Juan was a serving officer in the Royal Navy on HMS *Enterprise*, anchored in Bombay. Because he realized that his new role would eventually involve him leaving his beloved naval career, he accepted only after some delay. In May 1934, he was promoted to sub-lieutenant and in September, he joined the battleship HMS *Iron Duke*. In March 1935, he passed the examinations in naval gunnery and navigation which opened the way to his becoming a lieutenant and being eligible to command a vessel. However, that would mean renouncing his Spanish nationality, something he was not prepared to do. His uncle, King George V, granted him the rank of honorary Lieutenant RN.[13]

Don Juan did not emulate his elder brothers' disastrous marriages. On 13 January 1935, at a party given by the King and Queen of Italy on the eve of the marriage of the Infanta Doña Beatriz to Prince Alessandro Torlonia, Prince di Civitella Cesi, Don Juan had met the 24-year-old María de las Mercedes Borbón Orléans. Having faced the problem of his eldest son's unsuitable marriage, Alfonso XIII was delighted when Don Juan began to fall in love with a statuesque princess who was descended from the royal families of Spain, France, Italy and Austria. They were married on 12 October 1935 in Rome. Several thousand Spanish monarchists made the trip to the Italian capital and turned the ceremony into a demonstration against the Spanish Republic. By this time, Queen Victoria Eugenia had long since left Alfonso XIII and she refused to attend the wedding.[14] The newly appointed Príncipe de Asturias and his new bride settled at the Villa Saint Blaise in Cannes in the south of France. There, he quickly made contact with the leading monarchist politicians who were involved in anti-Republican plots.

Unsurprisingly, when on the evening of 17 July 1936 units of the Spanish Army in Morocco rebelled against the Second Republic, the coup d'état was enthusiastically welcomed by both Don Juan and his father. They avidly followed the progress of the military rebels on the radio, particularly through the lurid broadcasts of General Queipo de Llano. A group of Don Juan's followers, who had been avid conspirators against the Republic, including Eugenio Vegas Latapié, Jorge Vigón, the Conde de Ruiseñada and the Marqués de la Eliseda, felt that it would be politically prudent for him to be seen fighting on the Nationalist side. He had already discussed the matter with his aide-de-camp, Captain Juan Luis Roca de Togores, the Vizconde de Rocamora. Don Juan left his home for the front for the first time on 31 July 1936, despite the fact that only the previous day Doña María de las Mercedes had given birth to their first child, a daughter, Pilar. His mother, Queen Victoria Eugenia, was present, having come to Cannes for the birth. To the delight of Don Juan's followers, she declared: 'I think it is right that my son should go to war. In extreme situations, such as the present one, women must pray and men must fight.' Pleasantly surprised by this, they were, nevertheless, worried about the possible reaction of Alfonso XIII who was holidaying in Czechoslovakia. However, when Don Juan telephoned him, he too agreed enthusiastically, saying, 'I am delighted. Go, my son, and may God be with you!'

The following day, 1 August, the tall and good-natured Don Juan duly crossed the French border into Spain in a chauffeur-driven Bentley, ahead of a small convoy of cars carrying his followers. They arrived in Burgos determined to fight on the Nationalist side. However, the rebel commander in the north, the impulsive General Emilio Mola, was in fact an anti-monarchist. Without consulting his fellow generals, he abruptly ordered the Civil Guard to ensure that Don Juan left Spain immediately. This incident inclined many deeply monarchist officers to transfer their long-term political loyalty from Mola to Franco.[15]

After his return to Cannes, the presence of important supporters of the Spanish military rebellion attracted the attention of local leftists. Groups of militants of the *Front Populaire* took to gathering outside the Villa Saint Blaise each evening and shouting pro-Republican slogans. Fearful for the security of his family – his wife was pregnant once more – Don Juan decided to move to Rome. His father was already resident there and the Fascist authorities would ensure that there would be no unpleasantness of the kind that had marred their stay in France. At first they lived in the Hotel Eden until, at the beginning of 1937, they moved into a flat on the top floor of the Palazzo Torlonia in Via Bocca di Leone. The palazzo was the home of Don Juan's sister Doña Beatriz and Alessandro Torlonia.[16]

At the beginning of January 1938, Doña María de las Mercedes was coming to the culmination of her second pregnancy. However, when Don Juan was invited to go hunting, her doctor assured him that it was safe to go as the baby would not appear for at least another three weeks. Doña María was at the cinema with her father-in-law, Alfonso XIII, when her labour pains began. Juan Carlos was born at 2.30 p.m. on 5 January 1938 at the Anglo-American hospital in Rome. He was one month premature. When Doña María was taken to hospital, her lady-in-waiting, Angelita Martínez Campos, the Vizcondesa de Rocamora, called Don Juan back to Rome by sending him a telegram which read '*Bambolo natto*' (Baby born). On receiving the telegram, he set off, driving so furiously that he broke an axle spring on his Bentley. Arriving before his son, Alfonso XIII played a trick. As he welcomed Don Juan, he held in his arms a Chinese baby boy – who had been born in an adjoining room to the secretary at the Chinese Embassy.

Don Juan knew at once that the child was not his, yet, on seeing his own son, he confessed later, for a moment, he would have almost preferred the Chinese baby. Doña María, unlike most mothers, did not think her baby was the most beautiful creature on earth. She later recalled that, 'The poor thing was a month premature and had big bulging eyes. He was ugly, as ugly as sin! It was awful! Thank God he soon sorted himself out.' The blond baby weighed three kilograms. The earliest photographs of Juan Carlos were taken, not at his birth, but when he was already five months old.[17] Despite his mother's initial alarm, Juan Carlos did not remain 'ugly' for long. His good looks would always be a major asset – they would, indeed, be a major factor in his eventually winning the approval of Queen Frederica of Greece, his future mother-in-law.[18]

On 26 January 1938, the child was baptized at the chapel of the Order of Malta in the Via Condotti in Rome. The choice of the chapel was made because of its proximity to the Palazzo Torlonia, where the reception took place. The baptism ceremony was conducted by Cardinal Eugenio Pacelli, then Secretary of State to the Vatican, and the future Pope Pius XII. At the christening, the baby Prince's godmother was his paternal grandmother, Queen Victoria Eugenia. His godfather in absentia was the Infante Carlos de Borbón-Dos-Sicilias, his maternal grandfather. As a general in the Nationalist army, at the time engaged in the battle for Teruel, he was unable to travel to Rome. He was represented at the baptism by Don Juan's elder brother, Don Jaime. Very few Spaniards were able to travel to Rome for the occasion and the birth of the Prince went virtually unnoticed even in the Nationalist zone of Spain.[19]

The boy was christened with the names Juan, for his father; Alfonso, for his paternal grandfather, the exiled King Alfonso XIII; and Carlos, for his maternal grandfather, Carlos de Borbón-Dos-Sicilias. Juan Carlos's family and friends would, however, usually call him Juanito, at first because of his youth and later in order to distinguish him from his father. It was only after his emergence as a public figure that he began to use the name of Juan Carlos. There were, of course, political reasons behind the choice of the Prince's public name. Don Juan told his lifelong adviser, the monarchist intellectual, Pedro Sainz Rodríguez, that the choice was Franco's. The idea may also have emanated from the conservative monarchist Marqués de Casa Oriol, José María Oriol, although the future King himself could not remember this with any certainty.[20] 'Juan Carlos' would distinguish the Prince from his father, Don Juan, and perhaps ingratiate him with the ultra-conservative Carlists whose pretender always carried the name Carlos. The elimination of his middle name, Alfonso, would certainly have been to Franco's liking since it was central to the Caudillo's rhetoric that it was the misguided liberalism of Alfonso XIII that had rendered the Spanish Civil War inevitable.

Don Juan de Borbón continued to harbour a desire to take part in the Nationalist war effort. He had written to the Generalísimo on 7 December 1936 and respectfully requested permission to join the crew of the battlecruiser *Baleares* which was then nearing completion: '. . . after my studies at the Royal Naval College, I served for two years on the Royal Navy battlecruiser HMS *Enterprise*, I completed a special artillery course on the battleship HMS *Iron Duke* and, finally, before leaving the Royal Navy with the rank of Lieutenant, I spent three months on the destroyer HMS *Winchester*.'[21] Although the young Prince promised to remain inconspicuous, not to go ashore at any Spanish port and to abstain from any political contact, Franco was quick to perceive the dangers both immediate and distant. If Don Juan were to fight on the Nationalist side, intentionally or otherwise he would soon become a figurehead for the large numbers of monarchists, especially in the Army, who, for the moment, were content to leave Franco in charge while waiting for victory and an eventual restoration of Alfonso XIII. There was the danger that the Alfonsists would become a distinct group alongside the Falangists and the Carlists, adding their voice to the political diversity that was beginning to come to the surface in the Nationalist zone. The execution of José Antonio Primo de Rivera, founder of the Falange, in a Republican prison had solved one problem, and Franco was now in the process of cutting down the Carlist leader, Manuel Fal Conde. He did not need Don Juan de Borbón emerging as a monarchist figurehead.

Franco's response was a masterpiece of duplicity. He delayed some weeks before replying to Don Juan. 'It would have given me great pleasure to accede to your request, so Spanish and so legitimate, to serve in our Navy for the cause of Spain. However, the need to keep you safe would not permit you to live as a simple officer since the enthusiasm of some and the officiousness of others would stand in the way of such noble intentions. Moreover, we have to take into account the fact that the place which you occupy in the dynastic order and the consequent obligations impose upon us all, and demand of you the sacrifice of desires which are as patriotic as they are noble and deeply felt, in the interests of the *Patria* ... It is not possible for me to follow the dictates of my soldier's heart and to accept your offer.'[22] Thus, with apparent grace, he deflected a dangerous offer.

Franco also managed to squeeze considerable political capital out of so doing. He arranged for word to be circulated in Falangist circles that he had prevented the heir to the throne from entering Spain because of his own commitment to the future Falangist revolution. He also publicized what he had done and gave reasons aimed at consolidating his own position among the monarchists. 'My responsibilities are great and among them is the duty not to put his life in danger, since one day it may be precious to us ... If one day a King returns to rule over the State, he will have to come as a peace maker and should not be found among the victors.'[23] The cynicism of such sentiments would be fully appreciated only after nearly four decades had elapsed, during which Franco dedicated his efforts to institutionalizing the division of Spain into victors and vanquished and failing to restore the monarchy. When the *Baleares* was sunk on 6 March 1938, Franco is said to have commented with an ironic smile, 'And to think that Don Juan de Borbón wanted to serve on board.'[24]

In the meantime, in the autumn of 1936, believing that the military uprising would, if victorious, culminate in a restoration of the monarchy, Alfonso XIII had telegraphed Franco to congratulate him on his successes. In his suite in the Gran Hotel in Rome, the King kept a huge map of Spain marked with little flags with which he obsessively followed the progress of the rebel troops on various fronts.[25] In his confidence that Franco would repay earlier favours by restoring the monarchy, he misjudged his man. Had he and his son been a little more suspicious, they might have been alarmed to note that the newly installed Head of State had already begun to comport himself as if he were the King rather than simply the praetorian guard responsible for bringing back the monarchy. With the support of the Catholic Church, which had blessed the Nationalist war effort as a religious crusade, Franco began to project himself as the saviour of Spain and the defender of the universal faith, both roles associated with the great kings of the past. Religious ritual was used to give legitimacy to his power as it had to those of the medieval kings of Spain. The liturgy and iconography of his regime presented him as a holy crusader; he had a personal chaplain and he usurped the royal prerogative of entering and leaving churches under a canopy.

The confidence in himself and his office generated by such ceremonial was revealed when Franco celebrated the first year of his *Movimiento*. His broadcast speech was, according to his cousin, entirely written by himself. He spoke in terms which suggested that he placed himself far higher than the Borbón family, as a providential figure, the very embodiment of the spirit of traditional Spain. He attributed to himself the honour of having saved 'Imperial Spain which fathered nations and gave laws to the world'.[26] On the same day, an interview with the Caudillo was published in the monarchist newspaper *ABC*. In it, he announced the imminent formation of his first government. Asked if his references to the historic greatness of Spain implied a monarchical restoration, he replied truthfully while managing to give the impression that this was his intention, 'On this subject, my preferences are long since known, but now we can think only of winning the War, then it will be necessary to clean up after it, then construct the State on firm bases. While all this is happening, I cannot be an interim power.'

For Franco, and indeed many of his supporters within the Nationalist zone, the monarchy of Alfonso XIII was irrevocably stigmatized by its association with the constitutional parliamentary system. In his interview, he declared that, 'If the monarchy were to be one day restored in Spain, it would have to be very different from the monarchy abolished in 1931 both in its content and, though it may grieve many of us, even in the person who incarnates it.' This was profoundly humiliating for Alfonso XIII, all the more so coming from a man whose career he had promoted so assiduously.[27]

The Caudillo's attitude to the exiled King, and by implication, to the Borbón family, was underlined in a harshly dismissive letter sent to Alfonso XIII on 4 December 1937. The King, having recently donated one million pesetas to the Nationalist cause, had written to Franco expressing his concern that the restoration of the monarchy seemed to be low on his list of priorities. The Generalísimo replied coldly, insinuating that the problems which caused the Civil War were of the King's making and outlining both the achievements of the Nationalists and the tasks remaining to be carried out after the War. Expanding on his *ABC* interview, the Caudillo made it clear that Alfonso XIII could expect to play no part in that future: 'the new Spain which we are forging has so little in common with the liberal and constitutional Spain over which you ruled that your training and old-fashioned political practices necessarily provoke the anxieties and resentments of Spaniards.' The letter ended with a request that the King look to the preparation of his heir, 'whose goal we can sense but which is so distant that we cannot make it out yet'.[28] It was the clearest indication yet that Franco had no intention of ever relinquishing power, yet the epistolary relationship between Franco and the exiled King remained surprisingly smooth. (Indeed, in December 1938, Franco revoked the Republican edict that had deprived the King of his Spanish citizenship and the royal family of its properties.) Throughout the Civil War, after each victory, the Generalísimo had sent a telegram to Alfonso XIII and, in turn, received congratulatory messages from both the exiled King and his son. However, after the final victory, and the capture of Madrid, Franco had not done so. The outraged Alfonso XIII rightly took this to mean that Franco had no intention of restoring the monarchy.[29]

If the future of Alfonso XIII's heir was unclear to Franco, even less certain was that of his grandson, Juan Carlos. For the first four and a half years of his life, the boy lived with his parents in

Rome. Soon after his birth the family moved from the modest flat on the top floor of the Palazzo Torlonia in Via Bocca di Leoni to the four-storey Villa Gloria, at 112 Viale dei Parioli in the elegant Roman suburb of Parioli.[30] This was a happy time for the Borbóns – a period during which it was possible to live as a relatively normal, as opposed to a royal, family. Juan Carlos's younger sister Margarita was born blind on 6 March 1939. Even so, the degree of family warmth was limited. All three children were looked after by two Swiss nannies, Mademoiselles Modou and Any, under the supervision, not of their mother but of the Vizcondesa de Roca-mora. The young Prince was often taken out for walks by his parents or by his nannies, sometimes to the Palazzo Torlonia, sometimes to the private park of the Pamphili family or to the park of Villa Borghese. Don Juan showed some affection for his eldest son, often carrying him in his arms when they visited Alfonso XIII at the Gran Hotel.

However, such signs of warmth were rare. The young Prince was soon being schooled in the harsh lesson that his central pur-pose in life was to contribute in some way to the mission of seeing the Borbón family back on the throne in Spain. Don Juan had already started to make demands that the child found difficult to meet. Miguel Sánchez del Castillo (a film actor working in Rome at the time) recalls that, on one occasion, Juan Carlos was given a cavalry uniform as a present from several Spanish aristocratic ladies. 'An Italian photographer spent over an hour taking pictures of him. Don Juan Carlos, who was only four years old at the time, endured having to stand to attention on a table. When they finally took him to the kitchen and one of his nannies took his boots off, his feet had been rubbed raw, because the boots were too small for him. That is when he shyly started to cry. I later learnt that his father had taught him from a very young age that *a Borbón cries only in his bed*.'[31]

Two events soon disturbed the royal family's tranquillity: the first was Queen Victoria Eugenia's departure from Rome; the second was Alfonso XIII's death. Victoria Eugenia had been spend-ing increasing amounts of time in Rome. When Italy entered the Second World War on 9 June 1940, her position as an English woman became difficult and thereafter she divided her time between Lausanne in neutral Switzerland and the outskirts of Rome. She and her husband had been effectively separated for more than a decade but, as his health deteriorated, they spent more time together. In 1941, she returned to Rome in order to care for him, moving into the nearby Hotel Excelsior, where she stayed until his death.[32]

Alfonso XIII died on 28 February 1941. A few weeks earlier, on 15 January, he had abdicated in favour of his son and heir, Don Juan. Speaking with the American journalist, John T. Whitaker, shortly before his end, the exiled King said, 'I picked Franco out when he was a nobody. He has double-crossed and deceived me at every turn.'[33] Alfonso was right. During his final agony, he kept asking whether Franco had enquired about his health. Pained by his desperate insistence, his family lied and told him that the Generalísimo had indeed sent a telegram asking for news. In reality, Franco showed not the slightest concern. At Alfonso XIII's bedside, Don Juan made a solemn promise to his father to ensure that he was buried in the Pantheon of Kings at El Escorial. His promise could not be fulfilled while Franco remained alive, and Alfonso XIII's body would remain in Rome until its transfer to El Escorial in early 1981. Franco was reluctant even to announce a period of national mourning for the King. He grudgingly agreed to do so only when faced with the sudden appearance of black hangings draped from balconies in the streets of Madrid. He limited himself to sending a red and gold wreath. Amongst the many other floral tributes that adorned Alfonso XIII's funeral on 3 March 1941 was one from Juan Carlos. It was a simple arrangement of white, yellow and red flowers tied together with a black ribbon on which someone had sewn with a yellow thread the dedication *'para el abuelito'* (for granddad).[34]

The death of Alfonso XIII seemed, in all kinds of ways, to free Franco to give rein his own monarchical pretensions. He insisted on the right to name bishops, on the royal march being played every time his wife arrived at any official ceremony and planned, until dissuaded by his brother-in-law, to establish his residence in the massive royal palace, the Palacio de Oriente in Madrid. By the Law of the Headship of State published on 8 August 1939, Franco had assumed 'the supreme power to issue laws of a general nature', and to issue specific decrees and laws without discussing them first with the cabinet 'when reasons of urgency so advise'. According to the sycophants of his controlled press, the 'supreme chief' was simply assuming the powers necessary to allow him to fulfil his historic destiny of national reconstruction. It was power of a kind previously enjoyed only by the kings of medieval Spain.[35]

The 27-year-old Don Juan – now, in the eyes of many Spanish monarchists, King Juan III – took the title of Conde de Barcelona, the prerogative of the King of Spain. He faced a lifelong power struggle with Franco, who held virtually all the cards. For the task of hastening a monarchical restoration, he could rely only on the support of a few senior Army officers. However, the Falange was fiercely opposed to the return of the monarchy and Franco himself had no intention of relinquishing absolute power. In the aftermath of the Civil War, many conservatives who might have been expected to support Don Juan were reluctant to face the risks involved in getting rid of Franco. Accordingly, Don Juan began to seek foreign support. With an English mother and service in the Royal Navy, his every inclination was to look to Britain. But he was resident in Fascist Italy and the Third Reich was striding effortlessly from triumph to triumph. Accordingly, his close adviser, the portly and foul-mouthed Pedro Sainz Rodríguez, pressed him to seek the support of Berlin or at least secure its benevolent neutrality towards a monarchical restoration in Spain.[36] On 16 April 1941, Ribbentrop instructed the German Ambassador in Spain, Eberhard von Stohrer, to inform Franco – lest he hear of it through other channels – that Don Juan de Borbón had tried to contact the Germans through an intermediary in order to get their support for a monarchist restoration. The intermediary had approached a German journalist, Dr Karl Megerle, on 7 April and again on 11 April 1941. In the early summer of 1941, the Italian Ambassador in Spain, Francesco Lequio, recounted rumours circulating in Madrid that Don Juan was about to be invited to Berlin to discuss a restoration. Lequio reported that the intensification of efforts to accelerate the restoration were emanating from Don Juan's mother – 'an intriguer, eaten up with ambition'.[37]

In response to the approaches made to the Germans by Don Juan's supporters, Franco wrote an impenetrably convoluted letter to him at the end of September 1941. The tone was deeply patronizing: 'I deeply regret that distance denies me the satisfaction of being able to enlighten you as to the real situation of our fatherland.' The gist was a tendentious summary of Spain's recent history which permitted Franco to combine the apparently conciliatory gesture of recognizing Don Juan's claim to the throne with the threat that he would play no part in the future of the regime if he did not refrain from pushing that claim. What was quite clear was Franco's total identification with the cause of the Third Reich – unmistakably referring to Britain and Russia when he spoke of 'those who were our enemies during the Civil War . . . the nations who yesterday gambled against us and today fight against Europe'. Warning Don Juan against any action that might diminish Spanish unity (that is to say, threaten the stability of Franco's position), he underlined the need 'to uproot the causes that produced the progressive destabilization of Spain' – a sly reference to the mistakes of the reign of Alfonso XIII. This task could be fulfilled only by his single party, the great amalgam known as the *Movimiento*, which was dominated by Falangists. Don Juan was warned that only by refraining from rocking Franco's boat might he, 'one day', be called to crown Franco's work with the installation – not restoration – of Spain's traditional form of government.[38]

Don Juan waited three weeks before replying. The delay may have been caused by the fact that, on 3 October 1941, his second son had been born. Christened Alfonso after his recently deceased grandfather, he would soon be the apple of his father's eye. When he did write to the Caudillo, Don Juan seized on the recognition of his claim to the throne and suggested that Franco convert his regime into a regency as a stepping stone to the restoration of the monarchy.[39] Subsequently, knowing that Franco was in no hurry to bring back the monarchy, and as part of their ongoing power struggle with the Falange, a group of senior Spanish generals sent a message to Field-Marshal Göring in the first weeks of 1942.

They requested his help in placing Don Juan upon the throne in Madrid in exchange for an undertaking that Spain would maintain its pro-Axis policy. Pressure on Franco was stepped up in the early spring, when, at the invitation of the Italian Foreign Minister, Count Galeazzo Ciano, Don Juan attended a hunting party in Albania where he was received with sumptuous hospitality and full honours by the Italian authorities. In May, it was rumoured in Madrid that Göring himself had met with Don Juan in Lausanne (where he and his family were now resident) to express his support for his ambitions. Johannes Bernhardt, Göring's unofficial representative in Spain, arranged at the end of May for General Juan Vigón to be invited to Berlin to discuss the matter. Vigón was both Minister of Aviation and one of Don Juan's representatives in Spain. At the same time, Franco's Foreign Minister, Ramón Serrano Suñer, had come to favour a monarchical restoration in the person of Don Juan. In June 1942, Serrano Suñer told Ciano in Rome that he believed that the Axis powers should come out in favour of Don Juan in order to neutralize British support for him. Serrano Suñer was planning to visit Don Juan in Lausanne. A somewhat alarmed Franco prohibited the trips of Vigón and of Serrano Suñer.[40]

In fact, the brief flirtation between some monarchists and the Axis soon came to an end. It was clear that the fate of the monarchy would be better served by alignment with the British. Soon after her husband's death, Victoria Eugenia had returned to her home in Lausanne, La Vieille Fontaine. In the summer of 1942, Don Juan moved his family there too and, shortly afterwards, appointed the four-year-old Juan Carlos's first tutor. His strange choice was the gaunt and austere Eugenio Vegas Latapié, an ultra-conservative intellectual. In 1931, appalled by the establishment of the Second Republic, Vegas Latapié, for whom democracy was tantamount to Bolshevism, had been the leading light of a group which set out to found a 'school of modern counter-revolutionary thought'. This took the form of the extreme rightist group, *Acción Española*, whose journal provided the theoretical justification for violence against the Republic, while its well-appointed headquarters in Madrid served as a conspiratorial centre.[41] Shortly after the creation of *Acción Española*, Eugenio Vegas Latapié had written to Don Juan and a friendship had been forged. Ironically, Vegas Latapié had helped elaborate the idea that the old constitutional monarchy was corrupt and had to be replaced by a new kind of dynamic military kingship, a notion used by Franco to justify his endless delays in restoring the Borbón monarchy. Now, as a faithful servant of Don Juan, his outrage at this was such that, despite having served in the Nationalist forces during the Civil War, he turned against Franco. In April 1942, Don Juan asked Vegas Latapié to join a secret committee with the task of preparing for the restoration of the monarchy. When Franco found out, he ordered both Vegas Latapié and Sainz Rodríguez exiled to the Canary Islands. Sainz Rodríguez took up residence in Portugal and Vegas Latapié fled to Switzerland where he became Don Juan's political secretary.

Deeply reactionary and authoritarian, Vegas Latapié had a powerfully sharp intelligence but seemed hardly suitable to be mentor to a four-year-old child, particularly one who was far from intellectually precocious. Inevitably, Vegas Latapié's nomination as the boy's tutor did little for the rather introverted Juan Carlos. Neither his tutor nor his father took much notice of him, their attention being absorbed by the progress of the War and plans for the return of Don Juan to the throne. Initially, Vegas Latapié's role was, at Don Juan's request, to give Spanish classes to Juan Carlos because the boy spoke the language with some difficulty, having a French accent and using many Gallicisms. When Juan Carlos reached the age of five, he began to attend classes at the Rolle School, in Lausanne. Vegas Latapié would accompany him to school in the morning and pick him up in the afternoon, using the trip to give the boy his extremely partisan and reactionary view of Spain's past.[42]

The relationship between Don Juan and Franco was developing in such a way as to dictate the direction of the young Prince's later childhood, his adolescence and his adulthood. Fearful that the approaches made to the Germans by Don Juan's supporters might bear fruit, on 12 May 1942, Franco had written him another patronizing letter based on his bizarre interpretation of Spanish history. In it, he rejected the notion that there was support in Spain for a restoration and reiterated his rejection of everything associated with the constitutional monarchy that fell in 1931. Linking the greatness of imperial Spain with modern Fascism, he stated that the only monarchy that could be permitted was a totalitarian one such as he associated with Queen Isabella I of Castile. He made it clear that there would be no restoration in the near future, and none at all unless the Pretender were to express his commitment to the Spanish single party, *FET y de las JONS* (*Falange Española Traditionalista y de las Juntas de Ofensiva Nacional Sindicalista*), created in 1937 by the forced unification of all right-wing parties.[43]

Don Juan did not reply to Franco's letter of May 1942 for ten months. The outbreak of violent clashes between monarchists and Falangists – and the consequent removal of Ramón Serrano Suñer – in mid-August 1942 boosted his confidence. The Allied landings in North Africa on 8 November 1942 convinced him that the best chance of a restoration was to distance himself from Franco and persuade the Allies that, after the War, the monarchy could provide both stability and national reconciliation. On 11 November 1942, barely three days after the landings, Don Juan's most powerful supporter, General Alfredo Kindelán, the most senior general on active service and Captain-General of Catalonia, travelled to Madrid. After discussing recent events with the rest of the high command, Kindelán informed the Caudillo in unequivocal terms that if he had committed Spain formally to the Axis then he would have to be replaced as Head of State. In any case, he advised Franco to proclaim Spain a monarchy and declare himself regent. Franco swallowed his fury and responded in a conciliatory – and deceitful – way. He denied any formal commitment to the Axis, implied that he was anxious to relinquish power and confided that he wanted Don Juan to be his ultimate successor. Franco was seething. After a cautious interval of three months, he replaced Kindelán as Captain-General of Catalonia.[44]

When Don Juan did finally reply to Franco's letter, in March 1943, his tone was altogether more confrontational than before. He questioned Franco's exercise of absolute power without institutional or juridical basis and expressed alarm at both the continued divisions within Spain and the international situation. He firmly informed Franco that it was his patriotic duty to: 'abandon the current transitory and one-man regime in order to establish once and for all the system which, according to Your Excellency's oft-repeated phrase, forged the greatness of our fatherland'. He bluntly stated that he found entirely unacceptable Franco's vague formula of delaying the return of the monarchy until his work was done. Then, in terms that can only have horrified Franco, Don Juan roundly rejected the Caudillo's call for him to identify with the Falange, asserting that any link with a specific ideology 'would mean the outright denial of the very essence of the value of monarchy which is radically opposed to the provocation of partisan divisions and domination by political cliques and is rather the highest expression of the interests of the entire nation and the supreme arbiter of the antagonistic tensions inevitable in any society'.

In his letter, Don Juan outlined the formula for the eventual restoration of a democratic monarchy in Spain on the basis of national reconciliation– although he cannot have imagined that it would take a further 32 years. Recalling Alfonso XIII's declaration in 1931 that he was *'Rey de todos los españoles'* (King of all Spaniards), Don Juan presented Franco with a slap in the face for which he would never be forgiven: 'In fact, my arrival on the throne after a cruel civil war should, in contrast, appear to all Spaniards – and this is precisely the transcendental service that the monarchy, and only the monarchy, can offer them – not as an opportunist government of a particular historical moment or of exclusive and changing ideologies, but rather as the sublime symbol of a permanent national reality and the guarantee of the reconstruction, on the basis of harmony, of Spain, complete and eternal.'[45]

Franco's outrage can be discerned both in the unaccustomed (for him) rapidity (19 days) in which he replied and in the unconcealed contempt of his tone. 'Others might speak to you in the submissive tone imposed by their dynastic fervour or their ambitions as courtiers; but I, when I write to you, can do so only as the Head of State of the Spanish nation addressing the Pretender to the throne.' He went on, condescendingly, to attribute Don Juan's position to his ignorance and to lay before him a petulant list of what he regarded as his own achievements.[46]

In the wake of Allied success in expelling Axis forces from North Africa in June 1943, Don Juan remained on the offensive. He could draw confidence from the fact that monarchists within the regime were beginning to fear for their own futures. At the end of the month, a group of 27 senior *Procuradores* (parliamentary deputies) from Franco's pseudo-parliament, the Cortes, appealed to the Caudillo to settle the constitutional question by re-establishing the traditional Spanish Catholic monarchy before the War ended in an inevitable Allied victory. They believed that only the monarchy could avoid Allied retribution for Franco's pro-Axis stance throughout the War. The signatories came from right across the Francoist spectrum, with representatives from the banks, the Armed Forces, monarchists and even Falangists. The Caudillo reacted swiftly. Even before the manifesto was published, he had ordered the arrest of the Marqués de la Eliseda who was collecting the signatures. As soon as it was published, showing how very little he was interested in his much-vaunted *contraste de pareceres* (contrast of opinions – his substitute for democratic politics), he dismissed all the signatories from their seats in the Cortes immediately and sacked the five of them who were also members of the *Movimiento*'s supreme consultative body, the *Consejo Nacional*.[47]

The Caudillo's sense of being under siege by Don Juan was intensified by the fall of Mussolini on 25 July 1943. Don Juan sent Franco a telegram recommending the restoration of the monarchy as his only chance to avoid the fate of the Duce. It embittered even further the tension between the two. Thereafter, Don Juan believed that Franco never forgave him: 'he always had it in for me after that telegram.' It was a bizarre measure of Franco's self-regard that he regarded Don Juan's action as high treason.[48] Mortified, but aware of his own vulnerability, he shelved his resentment for a better moment. Instead, Franco replied with an appeal to Don Juan's patriotism, begging him not to make any public statement that might weaken the regime.[49] The Caudillo had every reason to be worried – his senior generals were swinging more openly behind the cause of Don Juan. Pedro Sainz Rodríguez was informed that a number of them were ready to rise to restore the monarchy, provided that immediate Allied recognition could be arranged by Don Juan. The Caudillo's anxiety – and his resentment of Don Juan – was exacerbated when he discovered in the late summer that the generals were conspiring. Prompted by Don Juan's senior representative in Spain, his cousin Prince Alfonso de Orleáns Borbón, they met in Seville on 8 September 1943 to discuss the situation and composed a document calling upon Franco to take action to bring back the monarchy.[50]

Signed by eight Lieutenant-Generals, Kindelán, Varela, Orgaz, Ponte, Dávila, Solchaga, Saliquet and Monasterio, the letter was handed to the Caudillo by General Varela at El Pardo (Franco's official residence just outside of Madrid) on 15 September. In fact, the Caudillo had already been alerted to its contents by a member of Don Juan's Privy Council, Rafael Calvo Serer. Calvo Serer was a talented, if somewhat erratic, young intellectual, and a convinced monarchist, but he was also a high-ranking member of the Opus Dei. He had insinuated himself into the inner circle of Alfonso de Orleáns Borbón and when he got hold of the draft, hastened to Franco's summer residence, the Pazo de Meirás in Galicia. In fact, respectfully couched – 'written in terms of vile adulation' according to one of Don Juan's principal advisers, the exiled José María Gil Robles – the letter was more annoying than threatening to Franco. However, it did nothing to improve his attitude to Don Juan.[51]

At the end of 1943, Don Juan wrote a letter to one of his most prominent followers, the Conde de Fontanar. The inflammatory text referred to Franco as an 'illegitimate usurper' and called upon Fontanar to break publicly with the regime. The letter fell into Franco's hands. Don Juan had chosen as his intermediary the sleekly ambitious Rafael Calvo Serer. Later Don Juan came to believe erroneously that the letter had been given by Calvo Serer to his spiritual adviser, Padre Josemaría Escrivá de Balaguer, the Aragonese priest and founder of the Opus Dei, who had then handed it to Franco. It has also been alleged that the letter was actually given by Calvo Serer to Franco's cabinet secretary and a key adviser, Captain Luis Carrero Blanco, with the request that its 'interception' be attributed to the dictatorship's intelligence services. However, the allegation remains unproved.[52]

The Caudillo responded to Don Juan with disdain. After a feeble lie about the letter falling into the hands of an enemy agent 'from whom we were able to retrieve it', he went on to patronize the Conde de Barcelona in imperious terms. He asserted that his own right to rule Spain was infinitely superior to that of Juan III: 'among the rights that underlie sovereign authority are the rights of occupation and conquest, not to mention that which is engendered by saving an entire society.' To devalue Don Juan's claims, Franco stated that the military uprising of 1936 was not specifically monarchist, but more generally 'Spanish and Catholic' and that his regime therefore had no obligation to restore the monarchy. This sat ill with his own published justification for preventing Don Juan serving on the Nationalist side in 1937. In further defence of his legitimacy, he cited his own merits, accumulated during a life of sacrifice, his prestige among all sectors of society and public acceptance of his authority. He went on to state that Don Juan's actions constituted the real illegitimacy because they were impeding the monarchical restoration to which the Caudillo ostensibly aspired. Franco ended by recommending that Don Juan leave him, without any time limit, to his self-appointed task of preparing the ground for an eventual restoration.

Don Juan's reply was not without its ironic undertones. In response to Franco's insinuation that he was out of touch with the situation in Spain, he pointed out that in 13 years of exile, he had learned more than he might living in a palace, where, he said in a pointed reference to life at El Pardo, the atmosphere of adulation so often clouded the vision of the powerful. Regarding their conflicting visions of the international situation, Don Juan pointed out that Franco was one of the very few people in 1943 to believe in the long-term stability of the National-Syndicalist State. He suggested that Franco and his regime would not survive the end of the War. To avoid a stark choice between Francoist totalitarianism and a return to the Republic, Don Juan appealed to the

Caudillo's patriotism to restore the monarchy. Once more, he repeated his argument – an anathema to Franco – that the monarchy was a regime for all Spaniards and how, for that reason, he had always refused Franco's invitations to express solidarity with the Falange.[53] Don Juan's crystalline letter had all the logic, common sense and patriotism that was lacking in Franco's convoluted effort. However, the Caudillo was the sitting tenant and he was determined to brazen out the situation, confident that the Allies had too many other things to worry about. His optimism was in part fed by the conviction that the Americans regarded him as a better bet for anti-Communist stability in Spain than either the Republican opposition or Don Juan.

Despite his virtually limitless confidence in his own superiority over the House of Borbón, and his belief in the legitimacy of his power by dint of the right of conquest, Franco did feel seriously threatened by Don Juan's so-called Manifesto of Lausanne. This momentous document was issued just as the Caudillo's faith in Axis victory was finally beginning to ebb. With Pedro Sainz Rodríguez and José María Gil Robles in Portugal, and communication with Switzerland extremely difficult, the Manifesto was drawn up largely by Don Juan himself with the assistance of Eugenio Vegas Latapié. It was a denunciation of the Fascist origins and the totalitarian nature of the regime. Broadcast by the BBC on 19 March 1945, it called upon Franco to withdraw and make way for a moderate, democratic, constitutional monarchy. It infuriated Franco and set in stone his prior determination that Don Juan would never be King of Spain. Only the tiniest handful of monarchists responded to the Manifesto's call for them to resign their posts in the regime.[54] For many monarchists, Francoist stability had come to be worth much more than the uncertainties of a restoration. Fearful that Don Juan's confidence in Allied support threatened the overthrow of the dictatorship and the possible return of the exiled left, they were not inclined to rally actively to his cause.

Franco's *éminence grise*, the naval captain Luis Carrero Blanco, short, stocky, his face overshadowed by his thick bushy eyebrows, advised him how best to exploit this sentiment. The dourly loyal

Carrero Blanco recommended that he refrain from lashing out immediately against Don Juan. Instead, he counselled a process whereby the Pretender would be weaned away from his more radical advisers and coaxed into the *Movimiento* fold. His memorandum to Franco was astonishingly prophetic and it did not bode well for Don Juan's future or for Juan Carlos's happiness: 'It is crucial to get Don Juan on the road to radical change so that, in some years, he might be able to reign, otherwise he must resign himself to his son coming to the throne. Moreover, it is necessary to start thinking about preparing the child-prince for Kingship. He is now six or seven and seems to have good health and physical constitution; if properly brought up, principally in terms of Christian morality and patriotic sentiments, he could be a good King with the help of God, but only if this problem is faced up to now. For the moment, it would be prudent, 1) given that new clashes are not in our interests and nothing good can come of them, not to react violently against Don Juan nor give up on him altogether even though we believe that he cannot now be King; 2) to send some trustworthy monarchists to Lausanne; 3) to put the greatest care into selecting a perfectly prepared tutor for the young Prince; 4) to face up determinedly to the problem of the fundamental laws that we need, and define the Spanish regime. With regard to choosing our definitive form of government, since nations can be only republics or monarchies, and in Spain the republic is out of the question since it is a symbol of disaster, the form of government has to be a monarchy.'[55]

Without the military support of the Allies or the prior agreement of the military high command and the ecclesiastical hierarchy, Don Juan was naïvely depending on Franco withdrawing in a spirit of decency and good sense. The Caudillo's determination never to do so was revealed in his comment to General Alfredo Kindelán: 'As long as I live, I will never be a queen mother.'[56] Despite Carrero's counsel of moderation, Franco was deeply stung by the Lausanne Manifesto. He began to take practical steps to give substance to his claims to be the best hope for the monarchy. Two prominent regime Catholics, Alberto Martín Artajo, President of Catholic Action, and Joaquín Ruiz Giménez were despatched to tell Don Juan that the Church, the Army and the bulk of the monarchist camp remained loyal to Franco. They had no need to tell him that the Falange was deeply opposed to a restoration.[57] To neutralize any resurgence of monarchist sentiment in the high command, Franco summoned his senior generals to a meeting which remained in session for three days, from 20 to 22 March. He brazenly informed his generals that Spain was so orderly and contented that other countries including the United States were jealous and planned to adopt his Falangist system. He tried to frighten his generals off any monarchist conspiracy by brandishing the danger of Communism for which he blamed Britain, Don Juan's best chance of international support. It did not bode well for the Borbón family that, Kindelán aside, the generals seemed happy to swallow the Caudillo's absurd claims.[58] The controlled press praised Franco for having saved the Spanish people from 'martyrdom and persecution', the fate, it was implied, to which the failures of the monarchy had exposed them.[59] Even more space than usual was devoted to the annual Civil War victory parade. Slavish tribute was paid to Franco's victory over the 'thieves', 'assassins' and Communists of the Second Republic – the barely veiled message being that these same criminals – and with them, Don Juan – were even now plotting their return with the help of the Allies.[60]

All this time, the young Juan Carlos had been brought up by nannies and tutors, seeing more of his mother than his father, who was absorbed by the struggle to restore the throne. Now he was seven and oblivious, as were his parents, to the momentous implications of Carrero Blanco's report on the Lausanne Manifesto. Thirty years before the death of Franco, Carrero Blanco was proposing that his master's eventual successor be Juan Carlos. For that to be a feasible option, it would be crucial, from the dictator's point of view, that Juan Carlos received the 'right' kind of political formation, or indoctrination. Don Juan's acquiescence was crucial, yet Franco made little effort to avoid unduly antagonizing him. When the chubby Martín Artajo returned from his mission to Lausanne, Franco grilled him on 1 May for two and a half hours about his conversations with Don Juan. Still furious about the

Manifesto, Franco snapped, 'Don Juan is just a Pretender. I'm the one who makes the decision.' The Caudillo made it patently clear that he did not believe in one of the basic tenets of monarchism – the continuity of the dynastic line. In coarse language that must have shocked the prim Martín Artajo, he dismissed what he considered to be the decadent constitutional monarchy by reference to the notorious immorality of the nineteenth-century Queen Isabel II. He said, 'the last man to sleep with Doña Isabel cannot be the father of the King and what comes out of the belly of the Queen must be examined to see if it is suitable.' Clearly, Franco did not regard Don Juan de Borbón as fit to be King. He made critical comments about his personal life and dismissed Martín Artajo's efforts to defend him – 'There's nothing to be done . . . He has neither will nor character.' Franco would produce a law which turned Spain into a kingdom but that would not necessarily mean bringing back the Borbón family. A monarchical restoration would take place, declared Franco, 'only when the Caudillo decided and the Pretender had sworn an oath to uphold the fundamental laws of the regime'.[61]

Nevertheless, the imminent final defeat of the Third Reich, together with Don Juan's pressure, impelled Franco to make a crudely cynical gesture aimed at undermining the Pretender's position among monarchists inside Spain. Over several days in the first half of April 1945, he discussed the idea of adopting a 'monarchical form of government'. Monarchists within the Francoist camp were thus offered a sop to their consciences, together with an assurance that they need not face the risks of an immediate change of regime. At the same time, the cosmetic change would help the Allies forget that Franco's regime had been created with lavish Axis help. A new *Consejo del Reino* (Council of the King) would be created to determine the succession. Grandiosely billed as the supreme consultative body of the regime, its function was simply to advise Franco, who would have no obligation to heed its advice. Moreover, the emptiness of the gesture was exposed by the announcement that Franco would remain Head of State and that the King designated by the *Consejo* would not assume the throne until Franco either died or abandoned power himself.

A pseudo-constitution known as the *Fuero de los Españoles* (Spaniards' Charter of Rights) was also announced.

Given his messianic conviction in his own God-given right to rule over Spain, Franco could never forgive Don Juan for trying to use the international situation to hasten a Borbón restoration. He believed that, if he could buy time from his foreign enemies and his monarchist rivals with cosmetic changes to his regime, the end of the War would expose, to his benefit, the underlying conflict between the Western Allies and the Soviet Union. His confidence was well-founded. On 19 June, at the first conference of the United Nations, which had been in session in San Francisco since 25 April, the Mexican delegation proposed the exclusion of any country whose regime had been installed with the help of the Armed Forces of the States that had fought against the United Nations. The Mexican resolution, drafted with the help of exiled Spanish Republicans, could apply only to Franco's Spain and it was approved by acclamation.[62] Within the Spanish political class, it was assumed that there would now be negotiations for the restoration of the monarchy.[63] However, aware that, in Washington and London, there were those fearful that a hard line might encourage Communism in Spain, Franco and his spokesmen simply refused to accept that the San Francisco resolution had any relevance to Spain, making the most bare-faced denials that his regime was created with Axis help.[64]

Shortly afterwards, Franco would adopt a strategy aimed at reversing Don Juan's advantage in the international arena. The *Fuero de los Españoles* was introduced with a speech that implied to Spaniards and Western diplomats alike that any attempt to remove or modify the regime would open the gates to Communism.[65] Within one month, he reshuffled his cabinet in order to eliminate the ministers most tainted by the Axis stigma and brought in a number of deeply conservative Christian Democrats. They, and particularly the most prominent of them – Alberto Martín Artajo as Foreign Minister – permitted Franco to project a new image as an authoritarian Catholic ruler rather than as a lackey of the Axis.[66]

A fervent Catholic, Martín Artajo owed his appointment to

the recommendation of Captain Carrero Blanco, with whom he had spent nearly six months between October 1936 and March 1937 in hiding in the Mexican Embassy in Madrid. He accepted the post after consultation with the Primate, Cardinal Plá y Deniel, and both were naïvely convinced that he could play a role in smoothing the transition from Franco to the monarchy of Don Juan.[67] Franco was happy to let them believe so, but intended to maintain an iron control over foreign policy. The subservient Artajo would simply be used as the acceptable face of the regime for international consumption. Artajo told the influential right-wing poet and essayist, José María Pemán, a member of Don Juan's Privy Council, that he spoke on the telephone for at least one hour every day with Franco and used special earphones to leave his hands free to take notes. Pemán cruelly wrote in his diary: 'Franco makes international policy and Artajo is the minis-ter-stenographer.' In the first meeting of the new cabinet team, on 21 July, Franco told his ministers that concessions would be made to the outside world only on non-essential matters and when it suited the regime.[68]

While nonplussed by the clear evidence that Franco had no immediate intentions of restoring the monarchy, Don Juan was encouraged by the appointment of Martín Artajo, whom he trust-ingly regarded as one of his supporters. It was the beginning of a process in which Don Juan was to be cunningly neutralized by Franco. As part of a plan to drive a wedge between Don Juan and his more outspoken advisers, Gil Robles, Sainz Rodríguez and Vegas Latapié, Franco encouraged conservative monarchists of proven loyalty to his regime to get close to the royal camp. One of the most opportunistic of these was the sleekly handsome José María de Areilza, a Basque monarchist who had been closely linked to the Falange in the 1930s. Areilza had acquired the aristo-cratic title of Conde de Motrico through marriage and his impec-cable Francoist credentials had been rewarded when he was named Mayor of Bilbao after its capture in June 1937. In 1941, he wrote with Fernando María Castiella, the ferociously imperialist text *Reivindicaciones de España* (Spain's Claims) and had aspired to be Ambassador to Fascist Italy. After the War, he moved back to the pro-Francoist monarchist camp, and would be named Ambassador to Buenos Aires in May 1947. His visits to see Don Juan were dutifully reported to the British Embassy to give the impression that Franco was negotiating the terms of a restoration and so buy him more time.[69]

The wisdom of Franco's policy, and the waning prospects of Don Juan, were both illustrated by the relatively toothless Potsdam declaration which reiterated Spain's exclusion from the United Nations but made no suggestion of intervention against the Caudillo. Statements from the British Labour government that nothing would be done that might encourage civil war in Spain heartened the Caudillo further.[70] Don Juan would have been even gloomier had he known of a report on the regime's survival drafted at this time by Franco's ever more influential assistant, Captain Carrero Blanco. It was a brutally realistic document which rested on the confidence that, after Potsdam, Britain and France would never risk opening the door to Communism in Spain by supporting the exiled Republicans. Accordingly, 'the only formula possible for us is order, unity and hang on for dear life. Good police action to anticipate subversion; energetic repression if it materializes, without fear of foreign criticism, since it is better to punish harshly once and for all than leave the evil uncorrected.' There was no place for Don Juan in that future.[71] On 25 August 1945, Franco sacked Kindelán as Director of the *Escuela Superior del Ejército* (Higher Army College) for making a fervently royalist speech predicting that the Pretender would soon be on the throne with the full support of the Army.[72]

Anxious to establish control over Don Juan, in the autumn of 1945, Franco through intermediaries suggested that if the heir to the throne took up residence in Spain, he would be provided with a royal household fit for a future King. The message, passed on by Miguel Mateu Plá, the Spanish Ambassador in Paris, made it clear that Franco had no intention of any sudden change. He was merely looking for a way of placating both the Great Powers and the monarchist conspirators in the Army. Don Juan had no desire to become the Caudillo's puppet and was still hopeful of military action to overthrow the regime. Accordingly, he rejected the offer out of hand – commenting 'I am the King. I do not enter Spain by the back door.' The refusal was underlined when Don Juan told *La Gazette* of Lausanne that the need to 'repair the damage done to Spain by Franco' made the restoration of the monarchy an urgent necessity. He denounced Franco's regime as 'inspired by the totalitarian powers of the Axis' and spoke of his intention to re-establish the monarchy within a democratic system similar to those of Britain, the United States, Scandinavia and Holland.[73]

On 2 February 1946, Don Juan and his wife moved to the fashionable but sleepy seaside resort of Estoril, west of Lisbon. An area of splendid mansions built for the millionaire bankers and shipbuilders of the nearby capital, its silent isolation was disturbed only by the click of chips falling in the casinos. The eight-year-old Juan Carlos, to his considerable distress, was left behind in Switzerland, where he was by now being educated by the Marian fathers in Fribourg. For the first two months in Portugal, his family lived in Villa Papoila, loaned by the Marqués de Pelayo, later moving in March 1946 to the larger Villa Bel Ver. They stayed there until the autumn of 1947 when they moved to Casa da Rocha, until finally in February 1949, they established their residence at Villa Giralda. In 1946, for many of Don Juan's supporters, his proximity to Spain seemed to shorten the distance that separated him from the throne. His mere presence in the Iberian Peninsula set off a wave of monarchist enthusiasm. The Spanish Foreign Ministry was inundated with requests for visas as senior monarchists set off to pay their respects.[74]

Franco's Ambassador to Portugal, his brother Nicolás, quickly established a superficially cordial relationship with Don Juan. However, when Nicolás suggested he drive him to Madrid for a secret meeting with the Caudillo, Gil Robles, Don Juan's senior adviser, was adamant: 'Your Majesty cannot go and see Generalísimo Franco on Spanish soil since he would be going there as a subject.'[75] Indeed, it had been the expectation of tension with Franco that had led Don Juan to decide that it was better for Juan Carlos to remain in Switzerland. The wisdom of his decision was underlined when the Caudillo lashed out in response to the publication on 13 February 1946 of a letter welcoming Don Juan to the

Peninsula, signed by 458 prominent establishment figures. Franco reacted as if he was faced with a mutiny by subordinates rather than an attempt to accelerate a process to which he had publicly committed himself. He told a cabinet meeting on 15 February, 'This is a declaration of war, they must be crushed like worms.' In an astonishing phrase, he declared, 'the regime must defend itself and bite back deeply.' He relented only after Martín Artajo, General Dávila and others had pointed out the damaging international repercussions of such a move. He then went through the list of signatories, specifying the best ways of punishing each of them, by the withdrawal of passports, tax inspections or dismissal from their posts.[76]

While these high political dirty tricks were going on, the eight-year-old Prince was sent to a grim boarding school at Ville Saint-Jean in Fribourg, run by the stern Marian fathers. Juan Carlos would later recall his distress at being separated from his family and from his tutor Eugenio Vegas Latapié, of whom he had become fond. 'At first, I was really very miserable, because I felt that my family had abandoned me, that my mother and father had just forgotten all about me.' Every day he waited for a telephone call from his mother that never came. It must have been the harder to bear because of the gnawing suspicion that his parents' favourite was his younger brother Alfonso, who remained at home with them. Only later did he discover that his father had forbidden his mother to phone him, saying, 'María, you've got to help him become tougher.' Later on, Juan Carlos tried to explain away his father's actions – 'It was not cruelty on his part and certainly not a lack of feeling. But my father knew, as I would later know myself, that princes need to be brought up the hard way.' Juan Carlos had to pay a terrible price in loneliness – 'in Fribourg, far from my father and my mother, I learned that solitude is a heavy burden to bear.' The most visible consequences of the apparent harshness of his parents' treatment would be his perpetually melancholy expression and a silent reserve.

In later endeavouring to explain away his father's motivation, Juan Carlos inadvertently shed light on his own life as an eight-year-old, far from his parents: 'My father had a deep sense of what being royal involved. He saw in me not only his son but also the heir to a dynasty, and as such, I had to start preparing myself to face up to my responsibilities.'[77] Despite such rationalizations, it is clear that it was difficult for Juan Carlos ever to reconcile himself to this early separation. (His own son, Felipe, would not be sent to boarding school at such a young age and did not leave home for the first time until he was 16, in order to spend his last year at school at the Lockfield College School in Toronto, Canada.) Indeed, in a 1978 interview for the German conservative paper *Welt am Sonntag*, Juan Carlos would describe his departure for Ville Saint-Jean in more heartfelt terms: 'going to boarding school meant saying goodbye to my childhood, to a worry-free world full of family warmth. I had to face that initial difficult period of separation from my family all alone.'[78]

Even when phone calls from home were finally permitted by Don Juan, they remained, for a long time, few and far between. This silence from his parents must have been very painful, since Juan Carlos was given no explanation. It was hardly surprising that he felt that they had simply forgotten him. His unhappiness at Ville Saint-Jean was intensified by the fact that he quickly fell foul of the school's rigid discipline. His teachers there would later remember him as a handsome but indisciplined eight-year-old of average intelligence, with a lively sense of humour. They considered him to have been spoilt by overindulgent nannies in the past: 'they had let him get away with virtually everything so that he considered himself as lord and master wherever he happened to be.' Father Julio de Hoyos, one of Juan Carlos's teachers, recalled how the Prince refused to attend his first class at the school: he had physically to carry the boy to the classroom and then to slap him in order to make him sit quietly and pay attention. No one seems to have considered that the boy's behaviour and poor academic performance were symptoms of his desperate unhappiness at being separated from his parents.[79]

In November 1980, Juan Carlos recounted to the English biographer of his grandmother his vivid memories of how important Queen Victoria Eugenia was to him during this period. She frequently visited him at his school. Although deeply conscious of the responsibilities of royalty, she had a warm relationship with him. Remembering her own difficulties with the Spanish language when she first arrived in Madrid at the turn of the century, she was determined that Juan Carlos would not suffer embarrassment or criticism as a result of having a foreign accent. Having been brought up in Italy and Switzerland, speaking French as much as Spanish, he had a noticeable accent, particularly in his pronunciation of the crucial letter 'r'. The majority of the pupils at Ville Saint-Jean were French and all classes were in French. Victoria Eugenia taught him to trill the 'r' in the Spanish style and to drop the French explosive 'r' which sounds so comical to Spaniards.[80]

At the beginning of the 1946 Christmas holiday, Victoria Eugenia accompanied Juan Carlos on his trip back to Estoril. On the boy's arrival, Eugenio Vegas Latapié, Don Juan's political secretary, resumed his duties as tutor, in order to prepare him for his future royal tasks, and would also accompany him back to Switzerland after the holidays. Astonishingly, Vegas was allowed to smack the Prince when he was naughty – although without hurting him. Despite Vegas Latapié's intellectually imposing and austere character, they had established a good relationship. He laid the basis for the boy's later conservatism – along with emphasis on Spain's one-time imperial glories, he taught him the anthem of the Spanish Foreign Legion, which Juan Carlos would find profoundly moving thereafter.[81] Before Don Juan had left Lausanne, Father Carles Cardó, the distinguished Catalan theologian, in exile in Switzerland, said to him, 'Sir, be careful that Eugenio Vegas Latapié doesn't turn the Prince into a new Philip II.' By this stage, Juan Carlos was already exhibiting an emotional (though naïvely expressed) concern for Spain's internal affairs. Vegas Latapié remembers that one day, the Prince told him that he had 'promised God not to eat chocolates again until an important political event takes place in Spain'. Vegas Latapié replied that this seemed rather too big a promise for a child to make and that he might not be able to eat chocolates for a very long time if he kept it. When Juan Carlos asked him what he should do, Vegas Latapié replied that he ought to go to confession. He then absolved him of his promise and told him not to make similar ones in the future.[82]

Franco's anger at the monarchist enthusiasm generated by Don Juan's arrival in Portugal continued to fester. He sent a note to Don Juan breaking off relations between them on the grounds that he had given his permission only for the Pretender to make a two-week visit to Portugal, yet he and his Privy Council were fomenting monarchist conspiracy against him. Franco acted out of pique, but there was a strong element of calculation in his reaction. The more daring monarchists now began to seek contacts on the left but many of the more opportunistic conservatives who had signed the letter welcoming Don Juan scuttled back to Franco.[83] In response, at the end of February 1946, Don Juan attempted to woo a broad spectrum of Spanish opinion, including the ultra-conservative Carlists, by issuing another manifesto, known as the *Bases de Estoril*. It was a draft constitution for the monarchy and contrasted with the earlier Lausanne Manifesto in promising a brand of Catholic corporatism. The *Bases de Estoril* did not succeed in convincing the Carlists, but the document did antagonize his more liberal supporters.[84]

In fact, all was not well within Don Juan's camp. Vegas Latapié tended to place considerable hopes on Allied intervention to restore the monarchy. On 4 March 1946, a Tripartite Declaration of the United States, Great Britain and France announced that: 'As long as General Franco continues in control of Spain, the Spanish people cannot anticipate full and cordial association with those nations of the world which have, by common effort, brought defeat to German Nazism and Italian Fascism, which aided the present Spanish regime in its rise to power and after which the regime was patterned.' Pedro Sainz Rodríguez, however, argued vehemently that the real significance of the Declaration lay in the statement that: 'There is no intention of interfering in the internal affairs of Spain. The Spanish people themselves must in the long run work out their own destiny.' Sainz Rodríguez would argue, against the views of Vegas Latapié and Gil Robles, that Don Juan must seek some rapprochement with the Caudillo.[85]

Don Juan was sufficiently concerned by the hostility emanating from Franco and the Falange to instruct Juan Carlos's teachers at Ville Saint-Jean to destroy any gifts of sweets, chocolates and other delicacies sent to the Prince by well-wishers, for fear of attempts to poison him. Eventually, Don Juan became uneasy about Juan Carlos being left alone in Switzerland and finally, in April 1946, called for his son to rejoin the family at Estoril. It opened a brief period of relative normality, with the boy able to attend a local school, the *Colegio Amor de Deus*. He made many friends and could spend time with his family and pursuing hobbies like horse-riding, sailing and football.[86] Juan Carlos's education at Estoril remained under the overall supervision of Vegas Latapié. In spite of his tutor's rigid conservatism and insistence on discipline and formality, the young Prince became increasingly attached to him, later describing him as 'a wonderful man'. According to Juan Carlos, Vegas Latapié believed that the heir to the throne: 'should be educated with no concession to the weaknesses that seem normal to commoners. Accordingly, he brought me up to understand that I was a being apart, with many more duties and responsibilities than anyone else.'[87]

In early December 1946, the United Nations denounced the Axis links of Franco and invited him to 'surrender the powers of government'. It was highly unlikely that there would be any Allied intervention against the Caudillo, but Franco responded as if there was such a threat by mounting a massively orchestrated popular demonstration in the Plaza de Oriente on 9 December. On 12 December, a plenary session of the General Assembly resolved to exclude Spain from all its dependent bodies, called upon the Security Council to study measures to be adopted if, within a reasonable time, Spain still had a government lacking popular consent; and called on all member nations to withdraw their ambassadors.[88] At the cabinet meeting on 13 December, Franco crowed that the United Nations was 'fatally wounded'.[89]

Nevertheless, Franco put considerable effort into making his regime more acceptable to the Western democracies. On 31 December 1946, Captain Carrero Blanco drafted a memorandum urging Franco to institutionalize his regime as a monarchy and then give it the veneer of 'democratic' legitimacy with a referendum. Building on the ideas first discussed in cabinet in April 1945, it was clearly an attempt to counter the threat of Don Juan as perceived by Franco. There could be no other interpretation to the central argument that the 'personal deficiencies' of any hereditary monarch could be neutralized by Franco remaining as Head of State and the King being subject to the advice of his vacuous consultative body, the *Consejo del Reino*, made up of loyal nominees of Franco. The Caudillo knew that an even simpler solution was never to restore the monarchy in his lifetime. Carrero Blanco's memorandum was thus refined further in another working paper presented on 22 March 1947, which suggested that Franco name his own royal successor.[90]

Franco quickly implemented Carrero Blanco's plans to give his regime the trappings of acceptability. Carrero Blanco's ideas formed the basis of a draft text of the *Ley de Sucesión* (Law of Succession) and were discussed in a cabinet meeting on 28 March 1947. The first Article declared that: 'Spain, as a political unit, is a Catholic, social and representative state which, in keeping with her tradition, declares herself constituted as a kingdom.' The second Article declared that: 'The Head of State is the Caudillo of Spain and of the Crusade, Generalísimo of the Armed Forces, Don Francisco Franco Bahamonde.'[91] The regime's Axis connections would simply be painted over with a monarchist veneer. The declaration that Franco would govern until prevented by death or incapacity, the Caudillo's right to name his own royal successor, the deafening silence on the royal family's rights of dynastic succession, the statement that the future King must uphold the fundamental laws of the regime and could be removed if he departed from them – all this showed that only the label had changed.

This elaborate deception aimed to buy time from both the Western Allies and monarchists inside Spain. Its success was dependent upon Don Juan speaking the right lines and not denouncing it. That part of the show was handled with notable clumsiness. On the day before the *Ley de Sucesión* was to be made public, Carrero Blanco arrived in Estoril. He carried an emolient message to Don Juan, implying that if he identified himself with the regime and were patient, he could be Franco's heir. Carrero Blanco had been ordered by Franco to seek an audience for precisely 31 March, in order to deny Don Juan the possibility of doing anything to impede the project that was to be announced that evening. Believing that he was being consulted about a draft, Don Juan candidly told Carrero Blanco that Franco could hardly pretend to be the restorer of the monarchy when he was prohibiting monarchist activities. Regarding the issue of his identification with the regime, he told Franco's emissary of his determination to be King of all Spaniards. This stung Carrero into a blunt statement of the Francoist view of politics: 'In Spain in 1936 a trench was dug; and you are either on this side of the trench or else on the other . . . You should think about the fact that you can be King of Spain but only of the Spain of the *Movimiento Nacional*: Catholic, anti-Communist, anti-liberal and fiercely free of any foreign influence in its policies.'[92] As he took his farewell, Carrero Blanco said nothing when Don Juan promised to read the text of the *Ley de Sucesión* and give him his opinion the next day.

When Don Juan had retired to his rooms, Carrero slipped back to the Villa Bel Ver and left a message with an official of the royal household that Franco would be going on national radio that night to announce the definitive text of the new law. He left hastily before Don Juan was given the message. At a dinner party attended by members of the Spanish Embassy in Lisbon, Don Juan gave vent to his fury at Carrero Blanco, saying, 'that bastard Carrero came to try to shut me up.' The remark was duly reported back to Madrid and ensured Carrero Blanco's undying resentment of Don Juan. In the medium term, this cheap deception inclined Don Juan and his advisers to strengthen their links with the left-wing anti-Franco opposition.[93] On 7 April 1947, Don Juan issued the 'Estoril Manifesto' denouncing the illegality of the succession law's proposed alteration of the nature of the monarchy without consultation with either the heir to the throne or the people. Franco, Martín Artajo and Carrero Blanco agreed that Don Juan had thereby eliminated himself as a suitable successor to the Caudillo.

On 13 April, the *Observer*, the BBC and the *New York Times* published declarations by Don Juan – drawn up by Eugenio Vegas Latapié and Gil Robles, in collaboration with the exiled Spanish scholar Rafael Martínez Nadal – to the effect that he was prepared to reach an agreement with Franco only if it was limited to the details of the peaceful and unconditional transfer of power. Since Don Juan had declared himself in favour of a democratic monarchy, the legalization of political parties and trade unions, a degree of regional decentralization, religious freedom and even a partial amnesty, Franco was livid. He later told his faithful confidant and head of his military household, his cousin Francisco Franco Salgado-Araujo 'Pacón', that it was the *Observer* interview that led him to contemplate Juan Carlos as his eventual successor. He unleashed a furious press campaign against Don Juan, denouncing him as the tool of international freemasonry and Communism. The fury of his reaction intensified the divisions within Don Juan's group of advisers. Against the anti-Franco line of Eugenio Vegas Latapié and José María Gil Robles, Pedro Sainz Rodríguez had come to the conclusion that Franco increasingly held all the cards and thus advocated a tactic of conciliation towards him. Distressed by the press assault, Don Juan began to incline towards Sainz Rodríguez's view. In consequence, in the autumn of 1947, Vegas Latapié resigned as his secretary.[94]

The *Ley de Sucesión* was rubber-stamped by the Cortes in June and endorsed by a carefully choreographed referendum on 6 July 1947.[95] Long before this plebiscite, Franco had been, in every respect, acting as if he were King of Spain, even dispensing titles of nobility. Ironically, as part of the campaign for the referendum, spectacular propaganda was made out of the visit to Spain by the glamorous María Eva Duarte de Perón (Evita) in June 1947. The publicity given to the visit implied that Evita had come just to see Franco, and the *Movimiento* press omitted to mention that she was also visiting Portugal, Italy, the Vatican, Switzerland and France. In Portugal, she visited Don Juan. Greeting him effusively – according to José María Pemán, she kissed him on both hands and part of his forearm – she had no hesitation in giving him a spot of advice about the *Ley de Sucesión*. 'Take the crown from whoever offers it,' she told him, 'you'll have plenty of time later to give him a good kick in the backside.' When Don Juan stopped laughing, he replied, 'There are certain things that a lady can say and a King cannot do.'[96]

Meanwhile, the now nine-year-old Juan Carlos exhibited a

precocious concern for events in Spain. In January 1947, shortly after his first communion, Don Juan had suggested to one of the monarchists who had come from Spain, José María Cervera, that he give the Prince an account of the Spanish Civil War. Juan Carlos reacted by asking: 'And why does Franco, who was so good during the war, treat us so badly now?'[97] However, Don Juan came to realize that sporadic contact with monarchists, fascinating though it might be for the young Prince, hardly added up to an education. Accordingly, the happy period, just 18 months, that Juan Carlos had been able to spend in Estoril came to an end. In late 1947, Don Juan sent his son back to the severe Marian fathers of Ville Saint-Jean, again under the supervision of Vegas Latapié.

The promulgation of the *Ley de Sucesión*, and its potential permanent exclusion of his family from the Spanish throne, led Don Juan to seek wider support for a restoration. In London for the wedding of Princess Elizabeth and Lieutenant Philip Mountbatten on 20 November 1947, Don Juan had a brief meeting with Ernest Bevin, the British Foreign Secretary. He also met State Department officials in Washington in the spring of 1948. He was forced to accept that, in the context of the Cold War, the Western powers had little stomach for the removal of Franco. In an effort to convince them that the departure of the dictator would not lead to another civil war, throughout the first eight months of 1948, Gil Robles and Sainz Rodríguez tried to negotiate a pact with the leader of the Socialist Party, the PSOE, Indalecio Prieto. Agreement was finally reached at St Jean de Luz on 24 August. The text was sent to Estoril for Don Juan's approval, but the days passed and there came no reply. Then to the consternation of both Prieto and the monarchist negotiators, the news arrived that Don Juan had met Franco on 25 August. Prieto said, 'I look like a total bastard in the eyes of my party. I've got such big horns that I can't get through the door,' a reference to the Spanish expression for sexual betrayal, *poner los cuernos*.[98]

Don Juan had been sufficiently impressed by the strength of Franco's position to consider some form of conciliation. The Caudillo, for his part, was now toying with the idea of grooming Juan Carlos as a possible heir. Although the tension between the two was not in the interests of either, all of the advantages lay with Franco. He knew that the United States would not risk provoking the fall of his regime through economic blockade, lest the left rather than Don Juan benefited. In mid-January 1948, messages had also been sent to Don Juan urging him to seek some agreement with Franco.[99] Pressure also came from Don Juan's most conservative supporters in Madrid – his senior representatives in Spain, the Duque de Sotomayor (also head of the royal household), José María Oriol, and two even more reactionary monarchists, the Conde de Vallellano and Julio Danvila Rivera, both of whom had been active members of the ultra-right-wing monarchist organization, *Renovación Española*, during the Second Republic. They hoped, with no concern whatsoever for the welfare of Juan Carlos, to negotiate with Franco by using the boy as a pawn.

In Switzerland, far from his family, Juan Carlos's loneliness was hardly mitigated by the company of Eugenio Vegas Latapié, for all his affectionate concern. In February 1948, the sense of being left alone was intensified when his parents went on a long trip to Cuba as the guests of King Leopold of Belgium. Juan Carlos began to suffer headaches and earache. It was not the only time that his distress at the separation from his parents would manifest itself in illness. Vegas Latapié took him to a clinic where he was diagnosed as having otitis, a severe inflammation of the inner ear. It was necessary that he have a small operation to perforate the eardrum. With the boy's parents entirely out of touch, this meant an enormous responsibility for Vegas Latapié. With the greatest difficulty, he finally managed to contact Queen Victoria Eugenia who granted permission for the operation to go ahead. Juan Carlos's ears suppurated so much that his pillow had to be changed several times during the first night. Juan Carlos had to spend 12 days in the clinic, his only regular visitor Vegas Latapié. His grandmother visited him only once. A sense of just how sad he was can be deduced from his anxiety to please. Vegas Latapié had spoken to him of the merit in eating what was put in front of him even if it was not exactly what he liked. He then discovered him eating, with the greatest difficulty, a plate of dry, indigestible ravioli. When Vegas asked why, he replied, 'I promised you I'd eat it.'[100]

Danvila and Sotomayor were suggesting to Franco the many advantages to be derived from having Juan Carlos in Spain. News of the monarchist negotiations with the PSOE galvanized the Caudillo into arranging a meeting with Don Juan on his yacht, the *Azor*. At first, precisely because of the negotiations with the Socialists in France, Don Juan fended off various invitations passed to him by the courtiers in Madrid. However, he was aware of the difficult situation in which the monarchist cause found itself and was also concerned about the education of his son. Danvila visited him in Estoril and finally Don Juan agreed to meet the Caudillo in the Bay of Biscay, on 25 August 1948.[101] Don Juan omitted to inform his own close political advisers, even Gil Robles.

When Don Juan came aboard the *Azor*, Franco greeted him effusively and, to Don Juan's bemusement, cried profusely. They then spoke alone in the main cabin for three hours. Apart from the short official account given to the Spanish press, the only detailed information derives from Don Juan's various accounts. The emotional outburst over, Franco quickly gave Don Juan the impression that he believed him to be an idiot, entirely in the hands of embittered advisers and totally ignorant of Spain. Barely allowing him to get a word in edgeways, the Caudillo counselled patience and blithely reassured Don Juan that he was in splendid health and expected to rule Spain for at least another 20 years. To the consternation of Don Juan, he spoke of his devotion to Alfonso XIII, and again wept. Franco claimed that there was no enthusiasm within Spain either for a monarchy or for a republic although he boasted that he could, if he wished, make Don Juan popular in a fortnight. He was nonplussed when Don Juan asked him why, if the creation of popularity was so easy, he constantly used popular hostility as an excuse for not restoring the monarchy. The only reason that the Caudillo could cite was his fear that the monarchy would not have the firmness of command necessary. In contrast to what he must have supposed to be Don Juan's practice, he declared, 'I do not allow my ministers to answer me back. I give them orders and they obey.' The meeting took a dramatic turn for the worse when, exasperated by Franco's patronizing distortions of history, Don Juan reminded him that in 1942, he had promised to defend Berlin with a million Spanish soldiers. As the temperature plummeted, Franco stared at him silently.

In fact, there were many reasons why Franco had already eliminated Don Juan as his successor. His real motive for arranging the meeting finally emerged when he expressed his desire for the now ten-year-old Prince Juan Carlos to complete his education in Spain. The advantages to Franco were obvious. Juan Carlos would be a hostage whose presence in Spain would create the impression of royal approval of Franco's indefinite assumption of the role of regent. It would make it easier for the Allies to accept that things were changing in Spain. Moreover, in Franco's hands, the Prince would also be an instrument to control the activities of Don Juan and the entire political direction of any future monarchical restoration. Speaking with his habitual combination of cunning and prejudice, Franco patronizingly instructed Don Juan about the dangers run by princes under foreign influence. Don Juan pointed out that it would be impossible for his son to go to Spain while it remained an offence to shout '¡Viva el Rey!' (Long live the King) and active monarchists were subjected to fines and police surveillance. Franco offered to change all that, but no firm agreement was made about the future education of Juan Carlos.[102]

Don Juan had agreed to meet Franco because he had already reached the conclusion that the Caudillo would survive and that a future monarchical restoration would happen only with his approval. He told an official of the American Embassy in Lisbon that before the *Azor* meeting, his relations with Franco were at an impasse and that now he had got 'his foot in the door'. The price was a serious weakening of his position. To the delight of Franco, secret police reports revealed that some of Don Juan's supporters were outraged at what they saw as treachery to the monarchy and were inclined to abandon his cause.[103] His most prominent representatives in Spain were deep in Franco's pocket. The Duque de Sotomayor and Julio Danvila, acting as intermediaries from El Pardo, pressed Don Juan for a decision about Juan Carlos's education. He hesitated on the grounds that any announcement about the issue would be used by Franco to imply that he had abdicated.

Juan Carlos did not know that an even more complete separation from his parents was under discussion. He had longed to return home to Estoril for the summer holidays and once there, he spent the time playing with friends, frolicking on the beach and horse riding. He had no desire to return to his boarding school in Fribourg and was thus delighted when he was allowed to stay on at Estoril. Since preparations were afoot for him to go to Spain, Don Juan saw no point in sending him back to school. Juan Carlos was in limbo, happy to be with his parents and unaware that his father was contemplating sending him as a hostage to Franco. At the beginning of October, Vegas Latapié advised Don Juan that this situation played into Franco's hands by making it obvious that the boy was eventually going to be sent to Spain. Within 12 hours, arrangements were made for Juan Carlos's rapid, and presumably upsetting, return to Fribourg accompanied by Vegas Latapié. In his heart, Don Juan was convinced that there could be no restoration against the will of Franco. He knew that the international situation totally favoured the Caudillo. So, the boy's interests were made subordinate to the need for a minor political gesture.[104]

The advantages of the uneasy rapprochement between the dictator and Don Juan were entirely one-sided. To Franco's satisfaction, the negotiations between monarchists and Socialists became meaningless. The so-called Pact of St Jean de Luz, so painfully constructed throughout 1948 and finally signed in October by Indalecio Prieto and Gil Robles, was the first serious attempt at national reconciliation since the Civil War. Now it was rendered stillborn. The *Azor* meeting completely discredited the democratic monarchist option for which moderate Socialists and Republicans had broken with the Communist Party and the Socialist left. It must have given Franco intense pleasure to read a letter, intercepted by his secret services, in which Indalecio Prieto referred to 'the little cutey of Estoril'.[105] In return, Franco merely gave Don Juan superficial respect and a stab in the back. The destabilizing effects on Juan Carlos – educational or emotional – played no part in the considerations of any of the players in this particular game.

On the occasion of Franco's 25th wedding anniversary, Don Juan sent a message of congratulation. He took the opportunity to say that he had decided to keep Juan Carlos at his boarding school in Switzerland until the arrangements were in place for him to go to Spain. He mentioned, 'the lively interest shown by his grandmother, Queen Victoria Eugenia, in having him with her before such a long separation'. What is remarkable is that the boy's own parents seemed not to need to spend time with their son prior to what was likely to be a gruesome experience for him.[106]

The real significance of the *Azor* meeting was brutally revealed on 26 October when Franco arranged for news to be leaked that Juan Carlos would be educated in Spain. With no concessions from Franco other than a promise that the monarchist daily *ABC* could function freely and that restrictions on monarchist activities would be lifted, Don Juan was forced to put an end to his hesitations.[107] On 27 October, he sent a telegram to Eugenio Vegas Latapié: 'It is urgent that you come with the Prince as soon as possible. Stop. There are SAS and KLM flights direct to Lisbon. Stop. I'll explain why when you arrive. Stop.' Vegas Latapié sent a cable to Estoril pointing out that they could save a day or more by taking a flight to Madrid and then changing for Lisbon. However, Don Juan sent categoric instructions that they were not to return via Spain. A somewhat bewildered Juan Carlos made the journey as instructed and then waited aimlessly in Estoril. He was distressed when told about the plans for his education in Spain. He was especially upset when he discovered that he was not to be accompanied by his tutor. The fact was that the Caudillo, eagerly backed by Don Juan's enthusiastically pro-Franco advisers, the Duque de Sotomayor and Danvila, did not want Vegas Latapié to have any influence on the Prince's education in Spain. At one point, the Prince said to Vegas, 'I'm sad that you're not coming to Spain with me!' Before Vegas could reply, Don Juan, perhaps feeling guilty about what he was doing to his son, interrupted brusquely 'Don't be stupid, Juanito!' Doña María de las Mercedes was deeply aware of how affected her son would be by the separation from his beloved tutor. Don Juan rather feebly suggested that Vegas Latapié return to Spain in a personal capacity in order to spend time with the Prince on Sundays. Vegas sadly pointed out that a ten-year-old boy could not be expected to give up his exiguous free time to go for walks with a crusty old man.[108]

Vegas Latapié took his leave of Juan Carlos on 6 November as if he would be seeing him the next day. He returned to Switzerland on 7 November. At Lisbon Airport, he gave Pedro Sainz Rodríguez a letter to deliver to the Prince. 'My beloved Sire, Forgive me for not saying that I was leaving. The kiss that I gave you last night meant goodbye. I have often told you that men don't cry and, so that you don't see me cry, I have decided to return to Switzerland before you go to Spain. If anyone dares tell Your Highness that I have abandoned you, you must know that it is not true. They didn't want me to continue at your side and I have no choice in the matter. When I return to Spain for good, I will visit Your Highness. Your faithful friend who loves you with all his soul asks only that you be good, that God bless you and that occasionally you pray for me. Eugenio Vegas Latapié.'[109] That such an austere and inflexible character as Vegas could be moved to write such a sad and tender letter testifies to his closeness to the Prince.

It serves to underline that, although there were many political reasons why Juan Carlos had to be educated in Spain, the entire episode could have been handled with greater sensitivity to his emotional needs. Gil Robles wrote in his diary: 'Vegas may have his defects – who doesn't? – but nobody outdoes him in loyalty, firmness of purpose, unselfishness and affection for the Prince. And, despite everything, with cold indifference, they just dumped him. How serious a thing is ingratitude, above all in a King!'[110]

It is a telling comment on Don Juan's attitude to what was about to happen that he did not spend the day before the journey with his son. A perplexed Gil Robles wrote in his diary: 'he's gone hunting as if nothing was happening.'[111] In an effort to ensure that there would be no demonstrations at the main station in Lisbon, the tearful ten-year-old Juan Carlos was waved off by his tight-lipped parents as he joined the Lusitania overnight express on the evening of 8 November at Entroncamento, a railway junction far to the north of the capital. If there was one thing that might have diminished a ten-year-old boy's sadness at having to leave his parents it was the possibility of a spell driving a train. However, that pleasure was monopolized by a grandee, the Duque de Zaragoza, decked out in blue overalls. For his journey into the unknown, the young Prince was accompanied by two sombre adults, the Duque de Sotomayor, as head of the royal household, and Juan Luis Roca de Togores, the Vizconde de Rocamora, as *mayordomo*.

At first Juan Carlos dozed fitfully but then slept as the train trundled in darkness through the drought-stricken hills of Extremadura. As they entered New Castile in the early light of dawn, he was awakened by the Duque. Burning with curiosity about the mysterious land of which he had heard so much but never visited, he pressed his face to the window. What he saw bore no resemblance to the deep greens of Portugal. Juan Carlos was taken aback by the harsh and arid landscape. Austere olive groves were interrupted by scrubland dotted with rocky outcrops. As they neared Madrid, the boy's impressions of the impoverished Castilian plain were every bit as depressing. He did not know it yet, but he was saying goodbye to his childhood. What awaited him the next morning could hardly have been more forbidding. The train was halted outside the capital at the small station of Villaverde, lest there be clashes between monarchists and Falangists. As he stepped from the train, shuddering as the biting Castilian cold hit him, his heart must have fallen when he saw the grim welcoming committee. A group of unsmiling adults in black overcoats peered at him from under their trilbies. The Duque de Sotomayor presented them – Julio Danvila, the Conde de Fontanar, José María Oriol, the Conde de Rodezno – and as the boy raised his hand to be shaken, out came the empty formalities, 'Did Your Highness have a good trip?' 'Your Highness is not too tired?' Their stiffness was obviously in part due to the fact that middle-aged men have little in common with ten-year-old boys. However, it may also have reflected their own mixed feelings regarding the rivalry between Franco and Don Juan. For all that they were apparently partisans of Don Juan, their social and economic privileges were closely linked to the survival of Franco's authoritarian regime.

The Prince came from Portugal deeply aware of his loneliness. Surrounded by such men, he can only have felt even more lonely.

The extent to which he was just a player in a theatrical production mounted for the benefit of others was soon brought home to him. Outside the small station at Villaverde, there awaited a long line of black limousines – the vehicles of members of the aristocracy who had come to greet the Prince and to attend the ceremony that followed. Without any enquiry as to his wishes, the Duque de Sotomayor ushered him into the first car and the line of cars drove a few miles to the Cerro de los Ángeles, considered the exact centre of Spain. There, his grandfather, Alfonso XIII, had dedicated Spain to the Sacred Heart in 1919. To commemorate that event, a Carmelite convent had been built on the spot. The sanctimonious Julio Danvila, ensuring that the boy should have no doubts about what Franco had done for Spain, hastened to tell him how the statue of Christ that dominated the hill had been 'condemned to death' and 'executed' by Republican militiamen in 1936. Still without his breakfast, the shivering child was then taken into the convent for what seemed to him an interminable mass. When mass was over, his ordeal continued. In a symbolic ceremony, he was asked to read out the text of his grandfather's speech from 1919. Nervous and freezing, he did so in a halting voice. Only then was he driven to Las Jarillas, the country house put at his disposal by Alfonso Urquijo, a friend of his father.[112]

It was an awkward moment since, on the same evening that Juan Carlos left Lisbon, Carlos Méndez, a young monarchist, died in prison in Madrid. A large group of monarchists, who had attended the funeral at the Almudena cemetery, came to Las Jarillas to greet the Prince.

Many monarchists were demoralized by what they saw as Don Juan's capitulation to Franco. The limits of the Caudillo's commitment to a Borbón restoration were starkly brought home to Don Juan when Franco refused to permit the young Prince to use the title Príncipe de Asturias. A group of tutors of firm pro-Francoist loyalty was arranged for the young Prince. Juan Carlos expected to be received by Franco on 10 November at El Pardo but because of the situation provoked by the death of Carlos Méndez, the visit was postponed. It finally took place on 24 November. The ten-year-old approached the meeting with considerable trepidation and, as he put it himself, 'understood little of what was being planned around me, but I knew very well that Franco was the man who caused such worry for my father, who was preventing his return to Spain and who allowed the papers to say such terrible things about him'. Before the boy's departure, Don Juan had given his son precise instructions: 'When you meet Franco, listen to what he tells you, but say as little as possible. Be polite and reply briefly to his questions. A mouth tight shut lets in no flies.'

The day of the visit was bitterly cold, and the sierra to the north of Madrid was covered with snow. The meeting was orchestrated with great discretion, with Danvila and Sotomayor driving Juan Carlos to El Pardo in the former's private car and without a police escort. The Prince found the palace of El Pardo imposing, with its splendidly attired Moorish Guard at all of the gates. He had never seen so many people in uniform. Franco's staff thronged the passageways of the palace, speaking always in low voices as if in church. After a lengthy walk through many gloomy salons, the Prince was finally greeted by Franco. He was rather taken aback by the rotund Caudillo who was much shorter and more pot-bellied than he had appeared in photographs. The dictator's smile seemed to him forced. He asked the boy about his father. To Juan Carlos's surprise, Franco referred to Don Juan as 'His Highness' and not 'His Majesty'. To Franco's visible annoyance, the boy replied, 'The King is well, thank you.' He enquired about Juan Carlos's studies and invited him to join him in a pheasant hunt. In fact, the young Prince was paying little attention since he was transfixed by the sight of a little mouse that was running around the legs of Franco's chair. Franco was, according to Danvila, 'delighted with the Prince'.

As the interview was drawing to a close, Sotomayor shrewdly asked whether Juan Carlos might meet Franco's wife. Doña Carmen appeared almost immediately, having been waiting for her cue. After being introduced, the Prince was taken by Franco for a tour of El Pardo, showing him, amongst other things, the bedroom in which Queen Victoria Eugenia had slept on the eve of her wedding, and which had been kept almost untouched ever since. Franco presented him with a shotgun and Juan Carlos then made his farewells. According to Danvila, in the car *en route* back to Las Jarillas, Juan Carlos said to him and Sotomayor, 'This man is really rather nice, and so is his wife, although not as much.' The Prince himself later claimed that the meeting had left no impression on him whatsoever. It is unlikely that the young Prince could have found Franco as 'nice' as Danvila reported after this first visit. Juan Carlos's family had often spoken about the Caudillo in his presence, and 'not always in complimentary terms'. In fact, as Juan Carlos's mother would later recall, the Generalísimo was often referred to as the 'little lieutenant' in their household.[113]

The publicity given to the visit was handled in such a way as to give the impression that the monarchy was subordinate to the dictator. That, along with the torpedoing of the monarchist–Socialist negotiations, had been one of the principal objectives behind the entire *Azor* operation.[114] At virtually no cost, Franco had left the moderate opposition in bitter disarray and driven a wedge between Don Juan and his most fervent and loyal supporters.[115] Danvila would later recall the furious reaction in Estoril when Don Juan heard of this first meeting between Juan Carlos and Franco. Danvila was instructed thereafter not to let the young Prince carry out visits or attend any events that could be regarded as being in any way political. That the very idea of sending the Prince to Spain was a gamble for the family was revealed in a letter from Victoria Eugenia to Danvila: 'I felt the greatest sorrow at having to be separated from the grandson that I love so much, but from the first moment that my son took the decision to send him to Spain, I respected his wishes without reservations ... I approve of the search for a new direction in our policy since what we were doing before had provided no success and I believe that without risk there can be no gain. I pray to God that my son's sacrifice produces a satisfactory result.'[116] There could be no more poignant evidence of the fact that in the Borbón family, the sense of mission stood far above political principle and emotional considerations.

Franco had created a situation in which many influential members of the conservative establishment who had wavered since 1945 would incline again towards his cause. The press was ordered to keep references to the monarchy to a minimum. In international terms, the Caudillo had cleverly made his regime appear more acceptable. In the widely publicized report of a conversation with the British Labour MP for Loughborough, Dr Mont Follick, Franco declared that it was his intention to restore the monarchy although he sidestepped the question of when.[117] In a context of growing international tension, the apparent 'normalization' of Spanish politics was eagerly greeted by the Western powers. Within less than a year, a deeply disillusioned Don Juan would order an end to the policy of conciliation.[118] By then it would be too late, Franco having squeezed all possible advantage out of the pretended closeness between them.

TWO

A Pawn Sacrificed

1949–1955

Juan Carlos's new home was Las Jarillas, a grand Andalusian-style house, 17 kilometres outside Madrid on the road to Colmenar Viejo. One reason for its selection was its proximity both to El Pardo and the military garrison at El Goloso. A special direct telephone line to the base was installed in Danvila's house in case of Falangist demonstrations against the Prince. Such daring would have been unlikely in Franco's Spain and the nearest thing to public opposition was the singing of a ditty whose chorus went: '*El que quiere una corona/que se haga de cartón/que la Corona de España/no es para ningún Borbón*' (He who wants a crown/ better get a cardboard one/for the crown of Spain/will go to no Borbón). Shortly after his arrival, the boy suffered an acute bout of flu, perhaps another occasion on which the pain of separation from his parents was manifested physically.[1] Used to absences from his family, Juan Carlos settled down relatively quickly at the school improvised for him at Las Jarillas. Although close to Madrid, it had not yet been overtaken by urban sprawl from the capital and still enjoyed an air of rural tranquillity. Its 100 hectares permitted hunting – mainly of rabbits. As it became obvious how much the Prince enjoyed shooting, he began to receive invitations to other hunts for larger prey such as wild deer and even wild boar.

Don Juan, with Franco's approval, had hand-picked a group of tutors and eight aristocratic students. Four had been chosen from amongst Spain's leading aristocratic families and others from the prosperous upper-middle classes: Alonso Álvarez de Toledo (son of the Marqués de Valdueza who, as an adult, would become an important figure in the Spanish financial world); Carlos de Borbón-Dos-Sicilias (Juan Carlos's first cousin on his mother's side, named for Juan Carlos's maternal grandfather and god-father); Jaime Carvajal y Urquijo (son of the Conde de Fontanar); Fernando Falcó y Fernández de Córdoba (later Marqués de Cubas); Agustín Carvajal y Fernández de Córdoba (who would become an airline pilot); Alfredo Gómez Torres (a Valencian who would become an agronomist); Juan José Macaya (from Barcelona, who would become an economist and financial counsellor); and José Luis Leal Maldonado (the son of naval officer who was a friend of Don Juan, he would later be an important banker and Minister of the Economy from April 1979 to June 1980).

Juan Carlos was especially fond of his cousin, Carlos de Borbón-Dos-Sicilias, and the fact that they were allowed to share a room took the edge off his initial loneliness. During the Christmas holidays after his first term at Las Jarillas, the Prince had to write an essay on his school. It revealed more than just his disregard for punctuation: 'On the day that I arrived, the boys were at the door waiting for me and I went in feeling really embarrassed with my Aunt Alicia and then we went upstairs it was a really nice room where we slept my cousin Carlos de Borbón is really nice because he is always saying daft things.'[2]

In his essay, Juan Carlos complained of how much he was obliged to study. Don Juan had given instructions that the work at Las Jarillas be hard and demanding. Years later, Juan Carlos would comment, 'Don't imagine that we were treated like kings. In fact, they made us study harder than in an ordinary school on the basis that "because we were who we were, we had to give a good example".' Certainly, Don Juan tried to ensure that his son's academic abilities were assessed as impartially as possible. At the end of the academic year, the boys would indeed sit, at the Instituto San Isidro of Madrid, the public examinations taken by all Spanish children at ordinary schools. Juan Carlos would soon grow particularly attached to two of his tutors: José Garrido Casanova, the headmaster at Las Jarillas and founder of the hospice for homeless children of Nuestra Señora de la Paloma, and Heliodoro

Ruiz Arias, the boys' sports teacher. Garrido, a good and fair man of liberal views from Granada, was a brilliant teacher and warm and sympathetic human being. He made a profound impression on the Prince. Years later, Juan Carlos would say, 'Sometimes, when I have to take certain decisions, I still ask myself what he would have advised me to do.' Heliodoro had, in the 1930s, been the personal trainer of José Antonio Primo de Rivera. He saw in the young Prince great athletic potential and set himself the task of converting him into an all-round sportsman.[3]

Jaime Carvajal later came to the conclusion that their headmaster was 'a key figure in the formation of Don Juan Carlos's personality, after his father or even at the same level as Don Juan'. It was inevitable that, having been sent away by his own father, the boy would latch on to an appropriate father figure. Garrido had the sensitivity to realize that the Prince would be disorientated and confused after the brusque separation from his family. Accordingly, he treated Juan Carlos with real affection. Each night, he would check that he was comfortable, make a sign of the cross on his forehead and, after asking if he needed anything, turn out the light. He was quickly made aware of the sadness that the boy felt as a result of his situation. His father had given him a letter to hand over to Garrido. In it, he gave the teacher instructions about how he wanted his son to be educated. They read it together and, when they reached the part in which Don Juan spoke of his son's responsibilities as representative of the family, tears appeared in the Prince's eyes. It was a brutal reminder that his official position as Prince took precedent over the needs of a little boy trying to be brave. Garrido often noticed Juanito gazing sadly into the distance and then, as if realizing that he had no right to nostalgia, suddenly jumping up and riding his bike or taking out his frustrations on a football.

The Prince always endeavoured to hide his feelings but Garrido later recalled how much Juan Carlos enjoyed reading *Platero y yo* by Juan Ramón Jiménez, carrying the book with him everywhere he went during his first months at the school. One evening, the boy recited by heart a passage from the book as they watched the sunset. He startled Garrido by saying, 'Mummy is on the other side.' Garrido was moved and grew very fond of him, commenting years later, 'This child radiated affection despite the fact that they only ever spoke to him about duties and responsibilities.' Garrido took particular interest in ensuring that the Prince's relations with his classmates and with servants and gardeners were as natural as possible. In 1969, when Juan Carlos was named royal successor by Franco, he wrote to Garrido the following note: 'I remember you with the greatest affection and every day allows me better to measure what I owe to you. You have helped me a lot with your example and your advice. And the counsels you gave to me were as good as they were numerous.'[4]

In contrast, Juan Carlos would later admit to an aversion for the dour Father Ignacio de Zulueta, an aristocratic Basque priest who visited Las Jarillas three times a week to supervise the children's ethical and religious education. Tall and gaunt as if he had stepped down from an El Greco canvas, Zulueta was a forbidding figure. He had been recommended to Don Juan by the Duque de Sotomayor and Danvila because he represented the most conservative strand of Francoist thinking. Deeply reactionary, obsessed with royal protocol, Zulueta insisted on the entire class calling the young Prince by the title of 'Your Highness'.[5] Juan Carlos, desperate to be treated as an equal by his classmates, preferred that they call him 'Juanito' and used the informal '*tú*' form of address. Accordingly, Zulueta's instruction was usually ignored by the boys.[6]

Juan Carlos's classmates at Las Jarillas remember him as a fun-loving child, who worked hard at his academic assignments, was an average student, excelled at sports, and was open and generous.[7] As a result, Juan Carlos made solid friendships at his new school. This was underlined by the fact that none of the boys from Las Jarillas would later try to exploit their relationship with the King. It was also shown in the warmth with which they still spoke of Juan Carlos, 50 years later. In 1998, on Juan Carlos's 60th birthday, a Spanish magazine interviewed the King's old school friends. Alonso Álvarez de Toledo recalled how, although they were aware of Juan Carlos's importance at the time (if only because he often received illustrious visitors), they soon accepted him as one of the gang. Jaime Carvajal y Urquijo agreed, describing the young Juan Carlos as 'an ordinary kid, joyful, naughty, with a heart of gold, a wonderful companion'. Juan Carlos's cousin, Carlos de Borbón-Dos-Sicilias, recalled being surprised at the time by Juan Carlos's acute intuition and by his already highly developed sense of responsibility. He also recalled how little spare time they had at Las Jarillas, spending, as they did, most of their hours studying or playing sports. According to Carlos de Borbón, Juan Carlos and Jaime Carvajal were the best sportsmen, the latter being the most academically gifted of the group.[8]

The day at Las Jarillas began with daily mass at which Juan Carlos often served as an altar boy. This was followed by the ritual raising of the Spanish flag. Although classes followed the general Spanish curriculum, there was – as might have been expected of a school whose teachers were all fervent monarchists – a degree of laxity when it came to Francoist political indoctrination. Fernando Falcó y Fernández de Córdoba remembered that, when they sat the exam for what the regime called 'Formación del Espíritu Nacional' (Formation of the National Spirit), none of the class knew the Falangist hymn 'Cara al sol' by heart. To avoid the scandal that this might provoke in Franco's Spain, the exam question was magically replaced by another. The children were also given the opportunity to experience some aspects of ordinary life at Las Jarillas. José Luis Leal Maldonado recalled that the Las Jarillas football team always lost to the visiting team of the Las Palomas school. Juan José Macaya recalled a day when the boys discovered a hen house in the grounds of the estate. In spite of – or perhaps in reaction to – the discipline enforced at the school, they proceeded to kill several hens.[9]

In spite of Juan Carlos's apparent contentment, certain aspects of his new life in Spain must have been difficult. Outside monarchist circles, his arrival in Spain had been greeted by some with a wave of ill feeling. With the exception of the monarchist daily ABC, the controlled press had marked his arrival with a series of articles featuring malicious and laconic comments about the young Prince, as well as carefully selected, mostly blurry photographs which made him look devious and sly.[10] Rumours were spread to the effect that the young Prince was a sadist who watered the plants at Las Jarillas with lime in order to kill them.[11] Already at the age of ten, he was obliged to devote many hours to replying to the many cards and letters that arrived for him. He also served an apprenticeship in the boring business of official audiences for the endless streams of monarchists who, after securing the appropriate permission from the Duque de Sotomayor, visited him. Among them was the ineffable General José Millán Astray who arrived accompanied by his permanent escort of Legionnaires. He startled the Prince by shouting, 'Highness! May the Virgin protect us.' The tedium was mitigated by the obligatory gifts which ranged from boxes of chocolates to a magnificent electric car.[12]

A week before the end of his first term, Juan Carlos was visited by the monarchist General Antonio Aranda, a Nationalist hero of the Civil War. Aranda took notes of their conversation: 'the boy is very likeable, lively and intelligent. I was utterly charmed by him since I thought he would be more sullen and he's quite the opposite. He asked me about the Army and aeroplanes. This is what excites him and when I explained things to him in detail, he was really pleased. Just then, from the downstairs room where we were talking, we spotted a group of overdressed ladies and gentlemen arriving and the Prince, with total spontaneity and frankness, burst out, "What a drag! They're coming to interrupt us! Weren't you really having a good time telling me all this stuff? I know I was enjoying listening to you. Why don't those people just go away?"' The Duque de Sotomayor glided in to inform the Prince that he had to receive these new visitors. It was indicative of the ambiguous loyalties of the supposed supporters of Don Juan that Aranda's notes soon found their way onto Franco's desk.[13]

At the end of term, Juan Carlos returned home to Estoril for the Christmas holidays. Towards the end of December, José María Gil Robles took his own children and Juan Carlos to the zoo in Lisbon. With great sensibility, he reflected on the power struggle between Don Juan and Franco, in which the Prince played the role of shuttlecock. Gil Robles was struck by Juan Carlos's subdued and sombre demeanour: 'He is still just a child and entirely

likeable, but I find him serious beyond his years and even rather
sad, as though he were aware of the battle being fought over him.
Watching him play in the park yesterday, and later at home, I
could not avoid a feeling of sorrow. He is a loveable child. When
I think about his future, I feel real compassion for him. What does
the future hold for this little boy who, at the age of ten, is the
object of such a bitter struggle?'[14]

In January 1949, Juan Carlos returned to Las Jarillas. However, his sojourn there was dependent on the continuing ceasefire
between his father and the dictator. Hostilities were once more
imminent. Gil Robles complained bitterly that Franco was failing
to fulfil any of the promises made to Don Juan on the *Azor*.
Instructions had been issued that any references to Don Juan had
to be to 'His Highness the Conde de Barcelona' which appalled
the monarchists who referred to him as 'His Majesty King Juan
III'. Juan Carlos was denied the right to use his proper title of
Príncipe de Asturias, and was to be referred to only as 'His Royal
Highness Prince Juan Carlos'.[15] Throughout 1949, the relationship
between Franco and Don Juan deteriorated and Juan Carlos would
be the victim. Although Gil Robles and Sainz Rodríguez continually urged Don Juan to recognize that Franco would never make
way for the monarchy, he continued to hope, on the basis of the
blandishments of Danvila.

The Caudillo made occasional token gestures to ingratiate himself with monarchists, by giving the impression that he was devoted
to their cause. Although determined never to cede power to Don
Juan, Franco wanted to maintain the credibility bestowed by the
link with him. At the end of February, for instance, he attended
a mass in El Escorial on the anniversary of the death of Alfonso
XIII and was extremely anxious to secure the presence of Juan
Carlos at the annual parade to commemorate the Nationalist victory in the Civil War. According to Gil Robles, 'He is determined
that the Prince should watch the parade from a special tribune,
lower than his own. The troops in the march-past will be ordered
to render him full honours.' Under intense pressure from Gil
Robles, Don Juan informed a disappointed Danvila that his son
would not be attending the parade.[16] On 18 May 1949, at the

opening of the Cortes, as if in retaliation, Franco made a long, rambling, self-congratulatory speech including, *en passant*, disparaging remarks about Alfonso XIII and his mother Queen María Cristina.[17] As a result, Don Juan's more militant supporters urged Juan Carlos's immediate return to Estoril.

Oblivious to the gathering storm clouds, Juan Carlos returned to Estoril at the end of May 1949 for summer holidays which would last for nearly 17 months. At the beginning of July, Don Juan wrote to Eugenio Vegas Latapié, inviting him to Portugal and commenting, 'Juanito is back from Spain full of the joys of spring. He always remembers you with great affection.' Juan Carlos himself wrote to Vegas Latapié on 17 July, repeating the invitation. After a cruise in the Mediterranean with the entire family, Don Juan left for a hunting party in Scotland on 23 August. Vegas arrived at about the same time and spent nearly a month with Juan Carlos, one day taking him to see a doctor because he had broken a finger. When asked how he broke it, the boy replied 'thumping my sister Pilar'.[18] In opposition to the views of Gil Robles and Sainz Rodríguez, Queen Victoria Eugenia believed that Juan Carlos should return to Las Jarillas after the summer holidays. She was concerned that the boy's life should not be turned upside down yet again although, in her determination to see her family once more on the throne in Madrid, she also inclined to Danvila's view that Franco should be placated at all costs. Juan Carlos remained in Estoril while Don Juan dithered.

However, many of his supporters, including the Duque de Alba, Franco's wartime Ambassador in London, expressed outrage at Franco's exploitation of his good will. Gil Robles and Sainz Rodríguez worked at persuading Don Juan to drop the duplicitous Danvila and to refuse to allow Juan Carlos to return to Spain. He finally made up his mind after a long conversation with Gil Robles on 26 September 1949. Attempting to put some backbone into his master, Gil Robles baldly pointed out that his collaboration with Franco had severely undermined his credibility. The same man who had been moved by Juan Carlos's sadness some months earlier now said, 'Your Majesty must consider that the Prince is the only weapon that he has left against Franco. If you agree in the same terms as last year, you will be disarmed for good.' Yet again it was obvious that, in Estoril, the needs of a future monarchical restoration would always be of far greater importance than the needs of the child. Don Juan was finally shaken out of his indecision when the plain-speaking Gil Robles made a prophetic warning: 'Do not think you are indispensable. Within a few years, many will be placing their hopes on the Prince: some in good faith; others out of sheer ambition.'[19]

At the end of September 1949, Don Juan sent a note, drafted by Gil Robles, informing Franco that, since the agreements made during the *Azor* meeting had not been fulfilled, the Prince could not remain in Spain.[20] Franco responded threateningly in mid-October, with a lengthy note, 'whose two principal characteristics,' noted Gil Robles, 'are overweening arrogance and bad grammar.' Denying that he had made any promises on the *Azor*, Franco stated that the benefits of Juan Carlos's presence in Spain were all on the side of the royal family but also made it clear that he had no plans to replace the dictatorship. His messenger, the servile Danvila, also passed on the Caudillo's demand that, during his forthcoming State visit to Portugal, Don Juan should pay him a courtesy call at the Palacio de Queluz. Made aware by Gil Robles that this would simply lead to his public humiliation, Don Juan declined. Franco insisted, even going so far as instructing his brother Nicolás to threaten Don Juan that the Cortes would pass a law specifically excluding him from the throne. Don Juan's snub was the only blot on a spectacular public relations success for Franco. He had arrived in Portugal on the battlecruiser *Miguel de Cervantes* at the head of a flotilla of 11 warships. The Caudillo's chagrin may be imagined when he discovered that, as the Spanish fleet left the Tagus estuary, Admiral Moreno, realizing that Don Juan was wistfully watching from the shore, had ordered the ship's company to form up and render him full honours.[21]

Don Juan felt troubled that his son would not be returning to Spain. After all, he believed that it was important that Juan Carlos should be educated as a Spaniard in the country over which, one day, he was destined to reign. At the back of his mind was the preoccupation, prompted by the insidious Danvila, that in keeping

Juan Carlos in Portugal he might be ruining the family's chance of a return to the throne. Gil Robles suspected that he was seeking any pretext to send his son back to Las Jarillas. Certainly, he had made no alternative preparations for the resumption of the child's education in Estoril. In consequence, the 1949–1950 academic year must have been a depressing one for the nearly 12-year-old Juan Carlos. It was good to be back with his family, although Don Juan was often away travelling or hunting. Having coped with separation a year before by becoming closely attached to his classmates at Las Jarillas, he had been torn away from them and now missed them. Kept together as a cohort in the hope that he would eventually rejoin them, they had been moved, for the 1949–1950 academic year, to the ground floor of the palace belonging to the Duque and Duquesa de Montellano in Madrid's Paseo de la Castellana.

In Portugal, Juan Carlos had to make do with work arranged by the stern Father Zulueta or sent by José Garrido and he rattled around Villa Giralda, missing the friends that he had made in Spain. He was too young to understand why he had been separated from them but not too young to resent it. The disruption to his education and his life again showed how little he mattered within the bigger diplomatic game. It is impossible to calculate how the callous exploitation of his person affected Juan Carlos's attitude to his father. However, the frequency with which he later spoke of certain individuals being 'like a second father' is revealing. Such references would include, bizarrely, Franco, and, much more understandably, José Garrido, and later, the man who would run his household in Spain, Nicolás Cotoner, the Marqués de Mondé-jar. Although he always spoke respectfully of Don Juan, perhaps subconsciously Juan Carlos felt that his father had not behaved towards him in the way that a 'real father' should.

The boy's depressing situation at Villa Giralda was exacerbated by anxieties about his godfather and grandfather, Carlos de Borbón-Dos-Sicilias, who was gravely ill. Doña María de las Mercedes was desperate to go to Seville to be at the bedside of her dying father. However, in a gratuitously humiliating gesture, Franco denied her permission to enter Spain until the very last moment. When Don Carlos's situation worsened, she set off anyway but arrived too late. Carlos de Borbón-Dos-Sicilias died on 11 November 1949, and Doña María would always hold a grudge against Franco. Years later, she said, 'I can forgive anything, but Franco, whom I defended in other things to the point of falling out with my friends, I could never forgive for the way he treated my father and for what he did to prevent me arriving in time to see him before he died.' While at Las Jarillas, Juan Carlos had often spent weekends in Seville with his grandfather. On 14 November, Juan Carlos wrote to one of his friends: 'I'm sad because of granddad's death and Mummy is in Seville.' He was slightly distracted by the arrival of his electric car from Las Jarillas.[22]

Don Juan continued to waver over his son's future. Gil Robles advised him not to send Juan Carlos back to Spain, since his presence would be exploited by Franco. Sainz Rodríguez suggested that arrangements for the 1950–1951 academic year could be proposed by the *Diputación de la Grandeza* (a kind of central committee of the Spanish aristocracy). To make matters worse for Juan Carlos and his father, in December 1949, Don Jaime de Borbón announced that he considered invalid his 1933 renunciation of his rights to the throne on the highly dubious grounds that his physical incapacity had been cured. He attributed this 'miracle' to the love of his new German 'wife', Carlotte Tiedemann, a hard-drinking operetta singer. Gil Robles was convinced that Franco was behind this manoeuvre. It was believed that the Caudillo had paid Don Jaime to make his announcement, resolving his immediate debts and providing him with a substantial allowance. Certainly, Franco was looking into ways in which he could make use of Don Jaime's ambitions.[23] His claim to the throne put pressure on Don Juan now, as it would later on Juan Carlos. In the short term, it seemed to determine Don Juan – shortly before disappearing on another hunting jaunt – that his son, who was still without teachers, would continue his education at Estoril, under the alternating supervision of Father Zulueta and José Garrido.[24]

During a stay in Rome in March 1950, Don Juan was visited

by Padre Josémaría Escrivá de Balaguer, the founder of the Opus
Dei. Escrivá believed that holiness could be achieved through ordinary work and had created a corps of militant Christians who
through austerity, celibacy and devotion to professional excellence
lived in a kind of virtual monastery within the real world. At the
time, Escrivá was residing in Italy while endeavouring to secure
full recognition from the Vatican for the Opus Dei. He was also
extremely keen to clinch the support of Franco, for whom he had
begun to supervise spiritual retreats at El Pardo in 1944. Now,
he reproached Don Juan for keeping his son in Portugal, saying
that he was badly advised and ill-informed about the real situation
in Spain. He urged him to return the Prince to Spain where he
could get a proper patriotic education. Escrivá's notes of the conversation were dutifully forwarded to Franco. It is probable that
at this encounter were sown the seeds of the Opus Dei's later
participation in the education of Juan Carlos.[25] Don Juan was
looking for a Catholic framework for his son's development.
Initially, he had hoped for the involvement of the Jesuits. Through
Danvila, contacts were made with the Spanish province of the
Society of Jesus and it was agreed in principle that Jesuits would
be chosen as teachers for the Prince. However, when permission
was sought from the Vicar General of the Society, the Belgian
Father Jean Baptiste Janssens, he issued categoric orders that the
proposal was to be rejected. When the request was repeated,
he explained that in the experience of the Society of Jesus, the
education of royal personages had been 'pernicious'.[26]

Finally, in the autumn of 1950, convinced that he had made
his point with Franco, Don Juan allowed Juan Carlos to resume
his education in Spain. This time, his eldest son was accompanied
by his brother, Alfonsito. A new school was set up, not at Las
Jarillas, but at the palace of Miramar, the old summer residence
of the royal family on the bay of San Sebastián, in the Basque
Country. Don Juan seemed to be hoping that distance might diminish the influence of Franco. Again, he made some effort to ensure
that his two sons' academic abilities would be evaluated impartially. The boys at Miramar were thus required to sit, at the end of
each academic year, the official exams taken by other children at

ordinary schools. Having said that, the 'normality' was relative. The examinations were oral and public. When Juan Carlos attended for examination at the Instituto San Isidro in Madrid, his answers had a large crowd breaking into enthusiastic applause. Afterwards, he was seen leaving the examination hall through a great throng of police and clapping well-wishers. The entire process was gushingly reported in the monarchist daily *ABC*.[27]

The 16 boys at the school were divided into two groups, one of Juan Carlos's age and the other of Alfonso's contemporaries. The older group contained several of Juan Carlos's pals from Las Jarillas – Jaime de Carvajal y Urquijo, José Luis Leal Maldonado, Alfredo Gómez Torres, Alonso Álvarez de Toledo, and Juan José Macaya. Aurora Gómez Delgado (the French tutor, nurse and housekeeper at Miramar) would later recall that the section of the Miramar palace that housed the school was very beautiful, but also extremely cold. There was no central heating, just one stove on each of the three floors. The permanent teaching staff resided with the boys at Miramar. José Garrido Casanova acted again as headmaster. The stern Father Ignacio de Zulueta taught Latin and religious education, and also organized their weekend outings. Father Zulueta said daily mass at which he would deliver a reactionary sermon. The children would later recall occasions on which Zulueta made them pray for the conversion of the Soviet Union or for the victory of the British Conservative Party in the 1950 elections. In the midst of this particular sermon, Juan Carlos stuck a needle into the bottom of one of his classmates, Carlos Benjumea, whose cry of pain secured him a ferocious dressing-down from the furious priest.

Aurora Gómez Delgado was the only woman on the full-time teaching staff. In addition, a group of non-resident part-time teachers came in a few hours a week to teach specialist subjects such as music, physics and gymnastics. Amongst them was Mrs Mary Watt, who started teaching English to the children in their third year at Miramar.[28] One of the reasons for Mrs Watt's late arrival at Miramar may well have been Juan Carlos's self-confessed reluctance to learn English – the consequence in part of the education he had received at the hands of Eugenio Vegas Latapié,

Julio Danvila, Father Zulueta and other Spanish reactionaries. In a 1978 interview for *Welt am Sonntag*, he explained that: 'For patriotic reasons I was predisposed against England and I refused to learn the language. My father used to reprimand me for this, as did my grandmother and my teachers. We had lunch with the Queen of England and my father said to Elizabeth II: "Sit next to him so that he feels ashamed at being unable to answer your questions." That is precisely what happened. I felt deeply ashamed at only being able to speak in French with the Queen, and realized that patriotism had to manifest itself in other ways and that I had to learn English no matter how much it outraged me to do so.' Juan Carlos would take a long time to master the English language. By his own admission, the early days of his engagement to Sofía were complicated by the fact that his English was still quite poor and she spoke no Spanish.[29]

Aurora Gómez Delgado claimed later that Juan Carlos's worst subject was mathematics – a view confirmed by his maths teacher, Carlos Santamaría. He remained indifferent to the Francoist doctrine imparted in the *Formación del Espíritu Nacional*, writing to his father on 31 January 1954: 'Today the text books for political formation have arrived and they are unbelievably boring, both for sixth and fourth year but, since we have to get stuck in whether we like it or not, we'll just have to study it all with patience.' Despite his block about English, Aurora was struck by the young Prince's extraordinary gift for foreign languages. She noted too a clear leaning towards the humanities, in particular towards history and literature. Juan Carlos remained passionate about Juan Ramón Jiménez's *Platero y yo* and allegedly showed a highly improbable predilection for Molière and French philosophers such as Descartes and Rousseau. During the holidays, like many boys of his age, he would, more appropriately, read adventure stories by Salgari. Juan Carlos also showed a keen interest in music. He enjoyed classical music, Rachmaninov, Beethoven, Bach as well as Spanish zarzuela, but also contemporary music, Mexican *rancheras* and the hit songs of the day. He would often be heard walking down the corridors singing popular tunes. Excursions within San Sebastián included trips to the stadium of Real Sociedad, where

Juan Carlos was able to indulge his support for Real Madrid when they played in the Basque city. His brother Alfonsito supported Atlético de Madrid. Juan Carlos was most notable at Miramar as a keen and gifted sportsman, who enjoyed horse-riding, tennis, swimming and hockey on rollerskates.[30] In 1951, the staff was joined by Ángel López Amo, a young Opus Dei member and professor of the History of Law at the University of Santiago de Compostela. This would be one of the first fruits of Don Juan's meeting in Rome with Padre Escrivá de Balaguer. It constituted the practical beginning of the strong Opus Dei influence in the life of the Prince.

Although it no longer interrupted his schooling, the tension between Don Juan and Franco did not diminish during Juan Carlos's stay at Miramar. The Caudillo's international position was improving through ongoing negotiations with the United States to bring Spain into the Western defensive system. As his confidence grew, Franco's tendency to behave as if he were King of Spain increased. On 10 April 1950, his beloved daughter Carmen married a minor society playboy from Jaén, Dr Cristóbal Martínez-Bordiu, soon to be the Marqués de Villaverde. The preparations and the accumulation of presents were on a massive scale. The press was ordered to say nothing for fear of provoking unwelcome contrasts with the famine and poverty which afflicted much of the country.[31] The wedding itself was on a level of extravagance that would have taxed any European royal family. Guards of honour, military bands, and hundreds of guests including all members of the cabinet, the diplomatic corps and a glittering array of aristocrats, took part in a full-scale State occasion.

The Soviet acquisition of the atomic bomb, the Chinese revolution and outbreak of the Korean War in June 1950 had increased Franco's value in the eyes of the Western powers. On the other hand, the regime had suffered considerable domestic erosion as a result of the recent massive strikes in Barcelona and the Basque Country in March and April. Feeling that the scale of domestic opposition might have made Franco open to negotiation, on 10 July 1951, Don Juan wrote him a letter that would have enormous repercussions both for himself and his son. In it, he managed to squander years of sacrifice and opposition to the regime yet gain nothing in return. Franco was outraged by Don Juan's comments about the 'attrition' inflicted on the regime by the strikes. Having blamed the strikes on foreign agitators, the Caudillo was even more annoyed by Don Juan's suggestion that they were the consequence of the economic situation and government corruption. Franco had no interest whatsoever in Don Juan's offer of a negotiated transition as a route that would allow him to consolidate his work within the stability of a monarchy that could unite all Spaniards. Don Juan's letter achieved the worst of both worlds. On the one hand, it merely stimulated the venom of Franco, because it criticized his regime and insisted on the need for national reconciliation – an idea that was anathema to the Caudillo. On the other, Don Juan was abandoning his past championship of a democratic monarchy and accepting the *Movimiento*. Despite the unctuous intervention of Danvila, Franco rudely delayed replying for two months. His long letter on 14 September 1951 was both disdainful and cruel.

Franco simply ignored the offer of negotiation within the *Movimiento*, expressing in the most patronizing terms his outrage that Don Juan had dared to criticize him. The scale of insult was breathtaking. Accusing Don Juan of 'ignorance of the Spanish situation', and dismissing his comments on the economy as 'inane', the Caudillo brushed aside his criticisms of the conditions in Spain with self-satisfied references to the 'indisputable triumph of Spain's policy in the international media'. He claimed that he had selflessly committed Spain to the idea of monarchy, but built in safeguards against the dangers of hereditary monarchy throwing up an incapable heir: 'Precisely because I consider the monarchical institution to be tied to our history and the best way to secure the revival and the greatness of our Fatherland, even though I was under no obligation to do so, I set the nation down that road and I recommended that Spain be constituted as a monarchy in the great plebiscite in which the nation unanimously endorsed the fundamental laws of the Fatherland. However, in so doing, I needed to guarantee the Spanish nation that the possible deficiencies of individuals would never bring about crises in our institutions as happened twice in the past' – references to the collapse of the monarchy on 11 February 1873 and 14 April 1931.

Having claimed that the *Ley de Sucesión* elevated the institution of monarchy above the defects of the hereditary principle (that is to say, by leaving the choice of king in his hands), Franco went on, rather bizarrely, to suggest that there was no support for the monarchy in Spain and claimed that the only reason there was any hope for a monarchical future was because the Spanish people had listened, as he put it, to 'the authoritative voice of he who gloriously led them in the Crusade and dexterously steered Spain through the stormy seas of the universal revolution in which we live'. Don Juan had referred to his efforts to join the Nationalist forces during the Civil War. Franco loftily scorned the idea that this constituted 'identification with the *Movimiento*'. His outrage was evident in the statement that: 'You are mistaken in thinking that the regime needs to seek a way out since it actually represents the stable way out of centuries of decadence. What other regime could have survived the harsh test of two wars and the international plot to which Spain was subjected?'

Regarding Don Juan's allusion to 'the historic laws of succession', Franco rejected the hereditary principle, stating that the *Ley de Sucesión* made no a priori assumptions about 'the dynasty or line with the best rights'. He went on to inform Don Juan of his hope that, 'when the time comes, if it were in the interests of our Fatherland or even of the monarchy itself, you would follow the patriot path of renunciation, of which your august father gave an example when he abdicated his rights in favour of Your Highness, just as the King of Belgium has done recently or as the King of England did'. He raised this matter because, 'a large number of Spanish monarchists, in the light of how your public acts are repelling great swathes of the country and undermining your good name, recognizing that the monarchy can come back only through the will of the *Movimiento*, begin to see in your renunciation in favour of your son a way, when the right time comes, of helping me perhaps to declare in favour of your dynasty, of your branch, when the dynastic problem is finally resolved.' Thus, after this devastating bombshell – that even if Don Juan were to abdicate, there would be no guarantees for Juan Carlos – he made it quite clear that his concern was simply the continuity of the regime after his death. That being the case, the Lausanne Manifesto and subsequent evidence of Don Juan's democratic proclivities had eliminated him as a possible successor.[32]

Utterly mortified by this letter, Don Juan cut off all communication with Franco for the next three years. During this time, the Caudillo decided on a strategy of encouraging the emergence of rivals to Juan Carlos and his father. This was to intensify the pressure on Don Juan, generally muddy the waters and diminish Falangist fears of an eventual Borbón restoration. In October 1952, through his Ambassador in Paris, the Conde de Casa Rojas, Franco approached Don Jaime, who, three years earlier, had reneged on his 1933 decision to renounce his rights to the throne. Franco had no difficulty in persuading the still impecunious Don Jaime that his son and heir, Alfonso de Borbón y Dampierre, should be educated in Spain, under the regime's supervision. Don Jaime was enticed by the prospect of permanent freedom from debt through regular financial support from the regime as well as by the possibility of re-establishing his own, or at least his son's, claim to the throne. Initially, Alfonso had no inclination to do what his father wished. His mother, Emmanuela Dampierre, had been estranged from his father long before they formally separated in 1946. Alfonso and his brother Gonzalo had been brought up by their mother, which effectively meant a life in boarding schools. Alfonso in particular resented his father. Nevertheless, he was even more deeply resentful at his penniless position, and in 1954 the now 18-year-old Don Alfonso finally accepted the plan and enrolled for a law degree at the Jesuit University of Deusto, in Bilbao.[33]

Meanwhile, Juan Carlos continued his education at Miramar. He was often homesick and looked forward to his holidays at Estoril. He admitted later to biting his nails as a result of his anxieties. Nevertheless, his four years at Miramar seem to have been reasonably contented ones. Originally, it was assumed that he would share a room with his brother but, because of the natural sibling rivalries between a 12-year-old and his younger brother, they ended up being separated, and Jaime Carvajal moved in with Juan Carlos. The routine at Miramar was harsh. The children had little time to themselves. They were woken each day at 7.30 a.m. with the ringing of a bell and required to go straight into the garden in order to hoist the flag. This was followed by mass and a sermon from Miramar's chaplain. Only then would the boys have breakfast and begin their morning classes. At the end of the morning, there was a short break before lunch. Lessons resumed at 4 p.m., until another brief break in the evening, followed by supper and study time. Discipline was strict. On one occasion, when he had been given lines for some infraction, he said to the maths teacher, Carlos Santamaría, 'When I'm King, I'm going to get so-and-so' (a reference to the teacher who had punished him). 'Not you. I'll make you Chancellor of the Exchequer.' The Prince had no doubts that one day he would succeed his father on the throne.

Aurora Gómez Delgado remembered Juan Carlos as an affable extrovert, who had his ups and downs like any ordinary boy, but who adapted easily to Miramar and was definitely not a 'difficult child'. When Juan Carlos was free from other obligations, he indulged his passion for photography or played chess. He enjoyed playing football and got into quarrels like other boys, but he was also very conscious of his status: 'He knew perfectly well that he was there in order to learn his profession.' In fact, Juan Carlos was, according to his French teacher, capable of showing an unusual degree of self-restraint when necessary, never allowing himself to cry in public. Juan Carlos also manifested a keen desire to talk to people of all walks of life, a taste that he was able to indulge during the weekend outings. None of the children at Miramar had much pocket money, and Juan Carlos was no exception. On occasions, the young Prince would write letters taking advantage of both the horizontal and the vertical space, so as to save paper.[34]

In a 1995 interview, Juan Carlos's mother suggested that Juan Carlos and his brother Alfonsito had always got on well. However, it is noteworthy that neither Juan Carlos himself nor those, like his French teacher, who recorded their memories of Miramar, had anything to say about the relationship during their time together there.[35] Aurora Gómez Delgado was however very aware of the deep attachment that Juan Carlos felt towards his mother. She telephoned him often from Estoril. When he was told that she was on the line, he would run down the corridor shouting, 'Mummy, Mummy!' Of Juan Carlos's relationship with his father at this time, the French teacher hinted at its stiff formality when she said only that, 'In addition to giving him fatherly advice, he behaved towards him as a friend.' There seems to have been a regular correspondence with his parents throughout his stay. The tone was loving if rather formal. Curiously those from Don Juan were somewhat more affectionate, ending, typically, 'Until the next, my beloved sons, with a big hug from your loving father,' or, 'With greetings to your teachers and classmates, and a hug for Alfonsito, and another for you with the love and affection of your father Juan.' Those from his mother were slightly more stilted – 'Good-bye, beloved children, hoping to see you soon, if God wills. A big hug from your Mummy who blesses you both. María.'[36] All things considered, Juan Carlos's four years at Miramar were relatively happy ones marred only by separation from his family and by attacks on his father in the press.

Franco had always given vent to his antipathy towards Don Juan through his total control of the Spanish press. *Arriba* and other *Movimiento* newspapers were free to make regular insinuations that the monarchists were disloyal to the regime. In January 1954, the hostility reached new heights. In December 1953, Don Juan's close friend and second cousin, Lord Mountbatten, at the time Admiral of the NATO Mediterranean fleet, had invited him to observe from the flagship major manoeuvres planned for January 1954. As an honorary Royal Navy officer, Don Juan was keen to accept. On the other hand, with tension growing between Britain and Spain over Gibraltar, he feared that the *Movimiento* press would distort the reasons for his presence and link anti-monarchist with anti-British propaganda. In the event, on the advice of Gil Robles, who reminded him that this was a NATO operation, he decided to attend. As had been expected, a hostile press campaign was unleashed in which the NATO dimension was totally ignored. The manoeuvres were presented as a threatening gesture by British naval forces and it was implied that Don Juan was selling out to London over Gibraltar. 'Don Juan de Borbón in the Royal Navy. The French press reveals that Don Juan de Borbón has arrived in Malta where he has boarded the twelve-thousand-ton cruiser HMS *Glasgow*, from which he will follow the English manoeuvres in the Mediterranean. Don Juan de Borbón has been an honorary lieutenant in the Royal Navy since 1936.' This 'news item' was accompanied by an editorial which described the manoeuvres as an outrageous provocation intended to remind the people of Spain that: 'Gibraltar is the thorn that has kept blood flowing since the iniquitous theft of 1704.' The pupils at Miramar followed the entire affair in the press. Juan Carlos was inevitably distressed and, for a time, it appeared as if the school might have to be closed down.[37]

By the summer of 1954, Juan Carlos had completed his second-ary education. Shortly afterwards, Don Juan received two assess-ments of the boy's character. The first was sent by Jesús Pabón y Suárez de Urbina, the distinguished monarchist historian who had chaired the board (tribunal) before which the Prince faced his oral examinations. The second came from the Conde de Fontanar, a close friend of Don Juan and a man free of personal political ambition. As father of Jaime Carvajal, the Prince's room-mate at Miramar, and having frequently welcomed the Prince as a guest in his home, he knew Juan Carlos well. The contrasts between these reports were illuminating. Pabón wrote: 'The impression that Juan Carlos produces and leaves behind him is of being, fundamentally, kind.' Fontanar went into more detail, describing the Prince as: 'generous, affectionate, biddable, kindly, unassum-ing, incapable of bearing a grudge, likeable, courageous, good-looking and with an aptitude for physical exercises'. Fontanar also underlined the fact that the Prince 'treats ordinary folk with simple affability'. Pabón noted Juan Carlos's 'genuine lack of pretence'.

Having seen Juan Carlos only in this formal setting, as a teacher examining him, Pabón naturally noted his nervousness and insecurity, and photographs of the boy from this period substan-tiate the professor's conclusions. Pabón wrote: 'The Prince is naturally shy and, like all shy people, he over-compensates for his shyness by reacting with a certain vehemence and even violence in his expressions, his gestures or his words.' Pabón saw the Prince's younger brother Alfonsito as being altogether more uninhibited and spontaneous, partly because of his great natural intelligence and also because he did not live weighed down by responsibilities. For Pabón, the cure for Juan Carlos lay in the acquisition of greater self-confidence. That, of course, was something in which his father could play a part, but Don Juan had a tendency to be critical and off-hand with his son.

For Fontanar, the problems with the Prince lay elsewhere. He had had far greater opportunity to observe the boy in his own home alongside his own son Jaime, who was academically outstanding. Like other observers of the schoolboy in Fribourg and at Las Jarillas, Fontanar perceived a degree of indiscipline – which may well have reflected a natural strength of character or a minor rebellion against the constant separations from his family. Contrary to the pious reflections of his teachers (made when Juan Carlos was King), Fontanar noted that the Prince had no interest in culture and read little, not even the press. At times, he complained, the boy seemed thoughtless, selfish and superficial. Accordingly, for Fontanar, what was required was to imbue him with a greater sense of duty.[38] Time and the boy's circumstances would take care of that.

The completion of the Prince's secondary education raised the question of where he would be sent next, since both Don Juan and Franco saw the decision as a weapon in their ongoing trial of strength. Already in the spring, Don Juan had discussed with Gil Robles the possibility of sending Juan Carlos to the Catholic University of Louvain in Belgium. Convinced that he had to differentiate the line of the monarchy from that of the Franco regime, Don Juan sent Gil Robles to Louvain in May to prepare the way.[39] Nevertheless, as Pedro Sainz Rodríguez pointed out, and Don Juan knew only too well, if acceptable terms could be negotiated, it made more sense for the Prince to be educated in Spain. Sainz Rodríguez advised Don Juan that Franco needed the Prince in Spain and could be manoeuvred into paying a price – a publicly acknowledged interview that would strengthen the image of the crown inside Spain. Thus advised, Don Juan threw down the gauntlet in a note sent to Franco on 16 June 1954. In it, he informed the Caudillo of his decision to send his son to Louvain. Juan Carlos later told his authorized biographer, the monarchist playboy José Luis de Vilallonga, that Don Juan was also toying with the idea of sending him to the University of Bologna.[40]

Coincidentally, when Don Juan's letter reached him, Franco was already engaged in composing a memorandum in which he outlined an elaborate scheme for the Prince's future education. Through the pompous language and cynical remarks could be discerned elements of common ground. Ignoring the fact that he was secretly encouraging the claim to the throne of Don Jaime and his son, Franco wrote that Juan Carlos: 'must prepare himself to be able, when the time comes, to deal with the duties and responsibilities involved in the leadership of a nation'. He claimed to be offering Don Juan a recipe for success based on 'thoughtful reflection on the conditions in which a Prince should be educated and the baggage of knowledge that is required today by the ruler of a nation if he is to awaken the respect, the trust and the love of the people that must sustain him'. His letter left no doubt that, if Juan Carlos were not educated in Spain and within the ambience of the *Movimiento*, he would never be allowed to ascend the throne. Moreover, various cruel asides about those who would probably never reign and about the 'shipwreck of the monarchy' made it clear that Don Juan did not figure in Franco's plans.

The Caudillo's scheme for the Prince's education was expressed in his inimitably grandiloquent and florid style. First, his philosophic and moral education would be assured by ensuring that he had at his side 'a pious, prudent person devoid of ambition'. Then, the Caudillo announced that for discipline and the moulding of his character, there could be 'nothing more patriotic, pedagogic and exemplary than his formation as a soldier in a military establishment'. This would mean a two-year period at the Zaragoza military academy, followed by shorter six-month periods in the Air Force and Navy academies. Then there would be two years at university studying politics and economics followed by three months each at the Schools of Agronomy, Industrial Engineering and Mining. This lengthy programme was to be adorned by regular contact with the Caudillo himself. Interestingly, he stated that: 'I consider it important that the people get used to seeing the Prince next to the Caudillo.' The letter was followed by a detailed – and revealing – summary of those aspects of the curriculum that Franco considered crucial. Needless to say, there was considerable stress on Franco's own interpretation of Spanish history and on the principles of the *Movimiento*.[41]

Don Juan's letter of 16 June arrived before this lengthy missive was sent and Franco therefore added a substantial postscript. Hurried and repetitive, its hectoring and threatening tone suggested that Don Juan's dart had hit its target. The constantly reiterated themes were that sending Juan Carlos abroad was not 'convenient' – presumably for Franco – and would cause a bad effect (for Don Juan). It was increasingly obvious in Franco's communications with Don Juan that, in the Caudillo's mind, what was at stake was not whether Don Juan should come to the throne but only whether Juan Carlos might do so. The unmistakable threat was directed against Juan Carlos. By implication, Don Juan had no future: 'You don't seem to appreciate the national mood and the damage that will be done to the political future of the Prince if he is removed from being educated within the thinking of the *Movimiento*.'[42]

While this correspondence was wending its way between Portugal and Spain, Juan Carlos and his brother Alfonso had gone to Madrid for the end-of-year examinations which led to Pabón's report. With the permission of Don Juan, they made a courtesy visit to El Pardo on 22 June to thank Franco for facilitating their time in Spain. The Caudillo ordered that the occasion be given massive publicity in the press. According to a French journalist, at the next cabinet meeting, Franco announced that: 'The two most important events in the history of Spain since 1939 are the signature of the agreements with the United States and the visit that the Infantes made me on 22 June.' He went on to comment that, 'One day Juan Carlos will be called upon to assume high responsibilities in the life of Spain.'[43]

Although urged by Gil Robles to send his son to Louvain, Don Juan was reluctant to see him educated outside Spain. However, he needed a bargaining chip in order to ensure that, if it was to be in Spain, it would be more on his terms than those of the Caudillo. Despite the outrageous way in which it simply brushed aside Don Juan's rights as father of Juan Carlos, much of what Franco suggested made good sense for the education of a future King of Spain. The danger was, as Sainz Rodríguez pointed out, that, 'the Prince will be definitively distanced from Your Majesty and will end up having a Franco-Falangist education.' However, the emphasis on the principles of the *Movimiento* aside, much of Franco's plan accorded with what Don Juan had in mind. In any case, as Pabón commented, 'to fight the bull, you have to stay in Spain.'[44] Nevertheless, Don Juan took his time replying, letting it be known that Franco's proposals were being submitted to the members of his Privy Council – a body containing several individuals whom Franco loathed. Most of those consulted realized that Franco's plan for the Prince signified the end of Don Juan's hopes of ever gaining the throne. Some, including Gil Robles and General Antonio Aranda, voted in favour of rejecting Franco's proposal, but the majority were in favour. This process was completed by the end of July. However, Don Juan waited until 23 September 1954 before responding to Franco. He used the excuse that he had been on a cruise of the Greek Islands organized by Queen Frederica of Greece. As a publicity stunt to foster tourism in Greece, she had arranged to bring together the younger generation of several European royal families. Don Juan's letter was sent from Tangier where Juan Carlos had just had an emergency appendectomy.

It was during the cruise, while on board a Greek destroyer, that Juan Carlos met his future wife, Sofía, the daughter of King Paul and Queen Frederica. Nothing came of this first meeting. Years later, Juan Carlos would relate how, the first time they met, the 15-year-old Sofía told him that she was learning judo. On hearing this, Juan Carlos said jokingly, 'That won't be much use to you, will it?' at which point she replied, 'Is that what you think? Give me your hand,' and proceeded to throw him to the floor.[45]

While sailing back from the cruise, Juan Carlos began to complain of stomach pains, which turned out to be appendicitis. Without his mother's prompt reaction, he might have suffered a possibly fatal peritonitis. Whilst the crew insisted on keeping the Prince warm, Doña María de las Mercedes, who had been trained as a nurse, remembered that, in the case of appendicitis, the affected area had to be kept cold with ice cubes. Don Juan's yacht, the *Saltillo*, put in at Tangier, where Juan Carlos was operated on at the Red Cross hospital by Alfonso de la Peña, a renowned Spanish surgeon who, luckily, happened to be in the town when they arrived.[46]

In the letter to Franco written in Tangier, Don Juan referred to himself 'as a father conscious of his duty'. This was a clear indication of his annoyance at Franco's attempt to usurp his role. His pique was evident too in the way that he deliberately 'misunderstood' Franco's scheme. With a dig at Franco's status, he expressed his satisfaction that: 'The view of Your Excellency, who is currently responsible for the government of Spain, agrees, essentially, with my own that it is entirely fitting that Don Juan Carlos receive a Spanish, religious and military education.' By deliberately sidestepping any reference to the Prince's education within the principles of the *Movimiento*, Don Juan was provoking the Caudillo. Franco pointedly delayed more than two months before replying. It seems never to have occurred to him that he would not be able to bend Don Juan to his will. On 2 October, he confidently told his cousin Pacón, head of his military household, 'Don Juan Carlos will be prepared for entry into the Zaragoza academy; and even though he won't have to undergo examinations, he should have some idea in mathematics, so as to be able to carry out his studies there on a reasonable basis.'[47] In the event, the young Prince would not get off so lightly.

The delay in resolving Juan Carlos's immediate future hardly mattered since, in the wake of his operation, he was in no fit state to be sent anywhere and spent the winter of 1954 convalescing in Estoril. Nevertheless, Gil Robles was appalled to learn that, while awaiting the reply to his letter of 23 September, Don Juan had permitted negotiations with the Caudillo to continue through the mediation of the Conde de los Andes, the recently appointed head of Don Juan's household. However, these talks would take place in the shadow of other events, and unexpectedly their eventual fruit would be the Caudillo's agreement to a private meeting with Don Juan to discuss the details of the Prince's education in Spain.[48]

Behind his apparent confidence, Franco still had concerns about monarchist opposition. Already, in February 1954, he had received a visit from several generals, including the influential Captain-General of Barcelona, Juan Bautista Sánchez. To his outrage, the generals touched on the forbidden subject of his eventual death and politely asked if he had made arrangements for the monarchist succession thereafter.[49] Then, while still contemplating Don Juan's letter of 23 September, Franco was alarmed to be informed that the coming out of Don Juan's eldest daughter, the Infanta María Pilar, had given rise to 15,000 applications for passports from Spanish monarchists who wished to travel to Portugal to pay homage to the royal family. Franco's oft-repeated claims that there were no monarchists in Spain were severely dented. Twelve thousand applications were refused but 3,000 monarchists made the journey to Estoril for the celebrations held on 14 and 15 October. Along with the cars of aristocrats and senior Army officers there were also charabancs packed with significant numbers of the more modest middle classes.

The Caudillo's brother Nicolás, the Spanish Ambassador to Portugal, was present at the spectacular ball given at the Hotel do Parque in Estoril, at which the great Amalia Rodrigues sang traditional Portuguese fados. He reported back to El Pardo about the warmth and spontaneous enthusiasm that had greeted the words of Don Juan when he spoke of his hope of seeing a Spain in which all were equal before the law and referred to 'the Catholic monarchy which is above any transitory circumstances'. Nicolás probably did not mention that he had clapped furiously when Don Juan took to the dance floor with his daughter or that his wife, Isabel Pasqual del Pobil, had eagerly joined in the shouts of '¡Viva el Rey!' Carmen Polo was quick to express her disgust to her husband when this was reported back to her.[50] Franco's fury was directed against the aristocratic guests, and he talked of removing the privilege of a diplomatic passport enjoyed by the highest ranking nobility, the *grandes de España*, 'because they use it to conspire against the regime'.[51]

The strength of the monarchist challenge was further brought home to Franco in the course of limited municipal 'elections' held in Madrid on 21 November 1954, the first since the Civil War. They were presented by the regime as genuine elections because one third of the municipal councillors would be 'elected' by an electorate of 'heads of families' and married women over the age of 30. Enthusiastically supported by the newspaper *ABC*, there were four monarchists up against the four *Movimiento* candidates put up by the regime. The monarchists were harassed and intimidated by Falangist thugs and by the police. The *Movimiento* press network mounted a huge propaganda campaign that presented these elections as a kind of referendum. The entire issue was seriously mishandled, exposing as it did the farce of Franco's claim that all Spaniards were part of the *Movimiento*. Monarchist publicity material was destroyed and voting urns were spirited away to prevent scrutiny of the count. Inevitably, official results gave a substantial victory to the Falangist candidates. It was clear that there had been official falsification and the monarchists claimed to have received over 60 per cent of the vote.[52] At first, Franco was happy to believe that the municipal elections constituted an outpouring of popular acclaim for him. However, a stream of complaints from prominent monarchists and a threat of resignation from Antonio Iturmendi, the traditionalist Minister of Justice, made even the Caudillo begin to doubt the official interpretation of events. He was shocked when General Juan Vigón, now Chief of the General Staff, but still a fervent monarchist, told him that military intelligence services had discovered that the bulk of the Madrid garrison had voted for the monarchist candidates. He was appalled to hear Vigón stating that: 'The regime lost the elections of 21 November.' This indication that support was gathering for Don Juan compelled Franco to take action.[53]

Instructions were sent to Nicolás Franco in Lisbon to inform Don Juan that he was now ready to meet him. Since Franco had never had any doubts about the kind of education that he wanted for the Prince, there was, from his point of view, no need for a meeting. The boy's personal needs were of no concern to him. His surprising agreement to meet the Pretender was merely a reaction to growing evidence of the strength of monarchist feeling within Spain. The encounter was to be no more than a propaganda stunt to neutralize that feeling. He had no intention of making any concessions. In his much delayed reply of 2 December 1954 to Don Juan's September letter, Franco wrote in dismissive terms, limiting the agenda for the meeting. He made it clear that Juan Carlos had to be educated according to the principles of the *Movimiento* in order to be in tune with 'the generations that were forged in the heat of our Crusade'. This was a matter on which, according to Franco, there could be no misunderstanding. If the Prince were not to be educated in this way, it would be better for him to go abroad, since: 'the monarchy is not viable outside the *Movimiento*.' Altogether better would be for the Prince to be educated in Spain under Franco's vigilance.

It was an irony – and one that Franco was anxious to conceal from Don Juan – that the neutralization of the monarchists and the consolidation of his own plans for the succession were probably now his greatest concern. Hitherto, his most effective weapon in silencing Don Juan had been to conjure up successive revivals of the Falange. This also served to strengthen his argument to Don Juan that, as Caudillo, he could tolerate no restoration of the line that fell in 1931, but rather only the installation of a Falangist monarchy. However, the unexpected success of the monarchists in the Madrid 'elections' showed that the Falange was increasingly anachronistic while the monarchist option seemed more in tune with the outside world. The policies of autarchic self-sufficiency favoured by both Franco and the Falange had brought Spain to the verge of economic disaster. At the very least, it would be prudent to convince the royalists among his own supporters of his own good faith as a monarchist – hence the meeting. Don Juan and his supporters might believe that they would be discussing ways of hastening a restoration but Franco's letter showed again that he would hand over power only on his death or total inca-

pacity and then only to a king who was committed to the unconditional maintenance of the dictatorship.

It was clear that Franco saw the education of Juan Carlos as
the preparation of precisely such a king. That did not necessarily
mean that there was certainty as to the Prince's eventual succession
to the throne. Apart from encouraging the claim of Don Jaime
and his sons, Franco now had another candidate nearer home. On
9 December, his first grandson had been born and his sycophantic
son-in-law, Cristóbal Martínez-Bordiu, suggested changing the
baby's name by reversing his matronymic and patronymic. The
formal agreement by a servile Cortes on 15 December to his name
being Francisco Franco Martínez-Bordiu made the new arrival a
potential heir to his grandfather. Alarm spread in monarchist
circles that Franco planned to establish his own dynasty.[54] This
was exacerbated when the Conde de los Andes reported on the
harshness of Franco's tone during their negotiations on the agenda
to be discussed in the forthcoming meeting between the Caudillo
and Don Juan. Outlining his own plan for the Prince's education,
he had told the astonished count that: 'If Don Juan does not accept
such an education for his son, or his son does not agree to it, the
Prince should not return to Spain and that will mean that he has
renounced the throne and that I will consider myself free of any
understanding with him.' Pacón noted in his diary that a meeting
was utterly pointless because he knew that nothing would make
Franco deviate from the plan that he had laid out. He bluntly told
Pacón, 'If Don Juan wants his son ever to reign in Spain, he must
submit to my wishes, which are for his own good and for that of
the fatherland, by entrusting the boy's education to me. It must
be without interference from anyone and handed over only to
people that I trust totally.'[55]

Don Juan set off for Spain by car on 28 December 1954.
Franco left El Pardo at 8 a.m. on the next morning in a Cadillac
and with a convoy of guards. Both were headed for a halfway
point between Madrid and Lisbon – Navalmoral de la Mata in
the province of Cáceres in Extremadura. Arriving in Spain that
evening was an emotional moment for Don Juan, the first time
that he had set foot in his homeland since his failed attempt to

join the Nationalist forces in 1936. The meeting – at Las Cabezas, the estate of the Conde de Ruiseñada, Juan Claudio Güell, the Pretender's new representative in Spain – lasted from 11.20 a.m. to 7.30 p.m. with a late lunch break. At the steps of the mansion, the ever-affable Don Juan greeted Franco cordially and had created a relaxed atmosphere by the time that they sat before a roaring fire. He felt confident, telling Franco that he had received thousands of messages of support from Spain including telegrams from four Lieutenant-Generals. However, such references to the current debate on the monarchist succession went over Franco's head as relating to a far distant and theoretical future. This became clear when he began to talk of the possibility of separating the functions of Head of State and Head of Government. He would do so only, he said, when his health gave out, or he 'disappeared' or because the good of the regime, with the evolution of time, required it, 'but, as long as I have good health, I don't see any advantages in change'.

Franco was clearly at his ease, talking without pause or even a sip of water, and he proceeded to give Don Juan an interminable, rambling history lesson. Don Juan commented later that it was like listening to an obsessive grandfather boasting about his past. In fact, Franco's reminiscences about his own military exploits could be seen as a sly attempt to humiliate Don Juan, who had not been allowed to fight in the Civil War. Efforts by Don Juan to get a word in edgeways and turn the discussion to the timing of the transition to the monarchy and the terms of the post-Franco future met with a frosty response. Franco did not hesitate to criticize many prominent monarchists as drunks and gamblers, accusing Pedro Sainz Rodríguez, about whom he had the most neurotic delusions, of being a freemason. When Don Juan praised Sainz Rodríguez as a faithful counsellor, in whom he had complete confidence, Franco replied, 'I have never trusted anyone.'

Don Juan's suggestion of the introduction of freedom of the press, an independent judiciary, social justice, trade union freedom and proper political representation merely reinforced Franco's conviction that he was the puppet of dangerous aristocratic meddlers who were probably freemasons. Through the impenetrable

and self-satisfied verbiage glimmered the Caudillo's message. As
he had already informed the Conde de los Andes: if Don Juan did
not bow to his demand that Juan Carlos be educated under his
tutelage, he would consider it as a renunciation of the throne. The
needs, let alone the wishes, of Juan Carlos simply did not enter
into the debate. Faced with Franco's ultimatum, Don Juan thus
agreed that his son be educated at the three military academies,
at the university and at Franco's side. However, he made it quite
clear that none of this constituted a renunciation of his own rights.
With the greatest reluctance, Franco accepted an anodyne joint
communiqué whose terms implicitly, if not explicitly, recognized
the hereditary rights to the throne of the Borbón dynasty. It
was a minor victory for Don Juan that his name should appear
alongside that of Franco.[56]

The joint communiqué aside, Franco had made no real concessions about a future restoration, or rather installation, as he
called it. Nevertheless, the theatrical gesture of meeting Don Juan
had, for the moment, drawn the sting of the monarchists and gave
the impression that progress was being made. In his end of year
message on 31 December 1954, he made it quite clear that he had
conceded nothing to Don Juan. Using the royal 'we', he stressed
that the monarchist forms enshrined in the Ley de Sucesión had
nothing to do with the monarchy of Alfonso XIII. In the wake of
the Las Cabezas meeting, the Caudillo was publicly affirming that
he did not renounce his right, enshrined in the Ley de Sucesión, to
choose a successor to guarantee the continuity of his authoritarian
regime.[57]

Chatting with Pacón on the same day, Franco claimed that, at
Las Cabezas, Don Juan had asked him if he thought it was necessary to abdicate in order that his son should have the right to
inherit the throne. The exchange is not recorded in other accounts
of the meeting. Indeed, those accounts suggest that what Don Juan
actually said was that allowing his son to be educated in Spain
did not constitute an abdication of his own rights. However, if it
was not just wishful thinking on Franco's part and Don Juan did
ask the question, it could be interpreted as a ploy to force Franco
to acknowledge the dynastic rights of the family. If, at Franco's

behest, Don Juan had abdicated in favour of his son, the Caudillo would have been committing himself to choosing Juan Carlos as his successor. It is unlikely that the question of abdication was raised in the precise terms recounted by Franco to his cousin. However the subject was raised, Franco's reply, at least in his own account to Pacón, was a masterpiece of cunning.

Unwilling to reduce his options, the Caudillo allegedly replied, 'I do not think that the problem of your abdication needs to be raised today, as we are here to discuss your son's education, but since you've mentioned it, I must tell you that I believe that Your Highness rendered himself incompatible with today's Spain, because against my advice that Your Highness remain silent and make no declarations, you published a manifesto in which you refused to collaborate with the regime and thus made yourself incompatible with it.' He went on to talk of his 'inclination' to name as his successor a direct heir to Alfonso XIII. However, he also mentioned the strong temptation to nominate a prince from the Traditionalist branch of the family as a reward to the Carlists for their role in the Civil War and their loyalty thereafter. If the conversation took place as he claimed, it revealed his determination both to humiliate Don Juan and to keep open his own options.[58]

At the point at which Juan Carlos was about to return to Spain to be educated as a possible successor to Franco, his own interests as a human being were being sacrificed for a gamble. Franco could choose between a Carlist, Don Juan, Juan Carlos, Don Jaime or his son Alfonso and, perhaps, even the newborn Francisco Franco Martínez-Bordiu. Neither Juan Carlos nor his father can have been unaware of this. It must have been difficult for Juan Carlos not to feel like a shuttlecock in someone else's game.

Before setting out for Las Cabezas, Don Juan had written to the Caudillo's wartime artillery chief, General Carlos Martínez Campos y Serrano (the Duque de la Torre), asking him to be the head of the Prince's household in Spain and thus charging him with the supervision of his son's military education. Stiff and austere, the 68-year-old Martínez Campos was known for his dour seriousness, his acute intelligence and his sharp tongue. His marriage had broken down, and by his own admission, he had failed in the education of his own children. Even Franco was moved to comment: 'God help the boy with that fellow!'[59] Nevertheless, it was a choice that provoked considerable satisfaction at El Pardo. Until recently, Martínez Campos had, after all, been Military Governor of the Canary Islands. The general reported to Franco on 27 December. Pacón noted in his diary: 'The Duque de la Torre is totally trustworthy and utterly loyal to the Caudillo.' In fact, this was not entirely true – Martínez Campos was loyal and obedient, but he had considerable reservations about Franco personally and about the way in which he treated Don Juan. Juan Carlos later commented that the Duke 'didn't get on' with Franco. Now, in the course of their conversation, Martínez Campos mentioned Don Juan's annoyance at the way in which Franco, in laying out his plans for the Prince's education, had ridden roughshod over his own rights as a father to educate his son. The Caudillo was unmoved, reiterating blithely his view that it was one thing to educate a son, another to train a Prince to reign. He added that, if Don Juan didn't like it, he could do whatever he liked but would lose the chance of ever seeing his son on the throne.[60] Once more, it was being made crystal clear that the personal interests of the 15-year-old adolescent mattered little in the wider political game being played out.

When General Juan Vigón, Chief of the General Staff and a fervent monarchist, heard of the choice of Martínez Campos and the arrangements for Juan Carlos, he was shocked, exclaiming, 'It's the wrong way to go about this! It's playing politics rather than educating the boy!'[61] Martínez Campos himself was hardly less critical of his own appointment. He remarked to a family friend, 'This is women's work.'[62] It is fair to say, therefore, that the selection of this rigid and irritable soldier was based not on any consideration of Juan Carlos's needs but on the fact that he had enjoyed good relations with Franco. It was typical of Martínez Campos's style that, once in charge, he would prevent Juan Carlos receiving visits from his beloved old tutor, Eugenio Vegas Latapié. In his eyes, the deeply conservative Vegas Latapié was a subversive.[63] The consequence of the meeting at Las Cabezas, as far as

Juan Carlos was concerned, was that, in early 1955, he would be obliged to leave Estoril once more and start preparing for the entrance examinations for the Zaragoza military academy.

The preparations for this began on 5 January 1955, when Martínez Campos telephoned Major Alfonso Armada Comyn, an intelligent aristocratic artillery officer, son of the Marqués de Santa Cruz de Rivadulla, to arrange a clandestine meeting. As they drove through Madrid, Martínez Campos passed him the letter from Don Juan. 'Congratulations, General,' said Armada as he handed it back. With a mixture of contempt and indignation, the general spat out: 'Are you just pretending to be stupid or are you really thick? Do you think it is possible that I would waste time just so you could congratulate me for something that I don't like, didn't ask for and is worrying the hell out of me? Can't you understand that they've dropped me in it?' A chastened Armada replied in a whisper, 'Then refuse.' 'No,' replied the general, 'that wouldn't be right. It's an honour, an uncomfortable one, full of responsibilities, especially being dumped on me now that I'm old and I was never any good at bringing up my own children. But let's not waste time. I don't have to give you explanations. You're young and have many children. Both you and your wife know palace life and its secrets.'

Martínez Campos's choice of Armada was understandable and one that would have profound effects throughout Juan Carlos's life. The young Major Armada's credentials, both as a monarchist and as a Francoist, were impeccable. Armada's father had been a childhood friend of Alfonso XIII, as had his father-in-law, the Marqués de Someruelos. As artillery generals, both were friends of Martínez Campos. At the age of 17, Armada had himself fought as a volunteer on the Nationalist side in the Civil War. In July 1941, shortly after graduating from the artillery academy in Segovia, he had joined the *División Azul* in order to fight alongside the Germans on the Russian front, for which he was awarded the Iron Cross. After completing his studies at the general staff college, he joined the general staff of the Civil Guard. Now, despite efforts to dissuade the general, Armada was overruled and told to report for duty the next day.[64]

Martínez Campos instructed Major Armada to prepare lists of officers from the various Army corps who might be recruited as teachers for the young Prince. He was also charged with organizing the staff of the Prince's residence, choosing suitable companions and arranging Juan Carlos's studies and even leisure-time reading. Martínez Campos cast aside some of Armada's suggestions and chose others. A daunting team of officers would supervise the boy's studies. The Prince's infantry professor was to be Major Joaquín Valenzuela, the Marqués de Valenzuela de Tahuarda, whose father had been killed in Morocco when he was Franco's immediate predecessor as head of the Spanish Foreign Legion. The teacher in charge of Juan Carlos's horse-riding, hunting and sporting development was to be the 50-year-old cavalry major Nicolás Cotoner, Conde de Tendilla, and later to be Marqués de Mondéjar. Brother-in-law to the Conde de Ruiseñada, Cotoner was a *grande de España* who had fought in the Civil War. He was a firm admirer of Franco which meant that he was viewed with some suspicion in Estoril.[65] The chaplain was Father José Manuel Aguilar, a Dominican priest who happened also to be the brother-in-law of Franco's Minister of Education, the Christian Democrat Joaquín Ruiz Giménez. The history teacher was Ángel López Amo, who had taught Juan Carlos at Las Jarillas. Mathematics was in the hands of a strict naval officer, Lieutenant-Commander Álvaro Fontanals Barón.[66]

A hint from Martínez Campos had led to the Duque and Duquesa de Montellano graciously putting at the Prince's disposal their palace in Madrid's Paseo de la Castellana, where in the 1949–1950 academic year his classmates from Las Jarillas had vainly awaited his return from Estoril. The cost of running the Prince's establishment was to be met by Carrero Blanco's *Presidencia del Gobierno* (the cabinet office). Juan Carlos travelled from Lisbon to Madrid in the company of Martínez Campos on 18 January 1955. This time, there was rather more pomp at his arrival than on his first trip to Spain in November 1948. The Prince travelled by train, in the well-appointed coach in which Franco had made the journey to meet Hitler at Hendaye in October 1940. It is to be supposed that repairs had been effected to the leaks that had blighted Franco's trip. Juan Carlos was no longer obliged to get off the train on the outskirts of the city. Now, he was met at the Delicias station by the Mayor of the capital, the Conde de Mayalde, by the Captain-General of the region, General Miguel Rodrigo Martínez, and a crowd of several hundred monarchists, most of them aristocrats. His arrival – and unfounded rumours that, at Las Cabezas, Franco had agreed to the return of Alfonso XIII's mortal remains to Spain – intensified tensions among hard-line Falangists. The council of the organization of party veterans, the *Vieja Guardia* (Old Guard), which attributed to itself responsibility for maintaining the ideological 'purity' of the regime, sent a delegation to protest to the Secretary-General of the *Movimiento*, Raimundo Fernández Cuesta.[67]

Falangist anger was largely due to the fact that the communiqué issued after the Las Cabezas meeting had immediately sparked off monarchist-inspired rumours that the Caudillo was now actively preparing an early transition to the monarchy. Franco responded quickly to the first mutterings of protest about such a prospect. Within a week of Juan Carlos's arrival, he gave a widely reproduced interview that dispelled any hopes of his early departure. 'Although my magistracy is for life,' he declared pompously, 'it is to be hoped that there are many years before me, and the immediate interest of the issue is diluted in time.' Franco was yet again making it clear, to his supporters and to Don Juan, that the monarchy would be a Falangist one in no way resembling that which had fallen in 1931.[68] In the face of potential opposition to what seemed to be the appeasement of Don Juan, Franco was asking the docile Falangist hierarchy to postpone the 'pending revolution' even longer in return for a Francoist future under a Francoist king.[69] Accordingly, in February 1955, he authorized the drafting of laws to block loopholes in the *Ley de Sucesión* and irrevocably shackle any royal successor to the *Movimiento*. At the same time, to make this more acceptable to his monarchist supporters, the Falangist edges of the *Movimiento* would be blurred, censorship of the monarchists would be relaxed, and Eugenio Vegas Latapié was reinstated to the *Consejo del Reino*.[70]

Within hours of the Prince's arrival in Madrid, a queue of

well-wishers, among them some aristocrats, had gathered outside the Palacio de Montellano. Like Franco, Martínez Campos was determined to ensure that there would be no entourage of courtiers at the palace. The Civil Guards on duty permitted those who came merely to sign the visitors' book and then leave.

The year and a half spent in the Palacio de Montellano preparing for the entry examination for the Zaragoza military academy would be a hard trial for Juan Carlos. This time, he had no friends to accompany him. In his austerely furnished room, the only personal items were some family photographs, a tiny triptych of Christ and a luminous statue of Our Lady of Fatima. Martínez Campos established an inflexible routine that left the boy little spare time. The Prince was woken at 7.45 a.m. and had three-quarters of an hour in which to wash, hear mass in the chapel, have breakfast and glance at the newspapers. The hour from 8.30 a.m. to 9.30 a.m. was devoted to private study. At 9.30 a.m., accompanied by his maths tutor, Álvaro Fontanals Barón, the Prince would set off for his classes at the naval orphans' college in Madrid where he followed a rigid timetable until 1.15 p.m. After lunch at the palace, there would be golf or horse-riding in the Casa de Campo until 5.00 p.m. Back at the palace, there would be more study until 9.00 p.m. at which time Juan Carlos was allowed an hour for letter-writing or telephone calls.

He had little free time since classes were held even on Saturdays and Father Aguilar often visited to impart religious and moral education. Other time was consumed by visits from distinguished academics who gave prepared talks on their specialities. The only glimmer of jollity in the otherwise stultifying atmosphere derived from the fact that a young friend, Miguel Primo de Rivera y Urquijo, the nephew of José Antonio Primo de Rivera, lived nearby and thus became the Prince's frequent companion. It was to develop into a lifelong friendship. At the time, it helped relieve the tedium of the regular lunch and dinner visits from important figures in the Church, the Falange, and the business world – including the head of the Opus Dei, Padre Josémaría Escrivá de Balaguer. This austere routine was rarely stimulating – indeed, if anything, it was utterly suffocating – for an adolescent. Asked by the diplomat

José Antonio Giménez-Arnau how he felt about his loneliness and the absence from his family, Juan Carlos replied sadly, 'If not resigned, I'm at least used to it. Just imagine! When I was six, I spent two years separated from my parents when they were first in Estoril. There was no choice.' Giménez-Arnau had been commissioned to write a feature article on the Prince. When it was published, Juan Carlos wrote him an informal note of thanks. The unaffected warmth and openness of the 17-year-old Prince's note guaranteed the lifelong loyalty of its recipient.[71]

Occasionally, the Prince was taken to El Pardo where the Caudillo subjected him to interminable history lessons about the mistakes made by various kings of Spain. He also gave him sententious advice about the need to avoid aristocrats and courtiers. Believing that the Prince was extremely pleased and grateful, Franco decided to see him at least once a month, 'to chat with him and carry on instilling my ideas in him'. The Caudillo was delighted by the severity of Martínez Campos who reported to him on 5 March 1955. When the Prince had begun to *tutear* (use the intimate '*tú*' form of address to) Major Valenzuela, the general had energetically forbidden it. He had refused the Prince permission to go to Lisbon for the wedding of one of the daughters of the ex-King Umberto of Italy, informing Don Juan that it would constitute an unacceptable interruption of the boy's studies. He insisted on speaking English with Juan Carlos. He also made every effort to ensure that no particular one of the Prince's friendships came to take priority over the others. That Martínez Campos felt it necessary to report to Franco gives some indication of the ambience in which the Prince was being educated. He was permitted, on occasions, to invite friends to lunch. Once, he was visited by the beautiful Princess Maria Gabriella di Savoia, King Umberto's other daughter, a friend and fellow-exile from Portugal, who later became his girlfriend. The Prince was usually short of cash, later recalling how Major Cotoner had to buy him a suit for the occasion.[72]

The tendency to high spirits that had characterized Juan Carlos as a schoolboy did not desert him despite his austere surroundings. One of the teaching staff, the Air Force Major Emilio García

Conde, had a Mercedes that the Prince loved to drive, even though he did not possess a driving licence. One day, on a trip to the headquarters of the *Sección Femenina* (the women's section of the Falange) at the Castillo de la Mota in the province of Valladolid, he had a minor accident involving a cyclist. Major García Conde resolved the problem by giving the cyclist some banknotes to get his wheel fixed and buy a new pair of trousers. After nearly being eaten alive by the enthusiastic women of the *Sección Femenina*, Juan Carlos and his party retired to lunch in a restaurant. The Prince delightedly recounted the bicycle incident and was astonished when Martínez Campos furiously ordered García Conde to find the cyclist, get the money back and oblige the unfortunate young man to report the incident to the Civil Guard. He was worried that if the young man was seriously injured, it would look as if the Prince was involved in corruptly trying to cover up his own involvement. He insisted that Juan Carlos return to Madrid in his car.[73]

General Martínez Campos's loyalty and deference to the Caudillo prevented him from complaining about the fact that Franco, partly to please the Falange and partly to bring the monarchists to heel, had encouraged criticism of Don Juan in the press. In consequence, as the general knew full well, hostility to the monarchy soon began to be directed against Juan Carlos. At the beginning of February 1955, the Mayor of Madrid wrote to Franco's cousin, Pacón. In response to the scattering of Falangist leaflets bearing the inscription 'We want no king!', the Mayor asked how it was possible, if Franco wanted Juan Carlos educated in Spain, that the regime's single party should be engaged in insulting the Prince. When Pacón mentioned this to the Caudillo, he brushed it aside as 'student antics'. However, the rumblings came from much higher in the Falange, including Pilar Primo de Rivera, the head of the *Sección Femenina*. Nevertheless, Franco brushed aside further reports about anti-monarchist activities from such dignitaries as the Captain-General of Valencia. The mutterings continued and, eventually, on 26 February, the Caudillo felt obliged to inform a concerned cabinet that 'a King would be nominated only if there were a Prince ready for the task'.[74]

Juan Carlos's presence in Spain and its possible implications were highlighted by the publication in *ABC* on 15 April 1955 of his interview with José Antonio Giménez-Arnau – the first press interview published since his arrival in Spain in 1948. A few days later, violence broke out between Falangists and monarchists at the end of a lecture on European monarchies given by Roberto Cantalupo, once Mussolini's Ambassador to Franco, at the Madrid Ateneo, the capital's leading liberal intellectual centre. In response to Cantalupo's enthusiastic advocacy of monarchy, Rafael Sánchez Mazas, a former minister of Franco, cried *'¡Viva la Falange!'* in reply to which shouts of *'¡Viva el Rey!'* or *'¡Viva Don Juan III!'* were heard from monarchists present. Falangists then showered the hall with leaflets ridiculing Juan Carlos and the police had to be called to put a stop to the fight that erupted. The Prince also faced the increasingly overt hostility of the then Minister for the Army, General Agustín Muñoz Grandes, whose sympathies lay with the Falange. Later on that spring, young Falangists roamed the streets of Madrid shouting: 'We don't want idiot kings!' Juan Carlos was also booed while he was giving out the prizes at some horse trials, and, in the summer, he was insulted during a visit to a Falangist summer camp.[75]

The noises coming from Falangists were the dying agony of a wounded beast. In reality, their organization could not have been more domesticated. On 19 June 1955, the Secretary-General of the *Movimiento*, Raimundo Fernández Cuesta, declared in a speech made in Bilbao that to ensure the survival of the regime after Franco's death, judicial, political and institutional guarantees would be necessary. The role of the *Movimiento* would be to sustain the monarchy that succeeded Franco and to keep it on the straight and narrow path of Francoism. It was the formal recognition by the Falange of the inevitability of a monarchical succession.[76] For their part, the monarchists had to accept that the monarchy would be restored only within the *Movimiento*. To hammer this home, Franco exploited the anxiety of the sycophantic Julio Danvila, the most Francoist of Don Juan's advisers, to further the establishment of a Francoist monarchy. At Franco's behest, the willing Danvila concocted the text of an 'interview' with Don Juan in which he apparently gave royal approval to Fernández Cuesta's speech. Franco agreed the text, which Danvila then took to Estoril where an indignant Don Juan refused to agree to its publication. Danvila then told the Caudillo that the Pretender had accepted the 'interview', at which point Franco amended the text to bring it even more into line with his own thinking and obliged *ABC* and *Ya* to publish it on 24 June 1955. Although outraged, Don Juan did not protest, since a public break between himself and Franco would have encouraged the anti-monarchical machinations of the extremist elements of the Falange. It might also have led to the termination of Juan Carlos's education in Spain.[77]

Franco was unconcerned about the Falangist rejection of his apparent choice of conservative monarchism as the future of the regime. At the November 1955 rally in El Escorial to commemorate the anniversary of the death of the Falange's founder, José Antonio Primo de Rivera, Franco rekindled Falangist anxieties about his Las Cabezas meeting with Don Juan and the presence of Juan Carlos in Spain. He had arrived for the ceremony in the uniform of a Captain-General instead of the usual black uniform and blue shirt of the *Jefe Nacional* (National Chief of the *Movimiento*). There was some nervous shuffling in the ranks of the assembled Falangists. As Franco walked across the square towards his car, a voice called out: 'We want no idiot kings.' It has also been alleged that a cry of 'Franco traitor' was heard. There were other minor incidents reflecting Falangist discontent with the complacency of the regime that Franco dismissed as of little consequence.[78]

The constant running down of the Borbón monarchy, together with Franco's assumption of royal airs, deeply annoyed Don Juan and his family. This was reflected in the indiscreet comments of Alfonso de Borbón, the second son of Don Juan. When he was 14 years old, Alfonsito was wont to refer to Franco as 'the dwarf' or 'the toad'. He said, 'That fellow won't leave. He has to be kicked out . . . Having to visit him makes me vomit and *la Señora*, always showing her teeth, kills my appetite.' It was an indication both of Don Juan's deteriorating relations with Franco and the fact that Alfonsito was such a favourite that his outbursts were tolerated and praised. Not many years before, Don Juan had smacked his daughter Margarita for repeating a joke about Franco. Things had changed and there can be little doubt that critical remarks about Franco or his wife would quickly have been relayed to El Pardo by the many monarchist visitors who maintained a dual 'loyalty'.[79]

THREE

The Tribulations of a Young Soldier
1955–1960

Despite Franco's readiness to excuse Juan Carlos the entry examinations for the Zaragoza military academy, General Martínez Campos insisted that he undergo the test just like any other prospective cadet. Having passed, Juan Carlos joined the academy in December 1955. As his companions from the academy would later recall, the exams were very difficult and they believed that, although the Prince was usually treated like any other candidate by the examiners, the mathematics test he sat must have been easier than the one they took: indeed, Juan Carlos would soon be shown to be well below average in this subject.[1]

Although Juan Carlos, in his public declarations at least, would later recall his years as a cadet with nostalgic fondness, his time at the military academies did not always go smoothly. When he took his oath of loyalty to the colours on 15 December 1955, the ceremony was chaired by the brusque General Agustín Muñoz Grandes, the Minister for the Army, who was much more inclined to the Falangist than to the monarchist cause. Accordingly, in his speech, he made no mention of the Prince.[2] In addition, Juan Carlos was saddened on this occasion by the fact that Franco had not permitted his father to attend the ceremony.[3] On 10 December, Don Juan wrote to him, reminding him of the tremendous responsibilities he would be undertaking when he swore his loyalty to Spain: '15 December will be a great day because it is the day on which you will knowingly consecrate the rest of your life to the service of Spain.' Juan Carlos sent his father a telegram: 'Before the flag I have promised Spain to be a perfect soldier and with tremendous feeling I swear to you that I will fulfil that oath.'[4]

It was Juan Carlos's fervent wish to be allowed to get on with life as an ordinary cadet. 'You can avoid a lot of problems by getting lost in the crowd.' That was rendered impossible because the campaign against Don Juan in the *Movimiento* press remained intense during this period. Juan Carlos found these constant attacks on his father upsetting. Some of his fellow cadets would derive a malicious pleasure from quoting the insinuations of the press. On several occasions, Juan Carlos was sufficiently provoked by remarks that his father was a freemason or a bad patriot (for serving in the Royal Navy) to get involved in fights. These were organized furtively in the stables at night, possibly even with the complicity of the teaching staff. When Juan Carlos eventually complained to Franco about the media's attacks on his father, the Caudillo replied, with his habitual cynicism, that the Spanish press was independent and that he had no influence over it. He stated that, 'it was impossible to do anything, since the press was free to express its opinions.' As Juan Carlos commented, 'it was such an outrageous lie that all I could do was laugh.'

Recounting this later, Juan Carlos was rather benevolent with regard to Franco. Reflecting on the fact that the Caudillo saw in Don Juan a dangerous liberal, he commented, 'When my father said "I want to be King of all Spaniards," Franco must have translated this as "I want to be King of the victors and of the vanquished." ' This puzzled Juan Carlos, because of the fact that Franco knew full well that Don Juan had tried to join the Nationalist forces against the 'reds'. Referring to the cunning letter with which Franco had refused Don Juan's offer, Juan Carlos commented rather uncritically, 'On that occasion, the General wrote my father a very beautiful letter to thank him for his gesture. In it, he told him that his life was too precious for the future of Spain and that he forbade him to risk it at the battle front. Why was my father's life precious if not because he was the heir to the crown? But, what can you say ... that was the General for you. At times, putting up with him was very difficult. But, as you know, I had totally convinced myself that to achieve my objectives I had to put up with a lot. The objective was worth the trouble.' The objective was the re-establishment of the Borbón family on the throne.[5]

Despite these occasional outbursts of hostility towards his father, Juan Carlos would later recall his years in the military academies as amongst the happiest in his life. In a brief letter to the readers of a Spanish magazine which published, in 1981, a feature on this period, he wrote: 'I remember my years at the military academies with genuine satisfaction and nostalgia ... Now that my post and occupations leave me hardly any time or freedom, I often think back to that distant period in which my life evolved in a way so different from the current one.'

Above and beyond the special status, of which none of his fellow students could remain ignorant, Juan Carlos soon became a genuinely popular cadet. His contemporaries at the academies would later describe him as a 'sensational companion', outgoing, generous, particularly gifted at sports and endowed with an extraordinary memory. His ability to remember people's names and faces would later enable him to recognize and greet comrades and teachers whom he had not seen in years. He had a good sense of humour and enjoyed playing practical jokes on his friends. He often participated, for instance, in the food fights that occasionally erupted at lunch times in the refectory. Academically, he was said to be of 'average intelligence', but above average in 'general knowledge', foreign languages, tactical thinking and military ethics. He struggled with mathematics, which was 'the subject dreaded by all'. Juan Carlos was also perceived as being deeply religious: every day, he would get up before reveille in order to attend the voluntary, early morning mass.

When it came to friendships, the Prince necessarily had to be careful, making every effort to avoid the creation of a circle of admirers or sycophants who wanted to be with him only out of self-interest. He tried to get to know as many people as possible, which was made easier by the fact that the class groups changed every term. He was aware of the dangers of nepotism: indeed, at the end of his military training, he refused to use his influence in order to get plumb postings for his friends from the academies. He did, however, strive to keep in touch with his old companions, attending and often even organizing reunions.[6] Not all of his contemporaries were keen to flatter him: 'Some thought that I was a spoilt brat, spoiled by destiny, a daddy's boy, the inhabitant of another planet. I had to use my fists to become one of them.'[7] To this end, he encouraged his peers to treat him with considerable informality. His close friends called him 'Juan' or 'Juanito', or even 'Carlos', whilst his other companions addressed him with the informal '*tú*' and jokingly called him SAR, an abbreviation of '*Su Alteza Real*' (His Royal Highness).[8]

This easy-going informality outraged General Martínez Campos who visited the academy each weekend to review the Prince's progress and have lunch with him. On one occasion, Martínez Campos allowed his tutee to invite a couple of his academy friends to join them for lunch. During the meal, when he heard one of these friends call the Prince 'Juan', he exploded. Red-faced with fury, he leapt to his feet, knocking his chair out of the way and shouted at the culprit: 'Gentleman cadet! On your feet and stand to attention! How dare you, gentleman cadet, address informally and by his first name someone that I, a Lieutenant-General, address as His Royal Highness!' Unsurprisingly, Juan Carlos was never again able to convince his friends to join him for lunch with Martínez Campos.[9] Juan Carlos soon came to dread these visits from his supervisor, turning pale and trembling as the meeting time came closer.[10]

The teaching staff at the academy addressed Juan Carlos as 'Your Highness' and, at roll-call, he was referred to by his full title – 'His Royal Highness Juan Carlos de Borbón'. That aside, in so far as it could be put aside, Juan Carlos was, according to his contemporaries, treated by the teaching staff just like any other student. He was disciplined like any other cadet when he broke the rules. Once, for instance, he was put under house arrest for being caught smoking indoors. The Prince was subject to the same timetable as the other students, which left them very little free time. Reveille was at 6.15 a.m., although Juan Carlos rose earlier in order to attend mass. By 6.30 a.m., all cadets had to be standing to attention in the corridors, where roll-call took place. The young men were then allowed to take their showers – in water usually either freezing or so hot as to be almost unbearable. Individual study time followed, then lessons, lunch, a half-hour break, further lessons, another half-hour break and dinner. According to his contemporaries, no one was ever asked by the teaching staff to make allowances for the Prince or to treat him with special deference. In his first year at Zaragoza, Juan Carlos was thus subjected to the same '*novatadas*' (initiation tests) and other pranks as the other newly arrived students. Years later, he remembered not only many of the pranks played on him on his arrival at Zaragoza, but also their names: 'I had to undergo everything. I had to do the "reptile" on the bedroom floor. I slept with the "nun" [with a sabre resting on his chest]. They "X-rayed" me [they made him sleep between two planks from the bedside table]. I also had to let them "clay pigeon shoot" me [he was left in a room blindfolded and, when he attempted to leave, he was battered with pillows].'[11]

Juan Carlos enjoyed being an ordinary cadet and even made an effort to prevent the teaching staff giving him preferential treatment. He once complained, for instance, that the mathematics tutor gave him an undeserved grade. According to his fellow students, the Prince had a 'natural sense of justice'. Prudently, he used his special status only in order to help others. For instance, when a companion had been punished for some misdemeanour by being deprived of pudding, Juan Carlos would complain that there was something wrong with his helping in order to get an extra one to pass to the friend.[12]

Nevertheless, it was inevitable that there would be differences in the way that Juan Carlos was treated at the Zaragoza military academy. He travelled into the centre of Zaragoza by car, a black SEAT 1500, whereas his contemporaries did so by tram. Although, while out on manoeuvres, he slept on the floor of a tent like everyone else, in the academy, he had an independent, though small, bedroom, while the others slept in communal dormitories. According to one of his Zaragoza companions, Juan Carlos's bedroom, which was situated above the infirmary, was Spartan. The only objects in it, besides a bed and a desk, were a multiple photograph frame displaying the pictures of all of the Borbón kings of Spain – including his father. He had pictures of his mother, his brother and his two sisters and a girlfriend, Maria Gabriella di Savoia. His book collection was small – a few textbooks and next to his bed usually was a novel by Marcial Lafuente Estefanía, from the 'Rodeo' collection of western stories popular at the time. Juan Carlos enjoyed less freedom than the others. He was obliged to have extra lessons and saw his private tutors during the morning period that should have been for individual study, during the afternoon breaks and sometimes at weekends. On the occasions when it was possible to go out for drinks in Zaragoza with his friends, they were delighted to be able to use his status and his unusual blond good looks as a ploy to get to know girls. When the cadets were on trains *en route* to camp, at each station women would come out to say hello to him. His ability to pick up girls was as unlimited as a capacity for falling briefly in love.[13]

In March 1956, there occurred an incident which totally diverted Juan Carlos from any thoughts of girls or even of the crown. He and his 14-year-old brother had travelled from Spain on the Lusitania Express to spend the Easter holidays in Estoril with their parents and sisters. It was the first time for some months that Don Juan and Doña María de las Mercedes had had all four of their children together. Alfonsito was a pupil at the lycée in Madrid and was about to become a cadet at the Spanish naval college at Marín near Pontevedra. Alfonsito was regarded as the family favourite, witty, intelligent and more *simpático* than his rather introspective elder brother. His passion for golf and sailing had brought him particularly close to Don Juan.[14]

On 29 March, Maundy Thursday, the entire family, dressed in black, attended morning mass and took communion at the small church of San Antonio de Estoril near the sea front. The principal Maundy Thursday service, which they also intended to attend, would not take place until the evening. In those days, Catholics still had to prepare for communion by fasting from midnight of the previous day. Rather than fast for 24 hours, the family had taken communion at the early mass. After a frugal lunch, Don Juan and Juan Carlos accompanied Alfonsito to the Estoril golf club where he was taking part in a competition (the *Taça Visconde Pereira de Machado*). Despite the cold blustery weather, Alfonsito won the semi-final and was looking forward to playing in the final on Easter Saturday. With no sign of a let-up in the cold wind and showers, the Spanish royal family went home. At 6 p.m. they attended the evening mass in the church of San Antonio and then returned home. At 8.30 p.m., the car of the family doctor, Joaquín Abreu Loureiro, screeched to a halt outside the Villa Giralda. Apparently, Juan Carlos and Alfonsito had been in the games room on the first floor of the house, engaged in target practice with a small calibre .22 revolver, while waiting for dinner. A recent gift, the pistol was, at any reasonable distance, relatively innocuous. Nevertheless, there had been an accident in which Alfonso was shot and died almost immediately.

On Friday 30 March, the Portuguese press carried a laconic official communiqué about Alfonso's death issued by the Spanish Embassy in Lisbon. 'Whilst his Highness the Infante Alfonso was cleaning a revolver last evening with his brother, a shot was fired hitting his forehead and killing him in a few minutes. The accident took place at 20.30 hours, after the Infante's return from the Maundy Thursday religious service, during which he had received holy communion.' The decision to make this anodyne statement and to impose a blanket of silence over the details was taken personally by Franco.[15]

Inevitably, however, there were rumours that the gun had been in Juan Carlos's hands at the time of the fatal shot. Within three weeks, these rumours were being stated as undisputed fact in the Italian press.[16] They were not denied by Don Juan at the time nor have they ever been denied by Juan Carlos since. Shortly after the accident, Gonzalo Fernández de la Mora, a monarchist and member of Opus Dei on Don Juan's Privy Council who later served Franco as Minister of Public Works, met Pedro Sainz Rodríguez and commented later: 'His short and portly figure was woebegone because a pistol had gone off in Prince Juan Carlos's hand and killed his brother Alfonso.' It is now widely accepted that Juan Carlos's finger was on the trigger when the fatal shot was fired.[17]

In her autobiography, Doña María de las Mercedes neither denied nor confirmed that it was Juan Carlos who was holding the gun when it went off. On the other hand, she directly contradicted the official statement. Doña María explained that, on the previous day, the boys had been fooling around with the gun, shooting at streetlamps. Because of this, Don Juan had forbidden them to play with the weapon. While waiting for the evening service, the two boys became bored and went upstairs to play with the gun again. They were getting ready to shoot at a target when the gun went off shortly after 8 p.m.[18] One possibility, later suggested by Doña María to her dressmaker, Josefina Carolo, is that Juan Carlos playfully pointed it at Alfonsito and, unaware that the gun was loaded, pulled the trigger. In similar terms, Juan Carlos apparently told a Portuguese friend, Bernardo Arnoso, that he pulled the trigger not knowing that the gun was loaded, and that it went off and the bullet ricocheted off a wall and hit Alfonsito in the face. The most plausible suggestion, possibly made by the boys' sister Pilar to the Greek author Helena Matheopoulos, is that Alfonsito left the room to get a snack for himself and Juan Carlos. Returning with his hands full, he pushed the door open with his shoulder. The door knocked into his brother's arm. Juan Carlos involuntarily pulled the trigger just as Alfonsito's head appeared around the door.[19]

Doña María de las Mercedes later recalled: 'I was reading in my drawing room, and Don Juan was in his study, next door. Suddenly, I heard Juanito coming down the stairs telling the girl who worked for us: "No, I must tell them myself". My heart stood still.'[20] Both parents ran upstairs to the games room where they found their son lying in a pool of blood. Don Juan tried to revive him but the boy died in his arms. He placed a Spanish flag over him and, according to Antonio Eraso, a friend of Alfonsito, turned to Juan Carlos and said, 'Swear to me that you didn't do it on purpose.'[21]

Don Alfonso was buried in the cemetery at Cascais at midday on Saturday 31 March 1956. The funeral service was conducted by the Papal Nuncio to Portugal, and was attended by prominent Spanish monarchists and royal figures from several European countries. The desolate Don Juan could barely contain his distress, his eyes full of uncomprehending sorrow. Yet he greeted them all with grace and dignity. The Portuguese government was represented by the President of the Republic. In contrast, the Caudillo was represented merely by the Minister Plenipotentiary of the Spanish Embassy, Ignacio de Muguiro. The Ambassador, Franco's brother Nicolás, was in bed, recovering from a car accident.[22] There were messages of sympathy from all over the world, including one each from General Franco and Doña Carmen Polo.

Juan Carlos attended in the uniform of a Zaragoza officer cadet. His look of vacant desolation masked his inner agony of guilt. After the ceremony, Don Juan took the pistol that had killed Alfonsito and threw it into the sea. There was considerable speculation about the gun's origins. It has been variously claimed that the weapon had been a present to Alfonsito from Franco or from the Conde de los Andes, or that someone in the Zaragoza military academy had given it to Juan Carlos. The autobiography of Juan Carlos's mother states discreetly that: 'The two brothers had brought from Madrid the small six-millimetre pistol and it has never been revealed who gave it to them.'[23]

Unable to support the presence of his elder son, Don Juan ordered Juan Carlos to return immediately to the Zaragoza academy. General Martínez Campos and Major Emilio García Conde arrived in a Spanish military aircraft in which the Prince was taken back to Zaragoza. The incident affected the Prince dramatically. The rather extrovert figure, so popular with his comrades in the academy for his participation in high jinks and chasing the local girls, now seemed afflicted by a tendency to introspection. Relations with his father were never the same again. Although he would return, superficially at least, to being a fun-loving young man, he was profoundly changed by the event. More alone than ever, he became morose and guarded in his speech and actions.[24]

The death of her younger son profoundly affected Doña María de las Mercedes who fell into a deep depression, began to drink, and turned ever more for company to her friend Amalín López-Dóriga. Doña María was held partly responsible for the accident by her husband because she had given in to her sons' repeated requests and allowed them to play with the gun despite their father's prohibition. According to one such report, by the French journalist Françoise Laot on the basis of interviews with Doña María, she personally unlocked the *secreter* (writing bureau) where the gun was kept and handed it to Juan Carlos. Françoise Laot would later state that, 30 years after the accident, María de las Mercedes told her, 'I have never been truly wretched except when my son died.'[25] So affected was Doña María that she had to spend some time at a clinic near Frankfurt.

His personal devastation aside, the death of Alfonso significantly weakened the political position of Don Juan. Henceforth, he would be more dependent on the vagaries of the situation of Juan Carlos in Spain. In the words of Rafael Borràs, the distinguished publisher and author of a major biography of Don Juan, the death of Alfonso: 'deprived the Conde de Barcelona, from the point of view of dynastic legitimacy, of a possible substitute in the event of the Príncipe de Asturias agreeing, against his father's will, and outside the normal line of succession, to be General Franco's successor within the terms of the *Ley de Sucesión*'. Borràs speculates that, had Alfonso lived, his very existence might have conditioned the subsequent behaviour of Juan Carlos in the struggle between his father and Franco.[26]

The Prince's uncle, Don Jaime, endeavoured to derive political advantage from the tragedy. His first reaction had been to send a message of sympathy. However, on 17 April 1956 when the Italian newspaper *Il Settimo Giorno* published an account of the accident which pointed the finger at Juan Carlos, he told his secretary Ramón de Alderete: 'I am distraught to see the tragedy of Estoril dealt with in this way by a journalist who has been used in good faith, because I refuse to doubt the veracity of my unfortunate nephew's version, as published by my brother. In this situation, and in my position as head of the Borbón family, I can only deeply disagree with the stance of my brother Juan who, in order to prevent future speculation, has neither demanded the opening of an official enquiry into the accident nor called for an autopsy on the body of my nephew, as is normal in such cases.' These words were reproduced in the French press, presumably via Alderete and with the permission of Don Jaime.

Given that neither Don Juan nor Juan Carlos responded to Don Jaime's demand, on 16 January 1957, he took the matter further and gave his secretary the following letter:

'Reuil-Malmaison 16-1-1957.

Dear Ramón,

Several friends have recently confirmed that it was my nephew Juan Carlos who accidentally killed his brother Alfonso. This confirms something of which I have been certain ever since my brother Juan failed to sue those who had spoken publicly of this terrible situation. It obliges me to ask that you request in my name, when you feel that the time is right, that the appropriate national or international courts undertake a judicial enquiry in order to clarify officially the circumstances of the death of my nephew Alfonso (RIP). I demand that this judicial enquiry take place because it is my duty as Head of the House of Borbón, and because I cannot accept that someone who is incapable of accepting his own responsibilities should aspire to the throne of Spain. With a warm embrace.

Jaime de Borbón.'[27]

There is no evidence to suggest that Alderete acted on the letter or, if he did, that a court showed an interest in the case. Nevertheless, the combination of insensitivity and ambition demonstrated by Don Jaime was breathtaking.

The Madrid authorities were shaken by the news of the accident. Rumours started to circulate in the capital to the effect that Juan Carlos had been so overcome by grief that he was thinking of renouncing his rights to the throne and joining a friary as penance. In fact, as his father had ordered, Juan Carlos was back in Zaragoza within 48 hours of the accident. Franco's relative silence on this issue was eloquent. Commenting on the tragedy to one of Don Juan's supporters, he said with a total lack of sympathy 'people do not like princes who are out of luck'. It was a recurrent theme. Two years later, he explained why he did not favour press references to Alfonsito: 'The memory could cast shadows over his brother for the accident and make simple folk dwell on the bad luck of the family when people like their Princes to have lucky stars.'[28] Perhaps most cruelly of all, within a year of the accident,

Franco had permitted the Ministry of Education to sanction the publication and use in secondary schools of a textbook entitled *La moral católica* (Catholic Morality) which used the incident to explore the limits of personal culpability.[29] Years later, Don Juan himself related that, when they met in 1960, Franco had justified keeping him off the throne by saying that the Borbón family was doomed: 'Just look at yourself, Your Highness: two haemophiliac brothers; another deaf and dumb; one daughter blind; one son shot dead. Such an accumulation of disasters in a single family is not something that could possibly appeal to the Spanish people.'[30]

Franco's lack of sympathy was a reflection of his hostility to Don Juan, of his own lack of humanity and perhaps too of the fact that, in March 1956, he was cooling on the idea of a monarchist succession. The scale of Falangist discontent that had been evident since the meeting at Las Cabezas seems to have led to him mulling over the mutual dependence between Caudillo and single party. This was manifested in the cabinet reshuffle of 16 February 1956. The liberal Christian Democrat Minister of Education, Joaquín Ruiz Giménez, was dropped, a punishment for his failure to control unrest in the universities. He was replaced by a conservative Falangist academic, Jesús Rubio García-Mina. Raimundo Fernández Cuesta, the Secretary-General of the *Movimiento*, was also removed for his failure to control Falangist indiscipline. He had been engaged in preparations to tighten up the Francoist laws lest any future king try to free himself from the ideals of the *Movimiento*. He was replaced by the sycophantic Falangist zealot, José Luis de Arrese. Alarmingly, for both Don Juan and for those who were looking forward to the eventual creation of a Francoist monarchy, the Caudillo commissioned Arrese to take over the programme of constitutional preparations for the post-Franco future.[31]

Arrese took his commission to be the preparation of an entirely Falangist future for the regime – one that would have no room for Don Juan nor even for Juan Carlos. The enthusiasm with which he went about his ambitious task would soon provoke a significant polarization of the Francoist coalition. Franco's cabinet changes were ill-considered reactions to a deep-rooted split at the heart of his coalition. The *Ley de Sucesión* had been a cunning way of neutralizing regime monarchists and outmanoeuvring Don Juan. However, the prospect of a future monarchy, even a Francoist one, alienated the Falange. And Franco had few options but to cling to the Falange. If the Falange were weakened, the Caudillo's fate would lie less in his own hands than in those of the senior Army officers who wanted an earlier rather than a later restoration of the monarchy. The situation required a complex balancing act and Arrese was more human cannonball than tightrope walker. The violent protests of Falangist students in February 1956 had been a symptom of a long death agony rather than of youthful vitality. With his mind elsewhere, occupied by the inexorable rise of Moroccan nationalism, and thus underestimating the seriousness of the crisis, Franco had responded instinctively by reasserting Falangist pre-eminence within his coalition. He was not controlling events but letting himself be driven by them.[32]

Some months earlier, prominent Falangists had presented Franco with a memorandum demanding the swift implementation of their 'unfinished revolution'. It was effectively a blueprint for a more totalitarian one-party State structure with no place for the monarchy of Don Juan.[33] Franco now seemed to be giving the green light for his new Secretary-General to implement the memorandum's recommendations. Arrese's plans were seen by Traditionalists, monarchists and Catholics as a totalitarian scheme which would block even limited pluralism under a restored monarchy.[34]

With the help of Rafael Calvo Serer, the Conde de Ruiseñada, at the time Don Juan's representative in Spain, elaborated a scheme to block Arrese's plans by hastening the restoration of the monarchy. Ruiseñada was equally devoted to both Don Juan and to Franco. For some time, he had been in contact with General Juan Bautista Sánchez, the Captain-General of Barcelona, an austere and eminently decent man who was appalled at what he saw as the corruption of the regime. Now, the so-called '*Operación Ruiseñada*' envisaged a bloodless, negotiated *pronunciamiento*, rather like that of General Miguel Primo de Rivera in 1923. The lead would be taken by the Barcelona garrison, with the agreement of the other Captains-General, and Franco would be persuaded to withdraw from active politics to the decorative position of 'regent'. While the restoration of the monarchy was implemented, day-to-day running of the government would be assumed by Bautista Sánchez. The involvement of Bautista Sánchez – the most respected professional in the Armed Forces – helped secure the support of other monarchist generals against Arrese. Don Juan had considerable doubts as to whether this wildly optimistic scheme had any hopes of success but, concerned by Arrese's plans, agreed to let it go ahead.[35]

Needless to say, Franco's intelligence services, which bugged most of Don Juan's telephone conversations with Spain, were aware of what was being plotted. It was thus all the easier for Arrese, on a tour of the south with the Caudillo, to persuade him that a Falangist future rather than a monarchist one would be truer to his legacy. Franco gave vent to his impatience with Ruiseñada and Don Juan in speeches to which he gave, according to a delighted Arrese, 'a twist of superfalangism and aggression that seemed to many to be announcing the beginning of the final triumphant era'. In Huelva on 25 April 1956, the Caudillo delighted his audience with an unmistakable and insulting reference to the monarchists and to Juan Carlos. He declared that: 'We take no notice of the clumsy plotting of several dozen political intriguers nor their kids. Because if they got in the way of the fulfilment of our historic destiny, if anything got in our way, just as we did in our Crusade, we would unleash the flood of blueshirts and red berets which would crush them.'[36] At a huge meeting of Falangists in Seville on 1 May, he passionately denounced the enemies of the Falangist revolution. In a passage of his speech that seemed to be directed at Don Juan personally, he referred openly to his own near-monarchical status. Describing the *Movimiento* with himself at the pinnacle, he said: 'We are a monarchy without royalty, but a monarchy all the same.' Stating that national life had to be based on the ideals of the Falange, he declared that: 'the Falange can live without the monarchy but what could not survive is a monarchy without the Falange.'[37] Many Francoists were happy enough to go along with the *Movimiento* as long as it remained a vague umbrella institution, but defining it so closely to Falangist terms led many to re-evaluate their own preferences.

One of them, the Minister of Justice, the Traditionalist Antonio Iturmendi, was sufficiently alarmed to commission one of his brightest collaborators to produce a critical analysis of Arrese's preliminary sketches for constitutional change. It was a decision that would have considerable impact on the later trajectory of Juan Carlos. The man given the job was the Catalan monarchist and professor of administrative law, Laureano López Rodó. His report was to be a blueprint of his growing commitment to the cause of Juan Carlos.[38] The deeply religious and austere López Rodó, who would quickly rise to a discreet but considerable eminence, was a typical senior member of Opus Dei, quietly confident, hard-working and efficient.

More immediately significant, at the beginning of July 1956, General Antonio Barroso Sánchez-Guerra protested to the Caudillo about Arrese's activities. He was just about to replace Franco's cousin Pacón as head of the Caudillo's military household. Along with two other monarchist generals, one of whom may well have been Bautista Sánchez, he discussed with Franco a version of the *Operación Ruiseñada*, in which a military directory would take over and hold a plebiscite on the issue of monarchy or republic, in the confident expectation that such a consultation would produce support for the monarchy.[39] While hardly likely to go along with *Operación Ruiseñada*, Franco was sufficiently sensitive to military opinion to begin gradually to restrain Arrese. Nonetheless, when he made a speech to the *Consejo Nacional de FET y de las JONS* on 17 July 1956, the 20th anniversary of the military uprising, he used notes provided by Arrese, 'to ensure that he did not say anything, either influenced by other sectors of the *Movimiento* or in an effort to calm liberal and monarchist anxieties, that might put us in an embarrassing situation later on'.[40] Essentially a long hymn of praise to his own achievements, although not without passing praise for Fascist Italy and Nazi Germany, the speech reassured Falangists that a future monarchical successor would not be allowed to use his absolute powers to bring about a transition to democracy.[41]

Unaware that the tide was turning against him, Arrese went ahead with his plans, distributing a draft to members of the *Consejo Nacional*, the supreme consultative body in the Francoist firmament. Although his text recognized Franco's absolute powers for life, it left the decision as to his royal successor at the mercy of the *Consejo Nacional* and the Secretary-General of the Falange. When the text was distributed, there was uproar in the Francoist establishment, and monarchists, Catholics, archbishops and generals joined together in outrage. There were protests from three cardinals, a government minister (the Conde de Vallellano, Minister of Public Works) and several generals, at what seemed to be an attempt to give the *Movimiento* totalitarian control over Spain and block the return of the monarchy.[42] By early January 1957, Arrese had been obliged to dilute his text sufficiently to satisfy his military and clerical opponents.[43]

Between the two poles of the proposal of *Operación Ruiseñada* for a negotiated transition to Don Juan and Arrese's plans for a resurgent Falangism, there emerged a middle option favoured by Luis Carrero Blanco, who had recently been promoted to Admiral. To the detriment of Don Juan and the benefit of Juan Carlos, this would ultimately be adopted by Franco. It consisted of an attempt to build on the *Ley de Sucesión* by elaborating the legislative framework for an absolute monarchy, in order to guarantee the continuity of Francoism after the death of the Caudillo. The legal expert commissioned to produce a blueprint was Laureano López Rodó. Carrero Blanco had been immensely impressed by López Rodó's critique of Arrese's text. Recognizing his talent and capacity for hard work, at the end of 1956 Carrero Blanco asked him to set up a technical secretariat in the *Presidencia del Gobierno* (the office of the President of the Council of Ministers) to prepare plans for a major administrative reform.[44] As Secretary-General of the *Presidencia*, the doggedly loyal Carrero Blanco was Franco's political chief of staff. As Franco began to relax his grip on day-to-day politics, Carrero Blanco was gradually metamorphosing into a Prime Minister. López Rodó, in his turn, would swiftly become Carrero's own chief of staff.

The Opus Dei was thus well placed for the future but was still hedging its bets. Just as Rafael Calvo Serer was banking on Don Juan being Franco's eventual successor, López Rodó was working on a long-term plan for a gradual evolution towards the monarchy in the person of Prince Juan Carlos. His plans would not come to fruition for many years. For the moment, Bautista Sánchez and other partisans of Don Juan were trying to implement the *Operación Ruiseñada* in order to marginalize Franco and place Don Juan upon the throne. Bautista Sánchez was under constant surveillance by Franco's intelligence services, and therefore did not attend, in December 1956, a meeting of military and civilian monarchists involved in the scheme who gathered under the cover of a hunting party at one of the estates of Ruiseñada, El Alamín near Toledo.[45] Nevertheless, Bautista Sánchez continued to be seen by the regime as dangerous, particularly when, in mid-January 1957, another transport users' strike broke out in Barcelona. Although not as violent as that of 1951, the coincidence of anti-regime demonstrations at the university alarmed the authorities.[46] Bautista Sánchez was highly critical of the Civil Governor of the province, General Felipe Acedo Colunga, for the brutal force with which demonstrations of workers and students were crushed. Franco perceived this as tantamount to giving moral support to the strikers.[47]

Madrid was buzzing with rumours and Franco quickly jumped to the conclusion that Bautista Sánchez was fostering the strike to facilitate a coup in favour of the monarchy. After his summer-time conversation with Barroso about *Operación Ruiseñada*, Franco was deeply suspicious of the monarchists. In fact, there was little or no chance of military action despite the wishful thinking of Ruiseñada, Sainz Rodríguez and others. However, the conversations between the royalist plotters and Don Juan's house in Estoril were being tapped by the Caudillo's security services, and Franco reacted to the transcripts of these optimistic fantasies as if they were fact.[48] He sent two regiments of the Foreign Legion to Catalonia, under his own direct orders, to join in military manoeuvres being supervised by Bautista Sánchez. Franco also sent Bautista Sánchez's friend, the Captain-General of Valencia, General Joaquín Ríos Capapé, to talk him out of his support for

Operación Ruiseñada. The Minister for the Army, General Agustín Muñoz Grandes, also appeared in the course of the manoeuvres and confronted Bautista Sánchez with the news that he was being relieved of the command of Captain-General of Barcelona. On the following day, 29 January 1957, Bautista Sánchez was found dead in his room in a hotel in Puigcerdá.[49] Wild rumours proliferated that he had been murdered – possibly even shot by another general, perhaps given a fatal injection by Falangist agents.[50] A long-term sufferer of angina pectoris, it is more likely that Bautista Sánchez had died of a heart attack after the shock of his painful interview with Muñoz Grandes.[51]

Meanwhile, Juan Carlos was undergoing the process of getting over the tragedy of Alfonsito's death. He seems to have adopted a forced gaiety and, understandably for a young man of nearly 19, spent as much time as his studies permitted in the company of girls. There were many of them and he had a readiness to think himself in love. He oscillated between being infatuated with, and just being very fond of, his childhood friend, Princess Maria Gabriella di Savoia. Neither Franco nor Don Juan approved of the relationship, among other reasons because she was the daughter of the exiled King Umberto of Italy, who had little prospect of recovering his throne.[52] However, in December 1956, during the Christmas holidays at Estoril, Juan Carlos met Contessa Olghina Nicolis di Robilant, an extremely beautiful Italian aristocrat and minor film actress, who was friendly with Maria Gabriella and her sister Pia. She was four years older than him. His infatuation was instant and, before the night was over, he had told her that he loved her. They began a sporadic affair that lasted until 1960. She found him passionate and impulsive, not at all what she expected after what she had heard about the tragedy of Alfonsito. 'Juanito,' she later recalled, 'did not show any signs of the slightest complex. He wore a black tie and a little black ribbon as a sign of mourning. That was all. I asked myself if it was a lack of feeling or if his behaviour was forced. Whatever the case, it seemed a little soon to be going to parties, dancing and necking.' After responding to his advances, she asked about his relationship with Maria Gabriella. He allegedly replied, 'I don't have much freedom of choice, try to understand. And she's the one I prefer out of the so-called eligible ones.'[53]

In 1988, the 47 love letters that Juan Carlos wrote to Olghina between 1956 and 1959 were published in the Italian magazine *Oggi* and later in the Spanish magazine *Interviú*. One of the letters was extraordinarily revealing both of the situation in which the 19-year-old Prince found himself and of his relative maturity and sense of dynastic responsibility. He wrote: 'At the moment, I love you more than anyone else, but I understand, because it is my obligation, that I cannot marry you and so I have to think of someone else. The only girl that I have seen so far that attracts me physically and morally, indeed in every way, is Gabriella, and she does, a lot. I hope, or rather I think it would be wise, for the moment, not to say anything about getting serious or even having an understanding with her. But I want her to know something about how I see things, but nothing more because we are both very young.' He repeated the message in another letter to Olghina in which he pointed out that his duties to his father and to Spain would prevent him ever marrying her.[54]

In her memoirs and in interviews following the publication of the letters, Olghina claimed that Don Juan had done everything possible to put obstacles in the way of the relationship. As she herself realized, Don Juan's opposition put her in the same position as Verdi's *La Traviata*, the courtesan abandoned because of the needs of her suitor's family. In view of the innumerable lovers whose names tumble through the pages of her memoirs, Don Juan's concern was entirely comprehensible. At one point, he stopped her being invited to the coming-out celebration in Portofino for Juan Carlos's cousin, Maria Teresa Marone-Cinzano. According to Olghina, this provoked a ferocious row between Don Juan and his son, who threatened not to go to the ball. Juan Carlos eventually agreed to attend, but when he left early to go to see Olghina, there was a scuffle with his father.[55]

Olghina provides an interesting testimony of the Prince's personality and convictions as he entered his twenties. She knew a passionate young man, who liked fast cars, motorboats and girls, although he never forgot his position. He was, she said, 'very serious albeit no saint'. She declared that 'he wasn't at all shy, but was rather puritanical' and that 'he was always very honest with me'. He disliked women whom he considered too calculating or 'of less than stringent morals'. His puritanical streak was perhaps typical of a Spanish young man of his generation – it did not prevent him ardently pressing on her his 'hot, dry and wise lips' nor spending nights in hotels with her. He was also very generous, even though he didn't have much money at the time. Interestingly, Olghina claims that Juan Carlos disliked hunting – one of Franco's favoured pastimes – because he had no desire to kill animals.[56]

When the interviewer suggested to Olghina that Juan Carlos's letters gave the impression that he had been more attached to her than she to him, she replied that this wasn't the case. The problem was, rather, that she was aware that he would never marry her. As a result, she tried to keep her distance from him. Juan Carlos, she said, 'was very clear on the fact that his destiny was to give himself to Spain and that, in order to achieve this, he needed to marry into a reigning dynasty . . . Juan Carlos was convinced that he would be King of Spain.'[57] It was later suggested that Olghina di Robilant blackmailed Juan Carlos. She was allegedly paid ten million pesetas by Juan Carlos for the letters, at which point she sent the originals to him but kept copies, which she then sold for publication.[58]

Despite his close relationship with Olghina, Juan Carlos had Maria Gabriella di Savoia's photograph in his room in the Zaragoza academy. He was ordered to remove it from his bedside table on the grounds that: 'General Franco might be annoyed if he visited the academy.' This ridiculous intrusion of the Prince's privacy may have been an initiative of the director of the academy rather than of Franco himself. However, Franco knew about it. That there was no respect for Juan Carlos's privacy would be seen again in 1958. When the Prince visited the United States as a naval cadet on a Spanish training ship, he took a fancy to a beautiful Brazilian girl at one of the dances organized for the crew members. He wrote to her, only to discover later that all his letters had ended up on Franco's desk. Again, in late January 1960, having been informed that Juan Carlos still had Maria Gabriella's photograph on his bedside table, the Caudillo would call in one of the Prince's closest aides, Major Emilio García Conde, to discuss the matter. Clearly preoccupied by the significance of the photograph, Franco said, 'We've got to find a Princess for the Prince.' He then went on to list a series of names whose unsuitability was pointed out by García Conde. When the latter suggested the daughters of the King of Greece, Franco replied categorically, 'Don Juan Carlos will never marry a Greek princess!' He had two objections – the fact that they were not Roman Catholics and his belief that King Paul was a freemason.[59]

The Caudillo felt that he had a right to interfere in the Prince's romantic affairs. He told Pacón that he regarded Maria Gabriella di Savoia as altogether too free and with 'ideas altogether too modern'. Newspaper speculation abounded about the Prince's relationship with Maria Gabriella, and Juan Carlos remained keen on her for some time. It was rumoured that their engagement would be announced on 12 October 1960 at the silver wedding celebrations of Don Juan and Doña María de las Mercedes. The Prince's choice of bride had enormous significance both for the royal family and the possible succession to Franco. The chosen candidate, irrespective of her human qualities, would have to be a royal princess, preferably of a ruling dynasty, financially comfortable and acceptable to General Franco. Sentiment would always take second place to political considerations. Some days before the anniversary party, the matter was discussed at a session of Don Juan's Privy Council. On the basis of having enjoyed herself rather publicly at the previous spring's *Feria de Sevilla*, Maria Gabriella was denounced as being frivolous – which José María Pemán thought ridiculous. In any case, Don Juan told Pemán: 'I don't think Juanito will be mature enough for at least a year or two.'[60]

Olghina di Robilant's view that, already by the late 1950s, Juan Carlos believed that he would succeed Franco and thus take his father's place on the throne was, of course, precisely the plan of Laureano López Rodó. On the reasonable assumption that there would be a monarchical succession to Franco, the Opus Dei was consolidating its links with both of the principal potential candidates. Thus, just as Rafael Calvo Serer remained close to Don Juan, so Juan Carlos was central to the far-reaching political plans of López Rodó.

In the wake of the internal dissent provoked by Arrese's schemes, the Barcelona strike, serious economic problems and the push for an accelerated transition to the monarchy that had culminated in the death of Bautista Sánchez, Franco reluctantly decided that the time had come to renew his ministerial team. His hesitation was not just a symptom of his lifelong caution but was also a reflection of his inability to react with any flexibility to new problems. The cabinet reshuffle of February 1957 was to be a major turning point in the road from the dictatorship to the eventual monarchy of Juan Carlos. It was to open up the process whereby Franco would abandon his commitment to economic autarky and accept Spanish integration into the Organization for European Economic Co-operation and the International Monetary Fund. The weary Caudillo was ceasing to be an active Prime Minister and turning himself into ceremonial Head of State, relying ever more on Carrero Blanco as executive head of the government. The recently promoted admiral, no more versed than Franco in the ways of governing a modern economy, relied increasingly on López Rodó who, at 37 years of age, had become technical Secretary-General of the *Presidencia del Gobierno*.[61] The long-term implications of López Rodó's growing influence could hardly have been anticipated by Franco or Carrero Blanco, let alone by Don Juan and his son.

The detail of the cabinet changes reflected Franco's readiness to defer to the advice of Carrero Blanco who, in turn, drew on the views of López Rodó. Indeed, such was López Rodó's closeness to Carrero Blanco that his own collaborators came to refer to him as 'Carrero Negro'.[62] Having witnessed the ferocity of internal opposition to Arrese's proposals, Franco now went in the other direction, clipping the wings of the Falange. The Falangists he appointed could scarcely have been more docile. Other key appointments saw General Muñoz Grandes replaced as the Minister for the Army by the monarchist General Antonio Barroso. While hardly likely to become involved in conspiracy, Barroso was infinitely more sympathetic to Don Juan than the pro-Falangist Muñoz Grandes. Most important of all was the inclusion of a group of technocrats associated with the Opus Dei. Together, López Rodó, the new Minister of Commerce, Alberto Ullastres Calvo, and the new Minister of Finance, Mariano Navarro Rubio, would undertake a major project of economic and political transformation of the regime. The implications of their work for the post-Franco future would dramatically affect the position of Juan Carlos.[63]

That was made clear in some astonishingly frank remarks made by López Rodó to the Conde de Ruiseñada shortly after the cabinet reshuffle. López Rodó claimed in effect that the marginalization of Franco was one of the long-term objectives of the technocrats. He told Ruiseñada that the 'Tercera Fuerza' (Third Force) plans of Opus Dei members like Rafael Calvo Serer and Florentino Pérez Embid (the editor of El Alcázar) were doomed to failure since, 'it is impossible to talk to Franco about politics because he gets the impression that they are trying to get him out of his seat or paving the way for his replacement.' He then made the revealing comment that 'The only trick is to get him to accept an administrative plan to decentralize the economy. He doesn't think of that as being directed against him personally. He will give us a free hand and, then, once inside the administration, we will see how far we can go with our political objectives, which have to be masked as far as possible.'[64]

At the end of March 1957, shortly before the first anniversary of the death of Alfonsito de Borbón, the Conde de Ruiseñada had a bust of him made and placed in the grounds of El Alamín. A number of young monarchists were invited and Luis María Anson, a brilliant young journalist and leader of the monarchist university youth movement, assuming that the bust would be unveiled by Juan Carlos, expressed concern that the occasion would be too painful for him. Anson was astonished to be told by Ruiseñada that the Caudillo had already instructed him to ask Juan Carlos's cousin, Alfonso de Borbón y Dampierre, to preside at the ceremony. 'I want you to cultivate him, Ruiseñada. Because if the son turns out as badly for us as his father has, we'll have to start thinking about Don Alfonso.' Anson reported the conversation to Don Juan. Until this time, the pretensions of Don Jaime and his son had not been taken entirely seriously in Estoril. Henceforth, there would be an acute awareness of the dangers of Franco applying the *Ley de Sucesión* in favour of Alfonso de Borbón y Dampierre.[65]

In May 1957, speaking with Dionisio Ridruejo, a Falangist poet who had broken with the regime, López Rodó revealed his concerns about the fragility of a system dependent on the mortality of Franco. López Rodó wanted to see the Caudillo's personal dictatorship replaced by a more secure structure of governmental institutions and constitutional laws. Allegedly declaring that, in the wake of the recent cabinet changes, 'the personal power of General Franco has come to an end', López Rodó hoped to have Juan Carlos officially proclaimed royal successor while Franco was still alive. It was rather like Ruiseñada's plan, except with Juan Carlos instead of Don Juan in the role of successor. Until 1968, when the Prince would reach 30, the age at which the *Ley de Sucesión* permitted him to assume the throne, Franco would remain as regent. To prevent the Head of State, King or Caudillo, suffering unnecessary political attrition, there would be a separation of the Headship of State and the position of Prime Minister.[66] López Rodó's optimism in this respect would be seriously dented in November 1957. At that point, he came near to being dismissed when Franco noticed that the decrees emanating from the *Presidencia del Gobierno* were limiting his powers.[67] López Rodó's plans for political change had to be introduced with extreme delicacy if the Caudillo were not to call an immediate halt to them. That, together with the hostility of the still powerful Falangists to the concept of monarchy, ensured that the realization of his programme would take another 12 years.

On 18 July 1957, Juan Carlos had passed out as Second-Lieutenant at Zaragoza. After showing off his uniform in Estoril, he went to visit his grandmother in Lausanne. While in Switzerland, he gave a press interview in which he stated that he regarded his father as King. His declaration of loyalty to Don Juan annoyed the Caudillo. Franco commented to Pacón, 'just like Don Juan, the Prince is badly advised and he should keep quiet and not speak so much.' Shortly afterwards, Juan Carlos visited Franco and the three military ministers of the cabinet. It may be supposed that the Caudillo's displeasure at his comments to the Swiss press was communicated to him because it was a mistake he would never repeat.[68]

On 20 August 1957, Juan Carlos entered the naval school at Marín, in the Ría de Pontevedra in Galicia, an idyllic spot marred only by the stench from the nearby paper mills. After facing initial hostility from some of his fellow cadets, his easy-going affability and capacity for physical hardship won them over.[69] While at Marín, he met Pacón, who wrote: 'I found him an absolute delight. It is impossible to conceive of a more agreeable, straightforward and pleasant lad.'[70] The Prince was unaware of López Rodó's schemes for his future. By now, the Catalan lawyer had been asked by Carrero Blanco to draw up a set of constitutional texts which would allow the eventual installation of the monarchy, yet still be acceptable to those who wanted the *Movimiento* to survive after the 'biological fact', as the death of Franco was coming to be called. The question of the transition from the dictator to an installed monarch, and López Rodó's draft texts, were discussed interminably in the cabinet. However, Franco had no interest in a process that he regarded as no more than fine-tuning the *Ley de Sucesión*. In any case, he was in no hurry to think about death.

Throughout the summer of 1957, Ruiseñada and López Rodó both tried to arrange an interview between Franco and Don Juan. Whether their agendas in doing so coincided is difficult to say. In any case, they had not consulted Don Juan previously. From Scotland, where he was on holiday, Don Juan refused on the grounds that he could see no sign of progress or reform in the regime. Indeed, on 25 June, he had sent Franco a letter and memorandum in which he stated that there was no point in a meeting until Franco was prepared to make a major step forward in planning for the future. 'The time for a new interview will be when Your Excellency judges that the opportune moment has arrived for a significant change. Such an interview should not be limited to a mere interchange of news and ideas but rather, unless you think otherwise, should deal with the fundamental issues of Spain's political future and this is not something that can be improvised in the course of a conversation.' It is not difficult to imagine how the Caudillo reacted to the suggestion that Don Juan might be in a position to negotiate about the political future. His role, if any, so far as Franco saw it, was simply to swear an oath to accept the Francoist system *in toto*.

A reference by Don Juan to 'the interim status of the present regime' might also have been designed to infuriate Franco. He was equally irritated by the suggestion that the monarchy under Don Juan would deviate from the essential bases of that regime. He replied in early September: 'The monarchy should be born as a natural and logical evolution of the regime itself towards other institutional forms of state; from a strong, authoritarian state that safeguards the national and moral values in defence of which the *Movimiento Nacional* emerged, and at the same time, opens the way to those new kinds of state demanded by the needs of the country and which can assure the consolidation and survival of the monarchical regime.'

Franco took the greatest offence at the implication that the future monarchy might change anything at all about his regime. He described Don Juan's points as 'unacceptable' and reminded him that while constitutional plans were in place for a monarchy, nothing had been settled about the individuals who might sit on the throne. The Caudillo made it clear that there was no question whatsoever of a different conception of the State succeeding his regime. As from on high, the all-powerful master lecturing the recalcitrant servant, he wrote: 'Herein lies the great confusion that has prompted your memorandum, not only in regard to the needs of the country and to the opinion of great sectors of the nation but also in regard to what it means to be able to forge a new legality. Our War of Liberation, with all its sacrifices, meant that the people won with their blood the situation and the regime that we now enjoy. The *Ley de Sucesión* came, nearly ten years later, to give written form to the legality forged by the man who saved an entire society, re-established peace and law and order and placed the nation firmly on the road to its resurgence. To call into question this long consolidated legality, to harbour reservations about what has been constituted and to try to open a constituent period, would signify a massive suicide. It would give hope to all the ambitions and appetites of the rebellious minorities and would offer foreigners and enemies from outside a new opportunity to besiege and destroy Spain.' Such a mixture of arrogance and paranoia left no room for dialogue.[71]

Don Juan had just returned from his holiday in Scotland and absorbed this thunderous rebuff when López Rodó arrived in Lisbon. He was in Portugal as part of a Spanish economic delegation. At a lunch given by the Portuguese Prime Minister, Marcelo Caetano, journalists asked the Spanish Ambassador, Nicolás Franco, if it was true that the Caudillo wished Don Juan to abdicate in favour of Juan Carlos. He replied in typical *gallego* (Galician) fashion, 'I've never heard my brother say anything about that. But I think that if he can have two spare wheels, he wouldn't want to make do with only one.' There can be little doubt that the exchange was reported back to Villa Giralda and can only have caused Don Juan considerable concern.

López Rodó took the opportunity of the trip to arrange a clandestine meeting with Don Juan in the centre of Lisbon at the home of a Portuguese friend. Unaware of Franco's high-handed letter, he endeavoured to reassure Don Juan that things were moving within the regime, albeit slowly. Without admitting, as he had to Dionisio Ridruejo three months earlier, that he saw Juan Carlos as the better bet, López Rodó himself explained to Don Juan his scheme for gradual evolution. Their conversation on 17 September 1957 lasted more than three hours. López Rodó told Don Juan that, although Franco wanted to put an end to the uncertainty surrounding his succession, he was obsessed with the fear that, when he died, his life's work could simply be jettisoned by his royal successor. Thus, in accordance with the *Ley de Sucesión*, whoever was chosen would have to accept the basic principles of the Francoist State. Don Juan made it clear that for him to take the first step would be, 'like being forced to take a purgative. I wouldn't want to be politically compromised.' As delicately as possible, López Rodó hinted that such an attitude eliminated him from the game.[72]

Later on the same day, perhaps influenced by his conversation with López Rodó, Don Juan wrote a conciliatory letter to Franco. His backtracking was a clear recognition of the fact that Franco held all the cards: 'I am deeply distressed that the interpretation which Your Excellency has given to the paragraph in my memorandum, in which I spoke of "the monarchy as a natural and logical evolution of the regime itself", should differ so much from the meaning that I put into my words. Evolution, for me, means *perfecting, completing* the present regime, but the idea of opening a constituent period, or of any discontinuity between the present regime and the monarchy, has never entered my mind.' He ended feebly by saying that, whenever Franco wished, he would be delighted to meet him.[73]

Revelling in the weakness revealed by this exchange, Franco twisted the knife further by fostering the claims to the throne of various Carlist pretenders. Accordingly, the ever-busy Pedro Sainz Rodríguez came up with a scheme to strengthen Don Juan's position. This took the form of an orchestrated ceremony at Villa Giralda on 20 December 1957 involving a delegation of 44 of the most prominent members of the rival dynastic group, the *Comunión Tradicionalista*. After a solemn mass, Don Juan, wearing the red beret of the Carlists, accepted the principles of the medieval absolute monarchy dear to the Traditionalists. They, for their part, declared that they regarded him as the legitimate heir to the throne. The consequence was that a majority of the Carlists lined up behind Don Juan, although a significant minority of hardliners would continue to push the claims of Don Javier de Borbón Parma and his son Hugo.[74]

The prize was insufficient to justify the fact that, as the paladin of a liberal monarchy, Don Juan was making two grave errors. Not only was he committing himself to principles inimical to the interplay of political parties, but he was also confirming to Franco the debility of his position. Far from being above partisan interests, he was showing that he had to wheel and deal in order to gain support. When he wrote to inform Franco officially, the Caudillo replied with a patronizing letter of considerable cunning, picking up precisely on this point. He expressed his satisfaction that Don

Juan had finally linked up with the only real monarchists (by which he meant those who rejected the liberal constitutional monarchy of his father, Alfonso XIII). He then went on to point out the contradiction of this new position with Don Juan's previously liberal stance. 'I refer to the repeated manifestation of your desire to be King of all Spaniards. There can be no argument that the Pretender to the throne of Spain might one day wish to feel that he could be King of all Spaniards. This is normal in monarchical situations in all countries. Everyone who accepts and respects an established order must respect its supreme authorities just as they must treat all citizens with the love given to subjects. But when there are citizens who, from abroad or inside the country, betray or combat their Fatherland, or declare themselves to be agents in the service of foreign powers, such words could well be erroneously interpreted.' The letter concluded with the condescending advice that Don Juan not make public declarations without first seeking his approval.[75]

Many of Don Juan's advisers, like Ruiseñada, believed that a rapprochement with Franco was the only route to the throne. Ruiseñada himself died in mysterious circumstances in France on 23 April 1958. His death in a sleeper compartment of a stationary train in the railway station of Tours, coming a year after the demise of his fellow conspirator Bautista Sánchez gave rise to suspicions of foul play. However, the death was almost certainly the result of natural causes.[76] Other monarchists thought that the growing unpopularity of the regime should incline the Pretender to keep his distance. In fact, their hopes were entirely misplaced. Every time that Franco spoke to his cousin Pacón about Don Juan, it was to lament his liberal connections. He muttered that if Don Juan were to accept the postulates of the *Movimiento* without reservations, there would be no legal impediment. However, it was clear that Franco had no confidence in Don Juan ever doing so. In early June 1958, he said to Pacón: 'I'm already 65 and it's only natural that I should prepare my own succession, since something might happen to me. For this, the only possible princes are Don Juan and Don Juan Carlos who are, in that order, the legal heirs. It's such a pity about Don Juan's English education, which is of course so liberal.' He would reveal his lack of trust in Don Juan even more clearly in mid-March 1959 when telling Pacón that Don Juan, 'is entirely in the hands of the enemies of the regime who want to wipe out the Crusade and the sweeping victory that we won'.[77]

In May 1958, while the 20-year-old Juan Carlos was still completing his course as a naval cadet, he sailed as a midshipman in the Spanish Navy's sailing ship, the *Juan Sebastián Elcano*. It was to cross the Atlantic, putting in at several US ports. At the same time, Don Juan was engaged in a dangerous adventure. In an effort to put behind him the tragedy of Alfonsito, he had decided to sail the Atlantic in his yacht, the *Saltillo*, following the route of Christopher Columbus. When he reached Funchal in Madeira, he was awaited by Fernando María Castiella, the Spanish Minister of Foreign Affairs. Castiella had been sent by Franco to persuade Don Juan to abandon the voyage.[78] It is likely that this was motivated less by concerns for Don Juan's safety than by fears that a successful journey might increase his prestige.

At the time, the Spanish Ambassador to the United States was José María de Areilza, the one-time Falangist who had only very recently become a partisan of Don Juan. As recently as 1955, Areilza had written to Franco protesting at the presence in Spain of Juan Carlos as a 'Trojan horse' whose presence delighted 'all the reds and separatists'.[79] Now, newly converted to liberalism, he informed the authorities in Washington of the fact that the Prince was aboard the training ship and alerted the American press. The Embassy was showered with invitations for the Prince in Washington, New York and elsewhere. Serious damage to the storm-battered *Saltillo* gave Areilza the excuse needed to arrange to have Don Juan picked up by the US coastguard and brought to the Embassy. Once Don Juan was installed there, Areilza was able to incorporate him into the various events arranged for Juan Carlos. The Ambassador requested permission from Franco to receive Don Juan and his son at the Spanish Embassy. However, to the delight of the Americans and the embarrassment of Madrid, Areilza went beyond his instructions and the presence of the two members of the Spanish royal family was converted almost into a State visit. There were much-publicized visits to the Library of Congress, the Pentagon and Arlington Cemetery, to West Point and, in New York, to Cardinal Spellman's residence, to the Metropolitan Opera, and to the offices of the *New York Times*.[80]

While Juan Carlos and Don Juan were in the United States, López Rodó was continuing to beaver away at his plan for the post-Franco monarchy. The first fruit of his work as head of Carrero Blanco's secretariat of the *Presidencia* was the *Ley de Principios del Movimiento* (Declaration of the Fundamental Principles of the *Movimiento*). The text was presented to the Cortes by Franco himself on 17 May 1958. It was clear that López Rodó had worked on the gradual reform to which he had referred in his conversations with Ruiseñada and Don Juan. The twelve principles were an innocuously vague and high-minded statement of the regime's Catholicism and commitment to social justice, but within them could be discerned the formal decoupling of the regime from Falangism. The seventh principle stated that: 'The political form of the Spanish State, within the immutable principles of the *Movimiento Nacional* and the *Ley de Sucesión* and the other fundamental laws, is the traditional, Catholic, social and representative monarchy.'[81] The biggest obstacle to Don Juan, or his son, ever accepting the idea of a monarchy tied to the regime was the Falange. Now it was shifting slightly. Of the *Movimiento Nacional* understood as being the *Falange Española Tradicionalista y de las JONS*, central to schemes such as that of Arrese, there was nothing in Franco's speech.

The text made it appear as if Franco was edging towards the idea of a monarchical restoration, and many monarchists eagerly interpreted the speech in those terms. So soon after Arrese's aborted plans, this constituted a puzzling u-turn that can be explained largely in terms of López Rodó's influence. Franco had left the drafting of his speech to Carrero Blanco and he in turn had left it to López Rodó. Either because he had not fully digested its implications, or else because they simply did not bother him, he had not discussed the text in cabinet before making the speech. In the Cortes, several ministers had revealed their dismay at its apparent departure from Falangism by ostentatiously failing to applaud. After a lengthy conversation with Franco in the wake of the speech, Pacón reached the conclusion that none of this mattered, since it was clear that Franco had no intention of leaving power before death or incapacity obliged him to do so. Pacón asked him if he excluded Don Juan as a possible successor in such a case. Franco replied: 'The designation of a King is the task of the *Consejo del Reino* but I certainly don't exclude him. If Don Juan accepts the principles of the *Movimiento* unreservedly, there is no legal reason to exclude him.' That Pacon had got it right was revealed on 6 June 1958, when Franco made Agustín Muñoz Grandes Chief of the General Staff replacing Juan Vigón. Muñoz Grandes was to ensure that the Caudillo's wishes would be carried out if he died or were incapacitated. The appointment made it unequivocally clear that Franco had no intention of handing over to any successor before that time.[82]

The promulgation of the *Ley de Principios del Movimiento* had taken place while Juan Carlos and his father were in New York. After their visit was over, Don Juan made the hazardous trip back across the Atlantic in the *Saltillo*. On reaching the Portuguese port of Cascais on 24 June, several dozen enthusiastic Spanish monarchists were waiting to congratulate him on his remarkable maritime exploits. On the quayside, Franco's new Ambassador to Portugal, José Ibáñez Martín, was jostled. When a Portuguese journalist asked the name of the man who had replaced Nicolás Franco in the Lisbon Embassy, several voices replied in unison '*sinvergüenza*' (scoundrel). As Don Juan posed for photographers, the Ambassador tried to insinuate himself into the frame. Ibáñez Martín was seized and dragged to one side by an ardent young monarchist who had to be restrained from throwing him into the water. When Ibáñez Martín protested to Don Juan, he was ignored. At the reception held afterwards, there was booing when someone announced that a delegation of *Procuradores* from the Cortes planned to ask Don Juan to accept the *Ley de Principios del Movimiento*. In his speech, Don Juan declared: 'I won't return as Franco's puppet. I will be King of all Spaniards.' He told the dissident General Heli Rolando de Tella that only prudence prevented him making a full public break with Franco. Full reports on the various incidents soon reached the Caudillo.[83]

Even without these declarations, the Caudillo now had yet another reason for resenting Don Juan. Franco always claimed that his real vocation was in the Navy. Only ten years earlier, on 12 October 1948, at the monastery of La Rábida where Christopher Columbus kept vigil on the night before setting out from Palos de Moguer on his historic voyage, Franco had awarded himself the title of *Gran Almirante de Castilla* (Lord High Admiral of Castile). Considering himself to be the twentieth-century Christopher Columbus, he must have been deeply irritated by the adulation showered on Don Juan for his real maritime achievements.[84] Franco was even more displeased when a report from the security services about Don Juan reached him. It consisted of a transcription of a lengthy conversation with a German journalist. Don Juan denounced the illegitimacy of Franco's tenure of power and stated categorically that the next King had to be committed to national reconciliation.[85]

It was hardly surprising that the Caudillo's determination not to hand over the baton for a very long time was reiterated in his end-of-the-year broadcast on New Year's Eve 1958. Despite the fact that the Spanish economy was on the verge of collapse, with inflation soaring and working-class unrest on the increase, he dedicated the bulk of his lengthy speech (30 pages in its printed version) to a hymn of praise to the *Movimiento*. In particular, he presented it as the institutionalization of his victory in the Civil War. The underlying message of his obscure ramblings was that the future succession would take place only in accordance with the principles of the *Movimiento*. Denouncing the failures of the Borbón monarchy in terms of 'frivolity, lack of foresight, neglect, clumsiness and blindness', he claimed that anyone who did not recognize the legitimacy of his regime was suffering from 'personal egoism and mental debility'. After these unmistakable allusions to his person, Don Juan could hardly feel secure about his position in the Caudillo's plans for the future.[86]

Franco's words made it clear that he was keen to dampen the ardour of those monarchists who had taken the *Ley de Principios del Movimiento* as implying that a handover of power to Don Juan was imminent. Their optimism was exposed at a monarchist gathering in Madrid on 29 January 1959. Progressive supporters of Don Juan held a dinner at the Hotel Menfis to launch an association known as *Unión Española*. The days of aristocratic courtiers like Danvila or Ruiseñada were now giving way to something altogether more modern. *Unión Española* was the brainchild of the liberal monarchist lawyer and industrialist, Joaquín Satrústegui. Although Gil Robles was present, he did not make a speech. Those who did – including the Socialist intellectual from the University of Salamanca, Professor Enrique Tierno Galván – made it clear that the monarchy, to survive, could not be installed by a dictator but had to be re-established with the popular support of a majority of Spaniards. The hawk-like Satrústegui directly contradicted Franco's end-of-year declaration that the Crusade was the fount of the regime's legitimacy.

To the outrage of the Caudillo, Satrústegui, who had fought on the Nationalist side in 1936, argued that the tragedy of a civil war could not be the basis for the future. He specifically confronted Franco's oft-repeated demand that Don Juan swear loyalty to the ideals of the uprising of 18 July 1936, saying 'a civil war is something horrible in which compatriots kill one another . . . the monarchy cannot rest on such a basis.' He brushed aside the idea of an 'installed' monarchy enshrined in the *Ley de Sucesión*, declaring openly that 'Today, the legitimate King of Spain is Don Juan de Borbón y Battenberg. He is so as the son of his father, the grandson of his grandfather and heir to an entire dynasty. These, and no others, are his titles to the throne.' Franco was livid when he read the texts of the Hotel Menfis after-dinner speeches and fined Satrústegui the not inconsiderable sum of 50,000 pesetas. That the penalties were not more severe, comparable for instance to those meted out to left-wing opponents, derived from the fact that Franco did not want to be seen to be persecuting the followers of Don Juan.[87] Given that victory in the Civil War, as he repeatedly stated, was the basis of his own 'legitimacy', Franco could not help but be appalled by what had been said and by the fact that Don Juan refused to disown Satrústegui. He told his cousin Pacón that the monarchy of either Don Juan or Juan Carlos, if not based on the principles of the *Movimiento*, would be the first step to a Communist takeover.[88]

If the Menfis dinner annoyed Franco, his outrage at a report from his secret service can be imagined. On the day before the Menfis event, Don Juan had received a group of Spanish students in Estoril. If the report written by one of the students was accurate, it presented either a misplaced attempt at humour or the indiscretions of someone who had had too much to drink at lunch. Allegedly, Don Juan had outlined his conviction that, in the event of Franco's death, all he had to do was head for the Palacio de Oriente in Madrid. Streams of monarchist generals would ensure that he was not challenged. He would abolish the Falange by decree and allow political parties, including the Socialists.[89] The report goes some way to explaining the contemptuous manner in which Franco referred to Don Juan in private.

The emergence of *Unión Española* was merely one symptom of unrest within the Francoist coalition. That Satrústegui could get away with such sweeping criticism of the regime suggested that Franco was losing his grip. Certainly, his inability to deal with the economic crisis other than by relinquishing control to his new team of technocrats suggested that his mind was elsewhere.[90] To dampen the speculation about his future, Franco permitted Carrero Blanco and López Rodó to continue their work on the elaboration of a constitutional scheme for the post-Franco succession. It would be called the *Ley Orgánica del Estado* and would outline the powers of the future King. The first draft was given to Franco by Carrero Blanco on 7 March 1959 together with a sycophantic note urging the completion of the 'constitutional process': 'If the King were to inherit the powers which Your Excellency has, we would find it alarming since he will change everything. We must ratify the lifetime character of the magistracy of Your Excellency who is Caudillo which is greater than King because you are founding a monarchy.' Once the law was drafted, Carrero Blanco proposed calling a referendum. Once this was won – 'people will vote according to the propaganda that they are fed' – 'we could ask Don Juan: do you accept unreservedly? If he says no, problem solved, we turn to the son. If he also says no, we seek a regent.'[91]

In the wake of the Hotel Menfis affair, Franco was hesitant. He reiterated to Pacón one week later that Don Juan and Prince Juan Carlos must accept that the monarchy could be re-established only within the *Movimiento*, because a liberal constitutional monarchy 'would not last a year and would cause chaos in Spain, rendering the Crusade useless. In that way, the way would be open for a Kerensky and shortly thereafter for Communism or chaos in our Fatherland.'[92] Unwilling to do anything that might hasten his own departure, he did nothing with the constitutional draft for another eight years.

To increase his freedom of action and to put pressure on Don Juan, Franco continued quietly to cultivate Alfonso de Borbón y Dampierre, the son of Don Juan's brother Don Jaime. Through the deputy chief of his household, General Fernando Fuertes de Villavicencio, an audience was arranged. Franco liked both Alfonso and his brother Gonzalo and discussed the succession question with them. After asking Alfonso if he was familiar with the *Ley de Sucesión*, he said, 'I have made no decision whatsoever regarding who will be called in the future to replace me as Head of State.' Hearing that Alfonso had been received at El Pardo, José Solís Ruiz, Secretary-General of the *Movimiento* and other Falangists began to promote the idea of meeting the conditions of the *Ley de Sucesión* with a *príncipe azul* (a Falangist prince).[93]

On 15 September 1958, Juan Carlos would move to the Air Force academy of San Javier in Murcia. He was delighted to be learning to fly and endeared himself to his fellow cadets with his pranks, ably assisted by his pet monkey, Fito, who wore Air Force uniform. Juan Carlos had taught him to salute and shake hands. The relationship with the monkey would see the Prince confined to barracks. Eventually Don Juan obliged him to part company with Fito.[94] In the course of the year, the Prince made a number of gestures aimed at consolidating his links with the regime. In the spring of 1959, while still a cadet at the academy, he took part in Franco's annual victory parade, to celebrate the end of the Civil War. That he was not treated exactly like all the other cadets may be deduced from the fact that, while in Madrid, he stayed at the Ritz where he received many visitors. At some points of the parade, Juan Carlos was applauded. However, at the Plaza de Colón, a group of Falangists and supporters of the Carlist pretender Don Javier, having arrived from the nearby head-quarters of the Falange in the Calle Alcalá, began to insult the Prince and shout 'We don't want idiot kings.' The police stood by without interfering. In order to diminish the hostility of the Falange, in late May 1959, Juan Carlos laid a laurel wreath in Alicante on the spot where José Antonio Primo de Rivera had been executed on 20 November 1936. It was to no avail. The *Movimiento* daily, *Pueblo*, criticized him for not visiting the historic sites of Francoism with greater frequency.[95]

On 12 December 1959, Juan Carlos's military training came to an end and he was given the rank of Lieutenant in all three armed services. At the official ceremony at the Zaragoza military academy, the new Minister for the Army, Lieutenant-General Antonio Barroso, in a speech that he had previously submitted for Franco's approval, paid a special tribute to Juan Carlos and to Queen Victoria Eugenia. Underlining the importance of the occasion for Juan Carlos's future, Barroso significantly spoke of how 'your fidelity, patriotism, sacrifice and hard work will compensate you for other sorrows and troubles'.[96] It is not clear whether this was a specific reference to the death of his brother or a more general comment on the situation of a young man separated from his family.

Juan Carlos was now 22 and he had matured during his time in the academies although his tastes were exactly what might have been expected in any young man of his age, particularly an aristo-crat – girls, dancing, jazz and sports cars. One of his instructors told Benjamin Welles, a correspondent of the *New York Times*, 'He is no older than his actual age.'[97] Nevertheless, Franco was happy with the progress made by Juan Carlos but ever more dis-trustful of his father. He told Pacón in early 1960: 'Don Juan is beyond redemption and with every passing day he's more untrust-worthy.' When Pacón tried to explain that the Pretender's objective was a monarchy that would unite all Spaniards, Franco exploded.

'Don Juan ought to understand that for things to stay as they were during the Second Republic, there was no need for the bloody Civil War . . . It's a pity that Don Juan is so badly advised and is still set on the idea of a liberal monarchy. He is a very pleasant person but politically he goes along with the last person to offer him advice . . . In the event of Don Juan not being able to govern because of his liberalism or for some other reason, much effort has gone into the education of his son, Prince Juan Carlos, who by dint of his effort and commitment has achieved the three stars of an officer in the three services and now is ready to go to university.'[98]

It is curious that while in public, Franco seemed to favour the cause of other pretenders, such as Don Jaime and his son, and the Carlists; in private, he had reduced the choice essentially to one between Don Juan and Juan Carlos. Although he harboured no hope of Don Juan accepting the principles of the *Movimiento*, he had little doubt in the case of Juan Carlos. The other candidates served both as reserves but also as a way of exerting pressure on Don Juan and his son. Franco's growing fondness for Juan Carlos was leading him to assume that he could rely on Don Juan to abdicate in favour of his son. It was a vain expectation. Don Juan wrote to Franco on 16 October 1959, reporting on an interview with General de Gaulle, in which they had discussed the future of Spain. He wrote: 'I believe that if one day, this situation were to be addressed using the present legal arrangements, it is to be hoped that a conflict will not be provoked by a rash attempt arbitrarily to alter the natural order of the succession which both the Príncipe de Asturias and myself are determined to uphold.'[99] The issue of Juan Carlos's university education was now about to bedevil even more the relationship between his father and the Caudillo.

Don Juan had originally planned for Juan Carlos to go to the prestigious University of Salamanca. This project apparently enjoyed the approval of Franco. For more than a year, the Prince's tutor, General Martínez Campos, had been making preparations to this end. He had discussed it with the Minister of Education, Jesús Rubio García-Mina, and the Secretary-General of the *Movimiento*, José Solís Ruiz. He had also been to Salamanca, for talks with the rector of the university, José Beltrán de Heredia. He had found suitable accommodation and had vetted possible teachers. Then, suddenly, without warning, Don Juan began to have doubts about his Salamanca project in late 1959. On 17 December, General Martínez Campos had travelled to Estoril to make the final arrangements. On the following day, there ensued a tense interview at Villa Giralda. The general began with a report on Juan Carlos's visit to El Pardo on 15 December. Apparently, after Franco had chatted to the Prince about what awaited him in Salamanca, he had told him that, once he was established at the university, he hoped to see him more often. Don Juan reacted by saying that he was thinking of changing his mind about sending his son to Salamanca. A furious Martínez Campos expostulated that any change in the arrangements at this late stage – after Juan Carlos had received his commissions in the three services – would be infinitely damaging for the prestige of Don Juan and of the monarchist cause. He was appalled that it might now look that he had lied in order to ensure that Juan Carlos received his commissions. He insisted that he would not leave Estoril until the issue was settled one way or the other.

On 19 December, the day after this disagreeable encounter, there was an informal meeting of several of Don Juan's Privy Council. One after another, the Marqués Juan Ignacio de Luca de Tena, Pedro Sainz Rodríguez and others spoke against the idea of the Prince being educated at Salamanca, implying that it was a dangerous place, full of foreign students and left-wing professors.[100] This was most vehemently the view of the Opus Dei members, Gonzalo Fernández de la Mora and Florentino Pérez Embid. Fernández de la Mora and Sainz Rodríguez proposed that Juan Carlos be tutored at the palace of Miramar, in San Sebastián, by teachers drawn from several universities. Martínez Campos pointed out that Salamanca had been chosen for its historic traditions and for its position midway between Madrid and Estoril. He explained that his meticulous preparations – including the nomination of military aides to accompany the Prince – obviated all of the problems now being anticipated. He was mortified when, with a silent Don Juan looking on, the others furiously dismissed his arguments. At this humiliating evidence of his declining influence over Don Juan, he resigned. This occasioned considerable distress for Juan Carlos, who had become increasingly attached to his severe tutor. Over the next three days, the Prince made great efforts to persuade him to withdraw his resignation, as did his father. However, the fiercely proud Martínez Campos was not prepared to accept an improvised scheme dreamed up by Sainz Rodríguez, Pérez Embid and Fernández de la Mora.

Martínez Campos pointed out the dangers inherent in what Don Juan was doing – after all, Juan Carlos was an officer in the Spanish forces and Franco could post him wherever he liked, including Salamanca. Don Juan responded by asking him to accept the formal nomination of head of the Prince's household, effectively the job that he had done for the previous five years. Concerned above all for his own dignity, Martínez Campos categorically refused to overturn his own plan and then supervise the implementation of the scheme of three men for whom he had little or no respect. He claimed that Don Juan's vacillations would constitute irreparable damage to the image of the monarchy within the Army and in Spain in general. Furthermore, he argued that Franco would see this as evidence that Don Juan was 'easily swayed by outside influences and pressures'. Don Juan ignored these warnings and gave him an envelope sealed with wax to take to El Pardo. It contained a letter to Franco explaining his change of mind. On the evening of 23 December 1959, General Martínez Campos took the overnight train to Madrid. On the following morning, he went directly from the station to El Pardo. Franco received him cordially and commented only that he was not surprised, 'bearing in mind those who were always in Estoril'. But, if he received the news with a shrug, his closest collaborators were in no doubt that he was mightily displeased.[101]

The entire episode provided further proof that Juan Carlos was little more than a shuttlecock in a game being played by Don Juan and Franco. In 1948, he had been unfeelingly separated from Eugenio Vegas Latapié, the tutor of whom he was deeply fond. Having come to like, respect and rely on Martínez Campos during their six years together, the process was now repeated. Once more to lose his mentor and to be reminded that his interests were entirely subordinate to political considerations carried considerable emotional costs for Juan Carlos. He said later 'The Duque's [Martínez Campos's] departure distressed me considerably, but there was nothing I could do for him. Nobody had asked for my opinion. It was as if I was on a football pitch. The ball was in the air and I had no idea where it was going to fall.' It is indicative of the Prince's relationship with his mentor that he made a point of spending time with him in the final days of his fatal illness in April 1975.[102]

There can be no doubt that the clash between Don Juan and Martínez Campos had enormous significance for the future of both the Prince and his father. Major Alfonso Armada Comyn, who had worked for Martínez Campos in overseeing the Prince's secondary education, wrote later that this episode was the definitive cause of Don Juan's elimination from Franco's plans for the succession. Luis María Anson, a declared admirer of Don Juan's senior adviser, claimed that the clash at Estoril had been deliberately planned by Sainz Rodríguez in order to provoke Martínez Campos's resignation, 'one of his most audacious and farsighted political masterstrokes'. In Anson's interpretation, Sainz Rodríguez believed that, in tandem with Martínez Campos, Juan Carlos would be highly vulnerable to the machinations of hostile elements of the *Movimiento*. By engineering the departure of the general, Sainz Rodríguez was manoeuvring Juan Carlos into the orbit of Carrero Blanco and López Rodó.[103] In fact, the efforts of Don Juan and Juan Carlos himself to get Martínez Campos to withdraw his resignation make this difficult to believe. Moreover, López Rodó had already begun to throw his efforts behind the candidacy of Juan Carlos as successor. Rather than a farsighted and cunning plan on behalf of Juan Carlos, the manoeuvres of Sainz Rodríguez, Fernández de la Mora and Pérez Embid suggest a desperate attempt at preventing the Prince from eclipsing Don Juan as Franco's successor. Sainz Rodríguez was concerned that, under the guardianship of Martínez Campos, Juan Carlos was being too smoothly integrated into Francoist plans for the future. In any case, whatever the aims of the choreographed ambush of Martínez Campos at Estoril, it merely consolidated Franco's conviction that Don Juan was too easily influenced by advisers.

Indeed, one of the first consequences of the break with Martínez Campos was that General Alfredo Kindelán would resign as president of Don Juan's Privy Council. A man of great dignity and prestige, Kindelán was replaced in early 1960 by the altogether more pliant and sinuous José María Pemán. The Opus Dei members Rafael Calvo Serer and Florentino Pérez Embid assumed key roles.[104] In the meantime, there ensued a lengthy correspondence that would give an entirely different tone to the contest between the Caudillo and Don Juan regarding Juan Carlos. If there had previously been any doubt, the interchange would make it unmistakably obvious that Franco was viewing the Prince as a direct heir while his father saw him as a pawn in his own strategy to reach the throne. The letter entrusted by Don Juan to Martínez Campos began with an expression of gratitude for Juan Carlos's passage through the three military academies and for General Barroso's generous speech in Zaragoza. Don Juan went on to refer to his deepening anxieties about the next stage of the Prince's education. He repeated most of the arguments that had been put to Martínez Campos over the previous few days. What he was saying echoed the advice received from Sainz Rodríguez, Fernández de la Mora, Pérez Embid and others, including Rafael Calvo Serer. He referred to this group as 'many people of great intellectual standing and healthy patriotism'. Alleging that Martínez Campos had hurried him into accepting the Salamanca scheme, he expressed the view that it would be better for the Prince to receive private classes from professors of many universities. Accordingly, he would prefer his son to be established in a royal residence with total independence.[105]

On the following day, Don Juan sent the Caudillo an explanatory note together with a new plan of studies. In it, Don Juan stated somewhat implausibly, 'I want to emphasize that the delay in making the final decision that the Prince should not follow his civilian studies in Salamanca is not in any way a sudden improvisation nor mere caprice on my part.' In justification of this statement, he alleged that Martínez Campos had gone ahead and made concrete plans despite his orders to the contrary. The plan itself, disparaging the University of Salamanca and its professors, was covered in the fingerprints of the same men who had confronted General Martínez Campos in Estoril.[106]

Franco's reply in mid-January was only mildly reproachful. He began by saying that he respected the Pretender's decision while pointing out that the grounds on which it was based were highly dubious. He went on to say that further delay would be damaging to the Prince since it would break the habit of study, 'to which I understand he is little inclined, preferring as he does practical activities and sport'. He then suggested that the Miramar palace in San Sebastián was totally unsuitable since it was too far removed from the great university centres and its damp climate would discourage hunting. Instead he proposed a location nearer Madrid, preferably the Casa de los Peces in El Escorial. 'This would allow me, at the same time, to be able to see the Prince more often and to keep an eye on his education, which, as far as possible, I want to look after personally.' He then announced that he had commissioned the Minister of Education, Jesús Rubio García-Mina, to draw up a full educational plan for the Prince and a team of professors from Madrid University to undertake the task.[107]

Don Juan discussed this letter with Pemán, who saw Franco's desire to see the Prince frequently as 'rather alarming'. Before talking to Pemán, Don Juan had already replied promptly at the beginning of February, accepting the idea of residence in El Escorial, suggesting a group of professors from all over Spain who might take charge of his son's education and naming the Duque de Frías, a non-political aristocrat who was best known as president of the Madrid golf club, as head of the Prince's household.[108] Franco was quick to point out that the proposed teachers were likely to provide something approaching a liberal education. While that might be fine for 'just any Spaniard', something altogether more specific was required for the Prince. 'It is necessary to complete the education of the Prince in those civilian subjects that are basic to his future decisions.' He went on to explain that the coldly abstract education provided by a group of unworldly scholars would be entirely unsuitable. What was necessary, he declared, was a plan based on the principles of the *Movimiento*. From this he went on to say that he had noted that Don Juan had advisers who seemed to harbour the absurd idea that the monarchy could change the nature of the regime. As far as Franco was concerned, the contrary was self-evidently the case. The Caudillo had chosen the monarchy to succeed him precisely in order to prolong, not alter, his regime.

Franco had not been concerned while the Prince was in one or other of the military academies, 'temples of patriotic exaltation and schools of virtue, of character-building, of the exercise of command, of discipline and of the fulfilment of duty'. 'In the light of all this, and given the age of the Prince, I believe that the education of Juan Carlos over the next few years is more a question of State rather than one concerning a father's rights and it is the State that should have priority in deciding the overall educational plan and the necessary guarantees.' He suggested that the Prince's director of studies should be a history professor who had fought in the Civil War with the *Requetés*, the ferocious Carlist militia that had played a crucial role in Franco's war effort, was a member of the Opus Dei and was now a priest – a reference to the deeply conservative Federico Suárez Verdeguer. Should Don Juan disagree, Franco was contemplating putting the entire matter of the Prince's education in the hands of the *Consejo del Reino*. Franco closed the letter with the ominous statement that he would consider a meeting to discuss the details only after certain misunderstandings had been cleared up, given that what separated them was a major issue of principle.[109]

Don Juan's reply was conciliatory. This reflected the role played in its drafting by the newly installed president of his Privy Council, José María Pemán. According to Pemán himself, he had been selected for the job precisely because he had no political ambitions of his own and he got on well with Franco. Now, to Don Juan's text, he added what he called 'the perfume so necessary for El Pardo'.[110] Don Juan seems not to have perceived that Franco's growing interest in the boy was as his direct successor not as the eventual heir to his father. The letter began by recognizing that 'it would be absurd for him not to receive an eminently patriotic education, inspired in the same loyalty to the fundamental principles of the *Movimiento* that he had imbibed in the military academies'. He recognized that the interests of the State should be paramount. He accepted Franco's suggestion of Suárez Verdeguer and other professors. Regarding the issue of whether the monarchy would try to alter the Francoist State, he engaged in an extraordinary juggling act. Recognizing that some of his supporters wanted a parliamentary monarchy, while others such as the Carlists were virulently opposed to it, he still claimed that his loyalty to the principles of the *Movimiento* was unquestionable. He also called, rather optimistically, for Franco to make a declaration that: 'the way in which the Prince's education is taking place does not prejudge the question of the succession nor alter the normal transmission of dynastic obligations and responsibilities.' Pemán had already begun some behind-the-scenes negotiations with a sympathetic Carrero Blanco. That they had borne fruit was revealed in Franco's reply nearly four weeks later in which he offered a meeting on 21 or 22 March at the Parador of Ciudad Rodrigo near the Portuguese border.[111]

News of the impending meeting stimulated rumours that major decisions about the future were imminent. Franco was now 67 and gossip was rife that his health was failing. On returning in his Rolls Royce from a hunting party in Jaén on 25 January 1960, a fault in the heating system had led to the rear of the car being filled with exhaust fumes. Noting his drowsiness, Doña Carmen had the presence of mind to order the car stopped before any serious harm was done. Wild rumours circulated within the regime, although Franco assured Pacón that he had suffered only a severe headache. Nevertheless, particularly after an announcement from the Rolls Royce Motor Car Company that exhaust gases could enter the car only if there had been deliberate tampering, the incident provoked speculation that something sinister had happened.[112] So, when news of the proposed meeting at Ciudad Rodrigo was broadcast on foreign radio stations and leaked in the press, gossip raced around Madrid that Franco planned to hand over power to Don Juan. Journalists, radio reporters and newsreel cameramen descended on the border town ready to flash the news to the world's capitals. Deeply irritated, Franco postponed the meeting for seven days and changed the venue.

Franco was infuriated by the rumours that he assumed to have emanated from Estoril and the change of venue was meant as a reprimand for Don Juan. Nevertheless, given the eager talk about Franco's mortality, enormous significance was read into Franco's third meeting with Don Juan, their second at Las Cabezas, on 29 March 1960.[113] Las Cabezas had been inherited, on the Conde de Ruiseñada's death, by his son, the Marqués de Comillas. Talking to Pacón before the meeting, Franco made it quite clear how little he planned to offer. He stated categorically, 'as long as I have my health and my mental and physical faculties, I will not give up the Headship of State.'[114]

Pedro Sainz Rodríguez was beginning to suspect that not only would Franco not relinquish power before his death but that he would also pick as successor someone other than Don Juan. Of the various competing candidates, Juan Carlos would be preferable, but Don Juan had no desire to lose the throne even to his son. Accordingly, in his preparatory notes for the Pretender, Sainz Rodríguez argued that he must insist that: 'the presence of the Prince must not be used to carry out manoeuvres suggesting that there is any agreement by which the order of succession can be altered.' This threat came to be referred to by Sainz Rodríguez as 'balduinismo' – a reference to King Baudouin of Belgium who had ascended the throne in 1951 after the abdication of his father, Leopold III.[115]

A grey-suited Franco arrived with a staff of 82 in a convoy of 11 Cadillacs. He was accompanied by the Ministers of Education and Public Works, as well as numerous security guards and aides, two cooks and a doctor. Apart from the driver, Don Juan was accompanied only by his private secretary, Ramón Padilla, and the Duque de Alburquerque. In contrast with their two previous meetings, the Caudillo manifested somewhat less interest in bringing Don Juan around to his point of view, having already eliminated him as a possible successor. In the event of ever needing to organize a rapid succession process, Franco had long since decided not to offer the throne to Don Juan. Rather, he would pick Juan

Carlos and simultaneously ask Don Juan to abdicate, confident that he would agree rather than risk a public break with his son. For some time to come, he would astutely refrain from making that decision public, convinced that if he did so, Juan Carlos would side with his father. Nevertheless, the notion underlay his agenda at Las Cabezas which went no further than criticism of Don Juan's collaborators and discussion of the details of the Prince's remaining education. Don Juan, for his part, firmly expressed his concern at the way Franco was seemingly fostering the claims of other pretenders to the throne. It was no small triumph when he successfully pressed Franco to admit that some of them (certainly Don Jaime) were receiving financial support from the Secretary-General of the *Movimiento*.

Don Juan complained vigorously about the continuing antimonarchist propaganda in Spain. In particular, he protested about a book, *Anti-España 1959*, published in Madrid by an obsessive regime propagandist, Mauricio Carlavilla, who was also a secret policeman. The book denounced the monarchist cause as the stooge of freemasonry and a smokescreen for Communist infiltration, as well as insinuating that Don Juan himself was a freemason. Hundreds of copies had been sent by the *Movimiento* to people in official positions. Don Juan knew that the censorship apparatus would not have permitted the book to be distributed while Juan Carlos was resident in Spain without the Caudillo's connivance. Now, Franco, who could plausibly have feigned ignorance, once again claimed evasively that he had no control over the press. He asserted that patriotic journalists must have seen the book as a reply to the memoirs of the monarchist aviator Juan Antonio Ansaldo, published in Buenos Aires in 1951.[116]

This revealed that, even if Franco had not commissioned Carlavilla's book, he certainly approved of its contents. Ansaldo's *¿Para qué . . . ?* (For What?) had referred to Franco as 'the usurper of El Pardo' and attacked his failure to restore the monarchy as a betrayal of the sacrifices made in the Civil War against the Republic. Don Juan pointed out that there was little need for a reply to a book that had been banned in Spain. He went on to complain about the constant attacks to which the monarchy had been subjected by the *Movimiento* press over the previous 15 years. Implying again that the press was beyond his control, Franco shiftily attributed these criticisms to indignation over the 1945 Lausanne Manifesto on the part of journalists. Franco exposed his identification with Carlavilla's views by referring bitterly to members of Don Juan's Privy Council as 'traitors'. He spent 25 minutes criticizing Pedro Sainz Rodríguez as a freemason, to which Don Juan replied that nothing that he had heard could persuade him that his piously Catholic adviser could be a mason. Somewhat rattled by this, Franco replied darkly that he knew of other masons in Don Juan's circle including his uncle 'Ali' – General Alfonso de Orleáns Borbón – and the Duque de Alba. When Don Juan burst out laughing at this, Franco finally desisted.

The remainder of the interview dealt with the education of Juan Carlos. Franco suggested that, while he would start off with a residence in El Escorial, he should soon move to the palace of La Zarzuela. Just outside Madrid, on the road to La Coruña, La Zarzuela was very near to Franco's own residence at El Pardo. The interest shown by the Caudillo in this respect led Pemán to note in his diary, 'La Zarzuela is being prepared for him and Franco is personally taking charge of its furnishing like a doting grandfather.' Franco also suggested that Juan Carlos should work in Admiral Carrero Blanco's *Presidencia del Gobierno* although nothing came of this suggestion. He agreed to the appointment of the Duque de Frías as the head of Juan Carlos's household. There was then a detailed discussion of a list of members of the 'study committee' that was to oversee the Prince's civilian education. Franco had brought a list with him, which included names such as that of Adolfo Muñoz Alonso, the Falangist head of the same censorship organization that had permitted the publication of Carlavilla's book and of endless attacks on the monarchy. In this part of the conversation, Don Juan commented later, Franco was more flexible than in previous meetings: 'he abandoned his usual dogmatic style of a schoolteacher dealing with an ignorant schoolboy.' Franco, in contrast, told Pacón later that: 'I said to Don Juan everything that I had to say to him and that he had to hear.'

Just before Franco rose to leave, Don Juan gave him the text of a proposed communiqué prepared by Sainz Rodríguez, in line with the notes that he had drawn up before the meeting. It stated that the talks had taken place in a cordial atmosphere and repeated once more that Juan Carlos's education in Spain 'does not prejudge the question of the succession nor prejudice the normal transmission of dynastic obligations and responsibilities'. It closed with the statement that 'the interview ended with the strengthened conviction that the cordiality and good understanding between both personalities is of priceless value for the future of Spain and for the consolidation and continuation of the benefits of peace and the work carried out so far'. A visibly displeased Franco read the text and discussed it at length with Don Juan. He argued the text point by point. He protested at a reference to Juan Carlos as Príncipe de Asturias. Acceptance of that title would have signified public recognition that Don Juan was the King, so Franco slyly claimed that it was inadmissible on the grounds that it had not been ratified by the Cortes. Don Juan conceded the point.

The discussion grew more conflictive over the statement that Juan Carlos's presence in Spain had no implications for the succession to the throne. Franco balked at this, saying it was '*duro*' (harsh). Don Juan replied that this was, for him, the central issue and he insisted that it, or a similar sentence, must appear in the communiqué. The Caudillo continued to make objections until Don Juan said with studied weariness, 'Well, General, if for whatever reason you find this note to be inopportune, I'm in no hurry. The academic year is well advanced, so I could keep the boy with me until October.' At that, Franco accepted the text with alacrity.[117] Don Juan returned to Estoril, convinced that he had scored an important victory. On the following day, his staff went ahead and issued the agreed text in good faith. However, to their astonishment, the version that every Spanish newspaper was obliged to publish contained significant variants from Don Juan's text. On arriving at El Pardo late on 29 March, Franco had unilaterally amended the agreed communiqué.[118]

He added a reference to himself as Caudillo, a title never acknowledged by Don Juan. To the phrase which made it clear that Juan Carlos's presence in Spain had no bearing on the transmission of dynastic responsibilities, he added 'in accordance with the *Ley de Sucesión*'. He thereby gave the impression that Don Juan now accepted the law, which in fact he repudiated. In the last sentence, he removed the phrase 'both personalities' lest he and Don Juan should be seen to be on an equal footing. Finally, he added to the reference to 'the work carried out so far' the words 'by the *Movimiento Nacional*', thereby implying that Don Juan was fully committed to it and that future relations between them would take place in that context.[119] This last phrase, and the reference to the *Ley de Sucesión*, were generally interpreted as clear acceptance by Don Juan of Franco's system. According to the British Ambassador, the entire political élite was 'scrutinising the communiqué as if it were a Dead Sea Scroll'.[120]

The Spanish censorship machinery blocked all attempts from Estoril to have the correct version published. To rub salt into the wound, the Spanish press printed accusations that Don Juan had dishonestly omitted the references that in fact Franco had added. Don Juan was understandably annoyed by Franco's underhand dealing. However, he wrote him an astute letter, drawing his attention to this apparent interference by third parties anxious to undermine the cordial relations between them. Giving Franco the perfect let-out, he wrote: 'I imagine that Your Excellency had nothing to do with these changes to what we agreed which, like me, you must have seen for the first time in print.' However, Franco replied quite brazenly that he had expressly authorized the changes, which he declared to be 'tiny' and merely clarifications of what they had agreed at Las Cabezas. Moreover, he reproached Don Juan for publishing the agreed text on the grounds that the communiqué was to be issued only in Madrid. Franco told his cousin Pacón, 'The note published by the press was brought already drafted by Don Juan. I made some objections. When I reached Madrid and I realized that it lacked a few words about the *Movimiento Nacional*, I had no hesitation about adding them since Don Juan had not objected when they were mentioned in our conversation. There was no need to consult with him since I knew that he would have to agree.'[121]

At some level, Don Juan must have known that Franco wanted

him to abdicate in favour of his son. Presumably hoping to dispel his own fears, at Las Cabezas, Don Juan had told Franco that he had been asked by Harold Macmillan, the British Prime Minister, if there was any truth in rumours that he was planning to do so. He told Franco that he had vehemently denied having any such intention but had no doubt that the gossip quoted by Macmillan had emanated from Madrid.[122] Don Juan had every reason to be concerned. In early April, just a few days after the publication of the communiqué, Carrero Blanco spoke to Benjamin Welles, the correspondent of the *New York Times*. Carrero dismissed monarchist claims that the Las Cabezas meeting had reasserted Don Juan's position. 'Juan Carlos will be King one day. If anything suddenly happens to Franco, he will have to ascend the throne.' The startled American journalist asked, 'What about Don Juan? Is he not first in line?' Carrero Blanco paused interminably before answering dismissively, 'He is already too old.'[123]

Juan Carlos returned to Spain in April 1960 to take up residence in the 'Casita del Infante', sometimes known locally as the 'Casita de Arriba', a small palace on the outskirts of El Escorial, which had been prepared for Franco lest he needed a refuge during the Second World War. It was also known as 'Casa de los Peces' (the House of the Fishes), because behind the house there was a pond full of baby carp. Once established there, it was not long before he was received in audience by the Caudillo. It was apparent that Franco's contempt for Don Juan was matched by a growing affection for the Prince. He continually muttered to Pacón that the Pretender was surrounded by evil influences, such as Sainz Rodríguez, whom he denounced as a leftist and a freemason. 'Don Juan lives with a coterie of enemies of the regime of whom the most dangerous is Sainz Rodríguez.' When Pacón innocently asked if Sainz Rodríguez had not once been one of his ministers, Franco replied that he didn't know him then and had appointed him only at the insistence of Ramón Serrano Suñer. This was a lie, since they had been friends in Oviedo when Franco was stationed there as a Major. On 27 April, he wrote to Don Juan: 'in the last few days, I had occasion to receive the Prince and talk with him at length. I found him much more grown up than in my last interviews with him and very sensible in his judgements and opinions.' He invited Juan Carlos to return soon for lunch. The writing on the wall for the Prince's father was clearer than ever.[124]

Sir Ivo Mallet, the British Ambassador in Madrid, was in no doubt that Franco had no intention of standing down until he had seen whether Juan Carlos was a suitable successor. It is hardly surprising that, in late May, Don Juan told Benjamin Welles of his anxiety that his son might be 'persuaded by the atmosphere, by flattery and by propaganda into abandoning his loyalty to his father and accepting the position of Franco's candidate for the throne'. To prevent this happening, he said, he had appointed as the head of the Prince's household the Duque de Frías. What is extraordinary is that Don Juan appears not to have discussed his fears with his son.[125]

Don Juan continued to resist his own dawning perception of the scale of Franco's deception. In late April, he told Sir Charles Stirling, the British Ambassador in Lisbon, that, at Las Cabezas, Franco had undertaken that there would be no further public attacks on members of his family.[126] The Caudillo's sincerity was revealed in May by a series of lengthy articles printed in *Arriba*, the principal Falangist newspaper. In laughably naïve terms, they blamed freemasonry for all the ills of Spain over the previous 200 years and managed to insinuate that the British royal family was responsible. Don Juan could hardly miss the implication for himself. The articles were signed by 'Jakin-Booz', a variant of Franco's own pseudonym. At the beginning of the 1950s, writing as 'Jakim Boor', the Caudillo had written a series of articles and a book denouncing freemasonry as an evil conspiracy with Communism. On the instructions of the Ministry of Information and Tourism, this new series of articles was republished in full by the entire Spanish press. It was believed that this time the author was Admiral Carrero Blanco. An official of the Ministry told a British diplomat that, as a follow-up to accusations that Don Juan was a freemason, these articles were intended to stress the royal origins of freemasonry and bring the monarchy into disrepute.[127]

The Spanish edition of *Life* magazine for 13 June 1960 carried an article on Don Juan in which he was quoted as saying that whatever form the restored monarchy might take, it would not be a dictatorship. Franco had thereupon communicated to Don Juan his displeasure at being called a dictator. Distribution of the magazine had been held up by the censors in Spain and Don Juan had been obliged to write and point out that he had merely stated that he himself would not be a dictator. Besides, he asked, how else could one describe Franco's form of government? Don Juan believed that Franco eventually agreed to its release only because this was the first thing he had ever asked of him. However, according to the account given to the British Embassy by Benjamin Welles, Franco had said that if Don Juan wanted to commit political suicide, he did not see why he should do anything to stop him by holding up the article.[128] In October, Franco showed Don Juan what he really thought. The Marqués de Luca de Tena, owner of *ABC*, gave a lecture to a monarchist club in Seville in which he extolled the *Ley de Sucesión* and the Franco regime. However, because he had pointed out that monarchists must accept the hereditary principle, saying: 'A king is king because he is the son of his father' and that, 'if a king comes, the only possible king is Don Juan III,' a report of the lecture in *ABC* was banned.[129]

In the early autumn of 1960, in his capacity as president of Don Juan's Privy Council, José María Pemán asked Franco to reveal his plans with regard to the succession. The Caudillo replied that he would be succeeded by the 'traditional monarchy', whose 'incumbent' he told Pemán with a straight face was Don Juan. He described him as 'a good man, a gentleman and a patriot'. Compounding this farrago of deception, he denied that Don Juan had been eliminated and claimed that the thought of choosing Juan Carlos instead had never crossed his mind. He said that the Prince, 'because of his age, is an unknown quantity'. In any case, he then went on to reveal that he had no intention of proclaiming the monarchy for a very long time: 'My health is good and I can still be useful to my Fatherland.'[130]

FOUR

A *Life Under Surveillance*

1960–1966

In October 1960, Franco received a perceptive report on Juan Carlos from one of his intelligence agents in Portugal. Commenting on the Prince's presence at the celebration of his parents' silver wedding anniversary, he wrote: 'It is certainly the case that Juan Carlos seems more mature by the day, despite the patience and the humility that he has to put on in front of his father. Don Juan treats him harshly, even more so when there is someone present, and is constantly saying "your place is behind me". It produces discord. The split probably won't come because there'll be a marriage and with it a new house, a new life and distance from his father who has got him tightly bound, like the feet of young Chinese girls in iron shoes. At the moment, and we know this from several sources, Juan Carlos is keen to get back to Spain and is fed up with his father and with his grandmother Doña Victoria Eugenia, whose company he finds every day more irksome. Marriage then is a political solution, a device so that the cord doesn't break altogether.' Franco must have been delighted to read that: 'Juan Carlos feels happy only when he is away from Villa Giralda and with his Spanish friends. He has two personalities, one serious, sad and submissive towards his father, and the other when he is out of Don Juan's sight, among his friends.'[1]

At the time, it was strongly rumoured that the announcement of his engagement to Maria Gabriella di Savoia was imminent. The persistence of these rumours provoked frequent denials from Estoril. In early January 1961, as part of this process, Don Juan gave a long interview to *Il Giornale d'Italia*. However, the bulk of his quoted remarks were aimed at reaffirming his indisputable right to the throne. He said that there was 'an indestructible accord' between himself and his son and that the royal family was 'firmly united in a single block'. The firmness with which he repeatedly asserted the unity between himself and his son suggested that he was protesting too much. The truth about the relationship surely lay nearer the disharmony cited in the secret service agent's report. 'Between us, there has always been total harmony: an unshakable faith and confidence. Therefore, there can be no thought of a solution contrary to these accords and to such a united firmness of wills and feelings. A different solution would break this block.' Such remarks could be read as directed more to Juan Carlos than to Franco.

Indeed, if Don Juan was trying to influence Franco in his own favour, he was going about it in a peculiar fashion. A few days later, in an interview with Jacques Guillemé-Brulon of *Le Figaro*, Don Juan lamented the fact that Franco 'has always been a lucky man'. He snorted that: 'General Franco thinks that he is a democrat with the naïve certainty of all those leaders who regard themselves as providential and irreplaceable.' He made it quite clear that, when he became King, he would loosen the rigid straitjacket of the regime. Franco did not need to read *Le Figaro* to learn of Don Juan's hostility to his person and his regime. Plenty of reports reached El Pardo from informers in Estoril recounting the Pretender's more unguarded comments.[2]

The contrast between the disdain that Franco displayed towards Don Juan and the warmth with which he spoke of Juan Carlos occasioned comment in Madrid if not in Estoril. In late February 1961, the Prince joined Franco's family for a hunting party at El Pardo. The regime issued photographs of Juan Carlos kissing the hand of Carmen Polo. They were printed in the *Movimiento* press and abroad. Franco was delighted. A few days later, at the Solemn Requiem Mass for the Kings of Spain at El Escorial, attended by the government and the heads of diplomatic missions, Juan Carlos was given the chair reserved for the representative of the royal family. To be seated so near the Caudillo was perceived by many as an honour implying 'almost equality of status'.[3] In a cabinet meeting, he had said 'tenderly, that the "boy" couldn't be left at the

Casa de Infante in El Escorial, that it was uninhabitable, that there were only two floors, that it had no sports facilities, that this wasn't right for the "boy" and that La Zarzuela was being prepared frenetically because the Prince could hardly live far from Madrid and La Zarzuela solved everything'.[4] Indeed, Juan Carlos himself would complain that he had to drive 50 kilometres every day to get from El Escorial to his classes in the university.[5]

In fact, the restoration work at La Zarzuela was supervised by Doña Carmen Polo, an activity she greatly enjoyed. In early August 1956, when the Mayor of El Ferrol had requested permission to open as a museum the family home in the Calle María where Franco had spent his childhood, Carmen, ashamed of the dingy house, had it completely restructured and refurnished. She did so with great taste and without concern for the expense. It was hardly surprising then that, in October 1960, José María Pemán would write in his diary that La Zarzuela 'was being furnished with exceptional luxury'. As a supporter of Don Juan, Pemán was, however, seriously alarmed when, in describing the layout of the house, Diego Méndez, the architect commissioned by Doña Carmen, made reference to the rooms of 'the Queen' and '*los infantitos*' (the little princes – but with the sense of 'the children of the King'). Pemán could not avoid the conclusion that the Francos were already thinking in terms of Juan Carlos as the future King.[6]

As we have seen, the idea of leaping a generation in the succession had long since been in Franco's mind. He commented to Pacón that he had plenty of people advising him that, given Don Juan's incorrigible liberalism, he should formally exclude him from the succession. Although determined to do so eventually, Franco regarded this as premature and likely to provoke a break with the entire Borbón family. 'I am sure that Prince Juan Carlos would follow his father and would not agree to rule. If a moment of real necessity arose and Don Juan was persisting in the same attitude as now, I would ask him to renounce his rights in favour of his son.' He made an explicit comparison between Don Juan and King Leopold III of Belgium, saying that he had no doubt that the Pretender would agree rather than lose the chance of seeing the monarchy back in Spain.[7]

Juan Carlos began his university level studies in El Escorial in September 1960. Franco's Minister of Education, Jesús Rubio García-Mina, a conservative Falangist with intellectual aspirations, made an important choice to head the committee of academics responsible for the Prince's education. He picked the 45-year-old Professor Torcuato Fernández-Miranda Hevia, Director General of University Education. He was chosen largely because he was considered an expert in the thinking of the founder of the Falange, José Antonio Primo de Rivera. A brilliant man, he had won a chair at the age of 30 and been rector of the University of Oviedo from 1951 to 1953. Despite his fierce intelligence, his political reliability seemed unquestionable. He had fought as an '*alférez provisional*' (acting lieutenant) on the Nationalist side in the Civil War. As Director General of University Education during the student disturbances of the mid-1950s, he had gained a reputation for firmness and decisiveness.[8] Elegantly dapper with an aquiline nose over a knowing smile, it hardly seemed likely that the Prince would get on with this apparently grey and dour individual. He was deeply religious, very conservative, and rather reserved. Yet, after General Martínez Campos and the tutors of the military academies, he was a blast of fresh air to Juan Carlos.

Torcuato Fernández-Miranda's powerful intellect and dry wit soon engaged the Prince. Each day, before the Prince went to Madrid for his classes, Fernández-Miranda would come to the Casita de Arriba and give him classes on politics. At first, Juan Carlos, who was used to the deadening Spanish custom of rote learning, was perplexed because Fernández-Miranda brought him no books. He felt unnerved to be told that he didn't need them: 'Your Highness must learn by listening and looking at what goes on around you.' Aware that one day, the Prince would be on his own, Fernández-Miranda encouraged him to think independently. In later life, he would be infinitely grateful for this but at the time it caused him considerable anguish. When they came to talk about all the things that he would have to do as King, he asked Fernández-Miranda: 'How am I going to get to know all these things? Who's going to help me?' 'No one,' replied his implacable teacher. 'You will have to do the same as the trapeze artists who work without a safety net.' Torcuato Fernández-Miranda taught Juan Carlos patience, serenity and not to trust appearances.[9] In the ruthless and cynical world of Francoist politics, these were crucial survival skills.

Fernández-Miranda stressed the value of debate and discussion, and downplayed the importance of formal learning and examinations. Hearing of this, Franco ordered that one or other of the Prince's military aides be present during his classes. The most senior of them, Nicolás Cotoner, the Marqués de Mondéjar, who had been with Juan Carlos since his secondary school days, was told by Fernández-Miranda that the presence of an officer was required 'so that His Highness and I don't talk about politics'. Mondéjar did not object to Torcuato's approach but his colleague, Lieutenant-Colonel Alfonso Armada, did not like the fact that his talks left the listener with questions unanswered.[10] Accepted by the Prince as his mentor, Fernández-Miranda would later become a crucial influence in helping him undo the constitutional constraints created by Franco to ensure that the regime could not be altered. At this time, Juan Carlos made the acquaintance of another major figure in the process of the eventual transition to democracy. This was Admiral Luis Carrero Blanco's collaborator, Laureano López Rodó, whose postgraduate classes on administrative law were attended by the Prince. Their relationship would be warm, with Juan Carlos frequently demonstrating that Borbón trait of affectionate affability which usually guaranteed the loyalty of those who surrounded him.[11]

When, on 19 October 1960, Juan Carlos first entered the faculty of law of the University of Madrid, accompanied by the Marqués de Mondéjar and a police escort, he faced a raucous ugly mob. Carlist students chanted 'Down with the idiot prince!', 'Long live King Javier!' and 'Get back to Estoril!' Hearing of this, Pedro Sainz Rodríguez telephoned Luis María Anson, leader of the Spanish monarchist university youth movement in Madrid, and asked him to organize some counter-measures. Anson managed to reach an agreement with Socialists, Communists and even Falangists, none of whom favoured Juan Carlos but who were not prepared to tolerate the antics of the Carlists. Juan Carlos himself showed considerable sang-froid, calmly restraining those of his own supporters who were eager to retaliate and relying on his own amiability to dissipate the tension. Franco hesitated before ordering General Camilo Alonso Vega, the hardline Minister of the Interior, and José Solís, the Secretary-General of the *Movimiento*, to put a stop to the incidents. The rector of the university intervened to impose discipline by threatening the Carlists with expulsion. Eventually, Juan Carlos became popular because of his unassuming air and his ability to give the impression of being just one of the crowd, in the bar or wandering the corridors chatting to other students. One was heard to cry with admiration, 'What a bloke! He smokes Celtas!', a reference to the cheap, fierce and highly popular brand of black cigarettes.[12]

Juan Carlos's reception in the university was a symptom of a much wider hostility. On 15 May 1961, at the annual Carlist gathering at Montejurra in Navarre, 50,000 Carlists acclaimed Don Javier de Borbón Parma and his son Hugo. This was part of a choreographed plan to disrupt the apparent inevitability of Juan Carlos being named successor. It was an open secret in government circles that, on the instructions of José Solís, the administration of the *Movimiento* was giving financial support to Don Hugo. When a well-placed supporter of Juan Carlos protested, Solís replied: 'We must keep various options open and we are thereby doing a great service for Franco.'[13]

Meanwhile, the Prince was more interested in girls than in his education. Olghina di Robilant later claimed that, after not seeing Juan Carlos for a year, they had met for one last fling in Rome in 1960. They spent the night in an hotel, and the next morning, he told her that he was engaged to marry Princess Sofía of Greece.[14] The flirtation ended amicably and he was thought to have resumed his interest in Maria Gabriella di Savoia. In July 1960, Maria Gabriella was Juan Carlos's partner at the wedding of the heir to the Duchy of Württemberg, and she accompanied him, later that year, to the Rome Olympics. There were rumours of an imminent announcement from Estoril in mid-October 1960. When by 8 November one had still not been made, the new British

Ambassador, Sir George Labouchere, asked the Duque de Frías and was told, 'Not for the present, at any rate.'[15] In fact, given the parlous state of the exiled Italian monarchy, Don Juan's closest advisers considered it an unsuitable match. Accordingly, Juan Carlos was put under great pressure to drop her. Eventually, he was prevailed upon to do so because, diplomats and journalists were told, she was too worldly.[16] In fact, it was surely another example of his being obliged to bend his will to his father's interests. Although Juan Carlos's relationship with Maria Gabriella would fail to prosper, it was later alleged that she had given birth to his illegitimate daughter.[17]

The first, inconsequential, meeting of Juan Carlos and Sofía had taken place when they were teenagers in 1954 during a cruise of the Greek islands with many European royal families. That enterprise had been arranged by Queen Frederica of Greece in order to boost tourism. It was organized, in the words of Doña María de las Mercedes, 'with Prussian efficiency'.[18] Subsequently, in July 1958, they had met again at the Castle of Althausen near Stuttgart at the wedding of the daughter of the Duke of Württemberg. On that occasion, the 22-year-old Prince began to take notice of the young Princess. It would appear that the relationship took off in Naples in September 1960. Sofía's brother, Constantine, was participating in the Greek Olympic sailing team. The Spanish and Greek royal families were staying at the same hotel and Juan Carlos and Sofía spent time together. Years later, Sofía recounted a scene that suggested a considerable degree of intimacy or at least of flirtation. At the time, Juan Carlos had a moustache and Sofía said to him, 'I don't like you one bit with that horrible moustache.' He replied, 'Really? Well I don't see what I can do about it now.' Taking him by the hand, she said, 'You don't? Well, I do. Come with me.' She took him into a bathroom, sat him down, put a towel around his neck and proceeded to shave off his moustache. On returning to Portugal, Juan Carlos told his Portuguese friend, Bernardo Arnoso, that they had become sweethearts (*novios*).[19] The relationship was further fostered when Don Juan's family was invited to spend the Christmas of 1960 in Corfu with the Greek royal family.[20]

It was not until June 1961, at the wedding of the Duke of Kent and Lady Katherine Worsley, that Juan Carlos showed an assiduous interest in Sofía in public. However, it was clear that there was an attraction dating back to the previous occasions on which they had coincided. Years later, Sofía would admit that, 'Previously, one or two things had gone on.'[21] At the ceremony in Westminster Abbey on 8 June, protocol apparently assigned Juan Carlos to escort Sofía. Nevertheless, it has been suggested that both Queen Victoria Eugenia and Queen Frederica of Greece used their influence with Lord Mountbatten to ensure that this would be the case.[22] 'We were alone there. We were there without our parents and we effectively became engaged in London.' The relationship seems to have resulted from genuine feelings of attraction, rather than from considerations of dynastic convenience.[23]

There were considerable obstacles to the relationship culminating in marriage. To begin with, there was a serious language barrier. Juan Carlos would later explain that, at the start, the relationship with Sofía was '*un jaleo*' (a muddle). He spoke no Greek and she spoke no Spanish. He spoke French, Italian and Portuguese well. She had fluent German, thanks to her mother and secondary education in Germany. The only common language was English: but his was still rather poor while hers was completely fluent. Her father had lived in exile in England from 1924 to 1935. She had been brought up by a Scottish nurse, Sheila MacNair. Her entire family had spent much of the Second World War exiled in South Africa.[24] The language problem would gradually be overcome, however, as Sofía learnt Spanish and Juan Carlos improved his English. Thereafter, the couple would, at home, speak to each other alternately in both languages. Things would be different when it came to their children, however, whilst their father would speak to them in Spanish, Sofía would do so in English and German – her mother tongue.[25] A greater obstacle was the fact that Juan Carlos was a less than ideal candidate for Sofía's hand. Whereas she was the daughter of a reigning monarch, the Spanish Prince was merely the disputed heir to the empty throne of a country where the very future of the monarchy remained uncertain. Even more important, perhaps, were the religious differences.

As Sofía herself would later explain: 'My parents had never contemplated the possibility of my marrying into the Spanish royal family. There was a difference in religion between our countries, the Roman Catholic and the Greek Orthodox.'[26] Juan Carlos knew only too well that the fact that Sofía was not a Roman Catholic would indeed be much criticized by the *Movimiento* press.

In other respects, however, Sofía was an ideal candidate for his wife. The Greek royal family seemed at the time to be firmly established on the throne. Moreover, Sofía possessed many of the virtues he favoured in a partner: she was attractive, highly cultured and, nevertheless, quite shy and unassuming. Furthermore, she had a rather puritanical streak, of which the Prince very much approved. It has been claimed that, during their stay in London for the wedding of the Duke of Kent, Juan Carlos was impressed by a detail which may well have been the catalyst for the relationship. One evening, several of the younger guests at the wedding, amongst which were Juan Carlos and Sofía, decided to have dinner at a famous restaurant. A show started at the end of the meal and, according to the story, it was to feature a striptease. When Sofía realized this, she decided to leave the restaurant and Juan Carlos, impressed by this gesture, accompanied her back to Claridges. Years later, Sofía denied this, saying that she had left the restaurant because it was late and Juan Carlos had accompanied her because they were both staying at the same hotel.[27]

When Sofía met Juan Carlos for the first time in 1954, she had found a boy who was 'scatter-brained, fun, a joker, funny . . . and a bit of a hooligan'. Now she encountered 'a taciturn man, with flashes of melancholy, who suddenly switches from a hearty laugh, from larking about, from a dirty joke, from eating watermelon in a London cab while wearing evening dress, to being plunged into a dark silence'. She quickly perceived that he was still carrying the pain of the loss of his brother Alfonsito. His sadness seemed to her also to be a symptom of a life in which, as a man, he was completely alone while, as a Prince, completely surrounded.[28]

Their mutual attraction led Sofía's brother, Prince Constantine, to telephone his parents in Athens to announce a great surprise. When King Paul I and Queen Frederica of Greece heard of their daughter's pleasure in the attentions of the Spanish Prince, the news 'delighted us and horrified us'. Queen Frederica was especially pleased because Juan Carlos was: 'good looking and elegant. He has curly hair, which irritates him, but is greatly pleasing to older women like myself. He has dark eyes and long eyelashes. He is tall and athletic and can turn on great personal charm. But the most important thing is that he is intelligent, has modern ideas and is kind and likeable. He is very proud of being a Spaniard, but has enough understanding and intelligence to forgive easily the offences and mistakes of others.' She was, however, 'horrified' by the upheaval that the religious issue was sure to produce: 'Before they could get married,' she wrote, 'there would be tremendous discussions on this relatively unimportant subject.'[29]

Juan Carlos obviously succeeded in gaining Frederica's wholehearted approval. With astonishing speed, she invited him and his parents to spend the rest of the summer with the Greek royal family in Corfu. They stayed once more at the palace of Mon Repos, where the Duke of Edinburgh had been born. There, according to Juan Carlos's future mother-in-law, the romantic atmosphere, the mysterious silences of the night, the great orange moon and the hum of cicadas helped intensify their love to the extent that they became unofficially engaged. Sofía, in contrast, remembered them having fierce arguments while they were out sailing and thinking that, if they could survive them, their marriage would have a chance of lasting.[30] The following autumn, the couple would become officially engaged. Years later, however, during the recording of a BBC documentary, Sofía would tease Juan Carlos by reminding him that he had never actually proposed to her. When Juan Carlos started to explain that he asked Sofía to marry him only years after meeting her for the first time, she interjected: 'Did you? Well, you describe it in your own way. I am still waiting. He gave me a ring and that was all. He never declared himself.' At that point in the interview, they both burst out laughing.[31]

The romance was proceeding while Franco was celebrating the 25th anniversary of the 1936 military coup. On 10 July 1961, Don Juan wrote to congratulate him. He recalled his own efforts to join the rising and evoked the memory of Alfonso XIII sticking tiny red and yellow flags in a map of Spain as he followed the progress of the rebels. He went on to proclaim the ties between the monarchy and the uprising of 18 July 1936 – in Francoist jargon, an unequivocal acceptance of the values of the Caudillo's regime. However, he also told Franco that the war had been fought to bring about the return of the monarchy. In reminding the Caudillo that it was time to do so, he also made his most explicit acceptance of the notion of the installation as opposed to restoration of the monarchy: 'It is not the repositioning of a past regime that we seek. With the name of monarchy, we aspire to a political creation which is built on the experiences of recent crises and the most modern thinking.' He suggested that they meet to discuss the future. Franco replied with a letter in which his delight was interleaved with cunning references to his recent triumphant tour of Andalusia and to his popularity in general. The hint was unmistakable: he had no need to consider stepping down. Moreover, the request for a meeting was brushed aside with an oblique remark about the tendentious views of Don Juan's advisers.[32]

It was hardly surprising then that Don Juan would be circumspect about apprising Franco of Juan Carlos's romantic adventures. Moreover, he saw it as an opportunity to assert his independence. Efforts had been made to ensure that no news of the burgeoning relationship between the Prince and Sofía should reach the Spanish Embassy in Greece. Inevitably rumours abounded. When Don Juan and his family returned to Estoril from Greece, he was visited by José Ibáñez Martín, the new Spanish Ambassador in Lisbon. On 28 July, Don Juan told Ibáñez Martín that rumours of a supposed idyll between Juan Carlos and Sofía were absolutely false. Ten days earlier, the Spanish Ambassador in Athens, Luis Felipe de Ranero, had written a report on the sojourn of the Borbón family in Corfu in complete ignorance of the relationship. There was considerable nervousness in El Pardo and at the beginning of September, with rumours proliferating, Ranero was informed that he would soon be moved to another embassy.[33]

Don Juan was clearly determined that Franco should be the

last to know about the relationship between Juan Carlos and Sofía. Early on 11 September, Ibáñez Martín visited Villa Giralda, and asked Don Juan point blank. Moreover, he reminded him that Franco should be the first to know. Ibáñez also pointed out that, according to the *Ley de Sucesión*, claimants to the throne had to report their marriage plans to the *Consejo del Reino* and seek the permission of the Cortes. Don Juan – who had not accepted the *Ley de Sucesión* – replied that the relationship between Juan Carlos and Sofía was in its early stages and that it was impossible to predict what might happen. Nonetheless, he made it clear that he did not object to the relationship. Carrero Blanco had also sent López Rodó to Lisbon to see if he could discover more. In the course of a long meeting on the same evening, Don Juan categorically denied that there was anything brewing. On the following morning, at Lisbon airport where he was seeing off Don Juan who was going to Lausanne, Ibáñez Martín asked: 'What news of this engagement and why are you going to Lausanne?' Don Juan repeated his denial: 'Nothing, Ambassador, absolutely nothing. Everything they're saying is pure fantasy.' What he had not told the Ambassador was that, in his mother's home in Lausanne, he would be meeting King Paul and Queen Frederica, as well as Juan Carlos and Sofía. At a dinner presided over by Victoria Eugenia, King Paul requested an early announcement of the engagement. He hoped thereby to boost the monarchist cause in Greece, where elections were imminent. Happy to assert his independence from Franco, Don Juan agreed to go ahead. On the morning of 13 September, the Greek and Portuguese newspapers splashed the news on their front pages. Alongside a beaming Sofía, Juan Carlos appeared nervous and apprehensive – if the photographic evidence is to be believed.[34]

At the time, Franco was fishing on his yacht, the *Azor*, and Don Juan managed to contact him on shore-to-ship radio to give him the news. On a line that went from Lausanne via Geneva, Paris, Madrid and San Sebastián, there was considerable interference and he had to shout to be heard. He explained through the crackling that he would rather have sent a letter but the King of Greece had requested that the news be announced early. When

Franco finally realized that this was an historic moment, he cried, 'Highness, wait, wait,' and disappeared for several minutes. He had gone off to consider his reply and write it down. As the minutes passed, an impatient Don Juan thrust the receiver into the hands of his private secretary, Ramón Padilla, and went off to get a drink. On his return, he heard Franco reading out, in typically slow and stilted manner, a lengthy message of congratulation.[35] The sugary felicities barely concealed Franco's annoyance. His intention had been to process Juan Carlos's eventual marriage through the clauses of the *Ley de Sucesión*, with consultation of the *Consejo del Reino*, and ratification by the Cortes. This would therefore have struck a severe blow against Don Juan because it would have confirmed that the monarchy derived its 'legitimacy' from the regime and not from dynastic continuity. Moreover, given the Caudillo's conviction that Sofía's father was a freemason, which he had confided in January 1960 to Emilio García Conde, the entire episode can only have poisoned further his relations with Don Juan.

On the day after the announcement, Juan Carlos and Sofía, accompanied by Doña María de las Mercedes, travelled to Athens to begin making arrangements for the wedding. The scale of their reception, huge crowds in streets decorated with Greek and Spanish flags, suggested considerable prior preparation and rather undermined Don Juan's claim that the announcement of the engagement had been precipitate. Nevertheless, when Don Juan returned to Estoril on 25 September, he assured Ibáñez Martín that he had not expected the announcement to take place when it did. He also informed the Ambassador that the wedding would take place in Athens with successive ceremonies in the Greek Orthodox and Roman Catholic rites.[36]

Two days later, Don Juan wrote to Franco with what seemed to be a considerable peace offering. First, he congratulated him on his 25 years as Head of State. He then announced his intention of awarding him the highest honour in the gift of the King of Spain, the *Toisón de Oro* (the Order of the Golden Fleece) on the occasion of the forthcoming wedding. It was to be bestowed as an: 'expression of recognition, by the Royal Family, of Your Excellency's great services to Spain throughout your life as a soldier and statesman'. Franco coldly declined. To accept would be to admit that Don Juan was King. He wrote that: 'for various reasons I judge it inappropriate and I could not accept. In this regard, I believe that you should request historical information on the subject' – a harsh and patronizing insinuation that only the King, and not a Pretender, could grant this honour.[37]

The news of the forthcoming wedding delighted monarchists in Spain. However, there was considerable disquiet at the way the *Movimiento* press ignored the Spanish royal family in its coverage of the engagement. In Estoril, it had been hoped that the engagement would stimulate a wave of publicity in favour of Don Juan. That it did not was hardly surprising. The Caudillo was now taking a petty revenge for the fact that he had not been consulted in the choice of bride or in the announcement of the engagement. More annoying for Franco was that Don Juan and his son had flouted the *Ley de Sucesión*. Most offensive of all in the dictator's eyes was the fact that the official announcement of the engagement read as follows: 'His Majesty the King and His Royal Highness the Conde de Barcelona have the exceptional pleasure to announce the happy event of the engagement to be married of their beloved children Her Royal Highness the Princess Sofía and His Royal Highness the Príncipe de Asturias, heir to the Crown of Spain.' Although this formula referred to Don Juan as 'His Royal Highness' – rather than as 'His Majesty' – which was acceptable to Franco, the reference to Juan Carlos as the 'Príncipe de Asturias, heir to the Crown of Spain' was a direct challenge. Franco had never permitted this title to be given to the Prince for the simple reason that its use would signify that Juan Carlos's father was the rightful King of Spain.

Nor can Franco have been unaware that Don Juan's Privy Council had been discussing ways of persuading him to withdraw from power. Among the fanciful ideas that had reached the British Embassy was that of offering the Caudillo an impressive title such as Príncipe de Vitoria or Conde de Castilla. Much debate went into the question of how to ask the Head of State to authorize his own ennoblement. Less consideration was given to the fact that

Franco considered himself to be above Don Juan and therefore unlikely to allow him to bestow any honour upon him. In the event, the deliberations led to the offer of the *Toisón de Oro* and Franco's scornful refusal.[38]

The Caudillo's irritation made itself manifest both in that rejection and in the Spanish press. Franco was fully aware that a royal wedding could be expected to intensify popular monarchist sentiment. When the engagement was announced, the press published several in-depth reports on the Greek royal family, but no information whatsoever on the Spanish royal family. This led to the publication of a '*Boletín del Consejo Privado del conde de Barcelona*' (Bulletin of the Privy Council of the Conde de Barcelona) lamenting the fact that: 'Unfortunately, not even the joyous news of the wedding has managed to break the sectarian silence imposed by the censorship on the press, which prevents Spaniards from knowing anything about how the Spanish royal family lives or what they look like.' In fact, the Falangist press did not simply ignore the wedding but soon went on to the attack, violently criticizing the notion of a mixed wedding (i.e. Catholic and non-Catholic) which, it claimed, was not: 'acceptable, nor would it be tolerated by the Spanish people'.[39]

On the first occasion that Juan Carlos visited Franco after the announcement, the Caudillo asked him, 'Are you pleased with your fiancée?' And, without waiting for his reply, added, 'You know, you don't have to marry a princess.' In similar vein, Franco said to Pemán, 'I shall be pleased if they are happy. But you know it wasn't essential for the bride to have royal blood. There are lots of girls in Spain who aren't royalty but deserve a throne.'[40]

Franco remained irritated by the implicit challenge of the engagement and the way in which it had been announced. As part of the celebrations of the 25th anniversary of his Headship of State, a cabinet meeting took place on 1 October in the Palacio de la Isla in Burgos, Franco's wartime headquarters. López Rodó had persuaded both Admiral Carrero Blanco and General Alonso Vega to press Franco to announce that the constitutional law which he had started to draft in 1957 would soon be submitted to the Cortes as the *Ley Orgánica del Estado*. But Franco was in no mood to commit himself irrevocably to a particular option for the succession and ignored suggestions during the short session.[41] On the following day, he addressed the *Consejo Nacional de FET y de las JONS* at the Monasterio de las Huelgas, where the first ever session had taken place in 1937. A clear message was being sent to Don Juan and to Juan Carlos when José Solís, the Secretary-General of the *Movimiento*, began the ceremony by addressing Franco simply as 'Señor', the form of address reserved for kings.

On 13 November, both Franco and Juan Carlos had been invited to a hunting party at El Alamín, one of the estates the Marqués de Comillas had inherited on the death of his father, the Conde de Ruiseñada. The Caudillo asked Juan Carlos what he planned to do after his wedding. Showing how much he had learned from Franco's own ability to keep his counsel, he replied, 'Up to now, everything has been agreed between you and my father.' Toying with the idea of eliminating Don Juan from the succession lottery, Franco said, 'Your Highness is getting old enough to make his own decisions.' With equal prudence, the Prince replied, 'But I still have a boss.' This conversation led Juan Carlos to meet Carrero Blanco and ask that his status be clarified before the wedding. He told López Rodó on 20 November that, for the previous three years, he had consistently got the impression that Franco planned to name him as his successor. Moreover, in that case, he was sure that his father, rather than risk the crown going to another dynastic branch, would tell him to accept.[42]

There were foreign media reports in late November 1961 to the effect that Juan Carlos, who had gone to Estoril, would not return to Spain unless he were recognized as Príncipe de Asturias. It is unlikely that there was any such pressure but, come what may, Juan Carlos would be disappointed in this regard.[43] Within weeks of the engagement becoming public knowledge, there was certainly speculation as to the Prince's future residence. The British Ambassador, Sir George Labouchere, reported to London, 'I am assured by some monarchists that the majority of them, supported by Don Juan, are most anxious that after his marriage Don Juan Carlos and his wife should live in Estoril. They fear that should he live in Madrid he will take all the limelight from his father and make it impossible for the latter to come back to Spain and reign.' He went on to say that the Greek Ambassador had learned that General Franco was determined that Don Juan Carlos and his wife should live in Spain for at least part of the year. 'I am, moreover, told by the Greek Ambassador's rather garrulous wife, and I have no reason to disbelieve it, that Don Juan Carlos has protested to her his great affection for General Franco and has assured her that the latter treats him like his son. I presume that another factor to be reckoned with is the Queen of Greece. From what I have heard of her I imagine that she is hardly the type of lady who would cheerfully allow her daughter to remain exiled from her new country and not at least take her rightful place for some periods of the year in Spain as the wife of the grandson of King Alfonso XIII. If only for this, I would presume that when married Don Juan Carlos will be seen rather more frequently about Madrid than is at present the case. He could hardly be seen less.' Labouchere was convinced that the Generalísimo had definitively turned against Don Juan, 'and intends now to wait to see whether the immature, if charming, Don Juan Carlos has it in him to attain the calibre to become King of Spain when he reaches the age of 30 in eight years' time'. Labouchere's reference to Queen Frederica was more discreet than the nickname 'the Prussian sergeant' by which she was known in Madrid.[44]

For all Frederica's determination to see her daughter married to Juan Carlos, the religious difference posed a major difficulty. Franco and the supporters of Don Juan were as one in expecting Sofía to convert to Catholicism before the wedding, just as Victoria Eugenia had done before marrying Alfonso XIII. They overlooked certain crucial differences. Sofía would not be marrying a reigning monarch. As a ruling dynasty, the Greek royal family was the senior partner in this particular liaison and held most of the cards. Because of Don Juan's precarious economic situation, there was no question of the wedding taking place in Estoril. It would have to be in Athens and, inevitably, the Greek government and royal family would expect a Greek princess marrying in the Greek capital to have a Greek Orthodox ceremony. The best that might be expected would be for Sofía formally to convert to Catholicism immediately after the Orthodox ceremony before proceeding to a second, Catholic, marriage service. This was a situation from which the press networks of the *Movimiento* derived the most malicious benefit, bizarrely accusing Sofía of being a *'hereje'* (heretic).[45]

In consequence, throughout the autumn and winter months of 1961, Don Juan was engaged in shuttle diplomacy with the Papal Nuncio in Lisbon, the College of Cardinals in Rome, Queen Frederica, the Greek government and the Metropolitan of the Orthodox Church. With Franco's permission, the Spanish Ambassadors to Italy (José María Doussinague), to the Vatican (Francisco Gómez de Llano), and Greece (the Marqués Juan Ignacio de Luca de Tena) did all that they could to help him. In Greece, the opposition had expressed outrage that Sofía might marry outside the Orthodox Church. Franco expected Sofía to convert to Catholicism before the marriage took place. In fact, from late 1961, she was discreetly taking instruction from the Catholic Archbishop of Athens. The Greek government insisted on a full-scale Orthodox wedding and refused Sofía permission to convert to Catholicism before leaving Greece. On 12 January 1962, Juan Carlos and Sofía accompanied his father to Rome where they were received in a lengthy audience by Pope John XXIII. Papal dispensation was granted for dual Orthodox and Catholic ceremonies, although the document did not arrive until 21 March. When Don Juan wrote to Franco to inform him of the visit to the Vatican, he ended: 'I'm not sure what I am supposed to do in terms of politics or protocol, but speaking from the heart, I hardly need to say how pleased we would be if Doña Carmen and Your Excellency could be present at the Prince's wedding.'[46]

In fact, there was never any possibility of Franco attending the ceremony. He travelled rarely – as Head of State, he left Spain only to see Hitler in 1940, Mussolini in 1941 and Salazar in 1949 – and to visit Greece he would have needed an invitation from the Greek government. Even if that were forthcoming, to be seen at Juan Carlos's wedding would tip his hand in the succession stakes. In any case, by the time that Franco got Don Juan's letter, a visit to Greece for a wedding was the last thing on his mind.

On Christmas Eve 1961, Franco had gone pigeon shooting in the hills behind El Pardo. At 5.15 p.m., he was hurt in a serious accident when his shotgun exploded, badly damaging his left hand.[47] Although the press played down the extent of his injuries – fractures of his index finger and his second metacarpal bone – panic ran through the *Movimiento*.[48] For Franco to be out of action under a general anaesthetic constituted a dramatic moment yet he used none of the complex mechanisms established in the *Ley de Sucesión*. Instead, he telephoned Carrero Blanco and ordered him to inform only the military ministers and the Chief of the General Staff. Then he sent for his lifelong friend Camilo Alonso Vega, the hardline Minister of the Interior. He made no provision for a diminished ability to govern other than to tell him *'ten cuidado de lo que ocurra'* (keep an eye on things).

Franco was considerably incapacitated by the consequent pain and unable to sleep at night for the first months of 1962 despite taking painkillers.[49] Even after the plaster was removed in April, he gingerly held his left arm to his chest. Much of the muscle and nerve tissue of the hand was destroyed and only extensive physiotherapy over the next three months returned him to near normal mobility.[50] Exhaustive tests indicated that the accident could not be attributed to a defective gun. This led to speculation that Franco had been the target of an assassination attempt with Alonso Vega especially convinced that the ammunition had been tampered with.[51] Inevitably, the incident propelled the succession to the top of the agenda.[52] The most worrying concern for both Don Juan and Juan Carlos was that the recourse to General Alonso Vega after the shooting accident implied that Franco favoured a kind of regency rather than a rapid passage to the monarchy. The accident and its aftermath revealed that Franco was likely to turn to a hardliner to guarantee that the eventual monarch would not stray from the *Movimiento*'s authoritarian path. The role of watch-dog of Francoist ideals would be successively entrusted, first to General Alonso Vega, then to the dour General Agustín Muñoz Grandes and finally to Admiral Luis Carrero Blanco. Ironically, Franco would outlive them all. In the meanwhile, despite Franco's close relationship with Carrero, who was committed to the mon-

archy of Juan Carlos, there remained considerable room for speculation and manoeuvre regarding the selection of a royal candidate.
The concerns of many Francoists for the survival and continuity
of the regime would be intensified when large-scale strikes swept
across the industrial north in the spring of 1962.

Over the winter of 1961–1962, visits to Estoril, Athens, Rome
and London, shopping and diplomacy in preparation for the wedding had left Juan Carlos little time for his university studies, but
by the end of February 1962, they were regarded as officially
complete. On 1 March 1962, Juan Carlos visited Franco for the
last time as a bachelor. He invited him to the wedding which had
now been scheduled for 14 May and suggested that he would like
also to invite the three armed service ministers. Franco declined,
saying that he would be adequately represented by the Minister
for the Navy, Rear-Admiral Felipe Abárzuza Oliva. The admiral
would sail to Athens aboard the Spanish Navy's flagship, the
battlecruiser *Canarias*, an ostentatious symbol of his Civil War
victory. Juan Carlos had tried to get the Caudillo to clarify his
own situation within Spain but, as he told López Rodó, 'Franco
gives nothing away.' It was inevitable that Franco would reject
this oblique request for Juan Carlos to be named Príncipe de
Asturias, since to do so would be to recognize that Don Juan was
King. However, to soften the blow, he said, 'I can assure you,
Highness, that you have far more chance of being King of Spain
than your father.' Where previously there had been hints, this
was the first unequivocal acknowledgement to Juan Carlos of the
elimination of Don Juan as possible successor. Deeply embarrassed, the Prince replied that he would inform his father of their
conversation since it was his duty to do so. Franco told Juan
Carlos that he should stay on in Spain after his marriage. 'Your
Highness should be in contact with the Spanish people so that
they get to know you and love you.'

The Caudillo was pleased by the meeting and found Juan
Carlos to be, 'very intelligent, with a lively imagination and already
well-informed about what is going on in Spain'. He reiterated to
Pacón his confidence that he could get Don Juan to abdicate: 'I
am sure that, when the moment arises, his father, for the good

of Spain and of the monarchy, will act with the patriotism that characterises monarchs such as Edward VIII of England and Leopold III of Belgium, renouncing the crown in the best interests of their country and their dynasty.' Nevertheless, he also commented that the entire question of the succession saw him currently 'embittered and worried'. On 3 April 1962, Carrero Blanco confirmed what Franco had said to Juan Carlos when he told López Rodó that the Caudillo had entirely eliminated Don Juan from his plans.[53]

Although the announcement of the wedding, with its various implications, had infuriated Franco, his fondness for Juan Carlos led him to make a number of gestures that facilitated its organization. Spanish diplomats helped resolve the various problems arising between Athens, Madrid and the Vatican over religion. He agreed that Luis Felipe de Ranero's successor as Spanish Ambassador to Greece be Juan Ignacio de Luca de Tena, the owner of the monarchist daily *ABC*, precisely to ensure that the wedding would go well. Luca de Tena's loyalty to the Caudillo was not in question. Nevertheless, this was a significant gesture since Franco was concerned that: 'he will seem more Estoril's ambassador than mine'. He prohibited Carlist meetings at the Valle de los Caídos, telling Pacón that Hugo, the son of the Pretender Don Javier, a French citizen, was: 'a foreigner whom nobody knows and has no support whatsoever'. Franco boasted to Dr Ramón Soriano, who was treating him for his injured hand, that: 'I personally oversaw all the arrangements for the wedding' and, 'I made the King of Greece confirm in writing everything concerning protocol and ceremonial,' commenting, 'I got it in writing because I don't trust the Greeks.' Franco gave Juan Carlos and Sofía the highest decoration in the gift of the Spanish government, the *Gran Collar y el Lazo con brillantes de la Orden de Carlos III*, an honour previously reserved for reigning sovereigns. He also sent, with Admiral Abárzuza, a magnificent wedding present in the form of a spectacular diamond brooch.[54] All of these attentions were unmistakable signs of the Caudillo's growing regard for Juan Carlos.

If Franco viewed Juan Carlos's marriage with almost paternal benevolence, he did nothing to discourage the elements in the *Movimiento* who were openly hostile to it. The Falangist press network had attacked Sofía by criticizing the announcement that she would be converting to Catholicism. In mid-February 1962, the Caudillo received José Luis Zamanillo, a prominent leader of the Carlist *Comunión Tradicionalista*. He encouraged Carlist activities in favour of Don Javier, telling Zamanillo to 'keep working away'. At the great Carlist gathering at Montejurra in May 1962, there were well-organized manifestations of support for Don Javier. Significantly, a number of well-known Falangist figures attended. Moreover, telegrams of support (*adhesión*) arrived from Miguel Primo de Rivera, the brother of José Antonio, and his sister Pilar, head of the *Sección Femenina*, and Raimundo Fernández Cuesta. All three of these major historic Falangists had had lunch on 3 May with José Luis Zamanillo and José María Valiente, President of the *Comunión Tradicionalista*, fierce advocates of Don Javier and Don Hugo.[55]

Even without signs of hostility emanating from the highest reaches of the *Movimiento*, the days immediately preceding the wedding were difficult ones for the couple. Sir Ralph Murray, the British Ambassador in Athens, found Juan Carlos 'in a rather gloomy state', which he attributed both to the nervous tension resulting from the wedding preparations and from the fact that he was in constant pain. On 20 April, he had broken his left collarbone whilst practising judo with Sofía's brother, Crown Prince Constantine. Until two days before his wedding, he would have his arm in a sling.[56] Juan Carlos's marriage took place in Athens on 14 May 1962. After the ceremony at the Catholic cathedral, the couple, now man and wife, returned to the royal palace. After a brief pause, they set off again in procession to the Greek Orthodox Metropole, travelling in separate carriages. Juan Carlos travelled with his mother, Sofía with her father in the State Coach drawn by six white horses with a cavalry escort. The Crown Prince Constantine rode at her side. The couple walked down the steps of the cathedral through an arch of sabres held aloft by 18 Spanish officers, friends of the Prince from his time in the three academies. Determined to outdo its Catholic rivals, the Orthodox

Church saw the Archbishop of Athens officiate with 22 other bishops in support.[57]

After toying with the idea of naval uniform, which would have pleased his father, the Prince sagely opted to wear the uniform of Lieutenant of the Spanish Army, which delighted Franco. The Caudillo watched the ceremony on television and told Dr Soriano that Juan Carlos 'was very military'. The occasion was turned into a major monarchist demonstration by the more than 5,000 Spaniards who made the journey. Franco had initially ordered that the occasion be given as little publicity as possible and that Don Juan should not figure in any photographs published. In the event, the press and television coverage provided massive publicity for Juan Carlos while managing to reduce Don Juan's participation to the minimum. He complained bitterly to Ibáñez Martín that Madrid wits were calling it: 'the wedding of the little orphan, because at the ceremony his parents are nowhere to be seen'.[58] The huge publicity unleashed by the wedding helped mask the labour problems faced by the regime.[59] Throughout April and May 1962, strikes spread from the Asturian mines and the Basque steel industry into Catalonia and Madrid. Despite massive repression, they were stopped eventually only by wage increases and thus marked the beginning of the end for the Falangist vertical syndicates and the emergence of a new clandestine working-class movement.[60]

Sofía was sharply aware that her chances of acquiring a throne depended on the good will of Franco. On the eve of her wedding, from the royal palace in Athens, she had sent a letter of thanks for his gifts. Typewritten in English, it seemed quite heartfelt by the standards of such things: 'My Dear Generalísimo, I was overwhelmed and deeply touched by the wonderful gifts, which the Admiral Abárzuza brought to me on your behalf and for which I thank you with all my heart. The decoration gave me much pleasure, as well as the magnificent diamond brooch which you sent me as a wedding present and I shall treasure them all my life. Sophie.' However, she seems to have been advised that the way to the Caudillo's heart was via flattery and attention to the ego of Doña Carmen. Accordingly, on 22 May she sent another letter, this time handwritten, in Spanish and drafted with the help of Juan Carlos. It was rather more personal in tone and pressed the right patriotic notes.

'My dear General,
Although I hope that, by now, Admiral Abárzuza has passed on my thanks for the signs of affection that you have shown on the occasion of my wedding, I don't want to let any more time go by without telling you personally just how thrilled I feel about everything. The beautiful jewel that you, General, and Doña Carmen gave me, as well as the high decoration, have made me feel already part of my new Fatherland which I burn with desire to know and to serve. A thousand thanks once more, General, and with affectionate greetings to your wife.
Yours truly,
Sofía.'[61]

After the wedding, the couple set off on the first stage of a very long honeymoon. Aboard the yacht *Eros*, they sailed to the idyllic island of Spetsopoula. The yacht and the island had been lent by the Greek shipping magnate Stavros Niarchos. From Spetsopoula, the *Eros* sailed to Corfu, where, on 31 May, Sofía was formally received into the Catholic Church at a private ceremony. On 3 June, the *Eros* landed at Anzio and the couple flew on to Rome. On the following day, they went to thank Pope John XXIII for all that he had done to facilitate their union.[62] From Rome, they flew to Madrid, with the approval of both Queen Victoria Eugenia and Queen Frederica, to thank Franco for his various attentions in relation to the wedding. It was impossible to consult directly with Don Juan, who was returning to Estoril aboard the *Saltillo* and out of touch because of a faulty radio. A delegation from Don Juan's Privy Council urged Sofía and Juan Carlos not to go to Madrid but they were determined to make the journey and the Duque de Frías was instructed to make the necessary arrangements. The Prince felt considerable trepidation about doing so. *En route*, he commented to his faithful aide and adviser, Emilio

García Conde, now promoted to an Air Force Colonel, 'This means a break with my father.' After arriving at the military airfield at Getafe, they went straight to El Pardo where Sofía was pleasantly surprised. She had expected the dictator to be '*duro, seco, antipático*' (harsh, dry and unpleasant). Instead, she found: 'a simple man, eager to please and very shy'.[63]

On the following day, they returned to El Pardo for lunch with Franco, his wife, his daughter Carmen and her husband, Cristóbal Martínez-Bordiu, the Marqués de Villaverde. In the course of the morning before receiving the newly weds, Franco also made a point of granting a long audience to the president of the *Comunión Tradicionalista*, José María Valiente. He thereby stressed that Juan Carlos was merely one of the several pretenders to the throne. Nevertheless, Sofía created a very favourable impression on the Caudillo. Doña Carmen Polo told her crony, Pura Huétor de Santillán, that the Princess 'has stolen Paco's heart'[64]. According to Pemán, Franco was entranced, 'by a beauty that was part childish, part malicious', by her religiosity and because he was pleasantly surprised by the quality of her Spanish. A beaming Franco subsequently told Pacón that Sofía: 'speaks Spanish quite well and is studying it intensively. She is very pleasant and seems intelligent and very cultured.'[65]

Monarchists in Madrid reported to the British Embassy their chagrin that Juan Carlos had found time to see Franco yet had not been able to receive any of the royal family's supporters.[66] What they saw as a slight was actually a major landmark on Juan Carlos's road to the throne. The enterprise showed very clearly how the situation had changed now that Sofía was part of Juan Carlos's life. Henceforth, gradually at first, but ever more perceptibly, Juan Carlos would act independently. Don Juan, now in Mallorca, immediately perceived the significance of the visit. As a reprimand, he dismissed the Duque de Frías as head of his son's household. Nearly a quarter of a century later, Sofía was asked if the visit had been arranged behind Don Juan's back. Her reply gives a hint of the steely determination that she brought to the marriage: 'Neither behind his back nor to his face. We didn't ask Don Juan's opinion because it wasn't necessary. I have no idea whether he opposed the visit roundly or not. All I know is that we told him about it but we didn't consult him.'[67]

After lunch with Franco, the couple flew back to Italy where they embarked once more on the *Eros* to continue their honeymoon with a short visit to Monaco. Despite the obvious benefits to the regime in terms of diverting attention from social tension, Franco insisted that minimum publicity be given to the couple's journey. When the new Minister of Information, Manuel Fraga Iribarne, took up office on Monday 23 July 1962, replacing Gabriel Arias Salgado, he demanded to see the so-called '*libro verde*' (green book) which contained the instructions given to the censor. To his astonishment, alongside bizarre directives about the prohibition of female bathing costumes '*con señora dentro*' (with ladies in them), he found the order that no publicity was to be given to the honeymoon of Juan Carlos and Sofía.[68]

After Monte Carlo, the newly weds returned to Italy where they left the *Eros*. Over the next four and a half months of globe-trotting, they would visit Jordan, India – where they met Pandit Nehru and Indira Gandhi – Nepal, Thailand, Japan, the Philippines, and finally the US. There the Spanish Ambassador, Antonio Garrigues y Díaz Cañabate, was perplexed by the fact that he received no instructions from Madrid about their status. On his own initiative, he informed the State Department that they represented Spain and Greece. In consequence, they met President Kennedy and were received with full military honours at West Point. According to an interview given years later by Sofía, no staff whatsoever (no security guards, policemen or even maids) accompanied them on their honeymoon and everything was set up through a travel agency. For part at least of the journey, however, they were accompanied as secretary by Rafael Calvo Serer, the smooth, urbane, intelligent Opus Deista. It will be recalled that Calvo Serer had met Don Juan in Lausanne during the Second World War and frequently shuttled back and forth between Madrid and Estoril, reporting to Franco in the process. In January 1963, he was back in New York and Washington with Juan Carlos and Sofía, canvassing powerful figures on Wall Street and on Capitol Hill for their future support for a monarchical regime in Spain.[69]

On the very day that Juan Carlos and Sofía were visiting El Pardo, the IV Congress of the European Movement began in Munich. Over the next three days, until 8 June 1962, monarchists, Catholics and repentant Falangists from inside Spain met exiled Socialists and Basque and Catalan nationalists. Franco's resentment of Don Juan was inflamed by the meeting and with it his sense of the greater trustworthiness of Juan Carlos grew. Although the general drift of the meeting was a moderate and pacific call for evolution in Spain, Franco was easily convinced that it was a conspiracy to undermine the regime by freemasons, Jews and Catholics. At one of the sessions, Joaquín Satrústegui sang the praises of a monarchy under Don Juan and asserted that there could be no question of Juan Carlos's loyalty to his father.[70] In response to this, at a marathon session of Franco's cabinet, it was decided to suspend the flimsy constitutional guarantees of the *Fuero de los Españoles*. The Caudillo was particularly incensed by the part played by Don Juan's adviser, José María Gil Robles.[71] Many of the Spanish delegates, including Dionisio Ridruejo and Gil Robles, were arrested and sent into exile for their part in what was denounced as the 'filthy Munich cohabitation' (*contubernio*). Franco's reaction severely damaged the Spanish case for entry into Europe.[72] Franco gave Gabriel Arias Salgado, then still Minister of Information, carte blanche to unleash a violent response in the press. The barrage of hysteria even extended to blaming Don Juan for what had happened.[73]

Several of those present were supporters of Don Juan and had also attended the wedding in Athens. In fact, Don Juan knew little about the preparation of the event and had learnt about the meeting while aboard his yacht, the *Saltillo*, returning to Portugal from Athens. Pemán issued a statement from Don Juan that no one present at the Munich sessions represented his views and that: 'if anyone there was a member of my Privy Council, they have in consequence ceased to be part of it.' The consequence was that a mortified Gil Robles, now in exile, resigned from the Privy Council. Bizarrely, Don Juan replaced him with Fernando Álvarez de Miranda who had been present at the wedding in Athens, at the meeting in Munich and was now – like Satrústegui – confined to the island of Fuerteventura in the Canaries.[74]

This and other categorical denials by Don Juan did nothing to diminish Franco's suspicion that he was behind the entire operation. He was outraged that Munich should come so soon after his shooting accident had posed the question of his mortality and while the strike wave was undermining the regime's image of invulnerability. He gave vent to his feelings about Munich in a series of speeches that he made in mid-June in Valencia. He denounced foreign criticism of his regime and derided liberalism as weak, useless and rotten. In words that summed up his attitude to Don Juan, 'weak spirits, timorous people, poor in spirit, faithless men, ambitious and bedazzled by what comes from abroad', he attacked those who went to Munich as 'the wretched ones who conspire with the reds to take their miserable complaints before foreign assemblies'.[75]

In the summer of 1962, it was reported in the Greek press that Queen Frederica had asked Victoria Eugenia to encourage Don Juan to abdicate in favour of his son. Although the Greek court issued a denial, there can be no doubt that Queen Frederica was determined to see her daughter on the Spanish throne. While in Athens for the wedding, Pemán had noted in his diary of Frederica: 'She can't be still. She's always giving orders. No wonder some believe that she will be plotting to see Juan Carlos leapfrog his father and Sofía crowned.'[76] Whatever the role of his mother-in-law, there was certainly a noticeable difference in the Prince after his marriage. Now enjoying the emotional security deriving from a supportive wife, he manifested a far greater confidence in himself. Sofía had known exile with the Greek royal family and brought a hard realism to her assessment of the Spanish situation. She surely reiterated what her husband already knew: that the only route to the throne was via a closer rapprochement with the Caudillo. Similar advice was being dispensed by the Marqués de Mondéjar.

The Prince and Sofía returned to Estoril in mid-September and within a month were back in Athens. Shortly afterwards, Sofía had to go into hospital for an operation. According to the official press release, it was for an appendectomy. Nevertheless, the presence of the royal gynaecologist led to speculation that she was suffering from an ectopic pregnancy. The British Ambassador to Greece reported to London: 'I understand that she was at the time pregnant and the operation caused a great deal of anxiety for this reason, but there has been no official confirmation of her pregnancy.' Sofía has subsequently denied that she was pregnant. Whatever her ailment, her recovery was swift and the Ambassador commented that he found Juan Carlos 'infinitely more cheerful, and indeed, almost boisterous'. He also reported that the couple remained uncertain as to where they were going to take up their permanent residence but were planning to stay in Greece until January or February to be present at the celebrations of the silver wedding of Sofía's parents. Juan Carlos had admitted to him that it was 'rather an embarrassing decision to make' and Sofía told him that 'they had reached one conclusion which was that they in any case did not want to live in Portugal'.[77] At the end of November 1962, the Spanish Ambassador, Juan Ignacio Luca de Tena, sent his farewell despatch to Madrid. He referred to the rumour that Sofía had had a miscarriage. Commenting on a lunch with the couple, Luca de Tena noted that the Prince spoke enthusiastically of his affection for the Caudillo. He also reported that Juan Carlos had recently sacked a Spanish member of his staff for speaking ill of the Generalísimo.[78]

In the wake of Munich, the Caudillo's hostility to Don Juan was greater than ever. In November 1962, Franco told Pacón that: 'Don Juan prides himself on being liberal and surrounds himself with enemies of the regime, placing himself in opposition to us. Naturally, I regret this and there's nothing I can do to avoid it. Accordingly, the responsibility before history is his.' Again, on 20 December 1962, Franco was even more explicit, albeit speaking as if the process were out of his hands: 'I am convinced that the Conde de Barcelona will not become King of Spain because his way of thinking would open the way to a Communist revolution like the one we defeated in 1939. If a king who guarantees the regime cannot be found, a regent will be appointed.' Franco even told an alarmed Carrero Blanco that he was thinking about putting the choice of his successor to a referendum.[79]

With the restoration of La Zarzuela now complete, Franco

was also growing ever more suspicious about Juan Carlos's absence from Spain. Despite being keen to take up residence there, the Prince and his wife were under intense pressure from his father to settle in Estoril. There was considerable tension when Don Juan was told by his son that his marriage was no reason for him to leave Spain. But Juan Carlos could see no reason to antagonize Franco after all the effort he had already put in. To please Don Juan, they spent a token period in Portugal but were quickly bored and were anxious to establish a home in Madrid. In late September 1962, hearing of the floods that had devastated parts of Catalonia, Juan Carlos immediately made the decision to visit the victims. General Martínez Campos made the arrangements with the Vice-President of Franco's government, General Agustín Muñoz Grandes. Juan Carlos and Sofía went to Tarragona and Tortosa, as well as the working-class shanty dwellings along the banks of the River Llobregat and in El Vallés near Sabadell. They were well received and the visit helped to establish them in the minds of the Spanish people. Rafael Calvo Serer endeavoured to present the initiative as a visit in representation of Don Juan. As he confided to Pacón, this deeply annoyed Franco. He was also irritated by the fact that Juan Carlos had visited the region before he had done so himself.[80]

Don Juan knew full well that Franco expected Juan Carlos and Sofía to live in the Spanish capital. The Caudillo had made that quite clear in his letter of April 1962. Ten months later, the Prince's failure to return to Spain was beginning seriously to irritate him and he was toying with other options for the succession. Although he had definitively eliminated Don Juan as a possibility, the uncertainty regarding Juan Carlos's place of residence was beginning to provoke doubts about his candidacy. In mid-January 1963, Franco told Manuel Fraga Iribarne: 'The Prince can come whenever he likes and I will receive him as always but I won't lift a finger to get him to come sooner or later.'[81]

On 4 February 1963, Franco revealed his annoyance in one of his very few critical remarks about the Prince, commenting to Pacón: 'I just don't understand why Juan Carlos lets himself be subject to the policy of his father who has declared himself incompatible with the principles of the *Movimiento Nacional.*' He was convinced, reasonably enough, that residence in Spain was essential if Juan Carlos were ever to be King. It was typical of his own egoism that Franco simply could not understand why the Prince should have more loyalty to his father than to him. 'Because of the *Ley de Sucesión*, the *Consejo del Reino* will decide who is going to be my successor and, if he lives in Spain, Don Juan Carlos would have more probability than anyone else.' The Lausanne Manifesto still rankled with Franco and this was the principal reason for eliminating Don Juan: 'It is unimaginable that the winners in a war should hand power to the losers.' Regarding any suggestion that his regime might be changed as 'treachery to the Fatherland and to the dead who fought in the crusade to save Spain', Franco was imposing very stringent conditions on Juan Carlos.

Hence his doubts and his readiness to toy with other candidates: 'The legal heir to the Crown, once Prince Don Juan de Borbón has been eliminated, is his son, Don Juan Carlos, who could successfully achieve the union of all monarchists. There are other princes, such as the Infante Don Alfonso de Borbón who is educated, patriotic and who could be a solution if things don't work out with Don Juan Carlos.' He went so far as to put his concerns in writing, noting the need to get Don Juan to abdicate and demand of: 'Don Juanito absolute identification with the regime and full commitment'. If this were not to be possible, 'we could look at Don Alfonso de Borbón y Dampierre. Try out his identification with the regime.'[82]

Aware of Franco's increasingly heated mutterings, General Juan Castañón de Mena, the head of his military household, sent an urgent warning to Juan Carlos. Colonel Emilio García Conde flew to Brussels in order to telephone the Prince, claiming that lines between Spain and Estoril were tapped. He passed on General Castañón's message that, if he and Sofía did not take up residence in La Zarzuela, the palace would soon be occupied by another prince. At the same time, Juan Carlos's father-in-law, King Paul of Greece, had encouraged Don Juan to let his son return to Spain.[83] Fraga had also kept Pemán informed about the Caudillo's mood. Thoroughly alarmed, Pemán urged Don Juan to write to

Franco to explain the Prince's absence and suggest that his return was imminent. Accordingly, the Pretender wrote in emollient terms to Franco in February. He explained the young couple's continued presence in Portugal in terms of his anxiety lest their life should become one of leisure and luxury. He was keen to keep them away from Madrid high society and declared his preference for short stays in the capital and plenty of visits to the provinces. He also expressed discomfort at the idea of the Prince and his wife living in La Zarzuela at the expense of the State while not having any official function. Suitably mollified, Franco replied to the effect that Juan Carlos's education had barely begun. He dismissed Don Juan's fears about the influences of Madrid and countered with the suggestion that things would be much worse in Portugal. It was therefore agreed that Juan Carlos would return to Madrid.[84]

By the end of February 1963, the newly weds had taken up permanent residence in the gilded cage of La Zarzuela. Relations with Franco quickly improved. Shortly after their return from Greece, Juan Carlos and Sofía visited the Caudillo and his wife at El Pardo. So attentive and deferential were the royal couple that both Franco and Doña Carmen were enchanted. When Pacón asked about his impressions, he replied: 'Wonderful. There is absolutely no truth in the rumour put about by his enemies that he is not very intelligent. That is not the case at all, because he's a lad who uses his brain and thinks for himself and not on the basis of what he's told by his family or his friends. I do not believe that in political matters he is in the hands of his father. There is no basis in the things that are said against the young Prince; they're just prejudice. Doña Sofía went in to say hello to Carmen and she stayed with her for nearly two hours. The meeting was really pleasant because the Princess is highly intelligent and charming. She now speaks Spanish quite well and when she can't think of a word, she falls back on French.'

Franco reiterated his conviction that Juan Carlos was independent of his father. His delight at the warmth of Princess Sofía's conversation with Doña Carmen was tempered only by his concern that she didn't mix with the high aristocracy lest she be contaminated by their patrician disdain for the regime. He was adamant that Don Juan's desire to see his son in the Spanish Navy was unrealistic, since his passage through the naval academy had been too brief to give him anything more than general knowledge. Convinced instead that the Prince should continue to study economics and political science in Spain, he told Juan Carlos that it was his task to make the monarchy popular, which meant constant contact with the people. He then treated the Prince to a long disquisition on the dangers of contact with the aristocracy: 'The atmosphere of frivolity of the highest classes, the great social gatherings of courtiers, the predominance of the aristocracy at the side of the royal family must all disappear completely.' To Franco's intense pleasure, the Prince listened 'very attentively and with great amiability'. Speaking of Juan Carlos so warmly brought to his mind the contrast with Don Juan. He repeated to Pacón that Don Juan stood no chance of being named as successor: 'There is no doubt that Don Juan is completely taken with liberalism. That would be a solution that would ensure that the defeated of yesterday would be the victors of tomorrow; that's what all the reds in exile want. Spain would be turned into the next Cuba.'[85]

The apparent warmth of Franco's feelings did not alter the fact that the royal couple were subjected to round-the-clock vigilance. The staff of La Zarzuela was appointed by the *Patrimonio Nacional*, the organization responsible for State property. Accordingly, every conversation, every telephone call, every letter was under scrutiny and likely to be reported back to Franco. The links between La Zarzuela and the office of Admiral Carrero Blanco were clinched when José María Gamazo Manglano, a senior functionary of the *Presidencia del Gobierno*, was given responsibility for liaison between the *Presidencia* and the office of the Prince.[86] Gamazo's loyalty to both of his employers was not in question but he was very much a López Rodó man. Inevitably, Gamazo's daily presence and his intimate knowledge of La Zarzuela's affairs must have put some strain on Juan Carlos, given the hostility between his father and Carrero Blanco. Caution was the order of the day and would remain so for the next 12 years. It was not just a question of espionage. The Prince knew that he was a pawn in the policy of López Rodó and Carrero Blanco. Even if he was still committed to the cause of his father, it made sense to go along with them. Moreover, his wife, ably seconded by the Marqués de Mondéjar, perceived that the route to the throne mapped out by López Rodó was the only road back to Spain for the monarchy. To have to cope with considerations of such moment was a heavy burden for any marriage. The couple were isolated and had reason to distrust many of those that they met.

It is likely that the inevitable anxiety and the consequent appearance of seriousness lay behind the rumours that had started to circulate in Greece to the effect that Juan Carlos and Sofía were no longer getting along. In March 1963, with Juan Carlos occupied in Spain, she visited Athens alone to attend the centenary celebrations of the Greek royal family. It was claimed that a separation was imminent. The politician Elias Bredimas went as far as asking in Parliament what would become of Sofía's dowry, were the marriage to fail. This was no more than journalistic speculation but it was deeply distressing for Sofía. She and Juan Carlos took it as a useful reminder that their every move was scrutinized by the media. The real strength of their marriage was suggested by the delight with which, on 17 April 1963, Juan Carlos told López Rodó that his wife was pregnant and expecting a child by the end of the year.[87]

The ambiguity of Franco's attitude – personal warmth and political suspicion – was to be seen in many ways. On taking up residence in Spain, the first official public appearance of Juan Carlos and Sofía had been the annual funeral service for the Kings of Spain at El Escorial on 28 February 1963, a date chosen specifically to commemorate the death of Alfonso XIII. Juan Carlos shared the presidency of the occasion with Franco. To the astonishment of Sofía, the news coverage later the same day wiped them out of the newsreel and their presence was not even mentioned. This snub had apparently happened behind the back of the Minister of Information, Manuel Fraga. General Castañón informed him that the Prince felt humiliated in front of his wife at having been eliminated from a ceremony to commemorate his own ancestors. This reflected anti-monarchist feeling within the *Movimiento* media apparatus. It must have been unpleasant for Juan Carlos to feel that Franco was using his presence to give a monarchist veneer to the regime yet did nothing to diminish Falangist hostility. In June 1963, Franco insisted that Juan Carlos occupied a prominent place at the funeral service for Pope John XXIII, at a time when the regime was still being excoriated internationally for the trial and execution of the Communist Julián Grimau García on 20 April. This occasioned some debate within Don Juan's Privy Council at Estoril over whether the publicity given to Juan Carlos should be welcomed as favourable to the cause of the Borbón dynasty or played down as damaging to Don Juan's chances of being successor.[88]

A bulletin of the Privy Council issued in February had announced that Juan Carlos was in Spain as his father's representative. Franco scoffed. He did not agree because: 'according to the *Ley de Sucesión*, Don Juan has no recognized right to the crown of Spain. His son could be the solution ... So, the longer he is at our side and the more he becomes part of the Spanish people, the better for everyone.' His affection for Juan Carlos seemed to be growing: 'Although he seems to be rather under the thumb of his father, I believe him to be intelligent and of kindly disposition. Many believe that he is a bit childish but that will pass as he gets more experience and gets to know the world better.'[89]

Sofía quickly became aware of the affection between Franco and her husband. She noted how the dictator's eyes would light up when he saw the Prince and felt that he was seeing in him the son that he had never had. Juan Carlos, having had to live without his own father, responded warmly. Franco's growing fondness for Juan Carlos was also noted by Fraga.[90] It was in contrast to the Caudillo's disappointment that the Carlists could produce only a Frenchman as their candidate for the succession. Moreover, he was annoyed by the Carlists' public demonstrations of hostility to Juan Carlos. One such incident, on 24 May 1963, rebounded in favour of the Prince. He and Sofía had been invited to the Teatro María Guerrero for a performance by the *Coros y Danzas*, the folklore troupe of the *Sección Femenina*. As they were leaving, a group of Carlists began shouting slogans in favour of Don Javier.

Juan Carlos ignored police advice to wait until they were dispersed. He and Sofía made their way through the hostile crowd which then surrounded their car. To their cries of *'¡Viva el Rey Javier!'*, Juan Carlos replied with a humorous *'¡Viva!'* The Caudillo was deeply touched to be told that Sofía had immediately chided her husband, saying that he should have shouted *'¡Viva Franco!'* Beaming with pleasure, he told Pacón: 'The Princess, as I told you, is highly intelligent. I was hurt by what happened, because it must not be forgotten that they reside in Spain because I wished them to and that their conduct is irreproachable in every way.'[91]

That the story should have been relayed to Franco with such alacrity reveals the level of surveillance to which they were subjected. It also shows that the new couple were conducting their affairs with a shrewd eye on the future. They were increasingly to be seen in public, usually at anodyne events. They visited hospitals and charitable organizations and were seen at the Holy Week celebrations in Seville. Sir George Labouchere invited them to dine at his ambassadorial residence on the grounds that he had spent a week shooting with Juan Carlos and that 'Great Britain stood in a rather special position towards the Spanish royal family'. The Prince replied that he did not feel able to accept 'just yet a while'.[92] Perhaps recalling the readiness of the *Movimiento* press to criticize his father for his British, and therefore liberal, connections, Juan Carlos was clearly not prepared to risk either adverse publicity or his personal relations with Franco.

As Franco grew more attached to Juan Carlos, his position in the succession stakes became the question of concern in Estoril. Labouchere visited Lisbon in April 1963 and had a long chat with Don Juan, who told him that he was aware that the Caudillo was fond of his son and he appreciated it. However, he confided in the Ambassador his anxiety that Juan Carlos not be drawn into the clique of Franco's son-in-law, the corrupt Cristóbal Martínez-Bordiu, the Marqués de Villaverde. He was concerned lest he might be tempted by their shady business deals and thus compromise his reputation. He claimed to have no worries that his son might be induced to occupy the Spanish throne in his place. Somewhat naïvely, in view of Franco's frequent remarks in private, Don Juan assured the Ambassador that: 'at no time had General Franco ever suggested to him, or as far as he knew, to anybody else, that Don Juan Carlos might ascend to the throne in preference to his father. Such an idea was unthinkable. Don Juan Carlos was too good a son ever to wish to take the place of his father.' Despite this display of confidence, Labouchere concluded that: 'my guess continues to be that in the long run it is Don Juan Carlos whom the Generalissimo [sic] is grooming, albeit in a somewhat half-hearted fashion, for king.'[93] According to Benjamin Welles, Don Juan frequently referred to his son as blindly loyal, and Juan Carlos ended all his letters to his father with the words 'always with you'.

Queen Victoria Eugenia knew full well that Franco was considering leaping a generation in the dynastic stakes. The point was put to her in Rome in early May 1963 by the recently appointed Spanish Ambassador to the Holy See, José María Doussinague. She expressed some enthusiasm for the notion of the monarchy being re-established in the person of Juan Carlos although she regretted the elimination of Don Juan. Her daughter, the Infanta Beatriz, told Doussinague of her conviction that Don Juan would make the sacrifice of ceding his rights to Juan Carlos.[94]

Given Franco's hostility to Don Juan, and given the existence of what Benjamin Welles called 'nuisance candidates' like Alfonso de Borbón y Dampierre and the Carlists, it made sense for Juan Carlos to do all that he could to maintain cordial relations with Franco. On 22 November 1963, Hugo de Borbón Parma, the son of the Carlist pretender Don Javier, changed his name to Carlos Hugo, thereby underlining his claim to the Carlist succession. On 29 April 1964, he was to marry the ambitious Dutch Princess Irene of Orange which led to him being called '*Jugo de Naranja*' (Orange Juice) by Madrid wits. At a symbolic level, it was a disastrous match for a Carlist pretender. The House of Orange was the historical enemy of Spain and Catholicism. Nevertheless, by way of slighting Juan Carlos, the press of the *Movimiento* gave Carlos Hugo much favourable publicity. The British Ambassador commented that *Arriba* and *Pueblo*, 'and to my surprise the Catholic newspaper *Ya* have taken to publishing rather gooey interviews of lady reporters in which Don Carlos Hugo tends to be referred to as Don Carlos and the couple generally described in terms of star-crossed lovers with an inordinate affection for Spain'. Carlos Hugo was a French citizen who had done his military service in France. He began the proceedings to seek Spanish nationality. This manoeuvre was supported by important Falangists such as Raimundo Fernández Cuesta. Franco let the process go through the Ministry of Justice where it was rejected. Moreover, he told Pemán in March that he had discounted Alfonso de Borbón y Dampierre and Carlos Hugo de Borbón Parma as pretenders to the throne. Nevertheless, at the annual requiem service for the Kings of Spain in El Escorial, Franco had Alfonso de Borbón y Dampierre seated in the royal family's tribune next to Juan Carlos. The implication that they were on the same level was to cause considerable anxiety for the Prince and his advisers. There were plenty of opponents of Juan Carlos only too glad to point out that Alfonso was the eldest grandson of Alfonso XIII and to question the validity of the renunciation of his rights made in 1933 by his father Don Jaime de Borbón.[95]

Juan Carlos frequently asked Franco to let him spend time with an Army regiment or aboard a naval vessel. He replied, 'What for? To play cards in the bar?' Instead, the Prince spent long hours visiting various ministries and learned about their workings. As a result of time spent with General Jorge Vigón Suerodíaz, the Minister of Public Works, he travelled all over Spain visiting major construction projects. López Rodó helped him understand the workings of the civil service. Although on occasions he had rotten vegetables hurled at him, his natural affability encouraged people to talk to him and he had the ability to listen.[96]

As 1963 wore on, the Prince's principal concern was the forthcoming birth of his first child. In July, Don Juan wrote a timid letter to Franco requesting permission for himself, his mother and his wife to attend the baptism. Delaying until Sofía's pregnancy entered its ninth month, Franco replied with an astoundingly patronizing letter: 'I have decided to write to manifest my indulgence to your being present with your children on such an important occasion, which must not lose its intimate and family dimension, in order to prevent your presence in Spain being exploited for partisan ends by your followers.'[97] On 20 December 1963, Sofía gave birth to a daughter, Elena. In the event, Queen Victoria Eugenia was unable to travel from Switzerland for the christening ceremony.

On 26 December, Don Juan, Doña María de las Mercedes and their two daughters, the Infantas Pilar and Margarita, set off for Madrid. Juan Carlos awaited them at the Portuguese frontier near Badajoz and then accompanied them to the capital. It was the first time that Franco had permitted them to come to central Spain. Even so, they were obliged to stay at El Soto, the estate of the Duque de Alburquerque in Algete to the north-east of the capital, and not allowed to enter Madrid. On the following day, as they drove from Algete to La Zarzuela, Doña María said to Don Juan 'If I'm introduced to Franco, the first thing I plan to say is just how badly he behaved with my father!' Don Juan managed to dissuade her. Elena's godparents were Doña María and her (and Don Juan's) uncle Ali (Alfonso de Orleáns Borbón) in the presence of the Caudillo and his wife. Nothing of moment was discussed and the meeting passed off with relative cordiality.[98]

It was no coincidence that Don Juan's first visit to central Spain should be preceded by the publication of a long interview with Franco by Jacques Guillemé-Brulon of *Le Figaro*. When asked whether he foresaw the re-establishment of the monarchy in the person of Don Juan or Juan Carlos, Franco hesitated. He then replied characteristically that he never tried to fix the frontiers of time and that the moment had still not arrived for a clear decision in favour of one or the other. He went on to say that the personal defects of individual monarchs often damaged the institution of monarchy. It was widely assumed in Madrid political circles that this was Franco's way of finally admitting publicly that Don Juan fell into the category of unsuitable monarchs and could therefore never be chosen. Presumably for this reason, the relevant paragraph of the interview was omitted in the version later published in Spain.[99] General Martínez Campos told Sir George Labouchere: 'that he was upset by the interview because it seemed once and for all to put a stop to any chance of Don Juan reigning here. Franco had in fact at last uttered what hitherto he had kept to himself.' In fact, Martínez Campos had long since deduced that Franco was grooming Juan Carlos for the throne and that, when the time came, he would give Don Juan the stark choice between seeing his son on the throne or the elimination of any kind of monarchical succession. The general was also certain that nothing would happen before Juan Carlos reached the age of 30, the age at which he would become eligible under the *Ley de Sucesión* for nomination as successor.[100]

1964 saw year-long celebrations of Franco's Civil War victory and the subsequent 25 years of peace. Accordingly, Juan Carlos's continuing travels around Spain inevitably saw him associated with the regime. López Rodó, Fraga and other reformist elements in the cabinet hoped that the euphoric nostalgia of the 25 years of peace might prompt Franco to clarify his plans for the future. They therefore pressed him to promulgate the regime's constitutional umbrella, the *Ley Orgánica del Estado*, and name his successor. It was to no avail. The Caudillo's ministers were beginning to notice, with some anxiety, how much he had aged. This was the consequence of the Parkinson's disease that would intermittently afflict him in his last years.[101] To the alarm of some of his own ministers, let alone the various royal pretenders, he reacted to the presentation, on 30 April 1964, of a medal to commemorate the 25 years of peace, by saying that he looked forward to a similar ceremony in another 25 years' time.[102]

Franco made little secret of his hopes that Juan Carlos would officially accept the *Ley de Sucesión* and swear to fulfil the principles of the *Movimiento*. He told Pemán as much in March 1964. Pemán discreetly passed the message on to Don Juan who did not want to hear it. Given the Prince's youth and inexperience, the Caudillo was in no hurry.[103] His ongoing concern – unnecessary, as it happened – was that Juan Carlos and Sofía would fall under the influence of the decadent aristocracy. Nevertheless, on 20 April, he told Pacón: 'I'm really sorry that Don Juan de Borbón has demonstrated his incompatibility with the regime. I'm hopeful that, given his patriotism, when the time comes, he will agree to abdicate in favour of his son and that his son will swear to uphold the fundamental laws and implement the postulates of the *Movimiento*.'

Musing on the existence of other candidates, he commented that Alfonso de Borbón y Dampierre 'is very committed to the *Movimiento*'. Nevertheless, he repeatedly commented dotingly on his pleasure at the patriotic way in which Juan Carlos and Sofía were behaving and his conviction that they were in contact with the people of Spain.[104]

Significantly, on 24 May 1964, at the spectacular annual Civil War victory parade, Prince Juan Carlos took the salute along with the Caudillo. To the obvious delight of Doña Carmen, she was accompanied by Princess Sofía. This 'presentation' of the Prince to the Armed Forces did not provoke universal approbation. In the early hours of the morning before the parade, Laureano López Rodó was awakened by a telephone call. An unknown voice growled: 'If the Prince is on the stand tomorrow, you will die.' Franco still gave no concrete indication of his plans for the succession. The pleasure that he derived from the 1964 celebrations increased both his reluctance to plan for the future and his conviction that he was indispensable. During the summer of 1964, Franco was greeted with frenetic applause on trips to Seville and Bilbao and at the final of the European Nations' Cup held at the Bernabeu stadium in Madrid.[105] He used this popular affection as the main argument for brushing aside his ministers' suggestions of the need for change.

Nevertheless, his ministers and others close to him were worrying more than ever because of unmistakable indications that Franco was deteriorating. He devoted significant amounts of time to hunting and fishing but there were signs of the intensifying effects of Parkinson's disease. The decline of his health was intermittent – as the year wore on, he seemed to liven up. Parkinson's disease and the consequent medication left Franco isolated from the real world. This was exacerbated by the manic enthusiasm of both the Caudillo and his wife for the television.[106] It was inevitable that many in the narrow circles of power would notice the symptoms of the disease – his rigid stance, his halting walk and a vacant, open-mouthed expression.

In the light of these health problems, his closest collaborators were emboldened to press him for action on the *Ley Orgánica*.

On 25 November 1964, Admiral Carrero Blanco presented Franco with a draft text. He reacted favourably, yet when his Minister of Education, Manuel Lora Tamayo, urged him to go ahead and promulgate the law, the Caudillo replied hesitantly, 'It's difficult.' On 14 January 1965, General Alonso Vega took advantage of his lifelong friendship with Franco to broach the topic of the succession. 'The country follows you and loves you,' he said, 'it will say yes to whatever you do. You must name a Prime Minister and define a political system which will guarantee the future. The other ministers think the same as me, but I am not speaking to you as their representative. If they don't say it to you, it is because they don't know you as well as I do. I can remember you in short pants and we've played together. If I can't speak to you like this, who can? Or maybe it's not allowed to say such things to you. Posterity will judge you by what you leave behind. People are worried about the future.' Franco listened with a benevolent smile, made a joke about their age and said that he was working on the *Ley Orgánica del Estado* and that it would be produced *'antes de lo que piensas'* (before you think).[107]

Despite the remark to Alonso Vega, Franco's sense of urgency was not like that of ordinary mortals. In the spring of 1965, there were serious student disturbances in Madrid and Barcelona. Unusually, at a cabinet meeting on 5 March 1965, the university troubles, labour problems and conflict with the Church were discussed. Carrero Blanco claimed implausibly that all such difficulties were the consequence of uncertainty about the post-Franco future and urged that the *Ley Orgánica del Estado* be propounded as soon as possible. Since Carrero Blanco had broken the ice with apparent impunity, the entire cabinet joined in and spoke in his support. Franco complained of the difficulty of finding a solution that could please all of the monarchist factions, by which he was hinting at his own reluctance ever to close off options. However, he ended the debate by saying, 'I have undertaken to do it and I will do it.' On 11 March, on entering the Caudillo's study, Carrero Blanco found him working on the *Ley Orgánica*.[108]

On the same day, the Minister of Finance, Mariano Navarro Rubio, spoke with Franco about the new constitution. In the course of their conversation, the 72-year-old Caudillo revealed that he anticipated ruling for some time to come. He said that he would have much preferred to leave the *Ley Orgánica* until later because the longer he left it the more in tune it would be with the future. However, he reluctantly recognized that he had no choice but to start the process now.[109] Leading regime figures paraded before Franco to press him to make his dispositions. On 25 March 1965, the Minister of Education, Lora Tamayo, also attributed difficulties in the universities to the uncertainty about the future. An irritated Franco snapped back, 'Do you think that the future doesn't worry me? It's difficult to find the right solution.'[110]

Franco had privately been tinkering with the text of the *Ley Orgánica* given to him in November by Carrero Blanco. On 1 April 1965, he read to his faithful collaborator a near-final draft. They debated whether it would be prudent to include the designation of his successor and decided against doing so. The urgency of resolving the future was brought home later the same day, when they both received news that the Vice-President of the Government, General Agustín Muñoz Grandes, had been diagnosed as having renal cancer. Muñoz Grandes was the man chosen in the last cabinet reshuffle to be guarantor of the post-Franco succession, to substitute for the Caudillo in the event of his incapacity or death. The cabinet meeting held on 2 April was dominated by the implications of the news. The question of the future was again raised by Navarro Rubio, closely seconded by Fernando María Castiella, Minister of Foreign Affairs, and Fraga. The debate became heated, with Fraga putting considerable pressure on Franco by claiming that thirty million Spaniards had a right to know about their future. Normally the silent arbiter, Franco was stung into giving rambling explanations about how difficult it was and how much time he needed. With typical impetuosity, Fraga pressed him further, saying: 'There's no time to spare and I beg you to make use of what we've got.' Franco exploded. 'Do you think I don't realize, do you think I am a circus clown?' Despite this outburst of annoyance, the storm passed. For the remainder of the session, Franco smiled knowingly. General Alonso Vega deduced this meant that he already had a draft of the law ready.[111]

On 8 April 1965 Franco and Carrero Blanco discussed submitting the law to a referendum. On 9 May, Juan Carlos was at his right hand when he took the salute at the annual Civil War victory parade. Later, as he returned to La Zarzuela along Madrid's Gran Vía, a group of Falangists came up to his car and shouted: '¡*Franco Sí, Don Juan No!*'[112] The Prince visited El Pardo the next day and asked Franco if there was any progress with the *Ley Orgánica del Estado*. 'I'm looking into it,' he replied enigmatically. He complained about pressures from various monarchist groups. 'They're prodding you, General, as they do me, saying that you should name me Príncipe de Asturias.' He reminded him that Sofía was pregnant again and expecting the child in June. With considerable delicacy and an acute sense of how to deal with Franco's sensibilities, he said, 'If it's a boy, I would like Queen Victoria Eugenia to be the godmother. But I don't want to cause problems. You know me, General. I need your advice and guidance. I wish you would call me more often.'[113] Juan Carlos's second child, Cristina, was born on 13 June 1965. To Juan Carlos's distress, following advice from his Privy Council, his father did not attend the christening.[114]

Despite the apparent progress being made on the subject of succession, Franco soon retreated into apathy. He was irritated by the incessant attempts of ministers and others to hasten him to settle the issue. Nevertheless, he did give occasional hints. In early July 1965, he named a new cabinet. In the course of the audiences that he gave to his appointees, the new Minister of Justice, Antonio María Oriol y Urquijo, spoke highly of Juan Carlos and Franco replied: 'He's the best solution. He has great self-assurance, with very sure reactions.'[115]

There was always someone ready to scurry to La Zarzuela to report on such conversations. They must have provoked both pleasure and foreboding in Juan Carlos. Since December 1964, Don Juan's Privy Council had been operating under the cautious presidency of Jesús Pabón, the monarchist historian who had written an assessment of Juan Carlos in 1954, after he had overseen the boy's oral examination at the end of his secondary education. Pabón had adopted what he called 'a parallel policy' towards

Franco, that is to say neither confrontation nor collaboration but discreet distance. Pabón enjoyed good relations with Juan Carlos and was thus profoundly aware of the Prince's agonizing moral dilemma. Juan Carlos remained deeply loyal to his father, but the continuing tensions between Don Juan and Franco put him in an appalling position. The more he heard that Franco was inclined to name him successor, the more he questioned the point of his own presence in Spain if it were not to be taken to this logical conclusion. At a meeting in August 1965, Pabón found the Prince 'weighed down, under pressure, anguished'.[116]

Carrero Blanco and López Rodó were making every effort to ensure that Juan Carlos would be seen popularly as Franco's successor. In what came to be known as *'Operación Príncipe'*, the various local authorities and ministerial functionaries with whom the Prince came into contact were requested to call him 'Your Highness'. There were many within the *Movimiento* who resented this. In the third week of November 1965, Manuel Fraga gave an interview to *The Times*, in which he stated that, 'It is now more and more accepted that when Franco's regime ends, Don Juan Carlos will become King of Spain,' and dismissed 'the extreme royalists and Falangists who might want to upset such arrangements' as too few to stop this happening.[117]

It was the clearest public statement ever made by a member of the government about the future. In Estoril, it was believed that Fraga could not have made such a statement without the authorization of Franco.[118] Certainly, when Fraga saw the Caudillo some days later, he suffered no reprimand. Senior Falangists responded by intensifying their partisanship for the rival royal pretender, Alfonso de Borbón y Dampierre. Two young monarchists, José María Ruiz Gallardón, and Torcuato, son of the Marqués de Luca de Tena, visited the Madrid correspondent of *The Times*. They presented him with a declaration from Don Juan denying that he had renounced any rights in favour of his son. Don Juan himself told the US Ambassador that he had no intention of abdicating and that Juan Carlos was entirely under his orders. Juan Carlos missed the consequent furore because he was representing Spain at the inauguration of the new President of the

Philippines. In January 1966, Franco said to General Alonso Vega, 'most people aren't monarchists'.[119] On the Prince's return to Spain, he hastened to reassure Don Juan by means of an interview in *Time* magazine in which he was quoted as saying, 'I will never, never accept the crown as long as my father is alive.'[120]

The chances of Franco ever permitting Don Juan to wear the crown were, of course, nil. In November 1965, General Rafael García Valiño, a Civil War hero deeply resentful of Franco's failure to make him Minister for the Army, had visited Estoril. He had claimed to be indignant about the 'conspiracy' by López Rodó and Carrero Blanco to alter the order of monarchical succession. To block these schemes, he said that he, with other senior generals, including most improbably the reactionary Captain-General of Madrid, General Rodríguez-Vita, had plans in place to depose Franco within the year. Jesús Pabón, through his connections with another general, the liberal Manuel Díez Alegría, knew that these were just empty boasts. Don Juan, however, was seduced by the notion. At about the same time, three police informers, posing as convinced monarchists, had penetrated the feeble defences of Estoril and gained the confidence of Don Juan. Never noted for his discretion, he had confided in them his belief that monarchist generals would soon overthrow Franco and install him in the Palacio de Oriente in Madrid. In January 1966, he told them about the recent visit by García Valiño. There was no chance whatsoever of a military coup against the Caudillo but to talk openly about the possibility was frivolous in the extreme. What is remarkable is that Don Juan seems to have taken García Valiño seriously. Reports of these conversations soon reached Franco. García Valiño was discreetly warned, the conspiratorial balloon burst and the Caudillo's contempt for Don Juan can only have intensified.[121]

Although there were no doubts in the Caudillo's mind regarding Don Juan, the question of the future continued to be the most divisive issue in the cabinet. On 9 February 1966, López Rodó had a long conversation with him about the need to pass from his personal power to what he called 'institutionalization'. When he pointed out that time was against them, Franco replied, 'Certainly, time is tight but I'm going to do it soon.' He then wandered off into minor details and López Rodó brought him back to the point by using the same arguments as Lora Tamayo had made the previous year. He pointed out that without clear plans for the future, when he died, 'the blind forces of chaos will take over.' Franco's eyes filled with tears and he said, 'Yes, it would be chaos, it would be chaos,' but then went on to lament the problems arising from the existence of the many competing candidates. This was totally disingenuous, since Franco himself had permitted the proliferation of candidates as a convenient excuse to keep his options open. In any case, he agreed that Don Carlos Hugo was French and therefore was not a possible successor, and went to say that, 'Don Juan must be discounted. He should long ago have abdicated in favour of his son.'[122]

Juan Carlos's dilemmas were not diminishing. He was as loyal as ever to his father in personal terms. He had a view of the eventual role of the democratic liberal monarchy that was similar to that of his father. On the other hand, his sense of how power functioned in Madrid was infinitely more realistic than that of Don Juan after 30 years in exile. Don Juan seemed oblivious to his son's problems. For him, like everyone in the Estoril entourage, he was still 'Juanito'. He treated his son as a child, yet 'Juanito' was now a 28-year-old married man, with two children, and a coolly realistic wife as companion and adviser. Both he and Sofía were fully aware of the extent to which he was a pawn in the strategy of López Rodó. Juan Carlos would have preferred to see his father on the throne but knew that the Caudillo had long since discounted Don Juan as a possible successor. To clash with Franco would merely have destroyed any chance of his family returning to the throne.[123] Increasingly, it must have seemed that the intelligent thing was to go with the flow and worry about the future as the possibilities became clearer. The likelihood of conflict with Estoril was intensifying.

Franco was delighted by signs that Juan Carlos might be wavering in his loyalty to Don Juan. The Prince had been invited to attend a lunch with his father's Privy Council on 5 March at the Hotel Palacio in Estoril. It was to be a commemoration of the 25th anniversary of the death of Alfonso XIII. At the meeting,

Don Juan would be declared 'the indisputable heir to the Spanish Crown'. Juan Carlos's presence at the event was meant to endorse the statement and would thus constitute a refusal to supplant his father. With unconcealed glee, Franco told Pacón what had happened. 'A few days ago, he refused to take part in a meeting of the Privy Council at Estoril under the chairmanship of his father, using the excuse that he was suffering from a slight stomach upset. It didn't prevent him visiting me, accompanied by the Princess. During our conversation, he told me that he did not want to attend that political meeting even though his father was especially keen for him to do so.'

Princess Sofía had urged Juan Carlos not to go to Estoril. His indisposition was used as an excuse. He sent a telegram to be read out, simply saying: 'On the occasion of the tribute in memory of my grandfather, I want to send you a warm embrace with all my affection, loyalty and respect.' Don Juan was deeply annoyed at his son's failure to attend. According to Anson who was present, when Juan Carlos rang to say he would not be arriving, Don Juan 'shouted terrible things and slammed the phone down'. He told his son that princes have no right to be ill. In his speech at the meeting, Don Juan had categorically reaffirmed his dynastic rights. He made it clear that he resented the title 'Pretender' given that the hereditary principle made his right to the throne indisputable. He saw in his son's absence, as did many others including Franco, a desire to avoid explicit commitment. This was a dramatic turn in the relations between father and son. He told his Privy Councillors, 'Today the Prince has rejected my authority and disobeyed an order. He is now 28 and in many questions his views are not the same as mine. I don't want to criticize, as you can all imagine, but to accept a new reality that has been coming ever since he got married and I, to please him, accepted his moving to La Zarzuela. The unity of the Dynasty, my friends, is broken, and that affects the way we must work. The policy that we have followed up to now has been entirely based on the unbreakable unity between my son and myself. This can no longer be the case. It would be ridiculous to maintain the fiction and, thus, the moment has arrived to seek a new policy.' One of the best-informed foreign correspondents in

Spain, Jacques Guillemé-Brulon, wrote in *Le Figaro* that Juan Carlos's diplomatic illness reflected the promptings of the Greek royal family.[124]

Now, the message sent by Juan Carlos's absence from Estoril led to Don Juan abandoning any efforts to ingratiate himself with the Caudillo. In April, he established a secretariat, a virtual shadow cabinet, headed by José María de Areilza, the Conde de Motrico. Eighteen months earlier, Areilza had resigned as Franco's Ambassador in Paris, appalled by the regime's reaction to the Munich gathering and the execution of Julian Grimau García. In early 1964, he had urged Franco to open up the regime and bring it nearer to the rest of Europe. The Caudillo had listened in glacial silence and then commented only that the Spanish temperament made liberal experiments disastrous. Since it had long been assumed that Areilza was the natural successor to Castiella, his gamble in going over to the monarchist opposition was a considerable blow to Franco. Given the scale of his ambition, the ex-Ambassador was a sensitive barometer of the political climate. Nevertheless, because of his Fascist past, his appointment by Don Juan provoked some ribaldry in more liberal monarchist circles.[125] In mid-April, Areilza visited the Prince at La Zarzuela for what he later described as an 'exploratory' meeting. According to Lieutenant-Colonel Alfonso Armada, he suggested a political strategy for the restoration of the monarchy. The Prince told him politely that La Zarzuela did not get involved in politics. If anything, the Prince was moving, apparently at least, nearer to Franco. In the spring of 1965, he appointed the Marqués de Mondéjar as the head of his household and in the autumn Lieutenant-Colonel Armada as his secretary. Mondéjar had enormous influence over Juan Carlos. His advice was crucial in helping the Prince establish good personal relations with Franco. Such was Juan Carlos's affection for Mondéjar that, on wishing him good night, he would often jokingly lean over and kiss him on his bald pate.[126]

On 6 May, the new secretariat discussed the dangers of Franco leaping a generation and Areilza suggested that there be '*un pacto de familia*' whereby both Don Juan and Juan Carlos would agree to accept the other's nomination by Franco. There was no question but that Juan Carlos would agree to the nomination of his father. The novelty lay in the idea of Don Juan's acceptance of his son's nomination. From this point, their positions began to diverge. A few days later, at a lunch given by the Greek Ambassador to Madrid, Areilza met the Prince, who asked him more about the new secretariat. He listened in silence to Areilza's long exposition. Thereafter they would meet periodically. Juan Carlos seemed to move ever closer to Franco while, under Areilza's guidance, Don Juan established closer relations with Socialists, a wide range of Basque and Catalan nationalists and other elements of the opposition, including the clandestine Communist trade union organization, the Workers' Commissions, and the PCE itself.[127]

As Don Juan became more explicitly anti-Francoist, the so-called '*Operación Príncipe*' gathered pace within Spain. Juan Carlos was at the 73-year-old Franco's side during the 1966 victory parade, which took place in torrential rain. There were anti-Juan Carlos protests from Carlists, and Franco told Pacón of his annoyance at this. At the end of April, Juan Carlos had gone to Barcelona to attend a motor show. A group of Carlists shouted insults and an egg was thrown at him. They distributed leaflets with the slogan: '*Ni Don Juan ni Don Juan Carlos.*' Although they were arrested, the Prince requested their immediate release. When Franco heard that Don Carlos Hugo and Princess Irene were planning to attend the annual Carlist assembly at Montejurra, he told the cabinet that they would be expelled from Spain, saying, 'Don Carlos Hugo is French and he has no right to carry on political activities here.'[128]

On 10 May 1966, the number two at the British Embassy, Nicko Henderson, had a remarkably revealing conversation with Juan Carlos. 'Juan Carlos was most eager to talk about his future and that of Spain and, so far as I could judge, frank in what he said.' Henderson found him, 'a not very mature or profound but extremely agreeable and straight-forward young man'. The Prince told the diplomat that: 'there was no widespread monarchical spirit in Spain. He had recently visited Barcelona and Bilbao and, over the years, had seen much of the rest of the country. He admitted that, "he had not been able to sense any strong instinctive feelings towards the monarchy on the part of the people of Spain anywhere". "I, after all," he said, with his hands on his chest, "would be able to experience such a pull when I go about the country if it existed, but frankly, it does not." Precisely because he could get no sense of there being widespread monarchical senti-ment in Spain, he was convinced that, "the monarchy would only be reinstated in accordance with, or perhaps as a continuation of, the present regime". Many people criticized him for living in Spain and appearing to condone Franco and his regime. But he did not think that there was any alternative. It would not be possible to force a monarchy on Spain against the will of the present rulers. He doubted whether there would be anything like a clamour for the return of his father or himself once Franco had gone.' Juan Carlos went on to speak in terms that betrayed a profound realism, if not cynicism, and an innate conservatism. 'The method of entry was therefore one of coming in to continue the stability and other good qualities which had been established over the past genera-tion.' According to Henderson, 'Juan Carlos was rather on the defensive about all this, as though he minded the criticisms that he was the tool of the present regime.'

Henderson then pressed him on the position of Don Juan. The British diplomat pointedly remarked that he understood that Juan Carlos, 'was not thinking of taking his father's place, should the latter wish to assume the throne'. Henderson commented that Don Juan's stance of opposition to the regime meant that a monarchical restoration would constitute a distinct change from the existing regime, albeit not a revolutionary one or 'a change that involved a return to the tumult of the thirties'. Juan Carlos replied that he had no intention of usurping his father's rights. Henderson got the impression that the Prince considered that: 'there would be an advantage in the monarchy being identified with advance to some form of representative government . . . He was pretty definite that, so far as his knowledge went, Franco had no intention of doing anything to nominate his successor during his lifetime. He admit-ted that he saw very little of Franco, but of course he was in touch with people who did see him. His view was that Franco, a hard-headed realist, knew that the meanest devolution of his power or position would undermine the whole edifice of his dictatorship. The moment another name was mentioned for the top, everybody would rush towards it as the symbol of the future and Franco's hold would be undermined.' Henderson concluded from their conversation that, 'the Spanish monarch, if he returns, will be reinstated, not in response to an overwhelming upsurge of popular emotion, but by cold decision of those in authority; and as a corollary, that what will matter for Spain will be less the person of the king than the nature of the system by which the country is governed.'[129]

Franco's continuing delay in naming a successor derived in part from the knowledge that Juan Carlos was not yet ready, and from a reluctance to admit that his own rule would ever end. He knew that once a successor was named there would be a rush of opportunists eager to ingratiate themselves with the nominee, something which could only diminish his own power. He continued to hope that Don Juan would make the task easier by abdicating. Franco complained to Pacón: 'In Estoril, they pursue a completely mistaken and biased policy against my plans for Alfonso XIII's heir to be Prince Juan Carlos who, by dint of his irreproachable political conduct and his personal prestige can bring days of glory and splendour to the Spanish monarchy. I have no idea if Don Juan Carlos and Doña Sofía will accept the crown when the moment comes but I still harbour hopes that the father, who when all is said and done is a good patriot, will come to his senses and realize that he must abdicate his rights in favour of his son, who is the one loved by the Spanish people.'[130]

To make sure that his conduct was remaining 'irreproachable', Franco devoured secret police reports on the Prince's activities. On 27 May 1966, Juan Carlos attended a dinner with progressive elements from within the regime at the home of the liberal lawyer, Joaquín Garrigues Walker. There were those present who hastened to report to Franco what had happened and they described the Prince as acting like a future King, showing a great capacity for dialogue and listening. The meeting lasted until the early hours of the next morning. There was general agreement from all the participants that the future monarchy should be a modern

European one with democratic institutions. Juan Carlos listened carefully but kept his counsel. He spoke of Franco with the greatest respect. The fact that Franco knew of this meeting has been cited as proof that he knew of Juan Carlos's democratizing intentions.[131] In fact, the report seemed not to bother him precisely because he would not proceed to name Juan Carlos as royal successor without his binding oath to uphold the principles of the *Movimiento*.

The Caudillo was now seeing Juan Carlos about twice each month. There was a widespread view shared by the left and many within the Falange that the tall, handsome, 28-year-old Prince was an empty-headed mediocrity comfortably installed as Franco's stooge. His diffidence and reserve did nothing to dispel that image. But what is known of his relations with Franco suggests considerable caution and thought. On 17 June 1966, for instance, he asked the Caudillo if the draft *Ley Orgánica del Estado* would introduce the separation of the powers of the Prime Minister and the Head of State. He was concerned about having to cope with more responsibility than was feasible. Some days later, visiting Barcelona with Franco, the Prince asked the Mayor, José María de Porcioles, for advice. Porcioles told him that if the Fatherland called him, he should be ready to abandon his father. In his formal speech, Porcioles spoke of Juan Carlos as signifying the continuity of the regime. The phrase would be picked up and do great benefit to Juan Carlos's cause. In fact, conversations with López Rodó about the need to hasten Franco's designation of successor had long since left Juan Carlos fully aware that he was likely to be selected instead of his father. However, he was always careful not to give Franco the slightest indication of his attitude to such an event.[132]

In private conversation Franco admitted to being concerned by the passage of time. Inevitably, the succession was assuming ever greater importance for him. On 13 June 1966, he gave Carrero Blanco the final draft of the *Ley Orgánica del Estado*. It was agreed that the text would be presented to the Cortes at the beginning of October. He publicly revealed his views on Don Juan on 21 July when he lashed out in response to an article by Luis María Anson in *ABC*. Entitled '*La monarquía de todos*' (The Monarchy for All), it outlined Don Juan's commitment to a democratic monarchy and repeated Juan Carlos's statement that he would not accept the throne while his father was alive. The quotation of Juan Carlos's remark outraged Franco more than the rest of the article. He ordered the police to seize all copies of the offending issue. Anson was forced into exile, going to Hong Kong as the *ABC* correspondent.[133] Solís and others tried to influence the Caudillo by keeping up the pressure against Juan Carlos. At the end of July, in a clear response to Anson's article, the *Movimiento* newspaper, *Pueblo*, printed an interview with Alfonso de Borbón y Dampierre under the headline '*El Príncipe prudente*'. The implication was that Juan Carlos was not prudent. Suggesting that Alfonso could well be named as successor, the article dismissed out of hand the idea that there was any validity to the renunciation of dynastic rights by his father, Don Jaime.[134]

But, after a long summer holiday, the Caudillo seemed to have slipped into apathy again. He and Carrero Blanco were unsure about whether to permit debate in the Cortes on the text of the *Ley Orgánica* and finally decided against it.[135] It would be submitted first to the Cortes in November and then to the Spanish people without any public examination of its advantages and disadvantages, or even much in the way of explanation. While the final touches were being put to the text, Franco avoided Juan Carlos. The Prince told Areilza that he had not seen Franco since 21 September and, 'he suspects that this is because he doesn't want him asking about the law until it is proclaimed or approved.' Juan Carlos had been told by López Rodó that the law was being made to measure for him. Inevitably, this increased his anxieties about his position relative to his father. He suspected that the law would require him to swear fidelity to the fundamental principles of the *Movimiento* even before he had been designated as successor. Areilza wrote to Sainz Rodríguez, 'it is really admirable and moving to hear the Prince speak about his father, the King. He does so with enthusiasm, with fidelity, with the desire that everything should turn out as well as possible for him.'[136] It is astonishing that the advisers of Don Juan seemed oblivious that Juan Carlos, for all his loyalty to his father, was painfully adjusting to the fact that the only way forward was to go with the

López Rodó–Carrero Blanco plan as encapsulated in the *Ley Orgánica*.

Franco's speech in the Cortes on 22 November 1966 to introduce the *Ley Orgánica del Estado* was of considerable significance for Juan Carlos. Franco had rarely appeared so aged and infirm in public – an inadvertent reminder of the urgent need for the completion of the arrangements for the succession. The halting, indistinct mumble with which the bespectacled Caudillo read out a speech created a gloomy atmosphere. His reflection on the past had an entirely valedictory tone, yet he gave no indication of considering retirement. In a premonitory way, the speech effectively laid out the inheritance that Juan Carlos, or any other selected prince, would be required to safeguard. Franco reviewed his own special relationship with God and what he regarded as the remarkable achievements of the 30 years of his rule. There was pride and a sense of being unappreciated in words that seemed directed to both Juan Carlos and to Don Juan. 'During these last 30 years, I have dedicated my life to the cause of Spain. And the distance was so great between the point of departure and the goal we had set ourselves that only faith and the help of God gave me strength to accept the high and grave responsibility of governing the Spanish people. Whoever takes on such a responsibility can never be relieved nor rest, but must burn himself out in finishing the task.'

Franco was making it quite clear why he could not bequeath his achievements to Don Juan and announcing to Juan Carlos what he would be required to undertake. 'Think of the Fatherland that I received, and bear in mind that from that anarchic and impoverished Spain has arisen a political and social order through which we have achieved a transformation of our structures, reaching a rhythm of perfection and progress never equalled . . . Night after night it was my job to keep watch at the deathbed of the invalid [Spain] who was dying, who had been led to war, to ruin and to hunger, who was surrounded by the Great Powers like birds of prey.' The reports on Juan Carlos's flirtation with liberal members of the regime were surely on Franco's mind as he justified the survival of his system well beyond his own death. When the

Caudillo's mumbled performance came to an end, the long and intractable text of the law was then read out by the recently appointed President of the Cortes, Antonio Iturmendi. It took him nearly two hours. There was no debate of the ten sections, 66 articles and many additional clauses of the law, which the *Procuradores* had seen for the first time when they were given copies at the beginning of the session. The Caudillo then called on the *Procuradores* to give their assent. They did so by acclaim.[137]

In fact, the *Ley Orgánica* had facilitated the eventual nomination of a monarchical successor although it brought the resolution of the question only a little nearer. Its function was, in Franco's words, 'to complete our institutional cycle'. It was thus essentially the crowning constitutional document of Francoism. It resolved minor contradictions between the previous 'fundamental laws' such as the *Fuero de los Españoles* and the *Ley de Sucesión*. Overall, it was a fine-tuning of what had gone before. There were, however, considerable implications for Juan Carlos. That the successor to Franco would be a monarch was emphasized. The future role of that monarch was laid out and distinguished from that of Franco in that there was to be a separation of the powers of the Head of State from those of the Prime Minister. Most significant were the warnings for the future with which Franco sprinkled his speech to the Cortes. He made it clear that no system should be contemplated which might unleash what he called 'Spain's family demons'. 'The Spanish people must remember that every people is surrounded by its family demons: those of Spain are anarchic spirit, negative criticism, a lack of cooperative endeavour, extremism and mutual enmity.' He dismissed 'the anarchic and artificial dialogue of parties' and denounced political parties as a threat to national unity. He offered in their stead merely what he called 'the legitimate contrast of opinions'. By this he meant no more than the tightly controlled rivalry between the factions within the *Movimiento*.[138]

At the end of November, prior to the referendum on the *Ley Orgánica*, Juan Carlos telephoned his father to ask for advice as to whether he should vote. As he had already said to Areilza, it was his legal obligation to vote, as a head of a family. Don Juan wrote to him to say that kings do not vote because they have to respect the laws whatever they might be. Nevertheless, he advised him to consult with Franco. Their meeting took place on 5 December. It was scheduled to last for one hour but they remained chatting for two. Franco was delighted with Juan Carlos and Sofía, praising the simplicity and austerity of their lifestyle. In contrast, he was spitting fire about Don Juan, referring to him as '*ese señor*' (that man). The Prince refrained from any comment about his father. Franco commented, 'Don Juan Carlos is sufficiently discreet and intelligent not to talk to me about this and I am certainly not going to ask him since it would be premature.'[139]

Seven days later, on 12 December, Franco addressed the nation on television and radio to seek a 'yes' vote in the forthcoming referendum. Again his speech made it clear that the future would be about safeguarding the past. The official slogan was '*¡Franco sí!*' and the Caudillo made the referendum a vote of confidence in him personally. He lamented that there were still those who dreamed of adopting foreign fashions, oblivious to the fact that democracy was a fiction. Some bitter ribaldry was provoked in Estoril and throughout the left-wing opposition by Franco's assertion, after 30 years of dictatorship, that: 'I was never motivated by the desire for power.'[140] Franco's speech was merely one part of a massive campaign mounted by Fraga with the full power of the media directed to securing a 'yes' vote. The propaganda emphasized that this was a vote for Franco, economic progress, and security. There was little mention of the *Ley Orgánica* itself and the opposition was silenced. On 14 December 1966, 88 per cent of the possible electorate voted in the referendum on the *Ley Orgánica* of whom fewer than two per cent voted 'no'. There had been a degree of manipulation of the vote – in some places, the 'yes' vote was 15 per cent higher than the number of voters.[141] Nevertheless, the referendum was a popular victory for Franco. Many had voted 'yes' in gratitude for the past and for growing prosperity, but many did so also in the hope that they would be bringing nearer the transition from Franco's dictatorship to the monarchy.

FIVE

The Winning Post in Sight
1967–1969

Within the Francoist establishment, the *Ley Orgánica* was perceived as a significant milestone for Juan Carlos. The *Movimiento* press was not slow to mount a counter-attack. Shortly after the referendum, *Pueblo*, under the headline 'Princes', carried interviews by journalist Tico Medina with Juan Carlos and his rather gloomy cousin, Alfonso de Borbón y Dampierre. Two days before publication, the front page of *Pueblo* carried photographs of the two and advertised the forthcoming interviews. By attributing to Alfonso the title of prince, to which he was not entitled, the clear implication was that when the time came for Franco to choose his successor, the two men had equally valid claims. The emergence of the rather insipid Alfonso de Borbón y Dampierre at precisely this time was no accident. In 1957, Santiago Bernabeu, the President of Real Madrid, introduced him to José Solís, who had just been appointed Secretary-General of the *Movimiento*. Seeing a way to weaken the position of Juan Carlos, Solís began to cultivate Alfonso, arranging for him to be invited to many sporting events. He encouraged him to study syndical law (the law pertaining to the regime's official trade unions).[1] It was certainly José Solís who encouraged Alfonso de Borbón y Dampierre, but the shadow of Franco could be seen behind the operation. Areilza had written to Estoril in October 1966 that Alfonso could be heard in Madrid speaking of 'promises, messages, suggestions' from people close to the Caudillo.[2] Having produced a law 'made to measure' for Juan Carlos, it would be typical of Franco to see benefits in giving publicity to the candidacy of Alfonso de Borbón y Dampierre and thereby reminding the Prince that he was dependent on El Pardo.

Needless to say, in his interview, Alfonso spoke admiringly of Franco and his achievements and stated, 'My obligation is to be at the service of Spain when I am called upon.' There could be no doubt that he perceived himself as a candidate to succeed Franco within the terms of the *Ley de Sucesión*. In contrast to the dourly serious image projected by Alfonso, Medina stressed the affability and approachability of Juan Carlos. Apparently, he had interrupted the interview to take a call from a fellow cadet from the Zaragoza military academy. He talked about his daily routines, from early morning sessions at the gymnasium of his old sports teacher from Las Jarillas, Heliodoro Ruiz Arias, to afternoons spent working in the Ministry of Finance. Juan Carlos was also quoted as saying, 'I sincerely admire the Caudillo,' before going on to list his achievements in terms that would have delighted Franco himself. This was immediately matched by comments on his father: 'I truly love and respect him. He has taught me how one should sacrifice oneself and love the Fatherland at all times. He is an admirable man who always wishes the best for Spain.' When Tico Medina asked how he would react if he was selected as Franco's successor, he responded with a pre-echo of his eventual response: 'More than ten years ago in Zaragoza, I swore an oath on the Spanish flag. That oath constitutes an unbreakable promise to serve my country totally. I do and I will stand by my promise and I assure you that I will know how to fulfil my duty.' There could be no clearer indication that, if offered nomination as Franco's successor, Juan Carlos would accept.[3]

1966 had seen Juan Carlos come to terms with the notion of superseding his father. There were numerous elements behind this development. Frequent contact with Carrero Blanco, López Rodó and other senior regime figures, as well as with Franco himself, had made it clear to him that his father would never be nominated as successor. And now he had a wife and a mother-in-law who wanted to see him on the throne. His education in Spain and his subsequent journeys around the country had given him a dramatically different view of the country and the regime from that held by his father. He knew nothing of the post-war Spain of abject poverty, concentration camps, prisons, torture and executions. His experience was of the massive infrastructural projects and the economic prosperity of the 1960s. If, for Don Juan, the Caudillo was the traitor who had cheated him of his throne, for Juan Carlos, the avuncular Franco seemed more benevolent than dictatorial. Inevitably, to accept the throne would mean a clash with his father. The Prince's situation made a degree of conflict inevitable – his needs and feelings had been ignored for years and, somewhere deep down, that must have left a degree of resentment. What had happened to him had been justified by reference to the higher need to re-establish the monarchy in Spain. It would hardly have been surprising if he stiffened his resolve with the thought that, ultimately, he would only be fulfilling that mission.

Having accepted in 1966 that, if a Borbón king were ever to rule again in Spain, it would have to be him, in 1967, Juan Carlos would see the emergence of a serious challenger to 'Operación Príncipe' in the form of Alfonso de Borbón y Dampierre. In mid-December 1966, the New York Times had reported that Alfonso was courting the 16-year-old María del Carmen Martínez-Bordiu, Franco's eldest granddaughter.[4] It will be recalled that shortly before the referendum on the Ley Orgánica, Juan Carlos had telephoned his father to seek advice. He was worried because he had learnt that Alfonso was intending to vote and he was being pressed to do the same. A letter from Don Juan shortly afterwards reflected his annoyance. 'When Sofía was in Estoril, I asked her if you had both received any hints that you should vote and she told me that you had to because Alfonso was going to do so. On the telephone, you said the same and this worries me because you cannot compare your situation with that of Alfonso who operates, on his own account, in open disloyalty to all that I represent and thus in opposition to you.' The letter was handwritten and of an entirely personal nature. Yet a copy was soon on Franco's desk. It must have been sent to the Caudillo by someone at La Zarzuela.[5]

There were always those who had contact with both Villa Giralda and La Zarzuela who were only too glad to run to Franco with tittle-tattle. They would usually be received in silence and get little more acknowledgement than a sage nod. However, the Caudillo took particular delight in knowing what was going on in the Prince's household before his ministers did. It gave him great pleasure to see them come in bloated with juicy gossip and then deflate them by saying, 'I already know and the reason is . . .' Once Juan Carlos and Sofía realized that this was the case, they were able to derive enormous good will from Franco by dint of keeping him informed of the details of who visited the palace.[6]

That they felt the need to do so was linked to the fact that Alfonso de Borbón y Dampierre was doing his best to get onto the starting grid for the race to the succession. Shortly after the referendum, Alfonso was interviewed by the correspondent of *Le Figaro*, Jacques Guillemé-Brulon. Asked if he regarded himself as an eventual pretender to the crown, he replied cunningly, 'No I do not, but, on the other hand, I have no right to forget that the conditions established in this regard by the *Ley de Sucesión* apply to me directly. In consequence, I consider it my duty to be at the disposal of my country should she one day need me.' For 'country', read Franco.[7] Within three months, Jacques Guillemé-Brulon would be expelled from Spain for a report on the totalitarian style of the Minister of Information.[8]

In January 1967, Juan Carlos and Sofía made an extended private trip to the United States. It was planned as part of a programme to raise their profile. At a press conference, the Prince was pressed by Benjamin Welles of the *New York Times* to accept that the future of the monarchy would depend on rapid democratization. The journalist was obviously putting the Prince in a difficult situation. To make declarations along those lines would seriously diminish his chances of being selected as successor. Not to do so would damage his image with the democratic forces in Spain. He had little choice and gave the reply that Franco would have wanted to hear. The Spanish Ambassador in Washington, Alfonso Merry del Val, reported to the Caudillo, 'He declared that any future monarchy could consolidate itself only if it was established as the continuation of the *Movimiento* and of the regime.' The Ambassador quoted the Prince as going on to say that, 'a rapid democratization would mean the definitive end of the monarchy in Spain and that, on the contrary, it was necessary to proceed with the caution that characterizes His Excellency's policy of which the *Ley Orgánica del Estado* is a perfect example'.

In his responses to other questions too, Juan Carlos gave stock Francoist replies. The Greek Ambassador in Washington told Merry del Val that Queen Frederica was pushing Juan Carlos to distance himself from his father. The advantages of such a line were obvious but the Prince was also made aware of the difficulties that it could bring. A meeting with Lyndon Johnson was limited to a perfunctory handshake across the President's desk. The Prince and Sofía were invited to tea by Lady Bird and Linda Bird. Juan Carlos muttered angrily to Merry del Val, 'For this my wife could just as well have gone on her own.'[9] Nevertheless, it was a timely reminder of the fact that a close association with Franco had its disadvantages.

With the arrangements for the succession now in place, the various factions in the *Movimiento* began to jockey for position with a quiet frenzy never before seen. Franco was now 74 years old, a distant and increasingly feeble patriarch. At public events, he was silent and morose, lost to the world, his speeches muttered incomprehensibly. Juan Carlos was in a strong position. The machinery of government was in the hands of his two great sponsors, Carrero Blanco and López Rodó. In private, Franco continued to speak dotingly of the Prince and his wife. On 27 March, he told Pacón, 'both he and the Princess are very good. Despite their youth, they show a great maturity. They are intelligent, serious and extremely sensitive. I am highly satisfied with their behaviour at all times. They both demonstrate the high regard they have for the mission that they have been called upon to fulfil. I am sure that when the day arrives, they will serve Spain with the greatest patriotism. Anyone who speaks ill of them just does not know their noble qualities and the life of sacrifice that they lead. I repeat, I am very pleased with them in every way.'[10]

Nevertheless, those who did not want Franco succeeded by a monarch who might liberalize the regime were not without power and influence. In March 1967, Solís gave Franco the text of a proposed *Ley Orgánica del Movimiento*, which authorized 'political associations' only within the strict confines of the single party. Solís's plan was a diluted version of Arrese's 1956 schemes to reassert the power of the Falange. Throughout April and May, Franco received hostile advice on the project from various ministers. Significantly, the partisans of Juan Carlos – Alonso Vega, Carrero Blanco, López Rodó, the Minister of Public Works, Federico Silva Muñoz, and others preferred the present vague *Movimiento* as an umbrella covering all Spaniards. Franco, convinced that the referendum had confirmed his personal power, liked the idea of constitutional obstacles to political parties and refused to squash Solís's project. It would be the basis of the so-called *inmovilismo* of the next few years – namely, a state of immobility, of stasis. This provided a safeguard to ensure that Juan Carlos could not change anything in the future but it did not in any way diminish Franco's commitment to him. In April, for instance, Franco refused permission for Carlos Hugo de Borbón Parma and his wife Irene to attend the annual Carlist celebrations at Montejurra. In June, he commented during a cabinet meeting, 'it's really boring having to keep reminding him not to play politics.'[11]

After his death, Franco's partisans claimed that he was benevolently aware of Juan Carlos's supposed long-term plan to democratize Spain. This is hardly sustained by his attitude to change at the time. During this period, his relationship with an ever more progressive Catholic Church deteriorated significantly. He was inclined, on the basis of secret service reports on his desk, to attribute progressivism in the Church to the sexual degeneration of individual clerics.[12] In fact, more than ever before, Franco accepted the most sinister theories about his enemies. A report from his Ambassador to Italy, Alfredo Sánchez Bella, about American financing of Socialist parties was behind a curious updating of the prejudice which blamed everything on international freemasonry. On 13 March 1967, Franco told Pacón: 'I believe that all the activities which have been carried out in the Western world against us have been carried out by organizations which receive funds from the CIA with the principal aim of establishing in Spain an American-style political system on the day that I cease to be around.'[13]

In April 1967, there took place a series of events in Greece which suggested that Franco was mistaken about the mission of

the CIA and that would obliquely have an influence on the thinking
of Sofía and, by extension, of Juan Carlos. In September 1964,
her father, King Paul, had died of cancer. The consequence was
that Greece lost a voice of moderation and her younger brother,
the rather impetuous Crown Prince Constantine, found himself
on the throne. Just 23 years old, an Olympic gold-medallist yachts-
man and a keen exponent of judo, he lacked the experience and
strength of personality necessary to reform an essentially corrupt
and highly conservative system. His mother Frederica was the
dominant force and she was conspiring to undermine the Centre
Union government of George Papandreou. The principal figure in
a group of conspirators was Colonel George Papadopoulos, a man
with links to the CIA. Eventually, with Constantine as a helpless
spectator, a coup aimed at forestalling an election victory in May
by Papandreou was hatched between the palace and the colonels.
It took place on 21 April. Three days earlier, Juan Carlos and
Sofía had been in Greece for the birthday of Queen Frederica. The
Prince had returned to Spain before the coup took place, but Sofía
was still in the royal residence of Tatoi to the north of Athens.
She was able to witness the somewhat hesitant performance by
her brother in contrast to the ruthless decisiveness of the conspirators. For the next two days, Juan Carlos suffered considerable
anxiety until Sofía was able to get back to Spain. King Constantine
would exist as an uneasy figurehead until 13 December 1967,
when he would launch a feeble counter-coup. Following its collapse, he would go into exile, to be replaced by a regent, General
Zoitakis.[14]

In the meantime, Franco avidly devoured reports of Juan
Carlos's activities around Spain. No doubt aware of this, the Prince
tried to give every indication that his thinking never strayed from
that of the Caudillo. In July, the Civil Governor of Barcelona,
Tomás Garicano Goñi, arranged for him to meet with prominent
Catalan figures of the *Movimiento*. At a working breakfast at the
yacht club, Juan Carlos spoke in terms that must have delighted
Franco when he read the report of the proceedings. He referred
to 'our common enemies'. When he was asked if he anticipated
a monarchical 'installation' or restoration, he replied that after

30 years of the Caudillo's rule, 'installation' was the only possibility. He spoke admiringly of Franco and with apparent enthusiasm about the *Movimiento* saying, 'to submit the monarchy to the free-play of parties would be a fatal mistake given that one monarchy has already perished at their hands.' Together, he said, the monarchy and the *Movimiento* would guarantee the continuity of the regime. These public declarations were at some remove from the conversations he was having with his mentor, Torcuato Fernández-Miranda, about a future democratization.[15]

Juan Carlos's position was strengthened yet again in mid-1967 when Franco finally allowed General Agustín Muñoz Grandes to resign as Vice-President of the government. It was a blow to those elements within the Falange that opposed the transition to the monarchy. Muñoz Grandes had been their champion. The move seemed to fulfil the hopes of the Opus Dei technocrats in the cabinet that, within the terms of the *Ley Orgánica*, the Caudillo would nominate Carrero Blanco as President of the Council of Ministers (Prime Minister). The doggedly faithful Carrero, however, did not want the post, believing that no one could do the job better than Franco. For two months, the Caudillo did nothing, to let time take any heat out of the situation. Finally, in the third week of September, after a cabinet meeting in San Sebastián, as they travelled by car to an official function, Franco casually told Carrero Blanco that he was to replace Muñoz Grandes. Fraga had entertained hopes that he might secure the post and thus hasten the succession of Juan Carlos and the eventual liberalization of the regime. With Franco looking ever more frequently to the past, that was unfounded optimism. Carrero Blanco was the logical choice. He had served the Caudillo loyally since 1941 and their views were almost indistinguishable.[16]

For most supporters of the Caudillo, Carrero Blanco was a guarantee of untrammelled Francoism. However, there were hardliners who were more Francoist than Franco himself and the admiral's determination to see Juan Carlos on the throne made him the object of their jealous suspicion. It was rumoured that Franco had been obliged to name a Vice-President because he had suffered a cerebral haemorrhage.[17] Anxious that an incapacitated

Franco was now entirely in the hands of Carrero Blanco and López Rodó, those who were determined to block change at all costs began to make their own plans. They were aware of Franco's affection for Juan Carlos and feared that, in backing the Prince, he risked opening the way to a liberal monarchy, and certainly one which would put an end to the monopoly of privilege previously held by the Falange.[18] They now unleashed a public war against the group associated with the Opus Dei through the *Movimiento*'s press network. Franco commented, 'the only newspapers which don't say what their owners tell them to are those of the *Movimiento*.'[19]

In 1967, Franco told his Minister of Finance, Juan José Espinosa San Martín (who had replaced Mariano Navarro Rubio in July 1965), one of the group associated with López Rodó, that he wanted the Prince to start learning about the workings of his ministry. Over the next three years, Franco would look on with pleasure as Juan Carlos spent about three afternoons each week working at the various departments of the ministry. He would regularly quiz Espinosa about the Prince's progress. When the minister told him that Juan Carlos was acquiring a considerable mastery of financial questions, his eyes would light up, like a doting grandfather hearing about the achievements of his favourite grandson. At other times, he gave the impression of protecting the Prince within the hostile environment of the *Movimiento*. For example, Espinosa suggested to Franco that Juan Carlos be given more responsible jobs than just opening exhibitions and visiting charities and be allowed to cease being 'a dumb Prince'. Franco replied, 'Everything will come to pass, and tell the Prince not to be in a hurry, it is better to be dumb than to stammer.'[20]

Ironically, given the dictator's attitude, the most effective opposition to Juan Carlos's prospects came from the group of right-wingers with the greatest access to Franco himself. The frequent indications that the Prince was acquiring ever more favour in the Caudillo's eyes spurred them into action. Their objective was to recruit an increasingly decrepit Franco for the cause of *inmovilismo*. Consisting of Cristóbal Martínez-Bordiu, Doña Carmen and hardline Falangists like José Antonio Girón de Velasco, the clique had close links with military hardliners known as the '*generales azules*' (blue generals), such as Alfonso Pérez Viñeta, Tomás García Rebull and Ángel Campano López. In his final years, largely because of Parkinson's disease and the drugs taken to mitigate the symptoms, Franco let himself be influenced by these people. He was fundamentally committed to the Carrero Blanco–López Rodó vision of the transition to an authoritarian monarchy. However, as he grew older, his instincts made him more prone to listen to the alarmist accounts of what was happening that were provided by this clique. He showed less political energy, and gave fewer signs of reading the press or even of knowing what his ministers had done. The extent to which he was out of touch was revealed in December 1967 when he asked Carrero Blanco, Fraga, Solís and other ministers for names to help him make senior appointments saying, 'I have been locked up here for so long that I don't know anyone anymore.'[21]

The narrow limits within which Franco expected Juan Carlos, or indeed any successor, to work were made clear in his speech inaugurating the new Cortes which met on 17 November 1967. He mocked those who wanted to bring back liberal democracy while describing the existing system as already democratic. There were hints that there would be some kind of *apertura* (opening) although he was at pains to stress the narrow limits within which that might happen. Using his favourite medical metaphor, he said, 'The illnesses of nations last for centuries and their convalescence many decades. Spain, with ups and downs, has been alternating between life and death for three centuries. She is just beginning to get out of her sick bed and have short walks in the hospital grounds. Those who want to send her to the gymnasium to do somersaults either don't know what they are talking about or else know only too well.'[22]

On 5 January 1968, Juan Carlos reached 30, the age at which the *Ley de Sucesión* made him eligible to be King. López Rodó and the Prince himself began to discuss the best tactics to follow to hasten his designation as successor. There can be no doubt that, by now, Juan Carlos was actively seeking his own nomination.[23] There were various efforts made by Falangists to trip him up. He was interviewed by Emilio Romero, the director of the most 'radical'

1 *Left* The four-year-old Juan Carlos in Rome, sports a cavalry uniform given him by a group of aristocratic ladies. After an hour of being photographed, one of his nannies took his boots off: his feet had been rubbed raw because the boots were too small for him. That is when he shyly started to cry. His father had taught him from a very young age that a Borbón cries only in his bed.

2 *Above right* Franco and Don Juan aboard the Caudillo's yacht, *Azor*, during their meeting on 25 August 1948.

3 *Right* A family portrait in 1945. From left to right, Don Juan, Alfonsito, Juan Carlos, Margarita, Doña María de las Mercedes, Pilar.

4 *Below* Juan Carlos arrives in Spain from Lisbon on 9 November 1948. Shuddering as the biting Castilian cold hit him, his heart must have fallen when he saw the grim welcoming committee. A group of unsmiling courtiers in black overcoats peered at him. Surrounded by such men, his loneliness can only have increased.

5 *Above left* Juan Carlos in his room in Las Jarillas. Don Juan had given instructions that the work at Las Jarillas be hard and demanding. Years later, Juan Carlos would comment 'Don't imagine that we were treated like kings. In fact, they made us study harder than in an ordinary school on the basis that "because we were who we were, we had to give a good example".'

6 *Above* Off the Portuguese coast near Estoril, on 28 September 1949, the eleven-year-old Juan Carlos at the helm of the yacht *Saltillo*, which had been loaned to Don Juan by a wealthy Basque monarchist.

7 *Left* Juan Carlos and his brother Alfonsito on 30 September 1950.

8 *Below* The two brothers talking to classmates and a teacher at the improvised school in the Palacio de Miramar in San Sebastian.

9 Juan Carlos as an officer cadet at the swearing-in ceremony at the Military Academy of Zaragoza on 15 December 1955. The Prince was saddened by the fact that Franco had not permitted his father to attend the ceremony.

10 The burial of Alfonsito at the cemetery of Cascais on Saturday 31 March 1956. Juan Carlos, in his cadet's uniform, is just visible behind Don Juan.

11 *Above* Juan Carlos in a training jet at the Spanish Air Force Academy of San Javier in Murcia, 1 January 1959.

12 *Above right* Juan Carlos oscillated between being infatuated with, and just being very fond of, his childhood friend, Maria Gabriella di Savoia, the vivacious daughter of the exiled King Umberto of Italy. Franco regarded her as altogether too free and with 'ideas altogether too modern'. Seen here together in Estoril in 1960.

13 *Below* To the astonishment of Franco, the engagement of Juan Carlos and Sofía of Greece is announced at the home of Queen Victoria Eugenia in Lausanne, 13 September 1961. From left to right, front: Queen Frederica of Greece, Queen Victoria Eugenia, Juan Carlos, Princess Sofía; rear: King Paul of Greece, Princess Irene and Don Juan.

14 *Left* The wedding of Juan Carlos and Sofía in Athens, 15 May 1962.

15 *Below* In early June 1962, encouraged by both Queen Victoria Eugenia and Queen Frederica, the newlyweds interrupted their honeymoon in the Mediterranean to fly to Madrid to thank Franco for his various attentions in relation to the wedding. Don Juan was appalled.

16 *Left* At the spectacular Victory Parade to celebrate the twenty-fifth anniversary of Franco's triumph in the Spanish Civil War, an uncomfortable Juan Carlos was 'presented to the Armed Forces' as the Caudillo's likely successor.

17 *Below* At the funeral of Queen Victoria Eugenia in Lausanne on 18 April 1969, Alfonso de Borbón Dampierre, Juan Carlos and Don Juan are among the pallbearers.

18 *Left* A religious ceremony held on 20 November 1974 at the Valle de los Caídos in memory of the execution of José Antonio Primo de Rivera. Franco and Torcuato Fernández-Miranda are in Falangist uniform, Admiral Carrero Blanco and Juan Carlos in military uniform.

19 *Below* Prince Felipe, Princess Sofía and Doña Carmen Polo in the presidential box at the annual Victory Parade in 1974.

20 On 30 August 1974, Juan Carlos, as acting Head of State, chaired a cabinet meeting held at the Caudillo's summer residence, the Pazo de Meirás in Galicia. Afterwards, Franco received the Prince, the prime minister – Carlos Arias Navarro and the ministers. On 2 September, under pressure from rightists suspicious of Juan Carlos's democratic intentions, the Caudillo decided to resume his powers.

21 On 1 October 1975, Franco made his last ever public appearance before a huge crowd at the Palacio de Oriente. He was accompanied by an embarrassed Juan Carlos and Princess Sofía, who both abstained from giving the fascist salute.

of the *Movimiento* newspapers, *Pueblo*, a paper committed to a Falangist future. The tone of the interview suggested an effort to drive a wedge between the Prince and his father. Asked what he would do if the mechanisms of the *Ley Orgánica* saw him named as Franco's successor, Juan Carlos replied, with an evasiveness worthy of Franco himself, 'my reaction would be whatever was in the best interests of the country at that time.' Not dismayed, Romero pressed on, asking if he could accept the nomination given that Don Juan represented dynastic legitimacy. With equally neat footwork, the Prince replied, 'I think that would depend on the political situation at that moment.' Running out of patience, Romero asked, 'Can your father abdicate or not?' and was driven back with heavy losses by the Prince's reply, 'He obviously has the ability to do so, no?'[24]

On 30 January, Sofía gave birth to a son and the Prince hastened to telephone Franco with the news. Two days later, he visited El Pardo to ensure that the date chosen for the baptism, 8 February, would be suitable for the Caudillo. For Franco, the birth of a male heir to the Prince confirmed him as the best candidate for the succession. Although the name Felipe had already been chosen for the baby, the Prince went through a charade of letting Franco make suggestions about names. He thus agreed with Franco that Felipe was preferable to Fernando. Franco said, 'Fernando VII is still very recent; the Felipes are more historic.' Juan Carlos asked if Franco would go to Barajas Airport to meet Queen Victoria Eugenia who was coming from Nice to be the godmother. 'You must realize, Your Highness,' he said to Juan Carlos, 'that I cannot compromise the State with my presence there.' Juan Carlos responded by asking with apparent innocence if he had not already committed the State to the monarchy in the *Ley Orgánica del Estado*. Franco agreed that this was indeed the case but that it was necessary to proceed slowly in search of the right psychological moment. No doubt, he had no wish to be present at an occasion that would be converted into a pro-Don Juan demonstration. He also refused a request from Juan Carlos to have a private meeting with Don Juan, commenting drily that everything that could be said had been said.[25]

Queen Victoria Eugenia was returning to Spain for the first time since the ignominious departure of the royal family on 14 April 1931. On 7 February, she was awaited at Barajas by her son, Don Juan, who had arrived earlier from Portugal. Her entry into the arrivals hall was greeted rapturously by many thousands of people shouting: 'Long live the King!' and 'Long live the Queen Mother!' Franco was represented at the airport by the Minister of Aviation, General José Lacalle Larraga. He also gave his permission for the presence of Antonio María Oriol, the Minister of Justice, who had formal responsibility for relations with the royal family. To his intense displeasure, however, three other ministers, Fernando María Castiella (Foreign Affairs), Juan José Espinosa San Martín (Finance), and Manuel Lora Tamayo (Education) went to the airport without asking his permission. Franco had expressly forbidden Alonso Vega, Minister of the Interior, to go. The entire road from Barajas back to Madrid was lined nose-to-tail with cars and another cheering crowd greeted Victoria Eugenia's arrival at the Liria palace, the home of the Duque de Alba, the head of her household. The monarchist press dwelt effusively on the reception given the Queen and about the popular demonstrations of warmth and respect that had greeted Don Juan's passage through Madrid and the University City on his way to La Zarzuela. In contrast, Spanish television, RTVE, devoted only 17 seconds to the item.[26]

The next day, after the Archbishop of Madrid, Casimiro Morcillo, had baptized the infant, there was a reception at La Zarzuela. Carrero Blanco ostentatiously snubbed Don Juan, whom he had loathed since their tense meeting in 1947. Victoria Eugenia spoke to Franco. She confided to the British Ambassador, Sir Alan Williams, that 'the thought of talking to Franco had given her a headache'. Nevertheless, speak she did and her account to the Ambassador coincides with that related by Jesús Pabón, president of Don Juan's Privy Council, who was at the reception and talked afterwards with both. 'General,' she said, 'this is the last time that we will ever see each other. I want to ask you something. You have done so much for Spain, so finish the job. Name a King of Spain. There are three of them. Choose. Do it while you are still alive: if not, there will be no King. Don't leave it until we're dead.

This is the last and only request of your Queen.' The conversation ended with Franco saying, 'It will be as Your Majesty wishes.' Reporting their conversation later to his ministers, Franco claimed that she had said that she would accept his choice of successor provided he chose a descendant of Alfonso XIII. He further alleged that she had indicated her own preference for Juan Carlos. She told him that she found Juan Carlos mature and well-prepared but she made no comment on the succession. In fact, her preferences had surely been made clear when, on greeting Don Juan at the airport, she had bowed before him as King.[27]

Nonetheless, while in Madrid, Don Juan made a gesture that appalled his more liberal followers and pleased Franco. He visited the Valle de los Caídos where he prayed before the tomb of the founder of the Falange, José Antonio Primo de Rivera. However, the symbolism was rather wasted since he also met two leaders of the clandestine Socialist Party, the PSOE, Carlos Zayas and Raúl Morodo. He also visited Antonio García Trevijano, a wealthy lawyer with links to the Socialists as well as being a friend and business associate of Rafael Calvo Serer. García Trevijano encouraged Don Juan in his belief that, on Franco's death, he had only to appear in Madrid for the Army to proclaim him as King. He claimed later that he had arranged for Don Juan to have a clandestine meeting with General Manuel Díez Alegría to discuss the attitude of the Army in the event of Franco dying before resolving the succession. At the home of the Duque de Alburquerque, Don Juan met many other officers. Reports on these encounters can only have confirmed all of Franco's prejudices against Don Juan.[28]

Juan Carlos was aware that these meetings were the fruit of José María de Areilza's efforts to consolidate Don Juan's relations with the left-wing opposition to the dictatorship. The Prince was also fully aware – and approved – of the determination of Carrero Blanco, López Rodó and the other technocrats to see himself named successor. Inevitably, these contradictory initiatives caused frictions between Juan Carlos and his father. In early May, Don Juan suggested that his son should come back to Estoril until the autumn. Juan Carlos responded sharply: 'I have followed the line that you laid down. General Martínez Campos, Duque de la Torre, opposed me being installed in La Zarzuela. He wanted me to go to Salamanca and it was you who put me in Madrid. When you did that, you made a choice. To be in La Zarzuela meant being near to Franco. In the last few years, I have done nothing to damage either you or the monarchy. I can't now insult him by leaving Spain for five months. You have played one card and I have played another, on your instructions. You stick with yours and I'll stick with mine. If your card wins, I'll take my hat off to you, but it doesn't seem likely. We have to think of Spain and of the monarchy.'[29]

López Rodó, Alonso Vega, Carrero Blanco, Federico Silva and others in the cabinet never missed an opportunity to urge Franco to go ahead and name Juan Carlos as his successor. Now aged 76, the Caudillo dithered, consistently citing the need to wait for 'the right psychological moment'. It seemed as if he was worried by the continued opposition to the Prince from within the *Movimiento*. This took various forms. There would be minor humiliations. For instance, when Juan Carlos travelled in Iberia, financial stringency obliged him to go tourist class. Very often, the captain or the purser of an aircraft would invite him to move into first class. On two occasions, pilots who happened to be Falangists, came into the passenger cabin and told Juan Carlos to return to his original seat. When the Prince visited a town, the Mayor and the Civil Governor would receive a call from General Alonso Vega, ordering them to stint nothing in his reception. Having done so, they would then receive a severe reprimand from the Minister-Secretary-General of the *Movimiento*, José Solís. In contrast, when Alfonso de Borbón y Dampierre travelled around Spain, it was Solís who telephoned ahead to the local authorities to demand that he be received with all pomp and ceremony.[30]

Franco made his views known only in the most oblique fashion. Juan Carlos was at his side for the annual victory parade in May and at the Navy week in Santander during the first week of July. On 2 July, he had a lengthy meeting with the Caudillo and discussed the difficulties of his situation *vis-à-vis* his father. He told Franco that he would not make any public statement of disagreement with Don Juan. Franco replied, 'Your Highness is doing the right thing. Be patient and keep calm.' Juan Carlos responded: 'My position gets ever more difficult because my status is not clear. Please, General, name your successor once and for all.' Franco's reply underlined his central concern: 'I will do it. I've got to find the psychological moment; I've got to test the mood of the new Cortes.' The implication was that he would be satisfied with nothing less than the acceptance of any nomination by unanimous acclamation. Yet when the Prince said, 'I'm not in a hurry,' Franco replied, 'Well, I am. Something could happen to me any day now.'[31]

With each indication of the Prince's closeness to Franco, his father became more distressed. Don Juan was still keen to see Juan Carlos return to Estoril. In mid-October, the Prince repeated to General Juan Castañón de Mena, the head of the Caudillo's military household, what he had already told his father: 'If I am in La Zarzuela it is because of what was agreed with the Generalísimo by my father. If I am asked to leave here, I will go, but not to Estoril. I will go to wherever I am posted by the Army, because that is my career.'[32] Reported to Franco, as it surely was, this apparent reaffirmation that, first and foremost, the Prince considered himself a Spanish soldier can only have delighted the dictator. Both father and son told various interlocutors that their political disagreements did not affect their family relationship. That is difficult to believe. In fact, Doña María de las Mercedes was having to work hard to smooth over the tensions between her husband and her son.

Inevitably, Pedro Sainz Rodríguez and Areilza were keen to undermine Franco's slow but sure progress towards the nomination of Juan Carlos. At their suggestion, Don Juan reluctantly wrote to his son on 12 October 1968. That he did so was a sign of weakness. Writing not as his father but as 'head of the Spanish dynasty', he called on Juan Carlos not to get involved in what he called 'dynastic upheaval'. His letter pointed out that, if he accepted nomination as successor, he would open himself to accusations of disloyalty and give the impression that the royal family was split. Rather brusquely, it stated that being 30 did not absolve the Prince of his duties of loyalty and discipline to the head of the royal family. Don Juan pointed out that, as his representative, it was the Prince's duty to seek a solution for the future that combined legitimacy and legality – that is to say to ensure that Don Juan would be Franco's successor. As an attempt to provoke the Prince into a public declaration in favour of his father, it was a failure. Juan Carlos was not prepared to do so and took some time thinking over his response. His eventual reply, some months later, would be a private one.[33]

Don Juan's admonitory letter to his son may even have helped resolve the Caudillo's private hesitations about the succession. In the course of October 1968, López Rodó and Oriol prepared a lengthy legalistic memorandum aimed at convincing him that the monarchy would guarantee the continuity of his regime. At the same time, in La Zarzuela, José María Gamazo Manglano, the Marqués de Mondéjar and Alfonso Armada prepared a 33-page curriculum vitae of Juan Carlos with the title 'Summary of the Prince's education and training'. This document was intended to provide Franco with proof of the Prince's identification with the regime. It contained details of the classes that he had taken, his time in various ministries and his journeys around Spain. Carrero Blanco took both documents to El Pardo and went through them in detail with Franco. He also gave the Caudillo a copy of Don Juan's letter to his son, presumably supplied by Juan Carlos himself. Carrero Blanco advised him that the announcement of Juan Carlos's nomination should come as a surprise, in order to prevent the partisans of Don Juan mounting a hostile publicity campaign in Spain and abroad. This would also require, he pointed out, the prior agreement of the Prince to maintain absolute secrecy. Franco listened in silence, then looked up and said, 'Totally in agreement.' After the meeting, Carrero Blanco asked López Rodó to prepare a draft of the Prince's acceptance speech of his nomination as successor.[34]

What was lacking was a date, but Carrero Blanco preferred not to push Franco too hard. Having made his decision, the Caudillo still hesitated about making it public. The small circle of those behind the '*Operación Príncipe*' began to talk of 'Operation Salmon', implying that having got Franco to take the bait, now they had to reel him in.[35] The apparent progress being made towards Juan Carlos's nomination alerted his opponents of the need to promote their own candidates. This led to a flurry of activity by, and the consequent eclipse of, the Carlist pretender Don Carlos Hugo de Borbón Parma. Before the end of 1968, Franco ordered the expulsion from Spain of Don Carlos Hugo, his father, Don Javier, and his sisters, as punishment for their political machinations.

With the Carlist claimants routed, many in the *Movimiento* had begun to place their hopes on Alfonso de Borbón y Dampierre. On 9 November 1968, *Pueblo* published yet another interview with the man who was coming to be a potential challenger to Juan Carlos. He was asked by the journalist Emilia González Sevilla: 'Do you regard yourself as having a right to the throne despite your father's renunciation of his rights?' He gave what he no doubt considered a cunning reply, although its main characteristic was its incomprehensible vagueness: 'Look, the only heir is the Spanish people, and if a referendum has been accepted by the Spanish people, in which it has voted yes to the monarchy, one must respect the thinking of the people.' The baffled young woman interjected, 'But the Spanish people cannot reign. There is a *Ley de Sucesión* which calls for a male, 30 years old, Catholic and of royal blood . . .' Alfonso finally revealed that he did indeed consider himself a candidate for the throne: 'Well then, if that law includes me, I can't say anything. Don't you think? There's no need for me to say anything. I repeat that I am very respectful of the thinking of the Spanish people and one must respect the laws and the votes cast by the people.'[36]

The letter from Don Juan on 12 October had been an attempt by Areilza and Sainz Rodríguez to undermine Juan Carlos's position. It was swiftly followed by another torpedo. The French journalist Françoise Laot published an interview with Juan Carlos and Sofía in the society gossip magazine *Point de Vue* on 22 November. In response to a question as to whether he was uncomfortable to be both Franco's designated heir and the son of the legitimate heir, his alleged reply was unequivocal: 'No, all the more so because there can be no problems between my father and myself. Dynastic law exists and can be changed by nobody. I will never, ever agree to rule while my father lives: he is the King. If I am here it is so that there will be a representative of the Spanish dynasty while my father is in Portugal.' The shock nearly knocked the fishing rod out of the hands of those engaged in 'operation salmon'.

Juan Carlos and his staff were even more surprised. They had been led to believe that the journalist would produce an anodyne 'human interest' piece about the family. Juan Carlos categorically denied having made the statement to Françoise Laot. He had, of course, been quoted as making an identical remark in *Time* magazine three years earlier and it had subsequently been repeated in the notorious *ABC* article for which Anson had been forced into exile. Certainly, had he planned to make such an explosive declaration, *Point de Vue* would have been an odd choice. The correspondents of the *New York Times*, *The Times* or *Le Monde* would have been only too glad to publish it. Jesús Pabón thought it impossible for the Prince to have made such a sweeping remark, simply because he knew full well that there were circumstances – his father's abdication or incapacity – in which he might legitimately ascend to the throne in Don Juan's lifetime. Now, the second-in-command of the royal household, Lieutenant-Colonel Alfonso Armada, telephoned the journalist in Paris and she admitted that the offending phrase was indeed apocryphal. Apparently, she had inserted it on the recommendation of 'friends' who had told her that it would please La Zarzuela. Fraga and others believed that one of the 'friends' was Areilza, although Alfonso Armada says that it was not. A damage limitation exercise was swiftly mounted. The Marqués de Mondéjar, the head of the Prince's household, went to see General Juan Castañón de Mena to make sure that Franco was informed of what had really happened. Armada claims that he went to see the Minister of Information, Manuel Fraga, his Under-Secretary, Pío Cabanillas, and his *chef de cabinet*, Gabriel Elorriaga. The diaries of both Fraga and López Rodó, much more plausibly, record the visit as being made by Mondéjar.

Fraga agreed to use his influence to try to prevent the publication in Spain of Laot's article but claimed that his own recent press law would make it difficult. He suggested that the best antidote would be some pro-Franco declarations by the Prince. Juan Carlos broached the matter with Franco when they met at a hunting party on 2 December. The Caudillo told him not to worry about what he saw as machinations emanating from Estoril. Some days later, Armada heard that *ABC* was intending to print a front page with a photograph of Don Juan and Juan Carlos and the headline: 'I will never reign in Spain while my father is alive. Prince Juan Carlos's words to the weekly *Point de Vue*.' Juan Carlos himself telephoned the paper's owner, Juan Ignacio de Luca de Tena, and persuaded him to drop the idea. However, on Thursday 26 December, the progressive pro-Don Juan evening paper, *Madrid*, ran an article about the alleged declaration. Closely linked to Opus Dei, *Madrid* was run by Rafael Calvo Serer and its lawyer was Antonio García Trevijano. On the next day, *ABC* reproduced the article.[37]

Some years later, Françoise Laot published a biography of Juan Carlos and Sofía. In it, the issue is fudged in such a way as to lend credence to Alfonso Armada's account of the falsification of the interview. She takes credit for what followed, suggesting that she was an inadvertent catalyst. The suspected 'friend', Areilza, also wrote a later account which insinuated that behind the entire issue lay a *'pacto de familia'* between father and son. This is so implausible as to seem a mere smokescreen.[38] After all, the reproduction in *Madrid* and *ABC* of the Prince's alleged declarations deeply alarmed La Zarzuela. It also clinched Fraga's determination that there be a response to the *Point de Vue* article. Over the last weekend of December, he drafted a statement with the help of Gabriel Elorriaga who took it to La Zarzuela. There it was revised by Mondéjar, Elorriaga and Juan Carlos himself, who added some lines.[39]

The Prince's reply was published as if it was the spontaneous outcome of an interview on Monday 6 January 1969 with Carlos Mendo, the director of the regime press agency, Agencia EFE. In fact, Mendo wrote up an account of an imaginary interview on the basis of the previously drafted declarations. His first visit to

La Zarzuela did not take place until two days after the interview was published. Nevertheless, in his widely circulated article, Mendo commented on the effusive good nature with which he was received. Juan Carlos's scripted answers to questions, naturally enough, reflected a considerable thoughtfulness. In defending the relevance of the monarchy, he spoke admiringly of 'peoples at peace with themselves' in which could be read a glimmer of discrepancy with Franco's division of Spain into victors and vanquished. Crucially, in response to the 'question' whether he would accept 'the application of the fundamental laws', a diplomatic reference to his likely nomination as Franco's successor, the Prince's reply was unequivocal. 'I have said several times that on the day that I received my commission, I swore on the flag to devote myself with all my strength to the service of Spain. I will fulfil my promise to serve her in the post in which I can be of most use, whatever the sacrifices it might cost me. You can surely understand that otherwise I would not be where I am. It is a matter of honour as I see it.' The reference to his sacrifice of family life in the past and of his relationship with his father in the near future was unmistakable.

On the issue of whether he believed that the fundamental laws should favour him, he 'replied': 'For me, it is not a question of rights but, simply, of being useful in the best interests of my Fatherland. This is what I have been doing in dedicating my life to the training necessary for such service, which requires the sacrifice of other activities and personal inclinations. I am where I have been placed by a series of circumstances, some of a historical nature and others to do with the present situation and I just try every day to do what I can to be more useful for the future of the Spaniards and to avoid anything that might stand in the way of my being useful.' The 'question' eagerly awaited by many Spaniards, posed in coded language, was whether acceptance of Franco's installed monarchy in accordance with the principles of the *Movimiento* was not a betrayal of dynastic rights. The Prince's 'reply' could not have been more pragmatic: 'The satisfaction of seeing the return of the monarchical institution is more than enough to justify both gratitude and a certain flexibility.'[40]

Fraga ensured that the declarations were given the maximum publicity in the press, on the radio and the television. Don Juan was appalled – not least because he was not mentioned in the interview.[41] However, he cannot have been totally surprised by its contents. His letter of 12 October and indeed the insertion of the apocryphal declarations in *Point de Vue* had been attempts to force the Prince into a public announcement that he would not accept nomination as Franco's successor. After discussing the *Point de Vue* article with Franco on 2 December 1968, Juan Carlos had replied to his father's 12 October letter. The text has never been published – not even by Alfonso Armada, who claimed to have kept the draft. According to Armada, in the rather ambiguous letter, the Prince reaffirmed his fidelity to his father, saying, 'above all else, I would prefer you to be named successor.' However, he went on to say that the most important thing was the future of the monarchy. That being the case, he had to make it clear that, 'If Franco nominates me, I will accept.'[42]

The unmistakable implication that the Prince would accept nomination as successor ensured that the article had enormous impact. According to Armada, 20,000 people wrote to La Zarzuela to congratulate Juan Carlos. One of them was Admiral Carrero Blanco who sent his 'enthusiastic congratulations on the declarations'. 'They are well thought-out, specific and forthright. And since they clearly reflect sincerity, a sense of responsibility, a spirit of service and patriotism, they have been received with open satisfaction by the immense majority of Spaniards.' The Prince's reply made it quite clear that he was fully aware of the implications of what he had just done. 'I am incredibly grateful for your letter. You know only too well how much effort I put into fulfilling my duty, both because my conscience demands it and because of my deep love for Spain. I understand the momentous nature of the declaration and I have weighed up the consequences. With each passing day, I need more help, and so when I receive proofs of affection like your letter I feel a great joy that makes up for inevitable unpleasantnesses.'[43]

The emphasis on the Prince's loyalty to Franco and to the *Movimiento* delighted the 76-year-old Caudillo. He was even more pleased to read secret reports on the consternation with which the declarations had been received in Estoril. After the cabinet meeting of 10 January 1969, he said to Fraga, 'I was struck by just how fitting were the Prince's declarations.' When Fraga came out of Franco's study, López Rodó congratulated him merely saying 'the perfect crime'. When López Rodó went in, he said to Franco: 'With these declarations, the Prince has burned his boats. Now all that is lacking is Your Excellency's decision.'[44]

On 15 January, Franco told the Prince that it was his intention to name him as successor at some point in the course of the year. Juan Carlos replied that as a Spanish soldier he was at the service of his country. Nevertheless, he asked the Caudillo to do things in such a way as to show some consideration for his father. Franco replied, 'I just don't understand your father's attitude; he simply doesn't take things on board. You need not worry, Your Highness. Don't let anything lead you astray now. Everything is done.' Juan Carlos replied, 'Rest assured, General, I have learned much from your *galleguismo* (Galician craftiness).' As they both laughed, Franco complimented him, 'Your Highness does it rather well.' Franco said that he would like the Prince to join him in cabinet meetings. After a pause, he said 'In about a year and a half . . .', but failed to finish the sentence. The implication was that he aimed to retire. Neither of these insinuations came to anything.[45] Juan Carlos had just made an unpleasant decision. Although he was pleased that Franco was edging towards his designation, he was distressed by the implications for his father. Jesús Pabón, who saw him shortly afterwards, commented, 'he dwells on it all with great sadness . . . He seems anxious, indeed heartbroken.'[46]

Painful though it was, Juan Carlos had long since decided that he would have no choice but to accept nomination as successor. However, delays in the process were made inevitable when, in response to university agitation, General Camilo Alonso Vega proposed a state of emergency at a cabinet meeting on 24 January 1969. Behind his benign appearance, the white-haired octogenarian retained his repressive instincts. He was supported by Carrero Blanco and by the opponents of Juan Carlos – Solís and the Minister for the Navy, Admiral Pedro 'Pedrolo' Nieto Antúnez, a lifelong crony of the Caudillo. In recent years, Spain had experienced vertiginous social change and it was clearly absurd for regime dinosaurs like Alonso Vega and Carrero Blanco to try to stamp out its consequences with repression. However, the tactful complaints of the Opus Dei technocrats went unheard by Franco. López Rodó's concern was that Solís and others wanted a state of emergency in place so that Franco would delay yet again the nomination of Juan Carlos as successor. Accordingly, he persuaded Alonso Vega that the situation was damaging Juan Carlos's prospects. Thus, at the cabinet meeting of 21 March 1969, Alonso Vega proposed that the state of emergency be lifted. Visibly annoyed, Solís opposed this, precisely because a successor could not be named while it remained in force. The technocrats used the argument that the regime should not approach its 30th anniversary in such conditions. Fraga argued that it would severely damage the tourist trade. Finally, Franco closed the debate saying, 'Given that the Minister of the Interior requests it, the state of emergency should be lifted.'[47]

In August 1968, in Portugal, the collapse of Oliveira Salazar's health had been so sudden as to catch him unprepared. Aware of this, the technocrats pressed the Caudillo to make a decision on the succession while he was still able. Juan Carlos also played his part by undermining a scheme hatched by Areilza to neutralize his declarations to Carlos Mendo. Doña María de las Mercedes was in a clinic in Nice, and her son planned to spend the weekend of 8 and 9 March 1969 with her. Don Juan was in Rome where he attended a requiem mass for his father and was received in audience by Pope Paul VI and by Monseñor Josémaría Escrivá de Balaguer, the founder of Opus Dei. Areilza proposed that, on his return journey, Don Juan coincide with his son in Nice. Areilza then intended to issue a statement to the effect that, having discussed the Spanish situation, father and son were totally in agreement and determined to act as a united front. This would give the impression that the declarations in *Point de Vue* were the authentic ones and those to the Agencia EFE insincere. Having already nailed his colours to the mast with regard to the succession, Juan Carlos was not prepared to contradict himself. Alerted to Areilza's wheeze, the Prince immediately cancelled his trip to Nice. Having done so, Juan Carlos was sufficiently frustrated by the continuing delays to ask Franco on 10 April, 'Don't you trust me, General?' Franco just replied, 'Why?'[48]

On 15 April 1969, Victoria Eugenia died in Lausanne. While in Switzerland for the funeral, Juan Carlos had a highly disagreeable confrontation with his father in the Hotel Royal. Don Juan criticized him roundly for his declarations to Carlos Mendo. Juan Carlos replied that he was in Spain to accept whatever was offered and Don Juan shot back saying, 'Yes, but not to take my place!' An agreement to meet soon in Estoril to clear the air temporarily defused the tension. Nevertheless, from now on, there would be suspicion and friction between father and son. Only the efforts of Doña María de las Mercedes prevented an irreparable rupture.

Franco sent Castiella, his Minister of Foreign Affairs, to represent him at the funeral. He decreed three days of national mourning and requiem masses were ordered for every provincial capital. Franco and his wife presided at the mass celebrated in Madrid on 19 April. In every respect, the Caudillo was responding to the news as if he took very seriously Spain's legal status as a monarchy. On 16 April, Carrero Blanco had taken advantage of this mood to press him hard about the need to hasten the nomination of the Prince. Three days later, López Rodó informed Juan Carlos of Carrero Blanco's conversation with Franco and handed him the draft speech for his acceptance, suggesting that he discuss the contents with Franco.[49]

Two weeks after the clash with Don Juan in Lausanne, Juan Carlos and Sofía arrived in Estoril. At a dinner at Villa Giralda that lasted until 3.30 a.m. the following morning, the situation in Spain was discussed. Hoping to bring his father round, the Prince had delegated Armada to explain 'the real situation in Spain and its future', the views of the Army high command and of the bulk of the Francoist political élite. Citing the efforts of Carrero Blanco, López Rodó and Camilo Alonso Vega, Armada made it quite clear that Franco was seriously disposed to name Juan Carlos his successor with the title of King. Don Juan, needless to say, was deeply reluctant to accept what was said. With a beaming smile, he said, 'Juanito, if they name you, you can accept, but you can rest assured that that won't happen.'[50] It must have been an embarrassing moment for Armada, and the Prince knew full well that it was now just a question of getting Franco to name the day.

Juan Carlos's allies continued to put gentle pressure on the Caudillo. On 7 May, Fraga spoke to him about his age and the growing political vacuum. Franco listened politely, said nothing, then left for a ten-day, salmon-fishing expedition in Asturias. Before leaving, he received from Carrero Blanco a long report on the political situation. In it, as well as dealing with a series of problems including the emergence of ETA in the Basque Country and deteriorating relations with the Church, the admiral claimed that uncertainty about the post-Franco future was causing anxiety for 'the immense majority of Spaniards who have blind faith in their Caudillo'. He played on Franco's fears when he said that the enemies of the regime were waiting to strike in the event of him dying before securing the perpetuation of his regime. He stressed that Juan Carlos could be the solution.[51] Later on the same day Franco listened in silence to Federico Silva's monologue in favour of the Prince, replying shortly, 'I'm working on it. I'll do it.'

On 22 May, it was López Rodó who urged the immediate designation of Juan Carlos to which Franco said that he was in total agreement. On 28 May, the eve of his own 80th birthday, Camilo Alonso Vega had a long conversation with Franco. He appealed to his old friend's pride in his achievements, saying, 'only those who are keen to see the destruction of the peace that we enjoy' wanted him to delay settling the succession in favour of Juan Carlos. He said that the wolves were ready to pounce when he died and that only the nomination of Juan Carlos could secure the survival of the regime. Franco said little but needed little convincing. Alonso Vega told López Rodó: 'Mission accomplished. I spoke to the Caudillo yesterday and my impressions couldn't be better. He reacted really well.' On the following day, Franco told Carrero Blanco that he would name Juan Carlos successor before the summer. A delighted López Rodó said to Silva Muñoz, 'It looks like the salmon has bitten.' By 6 June, López Rodó had given Carrero Blanco a draft nomination speech for Franco to use in the Cortes. Yet still he delayed, despite incessant pressure.[52]

This provoked gnawing anxiety for Juan Carlos. At the beginning of May, he had requested an audience in order to thank the Caudillo for his response to the death of Victoria Eugenia. He was still awaiting an answer from El Pardo six weeks later and he was due to spend a week in Estoril. López Rodó calmed his fears when they met on 16 June by telling him what Franco had said to Carrero Blanco about a nomination before the summer. At this, the Prince expressed concern about the likely hostility of his father. He tried to convince himself that all would be well by reflecting that Don Juan should surely have known that his own candidacy was doomed. Whatever his father's reaction, Juan Carlos had every intention of accepting the nomination. He clearly had plans for the future and asked the minister for his help in securing the evolution of Spain. Perhaps at this stage he genuinely believed that, once on the throne, he would turn to López Rodó as his Prime Minister.[53]

Just before leaving for Estoril with his family, the Prince finally got to see the Caudillo. Franco said, 'Come to see me when you get back because I shall have something important to tell you.' Juan Carlos must have had a very strong idea of what lay behind Franco's hint. Yet he claimed later that he put the dictator's words out of his mind and had forgotten them by the time he reached Estoril. Once there, his father mentioned rumours that Franco would soon name him as his royal successor. Juan Carlos told him that had heard the same from López Rodó. He sidestepped a potential row by dismissing the 'rumour' with the sophistry that, if a nomination were imminent, Franco would have told him when they met. When his father pressed him, 'So you know nothing specific?' he replied, 'No, absolutely nothing.' A suspicious Don Juan replied, 'You know something and you're hiding it from me. Won't you tell me?'

Don Juan wanted to believe his son because he remained confident that Franco would die before naming a successor and that the military would then place him on the throne. When Juan Carlos insisted that Franco's eventual plan was to nominate him, his irate father reminded him that he was the heir to the throne and reserved the right to revoke any decision by Franco. An exasperated Prince replied, 'You're absolutely right: I went to, and remain in, Spain because of your decision. And if you order me to leave or if you prohibit me from accepting, I'll pack my suitcases, and I'll get Sofi and the children and we'll come to Portugal, or I'll stay in the Army and just get on with my military career, but entirely outside of politics. I can't stay on in La Zarzuela if at the key moment, I'm called and don't accept. Just as long as you know that this would make it impossible for our family ever to regain the throne. I won't be King but nor will you. If I say no to Franco, he'll just turn to Alfonso. And then we can really say goodbye because he will put up with anything and swallow anything they put in front of him.'

Without fully realizing what his son was telling him about the situation in Madrid, Don Juan replied, 'Since your grandfather entrusted in me the rights of the dynasty, I have done nothing but sacrifice myself and fight so that the monarchy might be restored in Spain. For years, I've put up with all kinds; a wall of incomprehension and dirty tricks against me. And now it turns out that the problem is coming from my own son.' Juan Carlos responded hotly: 'I have not intrigued so that the nomination will fall on me. I agree that it would be better if you were the King, but if the decision is taken, what can we do about it? There is no possibility for you or rather, if there is, it is extremely risky.' Don Juan replied, 'Well in that case there's plenty you can do: make sure that nothing is done now, that everything is put off.'

This was, of course, ludicrous, since if Franco died before the situation was resolved, the chances of the monarchy being restored at all were slight in the extreme. Juan Carlos brutally pointed this out: 'It's not in my hands. And, if as I believe, I'm invited to accept, what will you do? Is there any solution other than what Franco decides? Are you capable of bringing back the monarchy?' Don Juan closed the discussion saying, 'Let's leave it. We're just talking for talking's sake. You'll see that they're pulling your leg and toying with you. There's no way that the General is thinking of designating a successor before he dies. It's an issue that, on his death, will have to be resolved by the generals.'[54]

Indeed, under pressure from Falangists and the supporters of both Don Juan and Carlos Hugo de Borbón Parma, Franco continued to dither, fearful, as he confided to Carrero Blanco, of deserting some of his loyal followers. With the technocrat ministers getting more impatient, finally Franco told Carrero Blanco on 26 June that he would make the announcement before 18 July 1969. However, on 30 June, when Antonio Iturmendi, the President of the Cortes, asked him when the ceremony would be, he said indecisively, 'It could be either before or after the summer.' At last, on 3 July, he told Carrero Blanco that on 17 July he would make the announcement and make Juan Carlos a Brigadier-General in the three armed services.

It was probably on the same day that Franco called the young Mayor of Jérez, Juan Carlos's old friend from his school days, Miguel Primo de Rivera y Urquijo, to El Pardo. Intriguingly, he informed Primo de Rivera of his decision and ordered him not to tell Juan Carlos. Perhaps the Caudillo did so because he felt that the approval of Miguel, as the nephew of José Antonio Primo de Rivera, the founder of the Falange, mattered. It is more likely that he did so because he knew that Miguel was a close friend of the Prince and would certainly be unable to keep the secret from him. When he finally informed the Prince, he intended to demand an immediate answer. Whatever the reason, Miguel Primo de Rivera jumped in his car and, constantly looking in his rearview mirror to see if he was being followed, sped to La Zarzuela. There he found Juan Carlos by the swimming pool. When the Prince heard his news, he gave a whoop of delight. Both jumped into the pool, although the Mayor of Jérez was still wearing the morning suit required for visitors to El Pardo.[55]

After Franco had informed Carrero Blanco, the delighted Vice-President told López Rodó. He too set off at high speed, determined to be the first to tell the Prince. López Rodó said simply that the announcement would be in the second half of July. When told about the proposed promotion, Juan Carlos expressed embarrassment about the likely reaction of his fellow cadets from the military academies when they saw him in a brigadier-general's uniform. Whether López Rodó or Primo de Rivera arrived first is difficult to say, not least because the Prince managed to give both messengers the impression that they were the first to bring him the news. It was a skill learned from Franco. Importantly, he had not heard the news from the one person who really mattered – Franco. Nevertheless, he quickly mobilized his staff to start the process of preparing his part and his acceptance speech in the probable ceremony.[56]

Knowing that the designation was imminent could only sharpen the Prince's anxieties about the probable repercussions within his family. His mother, Doña María de las Mercedes, was supporting him and frequently telephoned him to ask how things were progressing towards his nomination. Don Juan, in contrast, remained happily convinced that Franco would never name a successor. During his conversation with López Rodó on 3 July, the Prince told him that the acrimonious encounter in Estoril had left him no wiser about what action Don Juan might take when the announcement was made. By the following day, thanks to a leak emanating from the Minister of Industry, the technocrat Gregorio López Bravo, he knew the exact date. Juan Carlos had more pressing problems on his mind than just his father's reaction. Knowing that the designation still had to be accepted by the Cortes, he arranged to meet the veteran hardliner José Antonio Girón de Velasco, the man who could influence most Falangist votes. The intermediary was the Prince's lifelong friend, Nicolás Franco Pasqual del Pobil, whose father, the Caudillo's brother, had been for many years the Spanish Ambassador in Portugal. They had lunch in the famous Madrid restaurant, Mayte Comodoro. After some polite but indecisive skirmishing, Girón announced that he would do whatever Franco said. Just to make sure, the Prince's staff, his private secretary Jacobo Cano, Armada and the Marqués de Mondéjar also took Girón to lunch and reassured him of Juan Carlos's fidelity to the Caudillo and the regime.[57]

On 11 July, the Prince received the portly Pedro Sainz Rodríguez in La Zarzuela. Shrewdly, Don Juan's lifelong counsellor said that, if Franco made the offer, Juan Carlos must accept. The Prince had no need of this advice but he was perhaps reassured to be told that, back in Estoril, his mother would be doing everything possible to keep her husband calm. Sainz Rodríguez claimed that he would be able to restrain the inevitable anger of Don Juan. Nevertheless, knowing Sainz Rodríguez to be a leaky sieve, Juan Carlos said nothing about the imminence of the announcement, only that there were many rumours in the air.[58]

There is some confusion over the date on which Franco finally informed the Prince of his decision. Most historians have followed López Rodó who, in his memoirs, places it on 12 July but it is probable that this is an error. Alfonso Armada remembers the meeting as taking place on 15 July, as did Jesús Pabón. Moreover, both the Prince's letter of explanation to his father and his later narrative to José Luis de Vilallonga, date the meeting on 15 July. If the encounter did take place on the 12th, it would mean that the Prince then delayed three days before passing the news on to his father. Such a delay would obviously imply duplicity and cowardice on Juan Carlos's part, which would have been entirely uncharacteristic. In any case, it would provide an example of the most unusual carelessness on Franco's part. He was determined that the news should come as an utter surprise to Don Juan and it would therefore have been extremely imprudent to have told the Prince on the 12th and only then begin arrangements for informing the other key protagonists. Given the traffic in gossip between El Pardo insiders and the Madrid-based Privy Councillors of Don Juan, the news would have been out long before it was taken officially to Estoril. Accordingly, the following narrative is based on the assumption that it was at 4 p.m. on Tuesday 15 July, when Franco finally received the Prince and gave him the anticipated news.[59]

The Caudillo told him that, with this nomination, he intended to guarantee the continuity of his regime. Juan Carlos said later that he was staggered by the news and asked the Caudillo, 'But, General, why didn't you tell me when I came to see you before going to Estoril?' Franco replied sanctimoniously, 'Because I would have asked you to give me your word of honour not to reveal the secret and, if your father had asked you, you would have had to lie. And I preferred that you should not lie to your father.' He insisted that Juan Carlos gave him an immediate reply.

The Prince hesitated only briefly, knowing full well that if he said 'no', Franco would then turn not to his father but to another candidate, probably Alfonso de Borbón y Dampierre. As Juan Carlos had long known that he would, he accepted. It was an emotional meeting. Franco was particularly pleased by the Prince's repeated assertion that, when he had sworn on the flag, he had undertaken to serve Spain. As he took his leave, Franco embraced him.[60]

When Juan Carlos said that he must inform his father at once, Franco asked him not to do so and showed the Prince the letter that he had written to Don Juan. Worried about the impact on his father, Juan Carlos had asked that the letter be taken to Estoril by someone capable of softening the blow for his father. Franco said that there was no need. In fact, it was already on its way. Franco's apparently high-minded concern for the relations between Juan Carlos and his father barely concealed an element of cruelty. The last of his many delays had achieved his final revenge for the Lausanne Manifesto – a rupture between Don Juan and his son.[61] Juan Carlos was deeply apprehensive as to how to break the news of what could only seem like treachery. Having been instructed not to telephone his father, he did in fact call his mother to whom he briefly broke the news. Instantly perceiving the appalling situation for both her husband and her son, she understood that her role would be to try to safeguard the unity of her family.[62] Juan Carlos wrote a letter of explanation to his father while ordering the Marqués de Mondéjar to get a reservation on that night's Lusitania Express to Lisbon. It was a simple, affectionate letter asking for his father's blessing. In the hope of dissipating his father's expected anger, the Prince was anxious for his letter to arrive before the coldly formal one sent by Franco.

It would be touch and go. At around midday on the day before his meeting with the Prince, Monday 14 July, Franco had received José Antonio Giménez-Arnau, who in March had succeeded Ibáñez Martín as Ambassador to Portugal. The Caudillo handed over an open envelope containing his letter for Don Juan. There was a meeting of Don Juan's Privy Council scheduled for the following day in Estoril. To make sure that it would not be able to respond to Juan Carlos's nomination, Franco instructed

Giménez-Arnau not to deliver the letter until after the meeting was over. It took considerable insistence by the Ambassador to persuade Franco that a document of such historical importance should be sealed with wax. It was a minor detail that revealed Franco's insensitive disregard for Don Juan. The embarrassment of Giménez-Arnau was intensified in the course of his return to Lisbon that afternoon. Both at Barajas Airport and on board the plane, he had to make polite chit-chat with some of Don Juan's Privy Councillors who were *en route* to the meeting in Estoril. They were cheerfully unaware that Franco was about to make the announcement. For others, like Pabón, news of Giménez-Arnau's lightning visit to El Pardo was confirmation that the Prince's designation as successor was imminent. Fortunately for Juan Carlos, on the evening of 15 July, Don Juan would be hosting a dinner for the Privy Councillors who had attended the meeting earlier. Accordingly, he could not receive Giménez-Arnau until the morning of Wednesday 16 July. The Prince's letter would arrive before Franco's.[63]

When Don Juan returned from the dinner, Doña María de las Mercedes told him about their son's telephone call earlier that evening. When, at 9.40 a.m. on the following morning, Mondéjar arrived with Juan Carlos's letter, he was greeted by a dignified but saddened Don Juan. The letter, significantly signed not 'Juanito' as the Prince had always been known within the family, but 'Juan Carlos' as he was officially known, is worth quoting in full:

Madrid 15 July 1960.

Dear Papa,

I've just come back from El Pardo where the Generalísimo had sent for me. And since it's not possible to speak on the telephone, I hasten to write you these lines to be taken to you by Nicolás who is leaving in a moment on the Lusitania Express. The moment that I have so often told you might arrive has come and you will be able to appreciate the effect it had on me when Franco informed me of his decision to propose me to the Cortes as his successor with the title of King.

It is very hard to express my concerns at this moment. I really love you and you have given me the best lessons of how to serve and love Spain. These lessons are what obliges me, as a Spaniard and as a member of the dynasty, to make the greatest sacrifice of my life and, following my conscience and, in so doing, carrying out what I believe to be a service to the Fatherland, to accept the nomination so that the monarchy can return to Spain and guarantee our people, for the future, with God's help, many years of peace and prosperity.

At this time, so emotional and momentous for me, I want to reiterate to you my filial devotion and my immense affection, praying to God to maintain above all else the unity of our family and I want to ask you for your blessing so that it will help me always to fulfil, for the good of Spain, the duties imposed upon me by the mission for which I have been called.

I end these lines with a strong embrace and, loving you more than ever, I ask you again, with all my soul, for your blessing and your love.

Juan Carlos

To conceal his distress, Don Juan said little to Mondéjar. He did, however, ask him about the stance of the Army, to which Mondéjar replied, 'Sir, the Army has never said anything about you.' In contrast, shortly after returning to his hotel, Mondéjar received a telephone call from Doña María de las Mercedes who said, 'Tell Juanito that I am really pleased. Congratulate him. And let him know that I'll make sure that nothing silly happens here.'[64] Thus, by the time that the exquisitely elegant Ambassador reached Villa Giralda, there was nothing new for him to tell Don Juan. Luis María Anson, who was with Don Juan at the time, later described the neatly turned-out Giménez-Arnau as 'the lackey with the putrid smile'. Already defeated, Don Juan accepted Franco's letter and threw it on a table without opening it. His bitterness and disappointment were palpable. Clearly his son's letter had not diminished his inevitable sense of failure and betrayal. Giménez-Arnau tried to soften the blow with some prepared remarks about Alfonso XIII's abdication on 15 January 1941. With tears in his eyes and, in a voice of great sadness, Don Juan said, 'Don't bother, José Antonio. I know you and I know you're a decent person and you have no need to fear any rancour on my part, but, obviously, you can just imagine . . .'[65]

Franco's text was simple but devastating. He made the most fleeting acknowledgement of the distress that its contents would cause Don Juan. He then pompously and coldly reminded him that royalty was destined to make sacrifices and that therefore he should ignore any advice to oppose the Caudillo's will. He followed up with a patronizing explanation that this was not about the restoration of the old monarchy but about the 'installation' of a new monarchy to complete the political development of the regime. After reading this exquisitely humiliating text, Don Juan just said, 'What a bastard!' Desolate in his disappointment, he sat slumped in silence and refused to take calls from his son. Juan Carlos rang Villa Giralda three times without managing to speak to his father. Giménez-Arnau had hardly arrived back at the Embassy when Juan Carlos telephoned him. He was burning to know how Don Juan had reacted to Franco's letter. He was deeply upset by what the Ambassador had to tell him.[66]

Nevertheless, the preparations for his nomination were now moving apace. Late on 15 July, Carrero Blanco and the President of the Cortes, Antonio Iturmendi, went to La Zarzuela to show Juan Carlos the text of the law naming him as successor. He was delighted to see that there was an article granting him the title of Príncipe de Asturias. However, after years of being told that this title was unacceptable to Franco because it signified that his father was King, he doubted if it would be permitted. Doña Sofía, using the example of her own family, the House of Greece, suggested that an appropriate title would be 'Príncipe de España'. Simultaneously, López Rodó suggested to Carrero Blanco the same formula.[67]

At first, egged on by Areilza and Sainz Rodríguez, Don Juan believed that Juan Carlos had betrayed him. Areilza was quoted as saying, 'I never trusted that kid an inch.' Relations between father and son were strained for some time afterwards. Areilza, Sainz Rodríguez and García Trevijano drew up a declaration by Don Juan that was dated 19 July but published on the symbolic date of 18 July. Describing himself as a mere spectator of what had gone on, the declaration stressed his belief that the monarch should be King of all Spaniards, above groups and parties, based on popular support and committed to individual and collective liberties. He thus implicitly denounced his son's monarchy as irrevocably linked to the dictatorship. The declaration had been issued against the advice of Doña María de las Mercedes and confirmed Juan Carlos's worst fears about his father's negative reaction. Areilza continued to express his outrage to anyone who would listen and thus provided numerous police reports to amuse Franco. His disgust was perhaps with himself for having hitched his wagon to the wrong horse. Nevertheless, he published a statement denouncing the solution as inflicting irreparable damage on the monarchy. None of this shook the Prince's conviction that he was doing the right thing. Moreover, he could draw consolation from the fact that his father now dissolved his Privy Council. He had not raised a banner of opposition to his son.[68]

On the other hand, nor had he abdicated. In the event of things going badly for Juan Carlos, his father remained in play as the legitimate heir to the throne and the advocate of a democratic monarchy. Don Juan contemplated going to live in Canada in order to make things easier for his son but he was dissuaded by Sainz Rodríguez. He said, 'Don Juanito's monarchy will come when Franco kicks the bucket and, if we don't do something, it will last about as long as a bag of sweets at a school gate.' His view was that 'Operación Príncipe' as realized by Carrero Blanco and López Rodó had established a monarchical sequel to Franco, but that Don Juan had a part to play in ensuring that his son's tenure of the throne would be enduring. He suggested that Don Juan's task was to persuade the democratic left to be patient and give Juan Carlos time to prepare the transition.[69]

On 19 July, Juan Carlos visited Franco to read to him the acceptance speech that he planned to make before the Cortes. He was delighted and asked the Prince to read it again. He made him remove just one passage, in which he expressed filial devotion and paid tribute to Don Juan's patriotism.[70] Two days later, a beaming Franco announced his decision to the cabinet. He said: 'The years pass. I am 76, I will soon be 77. My life is in God's hands. I wanted to confront this reality.' After speaking in the warmest terms of Juan Carlos, he read out his letter to Don Juan. He then said, 'Don Juan's reaction was to be expected. He is someone who follows the last person to speak to him, and in this case, the last ones to speak to him are Sainz Rodríguez and Areilza. And we know what can be expected from them. So, Don Juan's declaration is the best proof for me that he was entirely useless.' The hardline Falangist opponents of Juan Carlos hastened to mount a last-ditch defence against his nomination. The device proposed by Solís in the cabinet was a secret Cortes ballot. He hoped to use his control of *Movimiento* patronage to engineer an unfavourable vote. This could then be interpreted flatteringly to Franco as an indication of Juan Carlos's inadequacy as a successor to such a providential figure. Franco, backed by Carrero Blanco, Alonso Vega and the technocrats, would have none of it. He wanted to see each *Procurador* vote individually.[71]

On the evening of 21 July, Juan Carlos finally managed to speak to his father on the telephone. Don Juan responded frostily: 'This all means that you knew when you came here and you chose not to tell me.' Juan Carlos protested his innocence but his father, for the moment, refused to believe him. The Prince made every effort to be affectionate and his father was still inconsolable.[72] Despite this small beginning of an improvement in their relations, Don Juan obliged his son to return to him the insignia of Príncipe de Asturias.[73]

The designation of Juan Carlos as Príncipe de España, and not Príncipe de Asturias, underlined the extent to which the *Ley de Sucesión* broke with both the continuity and the legitimacy of the Borbón line. The new monarchy was intended to be Franco's and Franco's alone. This would always cause bitterness for Don Juan. He might have been prepared to be King for a day and then abdicate in favour of Juan Carlos if only to safeguard the legitimacy and continuity of the Borbón dynasty. He reflected later: 'The truth is that each disappointment or defeat deepened my conviction that my aspirations as King were being blocked off. I began to think about a quiet life, watching my grandchildren grow. The last bastion of hope was that a formula could be found whereby I would be recognized as King and then immediately abdicate in favour of my son.' Franco could have negotiated such a solution but that would have meant renouncing his full revenge on Don Juan. And, with such a gesture, the monarchy in Spain would have been restored rather than installed, and thus less Francoist.[74]

The ceremony at the Cortes on 22 July took place in suffocating heat – there being no air-conditioning. In his emotional speech, tears running down his cheeks and audible sobs interrupting his mumbling delivery, Franco took pride in the precision of the instruments now created for the succession. 'Aware of my responsibility before God and before History, and having weighed with due objectivity the qualities found in the person of Prince Juan Carlos de Borbón y Borbón, who as a member of the dynasty that ruled Spain for several centuries, has given a clear demonstration of loyalty to the principles and institutions of the Regime, is closely tied to the Army, Navy and Air Force, in which he forged his character, and who, over the last 20 years, has been perfectly prepared for the high mission for which he might be called, and who, moreover, fulfils all the conditions laid down by Article 11 of the *Ley de Sucesión* regarding the Headship of State, I have decided to propose him to the nation as my successor.' The *Procuradores*, no doubt relieved to have their doubts finally resolved, interrupted his speech 11 times to applaud frenetically and, at the end, stood and chanted, 'Franco! Franco! Franco!' The proposal was accepted by 491 votes to 19 against, with nine abstentions. Those who risked Franco's hostility to vote against were Torcuato Luca de Tena, the editor of *ABC*, General Rafael García Valiño and a few Carlists and Falangists.[75] The event passed virtually unnoticed by the bulk of the population who were more interested in the televised film of the moonwalk by the astronauts of *Apollo XI* which had taken place two days earlier. No crowds gathered at the Cortes and there were only small Republican demonstrations in working-class areas of the large cities.[76]

The prospect of swearing fidelity to the fundamental laws had caused Juan Carlos considerable anxiety. With the encouragement of his wife, he had cultivated Franco and actively sought the nomination. At the same time, he intended to introduce some kind of future democratic reform. He had revealed this over several years in conversations with British diplomats, with Lord Mountbatten, with American journalists and with progressive Spaniards. Now, he wanted reassurance that the oath of loyalty would not chain him to the regime in its present form. His doubts were assuaged on 18 July in the course of a long visit to La Zarzuela by his one-time tutor and counsellor, Torcuato Fernández-Miranda. Both were heavy smokers and as the fumes got thicker, they went through the draft of the Prince's proposed speech. He reassured the apprehensive Juan Carlos that this oath would not prevent a future process of democratization and that Article 10 of the *Ley de Sucesión* permitted all the fundamental laws to be reformed or even repealed – although much would depend on arcane exegesis of Franco's often contradictory constitutional texts.[77]

On the morning of 23 July, at a private acceptance ceremony in La Zarzuela, in the presence of Antonio María Oriol, the Minister of Justice, and the President of the Cortes, Antonio Iturmendi, the Prince paid fulsome tribute to the Caudillo: 'Educated in the Spain that arose from 18 July, I have witnessed step by step the important achievements that have been attained under the magisterial command of the Generalísimo.' He swore to ensure that the principles of the *Movimiento* and the fundamental laws would be observed. He did so in the confidence derived from Torcuato Fernández-Miranda's assurance that these laws could be amended.[78]

Juan Carlos had invited Alfonso de Borbón y Dampierre to be one of his witnesses, by way of neutralizing him. Alfonso not only accepted but also successfully appealed to his father, Don Jaime, not to make any inopportune declarations. The Caudillo later rewarded him for this service by giving him the post of Ambassador to Sweden. The acceptance ceremony was attended by the editors of the principal Madrid newspapers, including Torcuato Luca de Tena of *ABC*. Somewhat nervous after his negative vote in the Cortes, he was greatly touched when Juan Carlos made a point of going up to him and saying, 'I want to thank you for what you did yesterday for my father by voting no.'[79]

In the afternoon, Juan Carlos accompanied Franco to the Cortes. Before leaving La Zarzuela, he sent a message to his parents saying he was off to do his duty but his heart was with them. His mother rang back to send her good wishes for his speech and reassuring him that his father would gradually accept the situation. The Prince was intensely nervous and, in the car, requested Franco's permission to light a cigarette. His speech was relatively short and simple. He began by saying, 'I receive from His Excellency the Head of State and Generalísmo Franco the political legitimacy born of 18 July 1936,' and ended with a plea for God's help.[80] He spoke strongly and naturally, having learned the speech by heart. The *Procuradores* and ministers present were delighted, and not just by the contrast with the marathon speeches of the Caudillo. The contents of the speech were entirely Francoist. Where Don Juan had made his slogan the determination to be King of all Spaniards, Juan Carlos was saying that he accepted nomination as King of the victors in the Spanish Civil War. The aplomb and assurance of his performance came as a surprise to all those who thought of him as shy.[81] The applause was prolonged. The weeping Caudillo was especially pleased. In the car returning to El Pardo, Franco said to him: 'I didn't know, Your Highness, that you spoke so well,' to which the Prince replied, 'General, you have given me so many surprises that I had to give you at least one.'[82] On the following day, Franco issued a decree naming Juan Carlos honorary Brigadier-General of the Army and the Air Force and Rear-Admiral of the Navy.[83]

Early that morning, an embittered Don Juan had wanted to be alone with his chagrin. He had gone out on his yacht and sailed far to the north. On reaching Figueira da Foz on Cape Carvoeiro, he had turned into the river Mondego towards Coimbra. Tying up at the village of Montemor O Velho, he had gone into a bar, ordered a bottle of whiskey and watched the Spanish broadcast of the speech. Afterwards he said, 'My Juanito has read very well,' a barbed reference to the fact that the speech had clearly been written by others. Nevertheless, he had the magnanimity to tele-phone his son that evening to congratulate him.[84]

The event had been an enormous triumph for the technocrats over the Falangists. Their euphoria was palpable. However, if they believed that Juan Carlos would be committed to their objective of an updated Francoism, they would be disappointed.[85] The sup-porters of Don Juan could not have been more outraged. José Luis de Vilallonga wrote dismissively of the 'impudence' with which Juan Carlos, 'in a few unhappy sentences, condemned himself and the monarchy'.[86] The reaction of the left could not have been more hostile. The Communist Party, *Partido Communista de España* (PCE), denounced the operation as Franco's effort to continue ruling after his death. Its newspaper, *Mundo Obrero*, claimed prophetically that the nomination, marking as it did the victory of the Opus Dei technocrats over the Falangists, would foster dissension within the upper reaches of the regime. Rather less prophetically, it declared that: 'The monarchy that Franco is "installing" is a reactionary and Fascist monarchy . . . By proclaim-ing Juan Carlos his successor and future king, Franco has destroyed every possibility that the monarchy had in Spain, ruining the illusions of certain sectors concerning the possibility of a democratic monarchy.'[87]

The PSOE issued a manifesto denouncing the nomination as the last desperate bid for survival by those who had destroyed democracy 30 years earlier. Juan Carlos was dismissed as 'an operetta prince' and the entire operation as an attempt to 'impose, in grotesque medieval theatre, a future cardboard king'. The Mao-ist faction *PCE-Marxista-Leninista* described the Prince as 'a Francoist abortion and a faithful lackey of his Yankee masters'. The influential sage, the exiled Salvador de Madariaga, wrote an article, '*Die spanische monarchie*', that was published in the *Neue Zürcher Zeitung* and reprinted in many other European and Latin American newspapers. In it, he said that: 'Spain will never accept a monarch who betrays his father and openly declares that he will be the King of the victors in a civil war.'[88]

Juan Carlos was euphoric in the following days, but he was fully aware that now his work had to begin in earnest. Two decades later, he revealed to José Luis de Vilallonga, now converted into a dedicated sycophant, how he felt about what lay ahead of him. 'I know that my father suffered during what was an unpleasant and frustrating time for him but very few people ever mention how I suffered before swearing fidelity to principles that I knew that I could never respect. What Torcuato [Fernández-Miranda] told me about every law carrying within itself the principle of its own reform and that nothing is eternal and that everything could be changed legally all sounded very nice, but one thing is to speak about it and another is to do it. If to that you add the pain that was caused me by having to go against my father, you will understand that all of that was pretty much a nightmare for me.'[89]

His task was to ensure that his nomination was not just the last act of one historical epic but also the first act of another. The reaction of the left was underlined by hostile slogans painted on walls in many Spanish cities. To succeed Franco, he needed to ensure that the machinery of government would work for him. That meant securing the support of the majority of the political class, of the civil service and the *Movimiento*. He was aware that the acclamation that he had enjoyed in the Cortes could be fragile. His position depended on the favour of Franco. He knew that he should not risk the prestige of the monarchy by combining, like Franco, the posts of Head of State and of the government. López Rodó advised him to consolidate his position and do nothing that might provoke the suspicion of the Francoist hierarchy. Shortly before his son's nomination, Don Juan had spoken to Giménez-Arnau about his belief that Franco would not designate a successor before he died. The Ambassador asked what he would do if the dictator died, as it were, intestate. With what can only be described as thoughtless optimism, Don Juan had replied, 'Within the hour, I'd be in Madrid.' After 20 years in Spain, his son had a greater awareness of the complications involved in taking over from Franco, with a political apparatus in which hostility to the monarchy was rife.[90]

1969 saw the 30th anniversary of Franco's victory in the Civil War. He had devoted those 30 years to keeping alive the divisions between victors and vanquished. Spain had changed massively in the latter half of that period, thanks to external circumstances and the efforts of the technocrats. Prosperity had taken some of the heat out of the simmering hatreds born of the war. Nevertheless, until barely four months before Juan Carlos's nomination, a state of emergency prevailed. The regime that Juan Carlos had just sworn to perpetuate remained every bit a dictatorship.

There can be no doubt that Franco had great faith in Juan Carlos and had come to like and respect him over the years. That faith was shared neither by the left-wing opposition nor by many on the Falangist wing of the regime, nor even, in the late 1960s, by Juan Carlos himself. Despite the support of López Rodó and Carrero Blanco, his uncertainty was reflected in a reserved and melancholic manner which gave the impression that he was 'a guest who wasn't sure if he was meant to stay to dinner'.[91] In fact, though in private conversation and public speeches Franco had made it obvious that he expected his successor to continue his work, he had never given any explicit instructions to Juan Carlos. He intended that Juan Carlos would be a figurehead, a ceremonial Head of State, with an iron chancellor, Admiral Carrero Blanco, to keep him on the path of true Francoism. A few days after his nomination, the Prince received a handwritten note from the dictator which said: 'I am certain that you will always serve Spain loyally and that you will honour and fulfil the oath to respect the fundamental laws of the kingdom that you made before the Cortes and that, when the time comes for your coronation, you must repeat.' Juan Carlos took the note as a warning that 'meant that I was being closely watched and that I better not leave the path marked out for me'.[92]

From now on, Juan Carlos visited Franco every week, usually in the late afternoon on Mondays. Whenever he asked for advice, the Caudillo would reply: 'What's the point of Your Highness expecting me to tell you? You will not be able to govern like me,' or 'I haven't the faintest idea, Your Highness. The only thing that you won't be able to do is act as I would.' What he meant was: 'You who didn't conquer power. You who didn't win a civil war. You who have power only because I gave it. You who will be watched over by Carrero and others. You who will be subject to the limitations imposed by the *Consejo del Reino* and the Cortes as I am not.'[93] When Franco spoke to Pacón about Salvador de Madariaga's article, he defended his choice of Juan Carlos as that which: 'provides me with the most guarantees of defending the regime which emerged victorious from the Crusade'. Referring to both the Prince and his wife, he affirmed his faith that they would not betray him with any democratic deviations. His words were almost exactly those of his note to Juan Carlos: 'I am certain that they will serve Spain with total loyalty and that he will honour the oath that he took before the Cortes, and which he will make again when he becomes King of Spain, to fulfil the fundamental laws.'[94]

Franco rarely gave the Prince direct advice other than through the oblique method of relating anecdotes of his own experiences.[95] The Prince had learned from the Caudillo the value of the dictum that, 'You are the master of what you don't say and the slave of what you do.' Juan Carlos commented later: 'Why did I always keep silent? Why did I never say anything? Because it was a period when no one, not even me, dared speak. Self-censorship – or prudence, if you like – was the norm.'[96] Don Juan had always maintained that the monarchy could not survive if it were too closely identified with Franco. Juan Carlos had risked rupture with his father precisely because he knew that, without such close identification, he would never have been nominated as King. It would soon become clear, through the fog of necessary discretion, that the Prince had not rejected his father's views. Rather, he was more sensitive to the problem of timing.

For some months after Juan Carlos's acceptance of the nomination, Don Juan was still not speaking properly to his son. He remained convinced that he had been betrayed. Finally, at the end of 1969, they met in Lausanne and had a frank discussion. Juan Carlos gave vent to a lifetime's bitterness when he said: 'Since I was eight years old I was nothing more than a minion. I was your pawn. I only ever did what you told me to. You wanted me to go and study in Spain and I studied in Spain. Then, because you fell out with Franco, you wanted me to leave Spain and I left Spain.

You renewed your relations with him and I went back again. Between the two of you, Franco and you, my life was planned out to suit you. No one asked me what I wanted or didn't want. It was given to me on a plate already decided. All I had to do was obey. I never did anything but obey you. In everything, I did what you told me. You helped make me what I am. It was from you that I learned to work for Spain and for the restoration of the monarchy. The fact that I was named "successor with the title of King" is a consequence of the fact that you put me in Spain. I didn't ask to go. You decided for me. And it is inevitable that what had to happen happened. But you, Papa, you don't see it because you have counsellors who don't let you see it. Anyway, if you believe something else, tell me. I'm listening.'

Don Juan brushed aside his son's remarks, obsessed only with the thought that he had deceived him. Juan Carlos replied, 'Papa, my situation is the consequence of your decision. I have always been a pawn. Objectively, I have a greater chance of being on the throne than you. But I am not sure. Franco could change his mind. What I can tell you is that we need each other. Me on the inside and you on the outside. Because here, on the inside, I am surrounded and watched all the time, I can't have contacts with the opposition. You, on the outside, can. And only in that way can I make a democratic monarchy, for all Spaniards, irrespective of the way that they think.' His father took a while to be convinced but he came around and embraced his son. Thereafter, according to Juan Carlos, Don Juan became his closest adviser. In fact, the tensions in their relationship were far from resolved.[97]

SIX

Under Suspicion
1969–1974

There now opened for the Prince the most difficult period of his long march to the throne. By accepting the nomination of Franco, he had earned the suspicion and contempt of the majority of the democratic opposition, including the supporters of his father. At the same time, his determination to carry out democratic reform could not remain entirely a secret within the regime. Accordingly, he was the object of outright hostility in many Francoist circles, especially within the Falange and within El Pardo. La Zarzuela was under intense vigilance. The delicacy of the Prince's situation was exacerbated as the regime itself came to feel besieged.

If Franco had hoped that, with the nomination of a successor, he could enjoy a period of tranquillity, he faced a rude awakening in the second half of 1969. ETA remained an ominous threat. More immediately, the Falangists within the *Movimiento* were about to wreak revenge for their defeat at the hands of the technocrats. In mid-August 1969, there erupted the political volcano known as the MATESA scandal. MATESA (*Maquinaría Textil del Norte de España Sociedad Anónima*) was, as its name suggested, a company manufacturing textile machinery in Pamplona in northern Spain. Under its director, Juan Vilá Reyes, MATESA had developed a shuttleless loom and exported it with great success to Europe, Latin America and the USA. To qualify for export credits, subsidiary companies were set up in Latin America which ordered large numbers of looms. Financial irregularities were discovered in late 1968, and it was alleged that the subsidiaries and their orders were a fraudulent device to secure the credits.[1] Vilá Reyes claimed that it was only the accusations themselves that caused genuine orders to his subsidiaries to be cancelled. The *Movimiento* press unleashed a stream of attacks on the techno-crats, with *Arriba* denouncing what it called 'a national disaster'.[2]

With Juan Carlos now named as successor, Solís was frantically seizing the last chance to break the hegemony of the group of Opus Dei technocrats before the post-Franco future began. Solís's operation backfired badly, since Franco did not believe that the ministers linked to Opus Dei acted as a sinister independent block. He boasted to Pacón that: 'Their loyalty to the regime and to me personally is absolute, and above all, they are perfect gentlemen.' He was outraged at the attempt by the *Movimiento* press to pro-voke a major political scandal.[3] In the event, the two ministers who had jurisdiction over the issues at stake, Espinosa San Martín in Finance and García Moncó in Commerce, resigned and the two ministers implicated in the generation of the scandal, Fraga at Information and Solís as Secretary-General of the *Movimiento*, were also dropped in the cabinet changes of 29 October 1969. The new cabinet was essentially picked by Carrero Blanco from a list supplied largely by López Rodó and Silva Muñoz.[4]

The sleek and dynamic 'regime pin-up', Gregorio López Bravo, previously Minister of Industry, for whom Franco had developed a paternal affection, was given his choice of ministries and selected Foreign Affairs. The appointment of greatest significance for Juan Carlos was the new Secretary-General of the *Movimiento*, the diminutive, dapper and sinuously intelligent Torcuato Fernández-Miranda, who had been his tutor and had become his close adviser. Many of the new ministers were López Rodó protégés and could therefore be expected to be totally loyal to Juan Carlos. This was especially true of the new Ministers of Industry, José María López de Letona; of Finance, Alberto Monreal Luque; of Commerce, Enrique Fontana Codina; of Housing, Vicente Mortes Alfonso; and of Agriculture, Tomás Allende y García Baxter. General Camilo Alonso Vega retired and his replacement as Minister of the Interior, the military lawyer, Tomás Garicano Goñi, already had close connections with the Prince from his time as Civil Gov-ernor of Barcelona. Since all the cabinet's members came from the two conservative Catholic pressure groups, Opus Dei and the

Asociación Católica Nacional de Propagandistas, and were all committed more or less to Juan Carlos, it was known as the 'monochrome government'. Even the new Minister for the Army, General Juan Castañón de Mena, was close to Juan Carlos.[5] Both Franco and Carrero Blanco were happy to have a technocratic team provided by López Rodó. However, as soon as it ran into problems, their essentially reactionary instincts would be reasserted.

Franco's hopes that the new cabinet could secure him some peace and quiet were soon shattered by Falangist tantrums. The intra-regime squabbles over MATESA went far beyond the immediate isssue. In part, it was a question of competition for the spoils of power. However, it also reflected growing unease about labour, student and regionalist unrest. Franco's supporters were beginning to break up into factions which reflected not the traditional divisions into Falangists, monarchists, Catholics and so on, but rather conflicting, and kaleidoscopically changing, perceptions of how best to survive the imminent disappearance of Franco. The technocrats hoped that prosperity and efficient administration would permit a painless transition to a Francoist monarchy under Juan Carlos. They were often called '*continuistas*'. Others, like Fraga, saw the scale of opposition as requiring reform of the political system. They were known as '*aperturistas*'. The boundaries between *continuistas* and *aperturistas* were constantly shifting. Others still believed that any modernization at all would destroy everything that they held dear, and so worked for a return to hardline Francoism. The readiness of these intransigent '*immovilistas*' to fight progress to the last led to them being known in Hitlerian terms as the 'bunker'. The bunker could count on sympathy among hardline Falangists of the older generation, the gilded youth that made up the terror squads and many extreme right-wing officers in the Armed Forces with the *generales azules* at their head.

Blind to the fact that the political instruments of his dictatorship were not adequate to cope with a dramatically different Spain, the Caudillo initially took it for granted that this cabinet would be capable of resolving the serious problems already on the agenda.

López Rodó's strategy of depoliticized adminstrative efficiency and economic prosperity was now in place, but it faced insuperable opposition from inside as well as outside the regime. There was unrest among the students and the workers. 1970 would be punctuated by increasingly fierce police violence against strikes and demonstrations. ETA was active. Priests who supported workers were attacked by parallel terror squads using various names, of which the best known were the *Guerrilleros de Cristo Rey* (Warriors of Christ the King). It was widely believed that they were organized within Carrero Blanco's more or less private intelligence service, the *Servicio de Documentación de la Presidencia del Gobierno*. The *Guerrilleros* were linked to the Neo-Fascist political association *Fuerza Nueva* (New Force), led by Blas Piñar, a member of the *Consejo Nacional* of the *Movimiento* and a friend of Carrero Blanco. The cabinet acquiesced in this violence because the existence of a wild extreme right let the government present itself as somehow belonging to the centre. Nonetheless, Tomás Garicano Goñi protested to Franco about the dangers of these extremists.[6] Inevitably, and soon, the inability of the 'monochrome' team to settle the ferment of Spanish society would open the way, with Franco's approval, to a return of the repressive brutality of the post Civil War period.

Juan Carlos would come under increasing pressure because, despite having originally sponsored the domination of the technocrats, when faced with the crises of the early 1970s, both Franco and Carrero Blanco instinctively returned to the siege mentality of the 1940s. This was, in Franco's case, a reflection of the success of the bunker in transmitting its ideas through the Caudillo's immediate circle. From the end of the 1960s onwards, they mounted a two-pronged assault in El Pardo against the planned Francoist monarchy under Juan Carlos. First, they started a whispering campaign against Opus Dei and the cabinet. Then, they began to try to undermine Juan Carlos's position by pushing the cause of Don Alfonso de Borbón y Dampierre, now Ambassador to Sweden. Alfonso was soon to be engaged to Franco's eldest grandchild, María del Carmen Martínez-Bordiu, a great favourite of Doña Carmen. They pointed to Alfonso de Borbón y Dampierre's status as eldest son of Alfonso XIII's eldest son, his enthusiastic Francoism and his friendship with Franco's son-in-law, Cristóbal Martínez-Bordiu.[7] Alfonso, the *príncipe azul* (blue prince – a pun on prince charming and Falangist prince), excited the hopes of many on the extreme right and especially within the Caudillo's family. In general terms, the dynastic question provided a focus for the intrigues that increasingly occupied, and divided, the Francoist factions. By having Juan Carlos at his side each year in the annual victory parade, and by officially naming Juan Carlos as his successor, Franco had made his position clear. Nevertheless, the bunker drew solace from the fact that the Caudillo stood studiously aloof when extreme elements in the top echelons of the Falange put pressure on provincial governors to play down visits from Juan Carlos and to inflate those by Alfonso de Borbón.

All of this put Juan Carlos in a difficult position. He had little or no popular support. Years of glum, mute appearances next to Franco had led to the widespread assumption that he had neither intelligence nor courage. Jokes proliferated about his alleged stupidity. Wits named him 'Juan Carlos the Brief'. While waiting for Franco's decision as to his royal successor, he had been obliged to keep a humiliating silence. Afterwards, he had hoped to go on travelling around Spain and begin to speak with a more distinctive voice. His brother-in-law, Constantine, had struck a powerful chord when he lamented his own failure to make himself better known to ordinary Greeks. However, Juan Carlos had become frustrated because he found that cabinet ministers were deeply cautious about letting him make the trips that he wanted to. Juan Carlos wanted to safeguard some of the economic achievements of the regime, but he felt that a political system born of the Civil War needed to be changed to meet the needs of the modern society and economy that he had come to know. It was widely assumed that he was closely tied to the 'monochrome' cabinet, yet he was irked by the fact that its members, fearful for their own positions, were hampering his efforts to establish even limited independence. Accordingly, he had started to break free of the tutelage of some of the technocrats. He was particularly irritated because Gregorio López Bravo seemed determined to prevent him speaking freely on foreign trips. Perhaps the minister was concerned that the Prince would reveal too much. Although his relations with his father remained tense, there could soon be little doubt that Juan Carlos's ambition was to establish the kind of democratic monarchy associated with Don Juan.

In mid-January, the Prince had an unexpectedly revealing meeting with Carrero Blanco. It had always been clear that Franco expected the admiral to watch over Juan Carlos and ensure that he would not betray the principles of the *Movimiento*. His reactionary views on liberalism and freemasonry made that a daunting prospect for the Prince. Accordingly, Juan Carlos was astonished by what Carrero Blanco had to say. Both knew that Franco intended to make Carrero Blanco Prime Minister sooner rather than later. Now, the admiral assured the Prince that if, as expected, he was President of the Government when Franco died, he would immediately resign. When, as a courtesy, Juan Carlos made the usual formulaic protests, the 77-year-old insisted that nothing would persuade him to accept the role. Carrero Blanco lived to serve Franco and was a born number-two. He did not want to be Prime Minister under Franco. He would accept the post in obedience to an order by the Caudillo but, when Franco died, that would be the end of it. Now he suggested that Juan Carlos start to think about names like Torcuato Fernández-Miranda, Laureano López Rodó or Gregorio López Bravo.[8] On balance, this was good news for the Prince but not without a worrying dimension. He was relieved to know that he would be liberated from inevitable clashes with the admiral. On the other hand, he knew that the most difficult period of his future reign would be the first six to eighteen months. In the aftermath of Franco's death, to have as Prime Minister a figure of such impeccable Francoist credentials might be crucial to deflect the hostility of regime hardliners.

In fact, the bunker was right to be concerned about Juan Carlos's intentions. In early February, the *New York Times* published a well-informed article by Richard Eder, the paper's Madrid correspondent. Eder revealed that Juan Carlos had 'begun to let his acquaintances know that he does not accept the role apparently chosen for him: that of docile successor', and had privately admitted 'that he has no intention of presiding over a dictatorship'. The article not only mentioned that he was receiving visits from independents and members of the opposition but also had told them of his determination to open up the political system. When he had said to a visitor, 'I am Franco's heir but I am Spain's heir as well,' the Prince was sending a message that he planned significant political evolution after Franco. Moreover, the journalist repeated some of the Prince's off-the-record remarks to the effect that: 'only under some form of democracy will he have any real chance of remaining Spain's King'.[9]

At this stage, Juan Carlos had vague aspirations rather than a specific blueprint for the future. Nevertheless, he gave Federico Silva Muñoz, the dourly efficient Minister of Public Works, the firm impression that the article accurately reflected his intentions. He told him that he would be unable to rule without at least two or three political parties.[10] Aware of the outrage provoked by the article in many regime circles, Torcuato Fernández-Miranda persuaded the Prince to make a gesture to the bunker. On 10 February, he presided at the closing ceremony of a meeting of one of the most hardline organizations of the regime. This was the *Guardia de Franco*, the reserve militia of the Falange. Juan Carlos was presented with a gold yolk and arrows and made a short speech. Under the circumstances, it was a masterpiece that avoided an outright endorsement of the goals of the *Guardia de Franco* but stressed merely that he, like the assembled Falangists in the audience, had sworn loyalty to Franco and to the service of Spain. Juan Carlos learned a lot from his contacts with the ultra-right. He became aware that, even within the regime, there was considerable hostility to Carrero Blanco. This was startlingly brought home to him when the new President of the Cortes and President of the *Consejo del Reino*, Alejandro Rodríguez Valcárcel, revealed his opposition to both the admiral and Torcuato Fernández-Miranda. Because of his post, Rodríguez Valcárcel was a man to be reckoned with. The arcane rules of the Francoist constitution would enable him to play a crucial role in choosing key personnel.[11]

The *New York Times* article left the Prince feeling that he had gone too far in showing his hand and, for many months, he withdrew into a cautious public silence. In private, he was altogether more forthcoming. On 24 February 1970, he had a lengthy conversation with the British Ambassador, Sir John Russell. The Prince told him that he was: 'beginning to get much more of a feel of the job. Lately he has stopped asking Franco every time he wants to go anywhere or do anything and has begun to make his own arrangements direct and then tell Franco – still giving him plenty of time to show the red light if he wants to. But so far, Juan Carlos says, Franco has let him go ahead with all his projects for provincial travel, visits to factories, opening of fairs, etc.' More significantly, the Prince revealed that he had been deeply distressed by the consequences of the *New York Times* article. The revelation of 'the much more liberal lines along which the Prince saw the role of the restored monarchy in Spain' had caused him problems with both López Bravo and with Alfredo Sánchez Bella, the reactionary who had replaced Fraga as Minister of Information, albeit not with Franco, who simply did not take them seriously. Nevertheless, there was concern in technocrat circles that it was far too risky to be revealing plans for the future which insinuated even a possible discrepancy, let alone an outright break, with the regime. Russell had no doubts about 'the democratic inclinations of the Prince and his views on the constitutional role of the Spanish monarchy' and wished to encourage them. For that reason, he supported a request from Juan Carlos for an invitation to England. The Foreign Office responded that a visit would be inappropriate as long as Gibraltar remained under blockade.[12]

The obstacles facing Juan Carlos's liberalizing aspirations were dauntingly obvious. With government collusion, ultra-rightist squads were assaulting liberal and leftist priests and lawyers. Carrero Blanco's government continued to silence even moderate opposition throughout 1970. Torcuato Fernández-Miranda knew that both Franco and Carrero Blanco regarded with intense suspicion his proposals to legalize political associations within the *Movimiento*. Franco had made it clear that he had no wish to see associations in his lifetime and that he would do everything possible to ensure that they would not exist after his death. Carrero

Blanco was hardly less opposed to reform of the system. This was made clear in the spring. On 24 March, José María de Areilza wrote an article on '*La via española a la democracia*' (The Spanish Road to Democracy) in *ABC*. He pointed out that the regime's objective of integration into Europe was unlikely to be fulfilled until Spain had real democracy complete with political parties. On 1 April, the Catholic daily *Ya* called for the democratization of Spanish life. Carrero Blanco himself replied in the crudest terms, under his pseudonym of Ginés de Buitrago, with an article entitled '*¡Un poco de formalidad!*' (Let's Be Serious). *ABC* was obliged to print his article. In it, Republican Spain was metaphorically represented as a helpless alcoholic, 'Sr Fernández'. Francoism had cured him and now the calls to democratize Spain were denounced as the equivalent of getting the reformed alcoholic 'Fernández' to take a drink. The message for Juan Carlos was that the principles of the *Movimiento* were unchangeable. The Prince can only have been profoundly relieved to have Carrero Blanco's offer to step down.[13]

In such a context, Sir John Russell consistently encouraged Juan Carlos in his hopes of liberalizing the regime after Franco's death. The Ambassador was in contact with both Areilza and Torcuato Fernández-Miranda, with whom he discussed the future regime once the Prince took over. On 9 April, Russell had discussed with Fernández-Miranda the constitutional implications of changing the role envisaged for the future King. The Ambassador visited Juan Carlos a week later and reported afterwards: 'I found the Prince in good heart and forthcoming as usual: but obviously rather lost and puzzled about his own future.' When asked if he had any indication of Franco's intentions, rather despondently, Juan Carlos 'replied, jerking his thumb over his shoulder at the direction of the Pardo, that "that old gentleman" never told him anything. He found that he got less and less guidance or suggestions about his own conduct from General Franco. He was accordingly going on feeling his own way, telling General Franco of his plans and awaiting the Generalísimo's reactions but not putting his projects in the form of requests for approval. He found that this worked well enough and that in practice General Franco left him very much to follow his own inclinations.' The Prince's meetings with the Caudillo could be perplexing. On some days, 'he was shrewd, quick and obviously on the ball'; on others, 'he was a tired old man, half gaga'.

In terms of a timetable for the succession, Juan Carlos said that he hoped that the handover would not come too quickly. He wanted at least another two to two and a half years in which to go on learning the job and establishing his own position. 'He felt that it was all going well, but he needed more time. He had no idea whether General Franco would hand over during his own active lifetime or whether he would hang on until his powers failed him: the Prince himself rather hoped for a final act something along Portuguese lines with Franco, like Salazar, obliged to hand over by failing health but still remaining alive in the background for a few months.' Juan Carlos's trepidation derived from concern that his liberal democratic intentions (of which Russell was convinced) would bring him into conflict with the government left behind by Franco. In particular, he made it clear that he was apprehensive about a future clash between his plans and the reactionary instincts of Carrero Blanco. This suggested that he was not convinced that he dared believe Carrero's offer to resign.[14]

During their meeting, the Prince continued to press for an invitation to London. An appropriate occasion would take place in late June in the form of the 70th birthday celebrations of Lord Mountbatten, a close friend of Don Juan. If that were not to be possible, in mid-November there was to be a meeting of the Council of the World Wild Life Fund of whose Spanish section Juan Carlos was president. The Gibraltar issue remained a stumbling block. Nevertheless, Sir John wrote to the Foreign Office: 'Here is the future King of Spain, filled with the most admirable pro-British and liberal sentiments, longing to pay a visit to England – prepared to that end to accept qualifications which for instance the Spanish Foreign Minister, as we know only too well, would never tolerate. In two years – in a year – next week, this young man may be of very considerable importance to us: is it politic to persist in cold-shouldering him?'[15]

The question of the proposed visit continued to preoccupy

both the Ambassador and the Prince. The Foreign Office was nervous of negative reaction in Gibraltar, all the more so because López Bravo was making repeated proposals for exchanges of official visits. In reply to Russell, the Foreign Office emphasized that any visit by Juan Carlos would have to be in response to a family invitation from the Queen and therefore entirely private.[16] By June 1970, it was agreed that Juan Carlos should visit Britain as the Spanish representative at the World Wild Life Fund meeting on 17–18 November 1970. However, in the event, on 9 November the Prince cancelled without explanation, although it is likely that López Bravo had prohibited the journey because of his frustrations over the lack of progress regarding Gibraltar.

At various points throughout 1970, the Prince asked Franco for advice and always got the answer: 'Your Highness can function on your own.' Perhaps the Caudillo was unwilling or unable to explain the instinctive cunning that characterized his own style. Juan Carlos also urged Franco to name a Prime Minister. He was worried by the prospect of having to cope with succeeding Franco as Head of State and, at the same time, with selecting his own Prime Minister. It would diminish right-wing opposition if the process of the succession could take place with a President named by the Caudillo. Franco always replied in the same way, 'All in good time, Your Highness.' With an eye on the future, both López Rodó and Torcuato Fernández-Miranda were trying to ensure the election of more monarchist members of the Cortes. Only a small number of *Procuradores* were elected, by heads of families, and only candidates from the *Movimiento* could run. Nevertheless, within these constraints, they still managed to get more pro-Juan Carlos *Procuradores*. With considerable foresight, López Rodó persuaded Carrero Blanco in July 1970 of the case for a law to establish that, in the event of the Caudillo's incapacity, the interim Headship of State should be assumed by Juan Carlos. Franco agreed.[17]

On 2 October 1970, Richard Nixon landed in Madrid. He was accompanied by Henry Kissinger, head of the National Security Council, who found Franco's Spain: 'as if suspended, waiting for a life to end so that it could rejoin European history'. The United

States retained a significant strategic interest in Spain. Although happy to see moderate evolution after Franco's death, the main priority for Washington remained the conservation of stability. Accordingly, US policy was to maintain a working relationship with the dictatorship while extending contacts within the moderate opposition. There was also discreet American pressure to persuade Franco to hand over to Juan Carlos before incapacity deprived him of control of the transition. When the President and Kissinger met Franco for what were meant to be 'substantive talks', they avoided any allusion to the post-Franco transition. However, the question was soon uppermost in their minds as they watched the dictator starting to doze off. Not long after, Kissinger joined the Caudillo in snoozing gently while Nixon talked to López Bravo.[18] Juan Carlos arrived later and had a long conversation with Nixon who was greatly impressed by the Prince.[19]

In accordance with his scheme for building up foreign support, Juan Carlos attended joint Spanish–French naval exercises during the week of 21–28 October. In the course of the event, he dined with President Pompidou and had lunches with the French Ministers of Defence and Foreign Affairs.[20] Potential support from the USA was consolidated in early November. At a spectacular banquet held at the White House in support of the United World Colleges, of which he was President, Earl Mountbatten spoke to Richard Nixon about Juan Carlos. When he began to explain how Washington could help the Prince and thereby contribute to long-term stability in Spain, Nixon called over Kissinger to join them. Mountbatten urged Nixon to use his influence to persuade Franco to hand over power while still alive. The consequence of their lengthy conversation was that Juan Carlos was invited to the United States in early 1971.[21]

The Caudillo would reach the age of 78 in December 1970 and was ever more debilitated by the progress of Parkinson's disease. He seemed oblivious to the fact that, within the regime, positions were being taken up for the aftermath of his demise. Various mutually hostile options emerged, ranging from the Fascist extreme right of Blas Piñar's *Fuerza Nueva* to progressive *aperturistas* like Fraga, who was organizing a political think-tank called GODSA to examine ways of opening up the dictatorship. Intra-regime tensions were heightened as ETA's terrorist activities shattered the regime's myth of invulnerability. Extreme rightists in the Army, the so-called *generales azules*, convinced Franco to respond with a show trial of 16 Basque prisoners, including two priests. That their narrowly vengeful views prevailed was a symptom of the decadence of the regime, Franco's declining judgement and the lack of political sensibility of Carrero Blanco. The trials began in December 1970 at Burgos. Violent clashes between the police and anti-regime demonstrators in Madrid, Barcelona, Bilbao, Oviedo, Seville and Pamplona led to the suspension of *habeas corpus*. Franco did not consult Juan Carlos.[22]

On the morning of 17 December, the *Movimiento* organized an anti-ETA demonstration. The press and the radio called on the population to go to the Plaza de Oriente in Madrid. Large numbers of rural labourers were bussed in from all over Old and New Castile. A multitude gathered outside the Palacio de Oriente shouting for Franco who, in principle, was not scheduled to make an appearance. Pacón entered the Palacio de Oriente to go to his office there and found himself surrounded by 'a group of ladies, close friends of Franco's wife, who made loud criticisms of the Opus Dei and passed opinions about what should be done'. He saw another friend of Doña Carmen, the Mayor of Madrid, Carlos Arias Navarro, as well as the Minister for the Navy, Admiral 'Pedrolo' Nieto Antúnez, and the head of the *Sección Femenina*, Pilar Primo de Rivera. Pacón telephoned El Pardo and urged the Caudillo to come. Franco's doctor, Vicente Gil, also drove to El Pardo and told Doña Carmen that 'the people awaited him in the Plaza de Oriente'. She went directly to her husband's office and told him in terms that invited no discussion, 'Paco, we have to leave immediately for the royal palace where a huge crowd has gathered.' A bewildered Franco and his wife immediately set out for Madrid in civilian clothes.[23]

The crowd was conservatively estimated at around 100,000 by the foreign press and 500,000 by the *Movimiento* press. On the many banners raised could be read slogans like '*Franco sí, Opus no*' and 'Long live the Sacred Caudillo of Spain'. While

Franco acknowledged the chants of the crowd by raising both hands, Doña Carmen gave the Fascist salute. A manifestly ill-at-ease Juan Carlos was present along with Princess Sofía. They had little choice since not to attend would have been taken as a betrayal of Franco and implied sympathy with ETA. They were obliged to listen to ultra shouts of 'Down with the monarchy!' and 'We want no idiot kings!' Lurking at the back of the balcony, Juan Carlos made every effort to seem invisible as he reflected on what kind of undertaking he had accepted.[24]

The trials ended with three of the ETA militants found guilty and each given two death sentences. The technocrats were appalled by the implications for Juan Carlos. On the evening before the cabinet meeting on 30 December 1970 at which the sentences were to be reviewed, López Bravo saw Franco and attempted to make him see that, if they were confirmed, Spain's international image would be badly damaged. The Caudillo listened to him for an hour, then said, 'López Bravo, you have not convinced me.' Carrero Blanco agreed that it would be politically disastrous for the Caudillo to approve the death sentences. On the following day, at the meeting, he and the technocrats mounted a desperate effort to convince Franco to commute the death penalties.[25] In the light of their arguments that executions would irrevocably smear the regime, he opted for clemency. However, the Burgos trials dramatically altered the balance of forces in Spain. The regime's clumsiness had united the opposition as never before, the Church was deeply critical and the Francoist clans began to polarize. The more progressive Francoists were beginning to abandon what they saw as a sinking ship. Under pressure, both Franco and Carrero Blanco inclined to the *immovilista* cause as, of course, did Doña Carmen and her clique of wealthy regime ladies.

The consequent deterioration of the regime's image had obvious implications for the Prince. In a rather pessimistic report on the events of 1970, the British Ambassador wrote glumly: 'Spain enters 1971 in a mood of retrogression to the late forties . . . The Prince of Spain continued to make halting progress towards what looks like being a very unsteady throne.'[26] Similar thoughts may well have been uppermost in Juan Carlos's mind as he spent Christmas not only waiting upon the results of the ETA trials but also entertaining his in-laws. He always got along well with Constantine. His domineering mother-in-law was altogether more of a trial. Sir John Russell commented: 'His Royal Mutter just about takes the biscuit! I have yet to meet a bossier, more pretentious, tactless and disagreeable woman. But I am glad to say that the Spaniards have her number: she started recently enquiring about buying property in Spain and was politely informed that she was welcome to pay occasional visits to her daughter but that residence was not on.'[27]

If Juan Carlos was to introduce some form of democratization, it was clear that he would need as much external support as possible when the time came. To secure it, he needed to put some distance between himself and the regime responsible for the Burgos trials. Accordingly, he seized the opportunity provided by an official trip to the US. On 25 January 1971, accompanied by Gregorio López Bravo, the Prince and his wife left for Washington to return the State visit made by President Nixon and his wife four months earlier. However, the scale of the welcome that they received went beyond simple protocol and was clearly intended to boost the Prince's image. The royal couple stayed at Blair House, the official residence for State visitors. The Prince was received by several cabinet members and a sparkling array of Capitol Hill dignitaries. He laid a wreath at the tomb of the unknown soldier at Arlington Cemetery. There was a State dinner at the White House. The Washington events were followed by visits to San Diego and Los Angeles, to Houston, Texas, to Cape Kennedy, Florida and to New York City. A special United States Air Force plane was at their disposal throughout. The atmosphere could hardly have been more different from the brusque reception accorded the Prince by President Johnson four years previously. When Sir John Russell saw the programme, he remarked approvingly, 'They are doing him up brown.'[28]

The Prince went to the White House on the morning of Tuesday 26 January. In the Oval Office, the President talked with him about what would happen when he succeeded Franco. Nixon advised Juan Carlos that his first priority must be law and order and that he should not concern himself about reforming the political system until stability had been guaranteed. He also urged him not to worry about presenting an image as a liberal and a reformer but rather to play on his youth, dynamism and amiability to project the message that things would change once he was in power. Nixon was even more impressed with the Prince than on their first meeting although he remained unsure whether he would be able to 'hold the fort after Franco's death'. Nevertheless, he was now inclined to put his weight behind the establishment of the monarchy in the person of Juan Carlos. George Landau, the Country Director for Spain at the State Department, told a British diplomat in Washington that the visit had been choreographed in order 'to express American confidence in the Prince not only in the context of US–Spanish relations in the future, but also as the best bet in securing the internal stability of Spain after Franco'. In the course of the visit, Henry Kissinger is alleged to have told Juan Carlos that, if he could ever be useful to him, he should not hesitate to get in touch.[29] Nearly five years later, in dramatic circumstances, he would take up Kissinger's offer.

Throughout the visit, Juan Carlos made discreet efforts to stress his independence from the Franco regime. This was particularly noticeable at the press conference that followed the White House meeting. His remarks about the future reflected the confidence that came from Nixon's approval of his plans. On 27 January, *The Chicago Tribune* published an article in which the Prince was quoted in terms reminiscent of his recent conversations with Torcuato Fernández-Miranda about using the Francoist constitution to provide more freedom: 'Franco has never, ever interfered in my life. He leaves me entirely free. I believe that the people want more freedom. It is all a question of knowing how fast. There will be no question of an explosion as long the constitution is in force. I am ready to use all means within the fundamental laws.' The accompanying commentary stated that Juan Carlos believed himself to be capable of leading the country along a more progressive path and appeared to be making a discreet effort to get out from under the long shadow of Franco. Quotation from this article was not permitted in the Spanish press. In an off-the-record briefing for Spanish journalists he made it clear that he hoped to use his power of appointing and dismissing prime ministers to give Spain more freedom.[30]

On 28 January, the Prince hosted a breakfast for US correspondents at Blair House. To some extent, he was inhibited by the frequent interruptions of López Bravo. It was clear to the State Department that the Prince had not wanted the Minister of Foreign Affairs to be present. Everything about Juan Carlos's statements at the breakfast signalled his intention to sponsor at least some cautious evolution in Spain once he was in power. Nevertheless, he was careful to keep repeating like a mantra, 'within the constitution'.[31] His evolutionary objectives were now an open secret. On his return to Madrid, an apprehensive Minister for the Army, General Castañón, told him that Franco had a copy of the *Chicago Tribune* article. Expecting Franco to be furious, he hastened to El Pardo. How much Franco assumed Juan Carlos to be of his way of thinking was revealed in his unexpected reaction.

To the Prince's surprise, Franco spoke in terms which recalled his own double-dealing with the Western powers during the years of international ostracism: 'There are things which Your Highness can and must say outside Spain and things which you must not say inside Spain. It may not be convenient for what is said abroad to be published here. And, sometimes, what is said here is better not known abroad.'[32] Franco's fondness for Juan Carlos, his 'grandfatherly' feelings, seem to have fostered a sense of identification with him. This could be seen in his inclination to attribute to the Prince his own cunning and secrecy about his real intentions. After all, he watched as Juan Carlos balanced his liberal declarations abroad with statements about his commitment to the fundamental laws and efforts to cultivate the extreme right. Franco thus believed that the Prince had absorbed some of his own skills of seeming to support various factions, playing them off against one another while pursuing his own goals. Accordingly, whatever Juan Carlos said, Franco felt that he 'really' had the same aims as himself.

The immediate consequence of his interview with Juan Carlos was that President Nixon decided to send General Vernon A. Walters, deputy chief of the CIA, to deliver a confidential letter to Franco. It is reasonable to presume that the decision intimated his support for Juan Carlos. Arriving in Madrid on 23 February 1971, Walters gained direct access to Franco via Carrero Blanco. Prior to the meeting, the admiral warned him that 'Franco was quite old and sometimes seemed feeble'. When Walters handed the Caudillo the letter from President Nixon, 'He reached out for it but his hand trembled violently and he motioned for the Minister of Foreign Affairs to take it.' Hesitant about asking the Caudillo about his death, Walters was surprised when Franco raised the matter himself. He was even more amazed by the calm and unemotional way in which the Caudillo discussed his own demise.

Franco assured Walters that the succession to Juan Carlos would take place without any disorder. He stated that 'the Army would never let things get out of hand'. He also 'expressed confidence in the Prince's ability to handle the situation after his death, saying that there was no alternative to the Prince. He said that he had created a number of institutions to ensure an orderly succession. He smiled and said that many people doubted that these institutions would work. They were wrong, the transition would be peaceful.' Surprised to hear the Caudillo speak so frankly about his own death, Walters came away convinced that it would not be long delayed. The American thought that he: 'looked old and weak. His left hand trembled at times so violently that he would cover it with his other hand. At times he appeared far away and at others he came right to the point.'[33]

Awareness of Franco's progressive physical deterioration led the Prince to think that the dictator would retire when he reached the age of 80, in December 1972. In the meanwhile, the frustrations were constant. Both López Rodó and Fernández-Miranda had seen the idea of political associations within the *Movimiento* as a possible vehicle for an eventual transition to real political parties. After an initial interest on Franco's part, by the spring of 1971, the possibility of such an evolution turned him against the idea. Accordingly, the Prince continued to push for the nomination of a Prime Minister, hoping that it would not be Carrero Blanco but prepared to accept that appointment if necessary. He revealed his impatience to López Rodó, saying, 'Franco needs a rocket under him.' During the summer of 1971, Juan Carlos spoke with Franco in the Caudillo's summer residence, the Pazo de Meirás. He left the Prince in no doubt about his opposition to any kind of liberalization, roundly squashing the idea that political associations might be the first step to something else: 'There will be no associations as long I live and I will do everything possible to make sure that there are none after: they would just be political parties.'[34]

Franco may well have refrained from giving Juan Carlos detailed advice about how he should rule in the future but he made no bones about his determination that his regime should not be reformed. Even in their own home, the Prince and his wife had to be cautious. The regime's intelligence services were spying on their every move. Sofía commented years later: 'Everyone who came here had a file on them opened. There was a doorman who sent a note every day to El Pardo saying who had come, what time they arrived, what time they left. We often found members of staff listening behind doors. And when we questioned them about it, we discovered that they did it because their orders came from above and they were expected to obey.'[35]

Despite the disagreeable uncertainties of his situation and the fact that he had to silence his ambitions for the dismantling of the regime, Juan Carlos was personally very fond of Franco. In March 1971, José María Pemán visited La Zarzuela and later wrote to Don Juan about their very frank conversation. 'My impression is that he places very little value on the entire official crew that pressures him and surrounds him and in whose words he almost always spots what is cliché, self-seeking or adulatory. I believe that the only one for whom he feels affection and in whom he has any faith is Franco, who has established with His Highness that "grandfather–grandson" relationship, while viewing the official politicans with the same suspicion and lack of affection as the Prince himself.' Pemán also commented on the recent tour of Andalusia undertaken by the Prince and Doña Sofía. He noted with pleasure their growing popularity and signs that ordinary people were beginning to place in them their hopes for the future.[36]

It was precisely because of fears deriving from his fondness for the Prince, as well as his physical infirmity, that Franco's immediate circle, with his wife at its centre, openly denounced the 'weakness' of the technocrats and made every effort to denigrate Juan Carlos. In fact, Franco's personal position was unequivocal. His speech on the opening of the Cortes on 18 November 1971 showed yet again that he had no toleration for any form of liberalization. His text was full of dark references to the enemies within and without, to the threat of chaos and to the need to maintain stability. The speech made a nonsense of the idea that somehow he benevolently approved of the Prince's ambitions for a democratic opening. 'Vain and sterile will always be the dream of certain groups that the mere passage of time can introduce into our institutions doctrinal or ideological elements alien to our system . . . Any political organization of whatever kind outside this representative system will be considered illegal . . . Those who believe that our process of political institutionalization could, sooner or later, lead to a fragmentation of social unity in multiple political parties are mistaken.'

He seemed to have been addressing his remarks directly to advisers of the Prince such as Torcuato Fernández-Miranda when he went on to say: 'I would like to stress this, so that no one can harbour any doubt, or using biased interpretations try to take our system along inappropriate roads and channels . . . The principles of the *Movimiento Nacional* are by their very nature permanent and unchangeable . . . Our representative system is open to improvement but the one thing for which there can never be room are political parties and anything that might lead to them in one way or another.'[37]

Nostalgic reminders from his wife about the good old days of the Civil War and its aftermath saw Franco become more susceptible to her whispered insinuations that salvation lay in a return to hardline Falangism. The danger to Juan Carlos emanating from the El Pardo clique was intensified when, on 20 December 1971, Don Jaime announced the engagement of his son to Franco's eldest granddaughter, María del Carmen Martínez-Bordiu y Franco. Hearing the news, Pedro Sainz Rodríguez said: 'Fucking hell, what are you saying? If Franco doesn't croak soon everything we've done up to now will go to hell in a bucket. We're fucked. What a cunt's trick!' He was convinced that the Prince would soon die in a mysterious accident. His fears were not diminished when, at the beginning of March, Don Jaime gave Franco the *Toisón de Oro*, the order which the Caudillo had rejected when it had been offered by Don Juan prior to the wedding of Juan Carlos and Sofía in 1962. Franco had refused the honour on the grounds that it could be conceded only by the King of Spain. The implications were clear, and a highly alarmed Juan Carlos asked López Rodó to persuade Carrero Blanco to intercede with Franco. The admiral successfully prevailed on his master not to wear the insignia.[38]

In the words of Franco's niece, 'A grandson of Alfonso XIII marries a granddaughter of the Francos. Doña Carmen is beside herself with joy.'[39] Doña Carmen's delight was not just about the social possibilities of the wedding: the challenge to Juan Carlos was evident. She and the Marqués de Villaverde issued wedding invitations which referred to 'His Royal Highness Prince Alfonso', a title to which the bridegroom had no right. Bursting with pride and snobbery, Doña Carmen presided over a wedding reception on 18 March 1972 even more sumptuous than that of her daughter in 1952 or that of Juan Carlos and Sofía. Two thousand guests filed into El Pardo down an avenue flanked by two lines of mounted lancers in long white capes and silver helmets. In order to enhance the status of the occasion, the Caudillo took the place of the bride's father to give away María del Carmen. He cut a pathetic figure, his eyes watering, his mouth open and his hands trembling while a stiffly upright, but beaming, Doña Carmen entered the chapel on the arm of Prince Juan Carlos.

At Barajas Airport, when the newly weds returned from their honeymoon, Doña Carmen made great play of curtseying formally before her granddaughter in full view of the assembled media. It was a message to them that her granddaughter was to be treated as if she were a princess – a message replete with political significance. This was a significant escalation of the bunker's challenge to Juan Carlos. In El Pardo shortly afterwards, at one of her frequent tea parties for the wives of top Francoists, there took place a bizarre, and probably rehearsed, scene. Doña Carmen genuflected like a courtier when María del Carmen entered the room and all the other distinguished guests, who had known her since she was a child, felt obliged to do the same. At dinners in El Pardo, María del Carmen, rather than her grandmother, was placed at the head of the table. Doña Carmen issued instructions to guests and servants that her granddaughter be called 'Your Highness' and insisted that María del Carmen be served at table before herself. Cristóbal Martínez-Bordiu, in a studied insult to Sofía, would make toasts to his daughter as: 'The most beautiful queen in Spain.' After a son, Francisco, was born to the couple, Doña Carmen was often heard to ask the household staff, 'Has Sire had his bottle?' After all, her great-grandson was also the great-grandson of Alfonso XIII. All these antics provoked the hilarity of María del Carmen's sisters.[40]

Social and political ambition combined in Doña Carmen's enthusiastic support for Alfonso's bid to secure a title matching that of Juan Carlos. Alfonso de Borbón's frequent presence in El Pardo so inflamed the ambitions of Doña Carmen and the Villaverde clan that they harboured hopes that the Caudillo might overturn his choice of monarchist successor. They encouraged Alfonso's desire to be Príncipe de Borbón and thus entitled to be called Royal Highness. Carmen urged her husband to grant his request. Don Juan de Borbón, as the head of the royal family, opposed it on the reasonable grounds that only the first son of the King had the right to be called a prince. Alfonso de Borbón y Dampierre's father was neither a King nor a Prince. Juan Carlos opposed it because he believed that it was a manoeuvre to put them on the same level and thus facilitate a future reversal of Franco's choice of successor. When he went to discuss the matter with Franco, he found him ill-humoured, his displeasure manifest. The Prince commented later, 'I have just been through one of the tensest moments in my life. I was sweating on the inside.'

Cristóbal Martínez-Bordiu and Doña Carmen easily convinced Franco that the objections were a petty and personal revenge for the many slights that Don Juan had suffered at the Caudillo's hands. A resentful Caudillo told his Minister of Justice, Antonio María Oriol, 'Don Alfonso had the title of prince and now, because he is marrying my granddaughter, they want to take it away from him.' Oriol had to explain to him that Alfonso de Borbón y Dampierre had never had any right to the title. In the end, to minimize the acrimony, Juan Carlos persuaded Don Juan to give Alfonso the title of Duque de Cádiz, with the right to be called 'Royal Highness'. Despite this compromise, relations between the Villaverde family and La Zarzuela were severely soured and this had extremely negative repercussions on Franco's attitude to Juan Carlos. Even if he did not seriously consider reversing the nomination of Juan Carlos as successor, he certainly shared his wife's desire to see their granddaughter become a princess.[41]

To counter the damage to his position, Juan Carlos stepped up his quest for foreign support. During Easter 1972, he visited England where he had a lengthy meeting with the British Labour Prime Minister, Harold Wilson. Given the deep hostility of the Labour Party to the Franco regime, it would be a difficult task to secure Wilson's support. Juan Carlos managed to bring it off. Having Wilson's good will would pay considerable dividends in the first months after the death of Franco. Juan Carlos also attended a dinner at the home of Princess Alexandra of Kent and Angus Ogilvy. There he convinced a group of financiers of his determination to bring a democratic regime to Spain.[42]

Back in Spain, Franco's health was failing and the Prince was worried for him. Juan Carlos still felt something bordering on filial concern despite the deterioration of their relations. In June 1972, for instance, he was taken aback by the harshness of Franco's complaints about some recent liberal declarations by Don Juan. The Prince commented afterwards, 'Franco is so hardline and he doesn't miss a thing!'[43] Juan Carlos was aware that their relationship was suffering consistent erosion at the hands of Doña Carmen. She would vehemently regale her husband with denunciations of 'all kinds of traitors and ingrates who are all around us', by which she tended to mean the technocrats. A much-used phrase was: 'We didn't fight the war just so some liberal or red could come along and steal our victory!'[44] Inevitably, frequent criticisms of Don Juan and protective feelings towards María del Carmen and Alfonso de Borbón y Dampierre fed doubts about Juan Carlos. In early November 1972, Franco anxiously asked his sister Pilar,

'How do you think Juan Carlos will treat you and our family when I die?' She reassured him that the Prince was fond of him and that there would be no problem.

The Caudillo simmered resentfully in the wake of Juan Carlos's opposition to the concession of a royal title to Alfonso de Borbón y Dampierre. He instructed the Minister of Public Works, Gonzalo Fernández de la Mora, not to invite him to the inauguration ceremonies of several major projects. In one case, the new container port in Barcelona, Franco relented because the company concerned and the municipal authorities of the city specifically requested the Prince's presence. However, the Caudillo issued instructions to Carrero Blanco that this was not to happen again. This was perhaps a reflection of pressure from powerful elements, like Alejandro Rodríguez Valcárcel and Admiral Pedrolo Nieto Antúnez, who were conspiring with the Martínez-Bordiu clan in favour of Alfonso de Borbón y Dampierre. Knowing this, the Prince's supporters wanted Alfonso out of Spain. Gregorio López Bravo offered him a choice of embassies, including Buenos Aires, but he refused. Alfonso aspired to a ministry but grudgingly accepted the presidency of the *Instituto de Cultura Hispánica*. Returning to Madrid, he and his wife moved into El Pardo while their new home was refurbished. Alfonso quickly established such a warm relationship with his wife's grandparents that Juan Carlos had good reason to be alarmed. With the encouragement of Doña Carmen, Alfonso de Borbón y Dampierre visited Carrero Blanco four times between October and December 1972. He pressed the admiral in vain to have him named as second in line to the throne after Juan Carlos.[45]

On 4 December 1972, Franco reached his 80th birthday. He appeared ever more decrepit, saying nothing in cabinet meetings and frequently nodding off. Juan Carlos remained hopeful that he might hand over power while still alive. Accordingly, in the early months of 1973, the Prince was thinking about the composition of his first government. He had no intention of maintaining Carrero Blanco as Prime Minister when the time came. Nevertheless, he realized that the transition from the Caudillo's last government to his first would go more smoothly if handled by conservative figures known to be loyal to Franco. He was convinced that this first government would be burnt out within six months to two years of the handover. Once this happened, he intended to name a government of altogether younger men more in line with his own way of thinking. Then, he would proceed to a thorough-going reform. In January 1973, he told Torcuato Fernández-Miranda: 'You know as well as I do that when I am King, there is no place for the *Movimiento* or its ministry. The monarchy of 18 July is meaningless. The monarchy cannot be blue, nor Falangist, nor even Francoist. The monarchy dates from way back, from other Kings, from history and it cannot be built on the present excessively partisan institutions. The monarchy must be democratic. That is the only way in which it can be accepted by Europe and by the world and by which it can survive.'[46]

Inevitably, despite the Prince's discretion, in El Pardo, suspicions about his intentions festered. In the earlier years of the regime, Doña Carmen had ventured her political opinions with some caution since she was as likely as not to be told by her husband that she 'didn't know what she was talking about'. However, as Franco grew more infirm, Doña Carmen had begun to express her opinions with more freedom. Her increasingly outspoken opinions were fomented in her weekly tea parties at El Pardo at which she entertained the wives of the '*generales azules*' and of hardline Francoists like José Antonio Girón – the women who had gathered for the demonstration at the Plaza de Oriente. As they sat, resolving the problems of Spain, anxiety and fantasy intermingled. The ambience of these tea parties spilled out at the beginning of February 1973. One day, as he left Franco's office, Carrero Blanco was called into a small ante-room by Doña Carmen. 'Carrero, I'm very worried. I can't sleep I'm so worried and that's what I wanted to see you about. Things get worse every day. I can't sleep because that Minister of the Interior [Tomás Garicano Goñi] worries me so much . . . and the Minister of Foreign Affairs, López Bravo, is not loyal . . . I already told you this. At our Paris Embassy, he spoke ill of Paco, with complete indiscretion. He spoke in front of the Ambassador, Pedro Cortina, who is loyal and told me everything. López Bravo went so far as to say that Paco no longer counted for anything. And that if he, the minister, wasn't present in the interviews with foreigners and ambassadors, Paco wouldn't know what to do or what to say . . . What can you expect from a minister like that? Carrero, you're the only one who can help Paco. You must persuade him to have a reshuffle. I keep telling you. This cabinet is full of weaklings and traitors.'

Carrero Blanco was shocked by the vehemence of her intervention, telling the Minister-Secretary-General of the *Movimiento*, Torcuato Fernández-Miranda, that he was 'frightened' and speechless because it was the first time that Doña Carmen had ever spoken to him in such terms. 'She had never interfered like that, so directly, with such irritation and certainty. It really worried me. Who can have put her up to it? I remember when Franco was in his prime, if Doña Carmen tried to say anything, he would shut her up immediately saying, "Shut up Carmen you know nothing about this".' To be thus accused of debility and surrender led Carrero Blanco to feel that his position was deeply compromised. There could be no doubt that Carmen and her son-in-law were trying to build the bunker at El Pardo to the detriment of Juan Carlos. Franco's friend, Admiral Nieto Antúnez, told Fraga that within the Caudillo's residence, Doña Carmen and Cristóbal Martínez-Bordiu openly criticized Carrero Blanco as weak and disloyal.[47] The implications for Juan Carlos were clear.

The fears provoked by Franco's health within the inner circles of the regime festered in an atmosphere of ever fiercer social and political tensions. In April 1973, the police killed a striking worker near Barcelona. Carrero Blanco himself had begun to lose confidence in the technocrats and was secretly encouraging the activities of the ultra-rightist terror squads of *Fuerza Nueva*. Franco too was uneasy that the government was not doing enough to combat the activities of ETA. The belief in El Pardo that events were slipping out of control came to a head on 1 May 1973 when a policeman was stabbed to death during a May Day demonstration. At the funeral of the murdered officer, 'ultra' policemen and Falangist war veterans howled for repressive measures. There were mass arrests of leftists. On 7 May, the Minister of the Interior,

Tomás Garicano Goñi, disappointed at the lack of will for reform and alarmed at the growing influence of extreme rightists, resigned.[48] The El Pardo clique finally convinced Franco that the cabinet had failed in its primordial task of maintaining public order. On 9 May, he again told an unwilling Carrero Blanco that he was going to be made Prime Minister and should start drawing up his cabinet.

Anticipating this moment, the Prince had been considering the names of the ministers that he would like for what was likely to be Franco's last cabinet and thus the one that he would inherit. His main concern was that the post of Minister of the Interior should not go to Carlos Arias Navarro, the Mayor of Madrid. Arias Navarro was a close confidant of Doña Carmen and, a year earlier, he had opposed the law which ensured that Juan Carlos would take over as interim Head of State in the event of Franco's incapacity.[49] It was no secret that Arias harboured suspicions of Juan Carlos's liberal aspirations. At a hunting party in October 1972, Antonio Guerrero, the editor of the hardline Falangist daily *Arriba*, had assured his companions that there was a secret agreement between Juan Carlos and his father to introduce democracy. Arias replied vehemently: 'Such agreements count for nothing here. The Prince has pledged himself to Spain. He has sworn an oath of fidelity to the values of 18 July and he has to fulfil that oath. In any case, when the time comes, we'll just throw his father out. There can be no playing with the Spanish people!' When this story was recounted to Franco, his face lit up and he said firmly, 'Absolutely right! Absolutely right!'[50]

At the beginning of June, when Carrero Blanco's cabinet list was approved, it provided mixed news for the Prince. The new government went some way to reversing the technocrat dominance of the cabinet of 1969. Gregorio López Bravo was dropped, which was pleasing to Doña Carmen, although Juan Carlos had also expressed a desire to see him go. López Rodó lost his crucial influence in domestic policy and was exiled, largely at his own request, to the Ministry of Foreign Affairs where he hoped he could do more to promote the Prince's cause in the international arena.[51] On the other hand, Juan Carlos's cause was strengthened by the fact that, as Vice-President of the Council of Ministers and Secretary-General of the *Movimiento*, Carrero Blanco chose Torcuato Fernández-Miranda – who had finally managed to persuade Franco to consider political associations. However, the El Pardo clique also derived great satisfaction from the further weakening of the technocrat monopoly in the nomination of several enthusiastic Falangists. Cruz Martínez Esteruelas as Minister for the Development Plan was a dynamic figure in the Fraga mould. José Utrera Molina at Housing was deeply loyal to Franco. Francisco Ruiz-Jarabo, Minister of Justice, was a close friend and follower of José Antonio Girón. Julio Rodríguez, the new Minister of Education, had been notorious for his violent methods as rector of the autonomous university of Madrid, when he had personally joined in police charges against left-wing students. According to Girón himself, the government 'would have been suitable for the 1940s or 1950s'.[52]

Despite the resurgence of Falangist influence in the government, the key figure was likely to be the sinuously intelligent Torcuato Fernández-Miranda. According to López Rodó, Fernández-Miranda told him: 'In Spain, there are three areas of power: the Prince, Franco and Carrero. I have the Prince in my pocket; Franco listens to me spellbound. I have him bewitched, and I have also won over Carrero.' It is difficult to imagine a man of Fernández-Miranda's discretion speaking in such crude terms of his relationship with Juan Carlos. Utrera Molina himself remembered the conversation in broadly similar terms, with the crucial difference that he recalled Fernández-Miranda saying in relation to the Prince merely that he had enormous influence over him.[53]

It was presumably the presence of both López Rodó and Fernández-Miranda that accounts for the Prince's curious reaction on seeing Carrero Blanco's cabinet list: 'All that is missing is the sign saying "Zarzuela Cabinet".' If that is what he said, he cannot have given the list his full attention. Carrero Blanco would always be a guarantee of Juan Carlos's own position, but some of the new cabinet list should have made disturbing reading for Juan Carlos. It was a reflection both of Franco's faith in Carrero

Blanco's reactionary instincts and of his own waning strength that the Caudillo accepted the list with only one change – and one that reflected his wife's preferences. Carrero's original choice as Minister of the Interior had been a firm partisan of the Prince, the technocrat Fernando de Liñán. The admiral was overruled. Having been persuaded by Carmen and the rest of the El Pardo clique that Carrero Blanco might be too soft, Franco insisted on the key ministry going to the man that Juan Carlos least wanted – the Mayor of Madrid. The hatchet-faced Carlos Arias Navarro was a tough law-and-order man who had started his career as a prosecutor during the repression of Málaga in 1937, where he had earned the nickname of 'the butcher'. From 1957 to 1965, he had been an implacable Director General of Security and was considered to be the protégé and natural heir of the then Minister of the Interior, General Camilo Alonso Vega. He was a business associate and a particular favourite of Doña Carmen as was his wife, María Luz del Valle, a frequent guest at El Pardo tea parties. The fact that Arias was also an anti-monarchist opponent of the Juan Carlos solution made him even more attractive to the El Pardo clique. On the evening of 6 June, Doña Carmen telephoned Arias and said, 'Thank God you've been appointed. Now I can rest easy.' A consequence of Arias's inclusion in the cabinet was that Carrero Blanco instead made Liñán Minister of Information. That post had been originally intended for a man expected to be a keen advocate of Juan Carlos, Adolfo Suárez González.[54]

Depressing as the cabinet was for those both inside and outside the regime who cherished hopes for progressive change, it was not the victory that it might have been for the group of ultra-Falangists who lurked around El Pardo. Carrero Blanco had been appointed Prime Minister for five years, yet he was 70 years old. He lacked both popular and military support. His authority depended entirely on the continued existence of his master. Madrid wits called it 'the funeral cabinet'.[55] Franco's physical decline was now acute. Fraga believed that he was 'ever more beyond the physical and mental demands of his great responsibilities'.[56] If Franco died first, it is unlikely that Carrero would have been able to rule for long thereafter since he lacked the will, the authority and the ideas.

As it was, by the end of the year, his cabinet was adrift in a sea of industrial unrest. Strikes in Catalonia, Asturias and the Basque Country had been provoked by austerity measures taken to stem inflation. With the first energy crisis brewing and Spain heavily dependent on imported fuel, the technocrat strategy of buying off political discontent with rising prosperity was doomed. Carrero Blanco's only response was intensified repression.

His return to the fierce authoritarianism of 1940s Francoism was encapsulated in a document that he planned to read to a cabinet meeting scheduled for 20 December 1973. In a paranoid interpretation of the difficulties faced by the government, he described Spain as besieged by a united front of international communism and freemasonry. His text fully reflected his identification with the ideas of Blas Piñar. Having infiltrated Spanish universities and the Catholic Church, these forces were now engaged in a subversive war. Carrero's response – which did not bode well for Juan Carlos's reforming aspirations – was to block any attempt at liberalization. He intended to propose the harshest possible repression to be supervised by the Ministries of Justice and the Interior. This would require: 'the maximum propaganda of our ideology and the total prohibition of enemy ideologies'. It would involve eliminating 'the enemies of the regime' from the staffs of universities and schools and from the clergy. Part of the 'enemy ideology' was transmitted by 'decadent dances and music'. The solution here lay with the television: 'The intention is to bring up men, not queers, and the long-haired weirdos that are sometimes seen gyrating on television do nothing to that end.'[57]

With Carrero Blanco in this mood, it is difficult to imagine him standing by passively while Juan Carlos endeavoured to liberalize the regime. In the event, the admiral never had the opportunity to inaugurate his plans for a more repressive policy. Just before 9.30 a.m. on 20 December, a squad of ETA activists assassinated Carrero Blanco. His car was blown up by explosives buried beneath the Calle Claudio Coello as he returned from daily mass. He was killed instantly.[58] Already weak from flu, Franco could not absorb the news. When he finally realized that Carrero Blanco had been assassinated, he was completely overwhelmed. Juan

278

Carlos and Sofía went immediately to the Madrid hospital where the admiral's corpse had been taken.[59]

Any plans that Franco might have had for withdrawing from political responsibilities were shattered. Aged and infirm, he was bewildered by the loss of his right-hand man and his response revealed the degree to which he was out of touch with contemporary reality. He told Fernández-Miranda, 'We must close ranks against this masonic attack.'[60] He was now more vulnerable to the El Pardo clique than ever. A kitchen cabinet emerged at his residence, headed by Doña Carmen, together with her son-in-law, Cristóbal Martínez-Bordiu, her and Franco's doctor, Vicente Gil, the second-in-command of Franco's military household, General José Ramón Gavilán and the highly conservative naval Captain Antonio Urcelay Rodríguez, one of Franco's aides-de-camp and a close friend of José Antonio Girón. Doña Carmen was immensely fond of Urcelay and also regularly visited Gavilán's home to take tea with his wife.[61]

With the various factions of the regime in disarray and tempers running high, the mood in La Zarzuela was of some trepidation. On the day after the assassination, Friday 21 December, Franco did not attend the requiem mass for Carrero. Immediately after the mass, the cabinet met for a brief meeting in El Pardo, during which the Caudillo wept disconsolately. He was too depressed to speak on television about Carrero's death. However, he did briefly receive a visit from the Falangist Alejandro Rodríguez Valcárcel, President of both the *Consejo del Reino* and the Cortes. Franco told Rodríguez Valcárcel that it was still too early to talk about Carrero's successor.[62] Shortly afterwards, at lunch on 21 December attended by members of the kitchen cabinet, Doña Carmen began her offensive. She repeatedly asked Urcelay to raise the issue of the appointment of the new Prime Minister. Never very articulate at the best of times, according to Vicente Gil, she appeared tense, nervous and confused. Accordingly, Urcelay pretended not to understand her, but did at last tentatively broach the question with the Caudillo. Franco was so entrenched in his misery that their hints had little effect. He did not silence Urcelay but nor did he answer directly, eventually changing the subject.[63]

If the implications of Carrero Blanco's death were disturbing for Juan Carlos, for Arias Navarro, as the Minister of the Interior, and the man responsible for the nation's security services, they were devastating. He assumed that he would be obliged to resign. As López Rodó commented, 'It is surprising that the State Security Services knew nothing about a tunnel being dug for several weeks under a street down which the President of the Government passed every day.' In fact the mystery was much more perplexing, since the ETA squad preparing the assassination had been working in Madrid for more than a year.[64] It is odder still that, after the assassination, there were no police controls on roads from Madrid to the Basque Country. Astonishingly, in fact, Arias Navarro, the only minister in Carrero Blanco's cabinet not chosen by the admiral, was to be the principal beneficiary of the crisis. For the moment, however, Torcuato Fernández-Miranda, as Vice-President of the Council of Ministers, took over as interim Prime Minister. With Franco too ill to attend the funeral, his place was taken by Juan Carlos. Demonstrating his courage at a time when fear was inundating the regime, he insisted on doing so, despite warnings about a further ETA attack. Wearing the uniform of Rear-Admiral, he walked alone at the head of the procession that followed the gun-carriage carrying the coffin. He refused to wear a bulletproof vest.[65]

At 6.30 in the bleak afternoon of 21 December, Doña Carmen, Franco and Captain Urcelay took tea. From the nearby cemetery of El Pardo could be heard the 21-gun salute that marked the burial of Carrero Blanco. Franco began to weep. Once again Doña Carmen pressed Urcelay to raise the subject of the choice of a new Prime Minister. This time, Franco was more receptive and a serious conversation ensued. All three were aware that, with the energy crisis deepening, social tension would intensify throughout 1974. ETA had targeted Carrero Blanco precisely because the Caudillo's plans for the continuity of the regime were built around him. At this point, Urcelay and Doña Carmen were pushing the candidacy of Girón. Franco seemed receptive to the idea although, when the subject was mentioned again at dinner, he stared vacantly and then just dozed off.[66]

It was an indication of the advanced state of Franco's physical and mental deterioration that Carmen and a mere adjutant could raise these issues, let alone influence the final resolution of the crisis. For Juan Carlos, it was deeply worrying that there was no call from El Pardo for discussions about the future Prime Minister. He was kept in touch with what was happening only through Fernández-Miranda, who was aware of the suspicion of the El Pardo clique and thus felt that his visits to La Zarzuela had to be clandestine. In fact, the initial consequence of the efforts of Doña Carmen and Captain Urcelay was the elimination of any possibility that Fernández-Miranda might continue in the post. They were able to persuade Franco that giving the presidency of the cabinet to Carrero Blanco had been enough of a mistake. Doña Carmen and the rest of the El Pardo clique had been appalled to learn that Carrero had promised Juan Carlos that, instead of remaining as the Francoist watchdog, he would resign. Apparently, a repentant Carrero Blanco had told Franco's daughter, Carmen, that he bitterly regretted the promise. In the words of José Utrera Molina, 'What Franco assumed to be tied down, and well tied down, was flapping in the wind.' Carrero Blanco seemed to have opened the way to what they feared would be Juan Carlos's secret liberalization plans under Fernández-Miranda. In their fevered imaginations, they seemed to fear that, if even a controlled and limited democratization took place under Juan Carlos, they would be treated with the same ruthless cruelty with which they had treated the left since 1939.[67]

After lunch at El Pardo on Saturday 22 December, Doña Carmen requested that one of the aides go to Admiral Pedrolo Nieto Antúnez's house to relate to him the previous evening's conversations. At this stage, she apparently hoped to recruit Nieto to use his own influence with Franco in favour of Girón or Arias as candidates for the presidency. Franco had suggested that the aide also visit Rodríguez Valcárcel to inform him and Nieto Antúnez decided to accompany him. They talked about the choice being one of the following three: Rodríguez Valcárcel himself, Arias Navarro or Girón de Velasco. When Rodríguez Valcárcel went to El Pardo in the evening of 22 December, he got the impression that Franco was pleased with these three candidates. It was left that later in the following week, they would proceed to the formal choice.[68]

In fact, Rodríguez Valcárcel was unaware that Franco had already told Pedrolo Nieto Antúnez that he wanted him to succeed Carrero Blanco. Nieto reluctantly accepted and began contacting possible ministers, including Fraga, whom he invited to be Vice-President, and López Bravo, whom he asked to be his Minister of Foreign Affairs. Equally in the dark, Fernández-Miranda still entertained hopes that he would be confirmed as Prime Minister. He did not know that a string of hardliners led by Girón and Rodríguez Valcárcel had convinced Franco that he was a treacherous liberal. So confident was Fernández-Miranda that he told Arias Navarro that he wanted him to continue at the Ministry of the Interior. Arias replied, 'I don't know, I don't know. My position isn't too rosy. Remember that they've just blown up the President on me.' However, when Torcuato Fernández-Miranda broached the subject on 24 December, he was shocked by the Caudillo's coldly dismissive response: 'Are you insinuating that I include you in the *terna* of the *Consejo del Reino*?' (Franco was referring to the procedure whereby the *Consejo del Reino* would provide him with a shortlist of names from which to choose a new President of the Government.) There were those in the *Consejo del Reino* who had already decided, prophetically, that Torcuato Fernández-Miranda would be the gravedigger of the regime.[69]

When she found out that her husband had opted for Pedrolo Nieto Antúnez, Carmen Polo was appalled, along with Vicente Gil and the rest of the El Pardo clique. She feared that the admiral was totally incapable of the firm government that she believed to be crucial. She passed a grim Christmas hoping to find a way of getting her husband to change his mind. In theory, Franco could not just appoint his old friend Pedrolo but had to choose the Prime Minister from the *terna* to be presented to him by the *Consejo del Reino*. This was the highest consultative body within the Francoist system, the duties of which were to assist the dictator in his most important decisions. In fact, ten of its 17 members were named directly by Franco and six were representatives of other major

Francoist institutions. There was no possibility that the *Consejo* would not include in the *terna* the name that he intended to pick.

Pedrolo was an apparently safe choice, a personal friend and fishing and card-playing companion, a senior military Francoist, not so self-effacing as Carrero Blanco and no friend to Juan Carlos. However, there were crucial disadvantages. Born in 1898, Pedrolo was only six years younger than the Caudillo himself and five years older than Carrero Blanco. He provided no guarantee that the problem of a replacement would not arise again in the near future. Moreover, although sufficiently Francoist in his credentials, he was likely to rely on the now openly reformist Fraga in the same way as Carrero Blanco had relied on the technocrat Laureano López Rodó. There were rumours of involvement in corruption. It was also said that he had a drink problem and was accompanied everywhere by a naval rating whose job it was to ensure that he came to no harm when in his cups. All in all, the El Pardo clique would do whatever was necessary to stop his nomination.

At 11 a.m. on 24 December, despite having decided to nominate Pedrolo, Franco went through the formal motions of asking Juan Carlos for his opinion on the next Prime Minister. In the course of a 45-minute meeting, the Prince suggested that it be Manuel Fraga or Torcuato Fernández-Miranda. Despite the apparent cordiality of the encounter, the Caudillo had no intention of accepting either suggestion. He dismissed Fernández-Miranda as impossible because he had too many enemies within the regime's upper reaches, including El Pardo and the *Consejo del Reino*. Later in the evening of Monday 24 December, a visibly exhausted Franco had a long meeting with Rodríguez Valcárcel. He still said nothing about his conversation with Pedrolo but Rodríguez Valcárcel was nonetheless shaken when he discovered that the Caudillo seemed to have retreated from the three names discussed on Saturday. They went through the charade of discussing 22 names, reducing them to 12, ranging from López Rodó to Falange hardliners like Girón, and José Luis de Arrese who, since leaving the government in 1960, had withdrawn from public life, living – as did all of Franco's ex-ministers – on various sinecures and his ministerial pension.[70] Doña Carmen and her son-in-law were still hoping that the choice would fall upon Rodríguez Valcárcel, Girón or Arias. To this end, they worked on Franco over Christmas Day and 26 December. However, when Franco spoke with Rodríguez Valcárcel on 26 December, it was made clear that he could not become Prime Minister since the post was incompatible with that of President of the *Consejo del Reino*. Franco did not want to have to go through another tedious process to find a successor. Girón was equally impossible, since he would first have to resign as a member of the *Consejo del Reino*.[71] Accordingly, Doña Carmen and the rest of the El Pardo clique now concentrated their efforts on pushing the candidacy of Arias Navarro.

When Rodríguez Valcárcel visited El Pardo on the morning of 27 December, Franco told him that he had reduced the list overnight to five: Torcuato Fernández-Miranda, Manuel Fraga Iribarne, Pedrolo Nieto Antúnez, Carlos Arias Navarro and the relatively liberal Minister of Finance, Antonio Barrera de Irimo.[72] Renowned for his hard line on public order matters, Arias Navarro was Doña Carmen's firm choice. He was one of Franco's card-playing cronies and a friend of Vicente Gil.[73] When Rodríguez Valcárcel came back at 7 p.m. on the same evening, he was convinced that he would leave with an instruction to arrange the *terna* so that Arias would be Prime Minister. To the chagrin of Doña Carmen, Cristóbal Martínez-Bordiu, Vicente Gil, Urcelay and Gavilán, Franco finally told Rodríguez Valcárcel that Pedrolo was his choice. When he pressed the candidacy of Arias Navarro, the Caudillo responded, 'But Valcárcel, how would it look? He's the Minister of the Interior who has had the misfortune of failing to prevent the assassination of his Prime Minister!' Accordingly, throughout the night of 27 December, Doña Carmen worked anxiously. Dinner took place in an icy silence as Carmen tried to get Urcelay once more to raise the subject of Pedrolo's unsuitability.[74]

Doña Carmen is alleged to have opened the operation by saying to her husband: 'They are going to kill us all just like Carrero Blanco. We need a hard President. It has to be Arias. There is no one else.' They went over the problem again and again until dawn, when they slept briefly. However, Franco had still not succumbed before his wife's advocacy of Arias. One of the Caudillo's aides later told Torcuato Fernández-Miranda that Doña Carmen had said to him: 'We spent the night in limbo, talking, thinking, going over things again and again.' When Franco called Urcelay on the morning of 28 December, his adjutant found him still in bed in his pyjamas and a haggard Doña Carmen in her dressing gown. Franco commented that they had not slept all night. Doña Carmen whispered to Urcelay that her husband had decided on Pedrolo. In consequence, she said, she was desperately worried and had spent the entire night crying.[75]

At this point, Vicente Gil took it upon himself to use his morning visit to tell Franco that Pedrolo Nieto Antúnez as Prime Minister meant the 'hecatombe' and accused Pedrolo of all kinds of corruption. Then Urcelay repeated the same accusations.[76] They seemed not to concern Franco, but the overnight and early morning pressure did persuade him that Pedrolo was as old and forgetful as himself. Finally, under the baleful eye of Doña Carmen, who sat doggedly knitting, he instructed Rodríguez Valcárcel to include Arias Navarro in the *terna*. Later on the same day, the *Consejo del Reino* 'elected' the *terna* which duly included Arias.[77]

In his end-of-year message on 30 December 1973, Franco's tribute to the assassinated admiral could hardly have been more tight-lipped. He amended the typed text of the message, adding by hand the words, 'It's an ill wind that blows nobody any good.' This was taken in the inner circles of the regime to be an acknowledgement that he now saw the Carrero Blanco period as a mistake.[78] When asked years later about his reaction to this, Juan Carlos maintained a pregnant silence.[79] The continuing suspicions of monarchists were expressed in the words of Luis María Anson: 'The death of Carrero was an evil. But Carrero with whom, for historical reasons, Franco could not easily dispense, signified a guarantee of the future for the Prince. His assassination has permitted Franco to appoint Arias. And Arias – it's an ill wind – signified a guarantee of the future for Franco's family.'[80] That Anson's speculation truly reflected Franco's thought processes is debatable but it almost certainly mirrored those of his wife.

The nomination of Arias as replacement for Carrero Blanco, in response to intense pressure, was Franco's last major political decision and it had not been his own. Even less had it been Juan Carlos's. Considering his position as official successor, and the proximity of Franco's inevitable demise, his exclusion from the decision-making process was both scandalous and humiliating. Nevertheless, he maintained his customary discretion. In contrast, Arias Navarro was, in the words of Girón, 'euphoric, exultant'. On 2 January 1974, he was sworn in as Prime Minister at El Pardo. Immediately afterwards, he was photographed with a laughing Doña Carmen who treated him to an alarmingly open-mouthed smile. Her apparent delight was splashed across the Spanish press on 3 January and caused considerable comment, given the rarity with which she manifested good humour in public. Moreover, such jollity was hardly in keeping with the nature of the occasion.[81]

The composition of Arias Navarro's cabinet can only have intensified Doña Carmen's delight. The remaining partisans of Juan Carlos from Carrero Blanco's cabinet – José María López de Letona (Industry), Gonzalo Fernández de la Mora (Public Works), Fernando de Liñán (Information), José María Gamazo Manglano (Under-Secretary of the *Presidencia*) – were removed *en masse*. The most notable, and damaging, absences were those of Laureano López Rodó and Torcuato Fernández-Miranda. When Arias proposed Manuel Fraga as his Minister of Foreign Affairs, this was vetoed by Franco who wanted to keep López Rodó. Arias was adamant that López Rodó was unacceptable. They compromised on the diplomat Pedro Cortina Mauri, the man who had informed on López Bravo's indiscretions about the Caudillo and a firm favourite of Doña Carmen. It would appear that Arias Navarro had good reason to want to reward Cortina Mauri. It has been alleged that, while Ambassador in France, Cortina did Arias a great service by refusing an offer from the French police to hand over the assassins of Carrero Blanco. Their interrogation in Spain might well have revealed Arias's security lapses.[82]

Nevertheless, it was not all bad news for the Prince. Arias Navarro categorically refused to have Girón as his Vice-President. Through the El Pardo clique, Girón's enormous influence was reflected in the number of hardliners in the cabinet. Nevertheless, to counteract that, Arias Navarro brought in two men who had pushed his cause within the *Consejo del Reino*, Antonio Carro, as Secretary-General of the *Presidencia*, and Pío Cabanillas, as Minister of Information. Both were followers of Fraga. Another progressive element in the cabinet was the liberal Minister of Finance, Antonio Barrera de Irimo. Arias had not wanted him to continue in his post, but Franco, who greatly admired Barrera's efficiency, had insisted. The ministers most opposed to change in the system were the two Falangist supporters of Girón from Carrero's cabinet: José Utrera Molina, now appointed Secretary-General of the *Movimiento*, and Francisco Ruiz-Jarabo, who remained as Minister of Justice. José García Hernández, the Minister of the Interior and Vice-President in charge of internal security, was, like Arias himself, a one-time assistant to General Camilo Alonso Vega. Joaquín Gutiérrez Cano, Minister for the Development Plan, was an economist who was utterly devoted to the Franco family. The Caudillo himself had insisted on his inclusion.[83]

Arias had wanted the chief prosecutor of the Supreme Court, Fernando Herrero Tejedor, to head the *Movimiento* – and it has been insinuated, without foundation, that this was in order to curtail his investigation into the assassination of Carrero Blanco.[84] In the event, Girón's influence in El Pardo ensured that Franco obliged Arias to appoint Utrera Molina. Utrera warned Arias that he would not permit the *Movimiento* to be an obedient herd of followers. The formal ceremony of his entry into the Ministry was attended by a number of hardline opponents of Juan Carlos – Arrese, Fernández Cuesta, Solís and Girón from the Falange and *generales azules* like Carlos Iniesta Cano, and García Rebull, the head of the Civil Guard.[85] In what was a calculated insult, Arias had not even spoken with Juan Carlos about his proposed new cabinet. Indeed, Arias made no secret of his lack of respect for Juan Carlos. The Prince was not pleased. He was furious that Alfonso de Borbón y Dampierre had been consulted about the appointment of ministers. This was to be an immensely worrying period for Juan Carlos. Although he could eventually take some consolation from the liberalizing intentions of Pío Cabanillas and Antonio Carro, for the moment he decided that he had to 'be like

Machiavelli'. His powerful allies in the government, López Rodó and Carrero Blanco, were gone. Carro manifested considerable hostility to López Rodó, telling him: 'Don't even think about setting foot in Alcalá!' (a reference to the offices of the *Presidencia del Gobierno*). Arias Navarro deprived Juan Carlos of a valuable adviser by sending López Rodó to be Ambassador to Austria. The posting was a humiliation for an ex-Minister of Foreign Affairs and particularly for someone so closely associated with the Prince. Juan Carlos took it as a personal slight.[86]

Moreover, the Prince's direct access to Franco was now deliberately impeded by the El Pardo clique. The Marqués de Villaverde was delighted by the fact that Arias had not consulted the Prince about the composition of the cabinet. At a hunting party in late January, he said with some confidence, 'For the moment, we've got five years in government, then we'll see.' At another hunt, Alfonso de Borbón y Dampierre commented on his satisfaction at the political turn of events since the death of Carrero Blanco.[87] Nevertheless, Juan Carlos's situation was benefited by the fact that Antonio Carro introduced into the government many of the Catholic reformist group known collectively as *Tácito*. They became under-secretaries in various ministries. Through his personal secretary, Jacobo Cano, the Prince was in close touch with many of them.[88]

The dictator's wife, his son-in-law and their bunker allies were initially delighted by Arias Navarro's marginalization of the Prince. However, the new Prime Minister would prove to be a big disappointment to them. The social problems of the regime would oblige an uncomprehending Arias to go further than Carrero Blanco had ever done in the direction of change. His instincts were entirely authoritarian, but the more liberal members of his team, particularly Pío Cabanillas, persuaded him that to defend the essences of Francoism it was necessary at least to change its image. Accordingly, he lent himself to reading out a declaration of progressive intent on 12 February 1974. The text was prepared in Antonio Carro's *Presidencia* by two of his subordinates from *Tácito*, Gabriel Cisneros and Luis Jaúdenes. Arias did not discuss its content with Juan Carlos nor was it discussed in cabinet. The first that Utrera Molina and the other partisans of Girón knew of it was when they heard Arias in the Cortes. They were inevitably alarmed by his declaration that: 'The Spanish people, and above all the government, must understand that it is not fair to go on unconsciously placing responsibility for political innovation on the noble shoulders of the Head of State.' The implicit threat of greater levels of initiative from the Prince and more popular political participation incited the fears of the bunker. Arias himself seems not to have perceived the full implications of what came quickly to be called the 'spirit of 12 February' – not least because Franco himself initially seemed unperturbed.[89]

It was symptomatic of the decadence of the regime that the cabinet became completely schizoid. The Prince, mistrustful of Arias himself, pinned his hopes on the reformers while the El Pardo clique banked on Utrera Molina and the Falangists who opposed change. The bunker had the advantage of being able to wheel out the increasingly uncomprehending Caudillo in an effort to block any progressive initiative. The process was facilitated by the fact that, as he aged and regressed, Franco was highly susceptible to accusations that some of Arias's ministers were freemasons. Franco relied for his interpretation of the general drift of politics on Utrera with whom he soon established a paternal relationship. Shortly after joining the government, Utrera was told by the Caudillo that: 'We have committed the error of lowering our guard but there is still time to make good the mistake.' After Arias's speech, the Caudillo asked Utrera to explain to him 'the spirit of 12 February'. Thoroughly alarmed by the explanation given, Franco said, 'There is no need to depart from the spirit of 18 July! If the regime allows its doctrinal essence to be attacked and its defenders fail to defend what is fundamental, we will be driven to think that some are contemplating a cowardly suicide.' The clear implication was that the liberalizing intentions of Juan Carlos and his partisans had to be blocked. The *Movimiento*'s intelligence services provided Franco with daily reports on the plans of the *aperturistas*. Seriously alarmed, he determined to block them.[90]

Juan Carlos was virtually ignored by the Prime Minister – something he did not forgive easily. He was obliged to watch helplessly as Arias Navarro drifted directionless through the waves of inflation and working-class militancy that were the fruit of the energy crisis. Arias lumbered into one conflict after another, his reactionary instincts soon making a mockery of the 'spirit of 12 February'. At the end of February, death sentences had been passed against a Catalan anarchist, Salvador Puig Antich, and a common criminal, Heinz Chez. Despite appeals from the European Commission and the Vatican, Franco refused to commute the sentences which were carried out by *garrote vil* (strangulation) on 2 March 1974. Aware of the importance of foreign opinion, Juan Carlos was appalled. The consequent international outcry was reminiscent of that which had accompanied both the Burgos trials in 1970 and the execution of Julián Grimau García in 1963.

Two days later, Arias Navarro ordered the expulsion from Spain of the Bishop of Bilbao, Monsignor Antonio Añoveros, for permitting the publication on 24 February of a homily in defence of ethnic minorities. Coming so soon after ETA's assassination of Carrero Blanco, the text was considered to be provocative. Añoveros was placed under house arrest and an aircraft was sent to Bilbao to transport him to Lisbon. The Bishop stood firm, declaring that only the Pope could order him to leave his diocese and that those using violence to remove him would suffer grave canonical sentences. There was a massive wave of support for Añoveros in the Basque Country and within the Church. The Cardinal-Archbishop of Madrid, and President of the Bishops' Conference, Cardinal Vicente Enrique y Tarancón, was uneasy about Añoveros's views but he could not permit arbitrary State action against a bishop. Accordingly, he prepared a decree of excommunication against the Prime Minister. Learning of this, Arias Navarro announced that he was perfectly prepared to break off relations with the Vatican. In the early days of the crisis, the inhabitants of El Pardo, including the Caudillo, encouraged Arias in his intransigence. On 6 March, Franco even went so far as to tell the Primate of Spain, the Cardinal-Archbishop of Toledo, Marcelo González Martín, that Añoveros was a subversive who had betrayed the fundamental laws of the regime. Tarancón and Pío Cabanillas were working on a compromise solution. To the relief of the Prince, finally Franco himself, alarmed at the prospect of his Prime Minister being excommunicated, obliged Arias to back down.[91] Juan Carlos complained to López Rodó, 'I never get to touch the ball. All I can do is smile, stay above petty politics, not push and be on guard.'[92]

In late April 1974, the fall of the dictatorship in Portugal sent shudders through El Pardo. Don Juan expressed his approval of the events, declaring himself to be a friend and admirer of General Antonio Spínola. Accordingly, the news from Portugal intensified the bunker's suspicions of Juan Carlos. The Spanish left was moving towards a united front. In Paris, Santiago Carrillo, the Secretary-General of the Spanish Communist Party, the PCE, was negotiating with various elements, including the Opus Dei monarchist Rafael Calvo Serer and the rich lawyer, Antonio García Trevijano. A frequent visitor to Estoril, García Trevijano optimistically believed that Don Juan would ride to the throne at the head of the opposition. The hope was that Don Juan might be persuaded to be the figurehead of what eventually became, in June 1974, the opposition coalition known as the *Junta Democrática*. Doña María de las Mercedes was alarmed by her husband's flirtation with the left. Juan Carlos was also concerned, since a declaration by his father of outright hostility to the regime would severely damage his own possibilities of reaching the throne. Don Juan met his son at his summer residence, the palace of Marivent in Mallorca in mid-June. As a consequence of their meeting, he pulled back from his connections with the *Junta Democrática*. It is likely too that Don Juan had realized that García Trevijano hoped for a referendum on the future form of the post-Franco State which might, of course, lead to the establishment of a Republic.[93]

On 28 April 1974, just three days after the cataclysm in Portugal, bypassing the censorship, Girón had launched in *Arriba* a savage broadside against 'false liberals'. The article was principally directed at Arias, and also Pío Cabanillas who had outraged hardline Francoists with an extremely liberal speech in Catalonia on 20 April. As Secretary-General of the *Movimiento*, Utrera thought that he would get the blame, but Franco confided in him that he was delighted by this so-called *Gironazo* because he was convinced that those pushing for the freedom of political associations were using the concept in order to introduce political parties.[94] As part of the same operation, there was a plot for crucial sectors of the Army to be taken over by generals close to the bunker. The scheme enjoyed the support of Girón and other members of the El Pardo clique, although Franco himself had not been informed. When it came to his attention, his concern for military regulations and seniority procedures ensured his backing for Arias and the plot came to naught. Nevertheless, the bunker scored a significant triumph over Arias when pressure from bunker generals obliged him on 8 June to dismiss the Chief of the General Staff, the liberal General Manuel Díez Alegría, as punishment for holding talks with President Ceaușescu of Romania. He was replaced by General Carlos Fernández Vallespin. Arias was told by Franco to make his peace with the bunker. Within a week, Arias went so far towards the appeasement of the bunker as to alarm Juan Carlos and his immediate advisers. On 15 June, at a meeting in Barcelona of the Catalan sections of the *Movimiento*, with his arm outstretched in the Fascist salute, Arias sang the Falangist anthem, '*Cara al sol*' and declared 'The "spirit of 12 February" exists but that spirit will not and cannot be different from the permanent and unchanging spirit of the regime from the moment of its foundation.' Franco was delighted and rang to thank him.[95]

By this time, the Caudillo's narrow circle of acquaintances had infected him with their own fears. According to a senior officer of his military household, Franco had started to keep a machine gun in his bedroom.[96] On 5 July, the El Pardo clique's anxieties for the future intensified dramatically when the Caudillo was taken seriously ill. He had phlebitis in the right leg, a problem attributed by Dr Vicente Gil to a combination of repeated pressure from a fishing rod and the fact that he had sat through every televised football match during the 1974 World Cup. Arias Navarro tried to prevent Franco being hospitalized but Gil and other specialists feared that the condition might develop into a pulmonary embolism. Accordingly, on Tuesday 9 July, he entered the Francisco Franco Hospital. The treatment of the phlebitis was complicated by the fact that the medication to alleviate the symptoms of Parkinson's disease was causing gastric ulcers. The anticoagulants needed to treat the blood clot associated with the phlebitis were incompatible with the treatment for his ulcers. When the Prince heard the news about Franco's hospitalization, he felt, with sinking heart, the reality of the tremendous responsibilities about to be placed on him.[97]

Before leaving El Pardo, Franco telephoned Arias Navarro and Rodríguez Valcárcel, President of the Cortes, and ordered them to prepare the decree permitting Juan Carlos to take over as interim Head of State – that is to say, without his being proclaimed King. Believing that he would have to undergo a life-threatening operation, Franco said, 'This is the beginning of the end.' The decree was ready by the next day. However, on Thursday 11 July, Juan Carlos suggested to Arias that he swamp Franco with cabinet files for decision, thereby hoping to provoke the Caudillo into recognizing that he was not fit to carry on as Head of State and thus retire fully. But Arias was adamant that Article 11 of the *Ley de Sucesión* be implemented. The Prince asked Franco not to sign the document, saying, 'General, you still have all your mental faculties. I wouldn't like to give the impression of being in a hurry. When the moment comes, I would like to succeed you as King and for you to be around to see it.' Juan Carlos pointed out to Rodríguez Valcárcel an ambiguity in Article 11 of the *Ley de Sucesión* which referred to the interim transfer of 'his powers' without clarifying whether this referred to the powers enjoyed by Franco or those to be eventually assumed by the King. The clarification of this point delayed matters for nearly ten days.[98]

Rumours proliferated to the effect that Arias wanted the Caudillo to hand over to Juan Carlos definitively. Regime hardliners were alarmed by talk that Arias Navarro himself wanted to assume Franco's title of *Jefe Nacional* of the *Movimiento* in order to facilitate this process and to push forward the idea of political associations. Girón immediately hastened to the hospital where he had a screaming row with Arias. Hearing the noise from his bed, Franco had Girón shown in. According to Girón's account, he found Franco fully determined neither to grant leadership of the *Movimiento* to Arias nor to hand over permanently to Juan

Carlos.[99] However, the fears of the bunker intensified when Franco was unable to preside at the regime's annual 18 July reception at the palace of La Granja near Segovia. His place was taken by the Prince. On the following day, the Caudillo took a dramatic turn for the worse.

A stricken Arias Navarro said to the cabinet, 'It looks really bad. I saw death in his eyes which were glazed over. He has surrendered.' The tearful ministers decided that Article 11 of the *Ley de Sucesión* should be implemented. Arias and Rodríguez Valcárcel returned to the hospital with the necessary papers. Cristóbal Martínez-Bordiu blocked the door in an attempt to prevent Arias and Dr Vicente Gil entering Franco's room, shouting that the nomination of Juan Carlos was treachery. Gil knocked him out of the way and Arias successfully urged the Caudillo to sign. Doña Carmen and Don Cristóbal were furious. Beside himself with rage, Don Cristóbal said to Gil: 'What a lousy trick you have played on my father-in-law! What a favour you have done for that snot-nosed kid Juanito.' The Marqués's fury was born of his recognition that the claims of his son-in-law, Alfonso de Borbón y Dampierre, were finally dead. When Doña Carmen realized that her granddaughter's prospects had been dashed, her anger was uncontained. She shouted at Gil that she would hold him responsible for the consequences of what he had done. When he explained his actions in terms of concern for Franco's health, she cut him short, snapping, 'Rubbish. You have done to Paco the worst thing you could have.'[100]

With the regime's international prestige still in tatters in the wake of the Puig Antich execution and the Añoveros affair, Juan Carlos remained extremely reluctant to accept the position of interim Head of State. He understandably had no desire to be tarnished by the actions of an unsympathetic government in whose selection he had played no part and whose Prime Minister never consulted him. Nor did he wish, as he put it, 'to be lumbered with a series of difficult problems' both economic and colonial (inflation was rocketing in the wake of the energy crisis and Morocco was pushing to recover Spanish Sahara). He was reluctant to take on such dangerous responsibilities before being made King. His plans for eventual reform of the regime could be compromised by even an interim period as Head of State during which he would have no capacity to change anything but have unlimited responsibility for everything. But his flimsy hopes that Franco would hand over to him on a permanent basis faced the determined opposition of Cristóbal Martínez-Bordiu and Doña Carmen.[101]

Arias and the hardliners in the cabinet were determined to make Juan Carlos accept in order to safeguard the continuity of the regime. The Prime Minister was quoted as saying, 'If he doesn't want to, he will be made to.' The Prince had no choice – to refuse outright would bring into question the entire constitutional edifice on which his succession was postulated. In the event, his period as interim Head of State would be short-lived. By 24 July, the Caudillo had made an unexpected recovery. Dr Manuel Hidalgo Huerta, Director of the Provincial Hospital of Madrid, declared that he was better and could go on holiday whenever he wanted. A new personal physician, Dr Vicente Pozuelo, an amiable man of great competence and sensibility, took over the Caudillo's care on 31 July 1974. In response to Franco's Parkinson's disease, Pozuelo prepared a programme of exercise therapy and rehabilitation. That, together with a more varied diet, saw a remarkable improvement in the Caudillo's health. On 4 August, Juan Carlos and Doña Sofía took their three children to El Pardo to see Franco. They found him rather lonely and forlorn. When the Prince asked Dr Pozuelo about Franco's health, the doctor replied with characteristic good nature and common sense, 'One of the key things that he needs is affection, the concern of all those that he thinks of as his family. And I think that, in that group, he includes Your Highness and your children.' Rather moved, Juan Carlos replied, 'Very good. I'll do what I can. Everything I have, I owe to him.'[102]

On 9 August, as interim Head of State, Juan Carlos had presided at a cabinet meeting in El Pardo. When it was over, one of Franco's aides said to Utrera, 'I know you are loyal, so I want to warn you that something is being cooked up. Be careful.' Utrera took this to mean a plan by the Prince's partisans to have Franco declared incapable of returning to the Headship of State. As the ministers went into the gardens to greet a convalescent Franco,

Cristóbal Martínez-Bordiu strutted about as if he had assumed, in all its ramifications, the role of head of the family. He was openly rude to Juan Carlos, ostentatiously ordering a whiskey for 'the Prince' and when Juan Carlos demurred, repeating the order, 'I meant for the Prince,' indicating his own son-in-law, Alfonso de Borbón y Dampierre. Franco brushed over the issue saying to the waiter, 'The Prince has got a drink. Take the whiskey to the Duke.' On 16 August, the Caudillo was able to fly to Galicia for his annual holiday at the Pazo de Meirás. There, he was subjected to a whispering campaign by his wife and son-in-law that awakened his suspicions of Juan Carlos. The family exaggerated secret service reports of the Prince's telephone conversations with his father to persuade Franco that he planned to recall Don Juan to Spain as King.[103]

The Marqués de Villaverde was reported to have travelled to Marbella to consult with Girón about how best to block Arias's drift into reformism. At the palace of Marivent, the Prince was deeply uneasy about the machinations of Martínez-Bordiu and Girón – 'I had a vague feeling that there was something fishy going on.' Accordingly, he concluded that it would be a good idea to spend time with Franco and try to counteract their influence. On 24 August, he telephoned Dr Pozuelo, and asked him if he considered it a good idea for him to visit Franco and, with typical diffidence, if there was room for him at the Pazo de Meirás. The good doctor suggested that he speak directly with Franco. Accordingly, the Prince arrived on 27 August. However, it was quickly clear that Cristóbal Martínez-Bordiu did not want him there. Indeed, even Dr Pozuelo felt a noticeable coolness from the family because of his excellent relationship with the Prince.

Seeing how well the Caudillo appeared, Juan Carlos said, 'I'm delighted to see that you are so much better, General. You'll soon be able to return to your normal activities again and I'll be able to withdraw.' Franco replied, with apparent warmth, 'No, Your Highness, carry on. You are doing very well.' The Prince's sixth sense told him that all was far from being as it seemed. He pressed on, 'General, you must understand that I am in a very difficult position. While you were ill, it was fine for me to replace you as

Head of State, but now that you're getting better, the Spanish people will not understand why there are two Heads of State: the real one, you; and the one who becomes pointless as soon as you are able to exercise power again, me.' Franco just looked at him silently. Forced to be slightly more blunt, the Prince said: 'I don't mind being Príncipe de España or King, but I refuse to carry out functions which are yours alone, General.' Franco replied simply, 'Believe me, Highness, you're doing very well. Carry on.' Everything about the atmosphere in the Pazo de Meirás, including Franco's cordiality, rang false with the Prince.[104]

Concerned by the ambitions of Cristóbal Martínez-Bordiu, Juan Carlos asked Dr Pozuelo about the situation of Alfonso de Borbón y Dampierre. The doctor took the liberty of suggesting to the Prince that, to counteract the influence of Alfonso, he should work on Franco's affections and even insinuate that he regarded him as a father figure. Pozuelo even went so far as to suggest that he stress the conflict between the Caudillo's desire to make him King and Don Juan's desires to impede the plans for the succession. With startling frankness, he said, 'Your Highness should play his cards better. Don't you realize that the children of the Duque de Cádiz are here all day calling Franco "grandad, grandad" nonstop? I recommend that you come and see him every day and bring your children to spend time with him so that he sees how fond of him you are.' Doña Sofía nodded agreement but the Prince asked, 'But, if we do that, won't it be misinterpreted?' Pozuelo replied, 'What does it matter? Don't you want a kingdom, Highness?'

Pozuelo later recounted this conversation to Franco, who seemed to be pleased by news of Juan Carlos's fondness for him. Alfonso de Borbón y Dampierre had the significant advantage of being married to María del Carmen Martínez-Bordiu, but the fact of being so aggressively sponsored by his father-in-law worked to his detriment. The Caudillo felt considerable disdain for Cristóbal Martínez-Bordiu, in part because of his boastful manner and his seedy business deals but, above all, because of his frequent marital infidelities. Franco was reported as saying, 'If someone betrays God in the sacrament of matrimony and deceives his wife, how can we be sure that he will not betray and deceive his Fatherland?'[105]

However, even if Franco was not inclined to favour Alfonso de Borbón y Dampierre over Juan Carlos as his eventual successor, he was not disposed to relinquish power. He was determined to block plans for the future liberalization of the dictatorship. On 28 August, in a long conversation in the garden of the Pazo de Meirás, Utrera Molina warned Franco about plans to have him declared incapable as the first step to democratization under Juan Carlos. The outraged Caudillo replied, 'That is not a political plan, it's a miserable ambition,' before making it clear that he had no intention of giving up. 'I have weighed up the necessity of retiring or staying on. Thank God, I feel better. I'm not a dictator who hangs on so as not to lose privileges, but this is not the first time that Spain has asked for my sacrifice. After a reasonable interval, and when I have made the changes which can be put off no longer, I will reconsider my decision.' Franco was not talking about changing the arrangements for the succession but about the need to change Arias's government precisely because of its perceived weakness. When asked for his opinion, Utrera replied, 'You should return and decide on changes, beginning with me,' to which Franco said only, 'It is necessary.'[106] Utrera's encouragement seems to have helped convince Franco that he must resume his functions.

The Prince presided at another cabinet meeting on 30 August. Underlining the provisional nature of his Headship of State, the session was held at the Pazo de Meirás. Utrera's interview with Franco had been the object of considerable press comment. That, plus the atmosphere in the Pazo convinced Juan Carlos that Franco would soon put an end to his interim status. When Franco received the ministers in the garden, the Minister of the Interior, José García Hernández, said to him, 'General, it is time for you to lighten your duties and leave the helm in other hands.' Franco stared at him and said ominously, 'You know that is not possible.'[107]

After the cabinet meeting, Juan Carlos left for Mallorca. By 31 August, the medical team had decided that Franco was restored to full health. Before leaving, Juan Carlos had asked Franco's daughter Nenuca if her father had any intention of resuming as Head of State, and she replied that his programme of convalescence rendered the prospect completely impossible. Nevertheless, fully aware of the machinations of Cristóbal Martínez-Bordiu, he was not convinced. Juan Carlos said later that Martínez-Bordiu, 'wasn't the only one gambling on that possibility. With that end in view, the members of Franco's entourage were bringing very strong pressure to bear on an old man weakened by pain and illness.'[108]

Franco's family having successfully worked on his anxieties about a conspiracy between Juan Carlos and Don Juan, on 2 September, the Caudillo decided to resume his powers. An exultant Martínez-Bordiu telephoned Arias Navarro at his holiday home at Salinas. Just before the official announcement, Franco himself spoke on the telephone to the Prince, who was now back at Marivent. He said, 'Highness, I just wanted to warn you that I have decided to assume my powers from tomorrow.' Juan Carlos, although delighted that his purgatory was over, for the moment at least, was furious at the dismissive way in which he had been treated. Franco merely wished him good night. Arias Navarro, however, did not bother to travel to Mallorca to tell Juan Carlos in person. The Prince, for his part, pointedly failed to be at the airport to greet Franco on his return from Galicia.[109]

Franco's precipitate and ill-advised return to power was a victory for the El Pardo clique over Juan Carlos. Efforts by Cristóbal Martínez-Bordiu to persuade the Prince that he had nothing to fear from El Pardo merely intensified Juan Carlos's suspicions. He commented to López Rodó, 'There's something going on in the family. Qui s'excuse, s'accuse.'[110] Now regarding Arias as a traitor, the bunker soon followed up Franco's return with an assault on the most liberal minister in the cabinet, Pío Cabanillas. Franco was given a dossier of Spanish magazine pages containing advertisements for beachwear and camping equipment featuring bikini-clad models skilfully interleaved with pages of foreign soft pornography to give the impression that such material was published in Spain. Already irritated by Cabanillas's reaction to the Portuguese revolution, Franco was infuriated by evidence that the minister was allowing the press to publicize the involvement of his brother Nicolás in a scandal concerning huge quantities of missing olive oil, the so-called *aceite de Redondela* case. The last straw was the publication in *El Correo de Andalucia* of an interview with Felipe González, the Secretary-General of the Socialist Party. On 24 October, Arias had his weekly meeting with Franco and was ordered to remove Cabanillas. In solidarity, Antonio Barrera de Irimo resigned. A feeble effort by Arias and Antonio Carro to maintain a balance by also removing Utrera and Francisco Ruiz-Jarabo was brushed aside by the Caudillo with praise for their loyalty.[111] Things were looking exceedingly bleak for the Prince.

SEVEN

Taking Over

1974–1976

By late 1974, Franco's health was deteriorating rapidly. He remained as determined as ever that political associations should never be a Trojan Horse to introduce political parties after his death. On 19 November, slack-jawed, his left hand trembling uncontrollably, he told Utrera Molina, 'Everybody knows my views on the pernicious nature of political parties and I'm sure the Government's scheme will prevent them degenerating to the point of becoming sectarian and adversarial groups.' It was the job of the *Consejo Nacional* of the *Movimiento* to control them, suspending or dissolving any that went beyond the provisions of the *Ley Orgánica* and showed signs of developing into political parties – 'they are incompatible with the Regime'.[1]

The *Estatuto de las Asociaciones Políticas* (Statute of Political Associations) was approved by the *Consejo Nacional*, after an 11-hour debate on 16 December 1974.[2] Three days later, Utrera confided in Franco his conviction that Juan Carlos was not committed to 'projects aimed at securing the continuity of the regime'. Outraged, the Caudillo fixed Utrera with a baleful glare and said, 'That is not true and what you are saying is very serious.' After a long hostile silence, he went on, 'I know that when I die, everything will be different, but there are oaths that have to be kept and principles which have to remain in place.' Utrera pressed on, insisting that, after the succession, Juan Carlos intended to return Spain to a liberal, parliamentary monarchy. Another tense silence followed, broken only when Franco said, 'The institutions will fulfil their task. Spain cannot return to fragmentation and discord.'[3]

Franco was not troubled by fears that Juan Carlos might use

associations as a stepping stone to political parties. In his end-of-year broadcast on 31 December 1974, he took pride in the solidity of the regime's institutions. He expressed confidence that political associations would not open the way to the divisions and egoism that were the hallmark of political parties.[4] He seemed blissfully unaware that the Francoist coalition was disintegrating around him. The bunker, led by Girón de Velasco and with powerful allies in El Pardo, was determined to defend the essences of the Francoist laws. The partisans of Juan Carlos hoped to use those laws to develop some kind of democratic regime. In the middle was Arias Navarro, aware that some kind of reform was necessary but determined to keep it to a minimum. His relations with Juan Carlos were tense, but with his one-time supporters of the bunker they were abysmal.

A group of politicians who regarded themselves as the Prince's men were planning for the future and, in the process, exposed the limitations of the Statute of Political Associations. Manuel Fraga Iribarne, Federico Silva Muñoz and José María de Areilza were cooperating in the preparation of a political association in the belief that Arias would hand over power to them when Franco died. When its draft programme was shown to Franco, he asked sarcastically for what country Fraga was writing. The plan came to nothing. When Fraga sought an audience with Franco to explain his plans, the Prince told a mutual friend, 'He shouldn't come; he'll be eaten alive by the beast.'[5] The Prince had been kept informed through the liaison of José Joaquín Puig de la Bellacasa, a brilliant young diplomat who joined his staff in May 1974. Puig de la Bellacasa would serve as a link between Juan Carlos and numerous figures of the opposition and the foreign press. In this way, he constituted a liberal counterweight in La Zarzuela to the conservative Marqués de Mondéjar and General Alfonso Armada.[6]

Through the *Movimiento* press, Utrera tried to undermine Arias. When the Minister of Labour, Licinio de la Fuente, resigned on 24 February 1975 in protest at obstacles put in the way of his plans to recognize the right to strike, Arias finally went onto the attack against the bunker. He told Franco on 26 February, and again on 3 March, that he wanted to take the opportunity offered by Fuente's resignation to replace other ministers. Juan Carlos urged Arias not to push too hard lest Franco end up replacing him with someone even more sympathetic to the bunker, such as Alejandro Rodríguez Valcárcel. In the event, by alleging that Utrera had plotted against him, and by threatening to resign himself, Arias was able to intimidate a weak and nervous old man into agreement. Franco was thus obliged to permit a ministerial reshuffle in which both Ruiz-Jarabo and Utrera were removed. Fernando Herrero Tejedor, the chief prosecutor of the Supreme Court, finally arrived as the great new liberal promise in the post of Secretary-General of the *Movimiento*.[7]

Despite the opposition of Girón, Franco accepted Herrero's nomination because of the highly competent investigative report that he had produced on the death of Carrero Blanco. Many, including the Prince, hoped that Herrero would be able to make something of the project for political associations. Juan Carlos also told Herrero that he saw him as a future Prime Minister and that he would be pleased if he named as his second-in-command the coming man in the Francoist political élite, the sleek and charming Adolfo Suárez González.[8]

Having become Herrero Tejedor's secretary in the mid-1950s, Suárez had risen on his coat-tails to become an archetypal *Movimiento* bureaucrat. Driven by a powerful ambition, Suárez joined the Opus Dei and made friends with important regime figures during the period of the early 1960s when Herrero was Vice-Secretary of the *Movimiento* under Solís. Thereafter, by carefully cultivating the then Minister of the Interior, General Camilo Alonso Vega, he became Civil Governor of Segovia in 1968. In that post, he had met the Prince and they had got on well, to the extent of *tuteándose* (using the intimate '*tu*' form of address). He was a good example of the professional politician who had grown up within the regime yet instinctively felt that it acted as a strait-jacket on a society that had outgrown its restraints. For the Prince, the 42-year-old Suárez had the attraction of being only six years older than himself and not having the paternal or patronizing attitudes of López Rodó or even Torcuato Fernández-Miranda. As he neared the top, Suárez used his connection with Herrero

Tejedor both to attract the attention of Franco and to consolidate his friendship with Juan Carlos.

Suárez was made Director General of the Spanish television and radio network, RTVE, in 1969 at the suggestion of Carrero Blanco who had, in turn, been given his name by Juan Carlos. He used his control of the media to promote Juan Carlos who, at that time, was the subject of popular jokes portraying him as Franco's puppet. He also fostered the image of ministers with whom he wanted to curry favour. He pleased the Prince greatly by failing to televise the wedding of Alfonso de Borbón y Dampierre with María del Carmen Martínez-Bordiu. During his period in television, he began to build a reputation as a man who enjoyed a special relationship with the Army. He began by establishing a close friendship with Colonel Andrés Casinello Pérez, second-in-command of Carrero Blanco's intelligence service, the SIPG, and ingratiated himself with senior generals by making television time available to them and by sending flowers to their wives. In consequence, when he became Vice-Secretary of the *Movimiento* himself in February 1975, the Secretary-General, Herrero Tejedor, had asked him to prepare a report on the Armed Forces and their attitudes to political change. In the course of this, he managed to consolidate his links with senior officers and with the Prince, who was impressed by the report and its conclusion that the Army would acquiesce in a mild political reform.[9]

On 31 May, President Gerald Ford arrived in Spain for a two-day visit. It was a reflection of the fact that State Department policy was planning for the future that President Ford spent considerably more time with the Prince than with Franco.[10] That endorsement of his position was soon followed by a reminder that his links with Francoism, although crucial to his ever securing the throne, placed him in a precarious position. The continuing activities of ETA and rightist terror squads, brutal repression in the Basque Country and death sentences passed against three ETA militants at the beginning of the summer provoked widespread fear and distaste. At the same time, the opposition was becoming more united by the day. The Communist-dominated front, the *Junta Democrática*, had been followed in June 1975 by the *Plataforma de Convergencia Democrática* which linked the PSOE with a group of Social Democrats and Christian Democrats. The *Plataforma* was somewhat more open to the notion of dialogue with the regime reformists than the *Junta Democrática*, which remained committed to a strategy of strikes and mass demonstrations. However, the regime's blood-lust helped overcome the Socialists' residual suspicions of the PCE to such an extent that both opposition fronts began negotiations for their ultimate unification.

The foundation of the *Plataforma* had been followed by a meeting of the moderate opposition held at Estoril on 14 June. Over 100 prominent liberal opponents of the regime, seated at tables decorated with Spanish flags and red carnations, were addressed by Don Juan de Borbón. He reaffirmed his rights as heir to the throne, accepted the need for the democratization of Spain and for popular endorsement of the monarchy, and asserted his commitment to human rights. By denouncing the arrangements for the succession as a device to guarantee the continuity of the regime, Don Juan provoked an outburst of panic among the regime reformists and no doubt caused many of them to reflect on the need to make a more serious commitment to democracy if they were to survive.[11]

Don Juan's closeness to the democratic opposition created a difficult situation for Juan Carlos. He told Lord Mountbatten that he was deeply embarrassed by the undermining of his own position.[12] He was equally hurt when the *Movimiento* press launched into savage attacks on Don Juan. On 16 June, an apprehensive Juan Carlos visited Franco who made no reference to the speech. When the Prince broached the subject, Franco brushed it aside, saying, 'We have come through similar circumstances in the past.' Deeply relieved, Juan Carlos embraced the now shrunken dictator and kissed him on the cheek. However, four days later, on the suggestion of Arias Navarro, Franco signed an order banning Don Juan from entering Spain, just at the moment when he would normally be sailing in the Mediterranean and put in at various ports. Juan Carlos had not been consulted. Indeed, in a further humiliating sign of the tension with Arias Navarro, the

Prince was not even informed of the decision. He was seriously displeased.[13]

On 12 June 1975, the new Secretary-General of the *Movimiento*, Fernando Herrero Tejedor, died in a car crash near Villacastín in the province of Segovia. Franco, who was attending a bullfight at the time, was given the news by Adolfo Suárez. The Caudillo was much affected, as was Juan Carlos who told Herrero's son: 'You have lost your father. I have lost my Prime Minister.' Arias Navarro also said to Luis Herrero Tejedor, 'With the death of your father, I have lost my successor as Prime Minister.'[14] The logical successor as head of the *Movimiento* should have been Herrero's second-in-command, Adolfo Suárez. However, Franco had taken the accident as a providential sign that the experiment with political associations did not have divine approval. Moreover, influenced by the poison dropped in his ear by Girón and Cristóbal Martínez-Bordiu, Franco now regarded Suárez as an ambitious traitor.[15] Instead, he obliged Arias to accept José Solís as the new Secretary-General.

In his farewell speech on 3 July 1975, Suárez made an astonishingly courageous plea for 'the construction of a democracy that manifests the legitimate pluralism that exists within society and the establishment of the social justice that is the basis of every real democracy', adding that, 'The monarchy of Don Juan Carlos de Borbón is the future of a modern, democratic and just Spain.' A delighted Juan Carlos showed his gratitude in various ways. He asked Luis María Anson, at the time editor of the weekly magazine *Blanco y Negro*, to do something for Suárez, who was made the magazine's 'politician of the month' shortly thereafter. The Prince also asked the Minister of the Interior, José García Hernández, to get Suárez a good job in the State telephone monopoly. He further requested Solís to make Suárez president of the political association, *Unión del Pueblo Español*, that Herrero Tejedor had been preparing.[16]

Despite the successful efforts of the El Pardo clique to imbue Franco with the fears of the bunker, it has been suggested that, in the summer of 1975, he contemplated standing down and proclaiming Juan Carlos as his successor on 1 October. Certainly, he showed every sign of being the doting grandfather when Juan Carlos and Sofía arrived with their children at the Pazo de Meirás in late July 1975.[17] But if Franco considered retirement, he certainly seems to have changed his mind very quickly after the royal family had returned to Mallorca. On 13 August, he received a group of wartime *Alféreces Provisionales* (Acting Second-Lieutenants in the Civil War) from La Coruña. With these ex-combatants standing rigidly to attention and declaring their loyalty to Franco and the values of the Civil War, the Caudillo began to sob uncontrollably. General José Ramón Gavilán, the second-in-command of Franco's military household, managed to pass him a pair of dark glasses and to bring the audience to an end. However, afterwards, Franco wept on the general's shoulder, sobbing, 'They want to destroy Spain, they want to destroy Spain.' Later the same day, he had a further emotional reminder of the Civil War. On his yacht, the *Azor*, he presided at a naval demonstration and, as the *Azor* entered the bay of El Ferrol, he was overcome with emotion by the sight of the battlecruiser *Canarias*, one of the symbols of his Civil War victory.[18]

In mid-August, Juan Carlos and his family unexpectedly returned to Galicia. Cristóbal Martínez-Bordiu had passed on reports of the Prince's contacts with the opposition. It was even whispered in the Pazo de Meirás that Juan Carlos had sent a message to Santiago Carrillo promising the eventual legalization of the Communist Party. Now Juan Carlos returned to counteract the insinuations of his disloyalty to Franco. Dr Pozuelo noted the acute tension in the atmosphere when Martínez-Bordiu and other enthusiasts for the bunker heard about the Prince's visit. They feared that the warmth between the Caudillo and Juan Carlos would neutralize their efforts. Certainly, over the next few days, the Prince spent every minute possible with Franco.[19]

A cabinet meeting held at the Pazo de Meirás on 22 August introduced a fierce new anti-terrorist law, whose blanket pro-visions covered all aspects of opposition to the regime. The first fruits of the law were a series of trials which would lead to the final black episode in Franco's life. On 28 August, a court martial in Burgos sentenced to death two members of ETA and, on

19 September, another in Barcelona passed a third death penalty. In between, two more courts martial on 11 and 17 September, held at a military base near Madrid, sentenced to death eight members of the *Frente Revolucionario Antifascista y Patriota* (Patriotic and Anti-Fascist Revolutionary Front). FRAP was a Maoist group dedicated to the violent overthrow of Francoism. A worldwide wave of protests, greater even than that occasioned by the trial of Julián Grimau García, provoked Franco's indignation. Fifteen European governments recalled their ambassadors. There were demonstrations and attacks on Spanish embassy buildings in most European countries. At the United Nations, the President of Mexico, Luis Echevarría, called for the expulsion of Spain. Pope Paul VI appealed for clemency as did all the bishops of Spain. Similar requests came from governments around the world. Don Juan asked his son to appeal to Franco on his behalf. Juan Carlos also received a moving plea for clemency from a Catholic lawyer, Juan Lozano Villaplana, who had been a fellow law student in the early 1960s. On 28 August in the Pazo de Meirás, the Prince pleaded with Franco not to proceed with the executions.[20] Franco ignored him as he ignored all the other pleas.

Extremely infirm, the Caudillo presided over the three-and-a-half-hour cabinet meeting held on 26 September at which five death sentences were confirmed. At dawn on the following day, the condemned were shot. Juan Carlos had not been consulted. The Pope took the lead in a series of international protests. The Spanish Embassy in Lisbon was sacked.[21] If, as the Caudillo himself had claimed, the pardons after the 1970 Burgos trials were a sign of the regime's strength, the executions of 27 September 1975 were a symbol of terminal weakness.

By now, Franco was losing weight and having trouble sleeping. On 1 October 1975, the 39th anniversary of his elevation to the Headship of State, he made his last ever public appearance before a huge crowd at the Palacio de Oriente. He was accompanied by an extremely solemn Juan Carlos and Princess Sofía, both looking shiftily ill-at-ease. The now diminutive, hunched Caudillo had evident difficulty in breathing as he croaked out the same paranoiac clichés as always. He took his leave of the crowd weeping and with both hands raised. On the balcony, only Juan Carlos and Sofía failed to give the Fascist salute.[22] Exposure to the stabbing autumn winds of Madrid on 1 October set off the escalation of medical crises that culminated in Franco's death. He was depressed by news on 6 October that King Hassan II of Morocco was planning a 'green march' by 500,000 Moroccans to take over Spanish Sahara. By mid-October, he had symptoms of influenza and, in the early hours of the morning of 15 October, he suffered a heart attack. He continued to work and chaired a cabinet meeting on 17 October. After the meeting, Cristóbal Martínez-Bordiu sidled up to Arias and said, 'I know that you are thinking about the transfer of power to Juan Carlos. My father-in-law needs tranquillity so that he can recover and, if he hears about your manoeuvres, it could worsen his illness. Just wait and in the fullness of time we will look at the situation when it's convenient.' Since the security services were tapping the telephones at La Zarzuela, Arias knew that the Prince would not accept another period as interim Head of State.[23]

Over the following days, Franco had a series of heart attacks and suffered abdominal distension as a result of stomach haemorrhage. However, on 20 October, he was well enough to discuss with Juan Carlos the replacement of Alejandro Rodríguez Valcárcel, whose period as President of the Cortes and of the *Consejo del Reino* would end on 26 November. When the Prince told him that he favoured Torcuato Fernández-Miranda for the position, Franco commented, 'Yes. He's intelligent but too many people dislike him.' In fact, later the same day, Franco informed Rodríguez Valcárcel that he intended to renew his mandate. The implications for the Prince could hardly have been more alarming. Like Arias Navarro, Rodríguez Valcárcel was one of the many Francoists who believed that it was the Prince's task to succeed Franco only in his ceremonial functions. That is to say, Juan Carlos was seen as having the stature to give dignity and decorum to the post of Head of State but was not expected to have political initiative. That would be the job of the Francoist élite who considered themselves to be the executors of the Caudillo's will. As Franco himself had often said, 'Your Highness will not be able to govern as I have done.' If Rodríguez Valcárcel were confirmed as President of the Cortes and of the *Consejo del Reino*, there was no chance of Juan Carlos getting a Prime Minister who could fulfil his reforming ambitions.

Making his immediate plans for the future, Juan Carlos had already telephoned Torcuato Fernández-Miranda on 17 October. They were unable to meet until the evening of Monday 20th, after the Prince's visit to Franco. The frankness with which the Prince spoke of his central concerns was revealed in the notes that Fernández-Miranda jotted down later: '1) Obsession with a purifying forgiveness. Determined to decouple himself from a politics that is going nowhere and to break free of Francoist politicians. 2) The monarchy cannot accept conditions or limits: no to narrowly partisan politicians, no to politicians who mean the acceptance of a line laid down long ago, or who link the monarchy to one specific group or another. 3) New faces: create surprise with the sheer novelty of the first government of the monarchy.' This clearly eliminated López Rodó, Fraga and Areilza and others who might harbour hopes of being the first Prime Minister once Juan Carlos was proclaimed King. Revealing his deep reluctance to continue with Arias Navarro, he told Fernández-Miranda: 'You are my candidate but I fear that is not going to be possible. You know I trust you more than anyone. I need you. I don't know where or how, but I need you. No one has ever spoken to me like you, nor known when to keep quiet like you.' If Fernández-Miranda was disappointed to see that he did not figure as a possible Prime Minister, he only had himself to blame. His advice about the reform of the Francoist constitution from within had already persuaded the Prince that he could better guide the process as President of the Cortes and the *Consejo del Reino*.[24]

Late at night on 20 October, the Caudillo suffered another heart attack. Finally Cristóbal Martínez-Bordiu was convinced that the time had arrived for the transfer of power. In fact, Martínez-Bordiu was interested only in the Prince accepting another period as interim Head of State. He urged Arias Navarro to seek the Prince's agreement. On 21 October, the Prime Minister, accompanied by Rodríguez Valcárcel, went to La Zarzuela to discuss the application of Article 11 of the *Ley de Sucesión*. To their astonishment, Juan Carlos refused outright. He said, 'The Sahara business could explode at any time and I will accept the responsibilities of Head of State only on the condition of having a free hand to act as I would if I were King.' Arias spoke to Franco about the need for a transfer of power but he just looked at him.[25] On 22 October Franco managed to tell Arias in a whisper to send Solís to Morocco to try to gain time from King Hassan.

Aware of Franco's dramatic turn for the worse, the Prince met Torcuato Fernández-Miranda again on the evening of that same day. Juan Carlos asked him if he would rather be Prime Minister or President of the Cortes. Torcuato Fernández-Miranda answered honestly that he would prefer to be Prime Minister but would be more useful as President of the Cortes and of the *Consejo del Reino*. The keys to changing the situation without contravening Francoist legality, and provoking opposition, lay in those two institutions. At the same time, the Prince was anxious to create an image of the monarchy as different from Francoism and the presence of Arias Navarro made that difficult. Neither Fernández-Miranda nor the Prince could see an easy way to remove Arias. He was entrenched in power and, despite the suspicions of the hardliners, was regarded in many regime circles as the executor of Franco's will. To remove him immediately would seem like the first step to dismantling the regime. The need not to antagonize the Francoist establishment made Juan Carlos accept, with the greatest reluctance, that he would have to keep Arias for the moment. It would be the necessary price for the greater prize of replacing Alejandro Rodríguez Valcárcel as President of the Cortes. After the meeting, Fernández-Miranda noted in his diary: 'I can see in the Prince clear appreciation, esteem and confidence in me. In none of the other politicians does he have the confidence that he has in me, but in a way I'm "awkward", he fears me. Although the phrase "he fears me" should not be taken literally: it's as if he sees in me too much his old teacher and thinks that I can "put one over on him".' The Prince trusted Fernández-Miranda's judgement and discretion totally but he perhaps feared for his own independence if his one-time professor were to become his Prime

Minister. Two years later, Torcuato would note: 'All this made him want me as an adviser but, deep down, even though perhaps even he didn't know it, he didn't want me as Prime Minister.'[26]

In the meantime, on 23 October, in the early hours of the morning, Franco suffered a third heart attack. Later in the day, Cristóbal Martínez-Bordiu asked Arias to get the Prince to accept the transfer of power. Knowing it was pointless, Arias said, 'I'm tired of begging the Prince. You speak to him and see if you can persuade him.' Martínez-Bordiu visited La Zarzuela and Juan Carlos told him what he had already told Arias. Accordingly, the Marqués de Villaverde invited him to a meeting at El Pardo where Franco's situation would be discussed by the medical team in charge of his care, the immediate family, Arias Navarro and Rodríguez Valcárcel. The Prince, already doubtful about the wisdom of accepting the invitation, was advised against attending by both General Alfonso Armada and by López Rodó. His old ally warned him that it might look like a cheap conspiracy and would damage his prestige to be involved. Reluctantly, he declined the invitation, agreeing with López Rodó that he should not be seen to play any part in hastening the succession. The decision should be either medical or political and thus should depend on the doctors or on the Prime Minister and the President of the Cortes. López Rodó advised the Prince to replace Arias Navarro and spoke of the need for the new Prime Minister to be someone who had long experience in the cabinet. In the face of this blatant hint, Juan Carlos sagely said nothing.[27]

Juan Carlos was anxious to ensure that he would be able to count on the support of the Army when Franco died. His own period as a cadet in the three military academies had given him a wide range of contacts which enabled him to take the military pulse. He also had help from the liberal General Manuel Díez Alegría. In the course of October, Díez Alegría held several crucial meetings, taking soundings of the Captains-General of the eight military regions, the three military ministers and the *Consejo Superior del Ejército* (Supreme Council of the Army).[28]

With Franco worsening by the hour, Juan Carlos had another long meeting with Torcuato Fernández-Miranda on 26 October.

His reluctance to have Arias Navarro as Prime Minister had resurfaced and he suggested that he should 'assert himself' at the beginning of his reign. He told Torcuato that General Armada had suggested that he keep Rodríguez Valcárcel as President of the Cortes and later name him (Torcuato) as Prime Minister. Torcuato was perplexed by this since he knew that Armada had long insisted that it would be a grave error to sack Arias immediately. He suspected, not unreasonably, that Armada's advice was motivated by his desire as a loyal Francoist to see nothing change and ensure Torcuato's elimination. Fernández-Miranda knew that if Rodríguez Valcárcel was confirmed as President of the Cortes, the confirmation of Arias Navarro's position as Prime Minister would be virtually automatic. Certainly with Rodríguez Valcárcel controlling the key institutions, it would be extremely difficult for the Prince to proceed with his plans for reform.[29]

By 30 October, Franco was manifesting signs of peritonitis. On being told by Dr Pozuelo of his heart attacks and his serious intestinal complications, Franco himself ordered the implementation of Article 11 of the *Ley de Sucesión*. Martínez-Bordiu and Arias, thrown together in alliance, still hoped to get Juan Carlos to accept an interim position, as he had reluctantly done a year previously. The Prince went to see Franco himself and was told by the doctors that the Caudillo had no chance of recovery. Accordingly, when Arias and Rodríguez Valcárcel visited La Zarzuela, the Prince agreed to the application of Article 11.[30] with Franco no longer Head of State, sections of the press began to build up the image of Juan Carlos and to talk of Franco in the past tense.[31] For the Prince, the situation could not have been more nerve-rackingly tense. He could take no decisions while Franco was alive yet had no wish to appear indecisive. Moreover, he was deeply apprehensive about the enormous responsibilities that awaited him. Through General Alfonso Armada, he kept a close eye on the situation in the Sahara.[32] The Portuguese example was very much on his mind. A democratic movement, the *Unión Militar Democrática*, was emerging within the officer corps and the international press was making comparisons with the Portuguese *Movimento das Forças Armadas*. The last thing that Juan Carlos wished to see at

the moment of his own assumption of power was the destabilization that would be provoked by a colonial war.[33]

On 31 October, Juan Carlos chaired a cabinet meeting at La
Zarzuela. The most crucial issue was the crisis in the Sahara.
General Carlos Fernández Vallespin, Chief of the General Staff,
attended the meeting to explain the military situation. As soon as
the meeting was over, Juan Carlos spoke to Arias, the Foreign
Minister, Pedro Cortina Mauri, and Fernández Vallespin. To the
astonishment of those present, he displayed an iron determination
to take control. He told them that he planned to fly to El Aaiún, the
capital of Spanish Sahara to explain the situation to the Governor
General, Lieutenant-General Federico Gómez de Salazar, and his
troops. He would outline to the garrison, 'what we've got to do
and how we're going to do it. We have to withdraw from the
Sahara but in good order and with dignity. Not because we've
been defeated, but because the Spanish Army cannot fire on a
mass of unarmed women and children.'[34] The politicians were
thunderstruck, but the soldiers present were delighted by this demonstration of courage and initiative by their new Commander-in-
Chief. It echoed the gesture of the dictator, General Miguel Primo
de Rivera, who, in October 1924, took personal responsibility for
a major Spanish withdrawal in Morocco.

The Prince had reason to believe that he could resolve the
Sahara crisis without bloodshed. What he did not tell those present
at the meeting in La Zarzuela was that he had decided to take
advantage of the promise made to him by Henry Kissinger in
January 1971. He had already sent a close friend, Manuel Prado
y Colón de Carvajal, to Washington to seek Kissinger's help. Prado
explained that a peaceful handover of power from Franco to the
Prince would be undermined if the Army, the key institution, were
to be involved in a colonial war. The potential parallels with what
had happened in Portugal were sufficient to persuade Kissinger to
intercede with Hassan II. Having agreed, Kissinger spoke not only
with Hassan, but with other Arab leaders and with French President Giscard d'Estaing. At that moment, Nixon's roving Ambassador, General Vernon Walters, was in Morocco. Walters was able
to talk to Hassan and make it clear that some reciprocation was

required. When Juan Carlos reached El Aaiún, the huge mass of Moroccan civilians was visible from the Spanish positions. He spoke to the Spanish forces and explained, to their intense relief, that there would be neither a slaughter of the innocents nor a dishonourable retreat but a negotiated withdrawal. The gesture not only boosted the morale of the garrison but firmly consolidated military loyalty to the Prince. On his return to Madrid, he called a cabinet meeting and announced his belief that the Moroccan King would soon telephone him to say that he would suspend the march. To the astonishment of the ministers, the call came through during the meeting. King Hassan announced that he was delighted with Juan Carlos's heroic gesture. Nevertheless, a week would pass before the suspension of the 'green march' by Hassan.[35] Although the entire episode had, to some extent, been skilfully choreographed, it demonstrated Juan Carlos's courage and initiative.

On 3 November, with Franco minutes from death, an emergency operation by Dr Manuel Hidalgo Huerta brought him back from the brink. He received extreme unction from his personal chaplain. However, with his situation again worsening, he left El Pardo for the last time on 5 November and entered the Madrid hospital, the Ciudad Sanitaria La Paz. Another operation on 6 November miraculously brought him back once more from the abyss.[36] The determination of the El Pardo entourage to keep Franco alive despite his intense suffering was commensurate with the alarm they felt at the prospect of Juan Carlos on the throne. Within days of the application of Article 11, the Prince had declared in *Newsweek* that he regarded himself as his own man and wished to be 'the symbol of national unity and reconciliation'.[37] Bunker hopes of blocking Juan Carlos's plans were not unrelated to the fact that the term of office of Rodríguez Valcárcel as President of the *Consejo del Reino* and of the Cortes was due to end on 26 November. If Franco could recover sufficiently to approve the automatic renewal of Rodríguez Valcárcel's mandate, the clique would have a key man in a position to ensure that the Prime Minister chosen by Juan Carlos would be 'reliable' and prevent the dismantling of the regime's structures. There was considerable manoeuvring going on within the *Consejo del Reino* to block the Prince's preferred candidate, Torcuato Fernández-Miranda.[38]

Aware of these machinations, on 7 November, the Prince discussed with Fernández-Miranda the best way of proceeding. Committed to the idea of Torcuato as President of the Cortes and of the *Consejo del Reino*, he hoped also to have as his Prime Minister someone loyal and committed to reform. His favoured candidate was José María López de Letona, an intelligent, liberal member of Opus Dei, who, as Minister for Industry between 1969 and 1973, had built up a reputation as a dynamic technocrat with excellent business contacts. Fernández-Miranda liked López de Letona but he had grave doubts about the possibility of securing his nomination as Prime Minister.[39]

On 12 November, Juan Carlos heard that his father was planning to issue a manifesto declaring that the succession process was illegal. Desperate to find a way of neutralizing Don Juan, he decided to send General Manuel Díez Alegría to Paris to speak to him. Once there, Díez Alegría told Don Juan that the senior generals were committed to a monarchical succession only in the person of Juan Carlos. He explained that the situation was precarious and that, in the interests of the monarchy, he should do nothing to impede his son's accession to the throne.[40] On entrusting this mission to Díez Alegría, Juan Carlos had taken the precaution of ensuring that he secured the prior permission of the Minister for the Army, Lieutenant-General Francisco Coloma Gallegos, who had replaced General Castañón in June 1973. On 13 November, Coloma discussed the proposal with the other two military ministers. However, when Arias Navarro heard about their meeting, he assumed that Juan Carlos was plotting with the Army and exploded hysterically, allegedly saying, 'He's going to hear me now. This snot-nosed kid needs putting in his place.'

Their relations had been at breaking point for months. Arias Navarro's tendency to treat the Prince in a dismissive manner had long infuriated him. Now, Arias went to La Zarzuela and brusquely offered his resignation, saying, 'If Your Highness wants a military dictatorship, why don't you name Admiral Pita da Veiga as Prime Minister? And I wish you lots of luck!' He adopted this confrontational tone in the confident knowledge that, in the context of the Sahara problem and facing the imminent difficulties of the transfer of powers, Juan Carlos would find it difficult to cope with an additional crisis. Gritting his teeth, the Prince apologized for not informing Arias of Díez Alegría's mission. The Prime Minister, seeing his vulnerability, stood his ground, determined to humiliate him. With tears of impotent rage, Juan Carlos appealed to his sense of responsibility and said 'you can't leave me alone now of all times', but Arias was obdurate. Juan Carlos sent Nicolás Franco Pasqual del Pobil, Franco's nephew, a friend of Juan Carlos since their childhood in Lisbon, to speak to him. Nicolás Franco told Arias that Franco himself would be appalled by his resignation. With characteristic obstinacy, Arias was unmoved. On 14 November, the head of the Prince's household, the Marqués de Mondéjar, undertook to try and get him to withdraw the resignation. He found Arias having his hair cut at the barbershop in the Hotel Palace. During their conversation, Arias made a remark to Mondéjar that underlined the difficulties of the Prince's position. In a clearly threatening tone, he said, 'Don't forget that we've got the Caudillo on ice.' It was only after Mondéjar had promised to get the three military ministers to explain, apologize and offer to resign that Arias changed his mind. He then patronizingly telephoned La Zarzuela to 'forgive' Juan Carlos. The entire episode provoked much delight in Francoist circles where Arias was praised for putting the Prince in his place. If he had any doubts before, Juan Carlos now knew that Arias Navarro was not to be trusted.[41]

On the following day, Franco's condition worsened. Faced with further evidence of peritonitis, the medical team operated again. Their intervention was initially successful. It seemed briefly that the Caudillo was getting better and the hopes of Cristóbal Martínez-Bordiu began to rise. However, within three days, Franco began to fail once more. Dr Pozuelo, ever realistic, telephoned La Zarzuela to tell Juan Carlos that the end would be soon. Martínez-Bordiu hopefully asked the brilliant surgeon Dr Hidalgo Huerta if he could operate yet again. Hidalgo refused.

With Alfonso de Borbón y Dampierre in close attendance, the indefatigable Dr Martínez-Bordiu continued feverishly to pump the Caudillo with antibiotics and sulphonamides.[42] While he tried to hold back the clock, the Prince continued to plan for the future. He asked Rafael Cabello de Alba, the Minister of Finance, if he had plans to issue commemorative coins to celebrate the forthcoming coronation. He also sent General Armada to negotiate with José María Sánchez-Ventura, the Minister of Justice, an amnesty for prisoners to be announced when he ascended the throne. Difficulties arose because the Prince wanted the amnesty to be more far-reaching than the cabinet was prepared to contemplate.[43]

With Franco barely alive and entirely dependent on complex life-support machinery, his daughter Nenuca insisted that he be allowed to die in peace. Although her husband initially agreed, pressure from the Caudillo's military staff, Alfonso de Borbón y Dampierre and some of the doctors, saw the initial order to cease treatment rescinded. The final crisis began in the early hours of the morning of 20 November. Despite frantic efforts at resuscitation, by 3.30 a.m. he was dead. However, loath to give up, Cristóbal gave Franco a last heart massage. It was to no avail. The official time of death was given as 5.25 a.m. on 20 November 1975.[44] As soon as the Caudillo was dead, Dr Pozuelo informed Juan Carlos. In contrast, neither Arias Navarro nor Alejandro Rodríguez Valcárcel, who became interim Head of State on Franco's death, had bothered to let him know. Juan Carlos telephoned Arias to protest that, although Franco had been dead for an hour, he had not been informed officially. The conversation ended in a shouting match.[45]

When he realized that he was dying, Franco had dictated his political testament to his daughter, Carmen. The document was given to Arias Navarro who, strictly speaking, should have passed it on to the acting Head of State, Rodríguez Valcárcel. Sobbing, he read it out on television, at 10 a.m. on 20 November. Arias seemed to feel that he was thereby enshrined as the Caudillo's executor. The text itself was a masterpiece of amnesia by Franco, wiping out at a stroke the politics of revenge, the vicious repression, the prisoners, the exiles and the executed. 'I beg forgiveness of everyone, just as with all my heart I forgive those who declared themselves my enemies even though I never thought of them as such. I believe and hope that I had no enemies other than the enemies of Spain . . . For the love that I feel for our Fatherland, I ask that you continue in unity and peace and that you surround the future King of Spain, Don Juan Carlos de Borbón, with the same affection and loyalty that you have given me and that you give him, at all times, the same support that I had from you. Do not forget that the enemies of Spain and of Christian civilization are on the alert.'[46]

Rodríguez Valcárcel certainly seemed to have Franco's words on his mind. Some weeks before the death of Franco, on 24 October, Juan Carlos had informed both him and Arias Navarro that Areilza had met a number of opposition leaders including Felipe González of the PSOE. The Prince was reassured to hear that González had assured Areilza that the Socialists would accept the monarchy. Rodríguez Valcárcel was outraged by the very idea of the opinions of such people being canvassed. His activities on the morrow of Franco's death were motivated by the fear that the opposition would be permitted some role under Juan Carlos. Accordingly, he was determined to get the political élite to help him ensure that Juan Carlos should be no more than a ceremonial Head of State. Since midday on 20 November, Rodríguez Valcárcel was acting Head of State. The mechanisms of the *Ley Orgánica* required the President of the *Consejo del Reino* to head a three-man regency committee, on which he would be joined by the senior Archbishop of the ecclesiastical heirarchy, Monsignor Pedro Cantero Cuadrado of Zaragoza, and the senior officer of the Armed Forces, the Air Force General Ángel Salas Larrazábal. As far as Rodríguez Valcárcel was concerned, the institutions of Francoism would be left to govern as before.[47]

During the rest of 20 November, Juan Carlos and Sofía behaved with great dignity, joining the Franco family in their mourning. The King had never concealed his essential affection for Franco. Now, he and his wife went several times to El Pardo and, with Doña Carmen Polo and Carmen Franco, presided at a *corpore insepulto* requiem at which Cardinal Enrique y Tarancón officiated. After enjoying untrammelled power for so long, the immediate Franco family feared reprisals from their victims, but Juan Carlos had reassured them repeatedly that he would ensure that no such thing occurred.[48] He told Doña Carmen that she could remain at El Pardo for the rest of her life.[49] Moreover, within several days of his investiture as King, he granted her the title of La Señora de Meirás and that of Duquesa de Franco for her daughter. Doña Carmen chose to remain in residence at El Pardo for only another two and a half months.

Within hours, however, Juan Carlos's principal preoccupation had to be the articulation of the process whereby he would be proclaimed King. Juan Carlos sent for Torcuato Fernández-Miranda on the evening of 20 November. With Doña Sofía, Armada and Mondéjar, they worked on his speech before the Cortes accepting the throne. In the meanwhile, the Prince's friend, the Duque de Arión, approached senior elements of the Communist Party inside Spain. Contact had long since been made with Santiago Carrillo through Nicolás Franco Pasqual del Pobil. One regular visitor to La Zarzuela was Luis Solana, a Socialist and friend of Juan Carlos's old schoolmate Jaime Carvajal. As a result of these contacts, Solana had been able to assure Felipe González that the PSOE would soon be legalized. With varying degrees of scepticism, the leaders of the opposition decided to give the Prince the benefit of the doubt. The message to all was that there was going to be significant political change and that the takeover should not be undermined. On Juan Carlos's behalf, the Minister for the Sindicatos (official trade unions), Alejandro Fernández Sordo, had made contact with both the Socialist and Communist clandestine unions. Assuring them that there would be rapid political reform, he had secured undertakings that the process of transition from Franco to Juan Carlos would not be disturbed by labour disputes. On the other hand, like so many politicians at the time, Fernández Sordo had his own agenda. He was hostile to Arias Navarro and apparently pushing the cause of López de Letona. However, he revealed to Torcuato Fernández-Miranda that he hoped to see Rodríguez Valcárcel brought into the next government as Secretary-General of the *Movimiento*, which would have done nothing for the new King's reforming ambitions.[50]

Juan Carlos was keen to put as much distance as possible between the funeral arrangements for Franco and his own coronation. Rodríguez Valcárcel was determined to link them as closely as possible. When the Prince sent emissaries to negotiate this, the Minister of Justice, José María Sánchez-Ventura, and the Minister of the *Presidencia*, Antonio Carro, were unceremoniously ejected from Rodríguez Valcárcel's office. Juan Carlos and his advisers were aware that attempts were being made to persuade Rodríguez Valcárcel to keep the Council of Regency in operation indefinitely. Finally, Girón, who was at the heart of the conspiracy, recognized that the extreme right lacked the force to bring it off.[51] While Franco's body lay in state on a dais in the Sala de Columnas of the Palacio de Oriente, there began to form queues several kilometres long of the hundreds of thousands of people who wanted to file past the body.[52]

Another major anxiety for the new King was the likely response of Don Juan. In mid-November, Juan Carlos had seen the draft of a declaration that his father was considering issuing on Franco's death. Referring to himself as '*Jefe de la Casa Real española*' (Head of the Spanish Royal House) and 'son and heir of Alfonso XIII and trustee of a secular treasure whose duties he considers cannot be renounced', Don Juan denounced Franco's rule as one of 'absolute personal power'. He stated that the duty of the monarchy now was to overcome the Civil War, establish a profound social justice, eliminate corruption, consolidate a real pluralist democracy and seek full integration into the European Community. He referred to Juan Carlos merely as 'his son and heir'. Juan Carlos was alarmed by the implication that Don Juan did not recognize him as King. Such recognition seemed to be conditional on his undertaking the total dismantling of the Franco regime. In consequence, the Prince did not sleep for several nights. The declaration was published in Paris on 21 November and led to outraged reactions in the press of the *Movimiento*.[53] It was not until 28 November that Don Juan sent Antonio Fontán with a secret message to La Zarzuela to the effect that he regarded his son as

King of Spain and head of the dynasty. He would abdicate formally as soon as his son was convinced that there was satisfactory progress towards democracy. The formalities were left up to Juan Carlos: 'We'll do the paperwork whenever he wants.' When the King received the message, he said only 'What a father I've got!'[54] Don Juan was to recognize his son, in fact, on 14 May 1977, when it was clear that the structures of the Franco regime were well on the way to disappearing.

On 22 November, there took place in the Cortes the ceremony at which Juan Carlos was to be proclaimed King. He was required to swear fidelity to the fundamental laws and the principles of the *Movimiento*. He was anxious that the occasion should be forward-looking and had asked Rodríguez Valcárcel not to link the proclamation to the Franco regime. After much reluctant heart-searching, Rodríguez Valcárcel produced a satisfactory compromise draft of his speech. It ended with the rousing proclamation: '*Señores Procuradores* [Members of the Cortes], *Señores Consejeros* [Members of the *Consejo del Reino*], from the emotion of the memory of Franco, a new era. Long live the King! Long live Spain!' In the event, to the annoyance of Juan Carlos, the stony-faced Rodríguez Valcárcel left out the phrase 'a new era' and thereby managed to identify the old regime and the new. Wearing the uniform of Captain-General of the Army, the King began his speech with respectful remarks about Franco's dedication to Spain. He then made it unequivocally clear that a new epoch was beginning. Declaring that the monarchy included all Spaniards, he called on the nation to participate in a national consensus. He used phrases that fitted in with the need to work within Francoist legislation but there could be no mistaking his intent – 'I am fully aware that a great people like ours demands the profound perfecting of the system. This moment of dynamism and change demands a creative capacity to pull different and desirable opinions into a common goal.' To the horror of many Francoists present, he paid tribute to his father for teaching him the concept of duty. The problems facing the King were illustrated starkly by the fact that this mildly progressive speech, which ostentatiously omitted references to 18 July 1936, was received coldly by the

Procuradores who then gave an ecstatic ovation to Franco's daughter.[55]

Under the circumstances, Juan Carlos's words to the Cortes could hardly have been more daring. Half an hour after the ceremony, the King appeared, dressed in mourning, at the catafalque of Franco. Later that afternoon, he visited Doña Carmen at El Pardo. Both gestures, while reflecting his sincere affection for both the Caudillo and his wife, were meant to calm the spirits of Francoists alarmed by his speech. Deeply aware that there were senior military figures who shared the views of the bunker, the so-called *generales azules*, he issued his first statement to the Army in his capacity as Commander-in-Chief: 'You are the trustees of the highest ideals of the Fatherland and the safeguard and guarantee of the fulfilment of the fundamental laws, the faithful reflection of the will of our people.' A few days later, a royal decree made the late Caudillo senior officer in perpetuity of the Army, Navy and Air Force. The King had fostered great sensitivity to military feelings since his time as a cadet. It was to be the foundation of a relationship with the Armed Forces on which a future democratic Spain would lean heavily.[56]

On the morning of 23 November, Franco's funeral cortège arrived at the Valle de los Caídos. The coffin was carried by Cristóbal Martínez-Bordiu, his son Francisco, Alfonso de Borbón y Dampierre and representatives of the Army, Navy and Air Force. Red-eyed, and clearly moved, Juan Carlos presided at the burial. Later that day, his first audience was granted to the leader of the bunker, José Antonio Girón de Velasco. It was part of a complex juggling act of different sets of symbols, those of the Francoist past and those of the democratic future.

It is impossible to exaggerate the pressures faced by Juan Carlos at the beginning of his reign. There was much hope and good will, both inside and outside Spain, but the obstacles awaiting his efforts to democratize the country were enormous. The legacy of bitterness and hatred that had politicized and embittered the Basque people would bedevil Spanish politics for years to come. The progressive forces that wished to advance towards democracy did not entirely trust him. After all, he had stood next to Franco for

15 years and remained silent about the crimes of the dictatorship. He had had no choice, but inevitably that compromised him in the eyes of the left. In that regard, Don Juan's prestige would be crucial. Yet, even if he could convince the left to give him time, there was still the bunker. Malevolent and reactionary, it remained powerful, entrenched in the Army, the police and the Civil Guard. Over 100,000 Falangists were still authorized to carry guns. Hard-line Francoists within the Army were working hard on several fronts to maintain control of the situation. General Francisco Coloma Gallegos captured the mood of the intransigent upper echelons when, on taking leave of his post as Minister for the Army, he declared on 15 December 1975 that: 'Today when we weep for the disappearance of our Generalísimo, today more than ever before, we must stay united to ensure that the torch picked up by the King should not be blown out by those who want to unleash storms.'[57]

Juan Carlos's proclamation as King before the Cortes was the institutional formality. The public celebration would be the coronation mass at the church of Los Jerónimos in Madrid. This had been delayed for two days, to the apoplectic fury of the bunker, in order to permit the attendance of Valéry Giscard d'Estaing and Walter Scheel, the French and German Presidents, plus Willy Brandt, the German Premier. Juan Carlos was determined to secure the symbolic presence of democratic leaders at the inauguration of his reign. Once more, he had recourse to his friend Manuel Prado y Colón de Carvajal. Prado went to Paris and managed to persuade a reluctant Giscard to commit his attendance. He had to be promised some gesture that would set him apart from the other guests. He insinuated that he would like to be given the *Toisón de Oro* but eventually settled for an exclusive breakfast with the King.[58] Securing the presence of prestigious democratic leaders was crucial to Juan Carlos's image-building for the future.

Some were more fastidious. The British Labour Prime Minister, Harold Wilson, for instance, although highly sympathetic to Juan Carlos, was aware of the bitter anti-Franco feeling within the trade union movement. Accordingly, as British representative at Franco's funeral, Wilson sent the Lord Privy Seal, Lord Shepherd, a relatively junior minister, a carefully calibrated gesture which still caused problems with the trade unions. In outright contrast, at the coronation, the Duke of Edinburgh represented Queen Elizabeth II.[59] Wilson told the US President, Gerald Ford: 'I recognize, even if it cannot be put bluntly in public, that King Juan Carlos has a very hard row to hoe. So we shall encourage him privately to move as fast as possible, but try to avoid public condemnation when we can, if the pace is slower than public expectation here may demand.'[60] The impression made by Juan Carlos on President Gerald Ford on his visit to Spain six months earlier ensured that the United States was represented by Nelson Rockefeller, the Vice-President.

In dramatic contrast, no significant Head of State, other than the Chilean dictator General Pinochet, attended the Caudillo's funeral. Thereafter, the King himself made it clear to Pinochet that he was not invited to the coronation mass on 27 November. The bunker was deeply outraged when, in his sermon at the mass, Cardinal Enrique y Tarancón gave the King's plans ecclesiastical endorsement in terms that implicitly condemned Francoism's vengeful spirit. 'I ask that you be King of all Spaniards. That your reign be a reign of life. Not one shaken by death and violence. May no one be enslaved by any kind of oppression. May all know and share freely the joy of life. May your reign be one of justice for all, without fear or favour, with everyone subjected to the rule of law, and with the law always at the service of the community.'[61]

Juan Carlos had given some evidence of the sincerity of his commitment to change in the form of the amnesty announced by José María Sánchez-Ventura, the Minister of Justice. In fact, on the left, it was perceived as the most minimal concession. Eventually extending to about 30 per cent of the prison population, it benefited many common criminals but released relatively few political prisoners – 235 out of a total of 4,000 released. Thus, at the very moment that Juan Carlos and Sofía drove down streets lined with cheering crowds, riot police were using baton charges, tear gas and water cannon to break up demonstrations outside the country's prisons. Many organizations, including *Colegios de Abogados* (Bar Associations), the Catholic *Pax et Justitia*, and the parties of the left protested at the limitations of the pardon and called for a full amnesty. Disappointment turned to anger when several released prisoners, including the Workers' Commissions leader, Marcelino Camacho, were immediately re-arrested. Huge amnesty demonstrations were held in Seville, Valladolid, Vigo, Barcelona and Madrid. Felipe González was harassed by police at Madrid's civil cemetery where he attended a tribute on the 50th anniversary of the death of the PSOE founder, Pablo Iglesias.[62]

For the next 18 months, Juan Carlos's future would be worked out in a context of drama and conflict on the streets and complex negotiations behind the closed doors of smoke-filled rooms. The elaboration of a guest list to adorn the coronation mass was just one of a number of fiendishly difficult negotiations that the King faced in his first days. One of the most delicate tasks was informing Rodríguez Valcárcel that he did not wish him to continue as President of the Cortes and of the *Consejo del Reino*. Under Franco, the selection in any Francoist institution of a *terna*, from which the Caudillo made his final choice, had always been a charade. Franco's preference was always ascertained beforehand and his candidate included in the *terna*. Now, Juan Carlos had to find a way of keeping Rodríguez Valcárcel out of the *terna* while ensuring the inclusion of the name of Torcuato Fernández-Miranda.[63]

In the event, Juan Carlos simply asked Rodríguez Valcárcel to ensure that his own name would not be included in the *terna* for the new Presidency of the Cortes. As might have been expected, Rodríguez Valcárcel was furious. However, with gritted teeth, he undertook to write a letter to all the members of the *Consejo del Reino* instructing them not to include his name. In his characteristically affable fashion, Juan Carlos then asked Rodríguez Valcárcel for the enormous favour of doing his best to ensure the inclusion of Torcuato Fernández-Miranda in the *terna*. Choking back his chagrin, he agreed. In fact, Torcuato, aware of the enmity that his own name was likely to provoke, had suggested to the King that he sought another candidate. Having already made up his mind, the King obstinately – and courageously – ignored him, determined to fight for what he knew was the crucial appointment. When it became clear that the resentful Rodríguez Valcárcel was hesitating about fulfilling his promise, Juan Carlos directly asked for the help of three men, two of whom might well be considered his enemies – José Antonio Girón de Velasco, Carlos Arias Navarro and the one-time Minister of Education, Manuel Lora Tamayo, who was the acting President of the Cortes and of the *Consejo del Reino* until a successor could be named. Such were the King's powers of persuasion that he convinced Girón and Arias to help him secure Fernández-Miranda's nomination. Girón, behind his aggressive bluster, had always had a sycophantic tendency where Franco was concerned and now the authority of the King reactivated it.

Even if his scheme to place Torcuato Fernández-Miranda in the Cortes came off, Juan Carlos still had to consider whom he wanted as his Prime Minister. He knew full well whom he did not want. On 30 April 1975, he had told López Rodó that: 'Arias is not the man for my first government; nor is Fraga; nor Silva who is "confessional" [too linked to the Catholic Church]. In monarchies, there shouldn't be any Catholic parties.' It should have come as little surprise to López Rodó to discover later that the Prince had said the same about him.[64] The King's attitude to Arias, hardened by the resignation episode, was expressed in a phrase eliminated from the Spanish edition of his interviews with José Luis de Vilallonga – 'He was far from being a fool, but he had no really long-term view of the problems of Spain. And he was obstinate as a mule. He substituted obstinacy for force of character.'[65] However, despite desperately wanting to see the back of Arias Navarro, Juan Carlos knew that to change both the President of the Cortes and the Prime Minister was an enormous risk while many of the most hardline of the Francoist political élite remained suspicious.

Recognizing that the chances of securing the nomination of López de Letona were extremely slim, he was coming to see the advantages, painful though it might be, of letting Arias stay on. To lose both of his candidates as Prime Minister and President of the Cortes would scupper the chances of a democratic monarchy. In turning to Arias for help in securing the nomination of Fernández-Miranda as President of the Cortes, the King was implicitly recognizing that he would have to let him stay on as Prime Minister.

Arias himself never entertained much doubt that he would keep the job and, always happy to patronize the King, he was delighted to have him asking for help. Seeing Fernández-Miranda as his great rival for the premiership, he was even more pleased to neutralize him, as he saw it, by helping send him to the Cortes. Initially then, Arias agreed to help.

Both Girón and Arias vacillated when Rodríguez Valcárcel warned them that, if Fernández-Miranda were to be elected, he would be the gravedigger of the system. In the event, Girón stood firm but Arias changed his mind. Rodríguez Valcárcel finally wrote the promised letter but in terms of such vague ambiguity as to leave the members of the *Consejo del Reino* free to name him. The King's plans were helped considerably by the fact that Rodríguez Valcárcel was no longer President of the *Consejo del Reino*. Despite the support of Lora Tamayo, the Opus Dei sympathiser and an old ally of Juan Carlos, the *Consejo*'s deliberations on 1 December were extremely tense. The large majority of the *Consejo*'s members had no wish to see a democratic monarchy. Until the very last minute of the meeting, Rodríguez Valcárcel maintained hopes of his appointment being renewed, thereby undermining the liberalization plans of the King. In the event, the machinations of various allies of the King, including Girón who insinuated that Rodríguez Valcárcel's health eliminated him as a realistic candidate, produced a *terna* with the names of Licinio de la Fuente, Emilio Lamo de Espinosa and Torcuato Fernández-Miranda. On 3 December, in La Zarzuela, Torcuato Fernández-Miranda was sworn in as President of the Cortes and of the *Consejo del Reino*. In his speech, he gave a clear hint that he would be an instrument of change when he said, 'I consider myself totally and absolutely responsible for my past in its entirety. I am faithful to it, but not tied down by it because the service of the Fatherland and of the King are an undertaking for the future.'[66]

Juan Carlos now had a crucial lever of power in the hands of one of his most faithful allies. However, it was far from seeming so. In his first plenary session as President of the Cortes, Torcuato Fernández-Miranda stated that the government was responsible for political action and the Cortes for the legal framework within which that action took place. Encapsulated in the statement was the determination to proceed to reform within the Francoist constitutional edifice. The King was determined not to be guilty of breaking his solemn oath to uphold the fundamental laws. Moreover, the strategy of proceeding within those laws was probably the only way of ensuring that the Francoist establishment did not use every means at its disposal to block reform. To the majority of Spanish and foreign observers, however, the idea of reform being channelled through the Francoist Cortes seemed to mean that democracy was impossible. After all, under Franco, the Cortes had been deeply reactionary and, in addition, had never had any power of initiative. All Franco's powers were theoretically subject to limitation by the Cortes and the *Consejo del Reino* but, in practice, both bodies acted as rubber stamps. They could not be expected to behave like that if faced with a reforming King. The task thus facing Juan Carlos and Fernández-Miranda – that of winning over the *Procuradores* to their project and of asserting the authority of the Cortes over the government – was awesome in its enormity.[67]

As has been stated, it has been suggested that Franco knew that Juan Carlos would endeavour to democratize Spain and that he approved.[68] If that is the case, it is odd that he did nothing to prepare his supporters for such an eventuality. In fact, everything about his behaviour after he named Juan Carlos as his successor demonstrated his confidence that the institutions of Francoism would prevent the future King straying from the principles of the *Movimiento* and of 18 July. That is the reason that the King faced such a dramatic situation in late 1975. Its resolution without large-scale bloodshed depended on his skill, on that of the ministers that he chose and on the delicacy of the leaders of the opposition. The King had no doubts about the advantages of democratization both for his nation and for his own dynasty. His closest advisers had kept him fully aware that important sectors of Spanish capitalism were anxious to ditch the obsolete political mechanisms of Francoism. He was deeply conscious of what had happened to the Greek royal family when it failed to go with the tide of popular democratic sentiment. The message from Estoril was also unequivocal. By opting boldly for progress, he would be assured of mass support for the monarchy. However, he was equally aware of the strength, determination and ill-will of the bunker. Moreover, the path out of the crisis was through the Byzantine labyrinth of that same Francoist constitution to which he owed his accession. His long-term aim was to be a constitutional monarch above politics but, for the moment, he would be obliged to play a dangerously active role in the political arena. Accordingly, in the early days of his reign, he manoeuvred with caution.

The bunker remained optimistic that Arias Navarro would be able to block the liberalizing schemes of the King. Extreme leftists continued to be rounded up. By excluding the monarchy from Spain for 40 years and by his arrogance in nominating his own royal successor, Franco seemed to have destroyed any political neutrality that Juan Carlos might have enjoyed, just as he had undermined the monarchy's other two central attributes of continuity and legitimacy. The bunker hoped that Franco's influence would still be felt from his tomb. Arias would later claim that he regularly visited the great basilica in the Valle de los Caídos to commune with the Caudillo and receive his instructions from beyond the grave.[69] It was hardly surprising that the left greeted the coronation with headlines in its clandestine press that proclaimed 'No to an imposed King!' and 'No to the Francoist King!'[70]

Having selected Torcuato Fernández-Miranda as President of the Cortes, the King now had formally to choose his Prime Minister. Despite strong rumours that he had resigned, Arias Navarro refused to make the process easy for the King. He failed to present the token resignation demanded by protocol because he believed that Franco had named him Prime Minister for five years. On top of that calculated slight, in a spirit of outright confrontation with the King, he ordered the members of the cabinet not to attend the ceremony at which Fernández-Miranda took up his post. Juan Carlos was deeply irritated but aware that, after the recent battle in the *Consejo del Reino*, it would be too risky to go back so soon in search of a new Prime Minister. Accordingly, having more or less insinuated already to Arias that he would ask him to stay on, on 4 December, Juan Carlos finally decided to do so. He had to send Torcuato Fernández-Miranda to persuade Arias to present his token resignation and to accept cabinet changes. Arias agreed only with the greatest reluctance. His view was that Franco had appointed him and the King remained subject to the Caudillo's will. He told Fernández-Miranda: 'I am bolted by the law to this chair.' Arias then omitted to announce that his position had been ratified by Juan Carlos, giving the impression that he remained in power not at the King's behest but by the grace of Franco. Juan Carlos telephoned Arias in the middle of a cabinet meeting on 5 December to ask why he had not announced his appointment. His astonishing reply was that he had just forgotten. He returned to the cabinet meeting and mentioned in passing that the King wanted him to continue. He thereby gave the impression that it was an irrelevant formality, an acceptance by Juan Carlos of Franco's will.[71]

The working relationship between Juan Carlos and Arias Navarro could not have started on a worse note. To some extent, Arias's cabinet reflected his Francoist inclinations and it contained names that would tranquillize the bunker. The new Minister of National Defence, General Fernando de Santiago y Díaz de Mendívil, was a fierce conservative. The King and his advisers had hoped that the Vice-Presidency of the Government with ministerial responsibility for defence matters, and therefore jurisdiction over the three service ministries, would go to the liberal commander of the Spanish enclave at Ceuta, Manuel Gutiérrez Mellado, a close friend of General Díez Alegría. A campaign was mounted against Gutiérrez Mellado by ultras infuriated by his moderate stance on the *Unión Militar Democrática* (UMD). He had made strong representations to the Minister for the Army and the Captain-General of Madrid for the UMD to be treated less hysterically. A dossier was drawn up by ultra generals, purporting to prove that Gutiérrez Mellado was in fact the spiritual leader of the UMD. Arias Navarro was sufficiently moved by the dossier to bow before the strength of feeling against Gutiérrez Mellado, giving the post instead to General de Santiago.[72] The new Minister for the Army, General Félix Álvarez Arenas, was marginally less reactionary than his predecessor, Coloma Gallegos. On the other hand, the Minister for the Navy was a survivor from Carrero Blanco's cabinet, the antediluvian Admiral Gabriel Pita da Veiga. The old Falangist José Solís moved from the headship of the *Movimiento* to the Ministry of Labour.

Although Arias's cabinet contained a sprinkling of hardliners, he had been persuaded by the King and Fernández-Miranda of the need for different, if not exactly new, blood. In the list announced on 10 December, there were a number of significant innovations. A suggestion emanating from the King led to the appointment of the young and dynamic Falangist, Rodolfo Martín Villa, as Minister for the Sindicatos. As Civil Governor of Barcelona, his openness and efficiency had eased much tension with Madrid and Juan Carlos had been greatly impressed by his contacts with the Catalan left. More crucially, the King had insisted, as his price for Arias's continuation in his post, on the appointment of three utterly crucial ministers. José María de Areilza became Foreign Minister, to the utter disgust of Don Juan who commented, 'He's ready to carry out for the new King exactly the same programme as the one that I drew up for my own reign. For others to do that would be fine. But that it should be Areilza whom I trusted at difficult moments, really disgusts me. It makes him just another who wants to sit in the glow of the warmest sun.'[73] It is indicative of Don Juan's ingenuousness that he had not previously noticed the frequency with which Areilza, in his path from Fascism to democracy, had betrayed other masters. Manuel Fraga became Minister of the Interior, and Antonio Garrigues y Díaz Cañabate, Minister of Justice – all three were of sufficient weight and personality to be able to make their voices heard against Arias. In any case, all three agreed to their postings once Arias Navarro had assured them that he accepted the King's project of complete democratization of the political system.[74]

Another crucial appointment was of the Christian Democrat Alfonso Osorio as Minister of the *Presidencia del Gobierno*, the post that effectively set the agenda for government business. This was another appointment that reflected the wishes of Juan Carlos himself. Since this ministry gave Osorio responsibility for the national patrimony, it gave him the perfect cover to hold regular meetings with the King. Osorio immediately named as his Under-Secretary, Colonel Sabino Fernández Campos, a protégé of General Alfonso Armada and thus very close to the royal household.[75] However, the key to all of Juan Carlos's plans lay in the appointment of Torcuato Fernández-Miranda as President of the Cortes and of the *Consejo del Reino*. His intelligence, his knowledge of Francoist constitutional law and his acquaintance with the entire Francoist political élite made him the perfect guide to the labyrinth through which Juan Carlos had to advance. He quickly ensured that he would have a mole in the cabinet by skilfully persuading Arias to accept his new protegé, Adolfo Suárez, in the key post of Secretary-General of the *Movimiento*. Arias believed that he was obliged by Franco's wishes to maintain José Solís in the post but Fernández-Miranda sidestepped the problem by suggesting that he gave Solís the Ministry of Labour.[76]

Perhaps most remarkable of all and most indicative of the King's independence – and ruthlessness – was the fact that López Rodó was not included in the cabinet. Despite his dedicated service to the monarchical succession, he was not even consulted by Juan Carlos. He had served his purpose and Juan Carlos clearly believed that the monarchy now needed ministers of his own generation. Indeed, he had said as much some weeks earlier. He told another of the technocrats, Gonzalo Fernández de la Mora, that he did not foresee a lengthy future for Arias Navarro and asked his view on possible Prime Ministers. When Fernández de la Mora suggested the name of López Rodó, the King replied coldly, 'He's no use to me because he's got Francoist lead in his wing.'[77]

With hindsight, it is possible to see what Juan Carlos had in mind with the various appointments. At the time, however, the presence of Falangist apparatchiks like Suárez, Martín Villa and Solís, of reactionary military men like General de Santiago and Admiral Pita da Veiga; and even of Fraga and Areilza led the ever-widening opposition coalitions to denounce what they saw as a poorly camouflaged exercise in continuity. They could hardly have thought otherwise, since Arias had now decided that he was Franco's representative on earth and behaved accordingly. At his first cabinet meeting, Arias Navarro said: 'I still firmly persevere in the objectives that I outlined in my 12 February speech. We are called, we come together, to continue and persist with the gigantic achievement of Francisco Franco.' Torcuato Fernández-Miranda was appalled at the lack of references to the King's reforming objectives or to the changed circumstances. He wrote in his diary: 'Could there be greater blindness? What about the King!' As his resignation on 13 November had shown, Arias Navarro would miss no opportunity to humiliate the King. Things went from bad to worse with Arias's speech to the *Consejo Nacional del Movimiento* on 19 January 1976. He announced 'his firm decision to be faithful to his origins' and assured his listeners that he 'accepted with honour the entire past of our regime from its first heroic and painful moments right up to yesterday and did so with the intention of keeping it going'. He went on to say that he harboured 'neither murky desires of revisionism nor suicidal aims of stirring up our institutional system because of an itch for novelty or out of crackpot irresponsibility'.[78] Ministers like Fraga, Garrigues and Areilza were left wondering what Arias had understood when he told them that he was committed to the King's democratic project.

On 28 January, Arias announced his programme in a televised speech to the Cortes. Fernández-Miranda asked him to stress that the government and the Cortes would be working together to bring the King's reformist plans to fruition. Arias ignored him. To the delight of the *Procuradores* and the despair of Juan Carlos, he made constant references to the Caudillo and stressed the maintenance of public order against the threats of the left. He addressed the *Procuradores* as the 'guardians of Franco's memory' and warned them that the enemies of Spain were prowling. What was clear was that the memory and legacy of Franco guided his every step. Arias, who for two years had oscillated wildly between talk of liberalization and deep instinctive reaction, was at it again. The most that could be hoped was that he might try to bestow upon Spain, in a paternalistic fashion, the minimum democratic gesture that might neutralize the left without provoking the bunker.[79]

This task was entrusted to a joint committee, or *Comisión Mixta*, of the senior cabinet ministers and members of the *Consejo*

Nacional under the chairmanship of Arias. At its first meeting, on
11 February 1976, Arias began by speaking of Franco, his will,
his funeral and the enemies of his legacy. He set out the limits for
liberalization as he saw it: some modification of the penal code,
liberalization of the law of political associations and an eventual
referendum on some kind of democratization. He was noticeably
displeased when Fernández-Miranda stated that the principles of
the *Movimiento* could be reformed. He then starkly revealed his
real attitude to change when he declared: 'What I want to do is
continue Francoism. And as long as I'm here or still in political
life, I'll never be anything other than a strict perpetuator of Francoism in all its aspects and I will fight against the enemies of Spain
who have begun to dare to raise their heads and are just a hidden
and clandestine minority.' He had not discussed the speech with
the King and did not send the text to him until the eve of its
delivery, thereby precluding any amendment. Symbolically, the
Prime Minister's office was belligerently dominated by an easel
supporting a large portrait of Franco that dwarfed the diminutive
photograph of the King.[80]

Arias seemed blithely unaware of the pressure for accelerated
change beyond the confines of his office. The growing threat of
popular militancy throughout Spain, and of violence in the Basque
Country, was building up dramatically. The first months of 1976
would see a trial of strength between Arias's intransigence and
the more flexible approach of Torcuato Fernández-Miranda and
the more liberal members of the government. They and Juan
Carlos himself were urgently aware that only a more positive
commitment to democratic change could prevent a serious challenge to the existing order. Mass demonstrations in favour of
amnesty for political prisoners and large-scale industrial strikes
spread during the first months of 1976. The political impact of
the strikes was magnified by the fact that so many of them affected
public services. The Francoist instincts of both Arias and Fraga,
as Minister of the Interior, were reflected in the violence of police
charges to break up amnesty demonstrations and groups of
strikers. The same could be said of the militarization of Madrid
underground and national railway workers and postmen. Labour

unrest was intensified even further by the government's imposition of a wage freeze, but remained as politically motivated as was the government's response. In some cases, the strikes were a response to Communist calls for a 'national democratic action' to overthrow the regime. They were much more a reflection of a general popular urge for political reform. In the Basque Country, strike action and mass demonstrations were inextricably linked, and reached a fever pitch unknown elsewhere. The frenzy of popular militancy in the North reflected the legacy of the violence used there by the forces of order during the state of emergency of 1975.[81]

The political and industrial unrest convinced the more liberal ministers of the urgency of the need for dialogue with the opposition. Arias himself remained doggedly opposed to any such contact and the only meetings were unofficial. The most important were those between Areilza and the left Christian Democrat, Joaquín Ruiz Giménez. An ex-Minister of Education under Franco, Ruiz Giménez was an idealistic Socialist Catholic. He had maintained close contacts with the Socialists through the liberal Catholic magazine, *Cuadernos para el Dialogo*, that he had founded in 1963. Universally respected for his total and transparent honesty, he had emerged as the opposition's most suitable interlocutor with the government. Ruiz Giménez arrived straight from mass to speak with Areilza who, as always the consummate cynic, noted in his diary: 'He is the sister of charity preaching chastity in a whorehouse.'[82] Areilza himself as Foreign Minister was undertaking a complex operation to secure the support of the Western democracies by convincing them of Juan Carlos's total commitment to political reform – for which he was accused by Girón of being a 'mendicant'.[83] He was thus as convinced of the need to reach a compromise with the opposition as he was appalled by the blind inflexibility of Arias Navarro. The problem for Juan Carlos was that the attitude of Areilza and the few other cabinet liberals did little to mitigate the opposition's view of the government's dogged inflexibility.

The King was alarmed to see the pressure being stepped up. Dialogue with Arias was difficult because the Prime Minister patronizingly believed, in the words of a senior US diplomat, that

Juan Carlos was 'an inexperienced young man who should be kept safely away from the serious day-to-day business of government'.[84] After the Madrid strikes of January, February was punctuated by amnesty demonstrations attended by as many as 80,000 people on successive Sundays in Barcelona.[85]

Juan Carlos thus found himself in a position in which the real institutional progress towards democracy – in the *Consejo del Reino* – was taking place in a way that was invisible to the bulk of the population. At the same time, he had a divided government under the erratic leadership of a recalcitrant Francoist. Accordingly, in the same spirit of energetic initiative displayed with the lightning visit to the Sahara in November, he decided to go out and make contact with the Spanish people. On 16 February 1976, he and Queen Sofía began a visit to Catalonia against the advice of General Armada and Salvador Sánchez-Terán, the Civil Governor of Barcelona, who were concerned by the intensity of labour disputes in the region. The King's speech at the official reception given at the beautiful Gothic Saló Tinell, once the seat of the Kingdom of Aragón, was televised. In the middle of his quite moving words about Catalonia, Juan Carlos suddenly switched from Castilian to Catalan. Given that, during the Civil War and after, Franco had endeavoured to annihilate Spain's regional nationalisms, this was a deeply emotional moment. Juan Carlos's gesture was a startling announcement that things were really changing and it provoked scenes of wild enthusiasm. That impression was confirmed on the second day of the visit, when Juan Carlos met the leading Catalan cleric, Cardinal Jubany, and visited the monastery of Montserrat, traditionally regarded as the fount of Catalan culture and thus of nationalist opposition to Madrid.

Juan Carlos had wanted to meet members of the Catalan opposition including Communists and Socialists. Both General Armada and Manuel Fraga had opposed this fiercely. However, contrary to the government's advice, Juan Carlos visited Baix Llobregat, a heavily industrialized area where a bitter general strike had just come to an end. In Cornellá, in front of an audience of several thousand workers, he declared: 'You can be certain that all your rights as citizens and as workers will be recognized and put into practice.' The entire visit massively increased the King's popularity. Indeed, a poll carried out at the end of May by the Catalan left-wing Republican group, *Esquerra Republicana de Catalunya*, placed Juan Carlos top of the list with 69 per cent of those interviewed declaring him to be the most popular political figure.[86]

These manifestations of popularity no doubt helped Juan Carlos during a period of great stress and anxiety. He was following a tortuous path with considerable courage and it took an enormous toll on him personally. Fully conscious of the need to pacify the bunker, he was equally aware that the democratic opposition's tolerance towards the monarchy required some nurturing. Many on the left regarded him as simply an instrument to ensure the continuation of the Francoist system. According to Santiago Carrillo, 'Within the democratic opposition, at least among the men that I had spoken with up to that time, there was no confidence in the Prince and they had extremely negative views on his intellectual capacity.'[87] One of Juan Carlos's most urgent tasks, therefore, was to find a way of weaning important sectors of the left away from their commitment to what was called the *ruptura democratica* (the democratic break), the swift and complete demolition of Francoism. The left's minimum demands were for full political amnesty, legalization of all political parties, free trade unions, the dismantling of the *Movimiento* and the Sindicatos, and free elections. The King was in the absurd position of having to rely on a Prime Minister for whom none of these goals were even negotiable.

In an attempt to counter the negative image being projected by Arias, in March 1976, the King once more turned to his friend and unofficial diplomatic envoy, Manuel Prado y Colón de Carvajal. He sent him clandestinely to Romania to speak with President Nicolae Ceauşescu. His mission was to persuade Ceauşescu of Juan Carlos's sincere democratic intentions in the hope that he in turn would urge Santiago Carrillo to be patient and to refrain from negative attacks on the crown. The message was not passed on to Carrillo until the beginning of May. While pleased to hear of the King's reforming aspirations, Carrillo made it clear that the PCE would continue to press for legalization at the same time as other parties. Carrillo determined to do everything possible to keep up the popular pressure for change – although in some extremely perceptive editorials in *Mundo Obrero* he revealed a readiness for compromise.[88]

Contacts with the Socialists were bearing fruit and the Communists were hinting at moderation. However, the greatest threats to the King's determination to establish a democratic monarchy were emanating from the Basque Country. The pardon issued on coronation day had affected fewer than ten per cent of the 750 Basque political prisoners. Rather than defusing the tension bequeathed by Franco, the pardon's inadequacy had provoked a feeling of popular rage. The bulk of the Basque population believed that ETA violence was a justifiable response to the institutional violence of Francoism, and disappointment with the pardon was quickly converted into an intensive amnesty campaign. In scope and intensity, Basque amnesty actions exceeded similar movements in the rest of Spain. Frequent demonstrations were backed by labour disputes, sit-ins, hunger strikes and mass resignations by municipal officials. Demands for freedom for prisoners were combined with calls for the legalization of the Basque flag, the *ikurriña*. To make matters worse, several Civil Guards lost their lives while trying to take down booby-trapped *ikurriñas*. Combined with ETA assassinations of informers and the kidnapping and murder of an industrialist, the tension in the Basque Country activated the fears of the bunker.[89]

Having to deal with this as Minister of the Interior, Fraga's Francoist instincts were soon engaged. Relations between Fraga and the Basques had been stretched to the limit already at the beginning of March. A two-month-long strike in the town of Vitoria culminated in a massive demonstration on 3 March 1976. As the workers left the church of San Francisco, they were charged by riot police. Three were killed immediately and over 70 badly hurt. Two more workers died as a result of their injuries some days later. In reply, a general strike was called throughout the Basque Country. Arias Navarro wanted to declare a state of emergency but was talked out of it by Adolfo Suárez, Alfonso Osorio and Rodolfo Martín Villa. The bitterness of the situation was illustrated during a visit made to the local hospital by Fraga and Martín Villa. A relative of one of the wounded asked the ministers if they had come to finish him off. The events of Vitoria destroyed any credibility that the government had had in the region, reinforced popular support for ETA and intensified the militancy of the Basque working class. In early April, Fraga declared war on ETA. Signifying a stepping-up of police activity and accompanied by the re-emergence of the ultra-rightist hit squads, this immeasurably worsened the situation.[90]

In fact, Fraga would soon begin a concerted policy of currying favour with the old Francoist élite, especially within the Army. On 8 March, he lunched with the three military ministers who were seeking reassurance that the progress to reform would not end in disorder or the division of Spain.[91] While the opposition elsewhere in Spain focused on the struggle for democracy, many Basques now had more far-reaching revolutionary nationalist aspirations. The King might reasonably harbour the hope that, once democracy was established, political militancy would diminish dramatically. In the Basque Country, however, pacification and a return to normal life were already near impossible.

Ironically, the sheer urgency of the situation gave a certain short-term advantage to the reform project of Juan Carlos and Torcuato Fernández-Miranda. Slowly but surely, Fernández-Miranda was changing the Cortes in such a way as to facilitate legal change. He had introduced the notion of parliamentary groups and, within the limits of a largely non-elected body, tried to turn it into a functioning parliament. Moreover, he convoked regular fortnightly meetings of the *Consejo del Reino* in order to give its deliberations an air of routine. He thereby hoped to introduce changes without provoking alarm within the Francoist establishment. The King used the Francoist prerogative of nominating *Procuradores* to replace deceased Francoists with trusted liberals such as José María López de Letona. The chairmanship of the *Comisión de Leyes Fundamentales* (Parliamentary Committee for Fundamental Laws) passed from the veteran Falangist Raimundo Fernández Cuesta to the progressive Opus Deista, Gregorio López Bravo. The committee had begun to examine projected bills introducing the right of meeting and association and a reform of the penal code. The latter had led to extremely stormy sessions of both the committee and the full Cortes, where it was defeated. These measures were the prelude to an eventual reform law opening the way to democratic elections for a constituent Cortes. That would require a two-thirds majority of the Cortes and a referendum.[92]

Perhaps the most remarkable feature of this period was the close attention with which the King followed and encouraged the entire process. When he presided at a meeting of the *Consejo del Reino* on 2 March 1976, he revealed an admirably detailed knowledge of the constitutional intricacies at stake. He also demonstrated a courageous determination. Before a potentially hostile audience of men who felt that it was their duty to prevent him dismantling Francoism, he declared: 'The King accepts with all its consequences the burden of the supreme authority of the State but he knows that it is essential for a true monarchy that the power of the King should not be arbitrary.' The words had been drafted in close consultation with Torcuato Fernández-Miranda. Not surprisingly then, the King went on to coat the strongest part of his speech with some seductive palliatives for the members of the *Consejo*: 'The will of the King cannot be put aside nor distorted, but it is precisely in such cases that the power of the King must not be personal nor arbitrary but rather institutional. That is the great role of the *Consejo del Reino*.'[93]

The left-wing opposition understandably regarded most of this activity in the Cortes as entirely irrelevant to the struggle for democracy. At the same time, most of the Spanish left was slow to appreciate the significance of what was happening in the Basque Country. The PCE leadership was forced to accept that the situation in the Basque Country was beyond its control and gradually came to terms with the fact that possibilities for its strategy of 'national democratic action' to overthrow the Francoist establishment were effectively limited to Madrid and Barcelona. In consequence, behind his continuing triumphalist rhetoric, Santiago Carrillo came to perceive the potential weakness of the PCE's position. The strategy based on the conviction that a nationwide strike would bring about the *ruptura democrática* was quietly acknowledged to be erroneous. If working-class militancy was to be incapable of defeating the Francoist establishment then the *ruptura* could only come from some process of negotiation between government and opposition. And this was precisely what the King and his advisers were hoping for.

Carrillo was desperate not to be marginalized from a process which was likely to favour the more obviously 'respectable' Christian Democrats and Socialists. Accordingly, he recognized the urgent need for closer unity between the two great opposition front organizations, the Communist-dominated *Junta Democrática* and the Socialist-dominated *Plataforma de Convergencia Democrática*. By dropping the PCE's insistence on the *ruptura democrática*, the total break with the Francoist system and the departure of Juan Carlos, Carrillo facilitated the fusion of the two organizations. At the end of March, they became *Coordinación Democrática*, popularly known as the '*Platajunta*'. Although the unwieldy width of the coalition was to dilute the opposition's capacity for decisive action, its formation paved the way for negotiation with the reformists within the system. On 28 March, the tenor of right-wing feeling about Juan Carlos's readiness to meet opposition demands was reflected in Blas Piñar's declaration that he would rather live in a bunker than a sewer.[94] The arrival on the agenda of the concept of '*ruptura pactada*' (negotiated break) exposed the divisions within the cabinet. Manuel Fraga announced that there would be no more tolerance. Horrified, Areilza was in despair as he watched Fraga undermine his own efforts in Bonn and Paris.[95]

More realistic and flexible ministers, like Adolfo Suárez and Alfonso Osorio, had come round to Areilza's position on dialogue. Fraga, on the other hand, reached deep inside and made contact with his inner Francoist self. Against the advice of the growing liberal camp in the cabinet, on 29 March, Fraga arrested Antonio García Trevijano, the Juanista lawyer, along with Marcelino Camacho and other leaders of the *Platajunta* when they met to announce the formation of the coalition.[96] At the beginning of April, the King himself counteracted the negative image being generated by Fraga and Arias when he visited Seville. He was delighted by a spectacularly enthusiastic popular reception. Areilza wrote in his diary: 'The government, having no political party to provide support, survives on the oxygen of the popular enthusiasm stimulated by the King on his trips.' However, Juan Carlos's political impotence was revealed when he presided at a cabinet meeting held in the Andalusian capital.

The recent arrests were discussed and Fraga stated categorically, 'They're Communists and so I won't release them.' Areilza, Suárez and Garrigues all mentioned the damaging repercussions of this, both at home and abroad. Fraga remained adamant. 'I won't release them. I'll keep them in jail until the beginning of May.' When Areilza spoke vehemently about the international dimension, Arias slyly passed the King a note saying, 'Areilza thinks he has Your Majesty's confidence.' It showed just how little he understood Juan Carlos's plans. In the room, there was a painting of a number of severed heads on a tray. As Arias supported Fraga, the King looked at Suárez and indicated the picture with a nod. It reflected his humour, his growing sympathy for Suárez and his disconformity with the line favoured by Fraga and Arias. On the following day, Fraga tried to persuade Areilza that his intransigence was a deliberate ploy to secure military tolerance for political reform.[97]

As Minister of the Interior, Fraga had been originally considered as one of the more reformist members of the cabinet. However, the events in Vitoria, which severely impaired the credibility of the government as a whole, particularly damaged Fraga's image. In fact, Fraga's alarming oscillations between liberal gestures, such as permitting the Socialist trade union, *Unión General de Trabajadores* (UGT), to hold a public meeting, and authoritarian outbursts completely destroyed the King's faith in him. The progressive Fraga who had joined López Rodó in pushing the cause of the Prince in the late 1960s seemed to be vanishing by the day. Typical of his abrupt and aggressive style was an incident that took place shortly after the Vitoria events. He was visited by the Valencian lawyer and Christian Democrat, Emilio Attard, who asked him to ensure that the police would be careful in controlling an impending amnesty demonstration in Valencia being organized by his friend, Manuel Broseta Pont. To the alarm of Broseta, Fraga informed Attard that it was the demonstrators in Valencia who would have to be careful, 'because I'm going to smash them to pulp'. Further evidence of Fraga's return to bellicose authoritarianism came a month later, on the eve of a projected PSOE May Day ceremony at the grave of the party's founder, Pablo Iglesias, in the Madrid civil cemetery. At a dinner held at the home of Miguel Boyer, who was later to be Minister of the Economy in Felipe González's first cabinet, Fraga managed to undermine much of the effort made by the King's emissaries to the PSOE. Fraga was outlining his plans for the future, unaware that he would not be playing the central role therein. In a threatening manner, he told Felipe González that the Socialists might be legalized in eight years and the Communists never. 'Remember,' he said with typical bluster, 'I represent power and you're nothing.' The dropping of the liberal veneer was a miscalculation from whose effects Fraga was not to recover until the elections of October 1982. In the spring of 1976, his assumption of a bullying authoritarian style alarmed Juan Carlos sufficiently to eliminate him as a possible successor to Arias.[98]

In contrast, the crisis of Vitoria, which so united the left, was to be a considerable boost to the career of the as yet unfancied Adolfo Suárez. Fraga being absent in Germany when the news broke, the Secretary-General of the *Movimiento* had assumed control of the Ministry of the Interior. The Captain-General of the Burgos Military Region, within which Vitoria lay, was urging the declaration of a state of emergency, but Suárez opted instead for a more discreet introduction of police reinforcements from neighbouring provinces. Subsequently, with the aid of Alfonso Osorio, Suárez convinced the King that his firm yet fastidiously careful handling of events had prevented more bloodshed.[99] The rise in Suárez's stock was curious. Areilza did not consider his young rival to be a convinced democrat, simply because of his apparent readiness to use the apparatus of the *Movimiento* to fabricate a merely cosmetic change. The view of Suárez as fundamentally reactionary was widely held within the *Movimiento*.[100] However, contact with the King's advisers, especially Torcuato Fernández-Miranda, were convincing Suárez that the future lay in the direction of more commitment to democracy. He was already establishing contacts with the 'tolerated opposition' of the Social Democrats and with the Christian Democrats linked to Fernando Álvarez de Miranda. Since this latter group was close to the King, Suárez became ever more the focus of royal hopes as a man who might be able to link disparate sectors of Spanish politics. Suárez himself got a hint of this at the 1975 cup final when, as the Minister in charge of the National Sports Delegation, he sat next to the King. Indicating the young president of Real Zaragoza, who contrasted markedly with the ageing president of their opponents, Real Madrid, Juan Carlos asked him if he had ever noticed how good young presidents were. Unlike Areilza and Fraga whom, given their massive political experience, he found somewhat patronizing, Suárez seemed more of an equal with whom Juan Carlos could be spontaneous.[101]

Meanwhile, the bunker was mobilizing. Arias, blissfully unmoved by the growing unity within the opposition, was tied to the past, his responses dictated by his long years as a hardened Francoist policeman. The furthest that Arias was prepared to go in terms of liberalization was some minor tinkering with a new law of political associations. Only he and the military ministers seemed unaware that his scheme for tightly limited reform had run aground. As his future replacement, however, Suárez faced the problem that his impeccable Francoist credentials could only provoke the suspicions of those on the left. He had few contacts within the illegal opposition and thus few opportunities to explain himself.[102] Both the King and the more openly liberal members of the government had already accepted the need for dialogue with the left. This was more possible than before now that the opposition had accepted the idea of the *ruptura pactada*. The creation of *Coordinación Democrática* had implied a realistic assessment of the limits of mass action. Now there would be a turn towards a more moderate programme aimed at widening the opposition front-to-centre and even right-of-centre groups while simultaneously isolating the government.[103]

The King was kept fully informed by his advisers of these developments on the left. His relations with Arias Navarro had always been tense but, in the course of the first half of 1976, they reached total breakdown. The Prime Minister's bizarre pro-Francoist declarations in mid-February were the last straw in his practice of simply ignoring what he knew to be Juan Carlos's will. Suárez later claimed that the only row he ever had with Arias Navarro was over his corrosive criticisms of the King.[104] On 8 March, Juan Carlos told a French journalist that he was deeply worried about the deteriorating situation. On the same day, he had received a visit from his father who told him, 'You either get rid of Arias or it will soon be the end.' Two weeks later, Areilza found the King weighed down by anxiety, concluding, 'In a few days, this man has aged I don't know how many years in experience, in wisdom, in bitterness and in scepticism.'[105]

Juan Carlos conveyed his exasperation to Torcuato Fernández-Miranda: 'I just don't know how to deal with Arias. I've tried to establish some connection but I haven't managed it. He doesn't hear what I say and in fact he doesn't let me speak, he doesn't want, or doesn't know how, to listen and I have the impression that he doesn't feel the need to tell me anything. It's as if he believes that he is absolutely safe, that he is Prime Minister for five years and that all I can do is keep him on. I think that at times he thinks he is stronger than me and that deep down he just doesn't accept me as King. He doesn't keep me informed, he talks and talks but the only thing he says is that, thanks to him, things are stable and that without him there would be chaos.' The big problem was that replacing Arias was easier said than done. Torcuato Fernández-Miranda urged the King to demand his resignation but Juan Carlos doubted that Arias would agree. To add to the King's doubts, General Armada consistently advised him not to dispense with Arias's services. In consequence, concerned that Arias might be able to provoke a backlash by the bunker, Juan Carlos was unable to sleep, wandering the palace at night – 'I'm like a ghost' he told Fernández-Miranda. He became increasingly tense and irritable, on one occasion driving the Queen to tears by shouting at her in front of his staff. His anxiety was that, if Arias could not be persuaded to resign, his dismissal would need the acquiescence of the profoundly Francoist *Consejo del Reino* and that would require all of the ingenuity of its President, Fernández-Miranda.[106]

Juan Carlos finally broke his silence on recent developments in an unequivocal interview with Belgian journalist Arnaud de Borchgrave on 8 April. He was greatly preoccupied by the damaging international effects of Fraga's assaults on the left and by Arias's slow progress on reform. The frankness of the interview revealed the depth of the royal heart-searchings. It was also a calculated risk in the hope of provoking Arias Navarro's resignation or at least gaining domestic and international support for the removal of the Prime Minister. Juan Carlos was now convinced that Arias's schizophrenic oscillations between vague nods in the direction of liberalization and instinctive recourse to repressive violence were turning both the left and the right against the monarchy. The King's Christian Democrat contacts – Joaquín Ruiz Giménez and José María Gil Robles – had complained that Arias simply refused to receive them. The interview was published in *Newsweek* on 26 April. The deadlock was underlined in the starkest possible form when Juan Carlos allowed himself to be quoted to the effect that his Prime Minister was: 'an unmitigated disaster, for he has become the standard-bearer of that powerful band of Franco loyalists known as "The Bunker"'. Furthermore, he went on to say that he was not opposed to the eventual legalization of the Communist Party. When the bulk of the interview was published in Spain, Arias Navarro obliged the Minister of Information, Adolfo Martín Gamero, to publish a statement that the interview with Borchgrave had never taken place.[107]

On Maundy Thursday, 15 April, Juan Carlos had discussed with Areilza his doubts about how to manage Arias Navarro's removal. At the same time, he had punctured Areilza's hopes, telling him that, according to Fernández-Miranda, the *Consejo del Reino* would not vote for him or even for Fraga. Arias was, of course, fully aware of the King's determination to get rid of him. Hanging on to power in desperation, he had allegedly attempted to blackmail Juan Carlos by threatening to publish tapes of his telephone conversations when he was still Príncipe de España. He demonstrated his contempt for the King at the end of April. Fully aware of the *Newsweek* interview, Arias did not respond with the expected resignation. About to make a televised address to the nation, he ostentatiously failed to send a copy to the King until the very last minute. Juan Carlos was outraged by this. In the event, the speech on 28 April had minimal content but was peppered with references to Franco and to the enemies of Spain. It was well received only by the extreme right-wing press. Arias was concentrating his efforts on provoking Areilza into resignation. When told, the King put his head in his hands but ordered Areilza not to respond: 'Just hang on, that's what I'm doing.'[108]

On 3 May, when Alfonso Osorio asked Arias Navarro if he would meet representatives of the opposition, he refused categorically. Osorio pressed on, 'Not even with those who are closest to us?', to which Arias snapped, 'Would Franco receive José María Gil Robles? No, he wouldn't. Neither will I.'[109] Two days later, Adolfo Suárez and Alfonso Osorio reproached Arias for not showing his speech to the King. He replied like a naughty child, 'Of course I don't show the King my speeches; he doesn't show me his.' When they told him that he was wrong not to talk to the King, Arias snapped back, 'How can I talk to him? It's like taking a five-year-old for a walk. After five minutes, I'm so bored I can't take any more. The King just talks rubbish.'[110]

On 21 May 1976, Juan Carlos received a visit from his parents at La Zarzuela. His sisters, the Infantas Pilar and Margarita, and their husbands were also present. It was the first time that the entire family was together since Juan Carlos's investiture. It appeared that father and son were finally coming to an agreement on the dynastic issue. The King's son Felipe had, a few days earlier, been officially granted the title of Príncipe de Asturias and Don Juan had recently declared that the content of a monarchy was more important than the identity of the person who wore the crown. Although La Zarzuela presented the occasion as a purely family affair, Don Juan and his son retired, after lunch, for a conversation judged by observers at the time to have centred on political, rather than dynastic, issues. Indeed, it was widely believed that he had urged Juan Carlos to remove Arias. The Barcelona daily *La Vanguardia* reminded its readers that Don Juan had made the possibility of his dynastic renunciation conditional on his son's proven commitment to be 'the King of all Spaniards' and noted that Don Juan saw Juan Carlos's meetings with the opposition as a measure of his progress.[111]

A few days later, an emissary of the King had lunch with senior members of the US Embassy. He stated that the future progress of political reform required the removal of Arias Navarro and requested American support for this during Juan Carlos's forthcoming visit to the United States. While expressing support for the King's project of liberalization, the American diplomats were anxious that the change of Prime Minister should not appear to have been organized in Washington.[112] By now, Arias had cut himself off completely from the King. He neither visited him at La Zarzuela nor reported by telephone. He did not even return calls.[113]

The situation was thus acute when, at the beginning of June, the King went to the United States. On 2 June, he was received by President Ford and then addressed a joint session of Congress and the Senate. His unequivocal declaration of commitment to democracy, made in excellent English and reported around the world, received a standing ovation. The principal US dailies, the *New York Times* and the *Washington Post*, hailed the King as the engine of change. The speech had an electrifying impact in Spain where the contrast with Arias's negative rhetoric was instantly perceived. Juan Carlos had a meeting with Henry Kissinger. The Secretary of State was concerned by the prospect of instability in Spain and recommended slow and steady progress towards reform. It is not known whether the specific issue of Arias Navarro was discussed, but Juan Carlos received strong assurances of American support during his visit. The warmth of the reception that he received both publicly and privately was a great morale boost. It strengthened his confidence and resolve. His determination to remove Arias was also no doubt intensified by the news from Spain received in New York. The police had arrested the liberal Opus Dei monarchist Rafael Calvo Serer on his return to

Spain from France, where he had been living in exile since 1971, and Arias had proposed to close down *Cambio 16*, the massively successful weekly news magazine.[114]

A few days after arriving back in Madrid, Juan Carlos attended Franco–Spanish military manoeuvres. Among the middle-ranking officers present were several who had been the King's contemporaries at the Zaragoza academy. An American journalist who was accompanying Juan Carlos was astonished by the warmth of the camaraderie displayed between the King and these officers. When Juan Carlos asked them if they wanted to dine with him, they replied that they would as long as they didn't have to dress for dinner. The group ended up eating at a transport café. Some of these officers would help the King dismantle the military coup of February 1981.[115]

Shortly after Juan Carlos's return from the US, the new law of political associations was to be presented to the Cortes. The initial assumption was that Fraga would speak in its favour, but Arias Navarro was jealously hostile. Osorio was asked to undertake the task but he argued that his Christian Democrat background would be a severe disadvantage and suggested instead that the Secretary-General of the *Movimiento* would be the appropriate speaker. Torcuato Fernández-Miranda agreed and, on the morning of 9 June 1976, Suárez defended the law with great style. Clearly and quietly, he defended political pluralism as a necessary reflection of the realities of Spanish society. The King was delighted and praised his eloquence by calling him '*pico de oro*' (literally 'golden beak', but with the sense of 'silver tongued'). After Suárez's charismatic speech, the Cortes passed the new law of political associations by 338 votes to 91 with 25 abstentions. However, on the afternoon of the same day, the Cortes balked at making the necessary amendments to the penal code to permit the legalization of political parties envisaged in the new law. Fraga was convinced that he could get the law passed, but Arias Navarro opted to withdraw it for further consultation. Arias was thus exposed as being as unable or unwilling to deal with the bunker as he was incapable of controlling the opposition. Juan Carlos knew that the transition to democracy would falter if it were not quickly placed in the hands of someone able to handle both bunker and opposition. Aware that dissatisfaction with Arias was also rife among senior Army officers, the King had to act before the military ministers formally requested that he dismiss the Prime Minister. In such an event, the preservation of his own authority would oblige him to keep on Arias if only to avoid a more reactionary figure.[116]

On the morning of 1 July, Areilza met the King whom he found relaxed and refreshed, 'as if a weight had been lifted from his shoulders'. Juan Carlos said, 'This can't go on without a risk of losing everything. The job of King is sometimes uncomfortable. I had to take a difficult decision but I've taken it. I will put it into effect suddenly and surprise everyone. You've been warned, so keep quiet and wait. It will be before anyone thinks. There's no choice.' The hint could not have been more blindingly obvious but Areilza claimed later not to have realized what was being hatched. At 1.15 p.m., Juan Carlos called Arias to the royal palace to ask for his resignation. When Arias reached the palace, he found the King with bags under his eyes and visibly nervous. He recalled later 'the distress revealed by the King whose embarrassed silence seemed to tell me how hard he found it to begin the conversation'.

The official version of what happened next is that Arias offered his resignation. He later described himself saying, with typical brusqueness, 'I understand what Your Majesty wants.' When Juan Carlos tried to soften the blow, Arias interrupted, saying, 'You will no doubt have important and adequate reasons.' Other versions have suggested that the King, in military uniform, simply informed him that he required his resignation and that a violent scene ensued. Whatever happened in La Zarzuela, that evening, the outgoing Prime Minister, with the darkest of expressions, manifestly furious, took his leave of his ministers in the cabinet room still dominated by a huge portrait of Franco. Arias could barely bring himself to shake Areilza's hand, believing him to have plotted his demise. After Arias left, the cabinet drew up a communiqué to the effect that Arias's resignation, at his own request, had been accepted by the King after he had taken the advice of the Consejo del Reino. It was, as Areilza commented, 'exactly the opposite of what had really happened'. Areilza and Fraga were both equally confident of being called by the King to succeed Arias.[117]

Both had too much personal ambition, too much historical baggage and too many enemies. During his long march from Fascism to democracy, Areilza had betrayed both Franco and Don Juan. As the previous months had shown, Fraga was a loose cannon with violent instincts. The man that the King and Torcuato Fernández-Miranda wanted would have to be loyal and capable of following a blueprint. Adolfo Suárez had energy and intelligence and a great capacity for dialogue. He was sufficiently young and unknown not to provoke the immediate hostility of the left yet enough of a regime figure not to excite the suspicions of the right. Ensuring that the *Consejo del Reino* would produce a *terna* including his name required some intelligent manoeuvring by Torcuato Fernández-Miranda. He called on the help of Juan Carlos's friend, Miguel Primo de Rivera y Urquijo, both to get Suárez included, 'not to be Prime Minister, of course', but ostensibly to present an image of youthful change and also to ensure that Federico Silva Muñoz did not receive unanimous support, 'because then we'd just be putting pressure on the King'. On 3 July, the *Consejo del Reino* produced a *terna* of Gregorio López Bravo, Federico Silva Muñoz and Adolfo Suárez.[118]

Areilza believed that the choice of Suárez as Arias Navarro's replacement had been planned since Easter and perhaps even since Henry Kissinger's visit to Madrid in January.[119] Indeed, it may well have been even earlier. When Gonzalo Fernández de la Mora visited Torcuato Fernández-Miranda in December 1975, he had asked him who he thought would eventually replace Arias Navarro. 'Someone who'll do what I tell him,' he replied.[120] The candidate with most votes in the *Consejo del Reino* had been Silva Muñoz. He might well have thought back to the day in 1969, 23 July, when Juan Carlos had been proclaimed successor. The Prince had embraced him and said, 'Thank you for all you have done to help me. I'll never forget it.' Gratitude, of course, could play no part in the King's decision. The stakes were higher than that. Silva was no more possible a candidate than López Rodó.

Soon after Suárez's appointment was made public, the King called Silva Muñoz to congratulate him on his inclusion in the *terna*. He explained that his decision had been painful, obliging him to disappoint two loyal friends. It was a typical gesture, both human and politically intelligent. Given his influence on the Christian Democrat right, Silva Muñoz's good will could facilitate Suárez's task of assembling a cabinet.[121]

In the six months since the death of Franco, the King's delay in replacing Arias Navarro had compounded doubts about his commitment to democratization. Convinced that the adjustment of Spain's political structure to the changed economic and social realities of the 1970s was inevitable, many observers tended to interpret hesitation as bad faith. However, such a view underestimated the residual power of the bunker in general and of the Armed Forces in particular. The subsequent emergence of the endemic military conspiracy (known as *golpismo*) puts Juan Carlos's slowness in a different perspective. The delicacy of his dealings with the military establishment was a crucial contribution to the coming of democracy. Similarly, the entire Arias experience was inevitable in that the early consolidation of the King's reign required some continuity with the Franco regime. It was possibly the most difficult period of his reign, during which the scale of tension and stress that he had to undergo aged him visibly. The left understandably regarded Arias as the continuation of Francoism. Juan Carlos had had to live with the opprobrium that came with Arias's presence as Prime Minister. Now he had a Prime Minister of his own choice. It was an enormous gamble but at least the King would now be playing his own cards.

EIGHT

The Gamble

1976–1977

At the halfway point of 1976, the future looked extremely uncertain for Juan Carlos. Trapped between a left pressing for rapid reform and a bunker determined to change nothing, he had had to cope with an erratic and obstructive Prime Minister in Carlos Arias Navarro. He had survived the seven months since Franco's death at the cost of much anxiety, many sleepless nights and a lot of hard work. He had put considerable effort into consolidating the loyalty of the Armed Forces. By dint of visits to Catalonia, Andalusia and Asturias, his popularity had increased. There had in fact been real progress to democracy. However, it was either hidden from the general view, as in the case of Torcuato Fernández-Miranda's behind-the-scenes efforts in the Cortes and the *Consejo del Reino*, or else apparently inimical to his cause. The fact that a freer press than ever before was active, that workers were striking and that students and nationalists had bravely taken to the streets demanding change was ostensibly a challenge to the King's position. For all Fraga's authoritarian reflexes, there was more real freedom than ever before. However, the demands for change were directed at a State of which Juan Carlos was the head, and held the position because he had been named by Franco. Much of the power of the Francoist establishment and, above all, of the Armed Forces remained undiminished. The monarchy could still be swept away in a catastrophic clash between the irresistible force of the left and the immovable object of the right. If that was to be avoided, it was essential that Juan Carlos do everything possible to facilitate more rapid progress towards the introduction of democracy, yet do so in such a way as to meet with the approval of the Armed Forces and the bulk of the Francoist old guard.

The King's choice of Adolfo Suárez as the man to take charge of the next, crucial, stage of the process seemed bizarre in the extreme. Suárez had once described himself to Laureano López Rodó as 'a foot soldier of politics'. Outside Spain, it had been widely assumed that the man chosen to work the miracle would be Areilza, who clearly regarded himself as a field-marshal of politics. Indeed, throughout April, in the belief that he might thereby secure nomination as Arias's successor, Areilza had made a concerted effort to ingratiate himself with Fernández-Miranda. However, neither the King nor Fernández-Miranda considered him to be sufficiently biddable. On the recent royal visit to the United States, Areilza had imposed himself on the proceedings with considerable arrogance and certainly with notably less deference than the King expected.[1] The other favourite for the job, Fraga, had long since ruled himself out by his belligerent style. In any case, both were too old and had sufficient prestige and support to try to impose their own views, perhaps in opposition to what Juan Carlos wanted. They would want their own governments, whereas what was required was a Prime Minister to lead the King's government. In fact, in agreement with the King, Fernández-Miranda had been sounding out the possible candidates. He came increasingly to see Suárez as someone who could follow a script although he was uneasy about the scale of his ambition.[2]

However, the qualities of freshness and approachability that the King saw in Suárez were not appreciated either by the left or by older rivals in the Spanish establishment who were convinced that his government would be short-lived. Yet Suárez had been Civil Governor of a province, a Director General in the government administration and head of the *Movimiento*. He was trusted by the Francoist establishment and knew the system inside out. The King observed Suárez closely, particularly during the Basque crisis in March when he had stood in for the absent Fraga. Juan Carlos asked Alfonso Osorio, 'Did Suárez do as well as he says he did?'[3] For the King, he signified someone who would be able, under the guidance of Fernández-Miranda, to use that system against itself and so initiate reform. In mid-1976, those assets were not widely perceived by either friends or enemies. Arias Navarro told Suárez that he was delighted with his appointment if only because it meant that neither Areilza nor Fraga would be Prime Minister. Indeed, Suárez's Francoist credentials pleased the bunker as much as they horrified the opposition. The response of the left to his appointment was to call massive demonstrations in favour of political liberties and amnesty for political prisoners in the second week of July. Their success left both the King and Suárez in little doubt that speedy and thorough reform was necessary if the crisis was to be resolved without violence.[4]

Responsibility for choosing Suárez belonged exclusively to Juan Carlos. The fate of the monarchy hinged on his success or failure. Suárez commented later that the King 'gambled the crown' on his appointment. Within a week, Suárez told a group of prominent journalists that, when Juan Carlos offered him the job, he told him that the consequence of the process of reform would be to leave the monarchy stripped of political power. The King had always known that this would be the case and he said nothing to limit his Prime Minister's objectives. However, he did tell him that he relied on two crutches – General Armada and Torcuato Fernández-Miranda. When he recommended that Suárez do the same, the Prime Minister replied that he would have no need of them.[5]

Just as the King had perceived the urgency of removing Arias Navarro, he knew that now time was even more pressing. For that reason, he can only have been glad of the olive branch intelligently held out by Santiago Carrillo in response to Suárez's televised denial that he wanted to perpetuate Francoism. Writing about 'the precarious rise of Suárez', Carrillo speculated on the possibility that Suárez might be the instrument of the *ruptura pactada*. 'As I write, there is still no cabinet or government programme and I would rather give the Prime Minister the benefit of the doubt. This is the dilemma in which both Suárez and King Juan Carlos find themselves.'[6]

The most difficult immediate task was the selection of a cabinet team. The spurned Areilza and Fraga both declined to continue in the government. They, like many others in the political élite and in the opposition, believed that Suárez's stay in power would be brief. This was particularly alarming for Juan Carlos, who had hoped to keep Fraga on board because of his credibility among the Francoist establishment and the considerable number of his devoted followers. On receiving his letter of resignation, the King, with typical determination, telephoned him to try and get him to change his mind. Fraga was adamant, claiming to have no faith in the new Prime Minister's capacity to take the reform project forward. Clearly believing this to be a job that only he could do, he made his position clear in terms that thoroughly discomfited his wife, who could hardly believe that he would speak so vehemently to the King.[7]

While an embittered Areilza actively tried to persuade influential figures not to accept posts in the cabinet, many of Fraga's collaborators simply made it clear that they wanted nothing to do with the new Prime Minister. Suárez was in danger of having to form a cabinet composed entirely of his cronies from the *Movimiento*. To the relief of the King, assistance was provided both by Alfonso Osorio and Torcuato Fernández-Miranda. A prominent member of the *Tácito* group of Christian Democrat functionaries, Osorio became Vice-President of the cabinet and Minister of the *Presidencia*. At the request of the King, he threw his considerable influence into persuading other '*Tácitos*' to accept posts.[8] The early days of Suárez's premiership required the King to have nerves of steel. He commented later, 'I didn't know it was possible to suffer so much.' The announcement of the final cabinet list could not have had a worse reception from the press. It was regarded as a collection of second-rank technocrats and progressive Falangists. Ricardo de la Cierva, Franco's self-styled official biographer, who was engaged in a short-lived operation to redefine himself as a liberal, denounced it as 'the first Francoist government of the post-Franco period'.

A notable feature of the new cabinet was Suárez's decision not to change the military ministers. This was particularly curious in the case of the highly reactionary General de Santiago y Díaz de Mendívil who remained as Vice-President for Defence Matters.

Fiercely Francoist, General de Santiago was monarchist in so far as he looked to Juan Carlos to guarantee the continuity of the Caudillo's regime. The fact that Santiago suffered ill-health would have provided Suárez with a good excuse to replace him. However, the King, conservative in military matters, thought it prudent to keep him on along with the other three Armed Forces ministers. The Minister for the Army, the rigidly austere General Félix Álvarez Arenas, had fought in the Civil War and felt utter veneration for Franco. He was loyal to Juan Carlos simply because that was what the Caudillo had ordered in his will. The same was true of the Minister for the Navy, Franco's crony, Admiral Gabriel Pita da Veiga, and the rather more progressive Minister for the Air Force, Carlos Franco Iribarnegaray. The King told Suárez that these men should not be replaced and he reluctantly agreed to keep them in the government. The military ministers aside, Suárez's team was dominated by young men. They were loyal monarchists who had been introduced to Juan Carlos in the early 1970s by his secretary, Jacobo Cano. Conservative Catholics like Osorio, Marcelino Oreja at Foreign Affairs, Landelino Lavilla at Justice, Eduardo Carriles at Finance and Leopoldo Calvo Sotelo at Public Works, gave Suárez a better chance to carry out reform than his critics believed possible.[9]

Juan Carlos presided at the first cabinet meeting on 9 July. By so doing, he was linking his prestige to the success or failure of Suárez. His speech called upon the new government 'to make possible the clear and pacific participation of all citizens in deciding our future'. He declared that he wanted all Spaniards to know that, 'The King is thinking about them because they make up the nation that I personify and the people that I serve.' He ended with a ringing command to the government – 'operate without fear!' They would certainly need courage to secure the good will of the left-wing opposition without provoking a backlash from the bunker. Feeling an uncommon sense of real solidarity as a consequence of the media hostility which had greeted their appointment, the cabinet responded by enthusiastically adopting the King's battle-cry. Suárez informed them that his strategy would be based essentially on speed. He would keep ahead of the game by introducing specific measures faster than the *continuistas* of the Fran-coist establishment could respond to them.[10]

On 14 July, Suárez returned to the Cortes to present once more the amendments to the penal code necessary to permit the legalization of political parties. Rejected on 9 June, the measure now passed by 245 to 175 votes by dint of a clause that seemed effectively to block any future legalization of the Communist Party. The clause referred to political associations 'that accept an inter-national authority and propose a totalitarian system'. López Rodó, however, told the King that, in his opinion, the modification of the penal code opened the way to the legalization of the Commu-nist Party. Juan Carlos was adamant that this was not the case.[11]

Suárez's programme, announced on television, gave some sub-stance to the promises made by the King on his accession. It recognized that sovereignty lay with the people, proclaimed the government's determination to introduce a democratic system and promised a referendum on political reform and elections before 30 June 1977. For the bulk of non-politicized Spaniards, fearful of losing the material benefits of the previous 15 years, but recep-tive to political liberalization, the combination of Juan Carlos and Adolfo Suárez was an attractive option. With all the skill that Juan Carlos had expected of him, Suárez cultivated a television appeal of energy and charm. Together, they presented an image of modernity and flexibility far removed from the sclerosis of late Francoism. The King and his Prime Minister projected dynamism, youth and sincerity in a way that consolidated political support among the silent majority by offering both to protect the economic and social advances of recent times and to advance peacefully and gradually towards democracy.

While Fernández-Miranda and Suárez worked on the details of political reform, Juan Carlos concentrated on touring the prov-inces and building support for democratic reform among ordinary Spaniards. On 24 July, accompanied by the Queen, he embarked on a six-day tour of Galicia – one of Spain's poorest regions. At first, the popular reception was cool, at times hostile. In Santiago de Compostela, groups of nationalists shouted slogans and waved banners in Gallego (the Galician language) demanding more jobs and schools. At the town hall, Juan Carlos made a speech from a balcony overlooking the Obradoiro square. Some of his remarks were in Gallego, which placated the crowd. On visits to Pontevedra, Vigo, Orense and Lugo, the King's openness to local issues melted the initially icy popular reception. In Vigo, he addressed a crowd of 60,000, promising to urge the government to look for solutions to the region's problems, and was enthusiastically greeted by workers at the Citroën Hispania factory. In Lugo, he declared to a delighted crowd, 'I promise you that the government will deal in depth and constantly with your problems. I will become your permanent advocate.' The reception was less enthusiastic in the poorer rural areas. The King could not fail to be aware that, at Arneiro in the Terra Cha, the heart of rural Lugo, banners demanding 'General Amnesty' and 'More justice for the countryside' were removed from the crowd.

By 29 July, the tour had moved on to La Coruña. At Pontedeume, Juan Carlos made a gesture to the right, inviting the town's most prominent citizen, the Caudillo's sister, Pilar Franco, to join him on the platform. In La Coruña itself, Juan Carlos inaugurated the 'Avenida del Ejército' (Avenue of the Army) before an enthusiastic crowd of 100,000 people. The King's local popularity was clinched when, during his speech, he recognized in the large crowd a sailor who had served under him aboard the battlecrusier *Canarias*. The Mayor of La Coruña, José Manuel Liaño, publicly asked for a general amnesty on political prisoners. On the following day, back in Madrid, the King chaired a cabinet meeting and successfully proposed a wide-reaching amnesty for political prisoners (but not including terrorists convicted of crimes of blood). The visit to Galicia was a considerable success for the King and greatly facilitated the reform process. According to *El País*, in drawing attention to the region's problems, Juan Carlos had shown himself to be 'the perfect interlocutor'.[12]

Despite the advantages brought by Suárez, the King continued to face the same difficulties as he had when Arias had been Prime Minister. Progress towards democracy had to take place under the hostile gaze of the bunker and the Army. The Galician tour was symptomatic of the effort that Juan Carlos put into securing the popularity of the monarchy while consolidating the loyalty of the Armed Forces. At the end of July, he made the decision personally to hand out the commissions to the cadets of the three service academies.[13] The problem of the opposition and its mass pressure for change was seen as Suárez's concern. The left-wing opposition quickly made it clear that it conceived of the *ruptura pactada* as signifying rapid negotiations for the opening of a constituent period. Bringing the opposition to collaborate in a process of democratization within Francoist 'legality' would come to be seen as one of Suárez's greatest challenges and consequently greatest triumphs.

Carrillo in particular was keeping up the pressure on the government by a calculated policy of bringing the PCE back to the surface, challenging the cabinet either to tolerate his party's existence or else to reveal its true colours by reverting to repressive action. He began by holding an open meeting of the PCE central committee in Rome at the end of July. Amply publicized by the media, it had considerable impact, revealing to the Spanish public for the first time that a significant number of well-known intellectuals and labour leaders were Communists. On 17 August, Suárez told López Rodó, 'You can be sure that, as long as I am Prime Minister, the Communist Party will not be legalized.' That seemed entirely plausible, since he had recently dismissed his Ambassador in Paris for personally receiving Carrillo when he applied for a passport. Expecting nothing from the Prime Minister, the PCE stepped up its challenge by openly distributing party membership cards to its militants.[14]

The struggle between Suárez and the opposition for control of the transition process intensified by the day. Accordingly, the King's success in building popularity for the monarchy would be crucial to the attempt to introduce reform from above. As an excuse for delay, Suárez could point to the Army; as an incentive to hurry, the opposition could point to the rising swell of popular feeling. Strikes had increased ten-fold in relation to the previous year.[15] To ensure a bloodless transition without economic or social dislocation, Suárez had to take the initiative away from the left. He began to make substantial concessions to the more moderate elements in an attempt to split the united front of the opposition and thereby force the Communists into defensively trying to prevent their own isolation rather than setting the pace of opposition demands.

Juan Carlos continued to work hard to facilitate the process of political reform even during the summer. Two days after beginning his holiday at Marivent in Mallorca, on 5 August, he made a private visit to Paris, where he publicized the recently announced political amnesty.[16] He also made considerable efforts to maintain US support. After returning to Marivent on 13 August, he received General Alexander J. Haig, NATO Supreme Commander and Chief of US forces in Europe. Although the meeting with Haig was portrayed as a mere courtesy in the course of a private holiday, there was inevitable speculation that Spain's eventual integration into NATO had been broached. Some days earlier, Haig had declared in Brussels that such a development was desirable. Then, after meeting Juan Carlos, Haig admitted that they had discussed security in the Western Mediterranean, and Juan Carlos went aboard the US aircraft-carrier *Nimitz*.[17] These gestures were not to the liking of Spain's left-wing opposition, but they were important in consolidating American support for the monarchy. It was not without significance that, shortly before the meeting with Haig, the *Washington Star* had published on 9 August a feature on Queen Sofía, praising her 'love for dialogue'.[18]

Throughout August, with the King's encouragement, Suárez had cordial interviews with a wide range of opposition personalities, including Felipe González. The PSOE leadership was already convinced that the Francoist system was unlikely to be overthrown by popular action and replaced with a provisional government and a constituent Cortes to decide on the form of regime. When Suárez met González on 10 August, the PSOE leader had already accepted that a constitution elaborated by a freely elected Cortes would in itself constitute a *ruptura*. González knew that, to get to that point, it would be necessary to negotiate with the government. Accordingly, he was delighted by the Prime Minister's openness and readiness to listen 'like a sponge' and convinced that Suárez was well-disposed to the creation of a genuinely democratic regime.[19] Through the King's friend, the lawyer and president of the Europa Press Agency, José Mario Armero, Suárez also made contact with Carrillo, urging him not to make the transition impossible.[20] By 'transition', Suárez meant a peaceful process that would leave the existing social and economic structure intact. Like González, fully aware that some kind of compromise with the reformist right was inevitable and that the imposition by popular force of a provisional government was unlikely, Carrillo assured Suárez of his commitment to pacific change.[21]

On Monday 23 August, Torcuato Fernández-Miranda gave Suárez a draft of the political reform law. It was a document that carried monumental political significance because it indicated a way in which Juan Carlos could fulfil his oath of loyalty to the principles of the *Movimiento* and yet remain true to his declared aim of bringing democracy to Spain. On the following day, the new Prime Minister presented the text to the cabinet, omitting to mention that it had been Torcuato's brainchild. It was received enthusiastically. A subcommittee was formed to work on the text and other proposals, such as that drafted by Miguel Herrero y Rodríguez de Miñón, the technical Secretary-General of the Ministry of Justice. The finally approved text would be presented to the nation on 10 September. On 26 August, the King called Fernández-Miranda and Suárez to La Zarzuela to discuss the situation. All three knew that they were walking a tightrope. The project had to be steered past the Francoist establishment and the Army while being exposed to the suspicious scrutiny of the opposition.[22]

Inevitably, there were incessant rumours of military subversion. Indeed, faced with the surging waves of opposition confidence, the Army and the bunker huddled together ever more defiantly. As Commander-in-Chief, Juan Carlos enjoyed a certain degree of respect but was still regarded with some suspicion by many senior generals. That had been shown by the efforts made to block, in the first cabinet of the monarchy, the King's candidate to be Minister of Defence, the liberal General Manuel Gutiérrez Mellado. Once he had been smeared as head of the *Unión Militar Democrática*, overall responsibility for defence affairs had passed to the reactionary General Fernando de Santiago. General de

Santiago had not felt the slightest hesitation about communicating to the King his disquiet at the rising tide of opposition. In February, Santiago had told him that if the wave of strikes and demonstrations continued, the Army would feel obliged to intervene. Juan Carlos, who maintained close contacts with younger officers of his own generation, told López Rodó on 24 February, 'the way of thinking of the older generals is not the same as that of the younger officers', a phrase that summed up Juan Carlos's dilemma regarding the military.[23] Confident that the younger members of the officer corps would accept democracy, he was equally aware that the presence of a large number of generals who had fought alongside Franco in the Civil War demanded several years of caution. Accordingly, his overriding concern was to keep the senior officers on board. As he later put it, 'I did not want at any cost that the victors of the Civil War should become the defeated under democracy.'[24]

General de Santiago sincerely believed that the Armed Forces were apolitical despite the intimacy of relations between senior military figures and the civilian bunker. For him, as for most military hardliners, there was nothing political about loyalty to the principles of Francoism, but rather just a basic patriotic duty. Throughout 1976, there had been contact between leading generals and Francoist ultras like José Antonio Girón de Velasco, president of the *Confederación Excombatientes* (Falangist Civil War veterans) and leader of the bunker, Blas Piñar, head of *Fuerza Nueva*, and the retired head of the Civil Guard, General Carlos Iniesta Cano. Their meetings aimed to bolster military intransigence in the face of democratic reform.[25] Juan Carlos was aware of the extent to which the hardliners were trying to block the transition. For that reason, the retention of General de Santiago in the cabinet had been tempered by the appointment of General Gutiérrez Mellado as Chief of the General Staff. The determined progress towards dialogue with the opposition caused first friction then rage among the diehard Francoists. The trend of the conflict was symbolized by General de Santiago's furious response to the fact that Suárez had removed Arias's life-size portrait of Franco from his office. They had also clashed dramatically in the presence of the King over the initial amnesty agreed on 30 July 1976 and Suárez had declared that he would not tolerate such outbursts.[26]

Given the atmosphere of military suspicion, the King thought it crucial that Suárez submit his reform project to a group of senior officers and appeal for their 'patriotic support'. He recalled later that he said, 'We have to act without hurting the feelings of the soldiers. We must not give them the impression of working behind their backs. I know the military. They hate surprises, subterfuge and petty secrets and will never tolerate lies.' Suárez was uneasy lest he be seen as excessively deferential and seem to be recognizing the military's right to determine the political direction of Spain. However, the King convinced him that it was better to make a good-will gesture towards the Armed Forces. Before the meeting, the King's one-time supporter but increasingly nostalgic Gonzalo Fernández de la Mora urged both Admiral Pita da Veiga and General de Santiago to oppose Suárez's plans.

Accordingly, tension and suspicion dominated the early stages of the meeting on 8 September 1976. The 29 officers invited to hear Suárez included the military ministers, the nine Captains-General and the Chiefs of Staff of the three services – all men steeped in the anti-Communism of a regime born of the Civil War. Stressing his determination to proceed at all times in accordance with the law, Suárez said that only if the law permitted it would the Communist Party be legalized. However, by reference to the recent amendment of the penal code, he was able to assure them that the international loyalties enshrined in the PCE's statutes would preclude any such legalization. Even so, Suárez's persuasively expounded plans were accepted cautiously in most cases and largely because they enjoyed the backing of Juan Carlos. A few received him enthusiastically – the ultra General Ángel Campano López, Director General of the Civil Guard, going so far as to say 'long live your mother!' – the ultimate approbation. It is likely that reactions would have been different had Suárez told them that, through his secret contacts with Carrillo, he was working towards a change in those statutes and an eventual legalization of the Communist Party. Curiously, eight years later, Suárez continued to insist that: 'I did not deceive any officer.' Most senior officers would later be convinced that they had been the victims of outright deception and came to regard Suárez with a bitter hatred until his departure from the political scene in 1981.[27]

Two days after the meeting with the high command, the cabinet approved the draft law for political reform without any opposition from the four military ministers. Within a matter of hours, Suárez announced the project on television. A few days later, to Juan Carlos's alarm, matters took a different turn when the Minister for Syndical Relations (a new ministry which recognized free trade unions), Enrique de la Mata, introduced a draft project for trade union reform. This provoked the outrage of General de Santiago y Díaz de Mendívil, for whom the trade unions were responsible for the disorder of the 1930s. So energetic was his protest on 21 September that Suárez obliged him to resign. The Prime Minister was asserting himself because he knew that he could not afford to have the reform programme slowed down. He was also happy to seize the opportunity to replace Santiago as Minister of Defence with General Manuel Gutiérrez Mellado. However, Suárez's resolve worried both the King and the Minister of the *Presidencia*, Alfonso Osorio. Shrewd, cautious and essentially very conservative, Osorio believed that General de Santiago's immense influence among the right-wing opponents of reform meant that he should have been brought around by persuasion. Juan Carlos agreed. Suárez, on the other hand, was blithely confident that he understood the Armed Forces sufficiently well to permit himself such firmness. He quickly paid the price.

General de Santiago circulated among his senior colleagues a letter explaining his position: 'The political evolution of our Fatherland is running along channels, and is based on premises, with which I have been able to identify myself. My deep conviction that a political intervention by the Armed Forces could only produce undesirable situations in the short term led me to eschew intransigent positions. However, I also consider, personally as well as in my capacity as the spokesman of the Armed Forces inside the government, that limits must be imposed on such restraint and understanding when they begin to be misinterpreted. The government is preparing a measure, which I have opposed in vain, authorizing trade union freedom. This means, in my opinion, the legalization of the CNT, UGT and FAI trade unions, responsible for atrocities committed in the red zone during the Civil War, and of the Workers' Commissions, the trade union organization of the Communist Party. I am convinced that the consequences of this measure will be immediate, and since neither my conscience nor my honour permit me to take responsibility for, nor implicate the Armed Forces in, such a measure, I have decided to present my irrevocable resignation.'[28]

This text, apart from masking the fact that General de Santiago had effectively been dismissed, implied that any other officer who accepted a ministry in Suárez's cabinet was both immoral and dishonourable. Santiago's stance, and perhaps also his distorted vision of Spanish history, gave rise to declarations of solidarity from other officers and expressions of delight from the bunker press. *El Alcázar*, the ultra-rightist newspaper whose board of directors was headed by the immensely prestigious right-winger, General Jaime Milans del Bosch, published a letter from the ineffable General Iniesta Cano thanking Santiago for his 'priceless lesson'. Iniesta had been enraged by café rumours that Santiago had not resigned of his own free will. Under the headline 'A Lesson In Honour', Iniesta built on Santiago's own circular by stating that his example had to be followed by any officer committed to the service of the Fatherland. This was effectively a declaration of war against General Manuel Gutiérrez Mellado, Santiago's successor and a man close to the King.

As if the King did not have enough to worry about, the emergence of *Alianza Popular*, a substantial political party of the right in potential opposition to Suárez, was equally worrying. It was the brainchild of 'the magnificent seven' – Manuel Fraga and six other prominent Francoist reformers. Rather irritated, the King described it, on 1 October, to one of them, López Rodó, as 'an explosive mixture'. It is hardly surprising then that Juan Carlos was sufficiently concerned to comment gloomily to him, 'If things go badly, I'm leaving.' Some days later, he received another of the 'seven', Gonzalo Fernández de la Mora, and reproached him for linking up with Fraga and Silva Muñoz (another member) rather than supporting Suárez. Fernández de la Mora was appalled by the disparaging way in which the King spoke about them, allegedly referring to Silva as an 'almighty bore' and saying of Fraga that even after his stint as Ambassador in London, 'he was still a wild man of the woods'.[29]

This meeting took place in La Zarzuela while the implications of the military crisis were being discussed by the government. At the cabinet meeting on 1 October, it was decided that both Santiago and Iniesta would be punished by being relegated to the reserve list – using a law introduced by Franco in order to repress monarchist officers. What Franco could do without hindrance was clearly no longer acceptable in a system of respect for the law. Osorio, who held a position in the juridical corps of the Spanish Air Force, believed that this was simply not legal without some kind of judicial hearing. The Under-Secretary at the Ministry of Information, Sabino Fernández Campo, telephoned Osorio after the cabinet meeting to express his opinion that the decision was improper. Fernández Campo had had long service in the Ministry of the Army and was an expert in military law. Both he and Osorio were concerned because the decree demoting Santiago and Iniesta would have to be signed by the King as *Jefe Supremo* (Commander-in-Chief) of the Armed Forces. To be associated with a measure that was likely to be overturned on appeal could only damage the prestige of the King. After vigorous protests from Iniesta and frantic consultations with military juridical experts, adjudication was entrusted to General Joaquín Fernández de Córdoba, a traditionalist and a close friend of Iniesta. Not only did he declare the government's decree improper but he also judged the conduct of both generals to have been blameless.[30]

It was understandable that Suárez wished to assert his authority over the Army, but he had acted precipitately. Prominent bunker figures like the sinister one-time head of the Francoist transport syndicate union, Juan García Carrés, General Jaime Milans del Bosch and José Antonio Girón de Velasco rallied around Iniesta and encouraged him to oppose the punishment. In the full glare of publicity, the cabinet had been made to look ridiculous and vindictive. General Gutiérrez Mellado was placed in an appalling

position. Having been only recently promoted to the rank of Lieutenant-General, he was regarded by many in the military establishment as insufficiently senior to occupy the post of Minister of
Defence. Now, he had to suffer the contempt of his comrades-in-
arms and the hostility of General de Santiago, perhaps the most
influential officer in the entire Army. The King's authority within
the Army had been undermined and the bunker was delighted.[31]
Generals Santiago and Iniesta had been exalted to iconic status as
courageous defenders of the eternal Francoist verities. Their
articles in *El Alcázar* over the next five years would reflect and
promote the growth of anti-democratic sentiment, or *golpismo*,
within the Armed Forces. Nonetheless, Santiago's removal deprived the bunker of a strategic position. Despite the hostile atmosphere in which he had to work, Gutiérrez Mellado was able to
begin the urgent task of promoting a new generation of officers
loyal to the coming democratic regime. In the short, and indeed
middle, term, rather than deep-rooted commitment to democracy,
the most that the Defence Minister could hope for from senior
officers was basic fidelity to Juan Carlos. Fortunately, that was
something that the King knew how to generate.

In the meanwhile, however, the task of steering the reform
project through the labyrinths of the Francoist establishment occupied most of Suárez's time. The reaction of the opposition was
mixed. The project allowed for the existing government to preside
over the elections promised before mid-1977 and there was no
question of Suárez resigning in favour of a provisional government.
Accordingly, a declaration of the executive committee of the Communist Party on 15 September had vehemently denounced the text
as 'an imposed law that attempts to defraud liberty and popular
sovereignty'.[32] Other groups within the opposition were, however,
pleasantly surprised by the extent to which daily life was being
liberalized, thereby giving substance to Suárez's claims. The press
was functioning normally, political groups to the right of the PCE
were unhindered and the PSOE was preparing to hold its XXVII
Congress. Now Minister of the Interior, Rodolfo Martín Villa had
issued provincial Civil Governors with instructions to prohibit
all public activities by the Communists.[33] Yet, to a certain degree,

even the PCE was unofficially allowed to go about its business. The initiative was swinging Suárez's way. He insinuated to the Socialists and the leftist Christian Democrats that he could make even greater concessions provided that they did not rock the boat and provoke the Army by prematurely insisting on the legalization of the PCE. With typical skill and cunning, Suárez was using the issue to drive a wedge into the opposition and to impose caution on Carrillo. Thus, in late September, Felipe González was adamant that legalization of the Communist Party was a non-negotiable prerequisite of democracy. Yet by the end of November, he was arguing that it was unrealistic to insist on it.[34] Faced with the obvious impossibility of imposing changes against the will of the Army and with the substantial evidence of progress under Suárez's guidance, the opposition could do little but acquiesce.[35]

While Suárez and Fernández-Miranda prepared the presentation of the political reform to the Cortes, the King worked hard both to generate foreign support and also to maintain the good will of Spanish public opinion. Shortly after a successful tour of Latin America, in late October 1976, Juan Carlos made his first official visit to France, meeting Giscard d'Estaing. On 29 October, while in Paris, the King gave a somewhat awkward interview to Feliciano Fidalgo from *El País*. In response to Fidalgo's questions about his contacts with the left-wing opposition, Juan Carlos went on the offensive and started asking questions: 'Do you consider France to be a democracy? What is a democracy?' Under the barrage of questions, Fidalgo finally interrupted him and said: 'Excuse me, Your Majesty, but I am the one asking the questions.' Juan Carlos laughed cheerfully and replied: 'Well, in any case think of other kings from European countries, and you will see that they do not easily lend themselves to dialogue.' Fidalgo replied: 'But Your Majesty knows that those monarchs do not rule. And Your Majesty does.' Juan Carlos brushed the questioning aside 'jovially'.[36]

Such public manifestations of affability and approachability by the King were crucial since the opposition remained distrustful, which was understandable after the empty efforts at reform witnessed successively from Solís, Carrero Blanco and Arias Navarro.

On 23 October, the *Platajunta*, the *Coordinación Democrática*, had united with five regional fronts from Valencia, Catalonia, the Balearic Islands, the Canary Islands and Galicia, to form the *Plataforma de Organismos Democráticos*. Meeting on 4 November in Las Palmas, the new organization rejected Suárez's plans for a referendum on his political reform project. The *Plataforma* called for abstention, arguing that the referendum would be meaningless while political parties were still illegal, while the government retained monopolistic control over radio and television, while there were still political prisoners, and while the huge apparatus of the *Movimiento* still existed as a mechanism of electoral pressure.[37] However, despite the apparent strength and firmness of the opposition stance, the pace would go on being dictated by Suárez and calibrated in terms of what the military would tolerate.

Juan Carlos knew that in order to complete his self-appointed task of returning democracy to Spain, the Communist Party would have to be legalized. He also knew that it would be necessary to advance as delicately as possible. This was demonstrated at a dinner party that he attended in Madrid on 10 November at the home of his sister the Infanta Doña Pilar. Apart from Juan Carlos and Queen Sofía, among the guests were Don Juan, José Mario Armero and the head of Suárez's private office, Carmen Díez de Rivera, an elegant blonde aristocrat to whom the King was greatly attracted. Juan Carlos had asked the willowy Carmen to broach the topic of the legalization of the PCE. Years later, she commented, 'I had been commanded to let it slip, to see what would happen.' When she did, a glacial silence fell over the room. To compound her embarrassment, she had also undertaken to talk to Don Juan about the need for him to abdicate.[38] The dinner conversation can only have reminded the King once more of the difficulty of the task facing both him and his Prime Minister. The reactions of those around the table were no doubt representative of Madrid high society and thus not wildly different from those of the military establishment. They would have to be reconciled with those of the opposition whose pressure for progress was reflected in continued industrial action.

The wave of strikes reached its peak in November without

seriously disrupting the government's timetable for gradual reform and then began to lose steam. Committed political or trade union activists aside, the broad mass of the people welcomed the changes introduced by Suárez and were likely to vote in favour of the reform project. In addition, the incorporation into the opposition factions of centrist elements had led to a softening of militant attitudes. Accordingly, the great general strike called for 12 November was posed in economic rather than political terms. Its slogans were protests against the wage freeze and redundancies, although the political implications were clear enough. In the event, more than a million workers were involved, but the strike never spilled over into the great national action against the Suárez reform that the Communists had hoped for. That was in large part because of the elaborate precautions taken by the Minister of the Interior, Rodolfo Martín Villa. By arresting workers' leaders in Madrid, Barcelona, Valencia, Bilbao and Seville, the police neutralized the nerve centres of the movement and so appreciably limited its impact.[39]

The relative failure of the planned general strike was also an indication of the success achieved by both the King and Suárez in persuading the mass of the population that the reform programme was genuine. Moreover, taking place only three days before the reform project was to be submitted to the Cortes, it strengthened the government's hand. Nevertheless, to be on the safe side, potential votes in the Cortes had, with the aid of Torcuato Fernández-Miranda, been nervously counted in advance. Every member of the cabinet had been given the task of sounding out a particular group of *Procuradores*. Suárez spoke to the most hardline members of the *Movimiento*. Many were persuaded by arguments to the effect that the process did not stray from Francoist legality, permitted a decorous end to the dictatorship and was the King's will. Fernández-Miranda approached, amongst others, the sourly suspicious Gonzalo Fernández de la Mora, and told him that, 'The King has made the decision and we are proceeding to a full-scale party system.' Juan Carlos himself saw Fernández de la Mora on 10 November and managed to dilute his hostility to the project, persuading him that *Alianza Popular*'s interests would be safeguarded in the future democratic system. Some votes were secured by promises of positions of influence in the post-election democratic regime.[40]

From 16 to 18 November, the law on political reform was discussed in the Cortes. The team to present the project had been carefully selected by Fernández-Miranda. All five were chosen in terms of their ability to appeal to different sectors of the Cortes. The cleverest choice was the King's lifelong friend, Miguel Primo de Rivera. As the political heir of the founder of the Falange, there was no one better to assume the defence of the reform project. Blas Piñar, the leader of *Fuerza Nueva*, denounced the project as contrary to the fundamental principles of the *Movimiento* and to the intentions of Franco. Virtuoso displays of sophistry using the entire panoply of Francoist political theories came from both sides. The prior backstage manoeuvres of Suárez and Fernández-Miranda bore fruit when the reform was approved by 425 votes, 59 against and 13 abstentions. Fifteen of the negative votes came from Army officers. Other military figures had left the Cortes in order not to have to vote.[41]

The likely outcome had been carefully calculated. Some possibly recalcitrant *Procuradores* were packed off to an official junket to Panama, via the Caribbean. Others were promised seats in the planned future Senate as a consolation prize. Suárez made much of the fact that the proposed democratic Cortes and Senate would have the same number of seats combined as the Francoist Cortes. This influenced many *Procuradores* who had come to believe that they were popular and genuinely 'represented' the areas on which they had been imposed. They therefore assumed that they would simply be re-elected by their grateful constituents or that Suárez would somehow 'fix' it. In general, the vote in favour of the political reform project was a collective suicide based on the ingrained habits of obedience to authority, an inflated sense of patriotism and, above all, tempting promises whispered in the ears of those to whom Suárez later referred as the '*Procuradores del harakiri*'.[42] The wisdom of the Suárez–Fernández-Miranda route to democracy was confirmed after the vote when the Minister for the Navy, Admiral Gabriel Pita da Veiga, a close personal friend of Franco, remarked, 'My conscience is clear because the democratic reforms will be carried out through Francoist legality.' Pita's confidence had been carefully nurtured by the King. With Franco's institutions in voluntary liquidation, the road was open to the elections. Suárez now had good reason to be confident that the left would be obliged to accept his version of reform bestowed from above.[43]

The failure of the 12 November general strike had persuaded many opposition groups to accept negotiation with Suárez as the best method to liquidate Francoism. The Prime Minister's conversations with moderate opposition figures were paying dividends. With more Liberal and Social Democrat groups joining the *Plataforma de Organismos Democráticos*, the readiness to negotiate prevailed over more maximalist positions. At the same time, however, the clear evidence of progress towards democracy was provoking a right-wing backlash. On 20 November, the first anniversary of Franco's death, a huge demonstration was held in the Plaza de Oriente. Indignant Francoists chanted: 'Suárez resign, the people don't want you; take note, government, Spain is not for sale; Juan Carlos, Sofía, the people don't trust you,' and 'Power to the Army.'

Elsewhere on the same day, fully aware of the need to placate right-wing opinion, the King was taking part in an important event in the basilica of the Valle de los Caídos. In the aftermath of the Cortes vote in favour of the reform project, it was a carefully calculated gesture towards those Francoist elements distressed by the signs that the dictator's legacy was being demolished. The royal household sent out invitations to a funeral mass to commemorate the first anniversary of the Caudillo's death on 20 November. Accompanied by Queen Sofía, the King presided at the ceremony which was attended by the entire cabinet, the *Consejo del Reino*, the *Consejo Nacional del Movimiento* and senior members of the Cortes. Special places were reserved for Franco's wife, his daughter Carmen, her husband, Cristóbal Martínez-Bordiu, Alfonso de Borbón y Dampierre and his wife María del Carmen Martínez-Bordiu Franco, as well as other members of the Franco, Primo de Rivera, Carrero Blanco and Calvo Sotelo families. The balancing act continued on 22 November, when Juan Carlos received the heads of the three armed services at La Zarzuela to commemorate the first anniversary of his reign. The Chief of General Staff of the Army, Lieutenant-General Carlos Fernández Vallespín, spoke of the 'unbreakable loyalty towards the crown of the three services'. On the following day, a Royal Decree promoted a Nationalist hero of the Civil War, Antonio Aranda, to the rank of Lieutenant-General. Having petitioned Franco for the establishment of a constitutional monarchy headed by Don Juan, Aranda had been held at the rank of Major-General for decades. His belated promotion was seen as correcting an injustice. In a coma in a hospital bed, Aranda was unable to derive much benefit from the gesture.[44]

A summit meeting of the *Plataforma de Organismos Democráticos* and other groups held on 27 November reaffirmed many of the demands of the *Plataforma*'s inaugural declaration. However, the crucial condition of a provisional government of 'democratic consensus' to oversee the forthcoming elections was dropped.[45] The way was now open for a 'committee of personalities' from the opposition to negotiate with the government. In the first week of December, the PSOE finally held its XXVII Congress. Inevitably, considerable pro-Republican rhetoric could be heard. Nevertheless, the German Socialist leader, Willy Brandt, visited La Zarzuela, which was seen as de facto evidence of the Socialist International's recognition of Juan Carlos's democratizing intentions.[46] In the wake of the PSOE Congress, the Spanish Communists were increasingly concerned about their position. Accordingly, on Friday 10 December 1976, Carrillo declared at a clandestine press conference in Madrid: 'Everyone knows we disapproved of the way the King came to the throne [but] the King is there, that is a fact . . . If a majority of the Spanish people vote for a constitutional and parliamentary monarchy, we Communists will respect as always the decision of the Spanish people.' With characteristic dry humour, Carrillo, who was being hunted by the police, offered to meet Juan Carlos in order to explain in person the Communists' position.[47]

On 15 December, despite the opposition's advocacy of abstention, the referendum on political reform saw the project approved by 94 per cent of the vote. The abstention calls were a tactical error. There was an unreal air about them and they were ignored by the left-wing rank-and-file. However, without more guarantees from Suárez regarding the legalization of political parties, neither the PSOE nor the PCE leaderships felt able to endorse his line publicly. In fact, both Carrillo and González knew that the referendum would be a success for Suárez and did not perceive the result as a defeat for themselves. Indeed, given that the government's progress towards democratization had been spurred along by opposition pressure throughout 1976, the referendum result was in a sense a victory for the left as well as for Suárez. Nonetheless, the boost to the position of both Suárez and of Juan Carlos was immeasurable. The monarchy was popularly regarded as the driving force behind the progress towards democracy. The referendum gave Juan Carlos a popular legitimacy signifying that he was no longer King only by dint of being Franco's successor. Flushed with success, Suárez now felt able to manifest his independence not only of Fernández-Miranda but also of the King.[48] In the case of Juan Carlos, this would pose serious difficulties in the future.

The minimal 'no' vote showed how small was the popular support for a continuation of Francoism. Nevertheless, opponents of democratization were often in evidence. On 20 December at a mass in memory of Admiral Carrero Blanco, Torcuato Fernández-Miranda was insulted by ultra-rightists chanting: 'Treacherous bastard government to the firing squad!' and 'We don't want the monarchy, neither Juan Carlos nor Sofía!'[49] On 17 December 1976, two days after the referendum, hundreds of policemen and Civil Guards held an anti-government demonstration in the centre of Madrid in protest against the political reform. Chants were heard demanding the resignation of Martín Villa. General Chicharro, who confronted the demonstrators, was violently jostled. In consequence, the Director General of Security and the Inspector General of the police were both replaced by Suárez. The sanction with the widest repercussions was the dismissal of the ultra Director General of the Civil Guard, Ángel Campano López. He was replaced by General Antonio Ibáñez Freire, a man close to Gutiérrez Mellado. The fact that Ibáñez Freire had to be promoted expressly to Lieutenant-General in order to take up the post provoked fury in reactionary segments of the military hierarchy for whom the most rigid seniority in promotions was sacrosanct.

The most vociferous critic of this irregularity was General Jaime Milans del Bosch, Commander of the *División Acorazada Brunete* (the Brunete Armoured Division), who, ironically, had also in his day been promoted out of turn. He was probably the most prestigious officer in the Spanish Army, as a cadet he had been besieged in the Alcázar of Toledo in 1936 and had fought with the *División Azul* on the Russian front. Now, he simply announced that he was 'going home' and ceased to attend his office. It took an intervention by the King to defuse the tension. Juan Carlos had an excellent relationship with Milans, whose grandfather had been head of Alfonso XIII's military household, and he was anxious to bring him back into the fold without obvious friction. In a private conversation, the King mitigated the exercise of his authority with his habitual charm in order to secure the return of Milans. On 6 January 1977, Juan Carlos made a further effort to calm military sensibilities with his speech on the occasion of the annual military festival, the *Pascua Militar*. Speaking in the Madrid royal palace to the high command of the three services, he referred to the assembled officers as 'my comrades in arms' and exhorted them 'to continue on the path of duty, honour, discipline and loyalty'. It was a brilliant speech, combining flattery, affection and leadership, and it had been drafted by Juan Carlos himself. The atmosphere created was illustrated on 31 January, when the King visited the *División Acorazada Brunete* accompanied by the Chief of Staff of the Army, General José Vega Rodríguez. A photograph of him eating a roll alongside a beaming Milans del Bosch was reproduced on the front page of all the newspapers.[50]

There was some disquiet over the fact that Milans had not been punished for his indiscipline. The conciliatory role of the King may have reflected the presence of the deeply conservative General Alfonso Armada as head of the secretariat of the royal household. Armada worked hard to ensure that the King's speeches would contain some laudatory reference to Franco. He also regarded it as his responsibility to keep Juan Carlos informed of opinion within the military high command. On his own admission, he was inclined always to stress the dangers of progress towards democracy and to emphasize the concerns of senior generals.[51] There is no reason to think that Armada was exaggerating the dangers. Certainly, in exercising his authority as Commander-in-Chief of the Armed Forces, Juan Carlos took serious note of Armada's warnings. Every Monday when he was in Madrid, the King received senior officers for lengthy conversations, both in order to assure them of his sympathy for their point of view and to keep in touch with the state of military opinion.[52]

After the referendum, Suárez still faced two issues, either of which could have upset the delicate balancing act that he and the King were performing. These were the unresolved dilemma of the legalization of the Communist Party and the problem of terrorism, particularly that of ETA, both of which threatened to undo Suárez's fragile truce with the Army. Thanks to his particular skills as backstage negotiator, the question of the Communist Party would eventually be solved, albeit at the cost of bitterly festering resentment in military circles. Basque terror, in contrast, was to prove insoluble and, in the long run, would be Suárez's undoing. Osorio wrote in his diary that Suárez simply did not understand the Basques. After all, immersed in the gargantuan task of creating a democratic polity, consumed by the problems of placating both bunker and opposition, neither Suárez nor the King could be expected to sympathize with the revolutionary nationalist aspirations that drove ETA to continue its guerrilla war. The turbulent months between July 1976 and June 1977 hardly permitted them to dedicate sufficient time to comprehending or resolving the Basque question. Suárez regarded the Basque problem as one of public order and left the 'technical' question of dealing with terrorism to his extremely competent Minister of the Interior, Rodolfo Martín Villa. Unfortunately, Martín Villa's Falangist background provoked intense hostility in Euskadi.[53]

By comparison with ETA, Suárez's other outstanding problem on the left, the legalization of the Communist Party, was relatively uncomplicated. Already in Madrid clandestinely, Santiago

Carrillo decided to force the pace by coming out into the open at a large press conference on 10 December. He was arrested on 22 December after a lengthy police manhunt. The Communist Party reacted with a massive campaign in favour of his release and a delegation of senior party members was received at Suárez's office by Carmen Díez de Rivera. To Suárez's discomfort, this was interpreted by the press as indicating his inclination to legalize the PCE. In any case, to keep Carrillo in custody, or to put him on trial, would have fatally undermined Suárez's credibility. He had to release him and that constituted a substantial step towards legalization.[54] However, the slightest hint that Communism might regain legal status in Spain could only intensify the problem of the military bunker whose nerves were kept on edge by terrorism. In fact, as soon as Suárez had made his first announcement of his commitment to change, a highly suspicious effort to destabilize Spain was made in the emergence of an allegedly Marxist-Leninist splinter group, GRAPO (*Grupos de Resistencia Antifascista Primero de Octubre*). GRAPO was suspected by Gutiérrez Mellado of being infiltrated by, or even the creation of, the extreme right and elements of the police. The success many years later of one of its leaders, Pío Moa, as a rightist commentator renewed these suspicions. After an initial bombing campaign, GRAPO managed to galvanize the extreme right. Four days before the referendum on the political reform project, they kidnapped Antonio María Oriol, President of the *Consejo de Estado* (the Council of the State, the advisory body which assessed the 'constitutionality' of proposed legislation, which was still at this time staffed entirely by Francoists). Their efforts to derail the transition would continue, on 24 January 1977, with the kidnapping of General Emilio Villaescusa Quilis, President of the *Consejo Supremo de Justicia Militar* (Supreme Council of Military Justice). Both remained in captivity until freed by the police on 11 February.[55]

The King was appalled. As Franco's Minister of Justice from 1965 to 1973, Oriol had been one of Juan Carlos's most loyal supporters and key collaborator of López Rodó in the operation to have the then Prince named as successor to the Caudillo. A fervent monarchist, Oriol had served in Franco's forces during the

Civil War. He was a conservative figure with important banking connections. It was suspected that he had been selected as a kidnapping victim as a provocation directly aimed at persuading orthodox Francoists that the reform project would open the way to disorder and violence of a kind not seen since the Civil War. The operation made no sense from a left-wing perspective. GRAPO claimed to be the armed wing of the previously non-existent *Partido Comunista de España (renovado)*. Since Suárez was in touch with the real PCE with a view to its eventual legalization within a democratic Spain, GRAPO was clearly intending to smear Santiago Carrillo and inflict major damage on the Prime Minister.

GRAPO's activities permitted the bunker to assert that Suárez's government was throwing away the achievements of the Civil War. A concerted campaign was launched against the reform process in general and against General Gutiérrez Mellado in particular. As part of the rightist strategy of tension, on the same day as the kidnapping of Villaescusa, right-wing terrorists murdered five people, four of whom were Communist labour lawyers, in an office in the Atocha district of Madrid. The PCE refused to be provoked and instead issued appeals for serenity. Initially, Suárez reacted nervously, failing to express sympathy for the families and refusing permission for a public funeral ceremony. Only after a fierce dispute with Carmen Díez de Rivera did Suárez authorize a funeral for the victims. In what was to be a key moment of the transition to democracy, Communist Party members and sympathizers marched in silence in a gigantic display of solidarity. Both Suárez and the King himself, who flew over the march in a helicopter, were deeply impressed by the demonstration of Communist strength and discipline. Certainly, much popular hostility to the legalization of the PCE was dissipated by the restraint with which its supporters responded to the tragedy. A delegation of opposition leaders negotiated with Suárez and, in return for promises of action against the bunker's violence, they offered him a joint government–opposition declaration denouncing terrorism and urging national support for the government. It was a significant advance for Suárez signifying his public acceptance by the left as belonging to the democratic forces in Spain.[56]

Thus, the poisonous situation in the Basque Country aside, Suárez was advancing along the path towards controlled democracy in the rest of Spain, dealing adequately with both the bunker and the Communists. Nonetheless, the ultimate objective was not merely to proceed to democratic elections that the better-organized left-wing parties might well win. Suárez did not intend to walk away once the immediate task was completed. His vision went far beyond the projected elections. Despite doubts expressed by the King, regular public opinion polls carried out by the government had convinced them that a centre-right party, not too tainted by Francoism, and backed by Suárez's control both of the apparatus of the *Movimiento* and of the media, would have a healthy electoral future. In fact, throughout the autumn of 1976, many progressive ex-Francoists began frantic preparation for political life under a democratic regime.[57]

One of the first off the mark was Manuel Fraga. He was convinced that 40 years of dictatorship had left the majority of Spaniards as convinced rightists. Accordingly, he had linked up with six other ex-Francoist dignitaries, Laureano López Rodó, Licinio de la Fuente, Federico Silva Muñoz, Cruz Martínez Esteruelas, Enrique Thomas de Carranza and Gonzalo Fernández de la Mora. Known collectively as the 'magnificent seven', four of them, like Fraga himself, had once been eager enthusiasts for Juan Carlos. They hoped to capture what they called 'sociological Francoism', a constituency they imagined to comprise the majority of Spaniards. Although Fraga underestimated the popular urge for change, he was successful in attracting large sectors of Suárez's political association, the *Unión del Pueblo Español*. It was to become eventually the focus of the ambitions of a wide spectrum of Francoist veterans ranging from Carlos Arias Navarro to Gregorio López Bravo. With substantial backing from the banks, Fraga's party, *Alianza Popular*, was created with breathtaking speed in the second half of September 1976, although its eventual electoral impact lay some way in the future.[58]

To some extent, the forging of *Alianza Popular*, together with the evidence of the opinion polls, confirmed Suárez's growing conviction that the most appropriate territory for his own political future was the centre. There existed centre-right parties and *grupu-scules* (tiny political groups) by the score. The process whereby they coalesced to become the *Unión de Centro Democrático*, or UCD, under the leadership of Adolfo Suárez was kaleidoscopic, confusing and involved some seedy wheeling and dealing. Both the King and Torcuato Fernández-Miranda had advised Suárez against the creation of his own political party.[59] It has been argued that their reluctance derived from the fact that they doubted Suárez's long-term future. They saw him as the ideal man to dismantle the Francoist system, not as the leader of a democratically elected party. It took the intervention of Alfonso Osorio in La Zarzuela before, in the spring of 1977, Juan Carlos finally gave a green light to Suárez's proposal that he lead the nascent UCD.[60]

UCD was the result, in the broadest terms, of an electoral alliance of five main groups, each in its turn composed of several others. The most numerous segment of the future party was constituted by a broad spectrum of conservative Christian Democrats, many of whom had attained senior positions in the Francoist civil service, while others had maintained their distance from the dictatorship. In the autumn of 1976, an important group of the former, Alfonso Osorio's own political association, the *Unión Democrática Española*, together with some *Tácitos*, combined with a group of the latter, Fernando Álvarez de Miranda's *Izquierda Demócrata Cristiana*. The resulting party was called the *Partido Popular Demócrata Cristiano*. A similar group composed of other *Tácito* functionaries and a variety of Christian Democrats was launched on 1 December 1976. Known as the *Partido Popular*, its early sponsors who included the Valencian lawyer, Emilio Attard, were rather overshadowed when the need for well-known figureheads led to the late inclusion of Pío Cabanillas and José María de Areilza. These two barely distinguishable parties, having merged as *Centro Democrático* in mid-January 1977, became the basis of UCD.[61]

Complex negotiations added two further, but small, groups to *Centro Democrático* in early 1977, the various Social Democrats led by Francisco Fernández Ordoñez and the several Liberal parties under Joaquín Garrigues. Neither Social Democrats nor Liberals were entirely natural partners for the Christian Democrats and both were eventually to be crucial to the fragmentation of UCD in the run-up to the military coup of 1981. However, in 1977, with elections on the horizon, the central requirement shared by all these groups was the urgent creation of an electable party. This meant that the search for profitable alliances would take precedence over ideological, personal or moral considerations. Accordingly, during February and March 1977, with his own *Unión del Pueblo Español* drifting into the orbit of Fraga's *Alianza Popular*, Suárez began to eye the nascent coalition as his own electoral vehicle. Given the government's control of the Spanish television and radio network, RTVE, and of local administrative machinery, he was confident of being an acceptable leader. Indeed, so attractive were his credentials in this regard that he had little difficulty in unseating the *Centro Democrático*'s leader, José María de Areilza.[62]

Similarly, practical rather than ethical considerations dictated the inclusion into UCD of its fifth and crucial component group, the *Movimiento* bureaucrats, rather like Suárez himself, who were coalescing around Rodolfo Martín Villa.[63] The final negotiations which brought all these, and many lesser, component groups together consisted of ruthless horse-trading. The formal agreement for the creation of the UCD electoral coalition was signed on 3 May 1977. Since the candidate lists had to be submitted by 9 May, the following five days saw the clinching of deals in which Suárez's control of the State electoral machinery gave him the edge. Inevitably, the UCD's final lists were dominated by men who had prospered in the government machinery of Franco.[64] Without a coherent ideology, UCD would eventually suffer from its clientelistic nature.

While UCD was still in the process of being forged, Suárez had yet to steer his reform project to its culmination. The process of legalizing political parties had begun in February 1977. The stumbling block remained the PCE. For the bunker and the Army, to legalize the Communists meant throwing away everything that they had fought for in 1936. General Gutiérrez Mellado's plans to liberalize the Army had already led to unrestrained verbal attacks on him. On 24 January 1977, the same day as the Atocha massacre, about 30 senior officers met at the *Casino Militar* in Madrid and called for the resignation of the government. The meeting was dissolved on the orders of General Milans del Bosch, at the time acting Captain-General of Madrid. This suggested that Juan Carlos's policy of keeping Milans close was paying dividends. Then the first of an escalating series of incidents took place at the funeral of a Civil Guard and two policemen who had been killed by GRAPO. As Gutiérrez Mellado was presenting medals to the families of the murdered officers, ultra slogans were chanted. When Gutiérrez Mellado endeavoured to impose silence, he was publicly insulted by the naval Captain Camilo Menéndez Vives, a close friend of Blas Piñar. Menéndez went virtually unpunished.[65] It was obvious that the rage of the ultras would be pushed onto an altogether higher plane if Suárez legalized the PCE. However, he had little choice. Democracy would simply be incomplete if it excluded a party of the significance of the PCE. In any case, Suárez was confident that, by delaying the PCE's entry into the game, he would diminish Communist electoral support.[66]

With characteristic shrewdness, Carrillo was prepared to make every possible concession to the crown. On 20 January 1977, at a dinner in the Ritz of Barcelona at which the magazine *Mundo* was giving awards to various politicians, a much-publicized meeting took place between Carrillo and the King's friend, Carmen Díez de Rivera. The consequent media furore embarrassed Suárez to the extent that she felt obliged to offer her resignation, which Suárez was astute enough to refuse. She then continued to act as intermediary between the Prime Minister and Carrillo. By the end of February, Suárez had agreed to a secret meeting with Carrillo at the home of José Mario Armero. In return for legal status, Carrillo undertook to recognize the monarchy, adopt the red-yellow-red monarchist flag of Spain and offer his support for a future social contract. Juan Carlos was aware that the decision to move ahead with the legalization of the Communist Party could have been deeply damaging to the monarchy, yet he supported his Prime Minister totally. He was kept fully informed by Suárez of the meeting with Carrillo. However, the disapproval of Torcuato

Fernández-Miranda was such that his relations with Suárez were irreparably damaged. Suárez allowed a Eurocommunist summit to take place on 2 March at the Hotel Meliá-Castilla in Madrid, knowing that a huge international scandal would ensue if he tried to block the entry into Spain of the leaders of the Italian and French parties, Enrico Berlinguer and Georges Marchais. Thus, with full press coverage, Carrillo was able to meet them. It was another step towards legalization.[67]

The PCE's statutes had been altered to enable Suárez to claim that, when it was legalized, he was not going back on the assurances given to the assembled generals in September. On Good Friday, 8 April, the Supreme Court issued a judgement to the effect that there was nothing in the statutes to prevent the PCE's inclusion in the Register of Political Associations. The King and Queen were on a brief private visit to France but, before leaving, Suárez had spoken at length to Juan Carlos about the step that he was about to take. The King was fully aware of the enormous risks involved. From her frequent conversations with him, Carmen Díez de Rivera was struck by the level of his anxiety about the military reaction. The scale of anti-Communist feeling within the Army was such that there was a real danger of a military coup and the overthrow of the monarchy. It was a massive gamble but one that he had to take. On Holy Saturday, 9 April, Suárez, mistakenly confident of Army acquiescence, announced the legalization of the PCE. Carmen Díez de Rivera heard the news at 6.45 p.m. when the King took the extraordinary step of telephoning to thank her for her contribution to the process.[68]

On 8 April, after the Supreme Court's judgement had been received, the Minister of the Interior, Martín Villa, had asked General Sabino Fernández Campo, the Under-Secretary of the Ministry of Information, to arrange the publication of the news. General Fernández Campo immediately enquired whether Suárez had informed the military high command that what he had told them on 8 September 1976 was about to be changed. He was certain that they could have been persuaded by an explanation of the impossibility of having a limited democracy and of the benefits of having the Communist Party in full view rather than in clandestinity. On the other hand, Fernández Campo believed that, if the top brass learned of the legalization through the media, they would be furious. Martín Villa went out to telephone Suárez, and returned saying 'that's already been dealt with'. Suárez was wrong and Fernández Campo was right. Most of the Madrid political and military élite were out of town for the Easter weekend but that merely delayed the negative reaction.[69]

On Easter Sunday, 10 April, a meeting took place in La Zarzuela of the King, Adolfo Suárez, the Marqués de Mondéjar and General Armada. Although Juan Carlos fully supported his Prime Minister's initiative, Armada took it upon himself to reproach Suárez. He accused him of endangering the crown because of the speed with which the measure was announced. Suárez was furious and made it clear that he would not tolerate challenges to his authority from the King's secretary. Armada's days in La Zarzuela were numbered.[70]

The sophistry over the PCE's statutes did not save Suárez from the unrelenting hatred of the bunker, although he was never to understand why. By legalizing the Communists, Suárez became guilty in the eyes of the ultras of a vile betrayal of the cause for which the Civil War had been fought. The Army, Navy and Air Force ministers believed that Suárez had betrayed them by issuing the announcement in their absence. Yet what lay behind the confidence of Suárez and Martín Villa was that General Gutiérrez Mellado, the Minister of Defence, had telephoned all three ministers to explain to them what was about to happen. Once the announcement was made, the Minister for the Air Force, Carlos Franco Iribarnegaray, returned to Madrid but noted no significant discontent among his subordinates. On Monday 11 April, he met the King and pragmatically accepted the legalization of the PCE. The Minister for the Army, the gaunt and moustachioed General Félix Álvarez Arenas, received numerous indignant protests from fellow officers. Despite grave misgivings, he now resisted calls for his resignation only because his senior colleagues made it clear that no one would replace him. The Minister for the Navy, Admiral Gabriel Pita da Veiga, was furious, claiming that he heard the news for the first time from the television news bulletin. On Monday 11 April, he resigned. A number of civilian ministers, headed by the Finance Minister Eduardo Carriles, were also ready to resign, but were dissuaded by Alfonso Osorio, who pointed out that to do so would irreparably damage the monarchy.

The threat of military subversion now seemed very real and both Suárez and Juan Carlos were seriously concerned. The King spent most of Sunday and Monday on the telephone to senior officers calming them down and heading off threats of indiscipline. On the one hand, he asserted his authority as Commander-in-Chief while, on the other, exercising his considerable gift for persuasion. Suárez met the high command on 11 April to justify to them what he had done. He even played them a tape-recording of the proceedings of their meeting on 8 September 1976. It was to little avail. On Tuesday 12 April, chaired by General José Vega Rodríguez, the senior generals of the *Consejo Superior del Ejército* met to discuss the situation. The mood was one of disgusted indignation and savage criticisms were made of both Suárez and Gutiérrez Mellado. A majority were in favour in demanding that the King issue a statement disowning his Prime Minister and Minister of Defence. Its communiqué referred to the widespread revulsion that the measure had caused, although it also accepted, in disciplined manner, that what had occurred was a *fait accompli*. A more extensive statement, strongly critical of both Suárez and Gutiérrez Mellado, was sent privately to the King. In consultation with the Prime Minister, General Antonio Ibáñez Freire, the Director General of the Civil Guard, drew up a note that was specifically designed to defuse some of the tension. As a further safety precaution, efforts had been made to keep key military units short of petrol in the preceding weeks.[71]

General Vega Rodríguez visited La Zarzuela on 14 April to explain what had happened. Alfonso Armada also spoke to senior officers in a personal capacity but did nothing to correct the impression that he was representing the King. Deeply conservative, with impeccably Francoist credentials, Armada played a valuable role in calming military sensibilities. However, over the years, the impression that Armada was the sole liaison between Juan Carlos and the high command would have dangerous consequences. Now, a rapid response to Pita da Veiga's resignation was crucial to avoid the government appearing weak. Apparently egged on by Manuel Fraga, no senior officer would agree to replace Pita. Only after much embarrassment were Suárez and Gutiérrez Mellado able to persuade a retired, but much decorated and immensely prestigious admiral, Pascual Pery Junquera, to take over as Minister for the Navy. There can be little doubt that the King's sangfroid was of crucial assistance to the government throughout an appallingly difficult week. On Friday 15 April at the swearing-in of Admiral Pery Junquera at La Zarzuela, a calm Juan Carlos, seeing the strained look on Osorio's face, went over and said, 'Alfonso, chin up.'[72]

The legalization of the PCE, inevitable and necessary part of the transition as it was, nevertheless constituted a gift for the ultras. Propaganda was stepped up in military barracks to exploit what was presented as Suárez's 'treachery'. A series of straw organizations, the Patriotic Juntas, the Patriotic Military Union and the Patriotic Military Movement, were rapidly invented. Their names headed the cyclostyled propaganda that was hastily improvised and stuffed into the mailboxes of military housing estates. Alongside virulent diatribes against the military reforms of General Gutiérrez Mellado, who was insultingly called Señor Gutiérrez, were accusations that an unpatriotic government was responsible for ETA terrorism. It was sneeringly insinuated that the King was a traitor to the legacy of Franco. This blanket propaganda gave the erroneous impression that the bulk of the Army wanted a military coup.[73] The same message was propagated daily by the bunker press, El Alcázar, El Imparcial and Fuerza Nueva. The King was increasingly obliged to impose his authority. He received one of the Captains-General, who expressed his disgust about the political reforms being introduced. Juan Carlos went onto the offensive, pointing out that he had heard that, in several regiments within the Captain-General's military region, both his portrait and his first message to the Armed Forces had been taken down from the walls. The Captain-General replied casually that he knew nothing about this. He was shocked into standing to attention when the

King ripped into him, saying, 'Well, find out and do something about discipline in the units under your command!'[74]

Inevitably, Basque aspirations gave a spurious plausibility to ultra-right claims that Spain was being torn apart by criminal separatists. Fortunately for Suárez, the bunker was unaware that his government had started to negotiate with ETA in November 1976. Those talks had led to a sporadic truce, with a trickle of released prisoners and a further partial amnesty on 14 March 1977. There were still 27 *Etarras* behind bars and the various left Basque nationalist (*abertzale*) parties declared that they would boycott the June elections unless all prisoners were released. With barricades going up in many Basque towns and clashes between *abertzales* and the forces of order a daily occurrence, the two wings of ETA, ETA-Político-Militar and ETA-Militar, renewed their terrorist activities. Alarmed at the prospect of the imminent elections being disrupted, the government then negotiated a cease-fire with both ETA factions and conceded total amnesty on 20 May. The slowness of Suárez to grasp the gravity of the Basque problem had thus led him to give both ETA and the bunker the clear impression that amnesty had been a capitulation in the face of armed violence.[75]

In the meantime, Juan Carlos worked hard to keep the officer corps loyal, using to the full both his authority as Commander-in-Chief and his own close contacts. On 14 May, for instance, he presided at the ceremony to mark the end of the academic year at the Army general staff college in Madrid. His speech on the role and virtues of the Armed Forces stressed his identification with military concerns.[76] On Saturday 28 May, the nine-year-old Príncipe de Asturias, Felipe, was made a member of the *Regimiento Inmemorial del Rey* (the King's Own Regiment). After the ceremony, the King and Queen, Prince Felipe and the entire cabinet watched a huge parade of the *División Acorazada Brunete*. Over 10,000 men and the tanks, armoured cars and other vehicles of the most powerful unit in the Army took part under the command of a delighted General Jaime Milans del Bosch. On the following day, the King presided at a great parade down Madrid's Castellana Avenue on the Armed Forces Day, an event that had replaced

Franco's annual Civil War victory parade. The King issued a pardon for all those sentenced for military offences except for members of the *Unión Militar Democrática* and those who had served the Second Republic during the Civil War. In defiance of the continual progress to democracy, the military bunker clung to the ostracism of both the UMD and Republican officers as if they were the last vestiges of the Civil War victory.[77] The King's sensitivity to the Francoist prejudices of the senior officer corps cannot be exaggerated. There was no artifice about the fact that Juan Carlos felt himself to be a soldier. It was entirely sincere and was at the heart of the combination of camaraderie, informed concern and authority that characterized his frequent contacts with the Armed Forces. Both his public appearances as Commander-in-Chief and his private meetings with officers were a crucial part of restraining military hostility to the democratic process.

After the Armed Forces Day parade, there took place an even more significant ceremony that passed virtually unnoticed by the bulk of the Spanish population. Don Juan fulfilled the promise that he had made to his son shortly after the death of Franco. He renounced his dynastic rights and recognized his son as King. It went some way to wiping out the 'original sin' of Juan Carlos's kingship – the fact that it was Franco's invention rather than the consequence of dynastic succession. Precisely because of the implications that such an act of renunciation might have for the legality of Juan Carlos's position, there had been considerable reluctance on the part of both Torcuato Fernández-Miranda and General Armada to arrange the ceremony. Originally, Don Juan had wanted to link three generations of the royal family by bringing the mortal remains of Alfonso XIII to a Spanish port in a warship and making his renunciation speech on the quayside. He later complained that the King's 'entourage' had suggested instead that he simply renounce his rights in a letter from Estoril.[78] In the event, a compromise was reached and a modest ceremony was held at La Zarzuela. Suárez believed that the King was less than enthusiastic about his father's renunciation. After all, his son Felipe had been given the title of Príncipe de Asturias in January 1977,

22 *Previous page*
The recently crowned
King Juan Carlos
and Queen Sofía
accompany Doña
Carmen Polo after
a requiem mass for
Franco at the Valle
de los Caídos on
20 December 1975.

23 On 30 October 1975, a desperately ill Franco had agreed to Juan
Carlos assuming the Headship of State. With Spanish Sahara facing the
'green march' by 500,000 Moroccans, the Prince flew to the capital, El
Aaiún, on 2 November. He explained the need for a dignified withdrawal
to the governor general, General Federico Gómez de Salazar, and his
troops. The Army were delighted by this demonstration of courage and
initiative by their new commander-in-chief.

24 Juan Carlos with the first government of his reign in mid-December
1975. To his right, Carlos Arias Navarro, and to his left General Fernando
de Santiago y Díaz de Mendívil.

25 On 9 July 1976, Juan Carlos chairs the first meeting of Adolfo Suárez's cabinet. The new prime minister is to his right.

26 On 31 January 1977, the King visited the Brunete Armoured Division whose commander, the fiercely right-wing General Jaime Milans del Bosch, was the most prestigious officer in the Spanish army. This widely reproduced photograph of them together reflected Juan Carlos's anxiety to reduce military hostility to democracy.

27 *Above* Shortly after the death of Franco, Don Juan promised his son that he would formally renounce his dynastic rights and recognise him as King if there was satisfactory progress towards democracy. On 14 May 1977, at La Zarzuela, Don Juan fulfilled his promise and went some way to wiping out the 'original sin' of Juan Carlos's kingship – the fact that it was Franco's invention rather than the consequence of dynastic succession.

28 *Right* On 24 June 1977, his saint's day, at a lavish reception at La Zarzuela for the members of the new Cortes, Juan Carlos welcomes the Secretary-General of the Communist Party, Santiago Carrillo. To be able to greet leading Socialists and Communists was a moving symbol of national reconciliation. The King had broken with Franco's policy of deliberately maintaining the hatreds of the Civil War and keeping alive the festering divisions between victors and vanquished.

29 The President of the Catalan government, the Generalitat, Josep Tarradellas, visits the Palacio de la Zarzuela on 5 April 1978.

30 In recognition of the King's acceptance of the constitution, after some debate within his executive committee, Felipe González became the first secretary general of the Socialist Party to request an audience. The meeting at the royal palace on 12 December 1978 sealed the Socialists' formal recognition of the monarchy.

31 *Left* Juan Carlos with Prince Felipe on 3 December 1979 at joint U.S.-Spanish military manoeuvres on the coast of Almería. Behind and to the Prince's left can be seen the Minister of Defence, Agustin Rodríguez Sahagún.

32 *Right* The military coup headed by Colonel Tejero was seen to have failed when Juan Carlos appeared on television at 1.15 a.m. on 24 February and declared his determination to defend the constitution, confirming that, several hours previously, he had ordered the conspirators to stand down.

33 *Below* In the evening of 24 February, at La Zarzuela, Juan Carlos received (from left to right) Santiago Carrillo, Agustin Rodríguez Sahagún, Adolfo Suárez, Felipe González and Manuel Fraga. In statesman-like language, he made it clear that 'my job should not be that of a fireman always ready to put out a fire'.

34 *Right* Sailing was always one of Juan Carlos's favourite hobbies.

35 *Below* The 1992 Olympic Games in Barcelona significantly boosted the public image of the entire Royal Family. The King's spontaneous demonstrations of enthusiasm and affection for the Spanish team were entirely in tune with the mood of the people. He was nicknamed 'King Midas' because it seemed that the Spanish competitors always did better when he was present in the stadium.

36 *Above* The King's
mother, Doña María de
las Mercedes, died on
2 December 2000 in
Lanzarote. On the
following day, a visibly
upset Juan Carlos,
accompanied by Queen
Sofía, attended a requiem
mass.

37 *Left* The King gave
away his daughter
Elena at her marriage
to Jaime de Marichalar
in Seville Cathedral on
18 March 1995.

38 *Below* The present
and future of the Spanish
monarchy – Juan Carlos
and his heir, Prince Felipe.

several months before Don Juan's official renunciation, making it clear that Juan Carlos had no doubts about the legitimacy of his position.[79] The mainstream Spanish press did not pick up on the implications of the ceremony but the bunker newspaper, *El Alcázar*, took the opportunity to remind its readers, many of whom were Army officers, that Juan Carlos's monarchy had been 'installed' by Franco, that Juan Carlos had, in 1969 and 1975, sworn to uphold the fundamental principles of the *Movimiento*, and that the monarchy could therefore only be regarded as legitimate if it remained true to those principles.[80]

On 23 May, Torcuato Fernández-Miranda presented the King with his resignation as President of the Cortes and of the *Consejo del Reino*. Juan Carlos was perplexed and told his mentor that he was making a mistake. The resignation was not announced until 30 May. Fernández-Miranda had more than fulfilled the immediate task entrusted to him by Juan Carlos but the reasons for his resignation remain unclear. He may have had doubts about his own capacity to function in mass politics. Certainly, his relations with Adolfo Suárez had deteriorated after the referendum on political reform. Before December 1976, the most important political decisions had been taken by the King, Fernández-Miranda and Suárez, who used to meet as a kind of super executive committee of the State. Once validated by the result of the referendum, Suárez had felt free to unleash his ambition and ignore the advice of Fernández-Miranda.[81] By the spring of 1977, they were barely on speaking terms, and Fernández-Miranda looked in vain to Juan Carlos for support. Gonzalo Fernández de la Mora, who missed no opportunity to portray the King in a bad light, claimed that a bitter Torcuato told him that, having fulfilled his purpose, Juan Carlos rarely received him at La Zarzuela. Although he was rewarded with a dukedom and the coveted order of the *Toisón de Oro*, Fernández-Miranda's relationship with the King cooled. Whatever the truth of the matter, it would be churlish not to recognize the astonishing achievements of Fernández-Miranda in helping the King reach his goal of Spanish democracy. He had both designed the political reform and guided the process of gaining Francoist acceptance thereof.[82] Nevertheless, the King had to make difficult decisions without considerations of personal loyalty. Like López Rodó before him, Fernández-Miranda had played his part and now was dropped. Adolfo Suárez was a better bet for the future. Yet, during the final stages of Torcuato's fatal illness in the summer of 1980, Juan Carlos would insist on being kept informed about his progress several times a day.

Great as had been the triumphs of Fernández-Miranda and Suárez, the King's equally remarkable achievement had been effectively to keep the Armed Forces from opposing the entire process of reform. The louring presence of the Army ensured that the joint commission of the opposition and the government had elaborated an electoral law in a spirit of some trepidation. Shortly before the elections, the Captain-General of Barcelona, Francisco Coloma Gallegos, had paraded a unit of tanks through the Catalan capital on the morning of a normal working day, bringing traffic to a halt. It was a threatening gesture that culminated in him taking the salute from the balcony of the Capitanía General (military headquarters) in the Paseo de Colón. Coloma Gallegos, who had been Franco's last Minister for the Army, was not even reprimanded. Moreover, on the day of the elections, he had heavily armed units, complete with armoured cars, ready to go into action if the left got out of hand.[83] However, despite such intimidation, the election campaign was carried out in an atmosphere of popular fiesta. The best attended meetings were those of the PSOE, followed by those of the PCE. The main thrust of the UCD's campaign was on television, press and radio where its resources were virtually unlimited.[84] Eighteen million people voted, nearly 80 per cent of the total electorate, and 90 per cent of them voted unmistakably for change.

In fact, Spaniards wanted change but not confrontation, and this favoured Suárez and Felipe González. In contrast, Carrillo and Fraga awakened memories of the conflicts of the past. Despite plentiful financing, *Alianza Popular*'s line-up of prominent Francoists did not help its cause, all the more so after an astonishing interview given by Arias Navarro to the journalist Pedro J. Ramírez, in which Arias claimed to make regular visits to Franco's tomb at the Valle de los Caídos in order to commune with the

Caudillo and to request his immediate return to life to sort things out. His meetings during the campaign were openly reactionary and nostalgic, provoking chants of 'Franco, Franco, Franco'. By giving one of *Alianza Popular*'s three television spots to Arias, who struck an unrepentantly Francoist note, Fraga almost certainly lost many votes.[85] The Communists were especially disadvantaged by memories of the Civil War. The Socialists, on the other hand, derived benefit from their Civil War record and from a hidden continuity of PSOE tradition in many families. Equally, the image of youthful honesty and energy generated by Felipe González and the prestige conferred by the support of European Socialist leaders made him a serious rival to Suárez.[86]

Suárez avoided confrontation by the simple device of refusing to take part in any debate with other party leaders, usually on the most specious grounds. His advantages were overwhelming. Above all, he was closely linked in the public mind with the King. In addition to UCD's exploitation of government control of the media, massive funding from the banks permitted a huge advertising campaign. UCD posters appeared on hoardings that had been set aside for government appeals for the population to vote. Sixty per cent of UCD voters were women, so the party's propaganda machine built on Suárez's filmstar looks to create an image of the devoted family man and practising Catholic. UCD won the elections, with 34.3 per cent of the vote; but the Socialists were not far behind with 28.5 per cent. *Alianza Popular* polled only 8.4 per cent, behind the PCE with 9.3 per cent.[87]

The Franco regime was laid to rest on 15 June 1977. From the late 1960s, many Francoists had pinned their hopes on Juan Carlos as a successor who might give the system a new lease of life, but few had actually shared his ambitions for far-reaching political reform. Accordingly, various half-hearted efforts were made to adapt Francoism without fundamentally changing it. The blind intransigence of the bunker eventually convinced larger and larger sections of the economic oligarchy, liberal monarchists and, in time, the more far-sighted Francoists that their survival depended on change. What Juan Carlos provided was the will and, with the guidance of Torcuato Fernández-Miranda, the formula whereby opposition demands for democracy could be met without violence or substantial loss of privileges. Suárez added a mixture of nerve, charm and determination to implement the formula. A crucial contribution was made in terms of the reason and moderation displayed by Felipe González, Santiago Carrillo and the other leaders of the opposition. The left sacrificed its hopes of significant social change in order to secure the urgent immediate goal of political democracy. Perhaps the greatest sacrifice was to accept the legality of the Francoist constitutional edifice on which the monarchy initially rested and out of which grew Fernández-Miranda's project of political reform.

On 22 July 1977, the eighth anniversary of his proclamation as Franco's successor, Juan Carlos addressed the recently elected Cortes. 'Today's solemn act has a concrete historical meaning: the recognition of the sovereignty of the Spanish people. The road that we have travelled until today has not been easy or straight, but the journey has been made possible by the sensible maturity of the Spanish people, by its desire for harmony, by the realism and capacity for change of the leaders today seated in this parliament and by the readiness of the highest bodies of the State to take on board the demands of society.' He went on to recognize the extent to which the achievement of democracy had been a collective effort. 'I am not, of course, going to praise the effort that allowed us to reach this goal, but I do want to say that between us all we have laid the foundations of a solid structure for coexistence in freedom, justice and peace.' After a bloody Civil War and 38 years of dictatorship, that achievement was truly remarkable. It was made up of many elements. The democratic spirit had been kept alive by the anti-Franco opposition in the interior and in exile. The intelligent self-preservation of progressive Francoists had also played a crucial part. Accordingly, the peaceful transition to democracy could not be thought of as the achievement of just one man. Yet Juan Carlos's words that day barely began to capture the scale of his contribution to the process.

The establishment of a constituent Cortes obviously signified the beginning of a process that would limit the considerable powers inherited by the King from Franco. That process began sooner than might have been expected. Victory in the elections emboldened Suárez to request that the King dispense with the services of Alfonso Armada. Relations between the general and Suárez had been deteriorating for some time. Armada considered himself the guardian of the monarchy and believed that the political reform had been too precipitate. He had made this clear to Torcuato Fernández-Miranda, to Manuel Gutiérrez Mellado and to Suárez. He permitted himself to talk down to Suárez because he remembered him from the days when, as Director General of RTVE, he had been anxious to secure the good will of La Zarzuela. Now the Prime Minister bitterly resented his readiness to exceed his authority and give him advice on matters that were strictly none of his business. He did not trust him, considered him to be dangerously conservative and saw him as an obstacle to his own relationship with the King. Certainly, given his long-standing collaboration with the King, Armada had considerable influence particularly as his intermediary with the high command of the Armed Forces.

Matters came to a head at La Zarzuela one day as Suárez awaited audience with the King. Armada vehemently criticized the government's plans to permit divorce and the consequent shouting match drew Juan Carlos out of his office. After accusations from Suárez's office that Armada had used palace notepaper to write letters in support of his son who had run as an *Alianza Popular* candidate, an accusation which he always denied, it was decided that General Armada should request a transfer back to active service. This was agreed at the end of July and he would be posted on 31 October to the *Escuela Superior del Ejército*. His successor in La Zarzuela was, at his own suggestion, General Sabino Fernández Campo. Armada would depart convinced that Juan Carlos shared his views and had let him go only at Suárez's insistence.[88]

The process that culminated in the democratic elections of 15 June gave an additional layer of legitimacy to Juan Carlos. He had progressed from the questionable 'legitimacy' of his nomination as successor by Franco to the dynastic legitimacy bestowed by his father's abdication in May. Now the elections completed the process begun with the referendum of December 1976 in securing popular legitimacy. He had moved from being the successor of Franco, sworn to perpetuate a dictatorship, to being King in a democracy, whose powers would be limited by the constitution about to be elaborated. This was symbolized on 24 June 1977, his saint's day, at a lavish reception at La Zarzuela for the members of the new Cortes. To be able to greet leading Socialists and Communists including Santiago Carrillo was a moving symbol of national reconciliation. The King had laid to rest Franco's policy of deliberately maintaining the hatreds of the Civil War and keeping alive the festering divisions between victors and vanquished.[89]

NINE

More Responsibility, Less Power:
the Crown and Golpismo
1977–1980

The elections of 15 June 1977 signified a monumental change in the life of Juan Carlos. His life since being taken to Spain in 1948 had been largely one of sacrifice and hard work. In the interests of the eventual return of the monarchy, his childhood and his adolescence were effectively taken from him. From the early 1960s, he had been obliged to live in a situation of acute tension. It is clear that he was convinced that, to survive, the future monarchy would have to be a constitutional, parliamentary affair. At the same time, in order to ensure that the successor to Franco would be either his father or himself, he had to manifest total commitment to the perpetuation of a dictatorship. As a young married man, he had been subjected to daily humiliation: intense scrutiny, every telephone conversation tapped, every visitor to La Zarzuela logged by servants in the pay of Franco. Eventual nomination as the Caudillo's successor required the heavy price of rupture with his father. In human terms, the 21 years from his departure from Estoril in November 1948 until his proclamation as Príncipe de España in July 1969 can only have been an appalling experience.

From 1969 onwards, his position was hardly less difficult. He was even more in the spotlight, subjected to the hostile man-oeuvring of an alliance of Falangists who distrusted his demo-cratizing intentions and of those in the Franco family who wanted to see him replaced as successor by Alfonso de Borbón y Dam-pierre. It requires a considerable effort of imagination to begin to understand what, in terms of stress and strain, it cost Juan Carlos, and his wife, to reach the ceremony in the Cortes on 22 November 1975 at which he was proclaimed King. That was an important landmark but, in many respects, after the moment that Juan Carlos had to swear fidelity to the fundamental laws and the principles of the *Movimiento*, the daily attrition was hardly less than before. He was caught between the two fires of a Francoist establishment determined to oppose change at all costs, and an opposition equally determined to see the dictatorship dismantled. Although he had an invaluable ally in the shadows in the form of Torcuato Fernández-Miranda, the man who should have been his closest support, his Prime Minister Carlos Arias Navarro, had been effectively a saboteur of his plans.

In an atmosphere of the greatest uncertainty, he undertook two crucial tasks. The first, as Commander-in-Chief of the Armed Forces, was to maintain the loyalty of the military. The second, as King, ably seconded by his wife, was to travel around Spain and establish the popularity of the monarchy. He did both with tireless energy, intelligence and good nature. However, it was only with the appointment of Adolfo Suárez that it could be said that he was fully in control of his own destiny. Working with Fernández-Miranda and Suárez, he played the pivotal role in the peaceful transition to democracy. It was a tribute to his vision and his efforts that the popular mood after the elections of June 1977 was one of palpable optimism. Yet this, his crowning achievement, left him in an ambiguous situation. On 17 June 1977, Adolfo Suárez informed the cabinet that the King had confirmed him in his position as Prime Minister. Immediately, the Vice-President, General Gutiérrez Mellado, in accordance with protocol, presented the collective resignation of the entire cabinet. Once Suárez formed a new government, the sweeping powers that Juan Carlos had inherited from Franco would begin to be stripped from him as a democratically elected Cortes set about elaborating a constitution. That process would require considerable effort and vigilance from the King because there were ominous clouds of unfinished business on the horizon.

The problems that lay ahead were strictly speaking now the business of the King's government and not of the King. Certainly, that would be the view of Suárez himself, who began to distance himself considerably from La Zarzuela, concerned that the crown should not be damaged by the attrition of day-to-day politics. Confronting the economic problems left by the dictatorship was a major, and daunting, long-term task for his government. However, there were immediate political issues that would be impossible to resolve without the assistance of the King. Until both the Army and the majority of the Basque people were brought into the fold, democracy would not be viable. Military subversion, terrorism and economic stagnation would erode Spain's new democracy over the next four years, and would absorb the political class to such an extent as eventually to provoke a certain disillusionment in the mass of voters who had expected that 15 June 1977 had heralded the birth of a new Spain.

Inevitably, popular hopes and expectations would not always be fulfilled. In the long run, Suárez faced the difficulties that would derive from the fact that UCD was an uneasy coalition which could fall apart as quickly as it had been cobbled together. Not all the members of his cabinet were up to the enormity of the tasks facing them. Suárez included close friends, most notably in the case of his new Vice-President for Political Affairs, the hitherto unknown agronomist Fernando Abril Martorell. Rodolfo Martín Villa had won his spurs at the Ministry of the Interior but even he would be swamped by difficulties to come. The most conservative of the Christian Democrats, and arguably the minister closest to the King, Alfonso Osorio, stayed out of the new cabinet. He did so partly because he felt that he had had enough of the day-to-day exhaustion of politics. His mind was made up when Suárez told him that he planned a government of the centre-left. The refusal of Osorio to join him exacerbated Suárez's tendency both to distance himself from La Zarzuela and to retreat into isolation. Osorio was a figure of considerable weight and of indisputable personal loyalty to the King. Particularly after the departure of Torcuato Fernández-Miranda, his presence might have added some wisdom and composure to the new cabinet.[1]

Things started well enough. On 22 July 1977, Juan Carlos opened the first session of the Cortes. On entering the chamber, he and Queen Sofía were greeted by applause from all the deputies present except for the Socialists. While the Communists clapped enthusiastically, with Dolores Ibárruri ('La Pasionaria') the most energetic, the Socialists remained seated and silent, awaiting clarification of the King's attitude towards a constitutional monarchy. His words made it clear that he recognized how much was left to do: 'Democracy has begun. Now we must try to consolidate it.' When Juan Carlos finished speaking, the PSOE deputies were the first to stand up and applaud in grateful recognition of the fact that he had explicitly defined himself as a constitutional monarch and acknowledged that the Cortes must draft a constitution capable of satisfying the entire Spanish people and of reflecting Spain's regional diversity. Suárez commented that Juan Carlos had made 'a speech that encompassed everyone'. Even the veteran Dolores Ibárruri was entranced by what she called 'a speech befitting a king'. The tension in the country at large would need leadership befitting a King, a fact underlined by the presence of armed police equipped with sub-machine guns staring stony-faced at the crowds of bystanders outside the Cortes.[2]

The anti-democratic violence of right and left would bedevil the task of constructing a widely acceptable constitutional framework. Although Suárez was keen to show his independence of the King, royal support was to be crucial for the consolidation of democracy. Suárez was inclined to a secretive style of backstairs dealing. His isolationism would be construed as helplessness as the threats of ETA and the Army were, by 1980, to convert the optimism of 1977 into disenchantment with Suárez and, by extension, with the King. Over the next four years, a spiral of terrorism and military conspiracy would bring apprehension and fear back into daily life. Indeed, as early as mid-August 1977, terrorism was to threaten the life of the King. A foreign intelligence service warned the Spanish police that an unknown group had planted a bomb in Palma de Mallorca, where both Juan Carlos and Suárez were on holiday. The police carried out a controlled explosion and exhaustive inspections were made of the King's yacht *Fortuna* and of his summer residence, Marivent. Among many suspects, GRAPO was the most plausible.[3]

In theory, the King wanted to keep out of politics but his commitment to the democratic process made that impossible. For precisely that reason, Juan Carlos had come to be reviled by the extreme right. It was asserted with increasing frequency that he had betrayed his oath to uphold the fundamental principles of Francoism. Shortly before the elections, Blas Piñar, leader of *Fuerza Nueva*, had launched a campaign against the crown. At a press conference, he declared that: 'If the issue of a liberal monarchy is raised one day, we will not be with it: we remain loyal only to the national monarchy that Franco wanted to restore.'[4] Cautious at first, *Fuerza Nueva*'s assaults on Juan Carlos would become ever more aggressive. In February 1978, during a rally in Tenerife, Blas Piñar told 800 supporters that: 'The monarchy must be Catholic, traditional, social and representative, as is laid down in Franco's constitutional laws, criteria that the current Spanish monarchy fails to satisfy.'[5]

Such attacks were inspired by the intertwined issues of military subversion and ETA violence. The bunker line was that terrorism was the fruit of the abandonment of Francoist rectitude. Blas Piñar and others knew that military loyalty could best be undermined by insinuations that the King was a traitor to Franco and had broken his solemn oaths. Whatever the King's preferences in terms of keeping out of politics, the government and indeed Spanish democracy needed his constant vigilance as Commander-in-Chief of the Armed Forces. In this respect, the most important minister in the government was General Manuel Gutiérrez Mellado. Retaining his position as Minister of Defence and as senior Vice-President, he took over the functions of the old separate ministries of the Army, Navy and Air Force. In organizational terms, this administrative streamlining made considerable sense. However, in political terms, it was not without risk. The old structure had kept the Armed Forces divided and easier to control, which was precisely why Franco had used it. Gutiérrez Mellado was, to many hardline Francoists, a conflictive figure. He was generally considered to be a democrat and specifically suspected of favouring the *Unión Militar Democrática* (UMD). In personal terms, he was neither emollient nor diplomatic and had a tendency to take precipitate action.[6] His success or failure would have dramatic repercussions for the position of the King.

In order to reassure the officer corps about the changes in Spanish politics and to underline the importance he attributed to the Armed Forces, Juan Carlos engaged in the first of many efforts to calm military fears. He interrupted his summer vacation in Mallorca in order to chair the first meeting of the new *Junta Nacional de Defensa* (National Defence Junta) at La Zarzuela on 28 July 1977. It was attended by Suárez, Gutiérrez Mellado, the newly appointed Head of the Joint Chiefs of Staff, Lieutenant-General Felipe Galarza Sánchez, and the Chiefs of Staff of the Army, Navy and Air Force. Juan Carlos's careful, and flattering, opening statement saw him express his satisfaction with the 'spirit of collaboration, commitment and calm vigilance' manifested by the Army in this crucial period of Spanish history. These were precisely the issues about which he felt most concern. Gutiérrez Mellado, in turn, carefully explained in a reassuring manner the changes that faced the Ministry of Defence and the restructured Armed Forces.[7]

Gutiérrez Mellado's sweeping responsibilities were compounded by the fact that the government's biggest problem was the neutralization of Basque nationalists, something that could be achieved only at the cost of flouting the wishes of the Army. Substantial sections of the *abertzale* left were increasingly committed to armed violence against the new democratic regime and persisted in arguing that the dictatorship still existed.[8] Their view that nothing had changed was vindicated for many by the behaviour of the government and the Spanish right throughout the summer of 1977. Once again, the battleground was the amnesty issue. At this stage, those few ETA prisoners still remaining in Spanish jails had been convicted of crimes of blood committed since the death of Franco. Demands for their amnesty could only provoke fury in Spanish right-wing circles. Accordingly, mass popular demonstrations in favour of amnesty were met by police brutality and the activities of armed *agents provocateurs*.[9] An area of mutual interest was emerging in which the extreme right used ETA terrorism as an excuse for military intervention, while ETA set out to provoke greater repression in order to generate anti-Spanish feeling among ordinary Basques.

On 5 October, a Fascist organization calling itself the Anti-Communist Apostolic Alliance bombed the offices in Pamplona of the *abertzale* weekly, *Punto y Hora*. ETA-Militar (ETA-M) responded with a terrorist offensive against the government, opening with the murder on 6 October of the President of the provincial council of Vizcaya, Augusto Unceta Barrenechea, and his two Civil Guard escorts.[10] The government now found itself at the centre of a constantly intensifying dialectic of terror and repression. ETA moved from executions of alleged informers and rank-and-file policemen to attacks on senior military officers, beginning with the assassination of the Pamplona police chief in late November.[11] Although it was never to provoke the desired military invasion of Euskadi, ETA-M's strategy did ensure that police methods continued to be characterized by indiscriminate brutality.

Spaniards had barely had time to take on board the implications of the elections before their new democracy came under threat from anti-democratic ferment in the Army. The triggers of resentment were all ones well understood by the King. Older officers deeply resented the legalization of the PCE and there was universal outrage at what was perceived as government weakness in the face of the Basques. Any efforts to replace the more reactionary Army officers would activate ingrained sensitivities about the rigid promotions structure. The King was anxious, as part of his project of ruling over a democracy for all Spaniards, to create Armed Forces for all Spaniards. Under Franco, the Army had played a very specific political role and Juan Carlos was aware of the need to depoliticize it. On the other hand, he was aware that without Franco's victory in the Civil War, the monarchy would never have been restored. Moreover, he felt a certain gratitude and respect for the military high command, all of whom had fought on Franco's side in the Civil War. However, the process of consolidation of democracy was one that was likely to provoke their suspicions. The depth of the problem was symbolized by the refusal of many officers to replace the portraits of Franco that dominated barracks and officers' messes with photographs of the new Head of State. Since Franco symbolized military power and Juan Carlos now symbolized democracy, it was hardly surprising that the Caudillo's portrait remained in place well into the 1980s.[12] Suárez and his ministers proceeded blithely, confident that loyalty to the King as Commander-in-Chief of the Armed Forces would keep the military in check. This constituted a monumental burden for Juan Carlos.

The cabinet's complacency was brusquely shattered in mid-September. General Fernando de Santiago hosted a meeting of senior generals who were on holiday in the province of Valencia. There is some debate as to whether the meeting took place in Játiva or Jávea, but general agreement that it was attended by three ex-Ministers for the Army, Antonio Barroso Sánchez Guerra, Francisco Coloma Gallegos and Félix Álvarez Arenas; and the ultra Generals Carlos Iniesta Cano, Ángel Campano López and Jaime Milans del Bosch. Several of them, notably Milans, Santiago and Iniesta, regarded themselves as close to the King but were beginning to feel exasperated by the inexorable progress of democratic politics. Between 13 and 16 September, the assembled generals discussed the political situation and drew up a memorandum to Juan Carlos. Widely circulated throughout the Armed Forces, this document called upon the King to place 'the spirit of order, discipline and national security higher than the misnamed constitutional order'. He was also requested to appoint a government of national salvation under the premiership of General Santiago. In the event of Juan Carlos refusing, he was to be asked to sack Suárez and suspend parliament for two years. The document was accompanied by the clear threat of outright military intervention 'even against the crown'. To agree to such 'requests' would amount to a bloodless coup d'état. Ministry of Defence spokesmen denied unofficially that any such memorandum had been presented to the King but there were widespread rumours about the meeting.[13]

The implications of this meeting led, after consultation with the King, to a series of strategic promotions of loyal generals. General Guillermo Quintana Lacaci was made Captain-General of Madrid and, most crucially, Milans del Bosch was removed as head of the *División Acorazada Brunete*, replaced by Antonio

Pascual Galmés. The *División Acorazada*, or DAC as it was known, would be the key to any coup attempt. The blow to Milans was softened, not to say rendered imperceptible, by his promotion to be Captain-General of the Third Military Region, centred on Valencia and well-equipped with armoured and motorized vehicles. In fact, this merely placed a determined enemy of the regime in a more powerful position without breaking his influence over the DAC at Brunete. The overall effect of the changes was merely to nourish military suspicions that the government was weak and interfering.

The Minister of Defence, General Manuel Gutiérrez Mellado, had declared, during a visit to Mexico, that 'the Army guarantees the advance of democracy'. Outraged, the bunker went onto the offensive. *Fuerza Nueva* distributed in barracks a statement that the protection of democracy was not recognized by the still current *Ley Orgánica del Estado*. *El Alcázar* declared that the Minister of Defence did not represent the Armed Forces. Disturbing rumours suggested that civilian support for such subversion went beyond the incitements of the bunker press. Gonzalo Fernández de la Mora was alleged to be one of the civilian ministers to be included in the government of national salvation proposed at the Játiva/Jávea meeting. Fernández de la Mora, a supporter of the monarchical succession to Franco, had been bitterly disappointed to be over-looked by Juan Carlos and had become an increasingly prominent figure in bunker circles. Civic support networks were also being organized. The usual ultra suspects, José Antonio Girón de Velasco, Blas Piñar, Juan García Carrés and José Utrera Molina, who were thought to be behind the propaganda campaigns of the 'patriotic juntas', were preparing for their followers to take over the civil service, local government and communications in the event of a coup. Such activities would continue over the next three years – fortunately with notable incompetence.[14] Given the enormous prestige within the Army of the generals involved in the Játiva/Jávea meeting, the government was reluctant to take dramatic measures that might have precipitated events.

Juan Carlos faced a situation whose demands on him must have been deeply galling after all that he had already done. A democracy had been established, in considerable measure as a result of his sacrifices. In theory, he should have been able to start the process of withdrawal to a position of ceremonial Head of State, able to leave the day-to-day business of government to his Prime Minister. Certainly Adolfo Suárez behaved as if that were the case. However, it would require the tireless efforts of the King to prevent Spain's new democracy from being crushed between the hammer of Basque terrorism and the anvil of military subversion. Juan Carlos could not simply leave his government to get on with it. As Commander-in-Chief, the political neutrality of the Armed Forces was his immediate problem. As a democratic monarch, popular commitment to the new democracy was also his concern. Far from being able to relax after years of tension and sacrifice, he had to be as alert as ever.

Evidence of the inadequacies of Suárez's government was provided by its reaction to an incident on 8 October 1977 in which Lieutenant-Colonel Antonio Tejero, a senior officer of the Civil Guard, came near to provoking a massacre in Málaga. Driven by his outrage at ETA-M's assassination of Augusto Unceta Barrenechea and his Civil Guard escorts two days previously, the volatile Tejero took out his anger on a legally authorized demonstration by local youth organizations in favour of a reduction in the voting age to 18. He encouraged his men, fully armed with live ammunition rather than with riot control gear, to break up the demonstration with great brutality. Only the pacific response of the young demonstrators prevented considerable bloodshed. An alarming signal was sent out when the authorities punished Tejero with just one month's confinement to barracks. During that time, he began to receive frequent visits by bus-loads of enthusiastic ultras who worked at inflating his ego and creating the myth that he was precisely the courageous officer 'necessary to save Spain'.

Although following the daily progress of military matters with close attention, the King played no part in detailed decisions. Accordingly, he could only look on with puzzlement as the velvet-glove treatment accorded Tejero contrasted dramatically with the apparently arbitrary sackings of more important officers. On 31 October, General Alfonso Armada had finally left his post in the secretariat of the royal household. Since his clash with Suárez in the wake of the elections, Armada had been preparing the handover within the royal household to his successor, General Sabino Fernández Campo. Armada was posted to the *Escuela Superior del Ejército* as professor of tactics. Nevertheless, he remained on the most cordial terms with the King who was, initially, less than pleased to have to get used to a new secretary-general. At about the same time, General Félix Álvarez Arenas, until recently Minister for the Army, was removed from his post as Director of the *Escuela Superior del Ejército*. Like Milans, he was being punished for his presence at Játiva/Jávea but the effect was botched by the announcement that he was being disciplined for extremist declarations against the amnesty law made by one of his subordinates, Captain Santiago Cabanas. Since Álvarez Arenas had already severely reprimanded the culprit, his removal now merely seemed to be an arbitrary and high-handed act on the part of General Gutiérrez Mellado. Such actions pushed generals who were lukewarm but not hostile towards democracy into the orbit of the bunker. Then, on 16 December, the eccentric and irrepressible General Manuel Prieto López was dismissed as Commander of the VI Zone (Galicia and León) of the Civil Guard for a speech made in Salamanca. Not an ultra, General Prieto was punished for condemning the use of Civil Guard units in inappropriate circumstances. The King was distinctly uneasy about sackings which could be seen as petty and provocative given the current state of feeling within the Armed Forces.[15]

Although unable to eradicate military subversion or Basque terrorism, Suárez could claim other achievements. Ironically, one of his greatest successes, the consolidation of the status of Catalonia within the new democracy, would provoke military neuroses about 'separatism'. In the case of Catalonia, the King helped forge a special relationship between Suárez and the 77-year-old exiled President of the Generalitat de Catalunya, Josép Tarradellas, that would eventually enable the Prime Minister to carry off a spectacular political coup. The Generalitat was the government of the autonomous region of Catalonia (comprising four provinces) under the Second Republic. Bringing back Tarradellas would open the way to the eventual restoration of the Generalitat. While not so conflictive as the Basque Country, Catalonia still constituted a significant problem for the government and was certainly an issue that greatly concerned the King. Even before his visit to Catalonia in February 1976, Juan Carlos had let Tarradellas know of his interest in the successful resolution of the Catalan question. The King's speeches during the visit were seen by Tarradellas as a symbolic break with the Francoist past.[16] Nevertheless, pressure for concessions to the area's nationalist aspirations had continued to grow throughout 1976 and could not be met without the cabinet appearing to lose the initiative, nor without provoking the resentment of the Armed Forces. A possible way out had emerged as early as October 1976. A prominent Catalan banker with important political connections in Madrid, Manuel Ortínez, suggested to Alfonso Osorio that Tarradellas could be the key to a peaceful resolution of the Catalan question.

At the time, Tarradellas seemed to be merely an eccentric anachronism. Yet, as Ortínez made clear to Osorio, the majority of Catalans accepted him as the legitimate embodiment of Catalanism. Tarradellas had never been properly elected as successor to the wartime President of the Generalitat, Lluis Companys. Nevertheless, he had proudly borne the standard of the Generalitat during a lonely and austere exile in France, where he still remained. He considered himself to be above parties and to be the spiritual leader of Catalonia. Ortínez persuaded Osorio that, if Tarradellas were invited to return as President of the Generalitat, he would accept the monarchy and the unity of Spain. Tension between Madrid and Catalonia would thereby be defused. Suárez was more inclined to talk to the moderate Catalan nationalist leader, Jordi Pujol, but reluctantly agreed to send an emissary, chief of the intelligence service of the Civil Guard, Colonel Andrés Casinello, to France to speak to Tarradellas. Although Casinello's report was sympathetic, Suárez decided that the Catalan leader's age made him a bad bet. Osorio discussed the situation with the King who was favourably disposed to the 'Tarradellas solution'. In the event, however, Suárez did not consider the Catalan situation sufficiently urgent to take the matter further.[17]

It took the elections of 15 June 1977 to revive Suárez's interest in Tarradellas. In Catalonia, the UCD had been swamped by the PSC and PSUC, the Catalan branches of the Socialist and Communist parties, and Pujol's *Convergencia i Unió* in a broad coalition of Catalanist parties, the *Pacte Democràtic*. After the elections, the various Catalan parliamentary deputies had formed the Assembly of Catalan Parliamentarians under the presidency of the leader of the PSC, Joan Reventós, in order to press for a statute of Catalan autonomy and the return of the Generalitat. In the name of the Assembly, Reventós requested meetings with both the King and Suárez. On 20 June, a Catalan delegation led by Reventós had a stormy meeting with Adolfo Suárez. On the following day, they were received by the King. The atmosphere could not have been more different. Affable and open-minded, he encouraged them to resolve the Catalan question and did much to defuse the effects of the previous day's encounter with Suárez. Publicly, Reventós declared that he was optimistic, although three days later he told Tarradellas that the meetings with the Prime Minister and the King had depressed him. He believed that Suárez had no inclination to make concessions about Catalan autonomy.[18]

In fact, with his unparalleled instinct for political advantage, Suárez had accepted the arguments of Carlos Sentís, the leader of the Catalan UCD, and of Manuel Ortiz, the new Civil Governor of Barcelona, that it might be possible to use Tarradellas to out-manoeuvre Reventós. On 27 June 1977, Tarradellas went to Madrid where his initial contact with the Prime Minister was awkward. Tarradellas would accept no solution that did not involve the re-establishment of the Generalitat. True to his origins as a Castilian Francoist, Suárez wanted a solution that smacked altogether less of Catalan autonomy and said threateningly, 'Do not forget that I am head of the government of a country of 36 million inhabitants and you were head of the Generalitat that lost the Civil War.' Tarradellas replied sharply, 'And don't you forget that a head of government incapable of resolving the Catalan problem puts the monarchy in danger.' Then the one-time Minister for the Army and present Captain-General of Catalonia, the fiercely reactionary and somewhat deranged

Francisco Coloma Gallegos, was said to have protested when he heard that Tarradellas, 'a defeated red', was about to be received by Juan Carlos.

It is revealing of the King's concerns about the military bunker that, despite this outrageous act of insubordination, he delayed his projected meeting with Tarradellas for 24 hours while he mollified Coloma Gallegos. When he arrived at La Zarzuela, Tarradellas was entranced to be greeted in Catalan by the head of the royal household, the Marqués de Mondéjar. He was equally impressed by the King's detailed knowledge of Catalonia and the Catalan question – about which he had been briefed by López Rodó. Moreover, the characteristic charm and affability with which Juan Carlos received him smoothed the way to a much more fruitful second meeting with Adolfo Suárez. In consequence, negotiations began that eventually culminated in early October in Juan Carlos's signature of a decree announcing the restoration of the Generalitat.[19] The re-establishment of the Generalitat was also an immense popular success although a price had to be paid in terms of resentment within the Army. Tarradellas had shrewdly insisted on being received in Barcelona with full military honours in order to underline publicly the military's acceptance of the Generalitat. The King had to work hard to placate Coloma Gallegos and thus ensure that, when he reached Barcelona on 23 October, Tarradellas be received as agreed. Nevertheless, when Tarradellas visited the military headquarters, Coloma Gallegos kept him waiting for a long time in a small side room and, when he eventually received him, failed to remove his gloves before shaking hands.[20]

Progress with the Basques was to be altogether slower. For Euskadi, there was no easy equivalent to the Tarradellas solution. The president of the Basque government in exile, Jesús María de Leizaola of the Basque Nationalist Party, lacked the moral authority enjoyed by the Tarradelles. Moreover, Suárez was hostile to the idea of concessions to what he considered to be the Basque bourgeoisie. In contrast, Juan Carlos tried to remain in touch with the Basque situation. Thus, in November 1977, he received at La Zarzuela the new leader of the Christian Democrat nationalist party, *Partido Nationalista Vasco* (PNV), Carlos Garaikoetxea. On leaving the palace, Garaikoetxea refused to discuss the details of the meeting; he told the assembled reporters that, 'The King was very understanding and conscious of the need to seek political solutions for the Basque people.'[21]

The single most conflictive issue bedevilling relations with the Basques was the question of political amnesty. Throughout the autumn of 1977, there was an intensification of united opposition pressure across the country for a wide-ranging amnesty to include not just members of ETA and even terrorists of the ultra-right responsible for the Atocha massacre, but also Army officers who had fought for the Republic during the Civil War and those involved in the *Unión Militar Democrática*. When a parliamentary commission began to prepare the text of an amnesty law, its secretary was called to La Moncloa, the Prime Minister's residence where the cabinet met. There, a sombre Gutiérrez Mellado, surrounded by a dozen other generals, told him that he would be unable to control the reaction of the Army if the scope of the amnesty was not limited. He even threatened to resign if the law encompassed the UMD. In the amnesty law passed in the Cortes on 14 October, both the Republican officers and those involved in the UMD were excluded.[22] These were all issues that struck raw nerves with many senior officers and their Commander-in-Chief sympathized with their sentiments with regard to terrorists. The UMD should have been a different matter, but such was the fear generated by the bunker that justice was sacrificed to political expediency.

Juan Carlos had long followed the development and difficulties of the UMD through his friend, Juan 'Tito' Más, a Captain in the Engineers. In consequence, in 1970, the Prince had asked him to arrange a meeting with Julio Busquets, one of the principal figures of what would later become the UMD. Busquets had found Juan Carlos to be liberal and open to change. Certainly, the Prince would be sympathetic to the UMD but, given his real fears about the power of the ultras, only up to a point. This had been revealed in February 1975 shortly after Busquets was arrested. A number of captains from the UMD surrounded the then Prince at a reception at the Capitanía General of Barcelona and told him of their distress at the arrest. Juan Carlos said, 'I'm really sorry but there's nothing I can do.' Captain Gabriel Cardona said to him, 'We command troops who are always about 20 years old. They have a different mentality and they want change. We have to change. Spain has to change.' The Prince had stood thinking for a moment, then replied, 'Yes, there has to be change, but it must be within the bounds of military discipline.'

Throughout 1975, Juan Carlos had continued to maintain contact with the UMD via the Duque de Arión. When confronted with the possibility of becoming provisional Head of State for a second time in mid-October 1975, he had been particularly interested to know whether he could count on the support of the UMD. In the event, he was forced to take his decision before meeting with UMD representatives. Nevertheless, shortly before Franco's death, when Juan Carlos made his celebrated lightning visit to El Aaiún, he had surprised many of the officers of the garrison there by making a point of speaking alone with Major Bernardo Vidal. Vidal, who had been a cadet with him in the military academy in Zaragoza, was someone that the Prince held in high esteem. He was the head of the UMD in the Sahara where he had been posted as a punishment for his liberal views. During their conversation, the Prince assured him that he intended to bring democracy to Spain. He also intervened to secure the release of three UMD officers arrested in November 1975.[23] Certainly, he believed at that time that the UMD was much more numerous than it was in reality. On 13 December 1975, he had said to José María de Areilza, 'There are more UMD than you might think.'[24]

Thereafter, however, perceiving that anti-UMD sentiment was overwhelming within senior ranks of the Army, he had stood aside during the trials of nine UMD leaders in March 1976. The defendants received sentences ranging from eight to two and a half years and were expelled from the Army. Their punishments were rather more severe than that which would be imposed upon many of those involved in attempted right-wing military coups between 1978 and 1981. As a result of various amnesties, the UMD officers were soon released from prison but efforts to secure their reinstatement in the Army ranks would be unsuccessful until much later and, even then, were limited.[25]

Whatever his real feelings about the members of the UMD, Juan Carlos was sufficiently in tune with the mentality of the more conservative members of the officer corps to incline towards caution. During the ceremonies of the *Pascua Militar* in January 1978, he witnessed at first hand the hostility of the Francoist hardliners towards any efforts to bring to an end Civil War hatreds. On 5 January, the Chief of the Army General Staff, General José Vega Rodríguez, made a speech in which, in passing, he commented on the military virtues of Enrique Líster and Juan Modesto, two Communist generals who had served with the Republican Army during the Civil War. His remarks, intended as a gesture of reconciliation, provoked the near apoplexy of several senior generals in his audience, most notably Carlos Iniesta Cano. The more conservative generals were already outraged by suggestions that the constitution being elaborated would concede the name 'nationalities' to Spain's regions. Accordingly, Gutiérrez Mellado had his work cut out when he insisted on the need for military discipline. He made a significant appeal to the centralist mentality of the military by speaking of the need to unite against 'the enemies of Spain', particularly separatists, and tried to dissipate fears about the constitution by stating that Spain would not be broken up.

The atmosphere was thus already tense on the next day when the grim-faced King presided at the principal ceremony at the old royal palace in the Plaza de Oriente. Sensitive to military doubts about the elaboration of the constitution, he appealed to the loyalty of the Armed Forces and called for acceptance and understanding of the need for the changes taking place. Nevertheless, alongside reassuring words were unequivocal assertions of authority. He declared that 'immobilism would be absurd and suicidal' and warned against those who attempted to politicize the Army. Stressing the need for discipline, he quoted, without naming the Caudillo, Franco's words on the occasion of his farewell speech to the cadets of the Zaragoza military academy on 14 July 1931. Franco had stated that discipline, 'acquires its full value when thought counsels the contrary of what is being ordered, when the heart struggles to rise in inward rebellion against the orders received, when one knows that higher authority is in error and acting out of hand'. Juan Carlos went on to say, in the same spirit as General Vega Rodríguez, 'We must show that we are capable of living in peace, in democracy and in freedom.'[26] The fact that Franco had ignored his own recommendations and risen against a democratic regime remained an unfortunate precedent.

Three months later, though, Juan Carlos would deliver a slightly more ambiguous speech at the Army Staff College, where he presided over the graduation ceremony. Here, he would declare that: 'The serene and understanding attitude of the Army should not be taken as meaning that it will not defend the essential rules or has abandoned its respect for high ideas.' Juan Carlos then spoke of the 'need to act within the strictest legality'. In words that applied to the majority of officers but certainly not to the entrenched Francoists, he commented that: 'Throughout this delicate period of transition, when the gaze of so many Spaniards has turned to the services, the Armed Forces have given a constant example of their prudence, understanding and patriotism.' His call for mutual respect between civilians and the military suggested that his perception of the rising tension within the officer corps required a more emollient tone.[27]

It was not without significance that, in his speech on 5 January, Gutiérrez Mellado had received such a favourable reaction when he said, 'Spain is a unity and we are not going to let them break it.' After all, the spectre of military resentment continued to hover in the background over the use in constitutional negotiations of the word 'nationalities' in relation to the regions. Negotiations over the eventual status of the Basque Country required the prior creation of a body to be called the General Basque Council consisting of parliamentary representatives of the PNV and of the Basque branches of the PSOE and of UCD. Since the left nationalists, the *abertzales*, were excluded from the process, they were hostile and suspicious. The most provocative issue as far as the military was concerned was the determination of the *abertzales* to incorporate Navarre within Euskadi. For the Army, UCD and the right in general, Navarre was a bulwark of Spanish unity and both the PSOE and the PCE were opposed to its inclusion within the Basque Country. After vociferously anti-Basque demonstrations organized by the ultra-right in Navarre throughout December, the General Basque Council came into being on 4 January 1978, its jurisdiction limited to the three indisputably Basque provinces of Vizcaya, Guipuzcoa and Alava.[28]

From the King's point of view, the problem of military subversion aside, the most important issue in this period was the drafting of the constitution. After nomination as Franco's heir, the succession in 1975, the referendum of 1976 and the elections of 1977, it would be the last great step towards the definitive consolidation of the monarchy. The threat of the Republican sentiments of the left still caused considerable concern in La Zarzuela. In the minds of many on the left, the King was still seen as the creature of the Caudillo. On the other hand, both the fear generated by military rumblings and appreciation of Juan Carlos's efforts in favour of democracy ensured that the bulk of the political élite would not question the position of the crown. That still left the problem of the extent of the monarchy's future powers. Juan Carlos was anxious to retain the power to call a referendum and, in the wake of elections, to propose Prime Ministers to the Cortes. It cannot have pleased him to learn that Suárez was keen on limiting his prerogatives as much as possible. Nevertheless, on 12 January 1978, he would tell José Oneto, one of Spain's best-informed journalists, 'I think that the way things are going, I will have fewer powers than the King of Sweden, but if that helps for all political parties to accept the monarchical form of the State, I am ready to accept it.' Then, at the beginning of March 1978, Juan Carlos told Manuel Fraga that he would maintain neutrality at all costs although he would follow the drawn-out process of the constitution's creation with close, if discreet, attention.[29]

Initially, Suárez had wanted his Minister of Justice, Landelino Lavilla, to arrange for a team of UCD's legal experts to produce a draft text that would then be submitted for debate in the Cortes. However, on the insistence of the PSOE and the PCE, an all-party committee, the *Ponencia*, consisting of seven parliamentary deputies, was elected by the new constitutional committee of the Cortes at the beginning of August 1977. Working for the most part in a spirit of collaboration and compromise, they had produced a first draft by mid-November – although the PSOE made it clear that it would initially defend the Republican form of State.[30] At the beginning of 1978, a somewhat more refined draft was placed before the 36 members of the parliamentary constitutional committee. Given that this text would lead to a significant reduction of royal prerogative relative to the powers inherited from Franco, Juan Carlos was kept informed by the committee's president, Emilio Attard, and cooperated fully in the process. When necessary, he used his influence to prevent discrepancies between the parties disrupting the entire process.[31] The King was relieved to be told that the Communist representative, Jordi Solé-Tura, did not question the position of the monarchy and that the Socialist, Gregorio Peces-Barba, made it clear that, once its symbolic Republican stance was defeated in the Cortes, the PSOE would accept the monarchy.[32]

In the final version, the most important clause in terms of the position of the crown was section 3 of Article 1, in which it was declared that: 'The political form of the Spanish State is the parliamentary monarchy.' This was achieved against the fierce enmity of both Basque and Catalan nationalists and the more discreet opposition of the PSOE. However, in the interests of political stability, and in recognition of Juan Carlos's contribution to the establishment of democracy, the Communists did not push for a Republic or even for a referendum on the nature of the State. During the debates on the powers of the crown, to the delight of the King, Santiago Carrillo had made a remarkable defence of the monarchy. He praised Juan Carlos's role during the transition as: 'the hinge between the apparatus of the State and the authentic democratic aspirations of civil society'. He absolved him of his Francoist past, describing him as, 'a young man who has shown that he is more identified with the Spain of today than with that of the past'. Carrillo also declared that: 'As long as the monarchy respects the Constitution and popular sovereignty, we will respect the monarchy.' Moreover, once the PSOE's Republican amendment was defeated in the Cortes on 11 May, the Socialists ceased to vote against the monarchy.[33]

Other clauses affected the King equally directly, and there has been some debate as to the extent to which his desires were taken into account in the final text. It is clear that some Senators who had been appointed directly by the King had been especially enthusiastic in defence of the powers of the monarchy. This was particularly manifest in the case of the philosopher, Julián Marías. Describing himself as 'an old Republican who hasn't given up on the use of reason', Marías denounced the PSOE's pro-Republicanism on the grounds that the Socialists had failed to make their position clear during the 1977 elections.[34] The secretary-general of the royal household, Sabino Fernández Campo, regularly met with representatives of all parties and the President of the Cortes, Antonio Hernández Gil, with whom he had a close relationship.[35]

Certainly, the King had good reason to be pleased by several of the clauses. He was reported to be delighted with Article 99, by which he was given the prerogative of proposing a Prime Minister to the Cortes, and with Article 62, Section H, which gave him supreme command of the Armed Forces. There were a number of contradictions that seemed to favour him. Article 14 recognized that all Spaniards were equal before the law irrespective of birth, race, gender, religion or opinion. Nevertheless, in the sections referring to the position of the crown, Article 56, Section 3 placed the King above the law with the words: 'The person of the King is inviolable and is not subject to liability.' Moreover, Article 57, Section 1, devoted to the royal succession, gave preference to the male line. Apart from a traditional preference for a male monarch, exacerbated by the scandalous reign of Queen Isabel II from 1833 to 1868, Juan Carlos's concerns in this respect are thought to have been driven by considerations over the ability of his firstborn, the Infanta Elena, to resist anti-monarchical pressures. This implied sexual discrimination led to considerable debate in the Cortes. Article 57 also referred to the King as the 'legitimate heir to the historic dynasty' which, at a stroke, wiped out the Francoist origins of the monarchy.[36]

In June 1978, the text was put before the full Chamber of Deputies, as the parliament was now officially called, and the Senate, and was ratified on 31 October. It was a further link in the chain establishing the monarchy in Spain. Apart from the failure to satisfy the Basques, the text's moderation and guarantee of basic liberties was broadly acceptable to all but the extremes of left and right.[37] To a large extent, the passing of the constitution was the high point of Suárez's political career, especially in terms of his relationship with Juan Carlos. In other areas, the Prime Minister's popularity was on the wane. In addition to the issue of political terrorism, the ultra press was exploiting a rise in the crime rate to generate middle-class panic about a collapse of law and order. An increase of street crime reflected spiralling unemployment, but the ultra-right claimed that delinquency was being perpetrated by leftists released from prison by amnesty measures. The law and order issue contributed significantly to the erosion of the popular credibility of the Suárez government, as did the poor performance of the economy. Inflation would be reduced somewhat by the social contract known as the *Pacto de La Moncloa* but high rates of unemployment remained a constant anxiety. It was, however, ETA terrorism and the military reactions provoked by it that would eventually destroy Suárez.

Nowhere was the Prime Minister's standing as low as among the senior ranks of the Army. The King's hope had been that tensions could be kept to a minimum until the more reactionary members of the high command reached retirement age. The Armed Forces' suspicions of the democratic regime had been intensified throughout 1978 by the apparent weakness of the government's response to ETA and even more so by the way Suárez and Gutiérrez Mellado seemed ready to interfere with sacrosanct traditions about promotion. This was revealed on 17 May by the resignation of the Chief of the General Staff, General José Vega Rodríguez, hitherto regarded as a reliable moderate. Since the elimination of the three service ministries, Vega Rodríguez had occupied the most senior position in the Army, having virtually the same status as the old Minister for the Army. A growing anxiety about the terrorist problem may have undermined his loyalty. He was certainly displeased about the circumstances in which the retirement of General Coloma Gallegos had led to the promotion out of turn of General Antonio Ibáñez Freire from Director General of the Civil Guard to Captain-General of the Fourth Military Region, Catalonia. The promotion of Ibáñez Freire was another case of General Gutiérrez Mellado bypassing the rigid seniority system in order to place loyal officers in key positions. Ibáñez Freire's earlier promotion to Lieutenant-General in December 1976 in order to permit his taking over the Civil Guard had already provoked outrage among senior generals. Vega Rodríguez and many other officers believed that political considerations should have no place in promotions. Vega Rodríguez was not a man of marked rightist sympathies but he was committed to entrenched and cherished traditions. Although the ultra-right was quick to attribute his resignation to hostility to Gutiérrez Mellado's policy, it owed more to a long history of poor personal relations between the two. They had clashed over the choice of candidates to be both president and secretary to the Joint Chiefs of Staff and now over candidates for the position of Captain-General of Catalonia.[38]

Whatever the motivation, Vega Rodríguez's resignation was a bitter blow for the government's military policy. As Vega's successor, Gutiérrez Mellado chose the most senior Lieutenant-General, Tomás de Liniers Pidal. It was a short-term appointment given his age. Hitherto apolitical, General de Liniers, like many officers, was being pushed to the right by the provocations of ETA. This was made apparent in a speech that he delivered in Buenos Aires on 15 June 1978. General Liniers praised the Argentine military's 'legitimate' use of violence in their 'dirty war' against the opposition. Despite the implication that similar methods would be appropriate in Spain, no action was taken against him.[39] Large increases decreed in military budgets, with salaries raised by 21 per cent, did little to consolidate military loyalty to the new regime. This had been brought home by a spectacular act of disrespect to the King at the end of May. On Sunday 28 May, he was to take the salute at the parade for the Armed Forces Day. Two days before, on 26 May, a unit of the Foreign Legion, without authorization, took part in a ceremony at Franco's burial place, the Valle de los Caídos, where the salute was taken by the Caudillo's widow, Doña Carmen Polo. Despite the insult to the Commander-in-Chief whose preoccupation was manifest, the man responsible, General José Ximénez Henríquez, received no more than a verbal reprimand. This was typical of the weakness displayed by Suárez towards the military.[40]

This official uncertainty was perhaps reflected in a series of royal gestures to the most conservative officers. In early June, while visiting Ávila, Juan Carlos spoke of the need to 'work in close unity, without hatred or resentments' but concluded with a statement that delighted Francoists: 'Politics is about flexibility, but one must not forget that this flexibility must be combined with inflexible stances on certain issues which are fundamental to the security of the nation and to respect for irrevocable historical values.'[41] An even more explicit gesture to the right was made on 18 July 1978, the 42nd anniversary of the 1936 military uprising. The King's military household published the following memorandum: 'National Uprising (18/7/1936): Today we commemorate the National Uprising which gave Spain its victory against hatred and misery, its victory against anarchy, a victory that would bring peace and well-being to all Spaniards. It emanated from the Army, the school of all national virtues, and, at its head, Generalísimo Franco, artificer of the great work of Spain's regeneration.'

This memorandum delighted the bunker press. *El Alcázar* wrote, 'We must sincerely thank His Majesty the King and his military household, from its highest echelons down to the last soldier, for such an opportune and moving reminder not just of a crucial date in the history of Spain and of its greatest protagonist, but also of those who revere it. At a time when this commemoration has met such official silence, we must underline this remembrance which represents the truth so accurately particularly because it comes from the military household of the highest authority in the nation.'[42]

The King was fully aware that, increasingly, senior officers were advising the government that the process of regional devolution would have to be slowed down in order to temper military hostility to the democratic regime. Pressure from ETA to accelerate the autonomy process was manifest in the steady stream of terrorist victims. The year 1978 saw a massive escalation in terrorism for which ETA was primarily, if not exclusively, responsible. Throughout 1978, the year of the constitution, 85 people were to die as a result of terrorist activities and the forces of order gave every appearance of being unable to do anything about it. Moreover, the intensification of terrorist violence provoked a retaliatory brutality from policemen and soldiers that maintained popular support for ETA. It also persuaded many generals that a firmer, more decisive, hand was necessary. Nevertheless, as tension heightened, in late July, the Joint Chiefs of Staff issued a statement to the effect that the terrorism would not weaken the Armed Forces' loyalty towards the King and the elected government.[43]

The inexorable wave of terrorism fed the government's image of paralysis and incapacity. ETA-M's determination to provoke a military intervention was starkly illustrated on 21 July, the day on which the Cortes was to finish its deliberations about the new constitution. At 8.30 a.m. General Juan Manuel Sánchez-Ramos Izquierdo, a senior Army bureaucrat, and his aide-de-camp, Lieutenant-Colonel José Antonio Pérez Rodríguez, were machine-gunned down in a Madrid street. Originally claimed by GRAPO, the killings were later and authoritatively attributed to ETA-M. The fact that neither officer was notably significant within the military structure marked the escalation of ETA-M's terrorist offensive, effectively announcing that all ranks were at risk in a democratic Spain. That risk extended to Juan Carlos who, as Commander-in-Chief, visited the chapel of repose where the victims' bodies awaited burial.

In July, an *Etarra*, Juan José Rego Vidal, was arrested in Palma de Mallorca, accused – not for the last time – of preparing a terrorist attack on Juan Carlos and, in early August, news emerged that ETA-M had been planning to kidnap Prince Felipe.[44] Adopting an air of scandalized horror, the ultra-right press drew comparisons with the situation prior to the military uprising of 1936. At the end of August, the ultra newspaper *El Imparcial* carried, on its front page, an open letter to Juan Carlos from Lieutenant-Colonel Tejero. He vehemently denounced the new constitution as Godless and eloquently presented the Civil Guards shot by ETA as heroic defenders of Spain. He then told the King how to resolve the situation. Tejero's recommendations were for 'a good and flexible anti-terrorist law, with every facility for those who have to implement it and rapid and exemplary punishment for the assassins', and for a press campaign against the terrorists. He declared that: 'It is necessary to do away with the apologists of this bloody farce even if they are parliamentary deputies.' He ended by affirming that: 'My God, my Fatherland, my Flag and my honour have obliged me to speak out.' The clear implication was that the King was not driven by similar devotion to God, Fatherland, Flag and honour. For this astonishing act of public disrespect, Tejero's only punishment was to be confined to barracks for two weeks. In fact, there was widespread discontent among older officers about the clauses in the constitution abolishing the death sentence, permitting conscientious objection to military service and prohibiting 'honour courts' (unofficial trials for offences against military honour).[45]

The second half of 1978 was characterized by a bloody counter-point of terrorism and rightist reaction. ETA-M and the ultra-right shared an interest in preventing the implementation of the new constitution. In late August, ETA-M embarked on a wave of murderous attacks on members of the security forces. The immediate objective was to disrupt both the parliamentary ratification of the constitution and the subsequent referendum to give it popular endorsement. On 13 October, *Etarras* attacked a police jeep in Basauri (Vizcaya), killing two policemen and seriously wounding a third. At the following day's funeral service, the Civil Governor of Vizcaya, the Director General of Security, and the head of the armed police, together with other senior officials, were barricaded in the Basauri barracks by enraged policemen who chanted insults against them and the democratic regime.[46] It was thus in an atmosphere of great tension that the Cortes gave its overwhelming approval for the constitution, voting on 31 October 1978 by 363 votes for, to six against, with 13 abstentions. In the Senate, similar results were announced: 226 votes for, five against and eight abstentions. Inevitably, an intensification of the ETA offensive destroyed the euphoria inspired by the unanimity of parliamentary support for the constitution. After claiming 13 victims in October, ETA-M would take another 13 lives in the course of November.[47]

Right-wing circles seethed with angry resentment. The descent into violence could hardly have served the interests of the ultra-right more directly. The backlash inevitably reached the King. The cover of *Fuerza Nueva* magazine featured, on 2 November 1978, a photograph of Juan Carlos over which had been printed the words 'Untouchable, but for how long?' Above, in smaller type, could be read the message: 'The Popular Front awaits.'[48] Even more worrying, at a rally in Zaragoza, on 6 November, Blas Piñar advocated a military coup. The emphasis was on the ETA offensive, with pictures of 155 victims of ETA displayed by the crowd. When Piñar asked rhetorically, 'What if they kill the King?' one of his followers shouted, 'Fat chance, unfortunately!' – a remark greeted with resounding applause.[49]

The deteriorating political situation had already swung many neutral officers over to the ultra camp. However, although the context favoured their plans, the shrewder heads within the bunker realized that Gutiérrez Mellado's policy of strategic promotions, timid though it seemed, was gradually undermining their positions. They had tried to counter his efforts by a tactic of applying for transfers to key operational and intelligence units. However, by the autumn of 1978, they felt that it was necessary to exploit their strength before the reformist efforts of Suárez and Gutiérrez Mellado received further legitimation in the constitutional referendum fixed for 6 December. The date chosen for a coup based on the kidnapping of Suárez and the entire cabinet at La Moncloa was 17 November. The plot had been hatched on 12 November by Tejero and Captain Ricardo Sáenz de Ynestrillas in the Cafetería Galaxia in Madrid. '*Operación Galaxia*', as it came to be known, constituted a sloppily improvised attempt to add force to the plans first mooted at the meeting of generals at Játiva/Jávea 14 months earlier. The King would be obliged to appoint a 'government of national salvation' that would then carry out some of the ideas outlined in Tejero's letter to *El Imparcial*, suspend parliament and launch a 'dirty war' against ETA.

The date of 17 November had been selected because the King was scheduled to be embarking on a lengthy tour of Latin America, the Minister of Defence and the Joint Chiefs of Staff to be out of Madrid, and a large number of senior generals to be on promotion courses in Ceuta and the Canary Islands. Furthermore, large contingents of Fascists, some of them armed and many in paramilitary uniform, were expected in the capital for the commemoration on 20 November of the third anniversary of Franco's death. The planned coup was preceded by an orchestrated campaign of propaganda in Army barracks.

The plot was exposed only when one of the conspirators, an infantry major attached to the police academy, informed the head of the police, General Timón de Lara. An investigation was undertaken and the Minister of the Interior, Rodolfo Martín Villa, informed Suárez. Distressingly for Suárez, the intelligence service CESID (*Centro Superior de Información para la Defensa*) had been extremely slow to pick up on what was happening and it would be even slower to seize the opportunity to gather information on the wider ramifications of the plot. Nevertheless, by 16 November, the Prime Minister had in his hands a full report by the chief of the intelligence service of the Civil Guard, Colonel Andrés Casinello. Suárez's first move was to hold a meeting with Juan Carlos and Gutiérrez Mellado in order to inform them and to develop a counter-strategy. It was decided not to postpone the King's departure for Latin America. Instead, Suárez would immediately meet 12 generals and senior military officers, and Lieutenant-General Gómez de Salazar, former Governor General of the Spanish Sahara, would be put in charge of further investigating the operation. Several interrogations and arrests followed that night, leading to the dismantling of the coup. Among those arrested were the two prime movers, Tejero and Sáenz de Ynestrillas. In general, however, the government showed alarming signs of wanting to brush the affair, and its more disturbing implications, under the carpet.

Nothing was done to prevent a series of events almost certainly linked with the projected coup. General Gutiérrez Mellado had decided to undertake a tour of garrisons to explain the constitution. This was a brave, if somewhat rash, decision given his unpopularity among the ultras. The meeting in Cartagena on 17 November, in a huge aircraft hangar, took place in an atmosphere of great tension. On the same morning, *Diario 16* had announced the arrest of Tejero and Sáenz de Ynestrillas. As Gutiérrez Mellado spoke, he was interrupted by the extremely short but fiercely Francoist head of the Levante region of the Civil Guard, General Atarés Peña, who shouted out that the constitution was 'a great lie', which brought forth a smattering of applause. Significantly, General Atarés had been Lieutenant-Colonel Tejero's commanding officer in the Basque Country in 1976. Gutiérrez Mellado ordered him, and anyone who agreed with him, to leave. No one moved except Atarés, who was accompanied by the Captain-General of the Third Military Region, Valencia, Jaime Milans del Bosch, who was endeavouring to calm him down. Atarés later called Gutiérrez Mellado, 'A freemason, a traitor, a pig, a coward and a spy.' The majority of the officers in the room, however, made it clear that they supported Gutiérrez Mellado, the government and the new constitution.

On 19 November, José Antonio Girón de Velasco's *Confederación de Excombatientes* held a rally in Madrid's Plaza de Oriente. Banners were unfurled in support of General Atarés Peña and insulting the King, Gutiérrez Mellado and Adolfo Suárez. Both Girón and Blas Piñar of *Fuerza Nueva* made speeches calling for a military uprising and their audience chanted insults against Juan Carlos as well as Suárez, and Gutiérrez Mellado. Five hundred officers attended a Fascist ceremony at Franco's tomb in the Valle de los Caídos on 20 November. Indeed, the way in which both the Atarés Peña incident and *Operación Galaxia* were handled did little to diminish the growing conviction in military circles that the democratic regime could be attacked with virtual impunity.

The low-key response of the government was born of the profound anxiety instilled by *Operación Galaxia*. It emerged, for instance, that nearly 200 officers had been contacted by Tejero and Ynestrillas. Using the excuse that they did not take the matter seriously, these officers failed, almost without exception, to report on the planned mutiny. It is difficult to avoid the conclusion that many of them were simply waiting on events. In particular, the intelligence services had played a disturbingly ambiguous role. Despite Tejero's notoriety as an hysterical opponent of the democratic regime, he had not been placed under surveillance. They were slow to discover the conspiracy and, when they did, even slower to inform the government. One senior intelligence and counterinsurgency expert, Lieutenant-Colonel Federico Quintero Morente, who was on a posting to the operations division of the General Staff of the Army, informed the head of the division, General Luis Saez Larumbe, who did not take the matter further. Subsequent investigations gave no grounds for complacency. Units in Burgos, Valladolid, Seville and Valencia were involved and on the alert the night before *Operación Galaxia* was due to take place. Only the energetic intervention of the liberal General Antonio Pascual Galmés prevented the crack DAC from joining in.[50]

In the immediate wake of the *Operación Galaxia* arrests, the King went ahead with the planned visit to Latin America in the course of which he made several symbolic gestures that widened support for the monarchy. In Mexico, he put further distance between himself and Franco's policy of maintaining the festering divisions of the Civil War. Many thousands of Republicans had been given refuge by Mexico immediately after the Spanish Civil War and had made their lives there, making a very significant contribution to intellectual, artistic, educational and economic life. Juan Carlos's olive branch of reconciliation to the exiles was symbolized by his generous words to Dolores Rivas Cherif, the widow of the Republican President Manuel Azaña: 'Your husband and you yourself are as much part of the history of Spain as I am.' Their meeting took place on the third anniversary of the death of Franco.[51]

The visit to Argentina was more conflictive but ultimately equally beneficial to the crown. Prior to the King and Queen's departure for the tour of Latin America, the news that they would be visiting Argentina had provoked considerable criticism from the Spanish left. In late August 1978, the PSOE had presented a Cortes motion opposing a royal visit to a country with such an appalling record on human rights. Gregorio Peces-Barba argued that to go to Argentina could be read as a tacit endorsement of General Videla's military dictatorship and thus risked damaging the crown. Videla had previously visited only his fellow military dictators, Augusto Pinochet of Chile and Hugo Banzer of Bolivia. The Socialist motion was defeated by only four votes. The government justified the tour by arguing that it would exert pressure on the military junta and possibly facilitate the release of missing Spaniards. In the event, Juan Carlos's performance in Argentina silenced the critics and went some way towards justifying UCD's arguments. His refusal to be seen as endorsing the ruling junta was manifest as soon as he stepped out of the aircraft at Buenos Aires Airport. General Videla stepped forward from the welcome party but his persistent efforts to embrace the King were thwarted by Juan Carlos's smart footwork. More importantly, at several official functions, Juan Carlos spoke in defence of democracy and human rights, to the visible annoyance of members of the junta. Videla also agreed reluctantly, at Juan Carlos's insistence, to allow him to meet the leading members of the Argentine opposition. As a result of these meetings, the Spanish King interceded in favour of many political prisoners, eight of them Spaniards.[52]

Back in Spain, ETA-M's leadership, far from being inhibited by the *Operación Galaxia*, stepped up its attacks on policemen and Civil Guards in Euskadi. Accordingly, the constitutional referendum was held on 6 December in an atmosphere of considerable tension. The result was a clear popular ratification of the constitution. The King affirmed that 'just as it is a constitution of all and for all, it is also the constitution of the King of all Spaniards' and expressed his determination to respect and serve it.[53] However, the results in the Basque Country were alarming. There was an abstention rate of 51.1 per cent and 23.54 per cent of votes cast were negative ones, dramatically underlining the need to elaborate a satisfactory statute of autonomy for Euskadi. In order to get parliamentary authority for such a course of action, Suárez dissolved the Cortes on 29 December 1978 and called general elections for 1 March of the following year. The twin tasks of winning the elections and negotiating with the Basques took place in the shadow of both terrorism and *golpismo*.

In 1979, the rate of ETA-M attacks on policemen and Civil Guards would be higher even than in the previous year. It was, however, the attacks on senior Army officers that drove the ultras to apoplexy. On 2 January, ETA-M murdered Major José María Herrera Hernández, aide-de-camp to the Military Governor of Vizcaya. On the following day in the capital itself, they assassinated the Military Governor of Madrid, General Constantino Ortín Gil, a highly competent professional considered to be close to Gutiérrez Mellado. The Minister of Defence presided at the funeral on 5 January. The ceremony was constantly interrupted by frenzied insults directed at both Rodolfo Martín Villa and Gutiérrez Mellado who was jostled and, on being hit from behind, blacked out. With the encouragement of General Iniesta Cano, the hearse was stopped and the coffin seized by a group of ultra officers, including Major Ricardo Pardo Zancada of the DAC. They took turns carrying it on their shoulders to the cemetery, while their supporters chanted 'the government is a murderer' and 'power to the Army!' The King and Queen were shocked, not just by the signs of insubordination, but also by the fact that Suárez and the cabinet had chosen not to attend the funeral.

At the *Pascua Militar* on 6 January 1979, a sombre Juan Carlos trod a careful path between expressing his sympathy for military sensibilities and his unequivocal condemnation of indiscipline. 'I assure you that I understand very well the feelings that drive you. And I realize perfectly that, even if they cannot always coincide with mine, they are, in my view, respectable in all cases . . . Indiscipline, a disrespectful attitude born of momentary passion, with tempers allowed to boil over and the serenity necessary in every soldier forgotten, is a disgraceful and shameful spectacle.' Measuring his words, he went on to say, 'The dangers of indiscipline are worse than the dangers of mistakes. A mistake can be put right but a soldier, an Army that has lost its discipline cannot be saved. They are no longer a soldier, no longer an Army.' Nevertheless, the King can only have been deeply frustrated to see that no action was taken against those who had attacked General Gutiérrez Mellado. In fact, with tension in barracks at boiling point, the ultra press ignored the King's words and made even more explicit calls for a military government. The prominent rightist, General Manuel Cabezas Calahorra, called for the King to take over direct control of the Armed Forces.[54]

Shortly afterwards, the campaign began for the elections that were to be held on 1 March 1979. The results threw up several surprises, most notably the emergence of an *abertzale* coalition known as *Herri Batasuna* which broadly supported ETA-M. Hardly less unexpected was the PSOE's failure to win. During the two months of the campaign, the opinion polls had placed the Socialists slightly in the lead. However, despite the fact that Suárez had suffered considerable attrition in the endless battles against military subversion, terrorism, unemployment and inflation, UCD won, increasing the number of its seats in the Cortes from 165 to 168, while the PSOE rose only from 118 to 121. Many factors had contributed to the result, including Church support for UCD and the hostility of Basque nationalists to the PSOE. Arguably, the key element was the television charisma of Suárez. His final speech on the eve of the elections, a swingeing attack on the PSOE as the Marxist party of abortion and divorce, was calculated to have swayed over one million undecided voters.[55] Greatest concern was generated by an abstention rate of 33.6 per cent on which the bunker eagerly seized as a popular rejection of democracy. That was not true, but the country's problems had dulled the excessive hopes and expectations of 1977. Moreover, after two referendums and two general elections, there was a degree of electoral fatigue.

The PSOE reacted to its disappointing results by a move towards the centre ground. Felipe González secured the elimination of the party's definition as exclusively Marxist at the extraordinary congress held on 28 and 29 September 1979. The ideological repositioning of the Socialists was a direct challenge to Suárez who had tried to occupy a centre-left space. In fact, the UCD leader's star was already descending. This was signalled by his party's disappointing performance in the municipal elections of 3 April 1979. In local contests, where the fear factor generated by the rumblings of the Army was less potent, the PSOE and the PCE between them gained control of 27 provincial capitals, representing 10,500,000 people.

In contrast, UCD, although gaining many rural municipalities, won only 23 provincial capitals, representing just 2,500,000 people. *Herri Batasuna* captured 15 per cent of the Basque vote and control of a number of small towns. When the new municipal authorities tried to change the symbols of the old regime, street names of Nationalist war heroes and statues of Franco, they were frequently prevented by the local military commanders.[56]

That depressing start was quickly compounded by the announcement of Suárez's new cabinet on 5 April. It was widely felt that his team lacked both the drive and the imagination needed to resolve the problems of regional autonomy, terrorism, unemployment and military subversion. It was dominated by Suárez's close friend Fernando Abril Martorell as second Vice-President with responsibility for Economic Affairs. Suárez believed that the build-up of hostility against General Gutiérrez Mellado made it essential to remove him from the firing line. Accordingly, he appointed as Minister of Defence a civilian, Agustín Rodríguez Sahagún, who had no previous experience of military matters. He was the first civilian in the post since 1936 and was never to win the respect of his military subordinates. General Gutiérrez Mellado was pushed upstairs to be Vice-President for National Security and Defence. An impression of second-rank mediocrity derived from the departure of some powerful figures. Rodolfo Martín Villa had asked to be replaced at the Ministry of the Interior after three years of intense and exhausting labour. The constant attacks on Civil Guards and policemen had seen him lose the loyalty of his senior officers. After difficulty in finding a suitable substitute, Suárez turned to General Antonio Ibáñez Freire, Captain-General of the Fourth Military Region, Catalonia. The use of a soldier, as had been the custom under Franco, did little for the prestige of the new government, despite Ibáñez Freire's liberal credentials. The Minister of Finance, Francisco Fernández Ordóñez, left in the wake of rumours that he was flirting with a move to the PSOE. In addition to the difficulties of forming a cabinet, Suárez was suffering pain and discomfort from a dental complication that made it increasingly difficult for him to talk.[57] Unsurprisingly, the press would soon be complaining about the Prime Minister's isolation and paralysis. Perceptions of his arrogance were summed up by graffiti on a Madrid wall which read: 'Franco was mad: he thought he was Suárez.'[58]

Even leaving aside his health, the problems faced by the Prime Minister were sufficiently daunting to provoke a desire to throw in the towel. It could be argued that Suárez's moment had passed. The historic task of steering democratic reform through the Francoist institutions had been fulfilled. The achievements of the two years since the elections of 15 June 1977 – the *Pacto de La Moncloa*, the constitution, the beginnings of autonomy legislation – were not inconsiderable. However, they had to be balanced against alarming daily headlines about terrorism, crime and military subversion. ETA-Militar was even more committed to violence than it had been two years before and now, through *Herri Batasuna*, enjoyed the support of at least 15 per cent of the Basque population. The dominance of the ultras in the Army, and especially in the intelligence services and key units such as the DAC at Brunete, was greater than ever. It is hardly surprising that the King was beginning to wonder if he, and Spain, needed new blood at La Moncloa. He was surely aware of his father's conviction that the monarchy would not be fully consolidated until it had coexisted with a Socialist government.[59] Certainly, he had already begun to establish cordial relations with Felipe González.

Initially, in contrast to the warmth of his contacts with Santiago Carrillo, their relations had been cool and the King was concerned by the fact that Felipe tried to avoid using the formula 'His Majesty'. However, given the essential affability of both men, the situation was easily improved. Suárez himself related to Federico Silva Muñoz a revealing incident. At a dinner for the President of Mexico in October 1977, Felipe had said to Suárez, 'How's your boss?', to which he had replied, 'Well, he's your boss as well as mine.' The Prime Minister had then brought the King into the conversation, saying, 'Sir, are you not also Felipe's boss?' When the King replied, 'Of course' Felipe conceded, saying, 'Yes, you are also my boss.'[60]

In his January 1978 interview with José Oneto, Juan Carlos told a story that revealed the subsequent improvement in the relationship: 'The other day, I saw Felipe González at a reception. He didn't see me and I came up behind him, took his arm and told him that I wanted to talk to him. He was surprised. I asked him what colour my eyes are. Perplexed, he looked at me and answered "grey". I let go of his arm and said, "So, next time, don't go around saying, as you did the other day, that the King is a tall, blond, blue-eyed lad."' He went on to tell Oneto, 'I think I can have a good understanding with Felipe. We are virtually the same age and have lots in common.'[61] Nearly 12 months later, after some debate within the party executive, Felipe González became the first Secretary-General of the PSOE to request an audience in the royal palace. On the day after the King's approval of the constitution, his meeting with the entire PSOE executive sealed the Socialists' formal recognition of the monarchy.[62]

After the elections of 1977, Juan Carlos might have felt that the time was rapidly approaching when he could relax. That had not been possible given the ongoing burden of consolidating democracy against the opposition of ETA and the bunker. However, after the constitutional referendum of December 1978 and the elections of March 1979, those hopes might well have resurfaced. Once more, it was not to be. The continuing pressure of terrorism and military subversion in a context of economic and social tension would see Suárez's government in increasing difficulties and the King frequently required to intervene to placate the Army. It became a media commonplace to talk of the '*desencanto*' (disenchantment) with Suárez and UCD. This extended to some degree to the King. It was most damaging as a consequence of the view spread by the bunker press, and eagerly accepted by ultra officers, that the '*desencanto*' implied a popular rejection of democracy and a desire to return to Francoism.

The military ultras were also emboldened by evidence that the government was in retreat. Gutiérrez Mellado had taken overall responsibility for Defence and National Security, but the authority that he had concentrated in the Ministry of Defence was now effectively devolved back to the general staffs of the three services. The new Minister of Defence seemed incapable of winning the respect of the military hardliners and their exasperation with the government quickly reached a new peak. The Chief of the General Staff of the Army, General de Liniers Pidal, was due to retire on 21 May. The choice of his replacement by strict seniority would have put this crucial post, the very pinnacle of the military hierarchy, into the hands of the ultras who still dominated the upper echelons of the Army.

The logical candidates, if seniority were the only qualification, – Ángel Campano López, Captain-General of Valladolid, Jaime Milans del Bosch, Captain-General of Valencia, and Jesús González del Yerro, Captain-General of the Canary Islands – were all extreme rightists. The normal appointments procedure called for consultation with the *Consejo Superior del Ejército*, which had duly produced a *terna* of these three. Campano, who loathed Gutiérrez Mellado, withdrew and neither Milans nor González del Yerro, each with the same number of votes, would concede. This put the choice in the hands of Rodríguez Sahagún who more or less left Gutiérrez Mellado to pick his own candidate. Given the stalemate, the choice of any lieutenant-general would probably have been seen as satisfactory. However, Gutiérrez Mellado decided to take advantage of the deadlock to put a reliable liberal in place. Furious indignation greeted his choice of General José Gabeiras Montero. Not only was Gabeiras known to be a close friend of Gutiérrez Mellado, but he also had to be promoted from Major-General to Lieutenant-General. In order that this promotion did not provoke even greater scandal in an Army obsessed with a rigid seniority structure, five other Major-Generals also had to be promoted. This, plus the fact that Gabeiras then leapfrogged all five, merely exacerbated the sense of outrage among the old guard in general and the deeply resentful Milans in particular. The King was on a visit to Algeria when Adolfo Suárez telephoned him with the news. Juan Carlos was thoroughly alarmed by what seemed like a provocation of the senior generals.[63]

As difficulties intensified, the various UCD factions became restless, the right inclining towards *Alianza Popular*, the UCD's Social Democrats, led by Francisco Fernández Ordóñez, even negotiating their transfer to the PSOE. To the alarm and annoyance of the King, Suárez responded by withdrawing into hermetic isolation. This was starkly underlined by his reaction to a bloody assault on the Army only a few days after Gabeiras's appointment. On the morning of 25 May, Lieutenant-General Luis Gómez Hortigüela, head of the personnel section of the Army General Staff, two Colonels and their driver were gunned down by an ETA-Militar hit squad. Two days before the Armed Forces Day, it was a viciously thought-out provocation. The new Minister of Defence, Rodríguez Sahagún, suspended the celebrations except in Seville, where the King and Queen were to preside over the parade. On the eve of their departure for Andalusia, Juan Carlos and Sofía visited the chapel of repose and gave their condolences to the families.[64]

Tension in the barracks could hardly have been greater. Rightist gangs roamed the streets of Madrid in search of victims for retaliation. At the funeral service held on 26 May, ultras provoked incidents and yet again there were chants against the King and against democracy and calls for the Army to take power. As he had done when General Ortín Gil was assassinated, Suárez failed to attend the funeral. The reason was his acute dental problems and a misplaced concern for how they might distort his image. His absence and the fact that he neither visited Army headquarters nor even appeared in the Cortes until the following week intensified the impression that Spain was not being governed. A few hours after the funeral service, a bomb exploded in a crowded Madrid cafeteria, the California 47, in the luxurious shopping area of the Calle Goya, which was bustling on a late Saturday afternoon. In an attack attributed to GRAPO, eight people were killed and another 50 injured. Calle Goya was near the *Fuerza Nueva* headquarters and right in the heart of the Barrio de Salamanca, such an ultra stronghold that it was nicknamed the 'Nationalist zone' in a reference to the Civil War. Unusually, none of the ultra regulars were in the café and the usual *Fuerza Nueva* souvenir stalls were suspiciously absent from the street outside. Nevertheless, on the next day they were out in force to shout insults at the King and Queen in Seville as they presided at the Armed Forces Day celebrations.[65]

Rumours of a coup d'état were deafening. On the same day

as the California 47 explosion, military intervention was discussed at a meeting between Generals Félix Álvarez Arenas and Luis Cano Portal and Lieutenant-Colonel José Ignacio San Martín, Chief of Staff of the DAC at Brunete.[66] The views of the military hierarchy on the promotion of General Gabeiras were now made starkly clear. On 28 May, General Atarés Peña was court-martialled for his attack on Gutiérrez Mellado during the attempted *Galaxia* coup in November 1978. Atarés Peña's offence had been committed, and therefore was to be judged, within the jurisdiction of the Valencia Military Region, whose Captain-General was the highly sympathetic General Milans del Bosch. Under the presidency of General Luis Caruana y Gómez de Barreda, the Military Governor of Valencia, who was later to play an ambiguous role in Tejero's 1981 coup attempt, the court absolved Atarés of the charge of indiscipline. This was clearly a judgement on General Gutiérrez Mellado rather than on the defendant, yet both government and opposition were silent about the acquittal of Atarés. Instead, politicians chose to assert their faith in frequent declarations by various generals that the Army would always respect Article 8 of the constitution, which defined its role as defender of Spain's constitutional order and territorial integrity. However, the affection of the high command for this Article derived from their erroneous belief that it constituted a legal justification for military intervention in politics.[67]

In fact, statements by generals about their readiness to defend the existing order were closely linked to fears that negotiations to concede Basque and Catalan autonomy threatened that order. The government was engaged in negotiating the draft texts of autonomy statutes for Catalonia and Euskadi, known as the 'Statute of Sau' and the 'Statute of Guernica'. Delays were inevitable, given divisions within UCD over the Basque text. An ETA bombing campaign against Spanish resorts was started and an abortive attempt was made to kidnap one of the more hardline UCD negotiators, Gabriel Cisneros, which left him seriously wounded. The extreme right took it as evidence of government concession to violence when, on the symbolically Francoist date of 18 July 1979, Suárez agreed the autonomy statute with the Basque leader or

Lehendakari, Carlos Garaikoetxea.[68] With a referendum to ratify the statute scheduled for 25 October, a prominent Francoist lawyer drafted a confidential analysis condemning the Catalan and Basque statutes as unconstitutional. It has been speculated that the author was either Gonzalo Fernández de la Mora or Laureano López Rodó. A copy was sent to La Zarzuela and another to General Armada who passed it to General Milans del Bosch. Against the opposition of General Gabeiras, Milans won a vote at the *Consejo Superior del Ejército*, permitting the document to be discussed. Needless to say, it inflamed the fears of the military ultras that Spain was about to be ripped apart by separatism.[69] After a highly conflictive campaign in the Basque Country, the referendum was held: 60.7 per cent of those entitled to vote did so and 89.14 per cent of them voted 'yes'.

The consequent disquiet within the high command was reflected in provocative declarations by the three most senior ultra generals still on active service, Jaime Milans del Bosch, Jesús González del Yerro and Pedro Merry Gordon, Captain-General of Seville. The first two were still fuming at the appointment of Gabeiras as Chief of the General Staff. In an interview with the columnist María Mérida, given some time before and now published in *ABC*, Milans denounced terrorism, insecurity, inflation, unemployment, pornography and the crisis of authority, all of which he blamed on democracy. González del Yerro, participating in a tribute to the Spanish Foreign Legion, denounced the failure of the government to reverse a process in which: 'Spain is dying on us.' General Merry Gordon, speaking to the garrison at Ceuta, was even more direct, referring to 'a series of murdering dwarves, sewer rats, who attack us from behind' and threatening in veiled terms that the Army would soon turn on its tormentors. Unperturbed, ETA-M replied on 23 September by murdering the Military Governor of Guipúzcoa, General Lorenzo González-Vallés Sánchez, in San Sebastián.[70] In November, shortly after the publication of Milans's remarks, there took place his first audience with the King as Captain-General of Valencia. It was a tense encounter. Acknowledging some understanding of Milans's complaints, the King had to insist on the need for the general to respect the constitution. Although he did so with great aplomb, shrewdly balancing affability and authority, it was clear that his good relationship with Milans was cooling.[71]

It was no accident that such outbursts came from the Captains-General of Valencia and Seville, two ultra strongholds. It was difficult to avoid the impression that they were directed at alerting ultra sympathizers to the fact that action was imminent. An unofficial intelligence service created by democratic officers, some of whom had been members of UMD, was aware of conspiratorial links between the Seville and Valencia headquarters, as well as of the existence of blacklists of journalists, leftist politicians and academics to be eliminated after a coup. The failure of *Operación Galaxia* had demonstrated to military ultras that success in such an undertaking depended on the participation of an important Madrid-based unit. Their thoughts centred on the DAC. The DAC was the key to the capital and, if it led, much of the rest of the Army would follow. Since mid-1979, it had been commanded by the highly popular General Luis Torres Rojas, who had endeared himself to his men and to ultras when, as commander of the Parachute Brigade, he had sworn to avenge any ETA attacks on his officers. In fact, Torres Rojas was merely the latest stage in a long process whereby the DAC had become an ultra fortress. Practically from the beginning of the transition to democracy, right-wingers had been requesting and obtaining postings to Brunete. Under the command of Milans del Bosch, who had a remarkable capacity to capture the unquestioning loyalty of his subordinates, the DAC had been brought into the bunker. Its Chief of Staff, Lieutenant-Colonel José Ignacio San Martín, had been the head of Carrero Blanco's intelligence service, the SIPG, and was working hard to turn the DAC into the élite force necessary to 'save Spain'. Significantly, San Martín's appointment in 1979 had partly been the result of a recommendation from General Alfonso Armada.[72]

Within a month of Torres Rojas taking command of the DAC on 1 June 1979, a series of unauthorized manoeuvres had begun, with patrols carrying out exercises in the control of the nerve centres of Madrid, armoured vehicles dominating the main access roads and troop carriers patrolling the industrial belt. Torres Rojas was at the heart of a planned coup to take place on the eve of the autonomy referendums. The Parachute Brigade, known as the BRIPAC, stationed at Alcalá de Henares near Madrid, planned to seize La Moncloa with helicopter support, while armoured vehicles of the DAC neutralized the capital. Once they had forced the government to resign, the conspirators aimed to form a military directory under either General de Santiago y Díaz de Mendívil or General Vega Rodríguez. The Cortes would be dissolved, the Communist Party banned and the regional autonomy process reversed. The continuity with the 1977 Játiva/Jávea meeting and the 1978 *Galaxia* attempt was obvious. The plan was for units of the BRIPAC to occupy La Moncloa on 21 October just before the referendums on Basque and Catalan autonomy took place. A full-blown coup was, however, still beyond the ultras' reach. Fuel and munitions were kept in short supply by a suspicious government. Nevertheless, desperately trying to calm the situation, Juan Carlos, after receiving Milans del Bosch for a private interview in November, now received a delegation from the DAC. The ostensible reason for their visit to La Zarzuela was to give the King the newly designed DAC beret. After expressing loyalty to the King, Torres Rojas passionately expressed his fury at what ETA was doing and declared that the DAC was ready to shed blood to defend the unity of Spain. Juan Carlos sympathized but insisted on discipline.[73]

The plotters were still in a minority within the Armed Forces. There were large numbers of officers who would not lightly go along with the enormity of an assault on the democratic regime. It was precisely to this majority that the King directed his emotional speech on the occasion of the 1980 *Pascua Militar* reception at the Palacio de Oriente. Unlike his 1979 speech, which had been a firm call for discipline, this was altogether softer and more personal. His words were aimed at demonstrating that Juan Carlos was a soldier just like them. 'You know full well that I am no stranger when I am with you, I am your comrade, and not because I am the Commander-in-Chief of the Armed Forces but because I was educated like you, and with many of you, in those military academies where tribute is paid to certain virtues and where a style is imposed that cannot be altered by the passage of time nor by changes in society . . . I have shared with you the most intense sorrow when our comrades have fallen, vilely murdered.' He went on to appeal to them not to fall into the trap of being exploited by the extremists of right and left, who for their own reasons wanted to provoke a coup. 'Let no one exploit your noble attitude as an instrument for their own convenience, let no one identify you with their own purposes or entice you into adopting entirely inappropriate roles.'[74]

The ultra press continued, however, to urge military intervention despite the missed opportunity of the October plot. Nevertheless, the conspiracy bubbling around Torres Rojas came to an abrupt end on 24 January 1980 when he was replaced as commander of the DAC by the liberal General Justo Fernández and sent to be Military Governor of La Coruña. Both the unofficial intelligence network set up by ex-UMD members and the CESID had informed Rodríguez Sahagún of the suspicious movements at the BRIPAC. Nevertheless, Rodríguez Sahagún publicly denied that Torres Rojas's posting had anything to do with any subversive activities. Informed by the ex-UMD officer, Fernando Reinlein, the editor of Diario 16, Miguel Ángel Aguilar, published the real reasons behind Torres Rojas's transfer. For doing so, Aguilar was prosecuted on the charge of insulting the Army. This, and the failure to initiate judicial proceedings against Torres Rojas, merely intensified military contempt for the Minister of Defence. Nevertheless, the dismissal of Torres Rojas effectively led to the neutralization of the DAC and thus removed a crucial element from the golpistas' armoury.[75]

Both Rodríguez Sahagún and Suárez were anxious to do nothing to offend senior Army officers. Their nervous anxiety was compounded by the trial of the Galaxia conspirators in early May 1980. Tejero and the newly promoted Major Sáenz de Ynestrillas were sentenced to only seven and six months' detention respectively. Given the time already served while awaiting trial, this meant their immediate release. A greater encouragement for plotters could hardly have been imagined. A week later, the Joint Chiefs of Staff rejected a petition for the return to the Army of the democratic officers who had led the *Unión Militar Democrática*. The Captain-General of Madrid, Guillermo Quintana Lacaci, by military standards a moderate, commented ominously that, 'The Army should respect democracy, not introduce it into its ranks.'[76] The failure of the government to press for the revindication of the UMD was a further act of weakness that helped to convince the rightists within the Armed Forces that they could act with impunity.

Thus, as soon as he was released from custody, Tejero entered into conspiracy with Milans del Bosch. Throughout the middle of 1980, the ultra press worked ever more openly to foment military discontent with the democratic regime. Considerable success in this regard was achieved through a spring campaign against the government's plans to bring the Civil Guard under civilian jurisdiction. Encouraged by the extreme rightist Juan García Carrés, Tejero played a major role in gathering petitions in barracks around Spain, in the course of which he widened the circle of enthusiasts for a coup. In the spring of 1980, Tejero was introduced by García Carrés to Lieutenant-Colonel Pedro Mas Oliver, the aide-de-camp of Milans del Bosch. The main focus of this and other rightist efforts was to intensify military pressure for the departure of Suárez – although Milans del Bosch slowed down the wilder hotheads by dint of his insistence that he would do nothing without the King's approval.[77] Terrorism, street crime, inflation and unemployment had all undermined Suárez's popularity sufficiently to lead *golpistas* to believe that they were interpreting the popular will. Under incessant attack from the Socialists, Suárez also had to deal with the disintegration of the UCD coalition. Internal divisions, the impression of incapacity and inactivity, together with a number of tactical errors contributed to a series of damaging reverses for UCD in regional elections in Andalusia, the Basque Country, Catalonia and Galicia. By the spring of 1980, the Prime Minister faced a major credibility problem.[78]

Opinion polls were turning against Suárez. The key to his decline was the popular feeling of *desgobierno*, of not being governed at all. A minor cut in inflation had been achieved by monetarist policies, but at the price of substantial increases in unemployment. The economy, however, was not an area that engaged Suárez's interest. He was, in any case, overwhelmed by the ongoing and interrelated problems of ETA terrorism, the military attitude to politics and the increasingly chaotic progress of the autonomy process. In part, he seemed to be trying to defuse the situation by treating ETA as if it were no more than a minor irritant and by ignoring the fact that the extreme right was virtually on a military footing. To most observers, however, it appeared as if his government had lost its sense of direction. Aware of this widespread perception, Juan Carlos decided to canvass the views of the leaders of the main opposition parties. He had a long interview at La Zarzuela with Felipe González on 24 April 1980. González told the King that the reins of government really were in the hands of Suárez's deputy and long-standing friend, Fernando Abril Martorell, and that this was eroding confidence in democracy.[79]

It cannot have pleased the King to hear yet again that Suárez was behaving as if he were Head of State and Abril Martorell the Prime Minister. This was an understandable criticism, since months passed between the Prime Minister's parliamentary appearances and press conferences. His absences even from cabinet meetings were increasingly frequent. Suárez was becoming the hermit of La Moncloa, reluctant to face parliament and isolated even from his own party some of whose deputies voted against him in the Cortes.[80] On 28 April, Juan Carlos saw Manuel Fraga at La Zarzuela for an hour. The *Alianza Popular* leader told the press only that Juan Carlos had been 'enormously generous, open and ready to listen to everyone' and that he had informed the King of his views on the current situation. In fact, Fraga had warned the King in alarmist terms that the country needed a new direction.[81] Inevitably, some of the criticisms aimed at Suárez had an impact on the image of the King. This was unfair. It was always the motto of Suárez's office that successes should be attributed to the crown and failures to the Prime Minister.[82]

The scale of dissent became apparent during the six painful weeks in the spring of 1980 during which Suárez cobbled together a new cabinet. Laborious and backstabbing, the negotiations were a rehearsal for the power struggle to come at the second UCD Congress scheduled for October. Announced on 2 May, the reshuffled cabinet was marked by the absence of Joaquín Garrigues's Liberals and of the more senior of Francisco Fernández Ordóñez's Social Democrats.[83] On 21 May, the PSOE tabled a motion of censure and Felipe González delivered a blistering attack on Suárez's failings. The Prime Minister survived the motion in the subsequent debate held between 28 and 30 May only because of the abstentions of *Alianza Popular* and Jordi Pujol's *Convergencia i Unió*. Nevertheless, it was the beginning of the end. The Prime Minister chose not to reply to the censure motion, but instead let his Vice-President take the brunt of the attack.[84] Suárez was now isolated from the barons of the various UCD factions. On 21 July, Abril Martorell resigned and, without his loyal support, Suárez was more vulnerable to the intrigue of his enemies.[85]

The decline of Suárez put the King in an appalling position. He had been able to ask for the resignation of Arias Navarro – and even then with some difficulty – because he was operating with the powers inherited from Franco. He did not have the same capacity to request Suárez's resignation. Adolfo Suárez was Prime Minister as a result of winning democratic elections and the King was scrupulous in his respect for the constitution. On the other hand, he was deeply sensitive to military feeling and was fully aware of the widespread popular discontent with the government's performance in respect of the economy and public order. Juan Carlos knew about the rumours circulating to the effect that the PSOE was prepared to enter a *'gobierno de gestion'* (caretaker coalition) under the presidency of a general. The Prime Minister dismissed the idea as absurd but he was clearly rattled and his discomfort was reflected in unease in La Zarzuela.[86] Josép Tarradellas – no longer President of the Generalitat, since being replaced by Jordi Pujol in May 1980, but now a respected elder statesman – reflected the general anxieties when he suggested in the summer that what was necessary was 'a touch on the rudder' – in other words, a change of direction.

There was no shortage of people, ranging from newspaper

editors to senior generals, insinuating to the King that such a touch on the rudder could only come from him. He had been through extraordinarily demanding experiences in reaching the goal of restoring the monarchy in a democratic setting. The years of humiliation under Franco had been followed by the tension-racked 18 months from the dictator's death to the first democratic elections. The King had then collaborated in the process whereby the monarchy was subjected to constitutional restraints. Despite his diminished powers, he had been obliged to work constantly to maintain military discipline and defuse threats to the democratic regime. There would be no respite yet. The prospect was opening up when awesome executive responsibilities seemed to be beckoning. The most daunting test now awaited him.

TEN

Fighting for Democracy
1980–1981

By the autumn of 1980, an anxious Juan Carlos saw Suárez isolated from his cabinet, his party and the press. The working agreement with the PSOE had collapsed. Felipe González declared that
the Prime Minister no longer had a meaningful contribution to
make. Unemployment had risen to one and a half million. The
government's policy on regional autonomies was bogged down.
Ill feeling in Andalusia remained intense after the referendum
fiasco. The slowness of the transfer of powers to the newly elected
Basque and Catalan regional governments was both an embarrassment and a provocation. In the Basque Country, the government's
delegate, General José Saenz de Santamaría, complained that by
dragging its feet, the government was generating support for ETA.
Indeed, at a time when public opinion in Euskadi was rallying
around the Statute of Guernica and moving away from commitment to the extreme nationalist programme known as the *Alternativa KAS*, the government's apathy with regard to Euskadi
bordered on criminal neglect. It reaped its reward in the re-
emergence of both wings of ETA in the second half of 1980. While
ETA-Político-Militar (ETA-PM) carried out a bombing campaign
on holiday resorts, ETA-Militar stole large quantities of explosive
and declared that it would unleash total war on the Spanish State
in order to get Navarre included within Euskadi. Despite the fact
that municipal election results in Navarre showed that the vast
majority of the province's population had no desire to be part of
the Basque Country, ETA-M began a campaign of grenade attacks
on Civil Guard posts and attempted to murder the editor of the
Diario de Navarra.[1]

The ETA claim to Navarre provoked fury among senior Army officers who regarded Navarre as an inalienable part of Spain as well as a symbol of patriotic values. Navarre had provided Franco with the *Requetés*, the ferocious Carlist militia that had played a crucial role in his war effort. Military discontent had, in any case, been near boiling point since the presentation to the Cortes in June 1980 of the draft military amnesty law, which aimed once more to open the way to the reintegration into the ranks both of UMD members and of officers who had fought for the Republic during the Civil War. Outrage in officers' messes was reported to be even more uncontrolled than after the legalization of the PCE. To make matters worse, military discontent had been kept at flashpoint throughout the spring and summer of 1980 by a series of assassination attempts on senior generals carried out by both ETA-Militar and GRAPO.[2]

Suárez gained some breathing space with a cabinet reshuffle on 9 September. The so-called 'government of the barons' secured the temporary loyalty of some his critics. However, the most vehement of them, Landelino Lavilla, used his position as President of the Cortes to organize the '*críticos*' as the internal UCD opponents of Suárez were known.[3] Moreover, some of the government's strengths turned out to be weaknesses. The immensely competent Rodolfo Martín Villa was made Minister for Territorial Administration but his earlier period as Minister of the Interior ensured that he still faced acute Basque hostility. The replacement of Abril Martorell, the President's erstwhile parliamentary shield, by the sinuous Pío Cabanillas with the novel title of Attaché to the Prime Minister backfired because of personal differences with Suárez's other principal supporter in the cabinet, Rafael Arias Salgado, the Minister of the *Presidencia*.[4]

Things improved slightly in October. Suárez met with Felipe González on 1 October, with Santiago Carrillo on 6 October, and with the Basque *Lehendakari* Carlos Garaikoetxea on 12 October. This led to speculation that a new *Pacta de La Moncloa* was in the offing. The meeting with Garaikoetxea was especially promising and reflected the injection of energy that Martín Villa had contributed to the autonomy process. Despite the fact that ETA-M, alarmed by the possibility of better relations between Euskadi and Madrid, murdered eight people in the course of Garaikoetxea's time in the capital, there was a generally positive outcome to the talks. Although there was no progress regarding the Basque call for an autonomous police force, agreements were reached over State funding for *Ikastolas* (Basque-language schools), for aid to the Basque steel industry and for the introduction of a Basque television channel.[5]

Unfortunately, Suárez's rally had come too late. The military situation was worsening by the day. Conspiracy was rife in the Army at various levels. On 7 August, the ultra magazine *Heraldo Español* had published on its cover a picture of a white horse under the title 'General wanted'. Inside, it was snidely insinuated that the King no longer had confidence in his Prime Minister. The author then listed the names of suitable military candidates to take over the government including Generals Álvaro Lacalle Leloup, Armada Comýn, Torres Rojas and Prieto López.[6] On 17 October, 26 of the most prominent civilian ultras in Spain met in a Madrid flat to discuss both the financing and the infrastructure of a projected coup. The ultra press was muttering darkly about a so-called '*Operación De Gaulle*'. This was almost certainly an obscure reference to the activities of General Armada, who was known to have become a great admirer of De Gaulle, during the two years that he spent at the *École de Guerre* in Paris from 1959 to 1961.

At the beginning of 1980, Armada had moved from the *Escuela Superior del Ejército* to become Military Governor of Lérida. Increasingly, he had concluded that the solution to what he, and other generals, regarded as an intolerable situation was a non-violent substitution of UCD by a government of national salvation under his own premiership. On 22 October, at a lunch in the home of the Socialist Mayor of Lérida, Antonio Ciurana, Armada went so far as to broach his ideas with two Socialists, Enrique Múgica, the PSOE official responsible for liaison with other parties, and Joan Reventós, the President of the Catalan parliament. They immediately informed Felipe González and he duly passed on the information to Suárez. As a result of the conversations that day, however, Armada seems to have convinced himself that he could count on the support of the Socialists for his scheme.[7] Over the next four months, Armada also had meetings with Leopoldo Calvo Sotelo, Rodolfo Martín Villa, Jordi Pujol, Josép Tarradellas, Pío Cabanillas and others. He enjoyed particularly cordial relations with Tarradellas, who described himself as a friend of the general. On 23 December, Manuel Fraga wrote in his diary: 'I have received solid information that General Armada has said that he would be prepared to head a coalition government.'[8]

With democracy trapped in the inexorable pincer movement constituted by the mutual interest of ETA and ultra subversion, political nerves were stretched to breaking point. The idea of a strong all-party coalition to replace Suárez had been in the air since the summer of 1980. Both Suárez and the King knew about the talk of broad coalitions, not least because of the fact that two of the people being proposed as leader of such a coalition were General Armada and the Christian Democrat Alfonso Osorio. Osorio had been hostile to Suárez since the legalization of the Communist Party and his own subsequent exclusion from the cabinet after the June 1977 elections. It was no coincidence that Osorio was a friend of Armada, nor that both maintained close relations with the King. In any case, in the summer, Armada gave the King a report, drawn up by an unnamed constitutional lawyer, examining legal ways of resolving the situation with a coalition possibly headed by a soldier. The hint was unmistakable. Moreover, in the course of the late summer and the autumn, Osorio had broached the idea of a strong coalition with Fraga's *Alianza Popular*, with the other Christian Democrat dissidents from within UCD, with leading figures from the PSOE and even with a representative of the PCE. Given the extreme nature of the situation, the idea had surfaced during these talks that such a coalition might be better led by a general than by the highly competent, but less than charismatic, Osorio.[9] This coalition came to be known as *Coalición Democrática*.

Undermined by the now deafening rumours of military conspiracy, Suárez also gave the impression of being besieged in La Moncloa by an increasingly aggressive PSOE. His public image was deteriorating badly and it was mortally damaged on 23 October 1980. On that day, 48 children and three adults were killed in an accidental propane gas explosion at the village school of Ortuella in Vizcaya. On the same day, ETA-M assassinated three Basque members of UCD. Whatever his real feelings, Suárez responded with what seemed like callous indifference. He made no parliamentary statement about either the disaster or the terrorist attacks. Nor did he visit the stricken village and he stayed away from the funerals of his party colleagues. In stark contrast, Queen Sofía flew immediately to Bilbao to be with the families of the victims of Ortuella. Suárez's coldness provoked damning criticism in the media and from the three main opposition parties.[10]

Whatever Juan Carlos's attitude to Suárez, he could not fail to be alarmed by the media's talk of 'paralysis' and 'putrefaction' nor by the descent into ever more indiscriminate violence in the Basque Country. The murders on 23 October were ETA-M's reaction to the appointment of Marcelino Oreja Aguirre to the newly invented post of Governor General of the Basque Country. One of the murdered UCD members, Jaime Arrese Arizmendiarreta, was scheduled to replace Oreja in the Cortes. Now, on 31 October, ETA-PM assassinated Juan de Dios Doval Mateos, a San Sebastián law professor who was next on the UCD candidate list for Guipúzcoa and thus due to replace Arrese Arizmendiarreta. Then, on 3 November, an ETA-M hit squad machine-gunned a bar in Zarauz, killing four Civil Guards and a PNV member and wounding six other customers. Astonishingly, Suárez chose not to attend the funeral of Professor Doval. The popular perception of *desgobierno* had reached its highest point and the King could not fail to be aware of this.

Juan Carlos was visited by a number of senior generals who complained bitterly about the situation. He listened attentively and, when they went too far, tried to make them see reason, making it quite clear 'that in no circumstances should they rely on me to cover the slightest act against a constitutional government like ours. Such actions, if they took place, I told them, would be considered by the King as a direct attack on the crown.' Shortly afterwards, in a private meeting with the ex-Communist intellectual Jorge Semprún, he similarly expressed his determination to oppose any assaults on the democratic system. Although not referring to any specific dangers, he spoke with such vehemence as to leave Semprún convinced that he had real threats on his mind and would have no doubts about opposing them.[11]

The year to the end of October 1980 had seen 114 deaths as a result of terrorism, an average of one victim every three days, including 57 civilians and 27 Civil Guards, 11 Army officers and nine policemen. Despite the fact that the spiral of violence had stimulated the creation of the wide-ranging Basque Peace Front, ETA-M continued to kill.[12] It was widely feared that the Army was about to lose its already threadbare patience. On 5 November, at a private party in a military housing estate in Madrid, 50 officers discussed ways of emulating the Turkish military coup led by General Kenan Evren in mid-September. They talked of prevailing upon the King to establish a junta to smash ETA. Alarmingly, one of the most prominent of these officers was Colonel José Ignacio San Martín, the Chief of Staff of the Brunete DAC. Even more alarmingly, Milans del Bosch's deputy chief of staff in Valencia, Colonel Diego Ibáñez Inglés, was in touch with San Martín. The officers meeting in Madrid based their discussions around an analysis of the Turkish events written and distributed by the Spanish military attaché in Ankara, Colonel Federico Quintero Morente, the US-trained counterinsurgency and intelligence expert who had exposed *Operación Galaxia*. His report, which discussed the effects of terrorism and economic stagnation on unstable Mediterranean democracies, was leaked to the press on 6 November.[13]

The intelligence services were inevitably following what was going on. Theoretically, the Defence Intelligence Centre (CESID) had no jurisdiction over internal military matters. However, since its creation in 1977, General Gutiérrez Mellado had encouraged its Director General, José María Bourgón López-Dóriga, as part of its function of defending the State, to investigate military conspiracy. Apart from creating a small department called 'Interior', little had been done. Thus, the CESID had been slow to pick up on *Operación Galaxia*. Nevertheless, within the CESID, there was circulating a file entitled *'Supuesto Anticonstitucional Máximo'*

(Greatest Hypothetical Threat to the Constitution). Another report, with the title 'panorama of operations under way', produced by the Ministry of Defence's own information office, was seen by Rodríguez Sahagún and Suárez and, it must be supposed, Juan Carlos himself. However, such information, arriving among so many other rumours and reports, was not taken entirely seriously.[14]

More enigmatically, the head of the special operations group of the CESID, Major José Luis Cortina Prieto, had taken it upon himself to follow the various conspiracies being hatched. A leftist as a young officer under Franco, at one time close to the UMD, Major Cortina had been a cadet at the military academy in Zaragoza in the same year as Juan Carlos. It seems clear that he was in touch with Armada and approved of the idea that the 'touch on the rudder' should take the form of a coalition government under his premiership. He may even have used his contacts with various conspirators to push the project along. However, that is a far way from recent suggestions that he was the brains behind 'a designer coup' and was manipulating all the other efforts in train. What is impossible to say is if Cortina's involvement constituted a genuine commitment to the plans of General Armada or if he was acting as an *agent provocateur*, hoping, somewhat irresponsibly, to provoke the failure of the various coups, or just fulfilling his function as an officer dedicated to intelligence gathering.[15]

Whatever the intelligence services may have been doing in the shadows, talk of the 'Turkish temptation' and the 'Ankara syndrome' became commonplace in the media and the corridors of parliament. Coming on top of the rumours about General Armada's *Operación De Gaulle*, both Manuel Fraga and Felipe González were sufficiently worried to tell the King of their readiness to join in a caretaker coalition government if the situation became sufficiently serious. That they should do so was the result of anxiety that some initiative was necessary to head off a full-scale *golpe a la turca* (Turkish coup).[16]

At the beginning of December, Osorio denied publicly that he had been in touch with any generals and asked Sabino Fernández

Campo to inform the King of this. Nevertheless, in the context of alarming rumours concerning the colonels' discussions about a violent coup, and faced with the apparent incapacity of the UCD government to resolve the problems of ETA and unemployment, a coalition led by a general had obvious attractions.[17] Suárez was aware of the fact that the King had recently met Fraga and Felipe González and took that fact to indicate that he had lost the royal confidence. He said to Fernando Álvarez de Miranda: 'I know full well that everybody wants my head and that the message from everyone including even the Socialists is a coalition government led by a soldier – General Armada. I won't bow to such pressures even if it means me leaving La Moncloa in a coffin.'[18]

On 17 November, Armada visited the Captain-General of the Valencia Military Region, Jaime Milans del Bosch. Fervent monarchists, they had been friends since both serving on the Russian front with the *División Azul*. In the course of their discussion, Armada managed to insinuate that he was acting on the King's behalf. According to Milans, Armada told him that: 'The King is worried about the situation in Spain. Things are going badly. Terrorism is shedding the blood of the Armed Forces and the autonomous regions are destroying our national unity.' As a convinced monarchist, such hints of royal approbation were just what Milans needed in order to edge nearer to action. When he asked what could be done, Armada allegedly replied, 'Plenty, General, we can do plenty. I have been with His Majesty the last few times he has been in Baqueira Beret. Violent actions are feared and we must point them in another direction. His Majesty has discreetly confided his worries to me.' (Baqueira Beret was a ski resort in the province of Lérida – where Armada was Military Governor – much frequented by the royal family.)

Armada's subtly ambiguous words were taken by Milans as a royal invitation to take action against ETA. The King may well, surely must, have talked to Armada about the rumours of a coup. However, when Armada quoted Juan Carlos as saying 'we must redirect them', taken by Milans to mean 'you (Milans), me (Armada) and the King', this was actually no more than Armada's own gloss on his conversations with Juan Carlos. Moreover, it should surely have struck Milans as odd that, if the King was hoping that he and Armada would lead a coup, Juan Carlos had not asked him directly. In fact, the opposite was the case and the King was actually avoiding him. If Juan Carlos had really sent Armada as an emissary then Milans should have asked himself why was it so hard to get an audience at La Zarzuela. On 25 November, the King came to the port of Cartagena to present a battle flag to the frigate *Infanta Cristina*. Milans was present as Captain-General of the region in which Cartagena lay. He took the opportunity to complain to General Joaquín Valenzuela, head of the royal military household, about the difficulty of getting an audience. Dissatisfied with Valenzuela's explanations, he raised the matter with Juan Carlos himself who responded, 'Don't worry, Jaime. I'll tell Sabino and he'll ring you.' The call never came.[19]

Nevertheless, the fact that the King and Alfonso Armada remained on the warmest terms inevitably permitted Milans and others to believe that there was real substance to the rumours about royal approval for a coalition government led by a general. On 18 December, Armada went to La Zarzuela where he discussed with Juan Carlos the text of his Christmas broadcast to the Spanish people. It was a rather sombre appeal on behalf of Spanish democracy. On 3 January, Armada visited the royal family at Baqueira Beret where they were taking their Christmas holidays. He again told the King that there was support across the political spectrum for a coalition government and talked of ways in which the various extremist conspiracies might be brought under control. Juan Carlos confined himself to listening and to suggesting that Armada do what he could to calm down Milans del Bosch. On the next day, Suárez also visited the royal family. It is not known what Juan Carlos and the Prime Minister talked about, but it is reasonable to assume that they discussed both the widespread mutterings about a planned bloody military coup and the implications of trying to head off the danger by means of a coalition government, possibly under a general. Suárez had, on occasion, said that 'a wink from the King would be enough' to secure his resignation and now there was inevitable speculation that Juan Carlos had talked to him about the advantages that would accrue from his departure. Certainly, after his return from Baqueira Beret, Suárez seemed to have lost much of the will to fight on.[20]

On 6 January, the royal New Year message to the Armed Forces, delivered at the *Pascua Militar* reception in the Palacio de Oriente, indicated the King's own acute preoccupation. Recognizing 'terrorism's absurd and painful bloodshed' and assuring his audience 'that the unity of Spain will be safeguarded', he went on to call for loyalty. He told the officer corps that, 'Happiness is total commitment to duty, with enthusiasm and dedication and no inclination to get involved in political activities other than that elevated endeavour which interests us all, the grand endeavour of the greatness of Spain and the permanent vigilance of its security.' In his final words, he made it quite clear that no conspiratorial activity would ever have his approval: 'If you stay united, committed to your profession, respectful of the constitutional norms on which our rule of law is based, with faith and confidence in your superiors and your Commander-in-Chief, and inspired always by hope and optimism, together we will overcome the difficulties inherent in any period of transition.'[21]

On 10 January 1981, Armada again visited General Milans del Bosch. It was their second meeting in two months. This time, on the basis of the fact that, one week earlier in Baqueira Beret, Juan Carlos had asked him to try to calm Milans's fears, Armada was able to announce that he came with a message from the King. However, it would appear that he went far far beyond anything that the King had said. During his later trial, Milans alleged that Armada told him that Juan Carlos 'was fed up with Suárez, that he was determined to replace him', and that, after discussing possible candidates, the King was looking for a civilian substitute but 'the Queen favours a military government' – which, given her Greek experience, was extremely implausible. Milans insisted that Armada had stressed the word '*reconducir*' (lead it in another direction). In this regard, Armada told Milans that he was about to take up a senior position in Madrid at the General Staff from which point he would direct the process, insinuating that the King approved. What Armada was taking upon himself to do suggested supreme arrogance on his part yet it fitted well with his conviction that he was merely protecting the monarchy. Thus, aware of Milans's inclination towards a violent coup, Armada was sounding him out, even subtly encouraging him to make the coup which he would eventually be in a position 'to redirect' (*reconducir*) to his own benefit. Milans was sufficiently convinced to agree that he would liaise with the 'active' groups and persuade them to put their plans on hold.[22]

The consequence of the meeting in Valencia was that, eight days later, on Sunday 18 January 1981, Milans del Bosch called together a group of conspirators in Madrid, at the home of his aide-de-camp, Lieutenant-Colonel Pedro Mas Oliver, in the Calle General Cabrera. Amongst others, those present included Milans del Bosch himself, Generals Carlos Iniesta Cano, Manuel Cabeza Calahorra and Luis Torres Rojas, Lieutenant-Colonels Mas Oliver and Tejero and, briefly, the civilian ultra Juan García Carrés. The proceedings made it clear that Milans was taking very seriously the mission given him by Armada, which he assumed to have come from the King, to redirect the activities of the more extremist hotheads. He reported on his recent conversation with Armada and assured his listeners that this meant that Juan Carlos was happy to see the military resolve the political situation. He was confident that Armada's manoeuvres would lead to a coalition government. He even went so far as to say that when Armada had taken his leave of the royal family in Baqueira Beret, the Queen had said, 'Alfonso, only you can save us!' Milans urged his fellow conspirators to stand aside to give Armada's scheme a chance. There then followed a discussion of contingency plans that had been made in case the scheme failed. It was decided that everything would be put on hold for one month. If by then Armada had not been named Prime Minister of a coalition government, Tejero would seize the government and the parliamentary deputies at a plenary meeting of the Cortes in mid-February. Using the excuse of the consequent vacuum of power in Madrid, Milans would then take over the Valencia region. Torres Rojas would come from La Coruña to take charge of the DAC and occupy key points in Madrid. Thereafter, they assumed, with the King's approval, Armada would direct operations from La Zarzuela and impose the solution of a coalition under his own leadership.[23]

On the following day, Monday 19 January, Milans's deputy chief of staff, Colonel Diego Ibáñez Inglés, travelled to Lérida to give General Armada a report of what had been agreed at the Madrid meeting. What Armada had told Milans was credible because Juan Carlos did indeed want to see him brought to Madrid. Having recently reached the rank of Major-General, Armada could reasonably aspire to be Deputy Chief of the Army General Staff. However, on 22 January, when Juan Carlos suggested Armada's appointment to Suárez, they clashed sharply. Partly because of the acrimony of his previous clashes with Armada and partly because of the rumours about the so-called *Operación De Gaulle*, Suárez opposed an appointment that would effectively make Armada head of military intelligence. Arguing vehemently on Armada's behalf, the King prevailed. It was extremely unusual for Juan Carlos to insist on a particular appointment. In part, this exceptional case reflected the affection and great esteem that he felt for Armada. Moreover, with rumours of conspiracy flying around, he wanted a trusted figure at his side in Madrid. His delight in securing Armada's appointment was revealed when he insisted on telling him personally. About to get on a plane to the Basque Country on 3 February, the King delayed leaving until he had been able to telephone Lérida from Barajas Airport to give Armada the news.[24]

Without knowing about the specific activities of Tejero, Milans and Armada, the situation was bad enough for both the King and for Suárez: juggling with the threats posed by military sedition, terrorism and a government party seething with conspiracy against the Prime Minister. The imminent UCD Congress in Palma de Mallorca was expected to see a major showdown in which Landelino Lavilla would launch an assault on Suárez's position.[25] Under intolerable pressure, Suárez began to look for a dramatic way out. He contemplated resigning as party president in the hope of securing a breathing space as Prime Minister but, physically and psychologically exhausted after leading Spain through the transition, he had little stomach to go on. Despite encouragement from his immediate entourage and the ever-faithful Abril Martorell, he was reaching the momentous decision to resign. The clash with the King over Armada's appointment had further undermined his morale. Then, on the day after that disagreement, 23 January, the intelligence services received information to the effect that 17 senior generals had discussed the passivity of the government and expressed a readiness to lead a military intervention. This was certainly a reference, albeit inaccurate, to the meeting held in the home of Lieutenant-Colonel Mas Oliver. Shortly before this news came in, the King had left Madrid for a hunting trip in Cazorla. Now, alerted by a telephone call from one of his aides, and despite dangerously stormy weather, he made a dramatic return to La Zarzuela by helicopter, determined to neutralize any such action. It was alleged that he was heard to mutter, 'Arias was a gentleman, when I hinted at resignation, he resigned.'[26]

On arriving back in Madrid, the King had several telephone conversations with his Prime Minister about the news that military intervention was being contemplated. It is likely that his resignation was discussed. The Church hierarchy was mobilizing to join the fray over divorce reform and the question of incorporating Catholic universities into the State system. On 24 January, the military threat that had provoked the King's rapid return to Madrid was underlined when *El Alcázar* published sinister ruminations to the effect that another *Galaxia*-style plot was on the horizon – presumably also a reference to the meeting at Mas Oliver's home. Suárez thus decided to make an announcement at the UCD Congress, perhaps hoping that the threat of his departure would frighten his party colleagues into supporting him.[27] On Monday 26 January, he discussed his decision with senior members of the cabinet and the party leadership. In the event, his plan was thwarted by an air traffic controllers' strike that forced the postponement of the Congress. It has been speculated that the strike was manipulated precisely in order to undermine his scheme.

Whatever the truth of the matter, on the following day, Suárez lunched with the King at La Zarzuela. Before entering Juan Carlos's office, he informed General Sabino Fernández Campo of his decision. He wanted there to be no suspicion that any suggestion of his resignation had emanated from the King, saying, 'No matter what happens, I want you always to be my witness and be able to say that no one sacked me.' Juan Carlos presented no more than token resistance to his Prime Minister's departure. The King turned to Sabino Fernández Campo and asked him what would happen next. Suárez was mortified by what he took as coldness.[28] The Prime Minister announced his resignation in a television broadcast on 29 January. The ultra-right was jubilant, crowing that Suárez had been forced to resign by the King and the Army generals together.[29]

The bombshell of Suárez's resignation led to speculation, which he always denied, that he was leaving in response to threats of military action. Certainly, he was fully aware of General Armada's conversation with various politicians about the formation of a coalition. Similarly, he knew about the intelligence reports that had curtailed the King's hunting trip. Public speculation was fed by one line in his resignation broadcast – 'I do not want to be responsible for the democratic regime of coexistence being once more a parenthesis on the history of Spain.' It may be that he was merely putting a high-sounding gloss on his own exhaustion.[30] However, on 26 January, when privately discussing his resignation with the UCD barons, he had said, 'I'm leaving you with the military problem resolved.[31] Above all, he was affected by a sense that he had lost the confidence of the King.[32] Whatever the reasons, his departure made it at least possible that the coalition might now be cobbled together. A process would open in which the King would take soundings from the leaders of the main parties before then proposing a new Prime Minister to the Cortes. If he were truly keen to see a coalition government presided over by General Armada, now would be the time to nudge the political élite in that direction.

After initial consultations with political leaders, Juan Carlos decided that, because the UCD Congress was imminent, he should delay his decision.[33] On 31 January, only two days after Suárez's resignation broadcast, the influential right-wing columnist Emilio Romero published an article in *ABC* discussing the choices to be made by the King in resolving the succession to Suárez. The hint was unmistakable. Rather than choosing another orthodox politician, Romero suggested that the King consider 'the idea of a politically blessed outsider' and went on to suggest the name of General Armada. Romero's article gave rise to widespread comment about the 'Solución Armada' (a pun on armed solution and Armada solution).[34] Although he later claimed to have been distressed by the article, the general himself was thrilled. Certainly, the article's publication could hardly have come as a surprise, given his friendship with Romero. On the following day, he met Josép Tarradellas to discuss the situation. The ex President of Catalonia, something of an enthusiast for Armada, was alarmed by his vehemence and commented, 'This guy's raring to go. He's got me worried.'[35] The fact that Juan Carlos did not take Emilio Romero's hint is a clear indication that he was not backing Armada's political ambitions. Indeed, three days after the publication of Romero's article, when the King spoke to Armada from Barajas, it was merely to congratulate him on his posting as Deputy Chief of the Army General Staff. If he had harboured hopes of having Armada as Prime Minister, it would have been logical for them to have had a very different conversation. Nevertheless, Armada was sufficiently heartened by news of his appointment to tell Colonel Diego Ibáñez Inglés, who visited him in Lérida, that his plans were going ahead successfully.[36]

To coincide with the Pascua Militar, Diario 16 had published a special supplement on the Armed Forces. In it, there was a long article by the one-time UMD officer, Fernando Reinlein, under the title 'Operation Zalamea: Objective, military coup. A fiction that one day could come true.' Ostensibly a piece of science fiction, in which the role of Armada was assumed by 'General Murillo', it gave an eerily accurate account of possible military coups in preparation. Reinlein's revelations caused some concern to the golpistas themselves and some irritation in La Zarzuela. In early February, Reinlein received a message through the Socialist Party, allegedly from the King, telling him 'not to write any more nonsense in Diario 16 about military coups'. The message had come via Enrique Múgica who had had an audience with the King on the previous day. It is highly unlikely that Juan Carlos would ever send such a direct message, but it is possible that Múgica was taking it upon himself to act upon concerns expressed by the King.[37]

Suárez's departure had long been the primordial object of military conspirators. However, far from neutralizing military discontent, it was merely the prelude to a process of political disintegration that encouraged the belief of many officers that their intervention was a patriotic duty. Since mid-December 1980, *El Alcázar* had been preparing the way for such an action by publishing more or less open appeals for a military coup. There had been three such articles under the byline of '*Almendros*' (almonds). The first had referred to a 'divorce between the government and the ranks of the military' and spoken of 'the urgent need for a corrective solution to permit the regeneration of the Spanish situation'.[38] The second declared blatantly that 'the democratic experiment has failed', and 'the constitution as it stands does not work'. General Mola, the 'director' of the military coup of 1936, was quoted admiringly and the article suggested that, given the incapacity of the government and the political parties, it was time to turn to other institutions, a reference to the King and Armed Forces.[39]

The most outspoken of the three articles was published on the day after Emilio Romero's hint about the *Solución Armada*. It too was unmistakably directed at the King and its text could also be seen to coincide exactly with the thinking of General Armada. 'We are at the critical point, the countdown has begun. Political irresponsibility has culminated in a sad process in which the crown is inescapably obliged to intervene.' The anonymous author lamented the constitution's reduction of the powers left to the King by Franco's fundamental laws and went on to incite Juan Carlos to exploit 'the great freedom of action' given him by his prestige. 'The crown finds itself with the historical opportunity to initiate a substantial change of direction, the oft-mentioned touch on the rudder that would permit the formation of a government of national regeneration, enjoying all the authority needed in the exceptional circumstances in which we live.' Such a government would be supported, it was hinted coyly, but unmistakably, by the

Army. If nothing was done about what was described as political paralysis, 'it would provide the opportunity for a legitimate intervention by the Armed Forces'. That the King was being invited to opt for the '*Operación De Gaulle/Solución Armada*' was made clear by an explicit comparison with what had happened in France in 1958.[40]

It was believed that the collective signature of the *Colectivo Almendros* was a coded message that something was being plotted for the second half of February which is when the almond normally blossoms. At the time, there was considerable speculation that the collective was made up of number of journalists from *El Alcázar*, the editor, Antonio Izquierdo, together with Joaquín Aguirre Bellver, Ángel Palomino and Ismael Medina, conservative politicians like Gonzalo Fernández de la Mora and Federico Silva Muñoz and prominent ultra officers, including Generals Iniesta Cano and Santiago and Colonel José Ignacio San Martín. However, it has recently been claimed that the articles were written by the now deceased General Manuel Cabeza Calahorra, a claim that conveniently absolves those previously believed to be involved. At the time, several hundred officers had agreed that, in the event of the newspaper being prosecuted for these seditious articles, they would all claim to have written them.[41]

Driven by a paranoiac fear of separatism, the most reactionary officers could hardly believe it when Juan Carlos and Queen Sofía undertook an official visit to the Basque Country from 3 to 5 February 1981. If anything could undermine the later accusations that the King had been in some way complicit with the *golpistas*, it was his readiness, at some personal risk, to initiate a direct dialogue between the crown and the Basque institutions. It was a generous gesture, recalling the historic situation before Basque privileges were lost. To emphasize the point, the government's official representative in the Basque Country, Marcelino Oreja, was marginalized from the proceedings. The King and Queen received a warm reception in many parts of Euskadi but the first royal visit to the area since 1929 was marred by desultory anti-Spanish demonstrations at Foronda, the airport at Vitoria. In Bilbao and elsewhere, Spanish flags and cries of ¡*Viva el Rey!* were challenged by the waving of *ikurriñas* (Basque flags) and chants of '*Erregeak, kampora*' (King and Queen go home!) and '*Gora ETA*' (Long live ETA).

The most dramatic and dangerous incident took place at the historic Basque Parliament, the tiny Casa de Juntas in Guernica. Sabino Fernández Campo had been warned in advance and had prepared some variants of the King's speech. Just as he began his remarks, saying, 'I had always hoped that my first visit as Head of State to this beloved Basque land . . .', the King was interrupted. The bare-chested deputies of *Herri Batasuna*, clenched fists raised, began to sing the Basque national anthem, the *Eusko Gudari* (the Basque warrior). Symbolic of the Basque struggle against Franco and his Nazi allies, it was a gratuitously offensive gesture towards Juan Carlos. Other deputies, UCD and Socialists, Communists and members of the Basque Nationalist Party began to applaud the now silent and impassive King. When the *Lehendakari*, Carlos Garaikoetxea, ordered the Basque security staff to remove the *Herri Batasuna* deputies, noisy scuffles broke out. It took nearly ten minutes before calm was restored.

When finally Juan Carlos was able to resume, Sabino Fernández Campo passed him an amended version of the prepared speech. The King now declared, 'Against those who make a practice of intolerance, who are contemptuous of coexistence and who have no respect for our institutions, I proclaim my faith in democracy and my confidence in the Basque people.' The dignity and aplomb with which the King handled the insulting outbreak, coming so soon after Queen Sofía's visit to the site of the Ortuella disaster, ensured that the royal visit had an immensely positive impact on much Basque public opinion although it did nothing to diminish the hostility of the *abertzales*. However, the military was appalled by what was seen as an outrageous challenge to the Spanish State.[42] To make matters worse, massive publicity was being given to two kidnappings by ETA. The first, of the Valencian industrialist Luis Suñer, the biggest taxpayer in Spain, was simply a crime of extortion, his release being secured by the payment of a gigantic ransom. The second was an attempt to blackmail the power company Iberduero into destroying the Lemoniz nuclear power station through the kidnapping, on 29 January, of José María Ryan, the chief engineer. Despite a wave of outrage throughout Spain and the Basque Country, Ryan was brutally murdered on 6 February.[43]

During the weekend following the visit to the Basque Country, the royal family took a skiing break at Baqueira Beret. It was normal protocol for Armada, who was still Military Governor of the province, to pay his respects to the King. They arranged to have dinner on the evening of 6 February. The occasion would be an excellent opportunity for the general to rehearse the benefits of the *Solución Armada* to the ongoing political crisis. However, the Queen was obliged to return to Madrid, having been told that her mother was fatally ill – in fact, Queen Frederica died that night. In consequence, Juan Carlos and Armada dined alone, then sat talking until 3 a.m. Apparently, Armada spoke about Tarradellas's remark about the need for 'a touch on the rudder', commented on the recent article by Emilio Romero and reminded the King about the pro-coalition report by the unnamed constitutional lawyer. Juan Carlos listened intently but his only response was to remind Armada of the royal duty to hear, and then act on, whatever the various leaders of the parliamentary parties might recommend.[44] Nonetheless, Armada clearly harboured great expectations since Ryan's death had triggered – as ETA-M apparently hoped – an intensification of anti-democratic fury within the Army.

That ETA-M's action could be construed as a valid excuse for military intervention was the theme of a provocative article in *El Alcázar* signed by the retired General Fernando de Santiago, albeit written with the help of Juan García Carrés. Under the headline '*Situación Límite*' (roughly, This Cannot Go On), he expressed his indignation at the recent events in the Basque Country. 'The spectacle of Guernica demonstrates the state of decomposition in which Spain finds itself. What is happening is intolerable and infuriating. Guernica was an insult to Spain and to the King, the Commander-in-Chief of the Armed Forces, and thus to those of us who are honoured to wear their uniforms. The event in Guernica did not turn into a full-scale tragedy thanks to the prudence, good humour and serenity of His Majesty. We can no longer remain impassive before such chaos.' He cited the long list of ETA kidnappings and assassinations as, 'the most obvious proof that here there is no authority and authority must be re-established'. Recent evidence of growing electoral abstention was used by General de Santiago to justify his assertion that Spaniards were collectively rejecting 'the political orgy' and were looking elsewhere for salvation. He made it clear that this lay, as in 1936, in military intervention: 'In our history we have lived moments every bit as difficult as these but always, in similar circumstances, there were Spaniards who came to the rescue and saved Spain.'[45]

On the same day, Sunday 8 February, that General de Santiago's article was published, the Congress of UCD elected Leopoldo Calvo Sotelo as their candidate for the premiership. He had been reluctantly chosen merely as the candidate who provoked least antipathy among the various factions.[46] On his return from Athens, where he and the Queen had attended the funeral of Queen Frederica, the King spent the next two days holding his consultations and Armada was confident that the final decision would favour his plans. His near certainty was revealed at a farewell dinner organized by the Catalan president at the Generalitat on 9 February. Marta Ferusola, the wife of Jordi Pujol, commented, 'It looks like Calvo Sotelo will be chosen as Prime Minister.' General Armada replied drily, 'I very much doubt it. I don't think that Calvo Sotelo will ever be Prime Minister.'[47]

On Tuesday 10 February, the King informed the President of the Cortes, Landelino Lavilla, of his decision to invite Calvo Sotelo to form a government. During the period of consultation, despite the hopes of Armada and the later accusations of the military conspirators, the King made no mention of a possible coalition led by Armada, confining himself, as was his constitutional duty, to listening to the views of the leaders of the various parliamentary groups. He was meticulous in his respect for the constitution despite the fact that it would have been easy enough to broach the possibility of a coalition government – the idea of which was in the air. This suggests that, with the resignation of Suárez and his replacement by Calvo Sotelo, the King believed the situation had received the 'touch on the rudder' that it required.[48] After all, Suárez was no longer there to be the target of ultra hostility, UCD squabbling was likely now to diminish and there would be in the Moncloa a much more conservative Prime Minister with an emblematic surname – that of the Francoist 'proto martyr' José Calvo Sotelo, whose assassination on 13 July 1936 had been used to justify the military uprising five days later.

Armada was bitterly disappointed yet, in the hope of reversing the situation, made a desperate effort to speak to the King. 10 February was his last day as Military Governor of Lérida and, on the following day, he attended a funeral service for Queen Frederica. Although the occasion was hardly appropriate for private matters, Armada surprised Sabino Fernández Campo by the vehemence with which he demanded an appointment to speak privately with the King. A meeting was set for two days later on Friday 13 February. However, when he arrived at La Zarzuela, Armada was surprised to be kept waiting for some minutes by a guard. The reason was simply a tightening up of security procedures. It showed that, despite Armada's insinuations to the conspirators about the closeness of his relations with the King, he no longer enjoyed privileged access to the palace. None of that would have mattered if Armada had been successful in the central purpose of his visit, which was to persuade Juan Carlos to change his mind about the appointment of Calvo Sotelo. He told the King that his prestige within the Armed Forces was at the lowest point since his accession to the throne. Juan Carlos replied that he should therefore inform the Vice-President of the government with responsibility for National Security and Defence, General Gutiérrez Mellado. Aware that he had failed in his mission, Armada duly went on, as instructed, to visit Gutiérrez Mellado who later recalled him frothing with rage, insisting that the King was mistaken in mechanically applying the constitution and just lengthening the crisis by replacing Suárez with another civilian. Gutiérrez Mellado was impelled to conclude that, 'In order to save the crown, as he saw it, he was ready to contemplate solutions inimical to the person of His Majesty the King.'[49]

Armada was now in a difficult position relative to Milans and Tejero. Still fuming after his abortive meeting with the King, in the evening, he drove to Logroño for a secret meeting with Terence

Todman, the right-wing US Ambassador. Todman, whose principal concern was the political instability that was afflicting Spain, was also in contact with Major Cortina of CESID.[50] Three days after the meeting with Todman, General Armada hosted a dinner at his home on 16 February. The guests included the Captain-General of Catalonia, Antonio Pascual Galmés, the Chief of the Army General Staff, José Gabeiras Montero, the head of the royal household, the Marqués de Mondéjar, and the Catalan Communist deputy, Jordi Solé Tura. The purpose of the dinner was to discuss preparations for the forthcoming royal visit to Barcelona. The King was to preside at the principal parade on Armed Forces Day, which for the first time was being held outside Madrid. It was obviously a subject that concerned all the guests, and it was the main topic of conversation. However, the mere fact of the dinner sent a message to Armada's fellow plotters. For them, such a gathering could only mean that he was getting support for his plans from the King, from the highest echelons of the Army and from politicians. Armada's political connections permitted them to go forward confident that the coup was surrounded by an aureola of political, and above all royal, legitimacy.

Whatever the results of the conversation with Ambassador Todman in Logroño, at some point between 14 and 16 February, Armada spoke to Diego Ibáñez Inglés, the man coordinating the various elements of the proposed coup. Armada agreed that the plans hatched in Madrid on 18 January but shelved for one month should now go ahead. Within 48 hours, on 18 February, Colonel Ibáñez Inglés spoke to Antonio Tejero by telephone and gave him the go-ahead for an action on 20 February, the day on which Calvo Sotelo would submit to a Cortes vote on his candidacy as Prime Minister. At his later trial, Tejero would allege that he had also been contacted by Major Cortina who had assured him that he was acting on behalf of both Armada and the US Embassy. Cortina, said Tejero, told him that the parliamentary deputies would accept the candidacy of Armada as Prime Minister once they heard the phrase: 'The white elephant has arrived.' Even with the assurance provided by the various prior negotiations, there was little time for adequate preparation. Tejero was relieved to learn that, since Calvo Sotelo was unlikely to receive sufficient votes on the 20th, there would be another plenary session on 23 February. It was therefore agreed that Tejero would launch his assault on the political élite on the evening of that day.[51]

Milans had been inclined to give Armada more time. After all, the decision to go ahead had been reached only after a flurry of further meetings between the plotters. Effectively, things went as expected in the Cortes on Friday 20 February. Calvo Sotelo addressed the chamber in a sombre atmosphere, darkened by rumours about an imminent military coup and the scandal provoked by the death at the hands of the police a week earlier of an ETA activist, Joseba Iñaki Arregui Izaguirre. Despite votes from Jordi Pujol's *Convergencia i Unió*, from small Aragonese and Navarrese regionalist groups and even from a section of *Coalición Democrática*, including Alfonso Osorio and José María de Areilza, Calvo Sotelo received only a simple majority of 169 votes to 158 against and 17 abstentions, seven short of the overall majority of 176 votes necessary to confirm him as Prime Minister.[52] It was agreed that there would be a second vote on 23 February at 6 p.m. At 9 a.m. and 5 p.m. on the following day, Armada and Milans had two telephone conversations in the course of which they discussed the plans for the coup and Armada also vouched for the reliability of Cortina. At 6 p.m., Milans told Tejero of his doubts about the speed with which things were advancing. Tejero replied, 'But I can't stop it now,' to which Milans responded, 'Well then, get on with it and I wish you luck.'

According to Tejero, later the same evening, in an apartment in Madrid (Pintor Juan Gris 5), he met Major Cortina and General Armada, both of whom later denied that any such meeting had taken place.[53] In Tejero's account, Armada assured him that, 'This is an operation backed by His Majesty the King to strengthen the monarchy.' Armada ordered him to stress, when he entered the Cortes, that he was doing so 'in the name of the King, the crown and democracy'. When Tejero asked where Armada would be, he allegedly replied, 'Well, since the King is fickle, even though he is backing this, from six o'clock onwards, I'll be at La Zarzuela to make sure that he doesn't change his mind.' It is difficult to credit that Armada, given his personal devotion to the King, would speak of him in such terms, particularly to an inferior officer. On the other hand, his outrage after what he saw as the royal brush-off on 13 February suggested that he now felt, as Gutiérrez Mellado had suspected, that he knew better than the King and was acting in his best interests, even though Juan Carlos might not see it that way.

On Sunday 22 February, Milans del Bosch ordered Major Ricardo Pardo Zancada of the DAC at Brunete to come to Valencia to discuss his unit's role in Madrid for the operation planned for the next day. Pardo Zancada expressed his concern that General Juste Fernández, the head of the DAC, would proceed with great caution. Milans assured him that this would not be a problem because the one-time DAC commander, General Torres Rojas, would travel from La Coruña to Madrid to take command of the unit. Milans also assured Pardo Zancada that the plan enjoyed the support of the United States and the Vatican and had royal backing. The proof was that General Armada would be directing operations from La Zarzuela. Milans's confidence on these points can have derived only from assurances given by Armada and possibly Cortina. Certainly, according to his later account, before Pardo Zancada set off back to Madrid, he was present while Milans spoke to Armada on the telephone. Armada apparently said, as he had the night before to Tejero, that he would be in La Zarzuela on the following day because the King was 'fickle'. Pardo Zancada was thoroughly alarmed by the utter precipitation of events, not least by the fact that key players in the plan, like Torres Rojas, had still not been informed of the role expected of them. The consequent level of improvisation would seriously hamper the coup. That was also the principal concern of the DAC's Chief of Staff, Colonel José Ignacio San Martín, when later that night, Pardo Zancada, back in Madrid, told him about what had been arranged in Valencia.[54]

Nevertheless, Monday 23 February seemed to start well enough for the conspirators. Milans del Bosch, splendidly attired in his Lieutenant-General's uniform, sporting all his many decorations, arrived early at his office and began work on his declaration of martial law. Its text revealed his belief that what he was doing would win the approval of the King. He also told the senior officers of his military region that the outcome of the operation would be a government presided by General Armada, with his own promotion to be President of the Joint Chiefs of Staff. Meanwhile, Lieutenant-Colonel Tejero was anxiously checking that he could count on sufficient Civil Guards for the assault on the Cortes and enough buses to get them there.

The most crucial events, however, took place in relation to the DAC. Pardo Zancada had managed to contact the Military Governor of La Coruña, General Torres Rojas, who informed his immediate superior, the Captain-General of the Eighth Military Region, Galicia, General Manuel Fernández Posse, that he had to go to Madrid on legal business. As Torres Rojas headed to the capital to take control of the DAC, its own commander, General José Juste Fernández, accompanied by San Martín, was *en route* to Zaragoza to attend manoeuvres being carried out by three units of the division. Their first stop was the headquarters of the Parachute Brigade (BRIPAC) in Alcalá de Henares to attend a ceremony celebrating the 27th anniversary of its foundation. Colonel San Martín hoped to see General Armada there and get confirmation of what he had been told the night before by Pardo Zancada – that Juan Carlos was behind the coup and that Armada would be directing operations from La Zarzuela. In the event, no meeting took place because, not having brought the correct uniform for this ceremony, San Martín and Juste were unable to go in. After waiting in vain for uniforms to be brought from Madrid, they continued on their journey towards Zaragoza. They stopped for lunch at the parador of Santa María de Huerta, between Medinaceli and Calatayud.

That is when things began to go wrong. San Martín had arranged with Pardo Zancada that he would find an excuse to return to Madrid to be close to the unfolding events. Now at Santa María de Huerta, San Martín telephoned the DAC headquarters at Brunete and learned that, as planned, Torres Rojas had arrived. Accordingly, San Martín told Juste merely that something unexpected had happened in Brunete, which could not be fully explained on the telephone and that, in consequence, they must return to Madrid. When they arrived at about 5.30 p.m., Juste was surprised to find Torres Rojas present and even more startled to discover that Pardo Zancada had called a meeting of senior officers. At the meeting, Pardo Zancada and San Martín announced that the DAC had to take part in a great patriotic operation that would resolve the political situation. Juste Fernández and his second-in-command, General Joaquín Yusti Vázquez, were thoroughly alarmed. However, their doubts were eased somewhat when they were told that the operation was being coordinated by General Milans del Bosch in collaboration with the Captain-General of Madrid. They were even more reassured to be told that the plan enjoyed the approval of both the King and the Queen and would be overseen from La Zarzuela by General Armada. Orders were then given for the DAC to occupy key points of Madrid.[55]

Meanwhile, the second vote of investiture for Calvo Sotelo was just beginning at the Cortes. After the failure on 20 February, this time only a simple majority was required. At 6.23 p.m., about 320 Civil Guards under Lieutenant-Colonel Tejero arrived at the Cortes. Tejero jumped from the first bus, waving his pistol and shouting, 'In the name of the King!' Approximately half the Civil Guards entered the Cortes. As he ran up the stairs, Tejero loudly repeated that he was acting on the orders of the King and General Milans del Bosch. The Civil Guards who burst into the chamber took hostage the government ministers and all of the nation's parliamentary deputies. General Gutiérrez Mellado bravely confronted the armed intruders and ordered them to leave. He was violently jostled and Adolfo Suárez courageously went to his assistance. Felipe González, Alfonso Guerra, the deputy leader of the PSOE, Santiago Carrillo, Gutiérrez Mellado, Suárez and Agustín Rodríguez Sahagún were locked in a bitterly cold room where they were obliged to remain in silence until the following morning. Tejero telephoned Milans del Bosch. His message was brief and incriminating: 'General. All quiet. Everything in order. Everything in order. All quiet.' Tejero then returned to the chamber where one of his men announced the imminent arrival of 'the competent authority, military of course' who would decide what happened next. This was later assumed to be the 'white elephant' referred to by Cortina in his conversation with Tejero. There has been immense speculation about the identity of this person. It was surely a reference to Armada – after all, he would be the person who would eventually fulfil this role. Moreover, with his large ears, baggy eyes and elongated nose, he had the look of a benevolent, if somewhat lugubrious, pachyderm.[56]

At 6.45 p.m., Milans del Bosch declared a state of emergency in the Valencian region. He ordered the Military Governor, General Luis Caruana y Gómez de Barreda, to take over the offices of the Civil Governor. On Milans's instructions, every 15 minutes, the local radio broadcast the proclamation that he had prepared that same morning. It began with the preamble, 'In the light of events in the capital and the consequent vacuum of power, it is my duty to guarantee order in the military region under my command until I receive instructions from His Majesty the King.' The unauthorized use of his name especially offended Juan Carlos. The proclamation ordered the militarization of all public service personnel, imposed a nine o'clock curfew and banned all political activities. Tanks took up positions alongside important public buildings. In the offices of trade unions and political parties, frantic efforts were made to destroy membership files and documents that might have facilitated a purge by the ultra-right. When the news reached the Basque Country, cars flooded across the border into France.[57]

As the DAC units were preparing to leave Brunete, the naturally cautious General Juste Fernández was still profoundly uneasy. He was particularly suspicious about Pardo Zancada's assurance that the Queen enthusiastically supported the coup. As military attaché in Rome in April 1967, he had been at Fiumicino Airport to meet the then Princess Sofía who was *en route* to Madrid from Athens where her brother King Constantine had just been overthrown by a military coup. Their conversation that night left him totally convinced that she would never approve of a military coup in Spain. However, he was concerned that if he openly opposed San Martín and Torres Rojas, he might simply be taken prisoner. Nevertheless, he managed to slip away and telephone the

Captain-General of Madrid, Guillermo Quintana Lacaci. Deeply conservative but fiercely loyal to the King, Quintana Lacaci would be one of the keys to the dismantling of the coup. He assured Juste that he was certainly not in touch with Milans del Bosch. Juste also managed to contact La Zarzuela and spoke to General Sabino Fernández Campo, a close friend. After discussing the difficulties of the situation, Juste said, 'But isn't Alfonso there?' Sabino, surprised, replied, 'He isn't here, he hasn't been here and he isn't expected.' The King, far from awaiting Armada or even news of what he had planned in his name, had just been changing to play squash with his friends Ignacio (Nachi) Caro and Miguel Arias, the owner of the skiing resort of Baqueira. Their preparations had been interrupted by Fernández Campo, who told the King about the dramatic news being reported on the radio. When Juste was told that Armada was not present, he had replied, 'That changes everything.' The DAC units were stood down. Torres Rojas did not interfere until he was ordered to return to La Coruña. Juste's neutralization of the DAC virtually guaranteed the eventual failure of the coup.[58]

After the first moments of drama, the Catalan Socialist, Anna Balletbó, managed to persuade the Civil Guards inside the Cortes to let her leave. She was four months pregnant with twins and thus wearing a maternity dress. Following some difficulty with the young guards outside, she managed to reach the nearby offices of the three Socialist parliamentary groups in Marqués de Cubas shortly before 7 p.m. Having telephoned home to arrange for her children to be taken to the house of relatives, and started arrangements for the Socialist Party to return to clandestinity in the event of the coup being successful, she decided that she must speak to the King. It turned out to be difficult to get the right number – at first, her secretary was given the number of the Teatro de la Zarzuela. It then occurred to her to ring Jordi Pujol. When she finally got through to him, the President of the Generalitat, who knew what was happening, was astonished that she had escaped and, at first, puzzled as to why she wanted to talk to the King. When it dawned on him, he said, 'It's a good idea. I'll ring him as well.'

When Anna Balletbó got through to La Zarzuela, which must have been at about 7.15 p.m., she asked for the Marqués de Mondéjar. When he realized who she was, he immediately put her through to the King. After her initial account, Juan Carlos immediately began to bombard her with questions about what she had seen, who were the officers in the Cortes, if she recognized them, what ranks they held, how many, if there were any wounded. He also commented, 'Someone has got nervous and has jumped the gun,' from which it might be deduced that he had good intelligence about what was likely to happen but had expected it still to be gestating for considerable time. Anna Balletbó asked him what he planned to do, and he replied with the phrase, 'The King is at the service of the highest interests of Spain.' When she replied, 'And?', he went on, 'And of democracy.' While they were speaking, he interrupted to say, 'Sorry, they're calling me from various military headquarters. Don't hang up.' After their conversation, Anna spent much of the night at various radio and TV stations broadcasting the message that the King was totally committed to the defence of democracy.[59]

The frenzied operation to dismantle the coup was coordinated from La Zarzuela by the track-suited King who contributed his authority and courage and Sabino Fernández Campo who was the decisive strategist. Key roles were played by the Marqués de Mondéjar and the head of the King's military household, General Joaquín Valenzuela. They were helped in manning the telephones by Manuel Prado y Colón de Carvajal, the King's close friend and now informal ambassador at large, who had carried out crucial missions for him in the past. The Queen and Prince Felipe were present throughout. Juan Carlos's squash opponents, Miguel Arias and Nachi Caro stayed on, glued to television and radio in search of useful information. The telephone lines were jammed by calls to and from military units and local authorities all over Spain, from politicians and foreign leaders offering help.[60]

There were three centres of action under the overall supervision of the King's office. Even before the call from Anna Balletbó, Juan Carlos had spoken to the highly competent Francisco Laína García, Director of State Security. To give the lie to the conspirators' claim about a 'vacuum of power', Sabino Fernández Campo suggested, and the King approved, the improvised creation of a provisional government consisting of the secretaries of state and under-secretaries of each ministry under the direction of Laína in the Ministry of the Interior. The members of the Joint Chiefs of Staff (JUJEM) – the President, General Ignacio Alfaro Arregui, and the Army, Navy and Air Force Chiefs of Staff – General José Gabeiras Montero, Admiral Luis Arévalo Pelluz and General Emiliano Alfaro Arregui – had initially assumed that they would take total control of the operation. However, the King realized that this would be to acknowledge the military's right to intervene in politics. Accordingly, the JUJEM was subordinate to the civilian government of under-secretaries and essentially given the job of controlling the major military nerve centres.

A communiqué was issued to reassure the country at large and to undermine the claims being made by General Milans. It stated that, since the government was being held hostage, the under-secretaries of each ministry: 'have gone into permanent session, on the instructions of His Majesty the King, to ensure the government of the country through civilian channels. They are in close contact with the Joint Chiefs of Staff who are similarly in continuous session.' The allegations of the conspirators that the King was involved in the conspiracy were rendered laughable by the statement that: 'Those who now assume full civil and military powers in Spain, on a temporary basis and under the direction and authority of His Majesty the King, can guarantee their fellow citizens that no act of violence will destroy the democratic coexistence that the people freely desire and which is enshrined in the text of the constitution that both civilians and the military have sworn to uphold.'[61]

The third centre of operations was established in the sumptuous Hotel Palace slightly down the hill of the Carrera de San Jerónimo from the Cortes. A command centre was quickly set up consisting of the Director General of the Civil Guard, General José Aramburu Topete, the Inspector General of the police, General José Saenz de Santamaría, and the head of the Madrid police, Colonel Félix Alcalá Galiano, and the Civil Governor of Madrid,

Mariano Nicolás. At various points, as Aramburu tried to reassert control over the Civil Guard, he was frustrated by the disingenuous claim that they were acting in the name of the King. In fact, Sabino Fernández Campo had also managed to speak briefly to Tejero by telephone and tell him that it was utterly untrue that the King supported his action. Tejero simply slammed down the receiver. At around 7.30 p.m., Colonel Alcalá Galiano entered the Cortes and was told by Tejero that his operation had been ordered by the King and General Milans del Bosch. While they argued, Aramburu crossed the road to the Cortes and tried single-handedly to make Tejero surrender. Tejero's response was, 'Before surrendering, first I'll kill you and then shoot myself.' Shortly afterwards, Laína managed to speak to Tejero and demanded that he surrender before special forces (GEO) were sent in. Tejero replied that he obeyed orders only from Milans del Bosch and Armada, thereby alerting Aramburu and Laína to the involvement of the latter.[62]

Meanwhile, La Zarzuela was a cauldron of telephonic activity. Juan Carlos, Fernández Campo, Mondéjar and Valenzuela were engaged in a frenetic battle to reassure political authorities around Spain, to clinch foreign support and to secure the loyalty of the Captains-General of the other military regions. From the first moment, they were able to count on the loyalty and assistance of Gabeiras Montero and of Guillermo Quintana Lacaci. Shortly after the King's initial conversation with Laína, Sabino Fernández Campo spoke to the Chief of the Army General Staff, Gabeiras Montero, and explained to him his suspicions about Armada. After an abortive attempt to persuade Milans to withdraw his troops, Gabeiras went to join the other members of the Joint Chiefs of Staff. It had initially been feared that Milans might have already gained crucial support by convincing his colleagues that there was royal backing for the *Solución Armada*. There was certainly much dithering and ambiguity as some Captains-General remained in contact throughout the night with Milans as well as with Quintana Lacaci and La Zarzuela. If the King had been prepared to abandon the constitution, there is little doubt that the Captains-General would happily have brought their troops out into the streets. In that sense, only he stood between Spanish democracy and its destruction.

Juan Carlos's task was rendered slightly easier by some early declarations of loyalty and support, most crucially from Quintana Lacaci. The Captain-General of the Sixth Military Region, Burgos, Luis Polanco Mejorada, also swiftly phoned La Zarzuela to declare his obedience to his Commander-in-Chief. Antonio Delgado Álvarez of the Ninth Region, Granada, was completely loyal. Once it was clear that Polanco was with the King, Manuel Fernández Posse, of the Eighth Military Region, Galicia, was also quick to declare his loyalty. Others were more doubtful. Antonio Pascual Galmés, the Captain-General of the Fourth Military Region, Catalonia, ultimately did remain loyal but provoked some concern. Quintana Lacaci regarded him as 'problematic'. In fact, at 11.20 p.m., Pascual Galmés telephoned Jordi Pujol to sound him out about a solution involving General Armada.[63]

Jesús González del Yerro, Captain-General of the Canary Islands, known to be a hardline reactionary, stood by his oath of loyalty to the King and the constitution. This reflected his long-term rivalry with Milans del Bosch. In the notes that he took in the course of the night, Quintana Lacaci noted about González del Yerro: 'Doubts. When he heard of Milans' role and that Armada wanted to be Prime Minister, he declared himself loyal. He asked why Armada and not another soldier [he meant himself].' Juan Carlos himself recalled that González del Yerro responded by saying, 'I will obey Your Majesty's orders, but it's a pity . . .' That he obeyed at all was a tribute to the authority enjoyed by Juan Carlos as Commander-in-Chief of the Armed Forces. González del Yerro's stance was to have considerable influence in inclining other doubtful Captains-General to adopt an attitude of wait-and-see.[64]

During the previous months, the Captain-General of the Fifth Military Region, Zaragoza, Antonio Elícegui Prieto, had held several meetings with the officers under his command and made clear his conviction that the Army should be ready to intervene to prevent further terrorism and separatism. Now, according to Quintana Lacaci's notes, 'He kept calling me to see what I was going to do, since "something ought to be done".' Laína knew Elícegui from his own period as Civil Governor of Zaragoza, and now pressured him to remain neutral while Milans urged him to join the coup. Only after considerable hesitation did Elícegui Prieto declare for the crown. The known ultra, Pedro Merry Gordon, Captain-General of the Second Region, Seville, was thought to be on the verge of taking tanks into the streets of the Andalusian capital. However, he drank too much Chivas Regal after dinner and was indisposed for much of the night. General Gustavo Urrutia, the Chief of his General Staff, and the Military and Civil Governors of Seville, General Manuel Esquivías Franco and José María Sanz Pastor, ensured that the Second Region remained loyal. The attitude of Ángel Campano López, Captain-General of the Third Region, Valladolid, did not inspire confidence. However, the shrewd intervention of his Chief of Staff, Colonel Rafael Gómez-Rico, and the Military and Civil Governors of the city, General Manuel María Mejía Lequerica and Román Ledesma, imposed caution on Campano. The King never managed to speak to the Captain-General of the Balearic Islands, Manuel de la Torre Pascual, a friend of Milans. However, Quintana Lacaci was convinced that he was merely 'waiting to see what happens, would happily join Milans'. De la Torre had prepared a proclamation similar to that issued by Milans and came near to broadcasting it.[65]

Perhaps the most crucial telephone conversation of the night was that between Sabino Fernández Campo and José Gabeiras Montero. Armada had been present, in his capacity as deputy Chief of Staff. The King then asked to speak with him and Armada offered to go to La Zarzuela to help deal with the crisis. Juan Carlos's instinctive reaction was to welcome this offer from his friend and mentor. Had he done so, it would have put Armada in the perfect position from which to control events while giving the impression that the King approved. However, Sabino Fernández Campo signalled for Juan Carlos to stall Armada and, while the King kept his hand over the receiver, managed to tell him about the earlier conversation with Juste. Thus alerted to Armada's involvement, Juan Carlos ordered him to remain at his post. Once

Gabeiras left to join the Joint Chiefs of Staff, Armada was in charge of the General Staff. He had to play a double role, giving the impression that he was trying to control the situation and yet looking for the opportunity to offer himself as the solution. To this end, he had a conversation with General Aramburu Topete and again offered to go and speak with Tejero, whom he claimed not to know. He contacted the various Captains-General to check on the situation and, at around 9.30 p.m., finally received a call from Milans del Bosch, who was anxious to know why he was not at La Zarzuela.

Given that there were witnesses, Armada spoke ambiguously. He managed to convey to the listeners the impression that, to his surprise, Milans was suggesting that he go to the Cortes and try to form a coalition government. Armada asked Milans to check out the response of the other Captains-General to this proposal. He then gave those present his version of the rest of the telephone conversation. Claiming to be highly dubious about the 'Milans proposal', he said that, if it was the only solution, he was prepared to give it a try. He again contacted La Zarzuela, speaking first with Sabino Fernández Campo, and saying that such a solution had to be attempted in order to avoid a massacre. Fernández Campo said, 'It's a ludicrous idea!' and instructed him to do nothing. When Fernández Campo questioned whether the parliamentary deputies would vote for him, Armada replied with utter confidence, 'Of course they'll vote for me!' Fernández Campo pointed out that, even if they did, such a vote given under duress would be valueless and said, 'As your friend, I beg you not to go there.' The King, who had been following the conversation, came on the line and said, 'I think you've gone mad.' Armada then telephoned the JUJEM and spoke to General Ignacio Alfaro Arregui, who also responded in much the same way. Shortly afterwards, he spoke to Gabeiras when he had returned to the General Staff headquarters and made the same suggestion without mentioning that the King had already rejected it. Gabeiras reaffirmed that the King would not accept such a solution.[66]

One of the key problems facing La Zarzuela during the night would be communication with the Third Military Region,

Valencia. Juan Carlos would eventually speak to Milans del Bosch on three occasions during the course of the crisis. The first would not be until approximately 10.30 p.m. When he demanded to know why Tejero was proclaiming that he was acting on the King's orders, Milans replied with fervent declarations of loyalty and assurances that he had brought his troops out only because of the 'power vacuum' in Madrid. The King then ordered him to withdraw his units from the streets, to oblige Tejero to surrender and to abandon any pretence that he was acting on royal authority. In the event, Milans would be extremely slow to obey.[67]

It had quickly occurred to the King and those who accompanied him in La Zarzuela that he should address the nation. However, the radio and television broadcasting studios at Prado del Rey had been taken over at 7.48 p.m. by a small renegade unit of communication engineers from the DAC led by Captain Martínez de Merlo. They insisted that the radio broadcast only military marches and were outraged when the Director General of the Radio, Eduardo Sotillos, responded with Baroque marches. A message was sent from La Zarzuela to the Director General of RTVE to send a mobile unit for the King to speak to the nation. With armed men in the principal offices, the Director General, Fernando Castedo, was unable to obey the request for some time. At 9.00 p.m., the Marqués de Mondéjar managed to speak to Captain Martínez de Merlo's commanding officer, Colonel Joaquín Valencia Remón, whom he knew. Mondéjar persuaded him to issue orders for Martínez de Merlo to withdraw his men from Prado del Rey. After considerable delay, he did so and, by 9.20 p.m., the occupiers had left.[68] Mobile units were then prepared. Since there was danger of being intercepted on the road to La Zarzuela, two separate units were sent in vehicles that did not carry the logo of RTVE. They arrived at 11.35 p.m. While an improvised studio was set up, Sabino Fernández Campo wrote the text to be recorded by the King who had changed from his tracksuit into the uniform of Captain-General. Since all concerned were reluctant to risk returning to Prado del Rey, the tape had then to be taken to a retransmission centre, known as La Bola del Mundo, near Barajas Airport.[69]

For Armada, the events in the Cortes constituted the '*Supuesto Anticonstitucional Máximo*' (Greatest Hypothetical Threat to the Constitution). The seizing of the entire political élite constituted the planned 'power vacuum' and thus provided the excuse for the actions of Milans del Bosch in Valencia and of the DAC in Madrid. At this point, Armada's offer to go to La Zarzuela would convince his fellow conspirators that the King was a party to the plot. When that possibility was blocked by Sabino Fernández Campo and the King, his next hope was to appear to acquiesce in the solution apparently just suggested by Milans. He would make a 'patriotic sacrifice', go to the Cortes, and persuade Tejero to release the Cortes deputies and, at a stroke, resolve the wider political situation by offering to form a government. Obviously, all of this had to be done without him ever seeming to have played any part in initiating the coup. It was a dangerous and ambiguous game. Armada may have had no intention of betraying Milans but there is little doubt that he was cunningly exploiting the blindly fanatical Tejero, for whom he can have felt little but patrician contempt. For the plan to work, the plebeian Tejero would have to be sacrificed as the 'spontaneous' madman who had provoked the crisis.

Behind Armada's behaviour was a strange mixture of hubris and paternalism which led him to believe that he could both interpret the unspoken wishes of Juan Carlos and then present himself to his brother officers as the King's spokesman.[70] The utter conviction of both Milans and Tejero that their actions had the King's approval can have come only from Armada. Armada seems to have been genuinely convinced that the parliamentary deputies, grateful for his intervention, would vote for his plan for an all-party government of national salvation. He may then have fulfilled his promise to make Milans del Bosch President of the Joint Chiefs of Staff but there could be no explaining away his previous contact with Tejero who would have to be persuaded to flee Spain or else be tried and imprisoned. The cunning of Armada's double game may be deduced from the fact that he was always careful never to meet more than one of the conspirators at a time. The consequent lack of witnesses would always enable him to claim to have had nothing to do with the plot and to present his 'solution' as a disinterested gesture.

Despite being refused royal approval to go to the Cortes, Armada had continued to argue with Gabeiras. His chance came as Tejero made it clear to the committee operating from the Hotel Palace that Armada was the only mediator other than the King himself with whom he would talk. Aramburu Topete informed Gabeiras of this. With Armada insisting that a massacre was likely, Gabeiras, after consulting La Zarzuela once more, finally gave him permission to go to the Cortes but for the sole purpose of trying to negotiate the surrender of Tejero. Both Sabino Fernández Campo and Gabeiras believed that it was essential to establish some kind of contact with Tejero to avert bloodshed. It has been claimed that Gabeiras sent Armada on his way with the words, 'At your orders, Prime Minister,' which may simply have been an ironic or frivolous reference to Armada's plan.[71] It may have been something more. After all, there is little doubt that, if Armada had put his scheme to the Cortes and it had been accepted by the deputies (a not impossible hypothesis), most senior military figures, even those utterly loyal to Juan Carlos, would have approved.

Armada reached the Hotel Palace at about midnight. Those present, Mariano Nicolás, the Civil Governor of Madrid, General Aramburu and General Saenz de Santamaría, were unsure about the basis on which he proposed to talk to Tejero but all were anxious to prevent a bloodbath. Armada entered the Cortes at 12.30 a.m. on the morning of 24 February and spoke to Tejero for nearly an hour. He explained that he proposed to address the deputies and offer them the solution of a government of national salvation under his own premiership. Tejero would then withdraw the Civil Guards and he and the ringleaders would be flown to wherever they wished, presumably to some South American dictatorship. As the next step in this 'constitutional solution', the Cortes would put the proposal to the King. Unfortunately for Armada, Tejero was outraged by the specifics of a proposed cabinet list that contained Socialists and Communists and quickly perceived that the offer of safe conduct abroad meant that he was to be the sacrificial lamb to justify Armada's actions. If Armada was the man who was saving the situation, then Tejero was the criminal. It has been argued that, if Tejero and Armada had met before, there would have been no disagreement. Given General Armada's capacity for ambiguity, it is perfectly possible that he had let Tejero assume that the deal was for a Pinochet-style junta that would crush the left and revoke regional autonomies. Nevertheless, in the midst of their heated argument, Armada suggested that Tejero speak with Milans del Bosch. Tejero did so and was flabbergasted when Milans, as might have been expected, told him to accept Armada's proposal. Since their earlier conversations, it had perhaps occurred to Tejero that a bland compromise government acceptable to the majority in the Cortes was the kind of government that would almost certainly want to try him for his crime.[72]

The coup had definitively failed when Tejero rejected Armada, although another ten and a half hours of tension would be necessary to secure the final surrender of Tejero and the release of the deputies. The nation as a whole breathed a sigh of relief when Juan Carlos appeared on television at 1.15 a.m. on 24 February. Given the hectic nature of what was going on, the delay was not as surprising or as sinister as has been subsequently claimed. There have been suggestions that the delay was because La Zarzuela was waiting to see the outcome of Armada's visit to the Cortes.[73] In fact, the decisive broadcast began while Armada was still crossing the road from the Cortes to the Hotel Palace. Moreover, Juan Carlos's declaration referred to the crucial measures that he had taken three hours earlier. He announced that he had sent the Captains-General the following order: 'Faced with the situation created by the events that have unfolded in the Cortes and to avoid any possible confusion, I confirm that I have ordered the civilian authorities and the JUJEM to take all necessary measures to maintain the constitutional order within existing legality. Any measure of a military character that might be necessary will require the approval of the JUJEM.' He ended with the words: 'The crown, symbol of the permanence and unity of the Fatherland, cannot tolerate any actions or attitudes by those who aim to interrupt by force the democratic process determined by the popularly ratified Constitution.' It is interesting to note that the *golpistas* insisted, during the coup and later during their trial, that they were acting on the orders of the King, yet took absolutely no notice of the real orders of the King given both individually to them and during the broadcast.[74]

The King's message to the Captains-General had been telexed at 10.35 p.m. although it was not received until nearly midnight in Valencia. Shortly before it was sent, Juan Carlos was finally able to speak to Milans del Bosch and repeated that he opposed the coup, that he would not abdicate nor abandon Spain and that in order to prevail the rebels would have to shoot him. The King told Milans that a telex was on its way and that he would soon be speaking on television. A further telex from La Zarzuela at about 1.45 a.m. confirmed the message in unequivocal terms: 'I tell you the following in the clearest possible terms. 1. I affirm my firm decision to maintain the constitutional order within existing legality. After this message, I cannot turn back. 2. Any coup d'état cannot hide behind the King, it is against the King. 3. Today more than ever, I am ready to fulfil my oath to the flag. Therefore, with full responsibility and thinking only of Spain, I order you to withdraw all the units that you have mobilized. 4. I order you to tell Tejero to desist immediately. 5. I swear that I will neither abdicate the crown nor abandon Spain. Whoever rebels is ready to provoke a new civil war and will bear responsibility for doing so. 6. I do not doubt my generals' love of Spain. First for Spain and then for the Crown, I order you to obey all that I have told you.' The phrase 'I cannot turn back' provoked subsequent speculation about the King's involvement. However, it was merely the consequence, in the midst of the crisis, of hurried drafting by the King's aide-de-camp, Major Agustín Muñoz-Grandes Galilea.[75]

Shortly after the King's broadcast, the Military Governor of Valencia, General Luis Caruana y Gómez, was ordered by Gabeiras to arrest Milans del Bosch. Milans threatened to shoot Caruana. As tension rose, the second call from the King was put through to Milans. He repeated what he said earlier and told Milans that any further delay in obeying the orders to withdraw his troops would be regarded as mutiny. Milans said that he would follow the King's instructions but pointed out that he no longer had any control over Tejero. He issued orders for his troops to return to barracks although the streets of Valencia were not entirely empty until after 4.30 a.m. At about 2.30 a.m., Milans received the third telephone call from La Zarzuela. The King demanded to know why his orders had still not been obeyed and insisted that the proclamation with which Milans had originally brought his troops out be rescinded. Within an hour, Milans issued a new proclamation, stressing his loyalty to the King and recognizing that there was no longer any need for a military presence in the streets.[76]

One reason for the prolongation of the crisis was that, after the King had been seen on television, Major Pardo Zancada arrived with a column of military police to join Tejero. Seeing things going wrong, he had decided, as the bulk of the country's senior *golpistas* did not, that he should stand by his commitments. Paradoxically, although his presence prolonged the crisis, his authority over the other occupiers may also have helped avoid a bloodbath. An effort was made in the early hours of the morning to secure his surrender. At the suggestion of Major Agustín Muñoz-Grandes Galilea, Colonel San Martín was sent to him at 3.30 a.m. but Pardo refused his entreaties. At that point, two of Pardo's friends tried to take a hand. Knowing Major Muñoz-Grandes Galilea, they rang him at La Zarzuela and discussed a possible intercession by one of them, Lieutenant-Colonel Eduardo Fuentes Gómez Salazar. In consequence, at 9.00 a.m. the following morning, a surrender was arranged by Eduardo Fuentes. Hammered out on the bonnet of one of the Land Rovers in which Pardo Zancada's column had arrived, it was later known as '*el pacto del capó*' (the bonnet/hood pact). Pardo insisted on being allowed to leave and hand himself over at his own unit and on immunity for his subordinates. Tejero also took full responsibility for his own actions but insisted that Armada come to receive the surrender, perhaps to show him in the most humiliating fashion that he had lost. Pardo Zancada and Tejero left the Cortes shortly after midday on 24 February, followed by the Cortes deputies.[77]

When news of the surrender was communicated to La

Zarzuela, Sabino Fernández Campo thought that it must be about midnight. He was astonished when he looked at his watch and discovered that it was in fact 12 hours later. Such had been the whirlwind of activity that had occupied him over the last 17 and a half hours.[78]

The military conspirators believed, on the basis of what they had been told by Armada, that Juan Carlos was behind the 'Solución Armada'. Subsequently, the accusation has been frequently repeated.[79] There is little doubt that, if the King had been involved, the coup would have succeeded. However, even leaving aside the obvious counter-argument about the role of the King in dismantling the coup of 23 February, there is another equally powerful reason for dismissing these accusations. The first ten days of February had given Juan Carlos the perfect opportunity to set up the Solución Armada. There is every reason to suppose that the bulk of the politicians consulted by the King would have supported the idea of a coalition government. If that is what the King had wanted, he could have secured his objective without the risks and ignominy of a military coup. Moreover, the idea that the King was involved is difficult to sustain in the light of Armada's anger on 13 February, expressed to General Gutiérrez Mellado, at his failure to persuade Juan Carlos to reconsider his decision to recommend the appointment of Calvo Sotelo as Prime Minister. Armada's anger was replicated after his abortive conversation with Tejero in the Cortes. At 2 a.m. on 24 February, Armada told Francisco Laína in heated terms that the King was wrong to have interfered in a matter that concerned only the Armed Forces: 'The King has made a mistake, the King has compromised the crown by divorcing himself from the Armed Forces, this is a military affair which we must resolve amongst soldiers, a solution must be found.'[80] The idea of collusion is also undermined by the unrestrained manner with which, a decade later, Juan Carlos condemned the treachery of Armada: 'It is infinitely sad to learn that a man in whom I had placed my trust for many years should betray me with such perfidy.'[81]

In the evening of 24 February, Juan Carlos received Adolfo Suárez, Felipe González, Agustín Rodríguez Sahagún, Santiago

Carrillo and Manuel Fraga at La Zarzuela. Believing Armada's presence at the end of the crisis to signify that he had played a part in securing the release of the deputies, Suárez said, 'I was wrong about Armada and Your Majesty was right.' Juan Carlos replied, 'No, Adolfo, you were right. Armada is a traitor.' It is a moot point whether Armada was a traitor or was guilty of extreme loyalty, acting on the assumption that he knew better than the King.

The extent to which the success or failure of the coup had been in the hands of Juan Carlos was underlined a few days later. When the new Minister of Defence, Alberto Oliart, called in the Captains-General to hear their versions of what happened on 23–24 February, the first to see him was Guillermo Quintana Lacaci. The Captain-General of Madrid said, 'Minister, before sitting down, I must tell you that I am a Francoist, that I adore the memory of General Franco. For eight years I was a colonel in his personal guard. I wear this military medal that I won in Russia. I fought in the Civil War. So you can well imagine my way of thinking. But the Caudillo gave me the order to obey his successor and the King ordered me to stop the coup on 23 February. If he had ordered me to assault the Cortes, I would have done so.'[82]

In November 1981, Quintana Lacaci made the same point in public when he delivered a speech at the end of military manoeuvres in Zaragoza. In response to accusations of the King's involvement in the so-called '23-F', Quintana declared, 'Many in the media have tried to implicate his Majesty the King. On this issue, gentlemen, I am an exceptional witness: a few moments after the storming of the Congress, I received a phone call from His Majesty King Juan Carlos, asking me how things were going and whether I had people under control. I told him that I did and he told me to keep them in their barracks.' To emphasize the extent to which it was the King's stance that saved the situation on 23 February, he said, 'Gentlemen, if, on that day, my King, my Captain-General of the Armed Forces, had told me to go out into the streets, I would have jumped to attention and gone out into the streets.'[83]

The defeat of the coup did not resolve the democratic regime's outstanding difficulties. This point was made by Juan Carlos on 24 February when he told the five political leaders that 'things could have gone either way'. He told them, as an illustration, that when the Marqués de Mondéjar had ordered Colonel Valencia Remón to instruct his men to leave Prado del Rey, he had replied, 'I obey your orders but what a chance we're missing here to impose order in Spain.' The King then read out a formal message to the assembled political leaders. It mixed paternal wisdom with personal exasperation, making it clear that, having been obliged to place his personal prestige and safety at risk, he had every right to suggest that it was time for Spain's political class to demonstrate greater moderation and prudence. In particular, he requested that they make every effort to ensure that the Spanish people did not assume the entire Army to be *golpistas*.[84]

In retrospect, the speech underlined the extent to which 23 February marked a turning point not only in the transition to democracy but also in the role of the King: 'I want to draw everyone's attention to the far-reaching implications of what happened. We cannot forget that even though the immediate problems that preoccupied us have been solved, we now have a delicate situation that must be faced with serenity and restraint ... The crown is proud to have served Spain steadfastly in the conviction that democracy and strict respect for constitutional principles is what the majority of the Spanish people want. However, everyone must look to their own responsibilities and be aware that the King cannot, and should not, be constantly taking responsibility for confronting circumstances of such tension and seriousness ... And, finally, I reiterate to all my call for loyal and unselfish collaboration, for you to put behind you secondary issues and unite in identifying the most serious and fundamental problems of the country so that we might consolidate our democracy within order, unity and peace.'[85] The first fruits of the King's exhortation to the politicians were harvested when, some hours after their release, the deputies returned to the Cortes. After a prolonged and heartfelt ovation for the King, they gave their approbation to Calvo Sotelo's investiture by a full majority of 186 votes to 158.

The real significance of the coup as far as the King was

concerned was revealed on 27 February. Three million people demonstrated across the cities of Spain in support of democracy and the King. In the evening, in pouring rain, one and a half million people marched through the capital, led by the leaders of Spain's major political parties. The crowds cheered, with equal enthusiasm, Carrillo and Fraga and all, including the most left-wing, shouted '¡Viva el Rey!' Fraga commented afterwards, 'I think that one should never use the clenched fist salute, but if it is done while shouting "Long Live the King" then it is acceptable.'[86]

On Saturday 28 February, the King made his first public appearance since the coup. He spoke at the Zaragoza military academy at the celebration of the 25th anniversary of the XIV promoción (the year in which Juan Carlos had entered the academy as a cadet). Despite the possibility of a negative reaction, the King insisted on attending. He was keen to be reunited with old friends and also to take the pulse of the middle-rank officers. Although there were many Civil Guard officers present, Juan Carlos and Sofía were the object of spontaneous applause. His speech was a warning to both the Army and to the political class. He told officers bluntly that 'thoughtless actions do nothing for the security of the State'. At the same time, he reminded the political class and the media to be careful about generating an atmosphere of discomfort, disquiet and concern within the Armed Forces. He called on the media not to 'apply analyses or moral sanction to an entire collectivity just because it contains those who believe erroneously that their precipitate impulses make them saviours of the Fatherland and that the only way forward is subversion and violence'. In the course of the ceremony, for the first time, the King made a solemn oath to uphold the constitution, which, in 1978, he had only signed.[87]

In his speech at Zaragoza, as in his message to the politicians, the King was laying down the guidelines for life in Spain after the coup of 23 February. It was a further call for civilians and soldiers alike to act with responsibility and patriotism. The applause with which the officers present greeted his words was a significant indication of the extent to which the Commander-in-Chief had acted in tune with the wishes of the majority of his men. That the

King had also interpreted the wishes of his people was graphically illustrated by the mass demonstrations in favour of democracy in Madrid and other cities. Because of the stance of *Herri Batasuna*, such unity was not possible in the Basque Country. The mood in most of Spain, however, was summed up in an article by the normally cynical commentator, Francisco Umbral, who wrote of the night of the 23-F, 'Whilst we Spaniards thought that we deserved something better than a king, it turns out that we have a king that we don't deserve.'[88] The King's own sense of exasperation was expressed in his later comment that, when speaking to the political leaders, what he had really wanted to say was: 'My job should not be that of a fireman always ready to put out a fire.'[89] The time was approaching when he could abandon that role, but it was still two years away.

ELEVEN

Living in the Long Shadow of Success
1981–2002

Juan Carlos had called on the political class to join in a spirit of post 23-F cooperation. In the words of Rodolfo Martín Villa: 'there was a kind of tacit armistice between all the political forces.'[1] The first fruit of this was the taciturn Leopoldo Calvo Sotelo's new cabinet, an attempt to distribute power evenly within UCD and thus create an image of harmony. However, the commitment to legalizing divorce of the Social Democrat Minister of Justice, Francisco Fernández Ordóñez, would eventually split the party, his position bitterly opposed by the Christian Democrats. In the short term, however, Juan Carlos's attention was concentrated on the Ministry of Defence. The first stage of the task of rooting out *golpismo* and rebuilding civil–military relations fell to a brilliant but little known lawyer, Alberto Oliart Saussol. A liberal, he quickly declared that his aim was to refine existing military legislation to make it subject to the constitution, a profoundly difficult and delicate task. However, in following the King's advice that the military should not bear blanket opprobrium as a result of the 23-F, Oliart would lay himself open to accusations that he was acquiescing in the military adjusting the constitution to its desires.

In a way that went far beyond the cabinet, the survival of democracy on the night of 23 February marked a new beginning. The mass demonstrations of 27 February marked the end of the *desencanto* (the disenchantment). The contempt for democracy shown by Tejero, Milans and Armada had the inadvertent effect of obliging the population as a whole to reassess the value of their democratic institutions. The change of mood was evident too in the offers made by Felipe González, Manuel Fraga and Santiago

Carrillo to support the government in the Cortes. Even ETA-PM announced an indefinite ceasefire. Juan Carlos's stand against *golpismo* had given Spanish democracy a second chance. The excessive expectations of 1977 had been stripped away by the years of terrorism and *golpismo* and there was a widespread acceptance that democracy was a deadly serious business, a matter of life and death for the entire nation. That, together with improvements in the international economic climate, heralded a brighter future. Unfortunately, the ongoing divisions in UCD ensured that Calvo Sotelo would not be the beneficiary of the new spirit of national cooperation.

Nevertheless, key elements of Calvo Sotelo's essentially moderate programme – entry into NATO, commitment to the market economy, reduction in the level of public expenditure, stimulation of private investment and wage restraint – would eventually contribute to controlling *golpismo* and improving the economic situation. With a view to appeasing the military, the bulk of the political élite also agreed that the relatively rapid progress towards regional autonomy should be slowed down. This led to an agreement between UCD and the PSOE for the elaboration of the notorious *Ley Orgánica para la Armonización del Proceso de las Autonomías*, LOAPA (Organic Law for the Harmonization of the Devolution Process), which aimed to limit the autonomous powers of all of the regions, especially Catalonia and the Basque Country. It was presented to the Cortes on 29 September 1981. Eventually, appeals made to the *Tribunal Constitucional* by the Basque and Catalan regional governments in 1982 managed in their turn to emasculate or at least freeze the LOAPA. Nevertheless, the existence of the LOAPA led to much speculation that the military was having some of the objectives of the 23-F handed to them on a plate. The same impression was given in April 1981 when the Army high command refused once more to readmit the democratic officers of the UMD to its ranks.

The element of the aftermath of the coup that most concerned the King was the trial of the *golpistas*. The fact that there were so few defendants and that they awaited trial in conditions of considerable physical comfort led to widespread comment that the military was getting off lightly and was, in some respects, the beneficiary rather than the scapegoat for the 23-F.[2] At the same time, the government, with the firm encouragement of Juan Carlos, began to press for rapid entry into NATO in the hope that the integration of the Spanish Armed Forces into the Western defence system would divert them from their constant readiness to interfere in domestic politics. This was interpreted in some circles as an indecent eagerness to appease the Armed Forces. The desire to curry favour with the military was understandable, since fear of what the Army might do was fuelled by the continuing terrorist activities of both ETA-M and GRAPO. The ceasefire offered by ETA-PM was not emulated by ETA-M.[3]

Calvo Sotelo revealed his determination to deal energetically with threats to democracy when his government presented to the Cortes a law for the defence of the constitution which permitted action to be taken against the press networks of both the bunker and ETA-M. This was followed by the announcement on 23 March of new measures to combat ETA. The Army was to be brought in to seal the Franco-Spanish frontier. A single anti-terrorist command was established in the Ministry of the Interior to coordinate the police, Civil Guards and the Army.[4] During the first three months of Calvo Sotelo's government, the post-23-F spirit of cooperation held firm amongst the political parties. Nevertheless, Calvo Sotelo faced the same problems as Suárez before him, ongoing terrorism and military subversion, while his party was being pulled apart by internal squabbling. The reappearance of GRAPO, one of whose gangs murdered the liberal General Andrés González de Suso on 4 May, underlined the coincidence of interest between terrorism and *golpismo*.

There was now, however, a new dimension in the wake of 23 February. The King himself was now a major target. On the morning of Thursday 7 May, in the Calle Conde de Peñalver in Madrid, an ETA-M *comando* placed a shrapnel bomb on the car of General Joaquín de Valenzuela. The explosion killed his aide-de-camp, Lieutenant-Colonel Guillermo Tevar Saco, his chauffeur, and a sergeant, wounded many passers-by and left Valenzuela gravely wounded. Ultra-rightists were quickly out on the streets chanting for military intervention and for the release of Tejero. The much-respected and immensely affable Valenzuela, the 68-year-old head of the King's military household, had worked closely with Juan Carlos for more than a quarter of a century, having been appointed as one of his teachers in January 1955. The King was devastated. However, the attempt on the life of Valenzuela suggested that, in ETA-M's determination to destroy Spanish democracy, Juan Carlos was also in their sights. The King must have taken some consolation from a remarkable action of mass solidarity in favour of democracy, recalling the demonstrations of 27 February. Two minutes' silence reigned in the streets, homes, universities and factories of Spain at midday on Friday 8 May.[5]

Nevertheless, the threat of *golpismo* had not gone away. Moreover, major efforts were being made to undermine the position of the King by leaks of statements by Tejero and others arrested after 23-F in which they claimed that he had been involved in the coup. On 21 June a series of arrests revealed that several rightist colonels had tried to organize another coup. Its ramifications emerged in the weeks following the arrest of Colonel Ricardo Garchitorena Zalba, who had been involved in the Tejero coup, Colonel Antonio Sicre Canut, a communications expert, and Major Ricardo Sáenz de Ynestrillas, who had been part of the *Operación Galaxia* in 1978. The idea behind the conspiracy was that a strategy of tension would be created by an escalating bombing campaign to be carried out by ultra-rightist militants. It was intended to culminate in Barcelona on 23 June at the Nou Camp football stadium where a huge Catalanist rally was scheduled. Simultaneously, the King would be seized and forced to abdicate. A military junta would be established. Blacklists of democrats to be liquidated had been drawn up.[6]

In part to soothe military sentiment, in July 1981, the Spanish monarchs declined, with great personal regret, to attend the wedding of Prince Charles and Lady Diana in response to the British decision that the couple's honeymoon should begin with them embarking on the royal yacht *Britannia* at Gibraltar. There can be no doubting the sincerity of Juan Carlos's unease at the continued

British presence in Gibraltar and, by refusing to attend the wedding, he was making an appeal to the more conservative sectors of Spanish civil society and, most importantly, of the Armed Forces. Certainly, the King's decision to put the interests of the Spanish State and national dignity above family commitments and links of friendship between royal families was widely praised in the Spanish media.[7]

Rumours of military conspiracies were apparently endless. However, Calvo Sotelo also had to face, as Suárez had done before him, the squabbling within his party. Both the right and the PSOE saw UCD as the obstacle to their own ambitions. Accordingly, Alfonso Osorio and *Coalición Democrática* were making efforts to attract the Christian Democrats of UCD and there was talk of a great right-wing coalition including Fraga's *Alianza Popular*. At the same time, the Socialists were attempting to pull Francisco Fernández Ordóñez into their orbit. UCD was crumbling and the PSOE was emerging as the inevitable alternative party of government. Felipe González consistently topped opinion polls as the nation's most popular leader, appearing approachable, sensible and open-minded in contrast with the gloomy image of Calvo Sotelo. The Socialists struck a chord with the nation in June when they unveiled their plan of action for the consolidation of democracy. The Socialist objective of a concerted battle against terrorism, the thorough-going investigation of 23-F and a moderate economic programme contrasted starkly with a UCD concerned less with the nation's problems than with its own internal haemorrhage. Throughout the autumn, UCD was rocked by effective Socialist attacks on the party's *desgobierno*. This was all the easier given the government's inept handling of the scandal over the sale of adulterated rapeseed oil (*aceite de colza*) as a result of which over 130 people had died.[8]

In October 1981, in search of external support for Spanish democracy, Juan Carlos and Sofía made an official visit to the United States. The main issue discussed during the visit was Spain's membership of NATO, an issue that Juan Carlos regarded as holding the key to eventual membership of the EEC and indeed to diverting the Spanish military from its obsession with domestic politics. In his private interview with President Ronald Reagan, Juan Carlos made no secret of his support for Spanish membership. Controversy was provoked in Spain, however, when the White House issued a statement to the effect that the King had expressed his personal commitment to NATO, thereby interfering with the political process. The Minister of Foreign Affairs, José Pedro Pérez Llorca, was obliged to make a public statement, five hours after the controversial interview with Reagan, clarifying that Juan Carlos had, throughout the interview, insisted on the fact that he was merely transmitting his government's views and that Spain's entry in NATO in any case depended on the outcome of the debate taking place at the Cortes at the time. Careful not to be seen as criticizing the King, the mainstream Spanish press blamed the incident on the US administration for its 'steamroller tactics' and the Spanish government for its slow reaction.[9]

On his return to Spain, the King found no slow-down in the deterioration of UCD. The scale of the party's decline was summed up by Adolfo Suárez, who commented: 'The scale of our deterioration is such that if we weren't all in UCD we wouldn't even vote for ourselves.'[10] In November, during a tour of Aragón, the King was sufficiently dismayed by the collapse of UCD to reiterate his rallying cry to the Spanish political class. Juan Carlos called on political leaders to avoid falling into the ineffectiveness that results from internecine struggles and from an obsession with their own political survival. His message was favourably received by González and Fraga but seems to have fallen on deaf ears within the UCD.[11] The Christian Democrats, Oscar Alzaga and Miguel Herrero Rodríguez de Miñon, were drawing ever closer to *Alianza Popular*. They refused posts in a cabinet reshuffle on 1 December which thus saw the government left significantly weaker. Rodolfo Martín Villa assumed the first Vice-Presidency and relinquished his responsibilities in the autonomy process. He was expected to oversee the reorganization of the party and prepare it for the next elections. It was an impossible task that fatally distracted him from the tasks of day-to-day government. He reflected in his memoirs that to accept the Vice-Presidency had been a serious error.[12]

The most disappointing feature of the cabinet was the continued presence at the Ministry of Defence of Alberto Oliart, since it was widely felt that he had demonstrated insufficient authority over the military. Consternation had greeted the appointment as Captain-General of Zaragoza on 20 August of General Luis Caruana y Gómez de Barreda, whose comportment as Military Governor in Valencia on the night of 23 February had been extremely ambiguous. Even greater astonishment had been provoked by the award of a medal for 'sufferings for the Fatherland' to General Milans del Bosch. Outrage greeted the imposition of a period of only one month's detention for his son, Captain Juan Milans del Bosch, for offensively insulting remarks made about his Commander-in-Chief, the King, to whom he referred as a 'useless pig'. On the same day, Colonel Alvaro Graiño Abeille was sentenced to two months' detention (reduced on appeal to one) for the offence of sending a letter to a newspaper warning of continued *golpismo* in the Armed Forces.[13]

Just as the country was gearing up for a major celebration of the anniversary of the approval of the constitution, military indiscipline, and its dimension of hostility to the person of the King, was disturbingly underlined by the reappearance of an ultra organization called the *Unión Militar Española* and the publication of an anti-constitutional manifesto signed by one hundred junior Army officers and NCOs, all stationed in Madrid, the so-called 'manifesto of one hundred'. It was an aggressively worded effort to build support for the 23-F plotters prior to their trial but it was also linked to the still festering coup being considered by a group of colonels. General Ignacio Alfaro Arregui, the President of the Joint Chiefs of Staff, reacted quickly to prevent the spread of revolt throughout the ranks. Five of the signatories – including Captain Blas Piñar, son of the leader of *Fuerza Nueva* – were arrested and all units were warned of the total prohibition of political statements by officers. Two days before its publication, José Antonio Girón de Velasco lunched with some of the more prominent signatories including Colonel Jesús Crespo Cuspineda of the DAC. In fact one of the principal authors, Crespo would later be arrested as the key man behind the revival of the colonels' coup planned to destroy the elections of October 1982. Oliart's declarations that there was nothing to worry about provoked Manuel Fraga to remark that the Ministry of Defence existed only on paper.[14]

The Minister of Defence's relaxed attitude contrasted with the determined display of authority by the King. Juan Carlos called a meeting of the Joint Chiefs of Staff (JUJEM) and issued a call for discipline in the Armed Forces.[15] Out of this meeting came a decision to replace the JUJEM in its entirety. The official explanation given was that, with many of its members coming up for retirement, total renewal was the only way to guarantee a coherent team to work together to oversee entry into NATO. Another view was that the JUJEM's authority was somewhat flawed after 23-F and that a fresh team would be needed to restore discipline especially with the trial of the conspirators on the horizon. Since General José Gabeiras Montero, Chief of the Army General Staff, was due to appear at the trial as a witness, it was feared that the authority of the JUJEM might be challenged in some way. The new president of the JUJEM announced in mid-January 1982, was General Álvaro Lacalle Leloup, a tough *Constitucionalista*.[16]

The King was utterly exasperated both by the ongoing evidence of *golpista* activities and by the continued insinuations that he had been involved in the 23-F. Even before the meeting of the JUJEM, at the January 1982 *Pascua Militar* reception at Madrid's Royal Palace, he made a particularly robust speech, condemning the smear campaign and urging the Armed Forces to adapt to change. After expressing gratitude for military loyalty during the night of 23 February, he called for mutual understanding between the military on the one hand and the government and other civil authorities on the other. Acknowledging that the changes currently faced by the Armed Forces were difficult ones, the King noted that: 'The will of the forces cannot differ from that of the nation,' and warned, 'Let no one attempt to set himself up as the saviour of his compatriots by going against their will.' He then, for the first time, publicly denounced the campaign against him, saying that it had: 'lies as its motto, confusion as its method and insult as its objective'. Speaking with remarkable frankness, he said, 'No one can have heard me make the slightest protest or the slightest effort to defend myself from calumnies which deserve only the most absolute contempt. No one can doubt my serenity and prudence, because I thought and think that I should not lower myself to counter falsehoods or to justify other people's actions . . . But allow me today, in this our *Pascua*, when I am speaking to beloved comrades in arms in a spirit of sincerity and trust, to leave a brief but profound testimony both of my pain at the lamentable devices used by some and of the gratitude I feel towards those who have rejected this insidious and deceitful propaganda.' Juan Carlos then expressed his absolute certainty that the truth would emerge from the 23-F trial and his confidence in democracy.[17]

As unease over the persistence of *golpismo* was exacerbated by a revival of ETA activity, 1982 saw the acceleration of the disintegration of UCD. Paradoxically, however, despite and perhaps even because of that situation, the popular mood was changing. Confidence in the King and in the country's democratic institutions was boosted by the *golpistas* themselves in the course of their trial. The proceeding began on 19 February 1982, and dominated Spanish politics until well into the spring. Juan Carlos followed the trial with the closest attention and was especially concerned when some of the accused confirmed their earlier claims that he had been actively involved in encouraging the coup. It had long since been leaked that, in his first statement to the examining judge on 14 April 1981, Tejero had openly accused the King of having endorsed and encouraged the coup. Sources described as totally reliable and close to La Zarzuela reacted by lamenting the fact that the *golpistas* were portraying Armada's decision to remain silent as proof of the King's involvement, both to reduce their own responsibility and to exact their revenge for his opposition to the coup. It is likely that the view of the King himself was expressed in the statement of these sources that all of the accused should say whatever they wanted, since there was 'absolute certainty that the monarch had been perfectly clear in his behaviour'.[18]

Inevitably, the defence lawyers did eventually base their strategy on the claim that the *golpistas* sincerely believed they were merely following Juan Carlos's orders. At the end of September

1981, when they produced their provisional conclusions, ten of the defence lawyers issued a joint statement to the effect that the 23-F operation was carried out 'in the firm conviction and certainty of following instructions emanating from His Majesty the King, Commander-in-Chief of the Armed Forces, as permitted by the constitution'. The lawyers went on to state that the operation was headed by Armada who recruited the others by claiming that the task had been a royal commission, a claim the other accused had no reason to doubt, given Armada's closeness to the King and his appointment as Deputy Chief of Staff.[19] During the trial, the defence lawyers went so far as to call for Juan Carlos to take the stand as a witness. Inevitably, La Zarzuela had to refuse, but the refusal could then be used against him. In a similar, if more subtle, fashion, General Armada let it be known that he had asked for royal permission to reveal the contents of his conversation with the King on 13 February. His letter went unanswered. Sabino Fernández Campo knew that to say yes would allow Armada to say what he liked without any possibility of it being denied. To refuse permission could be construed as the King having something to hide.[20]

In court, the defendants' bullying arrogance, disloyalty to one another, and moral bankruptcy was inadvertently to have a deep impact on civil–military relations. There was widespread public dismay at the sight of these self-appointed guardians of the nation's values boasting of their patriotism oblivious to the fact that their actions had brought international ridicule and shame on Spain and her military institutions. The trial provided the stimulus for debate in officers' messes about the rights and wrongs of *golpismo*. The loutish behaviour of those who projected themselves as the embodiment of honour and discipline and evidence of their disobedience of orders from superior officers undermined the certainties of the more thoughtful officers. After the trial, defence of the constitution, if not exactly fashionable, was less frowned upon within the ranks of the Armed Forces. Anti-democratic declarations which previously had enjoyed silent approbation if not open admiration were now more likely to draw severe rebukes from the military authorities.

The *golpistas* began to withdraw into the shadows, where they continued to work for the resuscitation of their coup. However, the bulk of the officer corps had slid over to what was known as the 'prudent sector', concerned above all to safeguard their careers. Moreover, the promotions policy first initiated by General Gutiérrez Mellado, and now firmly taken over by General Álvaro Lacalle Leloup, was beginning to bear fruit. Helped by the passage of time, the strategy of shifting Francoist generals to the reserve list, putting key units in the hands of loyal *Constitucionalistas* and awarding promotions on the basis of achievement rather than mere seniority was gradually producing dividends. Of profound symbolic importance was the King's signature on the document confirming Spain's entry into NATO on Sunday 29 May 1982. On that morning, Juan Carlos had presided at the great military parade that brought to an end the Armed Forces week, held that year in Zaragoza. Then, in the afternoon, despite the fact that there was a PSOE motion before the Cortes calling for a delay in Spain's entry until assurances could be secured from Britain about future negotiations over Gibraltar, the Spanish Embassy in Washington delivered the 'protocol of membership'. The decision had many ramifications, with a considerable boost for Spanish prestige being bought at the price of a limitation of its room for manoeuvre in international terms. Nevertheless, with the sentences in the 23-F trial expected over the next few days, the King's unequivocal support for NATO entry reflected his hopes of the military developing a more international outlook.[21]

NATO entry did little to halt the inexorable decline of UCD. Daily reminders about the 23-F through the media's blanket coverage of the trial and the apparently endless violence of ETA-M had fatally eroded the government's image. Opinion polls showed unmistakably that the PSOE would win the next general elections. Added proof came in the sweeping victory of the Socialists in the elections to the Andalusian parliament on 23 May.[22] Suárez had refused to take part in the campaign and, in the aftermath, UCD was torn apart by mutual recriminations. The banks were beginning to pump money into *Alianza Popular* and to treat UCD with a growing coolness. Calvo Sotelo's position was further weakened by the publication on 3 June of the sentences for the 23-F conspirators. Although Tejero and Milans del Bosch received the maximum possible 30 years, Armada, Pardo Zancada and Torres Rojas were sentenced to only six. Of the 32 defendants, 22 were condemned to less than three years. In consequence, they would be able to return to the ranks after they had served their sentences. The government would eventually appeal to the Supreme Court and some sentences would be substantially increased in 1983, most dramatically in the cases of Armada (increased to 30 years) and Torres Rojas (increased to 12 years). However, at the time, the benevolent sentences caused widespread dismay. It seemed, for the moment at least, as if nothing had changed.[23] In December 1988, Juan Carlos would sanction the Socialist government's proposal to pardon Armada, who was two months away from his 70th birthday, the age at which prisoners automatically became entitled to get conditional freedom.[24]

Faced with the inexorable rise of the PSOE and *Alianza Popular*, Leopoldo Calvo Sotelo announced on 30 July 1982 that he would not be the UCD's presidential candidate in the next elections.[25] UCD began to break up into its component parts. Even Suárez, angry at being offered only the third place on the party's electoral list for Madrid, decided to leave and form a new party, to be called *Centro Democrático y Social*. To prevent Suárez consolidating his new party and thus taking more votes away from UCD, on 27 August, Calvo Sotelo called general elections to be held within the legal minimum period of two months.[26]

The PSOE elaborated a moderate programme for the restructuring of Spanish industry, the stimulation of employment, the reform of Spain's cumbersome civil service and the development of a more positive and independent foreign policy. Most public attention focused on a promise to create 800,000 new jobs. The only serious challenge came from *Alianza Popular* with its altogether more conservative programme. The election campaign was carried out with a high degree of civic spirit. This was not unconnected with the fact that on 3 October, news broke of a projected coup. In the early hours of Saturday 2 October, Calvo Sotelo had held a meeting with the Ministers of Defence and

Interior, Alberto Oliart and Juan José Rosón, the Director General of the CESID, Emilio Alonso Manglano, and the Director of State Security, Francisco Laína García. Agents of the CESID had uncovered a plot for a coup d'état to take place on 27 October, the day before the polling was to take place. Now Calvo Sotelo telephoned the King to inform him of the imminent arrest of two colonels and a lieutenant-colonel involved in what came to be known as 'Operación Cervantes'.

It was a more thorough version of the long simmering 'coup of the colonels' albeit with the post-23-F refinement that the King was now a direct target. Three ultra-rightist colonels, closely connected with Fuerza Nueva, were involved in a conspiracy that had been coordinated from prison by General Milans del Bosch. Shortly after Calvo Sotelo's call to the King, the arrests were followed by the interrogation and imprisonment of Colonel Luis Muñoz Gutiérrez, whose wife was a Fuerza Nueva candidate for the Senate, Colonel Jesús Crespo Cuspinera of the DAC, one of the plotters behind the manifesto of one hundred published in December 1981, and his brother Lieutenant-Colonel José Crespo Cuspinera. While Muñoz Gutiérrez had had lunch with Blas Piñar, agents of the CESID had broken into his car and found immensely detailed plans for a coup involving several hundred artillery officers. The Zarzuela and Moncloa palaces, the Cortes, the headquarters of the JUJEM, various Ministries and key public buildings were to be taken over by commandos in helicopters. Railway stations, airports, radio and television transmitters and newspaper offices were to be seized by fast-moving units of armoured cars. The political élite was to be 'neutralized' in their homes. Central to the plan was the need for bloodshed in order to ensure no turning back. Manglano and Sabino Fernández Campo were to be executed and the King deposed for having betrayed his oath of loyalty to the Movimiento.[27]

The plotters had clearly taken on board the lessons of 23-F. The nation's politicians and the bulk of public opinion were appalled. There were, however, some grounds for cautious optimism. The CESID had acted swiftly and efficiently, in dramatic contrast to February 1981. Moreover, the indignation produced by the plans for the physical elimination of the Chiefs of Staff contributed to the isolation of the *golpistas*. On the other hand, only the three main protagonists were arrested despite the discovery of documents implicating at least 200 more. Nine more officers thought to be involved were posted away from Madrid, including Major Ricardo Sáenz de Ynestrillas and Colonel Antonio Sicre Canut, who had been involved in the manifesto of one hundred nine months earlier.[28] In the wake of the failed coup, on 12 October at the Day of Hispanity celebrations in Cádiz, the King responded with a forceful speech in defence of constitutional liberties.[29]

However, the era in which the King, as he commented bitterly, had had to be called out regularly as a 'fireman', the period of UCD appeasement of the military, was about to come to an end. Soon he would be able to leave the Socialists to deal with the problem of military subversion. Despite the shadow of military intervention, the population gave the PSOE a substantial parliamentary majority in the elections of 28 October 1982. It was massive public rejection of the canard that the *golpistas* were doing what was best for the people of Spain. The scale of the popular commitment to the democratic regime made it impossible for officers to claim that the military subversives interpreted the national will. The Socialists received 47.26 per cent of the votes cast and 202 seats. *Alianza Popular* came second with 25.89 per cent of the vote and 107 deputies. UCD was reduced to 6.17 per cent of the vote and only 11 deputies.[30]

On 23 November began the round of consultations at La Zarzuela as a result of which Juan Carlos would choose a candidate to propose to the Cortes as premier. Given the decisive verdict of the polls, it was obvious that he would have to select Felipe González. At the opening of the new parliament on 25 November 1982, Gregorio Peces-Barba, the new President of the Cortes, delivered a speech which offered a significant defence of the monarchy not just on account of Juan Carlos's role in the 23-F but also, importantly, on its own merit. The institution, he claimed, provided stability, equilibrium and the potential for progress. In reply, Juan Carlos praised the Armed Forces for their courage in the face of terrorism and reaffirmed that political violence could not be resolved by authoritarian means. He reiterated his determination to prevent the minority imposing its will upon the majority.[31]

The tasks awaiting Felipe González were enormous. The linked problems of ETA terrorism and military subversion required skill and authority. With good relations with both the conservative Basque PNV and the left *abertzale, Euskadiko Eskerra*, the PSOE had perhaps a better chance of success against ETA than UCD ever had. Under the immensely tactful and authoritative figure of the new Minister of Defence, Narcís Serra, the PSOE would inaugurate a programme of military modernization, redeployment, professionalization and depoliticization which would finally undermine the Third World *golpista* mentality in the Armed Forces. The restructuring of Spanish industry, with its obsolete sectors, its high energy dependence, its regional imbalances and its technological subservience, would require vision and sacrifice. The same was true of agrarian reform. No one expected short-term triumphs. However, the fact that the PSOE was prepared to confront tasks shirked by UCD ensured remarkable public tolerance for immediate measures like devaluation of the peseta, tax increases and fuel price rises. The Socialists had been elected by a serious electorate that had known the agonies of terrorism and military conspiracy. In return, they were expected to provide serious government.

Don Juan had once told his son that his task would be complete once he could rule with a Socialist government in power. The majority of the population had played its part in bringing that about. The political class too had worked in a spirit of compromise and sacrifice to establish democracy. Nevertheless, there was much of which Juan Carlos could be proud. As a democratic King who had risked his life in the service of the constitution, he had come a long way since his coronation as Franco's successor in 1975. His bravery and determination in defence of democracy on 23 February 1981 had added a de facto legitimacy to the dynastic legitimacy provided by his father's renunciation of his right to the throne and to the democratic legitimacy built on the two referendums of 1976 and 1978. With *golpismo* in retreat and a government in power with a large parliamentary majority, he could reasonably entertain hopes of being a constitutional Head of State in the manner of Queen Elizabeth II of England. However, the need for royal effort was only somewhat diminished. Over the coming years, the need for the exercise of the King's influence, if not direct intervention, would remain a constant of Spanish politics.

Neither of the problems of Basque terrorism or military subversion had been resolved. Over the next two decades, the King's commitment to the defence of Spanish unity would guarantee the direct hostility of ETA and the *abertzales* as well as the barely disguised antipathy of more moderate Basque nationalists. The *Lehendakari*, Carlos Garaikoetxea, was less than fulsome in his attitude towards the monarchy. The King was offended by Garaikoetxea's refusal, in May 1983, to attend the celebrations for Armed Forces Day, which were taking place in Burgos. Only after a strong message from Juan Carlos to the effect that his absence would be seen as an insult to the Spanish State, the crown and himself personally, did Garaikoetxea deign to attend.[32] When, on 19 December 1984, Garaikoetxea was forced to resign as a result of losing a vote of confidence in the Basque Parliament, Juan Carlos graciously telephoned him to express his sympathy.[33] The King's relations would be more cordial with Garaikoetxea's successor, José Antonio Ardanza, but a sense of hostility towards the monarchy would never entirely be dissipated and could be discerned in gestures such as the refusal of the Basque autonomous television station, *Euskal Telebista*, to broadcast the King's Christmas speech in 1995.[34] Moreover, it was the Basque newspaper *Egín* which, in mid-January 1996, published a piece accusing Juan Carlos's sister, Margarita de Borbón y Borbón, of having been involved in the illegal sale of paintings belonging to the State.[35]

Furthermore, relations with the extreme nationalists at this time could hardly have been worse. In 1983, *Herri Batasuna* had denounced the Armed Forces Week in Burgos as a 'provocative bluster' and as 'a military occupation by an Army opposed to the people'. This not only upset the King but also provoked plans for a coup among reactionary officers, which were dismantled in time by the police.[36] Viciously underlining the communion of interest between terrorism and *golpismo*, the escalation of terrorist activities by ETA-M would reach a peak of calculated brutality with the murder at the end of January 1984, of General Guillermo Quintana Lacaci, the Captain-General of Madrid who did so much to block the 23-F coup attempt, and a man of iron loyalty to the King.[37]

In October 1986, when Juan Carlos briefly visited Bilbao for the ceremony celebrating the centenary of the Jesuit university of Deusto, the city's *Herri Batasuna* councillors refused to attend. Similarly, on 8 February 1988, members of *Herri Batasuna* attempted to disrupt a two-day royal visit of Navarre. Moreover, security measures were intensified in response to fears of a terrorist attack. During a ceremony at the Palacio de la Diputación in the provincial capital Pamplona, Juan Carlos directly responded to the situation, saying that: 'The violent pressure on our democracy, on our system of autonomous regions and on our freedom, will provoke neither fear nor disunity.' He concluded with a challenge to ETA, saying, 'Today, as much as yesterday, to be Navarrese is to be Spanish.'[38] On 2 June 1989, when Sofía and her sister, Irene of Greece, attended a concert by Mikis Teodorakis at the Arriaga Theatre in Bilbao, they were greeted by a mixture of applause and abuse. When the Spanish national anthem was played, several *Herri Batasuna* town councillors chanted '*¡kampora, kampora!*' (out! out!)[39]

The 1980s would see the conversion of Spain into a semi-federal state through the evolution of what came to be called the State of the Autonomies. This had significant implications for the King who took extremely seriously the crown's constitutional role as 'symbol of the unity and permanence' of the Spanish State. He worked extremely hard to elaborate and popularize the idea of a Spain that was pluralistic and multicultural while remaining united. By stressing unity, he was consolidating the loyalty of the Armed Forces but also provoking the hostility of some regional nationalists.[40] His determination to champion the idea of Spanish unity against extreme Basque nationalism was illustrated during the *Pascua Militar* celebrations of 6 January 1994. In response to the claim made by the PNV that the Army stood in the way of Basque self-determination, Juan Carlos said, 'The diversity which enriches us should unite us rather than divide us.'[41] Iñaki Anasagasti, the PNV's spokesman, told the press that Juan Carlos's references to Spain's unity were 'crude and outdated'. Referring to the fact that the King's speech had been made to the highest military authorities, Anasagasti said, 'As Head of State, he should not depend only on bayonets.' In contrast, conservatives were delighted. Alberto Ruiz Gallardón of the *Partido Popular* declared that Juan Carlos's speech had been 'extraordinarily important' and Manuel Fraga claimed that the speech had been, 'absolutely correct in its content, in its form and in its timeliness because there are those who have been playing ambiguously with the concept of national unity'.[42]

Throughout the years following 1982, the hostility of ETA towards the King was manifested in several assassination attempts on Juan Carlos and his family.[43] In early August 1986, the press carried reports of ETA plans to assassinate Prince Felipe. At the end of the year, during the royal family's skiing holiday at Baqueira Beret, an ETA bomb exploded at the Hotel Montarto, where the King often met political figures. In late March 1989, security concerns redoubled when ETA let it be known that it possessed a number of SA-7 'Grail' land-to-air missiles manufactured in the USSR and it was assumed that these were for use against the King's aircraft.[44] Then, in October 1997, a few days before the arrival of the King and Queen to inaugurate Bilbao's Guggenheim Museum, the police uncovered a plan by an ETA cell to set off a bomb during the ceremony. In the event, when the glamorous occasion took place as planned on 18 October, the King and Queen were greeted by more than 10,000 cheering people.[45] In general, despite the hostility of the *abertzales*, the popularity of the King and Queen increased in the Basque Country, which they visited several times during the 1990s.[46] This process was greatly consolidated by the engagement in April 1997 of their daughter Cristina to the Basque handball star, Iñaki Urdangarín Liebaert. They were married in Barcelona Cathedral on 4 October. The.

wedding, together with the fact that she lived in Barcelona and spoke Catalan, saw 200,000 people in the streets to cheer the couple and their parents.[47]

The King's relations with Catalonia, while not without difficulty, were significantly easier than with the Basque Country. He was determined to do everything possible to consolidate Catalonia's presence within Spain's new democracy and, by the same token, to augment the popularity of the crown in the region. In mid-May 1985, he and Queen Sofía made their first visit to Barcelona since the restoration of the Generalitat in 1977. At the invitation of Jordi Pujol, the King chaired a meeting of the *Consell Executiù* (Executive Council), as well as visiting the Catalan Parliament, being received at the Town Hall by the Socialist Mayor, Pasqual Maragall, and encouraging the city's candidature to the Olympic Games of 1992. At the Olympic Office, Juan Carlos wrote in the guest book: 'To the Barcelona 92 Olympic bid committee, with affection and, above all, the promise of my firm support to obtain for Spain the Olympic Games of Summer 1992 to take place in Barcelona.'[48] On 22 April 1988, Juan Carlos presided over the celebrations marking the one-thousandth anniversary of Catalonia, at the Palau de la Generalitat.

As far as the military was concerned, one of the principal objectives of the Socialists was the definitive resolution of the problem of subversion. Given that the King was Commander-in-Chief, that task could not be fulfilled without his full collaboration and the new Minister of Defence, Narcís Serra, found it to be unstinting. At the *Pascua Militar* celebrations on 6 January 1984, for instance, Juan Carlos called on the Armed Forces to remain united and to collaborate 'without doubts or reservations' in the government's plans for military reform. The following year, he outlined the advantages of modernization within NATO.[49] Serra was aware that the fact that the constitution made the Armed Forces dependent on the wishes of the King rather than of the government gave a legal basis to the military pretension to autonomous power. Accordingly, Serra was anxious to incorporate the Armed Forces into the orbit of the State administration. His task was rendered somewhat easier by the fact that Spain was now in

NATO with the consequence that the Armed Forces would come into ever more regular contact with the officers of other democratic countries. He was also able to build on Oliart's determined effort to modernize the Armed Forces in terms of equipment. Nevertheless, even before he had begun the process, in the course of November he was obliged to overturn the decision of the *Consejo Supremo de Justicia Militar* to pardon those sentenced in the 23-F trial at Christmas 1982.

This was followed by the implementation of a series of laws that clearly established the supremacy of civilian power over the military. Although many senior officers rejected *golpismo*, they still believed that the link between the democratic State and the Army should be through the King as Commander-in-Chief. With great energy, and the full support of the King, Serra set about incorporating military administration into the civilian administration of the State. The JUJEM was converted from the highest body of the chain of command to being an advisory and consultative body at the service of the Prime Minister and the Minister of Defence. The post of Military Governor of each province was eliminated and, with it, connotations of an Army occupying enemy territory. The Captain-General of a region was no longer considered its highest authority, and the notion that autonomous institutions of military justice had jurisdiction over civilians was abolished. Of enormous symbolic importance was Serra's success, with the King's support, in securing the rehabilitation on 24 December 1986 of the officers expelled from the Armed Forces because of their membership of the UMD.[50]

In the long term, the military situation was destined to improve massively. Meanwhile, however, during Easter 1985, another reactionary coup, scheduled for 2 June 1985, was deactivated by the CESID. The Socialist government had decided not to give any publicity to *golpista* activities and the details of the planned coup and the names of those involved were kept from the press for nearly six years. The role of the King on 23 February 1981 ensured again that his name was the first of those to be assassinated during what was known as '*Operación Zambombazo*' (Operation Big Bang). The plan was for a bomb to be detonated under the structure from which the King would preside at the Armed Forces Day celebrations, due to be held that year in La Coruña. Had the plot gone ahead, Juan Carlos, Sofía and the Infantas, as well as Felipe González, Narcís Serra, the higher echelons of the Armed Forces and other invited guests would have been killed. The explosion would then be attributed to ETA and this would provide the excuse for the imposition of a military junta. Those involved included Major Ricardo Sáenz de Ynestrillas, of *Galaxia* fame, Major Ignacio Gasca Quintín and Colonel Jesús Crespo Cuspinera, who was still in prison for his involvement in *Operación Cervantes* in October 1982, together with a Galician shipbuilder, Rafael Regueira Fernández. One of those involved commented: 'After 1981, it was clear that a coup could not be made with the King nor even despite the King, but had to be against the King. For us, he was a traitor who had broken his oath to Franco.' This was the last serious plot against the King.[51]

The area in which the King was most active and most effective was in his tireless visits abroad. His visits to France and Germany were crucial in the process of Spain's integration into the European Community. Similarly, his cultivation of President Mitterrand helped secure French cooperation in the struggle against ETA. The King also did an enormous amount to consolidate the image of Spain in Latin America, as well as encouraging the transition from dictatorship to democracy in the region, especially in Argentina, Brazil, Chile and Uruguay.[52] His visit to Argentina in April 1985 was aimed not only at helping the Prime Minister Raul Alfonsín through a difficult time but also at giving new impetus to the King's efforts to locate 23 Spaniards who went missing during the military dictatorship.[53] Relations were improved too with Britain despite the ongoing issue of Gibraltar. Having secured the British government's agreement to include discussion of the sovereignty of Gibraltar on the agenda of future talks, Juan Carlos and Sofía made a spectacularly successful State visit to Britain in April 1986.

The King also had good relations with a number of Arab countries, Morocco, Jordan, Saudi Arabia, the United Arab Emirates and Kuwait, as a result of which Spain enjoyed secure oil supplies. He had extremely good relations with Yasser Arafat whom he received in La Zarzuela on 27 January 1989. Subsequently, Juan Carlos interceded with the Israeli President Chaim Herzog on behalf of Arafat. These efforts would be partly responsible for the decision to hold the October 1991 Middle East Peace Summit at the Royal Palace in Madrid.[54] On 8 November 1993, Juan Carlos and Sofía were the first European monarchs to visit Israel. On the second day of the visit, Juan Carlos gave, at the Knesset (the Israeli Parliament), a speech in which he strongly defended the right to self-determination of the Palestinian people. Shortly after returning from Israel, the Spanish monarchs acted as hosts to a grateful Yasser Arafat.[55]

The King's excellent relations with the Arab world were often connected to reports that he had received financial support from the richer Middle Eastern monarchies. This in turn would be linked, throughout the 1990s, to efforts to smear his image by association with the financial scandals that were to bedevil Spanish political life. The accusations against the King that would surface in the 1990s would have been inconceivable ten years earlier. His opposition to the military coup of 1981 had left Juan Carlos with enormous reserves of popularity and credibility. The national mood throughout the 1980s was one of serious collective collaboration in the consolidation of democracy, a process in which the King continued to work tirelessly. In doing so, he clinched his place in history.

Inevitably, what came thereafter was anticlimactic although, to some extent, the boring normality that went with Juan Carlos's role as an increasingly ceremonial monarch was a tribute to his achievement since 1975. Nevertheless, the prosperity that followed the success of the Socialist Party in the 1980s gave rise in Spain, as in much of the Western world, to an ambience in which the accumulation of wealth came to assume ever-greater importance. With it, the reputation of the King came into the firing line. No longer fighting daily to defend democracy, the King could legitimately look back over his life and reflect that he deserved some reward for the sacrifices made. His childhood and his adolescence had been stolen from him. As a young married man, he had seen his life distorted by the contradictory demands of Don Juan and General Franco. When he became King, the first six years were a ceaseless struggle to consolidate democracy. In 1981, he had risked his life to do so and, for the first half of the 1980s, he had wrestled with similar problems. Thereafter, he continued to travel indefatigably on behalf of Spain and to fulfil his constitutional duties to the full. However, with Felipe González's Socialist government presiding over a period of stability and prosperity, it is not surprising that he began to relax somewhat and give over more time to his pleasures.

Gossip magazines made much of his obsession with speed and wih expensive sports in which he risked his life and which frequently caused him serious accidents and injuries. On one occasion, as he was carried from an aircraft on a stretcher, Sabino Fernández Campo commented, 'A King should be seen in such a state only on his return from the Crusades.'[56] Skiing, driving fast cars and motorcycles, piloting helicopters and aeroplanes, along with yacht racing were all activities that enhanced his reputation in some circles and were the occasion of criticism in others. The same could be said of his enthusiasm for beautiful women which was the object of prurient attention in some parts of the weekly press and would eventually encourage attempts at blackmail by financiers who hoped to force him to intervene on their behalf when they were prosecuted for their criminal activities.

To some extent, the increased vulnerability of the King derived precisely from the fact that he was no longer the fireman, always on call to save democracy. He was able to dedicate more time to his own interests, his friends and his caprices, and that in turn would expose him to morbid, or even hostile, scrutiny. In this regard, his situation was rendered more difficult by the breaking up of the team that hitherto had worked successfully to protect his image. In January 1990, the now 84-year-old Marqués de Mondéjar retired. Always considered by Juan Carlos as a second father, Mondéjar was a powerful influence in favour of prudence, and his departure was the beginning of significant changes at La Zarzuela. On 22 January 1990, Mondéjar was replaced as head of the royal household by the extremely discreet and highly efficient

Sabino Fernández Campo, who since 1977 had been the secretary-general. As part of the process of renovation, the brilliant diplomat José Joaquín Puig de la Bellacasa, who had served in La Zarzuela between 1974 and 1976, returned as the new secretary-general. Prior to this appointment, Puig de la Bellacasa had enjoyed immense prestige as Ambassador in London and had master-minded the spectacularly successful Spanish royal visit of 1986. A great favourite of Queen Sofía, who was an assiduous visitor to London, the witty and urbane Puig, deeply religious and devoted to the monarchy, was to be groomed as successor to General Fernández Campo. However, after spending the summer with the royal family in Mallorca in 1990, Puig was shocked by the behaviour of the circle in which the King moved. His efforts to impose greater discretion on the King led to a clash with Juan Carlos that saw Puig removed less than a year after his appointment.[57]

Attempts were made to give the impression that the departure of Puig de la Bellacasa derived from rivalry with Sabino Fernández Campo. There may have been some friction over areas of responsibility but essentially they shared the goal of protecting the monarchy. To counter rumours that he had been in some way responsible for the demise of Puig, Fernández Campo let it be known that he was looking forward to his own eventual retirement. He was 71 years old, but his mental and physical faculties were unimpaired and he could easily have stayed in his post, as the Marqués de Mondéjar had done. In the event, Sabino Fernández Campo would also be forced out of La Zarzuela in a way that replicated what had happened to Puig. The circumstances of his removal and its consequences would be central to one of the most difficult periods faced by Juan Carlos.

One of Sabino Fernández Campo's immense services to the crown had been his ability to put obstacles in the way of the development in Spain of the voracious curiosity characteristic of the British tabloid press. From the late 1980s, the Spanish media had begun to show curiosity about the King's leisure activities in Mallorca and June 1992 saw the end of the taboo on investigating the private life of the King. Immense curiosity was provoked by a royal absence from Spain at a moment when his presence was required in order to give approval to the nomination of a new Minister of Foreign Affairs to replace Francisco Fernández Ordóñez, who was in the last stages of a fatal illness. *El País* reported that the King was in Switzerland having a medical check-up but, when asked by reporters, Sabino Fernández Campo denied that there was any health problem saying, 'What I have been told is that he is relaxing.' Rumours about matrimonial difficulties were fuelled by an interview given on the COPE radio station by Jaime de Peñafiel, one of Spain's most perceptive and best-informed royal-watchers. Peñafiel told the COPE presenter, Encarna Sánchez, that: 'The King is going through a very delicate emotional time which derives from an old marital problem which has finally reached crisis point. I am sure that, if he's left alone, he will manage to overcome it.'[58]

Meanwhile, on 25 July, the Summer Olympics opened in Barcelona. It coincided with a resurgence of radical Catalan nationalism. In March 1992, *Esquerra Republicana de Catalunya* (the Republican Left of Catalonia) had announced that, when Catalonia became an independent nation, the monarchy would be expelled. The impact of this declaration was mitigated somewhat when, in April, Pujol and Juan Carlos held a meeting at the end of which the President of the Generalitat described their relationship as one of 'mutual loyalty' and Pujol called for due respect to be shown to the royal family during the Olympic Games. When the games opened, the appearance of Prince Felipe, who led the Olympic parade as standard-bearer for Spain, provoked frenetic applause. The Olympic Games significantly boosted the public image of the entire royal family. The King's spontaneous demonstrations of enthusiasm and affection for the Spanish team were entirely in tune with the mood of the people. Juan Carlos was nicknamed 'King Midas' because it seemed that the Spanish competitors always did better when he was present in the stadium.[59]

However, after the Olympic Games closed on 9 August, there was a resurgence of interest in the reasons for the King's absence in June. The press and the radio had a field day, even going as far as to discuss his possible abdication. The media, with the sensationalist daily, *El Mundo*, leading the pack, then followed up its speculations by repeating allegations from the French and Italian press about the King's relationship with a Catalan woman who lived in Mallorca, Marta Gayá. Both Sabino Fernández Campo and Felipe González expressed their concerns about a campaign against the monarchy. Accusing eyes fell on the buccaneering financier Mario Conde, who was alleged to control *El Mundo*.[60] However, he managed to turn the King's understandable annoyance around. He apparently alleged that Sabino Fernández Campo was behind the leaks in *El Mundo* by way of a warning to the King about the dangers of his conduct. Conde had long since made an effort to win the favour of the King by means of expensive gifts – an assault that had initially been blocked by Sabino Fernández Campo. Nevertheless, Conde did win the gratitude of Juan Carlos through his attentions to the King's widowed sister, Doña Pilar and to Don Juan, who was dying of cancer. He also had financial links with the King's friend Manuel Prado y Colón de Carvajal. There can be little doubt that the ambitious Galician financier wanted to clinch a friendship with the King to adorn his vertiginous rise to the top of Spanish society, as an insurance policy and also in the hope of using him to push his political ambitions. It has been claimed that Mario Conde harboured the idea of a great government of national salvation with himself cast in the role of a Spanish Berlusconi. The removal of Sabino Fernández Campo seemed to be a first step towards the achievement of that goal.[61]

It was announced in January 1993 that Fernández Campo was to be replaced by Fernando Almansa Moreno-Barreda, the Vizconde del Castillo de Almansa. The fact that the highly intelligent and competent Almansa had been at university with Mario Conde led to speculation that he was Conde's man, although his subsequent fulfilment of his role made it quite clear that this was not the case. In part, the problem was that the King resented being under the tutelage of a man who, because of his age, felt able to tell him things that he did not want to hear. After all, Sabino Fernández Campo was the last in a line that had included General Martínez Campos, the Marqués de Mondéjar, and General Armada. Now, it was claimed, for instance, that Sabino Fernández Campo had been critical of the King's participation both in a BBC documentary with the beautiful and vivacious Selina Scott and in an authorized biography written by the playboy, José Luis de Vilallonga. The choice as his amanuensis of Vilallonga, a *roué* and hitherto malicious critic of Juan Carlos, caused many raised eyebrows, as did the uninhibited nature of what seemed to be a flirtation with Selina Scott, but both the book and the documentary had immensely positive consequences for Juan Carlos's popularity.[62]

Whatever the reasons for Fernández Campo's departure, there can be little doubt that it removed a barrier between the King and Mario Conde and other jetset financiers who wanted to exploit royal favour. One curious side-effect of the enormous prestige won by the King in the struggle for the survival of democracy in the early 1980s was the belief that he enjoyed a scale of influence that seemed to go beyond his strict constitutional powers. In consequence, there were those who hoped for royal favour in good times and royal intervention in bad. Along with Mario Conde, another who had tried, without notable success, to get close to the King was the Catalan financier Javier de la Rosa, the representative in Spain of the Kuwait Investment Office, large amounts of whose money went missing during the Gulf War. When both Conde and De la Rosa fell foul of the authorities from late 1993 onwards, they seemed to believe, because of their business dealings with Juan Carlos's friend, Manuel Prado y Colón de Carvajal, that they could somehow expect royal protection from justice.

Mario Conde's entry into La Zarzuela derived in large part from the fact that he had carefully cultivated the friendship of Don Juan de Borbón. In Pamplona, on 18 January 1993, Don Juan made his last public appearance when Juan Carlos presented him with the Gold Medal of Navarre in recognition of his efforts on behalf of democracy in Spain. By now, Don Juan was terminally ill with cancer and rarely left Pamplona's University Hospital. Don Juan was unable to make his acceptance speech, which was read out by Prince Felipe. In what was effectively his farewell address to the nation, he spoke for himself and Doña María de las Mercedes, expressing: 'Our good fortune, as subjects, and our joy, as parents, to see embodied in our son, for the good of Spain, the institution to which we have dedicated our life. Because of this, we can say with pride: "Lord, duty accomplished".'[63]

Don Juan died, two months short of his 80th birthday, on 1 April 1993, the anniversary of Franco's victory in the Civil War. A chapel of repose was set up at the Royal Palace and was visited by many thousands of ordinary Spaniards. It was a manifestation of popular affection that gave the lie to the Caudillo's sneers about Don Juan's desire to be King of all Spaniards. La Zarzuela received 4,000 telegrams of condolence from all over the world. Pasqual Maragall, the Mayor of Barcelona, announced that one of the city's avenues would be named after Don Juan. Don Juan's funeral mass took place at the basilica of the monastery of San Lorenzo de El Escorial and was attended by the royal family, the government, the entire diplomatic corps, the Portuguese President Mario Soares, and representatives of Europe's monarchies including Prince Charles. Juan Carlos's manifest sadness perhaps reflected his regrets about the frictions that had bedevilled his relationship with his father. He was moved by the presence of thousands of people who gathered outside the monastery to pay their last respects to Don Juan. The King issued a message expressing his gratitude for 'the innumerable displays of sympathy, solidarity and affection' received following Don Juan's death.[64]

The wave of sympathy that greeted the death of Juan Carlos's father was an effective barometer of the popularity of the monarchy. It was a moral capital that the King had earned in the years since 1975. That essential support would be crucial in helping Juan Carlos survive a difficult period in the mid-1990s. At the end of December 1993, grave doubts about the solvency of Mario Conde's Banesto saw the bank put into administration by the State. Javier de la Rosa was imprisoned in mid-October 1994, for massive embezzlement, and Mario Conde followed him into prison in December 1994 accused of large-scale fraud. The hopes of both that the King would save them were frustrated. Thereafter, it has been alleged that an enraged Javier de la Rosa planned to black-mail Prado y Colón de Carvajal over the funds missing from the Kuwait Investment Office. He backed up his attempts with vague threats against the King. It was similarly alleged that Conde saw an opportunity to blackmail the government over its involvement in the dirty war against ETA through documents provided by a renegade CESID agent, Juan Alberto Perote. In the rumour-laden atmosphere, there was no shortage of insinuations that the King was also likely to be smeared by both operations. The threat dissipated when the attempts to blackmail the King were exposed on 10 November 1995 by *Diario 16*. The consequence was a great wave of support for the King.[65] In fact, the adverse speculations in some areas of the press and in the sensationalist bestsellers of a number of investigative journalists did little to diminish the popularity of Juan Carlos. The popular image of the monarchy was consolidated even further by the media coverage of the weddings of Elena to Jaime de Marichalar in Seville Cathedral in March 1995 and of Cristina to Iñaki Urdangarín in Barcelona in October 1997.

The royal weddings merely clinched a popular perception of King Juan Carlos informed by a delight in his affability, in his popular touch and by pride in his bravery at key moments in the long process of transition from dictatorship to democracy between 1975 and 1982. It is a curious irony that this perception, perfectly reasonable and based on reality as it is, is not informed to any great extent by a sense of either the personal sacrifice and the considerable intelligence required of the King. His geniality during countless hundreds of public occasions and his bravery in his dealings with the threat of *golpismo* from 1976 to 1985, most particularly during the coup d'état of 23 February 1981, are the most public, but not the only, reasons for his success in re-establishing the monarchy in Spain.

As this book has tried to demonstrate, there is a less public, more meritorious, side to this success. No one can ever know what the rebuilding of the monarchy cost Juan Carlos de Borbón. The immediate price could hardly have been higher – it cost him much of his childhood and adolescence. The ten-year-old boy who boarded the Lusitania Express to travel from Lisbon to Madrid on 8 November 1948 was leaving his parents and his friends in order to be brought up under the doleful eyes of a series of humourless and puritanical aristocrats and generals. He was then subjected to a political education intended to prepare him for the task of perpetuating the regime of a man, Franco, who was the very antithesis of his own father. Not only could Franco never match the warmth, good humour and open-mindedness of the Conde de Barcelona, but he rarely missed an opportunity to mock Don Juan's desire to return to Spain as 'King of all Spaniards'. Long years under the vigilance of Franco, far from his family while being trained for an uncongenial task, go a long way to explaining why it was that, in so many photographs of the 1950s and 1960s, Juan Carlos appears so reserved and sad.

Juan Carlos knew that he was regarded by the left-wing opposition as no more than Franco's puppet and, at the same time, distrusted by many on the Falangist wing of the *Movimiento* as the representative of his father, Don Juan, and therefore a dangerous liberal contaminated by democratic leanings. In human terms, the 21 years from his arrival in Madrid until the final confirmation of his succession in his proclamation as Príncipe de España on 21 July 1969 can only have been an appalling experience. The six years from then until his coronation were hardly more pleasant – his home and his family were kept under constant hostile scrutiny. The idea of 'living like a king' was far from what he experienced. In material terms perhaps, it was not a bad life, but it was not his own. The choices about friends, education and career were imposed by Franco from outside in terms of training for the function that had been assigned him by the dictator. During the years of passage through various military and civilian academies, and immersion in the laws that made up the Francoist constitution and the objectives of the *Movimiento*, the young Prince had to present a public face that neither challenged Franco nor irrevocably undermined the possibility of consolidating the monarchy in a post-Franco democracy.

The necessary balancing act constituted a stress and a tension for him that easily explains his image as a melancholy and solitary individual. Inevitably he was misjudged by many since few could perceive the abnegation and sense of duty which lay at the core of his existence. Despite his belief in the legitimacy of the Borbón line, he accepted with dignity the many humiliations to which he was exposed by his position as just one of Franco's possible successors. It was a character-building experience that explains only too well how he was able to plan with his advisers the complex process of transition from the dictator's nominated heir to a King by his own right. The story of the removal of Carlos Arias Navarro, the collaboration with Torcuato Fernández-Miranda and Adolfo Suárez, the dealings with Santiago Carrillo and Felipe González, is a complex one but reveals a man who is intelligent, strong-minded and motivated by a deep patriotism. The way in which the King used his prestige with the military, even to the extent of risking his life, in order to combat *golpismo*, more than confirms that impression. However, what is often forgotten is that the maturity and wisdom that underlay these achievements and which has done so much for Spain were bought at a high price in human terms. For Juan Carlos at least, 'to live like a king' has meant sacrifice and dedication on a scale that has given the monarchy a legitimacy that was unthinkable in 1931, in 1939 and even in 1975.

BIBLIOGRAPHY

Abel, Christopher & Torrents, Nissa, editors, *Spain: Conditional Democracy* (London, 1984)

Abellán, José Luis, *Ortega y Gasset y los orígenes de la transición democrática* (Madrid, 2000)

Acqua, Gian Piero dell', *Spagna cronache della transizione* (Florence, 1978)

Agirre, Julen (Eva Forest), *Operación Ogro: cómo y porqué ejecutamos a Carrero Blanco* (Paris, 1974)

Agüero, Felipe, *Soldiers, Civilians and Democracy. Post-Franco Spain in Comparative Perspective* (Baltimore, 1995)

Aguilar, Miguel Ángel, *El vertigo de la prensa* (Madrid, 1982)

Aguilar Fernández, Paloma, *Memoria y olvido de la guerra civil española* (Madrid, 1996)

Aguilar Fernández, Paloma, *Memory and Amnesia. The Role of the Spanish Civil War in the Transition to Democracy* (New York, 2002)

Alba, Víctor, *La soledad del Rey* (Barcelona, 1981)

Alberola, Octavio & Gransac, Ariane, *El anarquismo español y la acción revolucionaria 1961–1974* (Paris, 1975)

Alcocer, José Luis, *Fernández-Miranda: agonía de un Estado* (Barcelona, 1986)

Alderete, Ramón de, *. . . y estos borbones nos quieren gobernar* (Paris, 1974)

Alonso-Castrillo, Silvia, *La apuesta del centro. Historia de la UCD* (Madrid, 1996)

Alonso de los Ríos, César, *La verdad sobre Tierno Galván* (Madrid, 1997)

Álvarez, Faustino F., *Agonía y muerte de Franco* (Madrid, 1975)

Álvarez de Miranda, Fernando, *Del "contubernio" al consenso* (Barcelona, 1985)

Amigo, Ángel, *Pertur: ETA 71–76* (San Sebastián, 1978)

Amodia, José, *Franco's Political Legacy. From Fascism to Façade Democracy* (London, 1977)

Amover, Francesc, *Il carcere vaticano: Chiesa e fascismo in Spagna* (Milan, 1975)

Amover, Francesc, *Stato cattolico e Chiesa fascista in Spagna* (Milan, 1973)

Anson, Luis María, *Don Juan* (Barcelona, 1994)

Antich, José, *El Virrey. ¿Es Jordi Pujol un fiel aliado de la Corona o un caballo de Troya dentro de la Zarzuela?* (Barcelona, 1994)

Apalategi, Jokin, *Los vascos de la nación al Estado* (San Sebastián, 1979)

Apezarena, José, *El Príncipe* (Barcelona, 2000)

Apezarena, José, *Todos los hombres del Rey* (Barcelona, 1997)

Aranguren, José Luis, *La cruz de la monarquía española actual* (Madrid, 1974)

Areilza, José María de, *A lo largo del siglo 1909–1991* (Barcelona, 1992)

Areilza, José María de, *Así los he visto* (Barcelona, 1974)

Areilza, José María de, *Crónica de libertad* (Barcelona, 1985)

Areilza, José María de, *Cuadernos de la transición* (Barcelona, 1983)

Areilza, José María de, *Diario de un ministro de la monarquía* (Barcelona, 1977)

Areilza, José María de, *Memorias exteriores 1947–1964* (Barcelona, 1984)

Arespacochaga, Juan de, *Cartas a unos capitanes* (Madrid, 1994)

Armada, Alfonso, *Al servicio de la Corona* (Barcelona, 1983)

Armario, Diego, *El triangulo: el PSOE durante la transición* (Valencia, 1981)

Aróstegui, Julio, *Don Juan de Borbón* (Madrid, 2002)

Arregi, Natxo, *Memorias del KAS: 1975/78* (San Sebastián, 1981)

Arrese, José Luis de, *Una etapa constituyente* (Barcelona, 1982)

Arteaga, Federico de, *ETA y el proceso de Burgos* (Madrid, 1971)

Attard, Emilio, *La Constitución por dentro* (Barcelona, 1983)

Attard, Emilio, *Vida y muerte de UCD* (Barcelona, 1983)

Azcarate, Manuel, *Crisis del Eurocomunismo* (Barcelona, 1982)

Balansó, Juan, *Los Borbones incómodos* (Barcelona, 2000)

Balansó, Juan, *La Familia Real y la familia irreal* (Barcelona, 1993)

Balansó, Juan, *La familia rival* (Barcelona, 1994)

Balansó, Juan, *Por razón de Estado. Las bodas reales en España* (Barcelona, 2002)

Balansó, Juan, *Trio de Príncipes* (Barcelona, 1995)

Balfour, Sebastian & Preston, Paul, editors, *Spain and the Great Powers* (London, 1999)

Balfour, Sebastian, *Dictatorship, Workers and the City. Labour in Greater Barcelona Since 1939* (Oxford, 1989)

Barciela, Fernando, *La otra historia del PSOE* (Madrid, 1981)

Bardavío, Joaquín, *Las claves del Rey. El laberinto de la transición* (Madrid, 1995)

Bardavío, Joaquín, *La crisis: historia de quince días* (Madrid, 1974)

Bardavío, Joaquín, *El dilema: un pequeño caudillo o un gran Rey* (Madrid, 1978)

Bardavío, Joaquín, *La rama trágica de los Borbones* (Barcelona, 1989)

Bardavío, Joaquín, *Sábado santo rojo* (Madrid, 1980)

Bardavío, Joaquín, *Los silencios del Rey* (Madrid, 1979)

Bardavío, Joaquín, Cernuda, Pilar & Jaúregui, Fernando, *Servicios secretos* (Barcelona, 2000)

Bardavío, Joaquín & Sinova, Justino, *Todo Franco. Franquismo y antifranquismo de la A a la Z* (Barcelona, 2000)

Bayod, Ángel, editor, *Franco visto por sus ministros* (Barcelona, 1981)

Ben Ami, Shlomo, *La revolución desde arriba: España 1936–1979* (Barcelona, 1980)

Benegas, Txiki, *Euskadi: sin la paz nada es posible* (Barcelona, 1984)

Benet, Josép, *El President Tarradellas en els seus textos (1954–1988)* (Barcelona, 1992)

Bernáldez, José María, *El patron de la derecha (Biografía de Fraga)* (Barcelona, 1985)

Bernáldez, José María, *¿Ruptura o reforma?* (Barcelona, 1984)

Blanco, Juan, *23-F. Crónica fiel de un golpe anunciado* (Madrid, 1995)

Blaye, Edouard de, *Franco and the Politics of Spain* (Harmondsworth, 1976)

Bonmati de Codecido, Francisco, *El Príncipe Don Juan de España* (Valladolid, 1938)

Borbón, Alfonso de, *Las memorias de Alfonso de Borbón* (Barcelona, 1990)

Borbón Parma, María Teresa de, Clemente, Josép Carles & Cubero Sánchez, Joaquín, *Don Javier, una vida al servicio de la libertad* (Barcelona, 1997)

Borràs Betriu, Rafael et al., *El día en que mataron a Carrero Blanco* (Barcelona, 1974)

Borràs Betriu, Rafael, *El Rey de los Rojos. Don Juan de Borbón, una figura tergiversada* (Barcelona, 1996)

Borràs Betriu, Rafael, *El Rey perjuro. Alfonso XIII y la caída de la Monarquía* (Barcelona, 1997)

Borràs Betriu, Rafael, *Los últimos borbones. De Alfonso XIII al Príncipe Felipe* (Barcelona, 1999)

Brassloff, Audrey, *Religion and Politics in Spain. The Spanish Church in Transition, 1962–96* (London, 1998)

Brooksbank-Jones, Anny, *Women in Contemporary Spain* (Manchester, 1997)

Bruni, Luigi, *ETA. Historia política de una lucha armada* (Bilbao, 1988)

Burns Marañón, Tom, *Conversaciones sobre la derecha* (Barcelona, 1997)

Burns Marañón, Tom, *Conversaciones sobre el Rey* (Barcelona, 1995)

Busquets, Julio, *Militares y demócratas. Memorias de un fundador de la UMD y diputado socialista* (Barcelona, 1999)

Busquets, Julio, *Pronunciamientos y golpes de Estado en España* (Barcelona, 1982)

Busquets, Julio, Aguilar, Miguel Ángel & Puche, Ignacio, *El golpe: anatomía y claves del asalto al Congreso* (Barcelona, 1981)

Busquets, Julio & Losada, Juan Carlos, *Ruido de sables. Las conspiraciones militares en la España del siglo XX* (Barcelona, 2003)

Cacho, Jesús, *Asalto al Poder. La revolución de Mario Conde* (Madrid, 1988)

Cacho, Jesús, *M.C. Un intruso en el laberinto de los elegidos* (Madrid, 1994)

Cacho, Jesús, *El negocio de la libertad* (Madrid, 1999)

Calleja, Juan Luis, *Don Juan Carlos ¿por qué?* (Madrid, 1972)

Calvo Serer, Rafael, *La dictadura de los franquistas: El 'affaire' del MADRID y el futuro político* (Paris, 1973)

Calvo Serer, Rafael, *Franco frente al Rey. El proceso del régimen* (Paris, 1972)

Calvo Serer, Rafael, *¿Hacia la tercera República española? En defensa de la Monarquía democrática* (Barcelona, 1977)

Calvo Serer, Rafael, *Mis enfrentamientos con el Poder* (Barcelona, 1978)

Calvo Serer, Rafael, *La solución presidencialista* (Barcelona, 1979)

Calvo Sotelo, Leopoldo, *Memoria viva de la transición* (Barcelona, 1990)

Campo Vidal, Manuel, *Información y servicios secretos en el atentado al Presidente Carrero Blanco* (Barcelona, 1983)

Cantarero del Castillo, Manuel, *Falange y socialismo* (Barcelona, 1973)

Caparrós, Francisco, *La UMD: militares rebeldes* (Barcelona, 1983)

Carcedo, Diego, *23-F. Los cabos sueltos* (Madrid, 2001)

Cardona, Gabriel, *Franco y sus generales. La manicura del tigre* (Madrid, 2001)

Carlavilla, Mauricio, *Anti-España 1959: autores, cómplices y encubridores del communismo* (Madrid, 1959)

Carol, Màrius, *Las anécdotas de Don Juan Carlos. El quinto rey de la baraja* (Barcelona, 2000)

Carr, Raymond, *The Spanish Tragedy: The Civil War in Perspective* (London, 1977)

Carr, Raymond & Fusi, Juan Pablo, *Spain. Dictatorship to Democracy* (London, 1979)

Carrero Blanco, Almirante, *Discursos y escritos 1943–1973* (Madrid, 1974)

Carrillo, Santiago, *El año de la Constitución* (Barcelona, 1978)

Carrillo, Santiago, *El año de la peluca* (Barcelona, 1987)

Carrillo, Santiago, *Demain l'Espagne* (Paris, 1974)

Carrillo, Santiago, *Después de Franco, ¿Que?* (Paris, 1965)

Carrillo, Santiago, *Libertad y Socialismo* (Paris, 1971)

Carrillo, Santiago, *Memorias* (Barcelona, 1993)

Carrillo, Santiago, *Memoria de la transición* (Barcelona, 1983)

Carrillo, Santiago, *Hacia el post-franquismo* (Paris, 1974)

Casals i Meseguer, Xavier, *Neonazis en España. De las audiciones wagnerianas a los skinheads (1966–1995)* (Barcelona, 1995)

Casals i Meseguer, Xavier, *La tentación neofascista en España* (Barcelona, 1998)

Castellano, Pablo, *Por Dios, por la Patria y el Rey. Una vision crítica de la transición española* (Madrid, 2001)

Castellano, Pablo, *Yo sí me acuerdo. Apuntes e historias* (Madrid, 1994)

Castells Arteche, Miguel, *El mejor defensor el pueblo* (San Sebastián, 1978)

Castells Arteche, Miguel, *Radiografía de un modelo represivo* (San Sebastián, 1982)

Cavero, José, *Poderes fácticos en la democracia* (Madrid, 1990)

Cebrian, Juan Luis, *La España que bosteza* (Madrid, 1981)

Cerdán Tato, Enrique, *La lucha por la democracia en Alicante* (Madrid, 1978)

Cernuda, Pilar, *30 días de noviembre. El mes que cambió la historia de España: las claves* (Barcelona, 2000)

Cernuda, Pilar, Jaúregui, Fernando & Menéndez, Manuel Ángel, *23-F. La conjura de los necios* (Madrid, 2001)

Cernuda, Pilar, Oneto, José, Pi, Ramón & Ramírez, Pedro J., *Todo un Rey* (Barcelona, 1981)

Chamorro, Eduardo, *Felipe González: un hombre a la espera* (Barcelona, 1980)

Chamorro, Eduardo, *Viaje al centro de UCD* (Barcelona, 1981)

Chamorro, Eduardo, *25 años sin Franco. La refundación de España* (Barcelona, 2000)

Chao, José, *La Iglesia en el franquismo* (Madrid, 1976)

Chao, Ramón, *Après Franco, l'Espagne* (Paris, 1975)

Christie, Stuart, *The Christie File* (Seattle, 1980)

Cid Cañaveral, Ricardo et al., *Todos al suelo: la conspiración y el golpe* (Madrid, 1981)

Cierva, Ricardo de la, *Crónicas de la transición. De la muerte de Carrero a la proclamación del Rey* (Barcelona, 1975)

Cierva, Ricardo de la, *La derecha sin remedio (1801–1987)* (Barcelona, 1987)

Cierva, Ricardo de la, *Don Juan de Borbón: por fin toda la verdad* (Madrid, 1997)

Cierva, Ricardo de la, *Francisco Franco: biografía histórica*, 6 vols (Barcelona, 1982)

Cierva, Ricardo de la, *Francisco Franco: un siglo de España*, 2 vols (Madrid, 1973)

Cierva, Ricardo de la, *Historia del franquismo: I orígenes y configuración (1939–1945)* (Barcelona, 1975)

Cierva, Ricardo de la, *Historia del franquismo: II aislamiento, transformación, agonía (1945–1975)* (Barcelona, 1978)

Cierva, Ricardo de la, *Juan Carlos I: misión imposible* (Madrid, 1996)

Cierva, Ricardo de la, *La lucha por el poder: Así cayó Arias Navarro* (Madrid, 1996)

Cierva, Ricardo de la, *No nos robarán nuestra historia. Nuevas mentiras, falsificaciones y revelaciones* (Madrid, 1995)

Clark, Robert P., *The Basque Insurgents: ETA, 1952–1980* (Wisconsin, 1984)

Clark, Robert P., *The Basques: The Franco Years and Beyond* (Reno, 1979)

Claudín, Fernando, *Santiago Carrillo: crónica de un secretario general* (Barcelona, 1983)

Claudín, Fernando, *Las divergencias en el Partido* (Paris, 1964)

Clavero Arévalo, Manuel, *España, desde el centralismo a las autonomías* (Barcelona, 1983)

Colectivo Democracia, *Los Ejércitos . . . más allá del golpe* (Barcelona, 1981)

Coverdale, John F., *The Political Transformation of Spain after Franco* (New York, 1979)

Cuadernos de Ruedo Ibérico, Horizonte español 1966, 2 vols (Paris, 1966)

Cuadernos de Ruedo Ibérico, Horizonte español 1972, 3 vols (Paris, 1972)

Debray, Laurence, *La forja de un rey. Juan Carlos I, de sucesor de Franco a Rey de España* (Sevilla, 2000)

Díaz, Elias, *Pensamiento español 1939–1973* (Madrid, 1974)

Díaz, Elias, *Socialismo en España: el Partido y el Estado* (Madrid, 1982)

Díaz, Elias, *La transición a la democracia (Claves ideológicas, 1976–1986)* (Madrid, 1987)

Díaz, Elias, *Los viejos maestros. La reconstrucción de la razón* (Madrid, 1994)

Díaz Cardiel, Victor et al., *Madrid en huelga: enero 1976* (Madrid, 1976)

Díaz Herrera, José & Durán Doussinague, Isabel, *Aznar. La vida desconocida de un presidente* (Barcelona, 1999)

Díaz Herrera, José & Durán Doussinague, Isabel, *El saqueo de España* (Madrid, 1996)

Díaz Herrera, José & Durán Doussinague, Isabel, *ETA. El saqueo de Euskadi* (Barcelona, 2002)

Díaz Herrera, José & Durán Doussinague, Isabel, *Los secretos del Poder. Del legado franquista al ocaso del felipismo: Episodios inconfesables* (Madrid, 1994)

Díaz Plaja, Fernando, *Anecdotario de la España franquista* (Barcelona, 1997)

Díaz Salazar, Rafael, *Iglesia, dictadura y democracia: Catolicismo y sociedad en España (1953–1979)* (Madrid, 1981)

Domínguez, José Ignacio, *Cuando yo era un exiliado* (Madrid, 1977)

Dunthorn, David J., *Britain and the Spanish Anti-Franco Opposition, 1940–1950* (London, 2000)

Durán, Manuel, *Martín Villa* (San Sebastián, 1979)

Eaton, Samuel, *The Forces of Freedom in Spain 1974–1979: A Personal Account* (Stanford, 1981)

Ekaizer, Ernesto, *Banqueros de rapiña. Crónica secreta de Mario Conde* (Barcelona, 1994)

Ellwood, Sheelagh, *Prietas las filas: historia de Falange Española 1933–1983* (Barcelona, 1984)

Elosegi, Joséba, *Quiero morir por algo* (n.p., n.d., but St Jean de Luz, 1971)

Enrique y Tarancón, Vicente, *Confesiones* (Madrid, 1996)

Equipo de Documentación Política, *Oposición española. Documentos secretos* (Madrid, 1976)

Equipo Mundo, *Los noventa ministros de Franco* (Barcelona, 1970)

Esteban, Jorge de et al., *Desarrollo político y constitución española* (Barcelona, 1973)

Esteban, Jorge de & Lopez Guerra, Luis, editors, *Las elecciones legislativas del 1 de marzo de 1979* (Madrid, 1979)

Esteban, Jorge de & López Guerra, Luis, *Los Partidos políticos en la España actual* (Barcelona, 1982)

Estévez, Carlos & Mármol, Francisco, *Carrero. Las razones ocultas de un asesinato* (Madrid, 1998)

Fabre, Jaume, Huertas, Josep M. & Ribas, Antoni, *Vint anys de resistència catalana (1939–1959)* (Barcelona, 1978)

Falcón, Lidia, *Viernes y trece en la Calle del Correo* (Barcelona, 1981)

Farràs, Andreu & Cullell, Pere, *El 23-F a Catalunya* (Barcelona, 1998)

Feo, Julio, *Aquellos años* (Barcelona, 1993)

Fernández de Castro, Ignacio & Martínez, José, editors, *España hoy* (Paris, 1963)

Fernández de la Mora, Gonzalo, *Los errores del cambio* (Barcelona, 1986)

Fernández de la Mora, Gonzalo, *Río arriba. Memorias* (Barcelona, 1995)

Fernández López, Javier, *Diecisiete horas y media. El enigma del 23-F* (Madrid, 2000)

Fernández López, Javier, *El Rey y otros militares. Los militares en el cambio de régimen político en España (1969–1982)* (Madrid, 1998)

Fernández López, Javier, *Militares contra Franco. Historia de la Unión Militar Democrática* (Zaragoza, 2002)

Fernández López, Javier, *Sabino Fernández Campo. Un hombre de Estado* (Barcelona, 2000)

Fernández-Miranda Lozana, Pilar & Fernández-Miranda Campoamor, Alfonso, *Lo que el Rey me ha pedido. Torcuato Fernández-Miranda y la reforma política* (Barcelona, 1995)

Fernández Santander, Carlos, *El Almirante Carrero* (Barcelona, 1985)

Fernández Santander, Carlos, *Los militares en la transición política* (Barcelona, 1982)

Figuero, Javier, *UCD: la 'empresa' que creó Adolfo Suarez* (Barcelona, 1981)

Figuero, Javier & Herrero, Luis, *La muerte de Franco jamás contada* (Barcelona, 1985)

Fishman, Robert M., *Working Class Organization and the Return to Democracy in Spain* (Ithaca, 1990)

Foltz, Charles Jr, *The Masquerade in Spain* (Boston, 1948)

Fontán, Antonio, editor, *Los monárquicos y el régimen de Franco* (Madrid, 1996)

Forest, Eva, *From a Spanish Jail* (Harmondsworth, 1975)

Forest, Eva, *Información número 179 – Testimonios de lucha y resistencia Yeserías 75–77* (San Sebastián, 1979)

Fortes, José & Otero, Luis, *Proceso a nueve militares demócratas: las Fuerzas Armadas y la UMD* (Barcelona, 1983)

Fraga Iribarne, Manuel, *En busca del tiempo servido* (Barcelona, 1987)

Fraga Iribarne, Manuel, *Memoria breve de una vida política* (Barcelona, 1980)

Franco Bahamonde, Pilar, *Cinco años después* (Barcelona, 1981)

Franco Bahamonde, Pilar, *Nosotros los Franco* (Barcelona, 1980)

Franco Salgado-Araujo, Francisco, *Mis conversaciones privadas con Franco* (Barcelona, 1976)

Franco Salgado-Araujo, Francisco, *Mi vida junto a Franco* (Barcelona, 1977)

Fuente, Ismael, *El caballo cansado. El largo adios de Felipe González* (Madrid, 1991)

Fuente, Ismael, Garcia, Javier & Prieto, Joaquín, *Golpe mortal: asesinato de Carrero y agonía del franquismo* (Madrid, 1983)

Fuente, Licinio de la, *"Valió la pena" Memorias* (Madrid, 1998)

Fuentes Gómez de Salazar, Eduardo, *El pacto del capó. El testimonio clave de un militar sobre el 23-F* (Madrid, 1994)

Gallagher, Charles F., *Spain, Development and the Energy Crisis* (New York, 1973)

Gallego-Díaz, Soledad & Cuadra, Bonifacio de la, *Crónica secreta de la Constitución* (Madrid, 1989)

García de Cortázar, Fernando & Azcona, José Manuel, *El nacionalismo vasco* (Madrid, 1991)

Garmendia, José María, *Historia de ETA*, 2 vols (San Sebastián, 1980)

Garriga, Ramón, *La España de Franco: de la División Azul al pacto con los Estados Unidos (1943 a 1951)* (Puebla, México, 1971)

Garriga, Ramón, *Nicolás Franco, el hermano brujo* (Barcelona, 1980)

Garriga, Ramón, *La Señora de El Pardo* (Barcelona, 1979)

Garrigues y Díaz Cañabate, Antonio, *Diálogos conmigo mismo* (Barcelona, 1978)

Garrigues Walker, Joaquín, *¿Qué es el liberalismo?* (Barcelona, 1976)

'Gasteiz', *Vitoria, de la huelga a la matanza* (Paris, 1976)

Gil, Vicente, *Cuarenta años junto a Franco* (Barcelona, 1981)

Gil Robles, José María, *La monarquía por la que yo luché: páginas de un diario 1941–1954* (Madrid, 1976)

Gillespie, Richard, *The Spanish Socialist Party. A History of Factionalism* (Oxford, 1989)

Gilmour, David, *The Transformation of Spain: From Franco to the Constitutional Monarchy* (London, 1985)

Gilmour, John, *Manuel Fraga Iribarne and the Rebirth of Spanish Conservatism, 1939–1990* (Lewiston, NY, 1999)

Giménez-Arnau, Joaquín, *Yo, Jimmy: mi vida entre los Franco* (Barcelona, 1981)

Giménez-Arnau, José Antonio, *Memorias de memoria. Descifre vuecencia personalmente* (Barcelona, 1978)

Girón de Velasco, José Antonio, *Si la memoria no me falla* (Barcelona, 1994)

Gómez Santos, Marino, *Conversaciones con Leopoldo Calvo Sotelo* (Barcelona, 1982)

González, Manuel-Jesús, *La economía política del franquismo 1940–1970: dirigismo, mercado y planificación* (Madrid, 1979)

González de la Vega, Javier, *Yo, María de Borbón* (Madrid, 1995)

González-Doria, Fernando, *Don Juan de Borbón, el padre del Rey* (Madrid, 1990)

González-Doria, Fernando, *¿Por qué la Monarquía?* (Madrid, 1976)

Gracia, Fernando, *Elena. Crónica de noviazgo real* (Madrid, 1995)

Gracia, Fernando, *La madre del Rey. La vida de doña María de las Mercedes: una causa histórica* (Madrid, 1994)

Gracia, Fernando, *Lo que nunca nos contaron de Don Juan* (Madrid, 1993)

Gracia, Fernando, *Objetivo matar al Rey* (Madrid, 1996)

Graham, Robert, *Spain: Change of a Nation* (London, 1984)

Granados Vázquez, José Luis, *1975: El año de la instauración* (Madrid, 1977)

(Grimau García, Julián), *¿Crimen o castigo? Documentos inéditos sobre Julián Grimau García* (Madrid, 1963)

Güell, Felipe Bertrán, *Preparación y desarrollo del alzamiento nacional* (Valladolid, 1939)

Gunther, Richard, Sani, Giacomo & Shabad, Goldie, *Spain After Franco. The Making of a Competitive Party System* (Berkeley, California, 1986)

Gurriarán, José Antonio, *El Rey en Estoril. Don Juan Carlos y su familia en el exilio portugués* (Barcelona, 2000)

531

Gutiérrez, Fernando, *Curas represaliados en el franquismo* (Madrid, 1977)

Gutiérrez Mellado, Manuel, *Un soldado para España* (Barcelona, 1983)

Gutiérrez-Ravé, José, *El Conde de Barcelona* (Madrid, 1963)

Harrison, Joseph, *The Spanish Economy. From the Civil War to the European Community* (London, 1993)

Harrison, Joseph, *The Spanish Economy in the Twentieth Century* (London, 1985)

Heine, Hartmut, *La oposición política al franquismo* (Barcelona, 1983)

Hernández Gil, Antonio, *El cambio político español y la Constitución* (Barcelona, 1984)

Herrero, Luis, *El ocaso del régimen. Del asesinato de Carrero a la muerte de Franco* (Madrid, 1995)

Herrero de Miñón, Miguel, *Memorias de estío* (Madrid, 1993)

Herrero de Miñón, Miguel, *El principio monárquico* (Madrid, 1972)

Heywood, Paul, *The Government and Politics of Spain* (London, 1995)

Heywood, Paul, editor, *Policy and Politics in Democratic Spain* (London, 1999)

Hidalgo Huerta, Manuel, *Cómo y porqué operé a Franco* (Madrid, 1976)

Hoare, Sir Samuel, *Ambassador on Special Mission* (London, 1946)

Hopkin, Jonathan, *Party Formation and Democratic Transition in Spain. The Creation and Collapse of the Union of the Democratic Centre* (London, 1999)

Huneeus, Carlos, *La Unión de Centro Democrático y la transición a la democracia en España* (Madrid, 1985)

Ibarra Güell, Pedro, *La evolución estratégica de ETA (1963–1987)* (Bilbao, 1987)

Ibarra Güell, Pedro, *El movimiento obrero en Vizcaya: 1967–1977* (Bilbao, 1987)

Iniesta Cano, Carlos, *Memorias y recuerdos* (Barcelona, 1984)

Iribarren, José María, *Mola, datos para una biografía y para la historia del alzamiento nacional* (Zaragoza, 1938)

Izquierdo, Antonio, *Claves para un día de febrero* (Barcelona, 1982)

Izquierdo, Antonio, *Yo, testigo de cargo* (Barcelona, 1981)

Izquierdo, Manuel P., *De la huelga general a las elecciones generales* (Madrid, 1977)

Jaraiz Franco, Pilar, *Historia de una disidencia* (Barcelona, 1981)

Jaúregui, Fernando & Menéndez, Manuel Ángel, *Lo que nos queda de Franco. Símbolos, personajes, leyes y costumbres, veinte años después* (Madrid, 1995)

Jaúregui, Fernando & Soriano, Manuel, *La otra historia de UCD* (Madrid, 1980)

Jaúregui Bereciartu, Gurutz, *Ideología y estrategia política de ETA* (Madrid, 1981)

Jérez Mir, Miguel, *Elites políticas y centros de extracción en España 1938–1957* (Madrid, 1982)

Juliá, Santos, Pradera, Javier & Prieto, Joaquín, coordinadores, *Memoria de la Transición* (Madrid, 1996)

Krasikov, Anatoly, *From Dictatorship To Democracy: Spanish Reportage* (Oxford, 1984)

Kindelán, Alfredo, *La verdad de mis relaciones con Franco* (Barcelona, 1981)

Laiz, Consuelo, *La lucha final. Los partidos de izquierda radical durante la transición española* (Madrid, 1995)

Lannon, Frances, *Privilege, Persecution, and Prophecy: The Catholic Church in Spain 1875–1975* (Oxford, 1987)

Lannon, Frances & Preston, Paul, editors, *Elites and Power in Twentieth-Century Spain: Essays in Honour of Sir Raymond Carr* (Oxford, 1990)

Laot, Françoise, *Juan Carlos y Sofía* (Madrid, 1987)

Lavardín, Javier, *Historia del último pretendiente a la corona de España* (Paris, 1976)

Lleonart y Anselem, A.J., *España y ONU II (1947)* (Madrid, 1983)

Lleonart y Anselem, A.J., *España y ONU III (1948–1949): La "cuestión española"* (Madrid, 1985)

Lleonart y Anselem, A.J., *España y ONU IV (1950): La "cuestión española"* (Madrid, 1991)

Lleonart y Anselem, A.J., *España y ONU V (1951): La "cuestión española"* (Madrid, 1996)

Lleonart y Anselem, Alberto J. & Castiella y Maiz, Fernando María, *España y ONU I (1945–46)* (Madrid, 1978)

Letamendia Belzunce, Francisco (Ortzi), *Historia del nacionalismo vasco y de ETA 1 ETA en el franquismo (1951–1976)* (San Sebastián, 1994)

Letamendia Belzunce, Francisco (Ortzi), *Historia del nacionalismo vasco y de ETA 2 ETA en la transición (1976–1982)* (San Sebastián, 1994)

Letamendia Belzunce, Francisco (Ortzi), *Historia del nacionalismo vasco y de ETA 3 ETA y el Gobierno del PSOE (1982–1992)* (San Sebastián, 1994)

Lieberman, Sima, *The Contemporary Spanish Economy: A Historical Perspective* (London, 1982)

Linz, Juan J., 'An Authoritarian Regime: Spain' in E. Allardt & Y. Littunen, editors, *Cleavages, Ideologies and Party Systems* (Helsinki, 1964)

Linz, Juan J. et al., *Conflicto en Euskadi* (Madrid, 1986)

Linz, Juan J. et al., *IV Informe FOESSA Volumen I: Informe sociologico sobre el cambio político en España: 1975–1981* (Madrid, 1981)

Lizcano, Pablo, *La generación del 56: la universidad contra Franco* (Barcelona, 1981)

López Pintor, Rafael, *La opinión pública española: del franquismo a la democracia* (Madrid, 1982)

López Rodó, Laureano, *Claves de la transición. Memorias IV* (Barcelona, 1993)

López Rodó, Laureano, *El principio del fin: Memorias* (Barcelona, 1992)

López Rodó, Laureano, *La larga marcha hacia la monarquía* (Barcelona, 1977)

López Rodó, Laureano, *Memorias* (Barcelona, 1990)

López Rodó, Laureano, *Memorias: años decisivos* (Barcelona, 1991)

López Rodó, Laureano, *Política y desarrollo* (Madrid, 1970)

López Rodó, Laureano, *Testimonio de una política de Estado* (Barcelona, 1987)

Lurra, *Burgos, Juicio a un pueblo* (San Sebastián, 1978)

Maravall, José María, *El desarrollo económico y la clase obrera* (Barcelona, 1970)

Maravall, José María, *Dictatorship and Political Dissent: Workers and Students in Franco's Spain* (London, 1978)

Maravall, José María, *The Transition to Democracy in Spain* (London, 1982)

Martín Villa, Rodolfo, *Al servicio del Estado* (Barcelona, 1984)

Martínez Campos, Carlos, *Ayer 1931–1953* (Madrid, 1970)

Martínez Cobo, Carlos & José, editors, *Congresos del PSOE en el exilio 1944–1974*, 2 vols (Madrid, 1981)

Martínez Cobo, Carlos & José, *¿República? ¿Monarquía? En busca del consenso. Intrahistoria del PSOE II (1946–1954)* (Barcelona, 1992)

Martínez Inglés, Amadeo, *23-F. El golpe que nunca existió* (Madrid, 2001)

Martínez Inglés, Amadeo, *La transición vigilada. Del Sábado Santo 'rojo' al 23-F* (Madrid, 1994)

Martínez Nadal, Rafael, *Antonio Torres de la BBC a The Observer: Republicanos y monárquicos en el exilio (1944–1956)* (Madrid, 1996)

Matheopoulos, Helena, *Juan Carlos I. El Rey de nuestro tiempo* (Madrid, 1996)

Melgar, Francisco, *El noble final de la escisión dinástica* (Madrid, 1964)

Meliá, Josép, *Así cayó Adolfo Suárez* (Barcelona, 1981)

Mérida, María, *Testigos de Franco: retablo íntimo de una dictadura* (Barcelona, 1977)

Mérida, María, *Un rey sin corte* (Barcelona, 1993)

Meyer-Stabley, Bertrand, *Juan Carlos. El Rey* (Barcelona, 1993)

Miguel, Amando de, *Sociologia del franquismo* (Barcelona, 1975)

Miguélez, Faustino, *La lucha de los mineros asturianos bajo el franquismo* (Barcelona, 1976)

Míguez González, Santiago, *La preparación de la transición a la democracia en España* (Zaragoza, 1990)

Moa Rodríguez, Pío, *De un tiempo y de un país* (Madrid, 1982)

Mohedano, José María & Peña, Marcos, *Constitución: cuenta atrás ETA-Operación Galaxia y otros terrorismos* (Madrid, 1978)

Mola, Emilio, *Obras completas* (Valladolid, 1940)

Mora, Francisco, *Ni heroes ni bribones: los personajes del 23-F* (Barcelona, 1982)

Morales, José Luis y Celada, Juan, *La alternativa militar: el golpismo después de Franco* (Madrid, 1981)

Morán, Gregorio, *Adolfo Suárez: historia de una ambición* (Barcelona, 1979)

Morán, Gregorio, *Los españoles que dejaron de serlo: Euskadi, 1937–1981* (Barcelona, 1982)

Morán, Gregorio, *El precio de la transición* (Barcelona, 1991)

Morán, Gregorio, *Testamento vasco. Un ensayo de interpretación* (Madrid, 1988)

Morodo, Raúl, *Atando cabos. Memorias de un conspirador moderado (I)* (Madrid, 2001)

Morodo, Raúl, *Por una sociedad democrática y progresista* (Madrid, 1982)

Morodo, Raúl, *La transición política* (Madrid, 1984)

Moya, Carlos, *Señas de Leviatán. Estado nacional y sociedad industrial: España 1936–1980* (Madrid, 1984)

Moya, Carlos, *El Poder economico en España (1939–1970). Un análisis sociológico* (Madrid, 1975)

Mujal Leon, Eusebio, *Communism and Political Change in Spain* (Bloomington, 1983)

Muñoz Alonso, Alejandro et al., *Las elecciones del cambio* (Barcelona, 1984)

Muñoz Alonso, Alejandro, *El terrorismo en España* (Barcelona, 1982)

Murtagh, Peter, *The Rape of Greece. The King, the Colonels and the Resistance* (London, 1994)

Naredo, José Manuel, *La evolución de la agricultura en España*, 2nd edition (Barcelona, 1974)

Navarro, Julia, *Entre Felipe y Aznar 1982–1996* (Madrid, 1996)

Navarro, Julia, *Nosotros, la transición* (Madrid, 1995)

Navarro, Julia, *Señora Presidenta* (Barcelona, 1999)

Navarro Rubio, Mariano, *Mis memorias. Testimonio de una vida política truncada por el "Caso MATESA"* (Barcelona, 1991)

Noel, Gerard, *Ena Spain's English Queen* (London, 1984)

Noticias del Pais, Vasco, *Euskadi: el último estado de excepción* (Paris, 1975)

Nourry, Philippe, *Juan Carlos. Un rey para los republicanos* (Barcelona, 1986)

Onaindia, Mario, *La lucha de clases en Euskadi (1939–1980)* (San Sebastián, 1980)

Oneto, José, *Anatomía de un cambio de régimen* (Barcelona, 1985)

Oneto, José, *Arias entre dos crisis, 1973–1975* (Madrid, 1975)

Oneto, José, *100 días en la muerte de Francisco Franco* (Madrid, 1975)

Oneto, José, *La noche de Tejero* (Barcelona, 1981)

Oneto, José, *El secuestro del cambio. Felipe año II* (Barcelona, 1984)

Oneto, José, *Los últimos días de un presidente: de la dimisión al golpe de Estado* (Barcelona, 1981)

Oneto, José, *La verdad sobre el caso Tejero* (Barcelona, 1982)

Ortuño, Pilar, *European Socialists and Spain. The Transition to Democracy, 1959–77* (London, 2002)

Ortzi (pseudonym of Francisco Letamendia), *Historia de Euskadi: el nacionalismo vasco y ETA* (Paris, 1975)

Osorio, Alfonso, *De orilla a orilla* (Barcelona, 2000)

Osorio, Alfonso, *Trayectoria política de un ministro de la corona* (Barcelona, 1980)

Palabras de su Alteza Real el Príncipe de Asturias Juan Carlos de Borbón y Borbón (Madrid, 1974)

Palacios, Jesús, *Los papeles secretos de Franco. De las relaciones con Juan Carlos y Don Juan al protagonismo del Opus* (Madrid, 1996)

Palacios, Jesús, *23-F: El golpe del CESID* (Barcelona, 2001)

Paniagua, F. Javier, *La ordenación del capitalismo avanzado en España: 1957–1963* (Barcelona, 1977)

Pardo Zancada, Ricardo, *23-F. La pieza que falta. Testimonio de un protagonista* (Barcelona, 1998)

Paricio, Jesús M., *Para conocer a nuestros militares* (Madrid, 1983)

Parti Communiste Français, *Dos meses de huelgas* (Paris, 1962)

Pasamar Alzuria, Gonzalo, *Historiografía e ideología en la postguerra española. La ruptura de la tradición liberal* (Zaragoza, 1991)

Payne, Stanley G., *Politics and the Military in Modern Spain* (Stanford, 1967)

Payne, Stanley G., *The Franco Regime 1936–1975* (Madison, 1987)

Pemán, José María, *Mis almuerzos con gente importante* (Barcelona, 1970)

Pemán, José María, *Mis encuentros con Franco* (Barcelona, 1976)

Peñafiel, Jaime, *¡Dios salve la Reina! Pequeña historia de una gran profesional* (Madrid, 1993)

Peñafiel, Jaime, *¡Dios salve . . . también al Rey!* (Madrid, 1995)

Peñafiel, Jaime, *El General y su tropa. Mis recuerdos de la familia Franco* (Madrid, 1992)

Peñafiel, Jaime, *¿Y quién salva al Príncipe? Los secretos mejor guardados de Felipe de Borbón* (Madrid, 1996)

Pérez Díaz, Víctor, *Spain at the Crossroads. Civil Society, Politics and the Rule of Law* (Cambridge, Mass, 1999)

Pérez Mateos, Juan Antonio, *Juan Carlos. La infancia desconocida de un Rey* (Barcelona, 1980)

Pérez Mateos, Juan Antonio, *El Rey que vino del exilio* (Barcelona, 1981)

Pérez Mateos, Juan Antonio, *Un Rey bajo el sol. El duro camino de Juan Carlos I hacia el Trono* (Barcelona, 1998)

Perote, Juan Alberto, *23-F; Ni Milans ni Tejero. El informe que se ocultó* (Madrid, 2001)

Pi, Ramon, *Joaquín Garrigues Walker* (Madrid, 1977)

Pla, Juan, *La trama civil del golpe* (Barcelona, 1982)

Platón, Miguel, *Alfonso XIII: De Primo de Rivera a Franco. La tentación autoritaria de la Monarquía* (Barcelona, 1998)

Platón, Miguel, *Hablan los militares. Testimonios para la historia (1939–1996)* (Barcelona, 2001)

Porcioles, José María de, *Mis memorias* (Barcelona, 1994)

Portell, José María, *Euskadi: amnistia arrancada* (Barcelona, 1977)

Portell, José María, *Los hombres de ETA*, 3rd edition (Barcelona, 1976)

Portero, Florentino, *Franco aislado: la cuestión española (1945–1950)* (Madrid, 1989)

Powell, Charles T., *España en democracia, 1975–2000* (Barcelona, 2001)

Powell, Charles T., *Juan Carlos. Self-Made Monarch* (London, 1996)

Powell, Charles T., *Juan Carlos. Un Rey para la democracia* (Barcelona, 1995)

Powell, Charles T., *El piloto del cambio. El Rey, la Monarquía y la transición a la democracia* (Barcelona, 1991)

Prego, Victoria, *Así se hizo la Transición* (Barcelona, 1995)

Prego, Victoria, *Diccionario de la Transición* (Barcelona, 1999)

Prego, Victoria, *Presidentes. Veinticinco años de historia narrada por los cuatro jefes de Gobierno de la democracia* (Barcelona, 2000)

Preston, Paul, *Franco: A Biography* (London, 1993)

Preston, Paul, coordinador, *España en crisis: evolución y decadencia del régimen franquista* (Madrid & México D.F., 1978)

Preston, Paul, *Palomas de guerra. Cinco mujeres marcadas por el enfrentamiento bélico* (Barcelona, 2001)

Preston, Paul, *The Politics of Revenge: Fascism and the Military in 20th Century Spain* (London, 1990)

Preston, Paul, editor, *Spain in Crisis: Evolution and Decline of the Franco Regime* (Hassocks, 1976)

Preston, Paul & Smyth, Denis, *Spain, the EEC and NATO* (London, 1984)

Preston, Paul, *The Triumph of Democracy in Spain* (London, 1986)

Prieto, Joaquín & Barbería, José Luis, *El enigma del "Elefante". La conspiración del 23-F* (Madrid, 1991)

Prieto, Martín, *Técnica de un golpe de Estado: el juicio del 23-F* (Barcelona, 1982)

Primo de Rivera y Urquijo, Miguel, *No a las dos Españas. Memorias políticas* (Barcelona, 2002)

Puell de la Villa, Fernando, *Gutiérrez Mellado. Un militar del siglo XX (1912–1995)* (Madrid, 1997)

Ramírez, Luis (pseudonym of Luciano Rincón), *Franco: la obsesion de ser, la obsesion de poder* (Paris, 1976)

Ramírez, Luis, *Nuestros primeros veinticinco años* (Paris, 1964)

Ramírez, Pedro J., *Así se ganaron las elecciones* (Barcelona, 1977)

Ramírez, Pedro J., *Así se ganaron las elecciones 1979* (Madrid, 1979)

Ramírez, Pedro J., *El año que murió Franco* (Barcelona, 1985)

Rayón, Fernando, *La Boda de Juan Carlos y Sofía. Claves y secretos de un enlace histórico* (Madrid, 2002)

Rayón, Fernando, *Sofía de Grecia. La Reina* (Barcelona, 1993)

Reina Federica de Grecia, *Memorias* (Madrid, 1971)

Reinares, Fernando, editor, *Violencia y política en Euskadi* (Bilbao, 1984)

Reinlein, Fernando, *Capitanes rebeldes. Los militares españoles durante la Transición: De la UMD al 23-F* (Madrid, 2002)

Ridruejo, Dionisio, *Casi unas memorias* (Barcelona, 1976)

Rincón, Luciano, *ETA (1974–1984)* (Barcelona, 1985)

Roa Ventura, Agustín, *Agonía y muerte del franquismo (una memoria)* (Barcelona, 1978)

Robilant, Olghina di, *Sangue blu* (Milan, 1991)

Rodríguez Armada, Amandino & Novais, José Antonio, *¿Quién mató a Julián Grimau?* (Madrid, 1976)

Rodríguez Jiménez, José Luis, *Reaccionarios y golpistas. La extrema derecha en España: del tardofranquismo a la consolidación de la democracia (1967–1982)* (Madrid, 1994)

Rodríguez Martínez, Julio, *Impresiones de un ministro de Carrero Blanco* (Barcelona, 1974)

Romero, Ana, *Historia de Carmen. Memorias de Carmen Díez de Rivera* (Barcelona, 2002)

Romero, Emilio, *Tragicomedia de España. Unas memorias sin contemplaciones* (Barcelona, 1985)

Rix, Rob, editor, *Thrillers in the Transition* (Leeds, 1992)

Rubbotom, R. Richard & Murphy, J. Carter, *Spain and the United States Since World War II* (New York, 1984)

Ruiz, David, coordinador, *Historia de Comisiones Obreras (1958–1988)* (Madrid, 1993)

Ruiz Ayúcar, Ángel, *Crónica agitada de ocho años tranquilos: 1963–1970* (Madrid, 1974)

Ruiz Moragas, Leandro Alfonso, *El bastardo real. Memorias del hijo no reconocido de Alfonso XIII* (Madrid, 2002)

Saez Alba, A. (seudónimo de Alfonso Colodrón), *La otra cosa nostra: la Asociación Católica Nacional de Propagandistas y el caso de EL CORREO de Andalucía* (Paris, 1974)

Sagardoy, J.A. & Leon Blanco, David, *El poder sindical en España* (Barcelona, 1982)

Sainz Rodríguez, Pedro, *Un reinado en la sombra* (Barcelona, 1981)

Salaberri, Kepa, *El proceso de Euskadi en Burgos. El sumarísimo 31.69* (Paris, 1971)

Salmador, Víctor, *Don Juan de Borbón. Grandeza y servidumbre del deber* (Barcelona, 1976)

Salmador, Víctor, *Don Juan. Los secretos de un Rey sin trono* (Madrid, 1993)

Sánchez Erauskin, Javier, *Txiki-Otaegi: el viento y las raices* (San Sebastián, 1978)

Sánchez Montero, Simón, *Camino de la libertad. Memorias* (Madrid, 1997)

Sánchez Soler, Mariano, *Los hijos del 20-N. Historia violenta del fascismo español* (Madrid, 1993)

Sánchez Soler, Mariano, *Villaverde: fortuna y caída de la casa Franco* (Barcelona, 1990)

Sánchez-Terán, Salvador, *De Franco a la Generalitat* (Barcelona, 1988)

San Martín, José Ignacio, *Servicio especial* (Barcelona, 1983)

Sanz, Benito, *Los socialistas en el País Valenciano (1939–1978)* (Valencia, 1982)

Sanz, Jesús, *La cara secreta de la política valenciana: de la predemocracia al Estatuto de Benicasim* (Valencia, 1982)

Sarasqueta, Antxón, *De Franco a Felipe* (Barcelona, 1984)

Sartorius, Nicolás & Alfaya, Javier, *La memoria insumisa. Sobre la Dictadura de Franco* (Madrid, 1999)

Satrústegui, Joaquín et al., editors, *Cuando la transición se hizo posible. El "contubernio de Munich"* (Madrid, 1993)

Seara Vazquez, Modesto, *El socialismo en España* (México D.F., 1980)

Segura, Santiago & Merino, Julio, *Jaque al Rey: las "enigmas" y las "incongruencias" del 23-F* (Barcelona, 1983)

Segura, Santiago & Merino, Julio, *Las vísperas del 23-F* (Barcelona, 1984)

Semprún, Jorge, *Autobiografía de Federico Sánchez* (Barcelona, 1977)

Semprún, Jorge, *Federico Sánchez se despide de ustedes* (Barcelona, 1993)

Silva, Pedro de, *Las fuerzas del cambio. Cuando el Rey dudó el 23-F y otros ensayos sobre la transición* (Barcelona, 1996)

Silva Muñoz, Federico, *Memorias políticas* (Barcelona, 1993)

Silva Muñoz, Federico, *La transición inacabada* (Barcelona, 1980)

Sinova, Justino, *Historia de la transición. 10 años que cambiaron España 1973–1983*, 2 vols (Madrid, 1983–1984)

Soriano, Manuel, *Sabino Fernández Campo. La sombra del Rey* (Madrid, 1995)

Soriano, Ramón, *La mano izquierdo de Franco* (Barcelona, 1981)

Sotillos, Eduardo, *1982. El año clave* (Madrid, 2002)

Suárez Fernández, Luis, *Francisco Franco y su tiempo*, 8 vols (Madrid, 1984)

Suárez Fernández, Luis, *Franco: la historia y sus documentos*, 20 vols (Madrid, 1986)

Sueiro, Daniel & Díaz Nosty, Bernardo, *Historia del franquismo*, 2 vols, 2nd edition (Barcelona, 1985)

Sverlo, Patricia, *Un Rey golpe a golpe. Biografía no autorizada de Juan Carlos de Borbón* (Pamplona, 2000)

Tácito (Madrid, 1975)

Tarradellas, Josép, *"Ja soc aquí". Recuerdo de un retorno* (Barcelona, 1990)

Tezanos, José Feliz, Cotarelo, Ramón & Blas, Andrés de, coordinadores, *La transición democrática española* (Madrid, 1989)

Tezanos, José Feliz, *Sociologia del socialismo español* (Madrid, 1983)

Threlfall, Monica, editor, *Consensus Politics in Spain. Insider Perspectives* (Bristol, 2000)

Tierno Galván, Enrique, *Cabos sueltos* (Barcelona, 1981)

Toquero, José María, *Don Juan de Borbón, el Rey padre* (Barcelona, 1992)

Toquero, José María, *Franco y Don Juan: La oposición monárquica al franquismo* (Barcelona, 1989)

Tusell, Javier, con la colaboración de Genoveva García Queipo de Llano, *Carrero. La eminencia gris del régimen de Franco* (Madrid, 1993)

Tusell, Javier, *Fotobiografía de Juan Carlos I. Una vida en imágenes* (Barcelona, 2000)

Tusell, Javier, *Franco y los católicos. La política interior española entre 1945 y 1957* (Madrid, 1984)

Tusell, Javier, *Juan Carlos I. La restauración de la Monarquía* (Madrid, 1995)

Tusell, Javier, *Juan Carlos I* (Madrid, 2002)

Tusell, Xavier, *La oposición democrática al franquismo (1939–1962)* (Barcelona, 1977)

Tusell, Javier, *La transición española a la democracia* (Madrid: Historia 16, 1991)

Tusell, Javier & Álvarez de Chillida, Gonzalo, *Pemán. Un trayecto intelectual desde la extrema derecha hasta la democracia* (Barcelona, 1998)

Tusell, Javier & Soto, Álvaro, editors, *Historia de la transición 1975–1986* (Madrid, 1996)

Unión Militar Democrática, *Los militares y la lucha por la democracia* (Madrid, 1976)

Urbano, Pilar, *Garzón. El hombre que veía amanecer* (Barcelona, 2000)

Urbano, Pilar, *Con la venia: yo indagué el 23 F* (Barcelona, 1982)

Urbano, Pilar, *La Reina* (Barcelona, 1996)

Urbano, Pilar, *Yo entré en el CESID* (Barcelona, 1997)

Utrera Molina, José, *Sin cambiar de bandera* (Barcelona, 1989)

Vázquez Montalbán, Manuel, *Cómo liquidaron el franquismo en dieciséis meses y un día* (Barcelona, 1977)

Vázquez Montalbán, Manuel, *Crónica sentimental de la transición* (Barcelona, 1977)

Vázquez Montalbán, Manuel, *Los demonios familiares de Franco* (Barcelona, 1978)

Vega, Pedro & Erroteta, Peru, *Los herejes del PCE* (Barcelona, 1982)

Vegas Latapié, Eugenio, *Los caminos del desengaño. Memorias políticas 2: 1936–1938* (Madrid, 1987)

Vilá Reyes, Juan, *El atropello MATESA* (Barcelona, 1992)

Vilallonga, José Luis de, *A pleines dents* (Paris, 1973)

Vilallonga, José Luis de, *El Rey. Conversaciones con D. Juan Carlos I de España* (Barcelona, 1993)

Vilallonga, José Luis de, *Franco y el Rey. La espera y la esperanza* (Barcelona, 1998)

Vilallonga, José Luis de, *La cruda y tierna verdad. Memorias no autorizadas* (Barcelona, 2000)

Vilallonga, José Luis de, *Le Roi. Entretiens* (Paris, 1993)

Vilallonga, José Luis de, *The King. The Life of King Juan Carlos of Spain* (London, 1994)

Vilar, Sergio, *La década sorprendente 1976–1986* (Barcelona, 1986)

Vilar, Sergio, *Historia del anti-franquismo 1939–1975* (Barcelona, 1984)

Vilar, Sergio, *La oposición a la dictadura: protagonistas de la España democrática. La oposición a la dictadura* (Paris, 1968)

Villacastin, Rosa & Beneyto, María, *La noche de los transistores* (Madrid, 1981)

Villamea, Luis F., *Gutiérrez Mellado: Así se entrega una victoria* (Madrid, 1996)

Viñas, Ángel, *Los pactos secretos de Franco con Estados unidos* (Barcelona, 1981)

Viver Pi-Sunyer, Carles, *El personal político de Franco 1936–1945* (Barcelona, 1978)

Walters, Vernon A., *Silent Missions* (New York, 1978)

Welles, Benjamin, *Spain. The Gentle Anarchy* (London, 1965)

Whitaker, Arthur P., *Spain and the Defence of the West: Ally and Liability* (New York, 1961)

Whitaker, John T., *We Cannot Escape History* (New York, 1943)

Woodworth, Paddy, *Dirty War, Clean Hands. ETA, the GAL and Spanish Democracy* (Cork, 2001)

Yale, *Los últimos cien días: crónica de una agonía* (Madrid, 1975)

Ynfante, Jesús, *El Ejército de Franco y de Juan Carlos* (Paris, 1976)

Ynfante, Jesús, *La prodigiosa aventura del Opus Dei: genesis y desarrollo de la Santa Mafia* (Paris, 1970)

Ynfante, Jesús, *El santo fundador del Opus Dei. Biografía completa de Josémaría Escrivá de Balaguer* (Barcelona, 2002)

Ysart, Federico, *Quien hizo el cambio* (Barcelona, 1984)

Zavala, José María, *Dos Infantes y un destino* (Barcelona, 1998)

Zavala, José María, *Matar al Rey. La Casa Real en el punto de mira de ETA* (Madrid, 1998)

Ziegler, Philip, editor, *From Shore to Shore. The Tour Diaries of Earl Mountbatten of Burma 1953–1979* (London, 1989)

Ziegler, Philip, *Mountbatten. The Official Biography* (London, 1985)

Ziegler, Philip, *Wilson. The Authorised Life of Lord Wilson of Rievaulx* (London, 1993)

NOTES

NOTES TO PAGES 1–7

ONE: *In Search of a Lost Crown*

1 From *Palabras del Rey Don Juan Carlos I*, quoted by Juan Antonio Pérez Mateos, *Juan Carlos. La infancia desconocida de un Rey* (Barcelona, 1980), p.11.

2 *ABC*, 17 April 1931.

3 Juan Antonio Ansaldo, *¿Para qué?... (De Alfonso XIII a Juan III)* (Buenos Aires, 1951), p.18; Alfredo Kindelán, *La verdad de mis relaciones con Franco* (Barcelona, 1981), pp.167, 225. Prince Alfonso de Orleáns Borbón's own account of his journey with the King from Cartagena to Paris is reproduced in Kindelán, *La verdad*, pp.166–8.

4 Ansaldo, *¿Para qué?*, pp.47–50; Felipe Bertrán Güell, *Preparación y desarrollo del alzamiento nacional* (Valladolid, 1939), p.84.

5 Gerard Noel, *Ena Spain's English Queen* (London, 1984), pp.238–40; Juan Balansó, *La Familia Real y la familia irreal* (Barcelona, 1993), pp.40–4.

6 Miguel Platón, *Alfonso XIII: De Primo de Rivera a Franco. La tentación autoritaria de la Monarquía* (Barcelona, 1998), p.82; Emilio Mola, *Obras completas* (Valladolid, 1940), p.239.

7 Ramón de Alderete, *...y estos borbones nos quieren gobernar* (Paris, 1974), p.41.

8 Luis María Anson, *Don Juan* (Barcelona, 1994), pp.129–31; Rafael Borràs Betriu, *El Rey de los Rojos. Don Juan de Borbón, una figura tergiversada* (Barcelona, 1996), pp.71–2.

9 Balansó, *La Familia Real*, pp.45–52; Borràs, *El Rey de los Rojos*, pp.68–72; José María Toquero, *Don Juan de Borbón, el Rey padre* (Barcelona, 1992), pp.84–5.

10 Alderete, *...y estos borbones*, pp.44–8; Balansó, *La Familia Real*, pp.62–7.

11 Toquero, *Don Juan*, pp.86–7.

12 Noel, *Ena*, pp.253–4; Balansó, *La Familia Real*, pp.52–6; Borràs, *El Rey de los Rojos*, p.315.

13 Toquero, *Don Juan*, pp.56–8.

14 Her absence was much noted in Spain – see Balansó, *La Familia Real*, pp.95–6.

15 Francisco Bonmati de Codecido, *El Príncipe Don Juan de España* (Valladolid, 1938), pp.224–37; José María Iribarren, *Mola, datos para una biografía y para la historia del alzamiento nacional* (Zaragoza, 1938), pp.166–7; Eugenio Vegas Latapié, *Los caminos del desengaño. Memorias políticas 2: 1936–1938* (Madrid, 1987), pp.34–44; Guillermo Cabanellas, *La guerra de los mil días. Nacimiento, vida y muerte*

de la II República española, 2
vols (Buenos Aires, 1973), I,
pp.636–7; *El País Semanal*,
6 February 1977; *Época*,
17 March 1997.

16 Vegas Latapié, *Caminos*, p.161.

17 Javier González de la Vega, *Yo,
María de Borbón* (Madrid, 1995),
pp.84–5; *El País Semanal*, 6,
22 February 1995. For Juan
Carlos's birth weight and lack of
baby photographs, see *El País
Semanal*, 6 February 1977.

18 Charles T. Powell, *Juan Carlos of
Spain. Self-Made Monarch*
(London, 1996), pp. 21–2; Reina
Federica de Grecia, *Memorias*
(Madrid, 1971), p.287.

19 José Luis de Vilallonga, *El Rey.
Conversaciones con D. Juan
Carlos I de España* (Barcelona,
1993), p.76; Powell, *Juan Carlos
of Spain*, p. 1.

20 Pérez Mateos, *La infancia*, p.35;
Pedro Sainz Rodríguez, *Un
reinado en la sombra* (Barcelona,
1981), p.276.

21 Don Juan de Borbón to Franco,
7 December 1936, Sainz
Rodríguez, *Un reinado*, p.347;
Vegas Latapié, *Caminos*, p.162.

22 Franco to Don Juan de Borbón,
12 January 1937, Sainz
Rodríguez, *Un reinado*, p.347.

23 *ABC*, 18 July 1937. [*Palabras de
Franco I año triunfal* (Bilbao,
1937), p.57.]

24 I am indebted to Gabriel Cardona
for this anecdote.

25 Vegas Latapié, *Caminos*, p.163.

26 Francisco Franco Salgado-Araujo,
Mi vida junto a Franco
(Barcelona, 1977), p.232;
Palabras de Franco I año triunfal,
pp.37–45.

27 *ABC*, 18 July 1937. (*Palabras de
Franco I año triunfal*, p.56.)

28 Vegas Latapié, *Caminos*,
pp.515–16.

29 Sainz Rodríguez, *Un reinado*,
pp.347–8; testimony of Doña
María Cristina de Borbón, *Hola*,
No.2478, 6 February 1992.

30 *El País Semanal*, 6 February
1977.

31 *El País Semanal*, 6 February
1977.

32 Noel, *Ena*, pp. 254–60; *El País
Semanal*, 6 February 1977.

33 John T. Whitaker, *We Cannot
Escape History* (New York,
1943), p.106.

34 *El País Semanal*, 6 February
1977; Anson, *Don Juan*, p.158;
Sir Samuel Hoare, *Ambassador
on Special Mission* (London,
1946), pp.292–3.

35 *Boletín Oficial del Estado*,
9 August 1939; *Arriba*, 9 August
1939; *Ya*, 9 August 1939.

36 Javier Tusell, *Juan Carlos I. La
restauración de la Monarquía*
(Madrid, 1995), p.53.

37 Ribbentrop to Stohrer, 16 April
1941, *Documents on German
Foreign Policy*, Series D, vol.XII
(London, 1964), pp.569–70;
Lequio to Ciano, 9 June 1941, *I
Documenti Diplomatici Italiani,
9a serie, vol.VII (24 aprile – 11
dicembre 1941)* (Rome, 1987),
pp.225–6.

38 Franco to Don Juan,
30 September 1941, Sainz
Rodríguez, *Un reinado*,
pp.349–50.

39 Don Juan to Franco, 23 October
1941, Sainz Rodríguez, *Un
reinado*, pp.350–1.

40 Lequio to Ciano, 13 April, 26,
29 May, 5 June, Colloqui Ciano–
Serrano Suñer, 15–19 June,
Fracassi to Ciano, 30 June 1942,
I Documenti Diplomatici Italiani,

9a serie, vol.VIII (12 dicembre 1941 – 20 luglio 1942) (Rome, 1988), pp.490–1, 617, 625, 651–4, 690–2, 725–7; Stohrer to Wilhelmstrasse, 8 May, 11 June, Stohrer to Wehrmann, 29 May, Mackensen to Ribbentrop, 17 June 1942, Documents secrets du Ministère des Affaires Etrangères d'Allemagne: Espagne (Paris, 1946), pp.96–108; Ramón Garriga, La España de Franco: de la División Azul al pacto con los Estados Unidos (1943 a 1951) (Puebla, México, 1971), p.287–90.

41 Paul Preston, 'Alfonsist Monarchism and the Coming of the Spanish Civil War' in Journal of Contemporary History, Vol.7, Nos 3/4, 1972.

42 Pablo Beltrán de Heredia, 'Eugenio Vegas Latapié: singularidades de un preceptor' in Antonio Fontán, editor, Los monárquicos y el régimen de Franco (Madrid, 1996), pp.81–97; Sainz Rodríguez, Un reinado, pp.29–30, 148–9, 268–9; Tusell, Juan Carlos, pp.67–8. I recall Eugenio Vegas Latapié's firmly reactionary views from my own conversations with him in 1970.

43 Franco to Don Juan, 12 May 1942, Sainz Rodríguez, Un reinado, pp.351–3.

44 Kindelán, La verdad, pp.32–6, 50–9, 125–7.

45 Don Juan to Franco, 8 March 1943, Sainz Rodríguez, Un reinado, pp.354–5.

46 Franco to Don Juan, 27 May 1943, Sainz Rodríguez, Un reinado, pp.355–8.

47 Pereira to Salazar, 24 June 1943, Correspondencia de Pedro Teotónio Pereira para Oliveira Salazar, IV (1943–1944) (Lisbon, 1991), pp.213–14; The Times, 7 July 1943. For the text of the document, see Xavier Tusell, La oposición democrática al franquismo (1939–1962) (Barcelona, 1977), pp.52–4.

48 Sainz Rodríguez, Un reinado, p.258.

49 Laureano López Rodó, La larga marcha hacia la monarquía (Barcelona, 1977), pp.515–19; José María Gil Robles, La monarquía por la que yo luché: páginas de un diario 1941–1954 (Madrid, 1976), p.55.

50 Gil Robles, diary entry for 23 August 1943, La monarquía, p.55; Sainz Rodríguez, Un reinado, p.161; Ricardo de la Cierva, Historia del franquismo: I orígenes y configuración (1939–1945) (Barcelona, 1975), pp.265–70.

51 Luis Suárez Fernández, Francisco Franco y su tiempo, 8 vols (Madrid, 1984), III, p.431; Ricardo de la Cierva, Don Juan de Borbón: por fin toda la verdad (Madrid, 1997), pp.306–11. For the full text, see López Rodó, La larga marcha, pp.43–4. For Gil Robles's comment, see diary entry for 18 September 1943, Gil Robles, La monarquía, p.60.

52 Sainz Rodríguez, Un reinado, p.299; Ricardo de la Cierva, Don Juan de Borbón, pp.320–4, 529–32; Jesús Ynfante, El santo fundador del Opus Dei. Biografía completa de Josémaría Escrivá de Balaguer (Barcelona, 2002), pp.167–9, 247.

53 Franco to Don Juan, 6 January, Don Juan to Franco, 25 January 1944, Sainz Rodríguez, Un

reinado, pp.359–62; López Rodó, *La larga marcha*, pp.520–3; Suárez Fernández, *Franco*, III, pp.478–81.

54 Tusell, *Juan Carlos*, pp.103–7; Anson, *Don Juan*, pp.222–6; *ABC*, 6 April 1945; López Rodó, *La larga marcha*, pp.48–54; Kindelán, *La verdad*, pp.229–36.

55 López Rodó, *La larga marcha*, pp.54–5.

56 Manuel Vázquez Montalbán, *Los demonios familiares de Franco* (Barcelona, 1978), p.105.

57 Bowker to Eden, 25 April 1945, FO371/49589, Z5249/1484/G41.

58 Bowker to Eden, 27 March 1945, FO371/49587, Z4137/233/41. For a list of those present, see Ricardo de la Cierva, *Francisco Franco: un siglo de España*, 2 vols (Madrid, 1973), II, p.406.

59 *Arriba*, 28 March 1945.

60 *Ya*, 1, 3 April; *ABC*, 3 April 1945.

61 Javier Tusell, *Franco y los católicos. La política interior española entre 1945 y 1957* (Madrid, 1984), pp.56–9.

62 Alberto J. Lleonart y Anselem & Fernando María Castiella y Maiz, *España y ONU I (1945–1946)* (Madrid, 1978), pp.30–3.

63 Bowker to Churchill, 26 June 1945, FO371/49589, Z7876/233/41.

64 Lleonart y Anselem & Castiella y Maiz, *España y ONU I*, pp.34–5; *The Times*, 18 June 1945.

65 *La Vanguardia Española*, 18 July; *The Times*, 18 July 1945; Francisco Franco Bahamonde, *Textos de doctrina política: palabras y escritos de 1945 a 1950* (Madrid, 1951), pp.15–25.

66 Tusell, *Franco y los católicos*, pp.63–77; Suárez Fernández,

Franco, IV, p.44; Gil Robles, diary entry for 21 July 1945, *La monarquía*, pp.126–7; Garriga, *De la División Azul*, pp.334–5.

67 Testimony of Alberto Martín Artajo, María Mérida, *Testigos de Franco: retablo íntimo de una dictatdura* (Barcelona, 1977), p.197; Tusell, *Franco y los católicos*, pp.61–2.

68 Tusell, *Franco y los católicos*, pp.84–94, 118; Florentino Portero, *Franco aislado: la cuestión española (1945–1950)* (Madrid, 1989), pp.106–10.

69 José María de Areilza & Fernando María Castiella, *Reivindicaciones de España* (Madrid, 1941). Bowker to Churchill, 5 June 1945, FO371/49589, Z7168/233/41; Gil Robles, diary entry for 11 October 1945, *La monarquía*, pp.134–5.

70 Paul Preston, *Franco: A Biography* (London, 1993), pp.540–2.

71 López Rodó, *La larga marcha*, pp.57–9; Tusell, *Franco y los católicos*, pp.99–100.

72 Ansaldo, *¿Para qué . . . ?*, pp.332, 336; Garriga, *De la División Azul*, p.295.

73 Suárez Fernández, *Franco*, IV, pp.53, 62–3; López Rodó, *La larga marcha*, pp.62–3; Sainz Rodríguez, *Un reinado*, pp.336–7; Anson, *Don Juan*, pp.239–40.

74 Mallet to Bevin, 15 February 1946, FO371/60373, Z2125/41/41; López Rodó, *La larga marcha*, pp.64–5; Tusell, *La oposición democrática* (Barcelona, 1977), pp.114–16; Anson, *Don Juan*, p.248.

75 José Antonio Gurriarán, *El Rey*

en Estoril. Don Juan Carlos y su familia en el exilio portugués (Barcelona, 2000), pp.198, 207–8; Anson, *Don Juan*, pp.241–7; López Rodó, *La larga marcha*, p.65.

76 Torr memorandum, 20 February 1946, FO371/60373, Z1741/41/41; Kindelán, *La verdad*, pp.128–30, 254; Tusell, *Franco y los católicos*, pp.150–1; Suárez Fernández, *Franco*, IV, pp.127–32, 153–7, 301.

77 Gurriarán, *El Rey en Estoril*, p.184; Vilallonga, *El Rey*, pp.53–4.

78 *Diario 16*, 6 March 1978 quoting extracts from the interview given by Juan Carlos to *Welt am Sonntag*.

79 *Cambio 16*, 3 November 1980; Pérez Mateos, *La infancia*, pp.91–2.

80 Noel, *Ena*, pp.266–8; Pérez Mateos, *La infancia*, p.116.

81 Pérez Mateos, *La infancia*, p.113; *Época*, 17 March 1997.

82 *Cambio 16*, 3 November 1980; Pérez Mateos, *La infancia*, p.172.

83 Tusell, *La oposición democrática*, pp.114–16; Gil Robles, diary entries for 15, 28 February 1946, *La monarquía*, pp.163, 168–9.

84 Gil Robles, diary entry for 11 March 1946, *La monarquía*, pp.172–3; Anson, *Don Juan*, 249–52.

85 *The Times*, 5 March 1946; Arthur P. Whitaker, *Spain and the Defence of the West: Ally and Liability* (New York, 1961), pp.25–7; Portero, *Franco aislado*, pp.151–5; Anson, *Don Juan*, pp.253–4.

86 Gurriarán, *El Rey en Estoril*, pp.162–8, 203–7.

87 Vilallonga, *El Rey*, pp.54–5.

88 *ABC*, 10, 11, 12, 13 December 1946; Lleonart y Anselem & Castiella y Maiz, *España y ONU I*, pp.310–89.

89 Tusell, *Franco y los católicos*, p.154.

90 López Rodó, *La larga marcha*, pp.73, 529–32; Gil Robles, diary entries for 5 November 1945, 15 March 1946, *La monarquía*, pp.138, 173–4.

91 López Rodó, *La larga marcha*, p.543.

92 López Rodó, *La larga marcha*, p.80.

93 Carrero's report to Franco is reproduced in López Rodó, *La larga marcha*, pp.75–89; Don Juan's reaction, *ibid.*, pp.89–99; Gil Robles, diary entries for 31 March, 1 April 1947, *La monarquía*, pp.206–9; Tusell, *La oposición democrática*, pp.161–2.

94 Gil Robles, diary entries for 6–15 April 1947, *La monarquía*, pp.209–14, 388–93; Tusell, *La oposición democrática*, pp.162–9; Tusell, *Franco y los católicos*, pp.161–2; Anson, *Don Juan*, pp.263–71; Rafael Martínez Nadal, *Antonio Torres de la BBC a The Observer: Republicanos y monárquicos en el exilio (1944–1956)* (Madrid, 1996), pp.91–140; Sainz Rodríguez, *Un reinado*, p.269; Tusell, *Juan Carlos*, pp.147–52.

95 On the manipulation of the referendum, see Preston, *Franco*, pp.570–2.

96 José María Pemán, *Mis almuerzos con gente importante* (Barcelona, 1970), p.255.

97 Pérez Mateos, *La infancia*, p.134.

98 Tusell, *Juan Carlos*, pp.159–64, 185–6; Carlos & José Martínez Cobo, *¿República? ¿Monarquía? En busca del consenso Intrahistoria del PSOE II (1946–1954)* (Barcelona, 1992), pp.143–86; David J. Dunthorn, *Britain and the Spanish Anti-Franco Opposition, 1940–1950* (London, 2000), pp.132–6.

99 Gil Robles, diary entries for 13 January, 15 February 1948, *La monarquía*, pp.253, 255–6.

100 Pérez Mateos, *La infancia*, pp.160–1.

101 Tusell, *La oposición democrática*, pp.197–202; Tusell, *Juan Carlos*, pp.164–70, 177–8; Suárez Fernández, *Franco*, IV, pp.249–51; Juan Antonio Pérez Mateos, *El Rey que vino del exilio* (Barcelona, 1981), pp.19–27.

102 Don Juan gave various accounts of the meeting: to José María Gil Robles on 1 September 1948 (Gil Robles, *La monarquía*, pp.265–73); to Pedro Sainz Rodríguez at about the same time (Sainz Rodríguez, *Un reinado*, pp.220–2); to an unnamed person (probably either Gil Robles or Sainz Rodríguez) 'close to Don Juan' who informed the US Ambassador in Lisbon, Lincoln MacVeagh; and directly to Theodore Xanthaky, Special Assistant to MacVeagh (*FRUS 1948*, III, pp.1050–1, 1059–63; *FRUS 1949*, IV, p.755); to Luis María Anson (Anson, *Don Juan*, pp.276–9). Cf. Alderete, *. . .y estos borbones*, pp.56–8; *The Times*, 28 August; *ABC*, 29 August 1948.

103 Jesús Palacios, *Los papeles secretos de Franco. De las relaciones con Juan Carlos y Don Juan al protagonismo del Opus* (Madrid, 1996), pp.39–40.

104 Gil Robles, diary entries for 1, 25 September, 5 October 1948, *La monarquía*, pp.272–5; Pérez Mateos, *La infancia*, pp.191–8.

105 Palacios, *Los papeles secretos*, pp.44–7; Martínez Cobo, *Intrahistoria del PSOE II*, pp.186–94; Tusell, *La oposición democrática*, pp.203–5.

106 *FRUS 1948*, III, p.1062; Sainz Rodríguez, *Un reinado*, p.368.

107 Gil Robles, diary entries for 8, 10, 11, 27 October 1948, *La monarquía*, pp.276–81.

108 Pérez Mateos, *La infancia*, pp.197–208; Ricardo de la Cierva, *Historia del franquismo: II aislamiento, transformación, agonía (1945–1975)* (Barcelona, 1978) p.73.

109 Pérez Mateos, *La infancia*, p.208.

110 Gil Robles, diary entry for 4 November 1948, *La monarquía*, p.281.

111 Gil Robles, diary entry for 7 November 1948, *La monarquía*, p.282.

112 Pérez Mateos, *La infancia*, pp.211–20; Gil Robles, diary entries for 8, 9, 10, 14 November 1948, *La monarquía*, pp.282–3; Vilallonga, *El Rey*, pp.37–44.

113 Vilallonga, *El Rey*, pp.49–50; *ABC*, 6 December 1981; Julio Danvila's notes, reprinted in Pérez Mateos, *El Rey que vino*, pp.94–6. On the derogatory remarks about Franco, see *El País*, 22 February 1995.

114 *ABC*, 10 November 1948; Gil

Robles, diary entries for
14 November, 19 December
1948, *La monarquía*, pp.284–6.
115 Testimony to the author of
Eugenio Vegas Latapié and José
María Gil Robles, Madrid,
1970; Gil Robles, diary entry for
6 August 1949, *La monarquía*,
p.302.
116 Victoria Eugenia to Danvila,
28 November 1948, reproduced
in Pérez Mateos, *El Rey que
vino*, pp.29–31.
117 *The Times*, 13 November 1948;
Follick in 460 H.C.DEB., 5s,
c.1757; Gil Robles, diary entries
for 12, 13 October, 2, 4, 10, 12,
13 November, *La monarquía*,
pp.278–83.
118 Gil Robles, diary entries for 4,
8, 30 June, 6, 18, 27 July 1949,
La monarquía, pp.298–301.

TWO: *A Pawn Sacrificed*

1 Pérez Mateos, *El Rey que vino*,
pp.30–2, 67.
2 *La Revista*, 4 January 1998;
Javier Tusell, *Juan Carlos*, p.193;
Vilallonga, *El Rey*, pp.50–1;
Pérez Mateos, *El Rey que vino*,
pp.39–40.
3 *Ya*, 14 June 1981 – interview
with the French teacher at
Miramar, Aurora Gómez
Delgado; Vilallonga, *El Rey*,
pp.50–1.
4 *Época*, 17 March 1997; Pérez
Mateos, *El Rey que vino*,
pp.55–60.
5 Pérez Mateos, *El Rey que vino*,
pp.61–2; Vilallonga, *El Rey*,
pp.51–2.
6 *La Revista*, 4 January 1998; Pérez
Mateos, *El Rey que vino*, p.40.
7 Pérez Mateos, *El Rey que vino*,
p.71; *Época*, 17 March 1997.

8 *La Revista*, 4 January 1998.
9 *La Revista*, 4 January 1998.
10 *La Revista*, 4 January 1998.
11 *ABC*, 6 December 1981.
12 Pérez Mateos, *El Rey que vino*,
pp.79–80.
13 Palacios, *Los papeles secretos*,
pp.57–8.
14 Gil Robles, diary entry for
28 December 1948, *La
monarquía*, pp.287–8.
15 Gil Robles, diary entry for
19 December 1948, *La
monarquía*, p.286.
16 Gil Robles, diary entries for 8,
11, 12, 13 March 1949, *La
monarquía*, pp.293–4.
17 Franco, *Textos de doctrina
política*, p.149.
18 Pérez Mateos, *El Rey que vino*,
pp.115–22.
19 Gil Robles, diary entries for 6, 8,
18, 27 July, 8 August, 18, 23, 25,
26 September 1949, *La
monarquía*, pp.299–306.
20 Sainz Rodríguez, *Un reinado*,
p.369.
21 *The Times*, 22, 24, 25,
28 October 1949; *Arriba*, 22, 23,
25, 26, 27 October 1949; Gil
Robles, diary entries for 19, 21,
23 October, 4 November 1949,
La monarquía, pp.308–13;
Franco Salgado-Araujo, *Mi vida*,
pp.327–8; Juan Antonio Pérez
Mateos, *Un Rey bajo el sol. El
duro camino de Juan Carlos I
hacia el Trono* (Barcelona, 1998),
pp.119–20.
22 González de la Vega, *Yo, María
de Borbón*, pp.107–8, 147;
interview with the French teacher
at Miramar, Aurora Gómez
Delgado, *Ya*, 14 June 1981; Gil
Robles, diary entries for 5, 11,
13 November 1949, *La
monarquía*, pp.313–14; Pérez

Mateos, *El Rey que vino*, pp.125–7.

23 Palacios, *Los papeles secretos*, pp.61–6.

24 Gil Robles, diary entries for 7, 8, 9 December 1949, *La monarquía*, pp.315–17; Pérez Mateos, *El Rey que vino*, pp.126–30.

25 Jesús Ynfante, *El santo fundador del Opus Dei*, pp.183–8; Víctor Salmador, *Don Juan. Los secretos de un Rey sin trono* (Madrid, 1993), p.52; Palacios, *Los papeles secretos*, pp.69–70.

26 Palacios, *Los papeles secretos*, p.80; Pérez Mateos, *Un Rey bajo el sol*, p.95.

27 *ABC*, 18 June 1952; Pérez Mateos, *El Rey que vino*, pp.182–3, 191–2, 196–8.

28 Interview with the French teacher at Miramar, Aurora Gómez Delgado, *Ya*, 14 June 1981; Pérez Mateos, *El Rey que vino*, p.201.

29 Extracts from the *Welt am Sonntag* interview were reprinted in *Diario 16*, 6 March 1978; *Diario 16*, 15 January 1981; BBC documentary about the Spanish Royal Household broadcasted in the UK on 23 January 1981; Pérez Mateos, *Un Rey bajo el sol*, pp.208–9.

30 Interview with the French teacher at Miramar, Aurora Gómez Delgado, *Ya*, 14 June 1981; Pérez Mateos, *El Rey que vino*, pp.144–6, 155, 194.

31 Madrid Embassy to FO, 16 April 1950, FO371/89487, WS1021/15.

32 López Rodó, *La larga marcha*, pp.112–13; 550–4; Sainz Rodríguez, *Un reinado*, pp.370–8.

33 Alderete, . . .*y estos borbones* pp.44–5, 89–91; Balansó, *La

Familia Real*, pp.144–6; Gil Robles, diary entry for 18 April 1953, *La monarquía*, p.321; Alfonso de Borbón, *Las memorias de Alfonso de Borbón* (Barcelona, 1990), pp.45–6, 49–53.

34 Interview with Aurora Gómez Delgado, *Ya*, 14 June 1981.

35 *El País*, 22 October 1995.

36 A selection of letters from Doña María de las Mercedes to Juan Carlos is reprinted in Pérez Mateos, *El Rey que vino*, pp.173–88; interview with Aurora Gómez Delgado, *Ya*, 14 June 1981.

37 Gil Robles, diary entry for 3 December 1953, *La monarquía*, pp.323–4; *Arriba*, 10, 20 January 1954; Pérez Mateos, *El Rey que vino*, p.207.

38 Tusell, *Juan Carlos*, pp.216–19.

39 Gil Robles, diary entries for 28 April, 13 May, 21 June 1954, *La monarquía*, pp.326–7.

40 Sainz Rodríguez, *Un reinado*, pp.378–9; Vilallonga, *El Rey*, p.93; Anson, *Don Juan*, pp.297–8.

41 Sainz Rodríguez, *Un reinado*, pp.379–82.

42 Sainz Rodríguez, *Un reinado*, p.382.

43 Gil Robles, diary entries for 22 June, 25 July 1954, *La monarquía*, pp.327–8; Jean Créac'h, *Le coeur et l'épée. Chroniques espagnoles* (Paris, 1958), p.333.

44 Tusell, *Juan Carlos*, p.226.

45 *Época*, 22 March 1993.

46 *El País*, 23 October 1995; Fernando Gracia, *La madre del Rey. La vida de doña María de las Mercedes: una causa histórica* (Madrid, 1994), pp.214–15.

47 Franco Salgado-Araujo, diary

entry for 2 October 1954, *Mis conversaciones privadas con Franco* (Barcelona, 1976), p.9.

48 Sainz Rodríguez, *Un reinado*, pp.383–4; Gil Robles, diary entries for 7 September, 25 October 1954, *La monarquía*, pp.328–9; Anson, *Don Juan*, p.298; López Rodó, *La larga marcha*, pp.115–17.

49 Créac'h, *Le coeur*, p.332.

50 *ABC*, 20 October 1954; Créac'h, *Le coeur*, pp.335–7; Suárez Fernández, *Franco*, V, pp.156–8.

51 Franco Salgado-Araujo, *Mis conversaciones*, pp.18, 23. It was rumoured that Amalia Rodrigues was Don Juan's lover.

52 *Arriba*, 23 November 1954; Rafael Calvo Serer, *Franco frente al Rey. El proceso del régimen* (Paris, 1972), pp.29–30; Franco Salgado-Araujo, *Mis conversaciones*, p.30; López Rodó, *La larga marcha*, p.117; Créac'h, *Le coeur*, pp.338–9; José María Toquero, *Franco y Don Juan: La oposición monárquica al franquismo* (Barcelona, 1989), pp.253–5.

53 Créac'h, *Le coeur*, pp.338–40; Suárez Fernández, *Franco*, V, p.159.

54 Franco Salgado-Araujo, diary entries for 9, 15 December 1954, 3 January 1955, *Mis conversaciones*, pp.46, 48, 65.

55 Franco Salgado-Araujo, diary entries for 20, 28 December 1954, *Mis conversaciones*, pp.52–3, 59.

56 Mallet to Eden, 11 January 1955, FO371/117914, RS1942/4; Sainz Rodríguez, *Un reinado*, pp.222–35; Franco Salgado-Araujo, diary entry for 30 December 1954, *Mis*

conversaciones*, pp.59–60; Créac'h, *Le coeur*, pp.341–5; Anson, *Don Juan*, pp.299–302.

57 Franco Bahamonde, Francisco, *Discursos y mensajes del Jefe del Estado 1951–1954* (Madrid, 1955) pp.551–3.

58 Franco Salgado-Araujo, diary entry for 31 December 1954, 1955, *Mis conversaciones*, pp.63–4.

59 Pérez Mateos, *Un Rey bajo el sol*, p.156.

60 Franco Salgado-Araujo, diary entry for 27 December 1955, *Mis conversaciones*, p.58; Carlos Martínez Campos, *Ayer 1931–1953* (Madrid, 1970), pp.411ff.

61 Alfonso Armada, *Al servicio de la Corona* (Barcelona, 1983), p.82.

62 I am indebted to José Francisco Yvars for this anecdote.

63 Pérez Mateos, *Un Rey bajo el sol*, p.160.

64 Anson, *Don Juan*, p.303; Armada, *Al servicio*, pp.17–18, 37–57, 79–82; Palacios, *Los papeles secretos*, pp.131–3.

65 On Mondéjar, see Pérez Mateos, *Un Rey bajo el sol*, p.163.

66 Armada, *Al servicio*, pp.83–4; José Antonio Giménez-Arnau, *Memorias de memoria. Descifre vuecencia personalmente* (Barcelona, 1978), pp.224–5.

67 Franco Salgado-Araujo, diary entries for 19, 21 January 1955, *Mis conversaciones*, pp.72–3; Créac'h, *Le coeur*, pp.347–8, 350–1.

68 *Arriba*, 23, 27 January 1955; *ABC*, 1 March 1955.

69 Mallet to Eden, 26 January 1955, FO371/117914, RS1942/6.

70 Franco Salgado-Araujo, diary entries for 1, 2, 5 March 1955,

Mis conversaciones, pp.89–90; Créac'h, *Le coeur*, p.351.

71 Author's conversations with Miguel Primo de Rivera y Urquijo; Giménez-Arnau, *Memorias*, pp.225–9; Créac'h, *Le coeur*, pp.348–9; Armada, *Al servicio*, pp.86–91.

72 Author's interview with Alfonso Armada; Franco Salgado-Araujo, diary entries for 5, 14 March 1955, *Mis conversaciones*, pp.90–4; Vilallonga, *El Rey*, p.88.

73 Armada, *Al servicio*, pp.87–8.

74 Franco Salgado-Araujo, diary entries for 1, 7, 22, 26 February 1955, *Mis conversaciones*, pp.74, 78, 83–5.

75 Franco Salgado-Araujo, diary entries for 22, 25 April, 17 May, 5 June 1955, *Mis conversaciones*, pp.100–2, 110, 115; Créac'h, *Le coeur*, pp.352–3.

76 *Arriba*, 20 June 1955; Mallet to Macmillan, 5 July 1955, FO371/117914, RS1942/21.

77 *ABC*, 24 June 1955; Mallet to Macmillan, 5 July 1955; Stirling to Macmillan, 26 July 1955; Balfour memorandum, 7 September 1955, FO371/117914, RS1942/21, RS1942/25, RS1942/27; Créac'h, *Le coeur*, pp.353–4; Anson, *Don Juan*, p.303; Sainz Rodríguez, *Un reinado*, p.294; Tusell, *Juan Carlos*, pp.240–3.

78 Franco Salgado-Araujo, diary entry for 19 November 1955, *Mis conversaciones*, pp.146–7; Créac'h, *Le coeur*, p.358.

79 Salmador, *Don Juan. Los secretos*, p.27; Borràs, *El Rey de los Rojos*, p.196; Gurriarán, *El Rey en Estoril*, p.199.

THREE: *The Tribulations of a Young Soldier*

1 *Sábado Gráfico*, 29 April 1981.

2 Franco Salgado-Araujo, diary entry for 31 December 1955, *Mis conversaciones*, p.196.

3 *Sábado Gráfico*, 29 April 1981.

4 Sainz Rodríguez, *Un reinado*, p.342.

5 Vilallonga, *El Rey*, pp.139–41.

6 *Sábado Gráfico*, 29 April 1981.

7 *Diario 16*, 6 March 1978.

8 Vilallonga, *El Rey*, p.140; reports of old companions from the military academies in *Sábado Gráfico*, 29 April 1981.

9 Vilallonga, *El Rey*, pp.52–3.

10 'Carlos B.' (Carlos Blanco Escolá), 'De cuando nuestro Rey era cadete', *Armas y Cuerpos. Revista de la Academia General Militar*, No.23, enero-febrero 1981, pp.5–12; *Sábado Gráfico*, 29 April 1981.

11 *Diario 16*, 6 March 1978; Pérez Mateos, *Un Rey bajo el sol*, pp.193–4.

12 *Sábado Gráfico*, 29 April 1981; Pérez Mateos, *Un Rey bajo el sol*, p.195.

13 Pérez Mateos, *Un Rey bajo el sol*, pp.178–9; *Sábado Gráfico*, 29 April 1981.

14 Gregorio Morán, *El precio de la transición* (Barcelona, 1991), p.145; José María Zavala, *Dos Infantes y un destino* (Barcelona, 1998), pp.112–14.

15 *El País*, 16 October 1992; Gurriarán, *El Rey en Estoril*, pp.408–9, 412–15.

16 Ezio Saini, 'Pasqua amara all'Estoril', *Settimo Giorno*, no.16, anno IX, 17 April 1956.

17 Gonzalo Fernández de la Mora, *Río arriba. Memorias* (Barcelona,

1995), p.97; Powell, *Juan Carlos*, p.17; Françoise Laot, *Juan Carlos y Sofía* (Madrid, 1987), p.48; Borràs, *El Rey de los Rojos*, p.209; Palacios, *Los papeles secretos*, p.152.

18 González de la Vega, *Yo, María de Borbón*, p.132; *El País*, 23 October 1995.

19 Gurriarán, *El Rey en Estoril*, pp.415–18; Helena Matheopoulos, *Juan Carlos I. El Rey de nuestro tiempo* (Madrid, 1996), pp.70–1.

20 González de la Vega, *Yo, María de Borbón*, pp.132–3; *El País*, 23 October 1995.

21 Gurriarán, *El Rey en Estoril*, pp.408–9; Juan Balansó, *Los Borbones incómodos* (Barcelona, 2000), pp.108–9.

22 Fernández de la Mora, *Río arriba*, p.230.

23 Powell, *Juan Carlos*, pp.17–18; *Daily Telegraph*, 11 April 1956; *El País*, 16 October 1992; *El Mundo*, 14 October 1992; Palacios, *Los papeles secretos*, p.152; Gurriarán, *El Rey en Estoril*, pp.416, 421; Pérez Mateos, *Un Rey bajo el sol*, p.213.

24 *El Mundo*, 14 October 1992; *El País*, 16 October 1992, 23 October 1995; José Gutiérrez-Ravé, *El Conde de Barcelona* (Madrid, 1962), pp.162–75; Gurriarán, *El Rey en Estoril*, p.408; Toquero, *Don Juan*, pp.199–201; Anson, *Don Juan*, pp.308–9; Tusell, *Juan Carlos*, pp.248–9.

25 See the eye-witness account by Jaime Miralles in Fontán, *Los monárquicos*, pp.133–4; *El País*, 16 October 1992, 23 October 1995; Laot, *Juan Carlos y Sofía*, pp.49–50.

26 Jaime Miralles in Fontán, *Los monárquicos*, p.134; Borràs, *El Rey de los Rojos*, p.211.

27 Alderete, ... *y estos borbones*, p.97; Balansó, *La Familia Real*, p.166.

28 Víctor Salmador, *Don Juan. Los secretos*, p.84; *Daily Telegraph*, 11 April 1956, quoted by Powell, *Juan Carlos*, pp.17–18; Palacios, *Los papeles secretos*, pp.153, 197.

29 Toquero, *Franco y Don Juan*, pp.384, 423.

30 Salmador, *Don Juan. Los secretos*, p.82.

31 José Luis de Arrese, *Una etapa constituyente* (Barcelona, 1982), pp.16–22; Equipo Mundo, *Los noventa ministros de Franco* (Barcelona, 1970), pp.249–53.

32 Mallet to Lloyd, 17, 18 February 1956, FO371/124127, RS1015/13, RS1015/14.

33 Madrid Chancery to Southern Department, 24 February 1956, FO371/124127, RS1015/18.

34 Preston, *Franco*, pp.651–5.

35 Sainz Rodríguez, *Un reinado*, pp.163–4; Calvo Serer, *Franco frente al Rey*, pp.36–7; Anson, *Don Juan*, pp.311–12; Suárez Fernández, *Franco*, V, pp.265–6; Federico Silva Muñoz, *Memorias políticas* (Barcelona, 1993), p.68.

36 Francisco Franco Bahamonde, *Discursos y mensajes del Jefe del Estado 1955–1959* (Madrid, 1960), p.165.

37 Arrese, *Una etapa*, pp.42–5; Franco, *Discursos 1955–1959*, pp.188–9; Madrid Chancery to Southern Department, 5 May 1954, FO371/124128, RS1015/23.

38 Laureano López Rodó, *Memorias* (Barcelona, 1990), pp.51–2;

López Rodó, *La larga marcha*, pp.124–30; Arrese, *Una etapa*, pp.71, 80.

39 Stanley G. Payne, *Politics and the Military in Modern Spain* (Stanford, 1967), p.443; Whitaker, *Spain and the Defence of the West*, pp.141–2; Gabriel Cardona, *Franco y sus generales. La manicura del tigre* (Madrid, 2001), pp.173–4.

40 Arrese, *Una etapa*, pp.82–3, 98–103.

41 Franco, *Discursos 1955–1959*, pp.214–15; Mallet to Lloyd, 20 July 1956, FO371/124128, RS1015/39A.

42 Arrese, *Una etapa*, pp.132–5, 144–92; López Rodó, *Memorias*, pp.65–77; López Rodó, *La larga marcha*, pp.133–5; Créac'h, *Le coeur*, pp.386–7; Tusell, *Franco y los católicos*, pp.409–25; Suárez Fernández, *Franco*, V, pp.306–12.

43 Mallet to Lloyd, 15 January 1957, FO371/130325, RS1015/3; Arrese, *Una etapa*, pp.234–42, 253–65; Suárez Fernández, *Franco*, V, pp.314–15; Tusell, *Franco y los católicos*, pp.426–8.

44 López Rodó, *Memorias*, pp.66–9; López Rodó, *La larga marcha*, pp.120–1.

45 Calvo Serer, *Franco frente al Rey*, p.36; Sainz Rodríguez, *Un reinado*, p.164; López Rodó, *La larga marcha*, pp.123–4; Toquero, *Franco y Don Juan*, p.266; Suárez Fernández, *Franco*, V, pp.319–20.

46 Madrid Chancery to Southern Department, FO371/130325, RS1015/5; Créac'h, *Le coeur*, pp.387–8.

47 Luis Ramírez, *Nuestros primeros veinticinco años* (Paris, 1964), pp.111–12; Franco Salgado-

Araujo, diary entry for 4 February 1957, *Mis conversaciones*, p.200; Jaume Fabre, Josep M. Huertas & Antoni Ribas, *Vint anys de resistència catalana (1939–1959)* (Barcelona, 1978), pp.208–11.

48 Franco Salgado-Araujo, diary entries for 11 August 1956, 30 January, 2 February 1957, *Mis conversaciones*, pp.176, 195–8; Suárez Fernández, *Franco*, V, pp.269, 319; López Rodó, *La larga marcha*, p.124; Sainz Rodríguez, *Un reinado*, p.166.

49 Calvo Serer, *Franco frente al Rey*, p.37; Cierva, *Historia del franquismo: II*, p.155, who quotes, without naming him, a minister; Serrano Suñer, *Memorias*, p.238.

50 Franco Salgado-Araujo, diary entry for 6 April 1957, *Mis conversaciones*, p.209 comments on the rumours having been picked up by the Cuban press. For speculation on what happened, see Ramírez, *Nuestros primeros veinticinco años*, p.117; Julio Busquets, *Pronunciamientos y golpes de Estado en España* (Barcelona, 1982), pp.140–1; Anson, *Don Juan*, pp.314–15.

51 Franco Salgado-Araujo, diary entry for 17 May 1955, *Mis conversaciones*, pp.107–10.

52 Gurriarán, *El Rey en Estoril*, pp.381–3.

53 Olghina di Robilant, *Sangue blu* (Milan, 1991), pp.173, 179, 243–52.

54 *Interviú*, 27 January 1988; *Época*, 8 February 1988. See also Jaime Peñafiel, *¡Dios salve la Reina! Pequeña historia de una gran profesional* (Madrid, 1993), pp.43–7.

55 Robilant, *Sangue blu*, pp.284–91.
56 Robilant, *Sangue blu*, pp.247–8; *Época*, 8 February 1988.
57 *Época*, 8 February 1988; Robilant, *Sangue blu*, p.247.
58 *Tiempo*, 11 September 1989; *Diario 16*, 10 November 1995; José Díaz Herrera & Isabel Durán Doussinague, *El saqueo de España* (Madrid, 1996), pp.86–7.
59 Peñafiel, *¡Dios salve la Reina!*, pp.47–8; Pérez Mateos, *Un Rey bajo el sol*, pp.243–4, 276–9; Fernando Rayón, *La Boda de Juan Carlos y Sofía: Claves y secretos de un enlace histórico* (Madrid, 2002), p.32.
60 Tusell, *Juan Carlos*, pp.347–50; Suárez Fernández, *Franco*, VI, pp.182, 299–300; Pérez Mateos, *Un Rey bajo el sol*, pp.251, 257.
61 López Rodó, *Memorias*, pp.89–99; Suárez Fernández, *Franco*, V, pp.320–1.
62 Conversation of the author with Fabián Estapé.
63 Preston, *Franco*, pp.666–71.
64 Toquero, *Franco y Don Juan*, p.267.
65 Anson, *Don Juan*, pp.314–15.
66 López Rodó, *Memorias*, pp.105–6; Jesús Ynfante, *La prodigiosa aventura del Opus Dei: genesis y desarrollo de la Santa Mafia* (Paris, 1970), pp.178–9.
67 Calvo Serer, *Franco frente al Rey*, pp.88–9.
68 Franco Salgado-Araujo, diary entry for 22 July 1957, *Mis conversaciones*, p.214; Suárez Fernández, *Franco*, V, p.339; Tusell, *Juan Carlos*, pp.260–1.
69 Pérez Mateos, *Un Rey bajo el sol*, pp.240–1.
70 Franco Salgado-Araujo, diary entry for 11 September 1957, *Mis conversaciones*, p.215.
71 Don Juan to Franco, 25 June, Franco to Don Juan, 4 September 1957, Sainz Rodríguez, *Un reinado*, pp.385–8.
72 López Rodó, *La larga marcha*, pp.145–8; Sainz Rodríguez, *Un reinado*, p.300; López Rodó, *Memorias*, pp.126–7; Toquero, *Franco y Don Juan*, pp.267–70.
73 Don Juan to Franco, 17 September 1957, Sainz Rodríguez, *Un reinado*, pp.388–9.
74 Francisco Melgar, *El noble final de la escisión dinástica* (Madrid, 1964), pp.147–57, 203–8; María Teresa de Borbón Parma, Josép Carles Clemente & Joaquín Cubero Sánchez, *Don Javier, una vida al servicio de la libertad* (Barcelona, 1997), pp.205–7; Juan Balansó, *La familia rival* (Barcelona, 1994), pp.188–9.
75 Don Juan to Franco, 22 December 1957, Franco to Don Juan, 18 January 1958, Sainz Rodríguez, *Un reinado*, pp.389–91; Anson, *Don Juan*, p.320; Borràs, *El Rey de los Rojos*, pp.212–21.
76 Anson, *Don Juan*, p.315.
77 Franco Salgado-Araujo, diary entries for 1 June 1957, 19 May, 2 June 1958, *Mis conversaciones*, pp.212–13, 236–7.
78 Gurriarán, *El Rey en Estoril*, pp.435–48.
79 Palacios, *Los papeles secretos*, p.138.
80 José María de Areilza, *Memorias exteriores 1947–1964* (Barcelona, 1984), pp.120–2; José María de Areilza, *A lo largo del siglo 1909–1991* (Barcelona, 1992), pp.144–5. It has been suggested that this caused some

embarrassment to the State Department, Powell, *Juan Carlos*, p.18. For Franco's reaction, see Franco Salgado-Araujo, diary entry for 2 June 1958, *Mis conversaciones*, p.237.

81 López Rodó, *Memorias*, pp.139–44.

82 Franco Salgado-Araujo, diary entries for 19 May 1958, 2 May 1959, *Mis conversaciones*, pp.236, 266.

83 Palacios, *Los papeles secretos*, pp.207–10.

84 *ABC*, 13 October; *Arriba*, 13, 14 October; *The Times*, 14 October 1948.

85 Palacios, *Los papeles secretos*, p.212.

86 Franco, *Discursos 1955–1959*, pp.557–68. Cf. Madrid Chancery to Southern Department, 2 January 1959, FO371/144927, RS1015/1.

87 Madrid Chancery to FO, 9 February 1959, FO371/144927, RS1015/3E; Report from Bank of London & South America, Madrid, 3 March 1959, FO371/144927, RS1015/9; Toquero, *Franco y Don Juan*, pp.297–300; Suárez Fernández, *Franco*, VI, pp.78–82; Tusell, *La oposición democrática*, pp.343–4; Enrique Tierno Galván, *Cabos sueltos* (Barcelona, 1981), pp.119–25.

88 Franco Salgado-Araujo, diary entry for 14 March 1959, *Mis conversaciones*, p.259.

89 Palacios, *Los papeles secretos*, pp.230–1.

90 Preston, *Franco*, pp.676–8.

91 Suárez Fernández, *Franco*, VI, p.96. For a slightly different version of Carrero Blanco's

words, see Javier Tusell con Genoveva García Queipo de Llano, *Carrero. La eminencia gris del régimen de Franco* (Madrid, 1993), pp.252–3.

92 Franco Salgado-Araujo, diary entry for 14 March 1959, *Mis conversaciones*, p.259.

93 Franco Salgado-Araujo, diary entry for 27 October 1960, *Mis conversaciones*, p.300; Alfonso de Borbón, *Memorias*, pp.63–4; Joaquín Bardavío, *La rama trágica de los Borbones* (Barcelona, 1989), pp.68–9.

94 Pérez Mateos, *Un Rey bajo el sol*, pp.249–54.

95 Franco Salgado-Araujo, diary entry for 2 May 1959, *Mis conversaciones*, pp.264–5; Toquero, *Franco y Don Juan*, p.279; Pérez Mateos, *Un Rey bajo el sol*, pp.257–9; Tusell, *Juan Carlos*, pp.285–6; Powell, *Juan Carlos*, p.19.

96 Franco Salgado-Araujo, diary entry for 23 December 1959, *Mis conversaciones*, p.274; López Rodó, *La larga marcha*, p.167.

97 Benjamin Welles, *Spain. The Gentle Anarchy* (London, 1965), p.360.

98 Franco Salgado-Araujo, diary entry for 16 January 1960, *Mis conversaciones*, pp.277–8.

99 Don Juan to Franco, 16 October 1959, Sainz Rodríguez, *Un reinado*, pp.391–2.

100 On the University of Salamanca during this debate, see Raúl Morodo, *Atando cabos. Memorias de un conspirador moderado (I)* (Madrid, 2001), pp.364–5.

101 Martínez Campos's detailed memoir of the meeting is

reproduced in Armada, *Al servicio*, pp.95–101, and in Ricardo de la Cierva, *Historia del franquismo: II*, pp.185–94. *New York Times*, 5 January 1960.

102 Vilallonga, *El Rey*, p.95; Pérez Mateos, *Un Rey bajo el sol*, pp.267–70.

103 Armada, *Al servicio*, p.100; Anson, *Don Juan*, pp.324–5.

104 Javier Tusell & Gonzalo Álvarez de Chillida, *Pemán. Un trayecto intelectual desde la extrema derecha hasta la democracia* (Barcelona, 1998), p.143; Welles, *The Gentle Anarchy*, p.361.

105 Don Juan to Franco, 22 December 1959, Sainz Rodríguez, *Un reinado*, pp.392–3.

106 Don Juan to Franco, 23 December 1959, Sainz Rodríguez, *Un reinado*, pp.393–4.

107 Franco to Don Juan, 15 January 1960, Sainz Rodríguez, *Un reinado*, pp.394–5.

108 Pérez Mateos, *Un Rey bajo el sol*, pp.273–4.

109 Don Juan to Franco, 22 January 1960, Franco to Don Juan, 2 February 1960, Sainz Rodríguez, *Un reinado*, pp.395–7; Tusell, *Juan Carlos*, pp.300–3.

110 José María Pemán, *Mis encuentros con Franco* (Barcelona, 1976), pp.195–8, 202–3; Tusell, *Juan Carlos*, p.304.

111 Don Juan to Franco, 19 February 1960, Franco to Don Juan, 12 March 1960, Sainz Rodríguez, *Un reinado*, pp.397–401.

112 Franco Salgado-Araujo, diary entry for 4 February 1960, *Mis conversaciones*, p.279; *The Times*, 29 March 1960; Jaime Peñafiel, *El General y su tropa. Mis recuerdos de la familia Franco* (Madrid, 1992), pp.70–2.

113 *The Times*, 30 March 1960.

114 Franco Salgado-Araujo, diary entry for 24 March 1960, *Mis conversaciones*, pp.277, 280.

115 Tusell, *Juan Carlos*, pp.307, 314.

116 Madrid Chancery to FO, 2 January 1960, FO371/153291, RS1941/1; Mauricio Carlavilla, *Anti-España 1959: autores, cómplices y encubridores del communismo* (Madrid, 1959), pp.117–24.

117 Ansaldo, *¿Para qué . . . ?*, pp.422–8; Sainz Rodríguez, *Un reinado*, pp.236–7; Franco Salgado-Araujo, diary entry for 2 April 1960, *Mis conversaciones*, pp.280–1; Toquero, *Franco y Don Juan*, pp.280–3; Anson, *Don Juan*, p.328; Tusell, *Juan Carlos*, pp.307–12.

118 *The Times*, 31 March 1960; Toquero, *Franco y Don Juan*, pp.280–4.

119 Stirling to Lloyd, 29 April 1960, FO371/153291, RS1941/4C; Sainz Rodríguez, *Un reinado*, pp.238–9.

120 Mallet to Lloyd, 5 April 1960, FO371/153291, RS1941/4.

121 Don Juan to Franco, 11 April 1960, Franco to Don Juan, 27 April 1960, reprinted in Sainz Rodriguez, *Un reinado*, pp.401–3; López Rodó, *Memorias,* pp.214–15; Franco Salgado-Araujo, diary entry for

18 April 1960, *Mis conversaciones*, p.286.

122 Franco Salgado-Araujo, diary entry for 2 April 1960, *Mis conversaciones*, p.282.

123 Welles, *The Gentle Anarchy*, pp.366–7.

124 Franco Salgado-Araujo, diary entries for 2, 9 April 1960, 9 November 1961, *Mis conversaciones*, pp.281–2, 284, 327; Sainz Rodríguez, *Un reinado*, pp.402–3.

125 Mallet to Lloyd, 25 April 1960, FO371/153291, RS1941/4B.

126 Stirling to Lloyd, 29 April 1960, FO371/153291, RS1941/4C.

127 Jakim Boor, *Masonería* (Madrid, 1952); Madrid Chancery to FO, FO371/153229, RS1011/9.

128 Madrid Chancery to FO, 12 July 1960, FO371/153291, RS1941/7.

129 Labouchere to Lord Home, 2 December 1960, FO371/153291, RS1941/10.

130 Tusell, *Juan Carlos*, pp.324–6.

FOUR: *A Life Under Surveillance*

1 Palacios, *Los papeles secretos*, pp.289–90.

2 Palacios, *Los papeles secretos*, pp.296–7, 300.

3 Labouchere to Sarell, 3 March 1961, FO371/160288, RS1941/3; Franco Salgado-Araujo, diary entry for 7 March 1961, *Mis conversaciones*, p.313.

4 Tusell, *Juan Carlos*, p.316.

5 Vilallonga, *El Rey*, p.95.

6 Tusell, *Juan Carlos*, p.343.

7 Franco Salgado-Araujo, diary entry for 17 December 1960, *Mis conversaciones*, p.304.

8 José Luis Alcocer, *Fernández-Miranda: agonía de un Estado* (Barcelona, 1986), pp.32–3; Equipo Mundo, *Los noventa ministros*, pp.489–93. For a fascinating account of Torcuato Fernández-Miranda as an intellectual, see Morodo, *Atando cabos*, pp.232–7.

9 Vilallonga, *El Rey*, pp.96–7.

10 Pilar Fernández-Miranda Lozana & Alfonso Fernández-Miranda Campoamor, *Lo que el Rey me ha pedido. Torcuato Fernández-Miranda y la reforma política* (Barcelona, 1995), p.51; Armada, *Al servicio*, p.138.

11 López Rodó, *La larga marcha*, pp.178–9; López Rodó, *Memorias*, pp.246–7, 267–8.

12 Anson, *Don Juan*, pp.330–1; Sainz Rodríguez, *Un reinado*, pp.93–9; Toquero, *Franco y Don Juan*, pp.284–6.

13 López Rodó, *Memorias*, p.274.

14 Robilant, *Sangue blu*, pp.351–2; *Época*, 8 February 1988.

15 Labouchere presented his credentials on 23 June 1960. Madrid Chancery to FO, 12 October 1960, FO371/153291, RS1941/8; *The Times*, 13 October 1960.

16 Hope to Heath, 29 September 1961, FO371/160786, CS1015/13; Welles, *The Gentle Anarchy*, pp.367–8.

17 *El Mundo*, 21 September 2001, 3, 7 April 2002.

18 Frederica, *Memorias*, pp.248–9; González de la Vega, *Yo, María de Borbón*, pp.127–9; Pilar Urbano, *La Reina* (Barcelona, 1996), pp.100–1.

19 Urbano, *La Reina*, p.115; Gurriarán, *El Rey en Estoril*, pp.460–4.

20 Rayón, *La Boda*, p.40.

21 Urbano, *La Reina*, p.116.

22 Víctor Salmador, *Don Juan. Los secretos*, p.83; Fernando Rayón, *Sofía de Grecia. La Reina* (Barcelona, 1993), p.85.

23 Interview of Sofía by Douglas Key, *Diario 16*, 14 August 1989.

24 *Diario 16*, 15 January 1981, previewing the BBC documentary on the Spanish royal household, broadcast in the UK on 23 January 1981.

25 *¿Qué?*, 27 February 1978; author's conversation with Alfonso Armada.

26 *Diario 16*, 14 August 1989.

27 *Tiempo*, 22 March 1993; Rayón, *Sofía*, pp.85–6; Urbano, *La Reina*, p.119.

28 Urbano, *La Reina*, pp.119–21.

29 Frederica, *Memorias*, p.287; Urbano, *La Reina*, p.122.

30 Frederica, *Memorias*, p.288.

31 *El País*, 24 January 1981, review of BBC documentary about the Spanish royal household, broadcast in the UK on 23 January 1981; Urbano, *La Reina*, p.125.

32 Don Juan to Franco, 10 July 1961, Franco to Don Juan, 22 July 1961, Sainz Rodríguez, *Un reinado*, pp.403–5.

33 Suárez Fernández, *Franco*, VI, pp.303–7.

34 Ibáñez Martín to Franco, 11 September 1961, reproduced in Suárez Fernández, *Franco*, VI, pp.307–10; López Rodó, *La larga marcha*, pp.182–5.

35 Welles, *The Gentle Anarchy*, p.368; Pemán, *Mis encuentros*, p.218; López Rodó, *La larga marcha*, p.187.

36 Rayón, *La Boda*, pp.86–7; Suárez Fernández, *Franco*, VI, pp.311–12.

37 Don Juan to Franco,

38 Hope to Heath, 29 September 1961, FO371/160786, CS1015/13.

39 López Rodó, *La larga marcha*, pp.188–9; *Diario 16*, 14 April 1987.

40 Welles, *The Gentle Anarchy*, p.369; Pemán, *Mis encuentros*, p.218.

41 López Rodó, *La larga marcha*, pp.189–90.

42 López Rodó, *La larga marcha*, p.193.

43 Suárez Fernández, *Franco*, VI, p.315.

44 Hope to Heath, 29 September 1961, FO371/160786, CS1015/13; Labouchere to Tomkins, 28 November 1961, FO371/160786, CS1941/5; Suárez Fernández, *Franco*, VI, p.351.

45 Rayón, *La Boda*, pp.163–5.

46 Suárez Fernández, *Franco*, VI, pp.315–18, 344–7; Frederica, *Memorias*, p.289; Don Juan to Franco, 18 December 1961, 23 January 1962, Sainz Rodríguez, *Un reinado*, pp.407–8; Rayón, *La Boda*, pp.96–102, 107–41, 170–5, 184–5.

47 *ABC*, 26 December 1961; Vicente Gil, *Cuarenta años junto a Franco* (Barcelona, 1981), p.131.

48 *ABC*, 27 December 1961; *The Times*, 27 December 1961; Ramón Soriano, *La mano izquierdo de Franco* (Barcelona, 1981), pp.14–20.

49 Franco Salgado-Araujo, *Mis conversaciones*, p.331.

50 Franco Salgado-Araujo, diary entries for 8, 15 January 1962, *Mis conversaciones*, pp.331–2; Soriano, *La mano*, pp.26–8, 47.

27 September, Franco to Don Juan, 31 October 1961, Sainz Rodríguez, *Un reinado*, pp.405–6.

51 López Rodó, *La larga marcha*, pp.195–6.

52 José María de Areilza, *Crónica de libertad* (Barcelona, 1985), pp.36–7; López Rodó, *La larga marcha*, pp.195–8; López Rodó, *Memorias*, pp.301–2.

53 López Rodó, *La larga marcha*, pp.202–3; Franco Salgado-Araujo, diary entry for 3 March 1962, *Mis conversaciones*, pp.333–4; Suárez Fernández, *Franco*, VI, p.349.

54 Madrid Chancery to FO, 7 December 1961, FO371/160786, CS1941/6; Franco Salgado-Araujo, diary entry for 14 December 1961, *Mis conversaciones*, p.329; Soriano, *La mano*, p.120; Suárez Fernández, *Franco*, VI, pp.350–2.

55 López Rodó, *La larga marcha*, p.201; López Rodó, *Memorias*, pp.288, 330.

56 Murray to Tomkins, 22 November 1962, FO371/163829, CS1941/2.

57 Philip Ziegler, editor, *From Shore to Shore. The Tour Diaries of Earl Mountbatten of Burma 1953–1979* (London, 1989), p.69; Rayón, *La Boda*, pp.251–2, 256–8.

58 Palacios, *Los papeles secretos*, p.347.

59 Soriano, *La mano*, pp.118–20; Peñafiel, *El General*, pp.126–8.

60 *Mundo Obrero*, 1 May 1962; *The Times*, 12 May 1962; Ignacio Fernández de Castro & José Martínez, *España hoy* (Paris, 1963), pp.67–97, 103–28, 140–92; Parti Communiste Français, *Dos meses de huelgas* (Paris, 1962), pp.41–95; Faustino Miguélez, *La lucha de los mineros asturianos bajo el franquismo* (Barcelona, 1976), pp.103–13.

61 Palacios, *Los papeles secretos*, p.340; Urbano, *La Reina*, p.146.

62 British Legation to Holy See to FO, 8 June 1962, FO371/163829, CS1941/3; Rayón, *La Boda*, pp.267–9.

63 Rayón, *La Boda*, p.272; Urbano, *La Reina*, p.148.

64 Paco means Frank, and was Doña Carmen's nickname for the dictator; Pacón (big Frank) was the family name for his cousin.

65 Peñafiel, *El General*, p.127; Urbano, *La Reina*, p.148; Pemán, *Mis encuentros*, pp.218–19; Franco Salgado-Araujo, diary entry for 7 July 1962, *Mis conversaciones*, p.345.

66 Hope to Tomkins, 13 June 1962, FO371/163829, CS1941/5.

67 Urbano, *La Reina*, pp.148–9.

68 Manuel Fraga Iribarne, *Memoria breve de una vida política* (Barcelona, 1980), p.37.

69 Rafael Calvo Serer, 'Los Príncipes y el Presidente', *ABC*, 20 November 1962; *Diario 16*, 14 August 1989; Welles, *The Gentle Anarchy*, pp.163–4; Franco Salgado-Araujo, diary entry for 2 March 1963, *Mis conversaciones*, p.375; Antonio Garrigues y Díaz Cañabate, *Diálogos conmigo mismo* (Barcelona, 1978), p.95; Suárez Fernández, *Franco*, VII, p.66; Pérez Mateos, *Un Rey bajo el sol*, pp.324–6.

70 Suárez Fernández, *Franco*, VI, p.377.

71 *ABC*, 9 June 1962; Franco Salgado-Araujo, diary entry for 23 June 1962, *Mis conversaciones*, pp.342–3; Soriano, *La mano*, pp.151–2;

López Rodó, *Memorias*, pp.335–6; Suárez Fernández, *Franco*, VI, p.357.

72 Areilza, *Memorias exteriores*, pp.170–82; Calvo Serer, *Franco frente al Rey*, pp.112–13.

73 *Arriba*, 9, 10, 12 June 1962; *ABC*, 9, 11, 12 June 1962.

74 Joaquín Satrústegui et al., eds, *Cuando la transición se hizo posible. El "contubernio de Munich"* (Madrid, 1993), p.16; Hope to Tomkins, 13, 20 June 1962, FO371/163829, CS1941/5.

75 *La Vanguardia Española*, 17 June 1962; *The Times*, 18 June 1962; Francisco Franco Bahamonde, *Discursos y mensajes del Jefe del Estado 1960–1963* (Madrid, 1964), pp.399–404, 412, 423–4, 427; Calvo Serer, *Franco frente al Rey*, p.112.

76 Palacios, *Los papeles secretos*, p.357; Tusell, *Juan Carlos*, p.357.

77 Murray to Tomkins, 22 November 1962, FO371/163829, CS1941/2; Urbano, *La Reina*, p.161; Rayón, *La Boda*, pp.289–90.

78 Palacios, *Los papeles secretos*, pp.357–8; Rayón, *La Boda*, pp.290–1.

79 Franco Salgado-Araujo, diary entries for 29 November, 20 December 1962, *Mis conversaciones*, pp.359, 362; López Rodó, *La larga marcha*, p.208.

80 Franco Salgado-Araujo, diary entry for 3 October 1962, *Mis conversaciones*, pp.350–1; Urbano, *La Reina*, pp.159–60.

81 Franco to Don Juan, 12 April 1962, Sainz Rodríguez, *Un reinado*, pp.408–9; Tusell, *Juan Carlos*, p.377.

82 Franco Salgado-Araujo, diary entry for 4 February 1963, *Mis conversaciones*, p.369; Suárez Fernández, *Franco*, VI, pp.383–4.

83 Tusell, *Juan Carlos*, pp.372–3; Pérez Mateos, *Un Rey bajo el sol*, p.332; Pilar Cernuda, *30 días de noviembre. El mes que cambió la historia de España: las claves* (Barcelona, 2000), pp.18–19.

84 Anson, *Don Juan*, p.340; Don Juan to Franco, 8 February, Franco to Don Juan, 18 February 1963, Sainz Rodríguez, *Un reinado*, pp.409–11; Tusell, *Juan Carlos*, pp.377–9.

85 Franco Salgado-Araujo, diary entry for 2 March 1963, *Mis conversaciones*, pp.374–5.

86 Pérez Mateos, *Un Rey bajo el sol*, pp.385–6.

87 Powell, *Juan Carlos*, pp.25–6; López Rodó, *La larga marcha*, p.208; Urbano, *La Reina*, p.162.

88 Fraga, *Memoria breve*, p.65; Peñafiel, *El General*, pp.127–8; López Rodó, *La larga marcha*, p.208.

89 Franco Salgado-Araujo, diary entry for 4 April 1963, *Mis conversaciones*, p.377.

90 Urbano, *La Reina*, p.166; Fraga, *Memoria breve*, p.74.

91 Franco Salgado-Araujo, diary entry for 25 May 1963, *Mis conversaciones*, pp.382–3.

92 Labouchere to Lord Home, 23 April 1963, FO371/169512, CS1941/1.

93 Labouchere to Lord Home, 23 April 1963, FO371/169512, CS1941/1; Welles, *The Gentle Anarchy*, p.372.

94 Suárez Fernández, *Franco*, VII, pp.122–5; Palacios, *Los papeles secretos*, pp.366–70za.

95 Labouchere to Dodson, 22 April 1964, FO371/174937, CS1015/10;

Welles, *The Gentle Anarchy*, p.372; López Rodó, *La larga marcha*, pp.211, 214–16; López Rodó, *Memorias*, p.531; Franco Salgado-Araujo, diary entry for 20 April 1964, *Mis conversaciones*, p.420; Suárez Fernández, *Franco*, VII, pp.130–4.

96 Vilallonga, *El Rey*, pp.82, 85; López Rodó, *La larga marcha*, p.212.

97 Franco to Don Juan, 14 November 1963, Sainz Rodríguez, *Un reinado*, p.412.

98 Labouchere to Dodson, 31 December 1963, FO371/174937, CS1015/1; González de la Vega, *Yo, María de Borbón*, pp.108, 147; López Rodó, *La larga marcha*, pp.211–12.

99 *Le Figaro*, 16 December 1963; Franco, *Discursos 1960–1963*, pp.599–609.

100 Labouchere to Dodson, 31 December 1963, FO371/174937, CS1015/1.

101 Fraga, *Memoria breve*, p.107; López Rodó, *Memorias*, pp.458–9.

102 Francisco Franco Bahamonde, *Discursos y mensajes del Jefe del Estado 1964–1967* (Madrid, 1968), p.43.

103 Labouchere to Butler, 25 March 1964, FO371/174937, CS1015/7; Tusell, *Juan Carlos*, pp.387–8.

104 Franco Salgado-Araujo, diary entries for 3 February, 20 April, 22 June 1964, *Mis conversaciones*, pp.409, 421–2, 426–7.

105 Hughes (Bilbao) to Labouchere, 23 June 1964, FO371/174937, CS1015/13.

106 López Rodó, *Memorias*, p.459; Franco Salgado-Araujo, diary entry for 20 January 1964, *Mis conversaciones*, p.407; Fraga, *Memoria breve*, pp.89, 99, 103, 123–5.

107 López Rodó, *La larga marcha*, pp.224–6.

108 López Rodó, *La larga marcha*, p.226; Fraga, *Memoria breve*, p.133.

109 López Rodó, *La larga marcha*, pp.226–7.

110 López Rodó, *Memorias*, p.512; López Rodó, *La larga marcha*, pp.227–8.

111 López Rodó, *Memorias*, pp.519–20; López Rodó, *La larga marcha*, pp.229–30; Fraga, *Memoria breve*, p.135.

112 Suárez Fernández, *Franco*, VII, p.197.

113 López Rodó, *Memorias*, p.522.

114 Urbano, *La Reina*, p.188.

115 Fraga, *Memoria breve*, pp.136, 138; López Rodó, *Memorias*, p.537.

116 On the role of Pabón, see Tusell, *Juan Carlos*, pp.395–417. See also Carlos Seco Serrano, 'A modo de prólogo', Jesús Pabón, 'Páginas de unas memorias perdidas', *Boletín de la Real Academia de la Historia*, Tomo CXCII, enero-abril 1995, Cuaderno 1, pp.1–8.

117 *The Times*, 20 November 1965.

118 Henderson to Dodson, 25 November 1965, FO371/180112, CS1015/9.

119 Henderson to Dodson, 7 December 1965, FO371/180112, CS1015/9(E); Toquero, *Franco y Don Juan*, pp.334–6; Bardavío, *La rama trágica*, pp.102–6, 111–14; López Rodó, *La larga marcha*, pp.237–9; Fraga, *Memoria breve*,

pp.150–1; Suárez Fernández, *Franco*, VII, pp.244, 280.

120 *Time*, 21 January 1966.

121 Tusell, *Juan Carlos*, pp.418–20; Palacios, *Los papeles secretos*, pp.400–1.

122 Laureano López Rodó, *Memorias: años decisivos* (Barcelona, 1991), pp.18–20; López Rodó, *La larga marcha*, pp.239–43; Bardavío, *La rama trágica*, pp.95–107; Franco Salgado-Araujo, diary entry for 26 March 1966, *Mis conversaciones*, p.465. On the Carlist claimants, see Javier Lavardín, *Historia del último pretendiente a la corona de España* (Paris, 1976), passim.

123 Urbano, *La Reina*, pp.174–6.

124 Suárez Fernández, *Franco*, VII, p.326–7; Franco Salgado-Araujo, diary entry for 26 March 1966, *Mis conversaciones*, p.466; López Rodó, *La larga marcha*, pp.243–7, 589–92; López Rodó, *Memorias: años decisivos*, pp.24–5; Anson, *Don Juan*, pp.351–2; Tusell, *Juan Carlos*, pp.440–4.

125 Pabón, 'Páginas de unas memorias perdidas', *Boletín de la Real Academia de la Historia*, pp.13–14.

126 Pérez Mateos, *Un Rey bajo el sol*, p.323.

127 Areilza, *Crónica*, pp.19–21, 42–54, 63–70; Toquero, *Franco y Don Juan*, pp.343–8; Suárez Fernández, *Franco*, VII, pp.171–2, 319–20, 327–8.

128 López Rodó, *Memorias: años decisivos*, pp.29, 32; Suárez Fernández, *Franco*, VII, p.342.

129 Henderson (Madrid) to Dodson (FO), 10 May 1966, FO371/185820, S1011/61/66.

130 Franco Salgado-Araujo, diary entry for 13 June 1966, *Mis conversaciones*, p.473.

131 Suárez Fernández, *Franco*, VII, pp.328–9; Palacios, *Los papeles secretos*, pp.407–10; López Rodó, *Memorias: años decisivos*, pp.41–2.

132 José María de Porcioles, *Mis memorias* (Barcelona, 1994), p.205; López Rodó, *La larga marcha*, p.247; Suárez Fernández, *Franco*, VII, p.343; Franco Salgado-Araujo, diary entry for 21 June 1966, *Mis conversaciones*, p. 479.

133 *ABC*, 21 July 1966; Anson, *Don Juan*, pp.358–62.

134 *Pueblo*, 30 July 1966.

135 Fraga, *Memoria breve*, pp.174–5; López Rodó, *La larga marcha*, p.248.

136 Tusell, *Juan Carlos*, pp.453–4.

137 Franco, *Discursos, 1964–1967*, pp.219–51; Williams to Brown, 2 December 1966, FO371/185768, CS1015/24; *Le Figaro*, 13 December 1966.

138 Franco, *Discursos, 1964–1967*, pp.231, 236, 240; Stanley G. Payne, *The Franco Regime 1936–1975* (Madison, 1987), pp.513–15.

139 Suárez Fernández, *Franco*, VII, pp.362–4; Franco Salgado-Aruajo, diary entries for 5, 27 December 1966, *Mis conversaciones*, pp.488, 491; Tusell, *Juan Carlos*, p.454.

140 Franco, *Discursos, 1964–1967*, p.259.

141 Madrid to FO, cypher telegram, Gordon-Lennox to Daunt, 15 December 1966, FO371/185768, CS1015/25A, CS1015/

25B; *Cuadernos de Ruedo Ibérico*, No.10, December 1966–January 1967, pp.27–63; Edouard de Blaye, *Franco and the Politics of Spain* (Harmondsworth, 1976), pp.236–8.

FIVE: *The Winning Post in Sight*

1 Alfonso de Borbón, *Memorias*, pp.67–8.
2 Tusell, *Juan Carlos*, p.460.
3 *Pueblo*, 21, 23 December 1966.
4 *Horizonte Español 1972*, 3 vols (Paris, 1972), I, p.63.
5 Suárez Fernández, *Franco*, VII, pp.362–4.
6 Armada, *Al servicio*, p.122.
7 *Le Figaro*, 27 December 1966.
8 *Horizonte Español 1972*, I, p.98.
9 Suárez Fernández, *Franco*, VII, p.374.
10 Franco Salgado-Araujo, diary entry for 27 March 1967, *Mis conversaciones*, p.500.
11 Lavardín, *Historia del último pretendiente*, pp.227–31; Silva Muñoz, *Memorias*, pp.146–52; López Rodó, *La larga marcha*, pp.262–3; Suárez Fernández, *Franco*, VII, pp.377–9, 392–3.
12 Suárez Fernández, *Franco*, VII, p.386.
13 'Franco: los archivos secretos IV', *Tiempo*, 14 December 1992; Franco Salgado-Araujo, diary entry for 13 March 1967, *Mis conversaciones*, p.498.
14 Peter Murtagh, *The Rape of Greece. The King, the Colonels and the Resistance* (London, 1994), pp.71–125, 157–61; Urbano, *La Reina*, pp.218–24.
15 Garicano Goñi, interview in Ángel Bayod, editor, *Franco visto por sus ministros* (Barcelona,

1981), p.202; Suárez Fernández, *Franco*, VII, p.395.
16 Cierva, *Historia del franquismo: II*, pp.250–1; López Rodó, *La larga marcha*, pp.263–5; López Rodó, *Memorias: años decisivos*, p.207.
17 Calvo Serer, *Franco frente al Rey*, p.171.
18 José Solís interview in Bayod, *Franco*, p.104.
19 Espinosa San Martín interview in Bayod, *Franco*, p.154.
20 Espinosa San Martín interview in Bayod, *Franco*, pp.159–60.
21 Fraga, *Memoria breve*, p.215.
22 Franco, *Discursos 1964–1967*, p.302.
23 López Rodó, *La larga marcha*, pp.266–7, 276.
24 *Pueblo*, 6 January 1968; Emilio Romero, *Tragicomedia de España. Unas memorias sin contemplaciones* (Barcelona, 1985), p.186.
25 Suárez Fernández, *Franco*, VIII, pp.24–6; López Rodó, *La larga marcha*, pp.267–8.
26 Williams to Beith, 8 February 1968, FCO9/406, CS1/6; Suárez Fernández, *Franco*, VIII, pp.26–8.
27 Williams to Beith, 14 February 1968, FCO9/406, CS1/6; Jesús Pabón, 'Páginas de unas memorias perdidas', *Boletín de la Real Academia de la Historia*, pp.17–18; Palacios, *Los papeles secretos*, pp.436–9; López Rodó, *La larga marcha*, pp.269–70; Franco Salgado-Araujo, diary entry for 3 May 1969, *Mis conversaciones*, pp.548–9. Anson, *Don Juan*, pp.20–2, disputes that the Queen spoke in this way to Franco.
28 Williams to Beith, 14 February

1968, FCO9/406, CS1/6; Franco Salgado-Araujo, diary entry for 12 February 1968, *Mis conversaciones*, p.518; Suárez Fernández, *Franco*, VIII, pp.28-9; Tom Burns Marañón, *Conversaciones sobre el Rey* (Barcelona, 1995), pp.74-5; Anson, *Don Juan*, pp.364-5.

29 Suárez Fernández, *Franco*, VIII, pp.59-60; López Rodó, *Memorias: años decisivos*, p.314.

30 Joaquín Bardavío, *Los silencios del Rey* (Madrid, 1979), pp.33-4; López Rodó, *La larga marcha*, pp.275, 288.

31 López Rodó, *Memorias: años decisivos*, pp.313-14.

32 López Rodó, *Memorias: años decisivos*, p.354.

33 Armada, *Al servicio*, pp.126-7; López Rodó, *La larga marcha*, pp.280-1, 295-7; Suárez Fernández, *Franco*, VIII, pp.61-5; Tusell, *Juan Carlos*, pp.475-8.

34 Tusell, *Carrero*, pp.336-7; Palacios, *Los papeles secretos*, pp.453-6; López Rodó, *La larga marcha*, pp.276-9, 596-600; López Rodó, *Memorias: años decisivos*, pp.358-9. There appears to be some confusion over the exact date of this meeting.

35 Suárez Fernández, *Franco*, VIII, p.66; López Rodó, *La larga marcha*, p.279.

36 *Pueblo*, 9 November 1968.

37 Pabón, 'Páginas de unas memorias perdidas', *Boletín de la Real Academia de la Historia*, pp.20-3; author's interview with Alfonso Armada; Armada, *Al servicio*, pp.124-5; Fraga, *Memoria breve*, pp.233-4; López Rodó, *Memorias: años decisivos*, pp.368-9.

38 Laot, *Juan Carlos y Sofía*, p.89; Areilza, *Crónica*, p.80.

39 Fraga, *Memoria breve*, pp.235-6; Armada, *Al servicio*, p.126.

40 *Pueblo*, 7 January 1969; Fraga, *Memoria breve*, p.236; author's interview with Alfonso Armada; Pérez Mateos, *Un Rey bajo el sol*, pp.417-18.

41 Sainz Rodríguez, *Un reinado*, p.313.

42 Author's interview with Alfonso Armada; Armada, *Al servicio*, p.124; Palacios, *Los papeles secretos*, p.461; Pabón, 'Páginas de unas memorias perdidas', *Boletín de la Real Academia de la Historia*, pp.33-4.

43 Tusell, *Carrero*, p.338.

44 Franco Salgado-Araujo, diary entry for 16 January 1969, *Mis conversaciones*, p.537; López Rodó, *La larga marcha*, pp.291-3; Suárez Fernández, *Franco*, VIII, pp.70-1; Fraga, *Memoria breve*, pp.236-7.

45 López Rodó, *La larga marcha*, pp.301-2; López Rodó, *Memorias: años decisivos*, pp.381-4.

46 Pabón, 'Páginas de unas memorias perdidas', *Boletín de la Real Academia de la Historia*, pp.34-5.

47 López Rodó, *Memorias: años decisivos*, p.386; López Rodó, *La larga marcha*, pp.303-11; Espinosa San Martín interview in Bayod, *Franco*, p.160.

48 López Rodó, *La larga marcha*, pp.311, 313; López Rodó, *Memorias: años decisivos*, p.403.

49 Sainz Rodríguez, *Un reinado*, p.314; Anson, *Don Juan*, pp.18-19; López Rodó, *La larga marcha*, pp.303-13.

50 Armada, *Al servicio*, pp.120, 173;

Palacios, *Los papeles secretos*, pp.472–4.

51 Fraga, *Memoria breve*, pp.245–6; López Rodó, *La larga marcha*, pp.316–18; López Rodó, *Memorias: años decisivos*, pp.423–6.

52 López Rodó, *La larga marcha*, pp.318–23.

53 López Rodó, *La larga marcha*, pp.324–5.

54 Víctor Salmador, *Don Juan. Los secretos*, pp.89–90; Urbano, *La Reina*, pp.204–5; López Rodó, *Memorias: años decisivos*, pp.449–50; López Rodó, *La larga marcha*, pp.331–3; Vilallonga, *El Rey*, p.79; Anson, *Don Juan*, p.24; Urbano, *La Reina*, p.339.

55 Author's conversation with Miguel Primo de Rivera y Urquijo.

56 López Rodó, *La larga marcha*, pp.325–31.

57 Armada, *Al servicio*, pp.120, 130; José Antonio Girón de Velasco, *Si la memoria no me falla* (Barcelona, 1994), p.208.

58 Anson, *Don Juan*, pp.28–9.

59 Pabón, 'Páginas de unas memorias perdidas', *Boletín de la Real Academia de la Historia*, pp.48–9; Armada, *Al servicio*, p.129 and in an interview with the author. Palacios, *Los papeles secretos*, p.483, makes a persuasive case for 15 July as the date of the meeting between Franco and the Prince.

60 Bardavío, *Los silencios*, p.35; Vilallonga, *El Rey*, pp.79–81; López Rodó, *La larga marcha*, pp.335–6.

61 López Rodó, *La larga marcha*, p.335; Anson, *Don Juan*, p.15.

62 Pabón, 'Páginas de unas memorias perdidas', *Boletín de la*

Real Academia de la Historia, p.50.

63 Giménez-Arnau, *Memorias*, pp.318–22; Pabón, 'Páginas de unas memorias perdidas', *Boletín de la Real Academia de la Historia*, pp.42–7; Areilza, *Crónica*, p.90; López Rodó, *La larga marcha*, pp.338–9.

64 Anson, *Don Juan*, pp.39–41; López Rodó, *Memorias: años decisivos*, pp.454–5.

65 Giménez-Arnau, *Memorias*, pp.322–4; Anson, *Don Juan*, pp.42–3; López Rodó, *Memorias: años decisivos*, pp.455–7.

66 *International Herald Tribune*, 24 July 1969; Giménez-Arnau, *Memorias*, p.323; Sainz Rodríguez, *Un reinado*, pp.414–15; Anson, *Don Juan*, pp.14–16, 32–3; Areilza, *Crónica*, p.91.

67 Vilallonga, *Franco y el Rey. La espera y la esperanza* (Barcelona, 1998), p.192; López Rodó, *Memorias: años decisivos*, p.453.

68 Areilza, *Crónica*, pp.91–4; Palacios, *Los papeles secretos*, pp.493–7; Urbano, *La Reina*, pp.234–5; Anson, *Don Juan*, pp.43–9; López Rodó, *Memorias: años decisivos*, pp.459–65; López Rodó, *La larga marcha*, pp.355–6, 360.

69 Suárez Fernández, *Franco*, VIII, pp.97–9; Anson, *Don Juan*, pp.65–77.

70 Anson, *Don Juan*, p.50; López Rodó, *La larga marcha*, pp.342, 357.

71 Bardavío, *Los silencios*, pp.35–6; López Rodó, *Memorias: años decisivos*, pp.471–6; López Rodó, *La larga marcha*, pp.362–5.

72 Vilallonga, *El Rey*, p.81; Anson,

Don Juan, pp.61–2; López Rodó, *La larga marcha*, p.335.

73 Sainz Rodríguez, *Un reinado*, p.276; Salmador, *Don Juan. Los secretos*, p.89.

74 Salmador, *Don Juan. Los secretos*, pp.91–5.

75 Francisco Franco Bahamonde, *Discursos y mensajes del Jefe del Estado 1968–1970* (Madrid, 1971), pp.85–97; Silva Muñoz, *Memorias*, pp.236–9.

76 *Horizonte Español 1972*, I, pp.159–60; *New York Times*, 23 July 1969.

77 Fernández-Miranda, *Lo que el Rey*, pp.52–5; Bardavío, *Los silencios*, pp.49–50.

78 *Palabras de su Alteza Real el Príncipe de Asturias Juan Carlos de Borbón y Borbón* (Madrid, 1974), pp.19–20.

79 Alfonso de Borbón, *Memorias*, pp.92–4; López Rodó, *La larga marcha*, p.378; Salmador, *Don Juan. Los secretos*, p.54.

80 *Palabras de Juan Carlos*, pp.21–3; López Rodó, *La larga marcha*, pp.372–6.

81 Pabón, 'Páginas de unas memorias perdidas', *Boletín de la Real Academia de la Historia*, pp.64–5.

82 Silva Muñoz, *Memorias*, p.240; Giménez-Arnau, *Memorias*, p.325; Anson, *Don Juan*, p.56.

83 Juan Luis Calleja, *Don Juan Carlos ¿por qué?* (Madrid, 1972), p.164.

84 Anson, *Don Juan*, pp.56, 61; Urbano, *La Reina*, p.437; Sainz Rodríguez, *Un reinado*, p.315; Areilza, *Crónica*, p.96; Vilallonga, *Franco y el Rey*, p.190.

85 Silva Muñoz, *Memorias*, p.240.

86 José Luis de Vilallonga, *A pleines dents* (Paris, 1973), p.79.

87 *Mundo Obrero*, 2 September 1969.

88 *Horizonte Español 1972*, I, pp.162–3; Suárez Fernández, *Franco*, VIII, pp.104–5.

89 Vilallonga, *Franco y el Rey*, p.191.

90 López Rodó, *La larga marcha*, pp.336, 379–80.

91 Bardavío, *Los silencios*, p.27.

92 Vilallonga, *Franco y el Rey*, p.192.

93 Vilallonga, *Franco y el Rey*, p.200.

94 Franco Salgado-Araujo, diary entry for 11 October 1969, *Mis conversaciones*, pp.549–52.

95 Armada, *Al servicio*, p.122; Bardavío, *Los silencios*, pp.50–2.

96 Vilallonga, *El Rey*, p.83.

97 Urbano, *La Reina*, pp.337–40.

SIX: *Under Suspicion*

1 Juan Vilá Reyes, *El atropello MATESA* (Barcelona, 1992), *passim*; Mariano Navarro Rubio, *Mis memorias. Testimonio de una vida política truncada por el "Caso MATESA"* (Barcelona, 1991), pp.345–431; López Rodó, *Memorias: años decisivos*, pp.494–521, 553–63; Suárez Fernández, *Franco*, VIII, pp.158–9.

2 *Arriba*, 24, 27 August 1969.

3 Franco Salgado-Araujo, diary entry for 11 March 1968, *Mis conversaciones*, pp.527, 530; López Rodó, *Memorias: años decisivos*, pp.507–9, 682–90.

4 López Rodó, *La larga marcha*, pp.390–5; López Rodó, *Memorias: años decisivos*, pp.520–3, 534–7.

5 *ABC*, 29 October 1969; Equipo Mundo, *Los noventa ministros*,

pp.420–500; López Rodó, *La larga marcha*, pp.392–5.

6 San Martín, *Servicio especial* (Barcelona, 1983), pp.23–42; 'Luis Ramírez' (pseudonym of Luciano Rincón), 'Morir en el bunker', *Horizonte Español 1972*, I, pp.1–20; Paul Preston, *The Politics of Revenge* (London, 1990), pp.165–74. Garicano's protest of 7 September 1972, López Rodó, *La larga marcha*, pp.424–5.

7 Ramón Garriga, *La Señora de El Pardo* (Barcelona, 1979), pp.235, 289–92, 297–301; Joaquín Giménez Arnau, *Yo, Jimmy: mi vida entre los Franco* (Barcelona, 1981), p.26.

8 Laureano López Rodó, *El principio del fin: Memorias* (Barcelona, 1992), pp.13–14.

9 *New York Times*, 4 February 1970.

10 Silva Muñoz, *Memorias*, p.279.

11 *Palabras de Juan Carlos*, p.41; López Rodó, *El principio*, pp.21–2, 25, 47, 180. On the *Guardia de Franco*, see Joaquín Bardavío & Justino Sinova, *Todo Franco. Franquismo y antifranquismo de la A a la Z* (Barcelona, 2000), pp.327–8.

12 Russell to Secondé, 25 February 1970, FCO9/1306, WSS26/1; Secondé & Greenhill minutes to same; López Rodó, *La larga marcha*, pp.399–403.

13 *Ya*, 1 April 1970; *ABC*, 24 March, 2 April 1970; *Mundo Obrero*, 29 April 1970.

14 Russell notes on conversation with Juan Carlos, 13 April 1970, FCO9/1306, WSS26/1.

15 Russell to Secondé, 13 April 1970, FCO9/1306, WSS26/1.

16 Russell to Bendall, 1 September 1970, FCO9/1281, WSS1/13–6.

17 López Rodó, *La larga marcha*, pp.404, 408–10.

18 Henry Kissinger, *The White House Years* (London, 1979), pp.930–2; López Rodó, *El principio*, pp.84–5; Russell to Brimelow, 29 March 1971, FCO9/1456, WSS3/313.

19 Vernon A. Walters, *Silent Missions* (New York, 1978), pp.570–1.

20 Russell Annual Review for 1970, FCO9/1451, WSS1/4.

21 Ziegler, *From Shore to Shore*, p.204; Philip Ziegler, *Mountbatten. The Official Biography* (London, 1985), p.678.

22 *Le Monde*, 16, 18 December 1970.

23 *Le Monde*, 18 December 1970; Gil, *Cuarenta años*, pp.98–103; Franco Salgado-Araujo, *Mis conversaciones*, p.560; López Rodó, *El principio*, pp.113–15.

24 *Le Monde*, 19, 21 December 1970; *Mundo Obrero*, 22 December 1970; Blaye, *Franco and the Politics of Spain*, pp.309–11; Philippe Nourry, *Juan Carlos. Un rey para los republicanos* (Barcelona, 1986), pp.176–7.

25 *Le Monde*, 29, 30 December 1970; López Bravo & Garicano Goñi interviews in Bayod, *Franco*, pp.124, 201–2; López Rodó, *La larga marcha*, pp.405–6; López Rodó, *El principio*, pp.122–9, 579–82.

26 Russell, Annual Review for 1970, FCO9/1451, WSS1/4.

27 Russell to Secondé, 13 January 1971, FCO9/1455, WSS3/304/1.

28 *The Times*, 26 January 1971; Russell to Secondé, 13 January 1971, FCO9/1455, WSS3/304/1;

Program for visit, State Department press release, copy in FCO9/1455, WSS3/304/1.

29 Crowe (Washington) to Thomas (FCO), 4 February 1971, FCO9/1455, WSS3/304/1; López Rodó, *El principio*, p.147; Walters, *Silent Missions*, pp.551–2. On Kissinger's promise, see Cernuda, *30 días*, p.21.

30 *New York Times*, 8 February 1971; López Rodó, *El principio*, p.146.

31 Transcript of Prince's breakfast with US correspondents, 28 January 1971, FCO9/1455, WSS3/304/1. On López Bravo, Crowe (Washington) to Neville-Jones, 24 February 1971, FCO1455, WSS3/304/1.

32 Urbano, *La Reina*, p.244; Bardavío, *Los silencios*, pp.53–4.

33 Walters, *Silent Missions*, pp.554–6.

34 López Rodó, *El principio*, pp.179, 195–6, 198.

35 Urbano, *La Reina*, p.245.

36 Tusell, *Juan Carlos*, pp.532–3.

37 *Discurso de Franco en las Cortes Españolas. Sesión de Apertura de la X Legislatura (18 de noviembre de 1971)* (Madrid, 1971), pp.20–2; Meyer to Baillie, 25 November 1971, FCO9/1452, WSS1/5; *Le Monde*, 20 November 1971.

38 López Rodó, *La larga marcha*, p.417; Anson, *Don Juan*, pp.379–80; Urbano, *La Reina*, p.248.

39 Pilar Jaraiz Franco, *Historia de una disidencia* (Barcelona, 1981), p.205.

40 Bardavío, *La rama trágica*, pp.163–72, 192; Peñafiel, *El General*, pp.166–8, 203–10; Fernando Díaz Plaja, *Anecdotario de la España franquista* (Barcelona, 1997), p.91.

41 Garriga, *La Señora*, pp.332–3; López Rodó, *La larga marcha*, pp.411–29; Suárez Fernández, *Franco*, VIII, pp.273–82; Bardavío, *La rama trágica*, pp.153–7, 181–92; Victoria Prego, *Así se hizo la Transición* (Barcelona, 1995), p.22.

42 Author's interview with Wilson's *chef de cabinet*, Joe Haines; Bardavío, *Los silencios*, pp.69–70.

43 López Rodó, *El principio*, p.296.

44 Jaraiz Franco, *Historia*, pp.156, 162–3, 174, 205.

45 Tusell, *Carrero*, p.421; López Rodó, *La larga marcha*, pp.426, 456; López Rodó, *El principio*, pp.333, 421–2; Alfonso de Borbón, *Memorias*, pp.131ff.

46 Fernández-Miranda, *Lo que el Rey*, pp.56–7; López Rodó, *La larga marcha*, pp.435–7.

47 Torcuato Fernández-Miranda, 'Diario inédito', *ABC*, 20 December 1983, pp.5–6; Carlos Fernández Santander, *El Almirante Carrero* (Barcelona, 1985), pp.238–9; Tusell, *Carrero*, pp.399–400; Fraga, *Memoria breve*, p.277.

48 See Garicano Goñi's note to Franco of 7 May 1973, López Rodó, *La larga marcha*, pp.440–2.

49 López Rodó, *El principio*, pp.296, 334.

50 Gil, *Cuarenta años*, pp.47–8.

51 López Rodó, *El principio*, pp.296, 334, 385–9.

52 Girón de Velasco, *Si la memoria no me falla*, p.228.

53 Author's conversation with José Utrera Molina, 20 August 2002;

López Rodó, *El principio*, p.180. See also Fernández-Miranda, *Lo que el Rey*, pp.300–1.

54 For the telephone call, see Carlos Estévez y Francisco Mármol, *Carrero. Las razones ocultas de un asesinato* (Madrid, 1998), p.117.

55 *Le Monde*, 4, 5–6, 7 August 1973; Ismael Fuente, Javier García & Joaquín Prieto, *Golpe mortal: asesinato de Carrero y agonía del franquismo* (Madrid, 1983), p.164; Carlos Arias interview in Bayod, *Franco*, p.308; Bardavío, *Los silencios*, pp.61–2; López Rodó, *La larga marcha*, pp.440–53.

56 Fraga, *Memoria breve*, p.298; López Rodó, *El principio*, pp.541–2; Cierva, *Historia del franquismo: II*, p.321.

57 Tusell, *Carrero*, pp.428–33.

58 Julen Agirre (pseud. Eva Forest), *Operación Ogro: cómo y porqué ejecutamos a Carrero Blanco* (Paris, 1974), *passsim*; Joaquín Bardavío, *La crisis: historia de quince días* (Madrid, 1974), pp.47–56.

59 Fuente et al., *Golpe mortal*, p.172; José Utrera Molina, *Sin cambiar de bandera* (Barcelona, 1989), pp.70–4; Cierva, *Historia del franquismo: II*, p.389; Rafael Borràs Betriu et al., *El día en que mataron a Carrero Blanco* (Barcelona, 1974), p.27; Pilar Franco Bahamonde, *Nosotros los Franco* (Barcelona, 1980), p.150.

60 Laureano López Rodó, *Claves de la transición. Memorias IV* (Barcelona, 1993), p.27.

61 Fuente et al., *Golpe mortal*, p.172.

62 Julio Rodríguez Martínez, *Impresiones de un ministro de Carrero Blanco* (Barcelona, 1974), pp.54–8, 80, 86; Utrera, *Sin cambiar*, pp.74–7; Gil, *Cuarenta años*, p.142; Fuente et al., *Golpe mortal*, pp.195–6.

63 Gil, *Cuarenta años*, p.144.

64 López Rodó, *El principio*, pp.523–5.

65 Vilallonga, *El Rey*, p.209; Prego, *Así se hizo*, p.48.

66 Gil, *Cuarenta años*, pp.145–6; Luis Herrero, *El ocaso del régimen. Del asesinato de Carrero a la muerte de Franco* (Madrid, 1995), pp.57–71; Santiago Carrillo, *Memorias* (Barcelona, 1993), pp.577–8.

67 Jaraiz Franco, *Historia*, p.208; Utrera Molina, *Sin cambiar*, p.83; Prego, *Así se hizo*, p.69; Herrero, *El ocaso*, p.27.

68 Gil, *Cuarenta años*, pp.147–8, 151; Javier Figuero & Luis Herrero, *La muerte de Franco jamás contada* (Barcelona, 1985), pp.29–30.

69 Fuente et al., *Golpe mortal*, pp.285–9; Utrera Molina, *Sin cambiar*, pp.79–80; Bayod, *Franco visto*, p.351.

70 Gil, *Cuarenta años*, p.152; Fuente et al., *Golpe mortal*, p.289.

71 Gil, *Cuarenta años*, pp.152–3; Fuente et al., *Golpe mortal*, p.290; Figuero & Herrero, *La muerte de Franco*, pp.30–2. There is an element of inconsistency in the dates and times given by the principal sources.

72 Fuente et al., *Golpe mortal*, p.290.

73 Borràs et al., *El día*, pp.252–6; *El Mundo*, 5 January 1974; Licinio de la Fuente, *"Valió la pena" Memorias* (Madrid, 1998), p.208.

74 Fuente et al., *Golpe mortal*, pp.291–5; Gil, *Cuarenta años*, pp.154–5; Estévez y Mármol, *Carrero*, p.201.

75 *ABC*, 20 December 1983, p.7; Gil, *Cuarenta años*, p.156.

76 Gil, *Cuarenta años*, pp.139–41, 156–9.

77 Gil, *Cuarenta años*, pp.160–1; Utrera, *Sin cambiar*, pp.83–5; Fuente et al., *Golpe mortal*, pp.293–5.

78 Francisco Franco Bahamonde, *Pensamiento político de Franco*, 2 vols (Madrid, 1975), I, pp.35–8; Bardavío, *Los silencios*, p.74; Fernando de Liñán interview in Bayod, *Franco*, p.319.

79 Vilallonga, *El Rey*, p.211.

80 Anson, *Don Juan*, p.385. Anson was a distinguished journalist. In 1975, he was made editor of the magazine *Blanco y Negro*, and in 1976 Director of the Agencia EFE. In 1982, he became editor of *ABC* (which is where he was when he wrote the comment cited above). In 1998, he founded the newspaper *La Razón*, of which he is still editor. See also the brilliant analysis by Herrero, *El ocaso*, pp.22–5.

81 Girón, *Si la memoria*, p.231; Borràs Betriu et al., *El día*, pp.250, 258–9; Rodríguez Martínez, *Impresiones*, p.87.

82 Estévez y Mármol, *Carrero*, pp.184–98.

83 *The Times*, 4 January 1974; *Le Monde*, 4 January 1974; Fuente et al., *Golpe mortal*, p.283; Girón, *Si la memoria*, p.231; interview with Carro Martínez, Bayod, *Franco*, pp.352–4.

84 For the insinuation, see Anson, *Don Juan*, p.385. For the definitive refutation by Herrero Tejedor's son, see Herrero, *El ocaso*, pp.64–71.

85 Utrera, *Sin cambiar*, pp.85–92; Cierva, *Historia del franquismo: II*, p.395.

86 López Rodó, *Claves*, pp.23–4, 28–9, 57; Prego, *Así se hizo*, p.74.

87 López Rodó, *Claves*, p.28.

88 Charles T. Powell, 'The "Tácito" Group and the Transition to Democracy, 1973–1977' in Frances Lannon & Paul Preston, coordinators, *Elites and Power in Twentieth-Century Spain: Essays in Honour of Sir Raymond Carr* (Oxford, 1990), pp.256–7.

89 *The Times*, 13 February 1974; *Le Monde*, 14 February 1974; Carlos Arias Navarro, *Discurso del Presidente del Gobierno a las Cortes Españolas, 12.11.1974* (Madrid, 1974); interview with Carro Martínez, Bayod, *Franco*, pp.348–9; Utrera, *Sin cambiar*, p.99.

90 Utrera, *Sin cambiar*, pp.98, 103–4; Cierva, *Historia del franquismo: II*, pp.395–6.

91 *Le Monde*, 26 February, 5, 9 March 1974; *El Alcázar*, 7, 8 March 1974; Vicente Enrique y Tarancón, *Confesiones* (Madrid, 1996), pp.627–92; José Oneto, *Arias entre dos crisis, 1973–1975* (Madrid, 1975), pp.63–77; López Rodó, *Claves*, pp.34–7; Audrey Brassloff, *Religion and Politics in Spain. The Spanish Church in Transition, 1962–96* (London, 1998), pp.66–7; Prego, *Así se hizo*, pp.101–14.

92 López Rodó, *La larga marcha*, p.462.

93 Carrillo, *Memorias*, pp.588–92; Anson, *Don Juan*, pp.388–92;

López Rodó, *Claves*, pp.50–1; Prego, *Así se hizo*, pp.145–8.

94 *Arriba*, 28 April 1974; *ABC*, 30 April 1974; *Cambio 16*, 13 May 1974; Utrera, *Sin cambiar*, pp.116–22; Herrero, *El ocaso*, pp.91–100; Prego, *Así se hizo*, pp.116–17, 127–34.

95 *Le Monde*, 15 May; *ABC*, 29 May, 16 June; *Ya*, 16 June; *Financial Times*, 29 May 1974; Manuel Gutiérrez Mellado, *Un soldado para España* (Barcelona, 1983), pp.47–9; Paul Preston, *The Triumph of Democracy in Spain* (London, 1986), pp.60–2; Prego, *Así se hizo*, pp.134–40.

96 Herrero, *El ocaso*, p.101.

97 Author's conversation with José Joaquín Puig de la Bellacasa.

98 López Rodó, *La larga marcha*, p.463; Gil, *Cuarenta años*, pp.172–84.

99 Girón, *Si la memoria*, pp.235–6.

100 Utrera, *Sin cambiar*, pp.139–40; Gil, *Cuarenta años*, pp.190–2; Herrero, *El ocaso*, pp.120–3.

101 López Rodó, *Claves*, pp.57–8; Bardavío, *La rama trágica*, pp.203–4.

102 Vicente Pozuelo, *Los últimos 476 días de Franco* (Barcelona, 1980), p.47.

103 Oneto, *Arias*, p.141: Bardavío, *Los silencios*, pp.95–101; Vilallonga, *El Rey*, p.215; Utrera, *Sin cambiar*, p.147. On the whiskey, Figuero & Herrero, *La muerte de Franco*, p.130.

104 Vilallonga, *El Rey*, pp.213–14; Pozuelo, *Los últimos 476 días*, pp.58–60.

105 Herrero, *El ocaso*, pp.145–6.

106 Utrera, *Sin cambiar*, p.159; author's conversation with José Utrera Molina.

107 Utrera, *Sin cambiar*, p.163.

108 These remarks are attributed to Juan Carlos himself in the English edition of José Luis de Vilallonga, *The King. A Life of King Juan Carlos of Spain* (London, 1994), p.165. In the Spanish edition, Vilallonga, *El Rey*, p.215, they appear as editorial comment by Vilallonga.

109 *ABC*, 3 September 1974; Pozuelo, *Los últimos 476 días*, pp.67–71; López Rodó, *La larga marcha*, pp.467–8; Garriga, *La Señora*, pp.343–6; Bardavío, *Los silencios*, pp.100–2.

110 López Rodó, *Claves*, p.74.

111 *Le Monde*, 4, 8, 18, 30, 31 October 1974; José Oneto, *Arias*, pp.149–53; Carro Martínez interview, Bayod, *Franco*, pp.354–6; Mariano Sánchez Soler, *Villaverde: fortuna y caída de la casa Franco* (Barcelona, 1990), p.100; Utrera, *Sin cambiar*, pp.173–5; Cierva, *Historia del franquismo: II*, p.402.

SEVEN: *Taking Over*

1 Pozuelo, *Los últimos 476 días*, pp.133, 177–8; Utrera, *Sin cambiar*, pp.183–91.

2 Fernández-Miranda, *Lo que el Rey*, p.71; Herrero, *El ocaso*, pp.165–8.

3 Utrera, *Sin cambiar*, pp.208–9.

4 Franco, *Pensamiento político*, I, pp.39–43.

5 Fraga, *Memoria breve*, pp.346–7, 362; Silva Muñoz, *Memorias*, pp.302–4.

6 Author's conversations with José Joaquín Puig de la Bellacasa. See also Bardavío, *Los silencios*, pp.70–1.

7 *Le Monde*, 5 March 1975; Carro

Martínez interview, Bayod, *Franco*, pp.356–7; Utrera, *Sin cambiar*, pp.226–33, 248–59; Fuente, *Memorias*, pp.220–8; Gregorio Morán, *Adolfo Suárez: historia de una ambición* (Barcelona, 1979), pp.286–7; Figuero & Herrero, *La muerte de Franco*, pp.19–21; Herrero, *El ocaso*, pp.176–9.

8 Herrero, *El ocaso*, pp.183–8.

9 Adolfo Suárez, testimony to private seminar on the transition organized by the *Fundación Ortega y Gasset* in Toledo, May 1984 (henceforth FOG/Toledo); Alfonso Osorio, *Trayectoria política de un ministro de la corona* (Barcelona, 1980), p.183; Javier Figuero, *UCD: 'la empresa' que creó Adolfo Suárez* (Barcelona, 1981), pp.19–22; Morán, *Suárez*, pp.74–5, 103–8, 121–7, 169–85.

10 R. Richard Rubbotom & J. Carter Murphy, *Spain and the United States Since World War II* (New York, 1984), pp.113–14.

11 *Cambio 16*, 23–29 June 1975; *Mundo Obrero*, 4ª semana de septiembre 1975; Fernando Álvarez de Miranda, *Del "contubernio" al consenso* (Barcelona, 1985), p.88.

12 Ziegler, *From Shore to Shore*, p.315.

13 López Rodó, *La larga marcha*, pp.477–80; Armada, *Al servicio*, p.188; Vilallonga, *El Rey*, p.218; Herrero, *El ocaso*, p.203.

14 Figuero, *UCD*, pp.21–2.

15 *Cambio 16*, 23–29 June 1975; Herrero, *El ocaso*, p.195; Pozuelo, *Los últimos 476 días*, pp.178–80.

16 Herrero, *El ocaso*, pp.194–9; Anson, *Don Juan*, p.403.

17 Herrero, *El ocaso*, pp.204–10; Pozuelo, *Los últimos 476 días*, pp.187–9.

18 Herrero, *El ocaso*, pp.210–12; Pozuelo, *Los últimos 476 días*, pp.196–7; Pedro J. Ramírez, *El año que murió Franco* (Barcelona, 1985), pp.51–2, 68–9; Morán, *Suárez*, pp.295–6.

19 Pozuelo, *Los últimos 476 días*, pp.198–9; Herrero, *El ocaso*, pp.212–13; Figuero & Herrero, *La muerte de Franco*, pp.50–1.

20 *Ya*, 30 September 1975; Vilallonga, *El Rey*, p.219; *Diario 16*, *Historia de la transición*, pp.130–7; Ramírez, *El año*, pp.197–9.

21 Pozuelo, *Los últimos 476 días*, pp.208–10; Ramírez, *El año*, pp.204–6.

22 *Arriba*, 2 October 1975; *Cambio 16*, 6 October 1975; Pozuelo, *Los últimos 476 días*, pp.210–12.

23 Franco, *Nosotros*, pp.167–8; Pozuelo, *Los últimos 476 días*, pp.218–21; Figuero & Herrero, *La muerte de Franco*, pp.26–7.

24 Fernández-Miranda, *Lo que el Rey*, pp.90–1.

25 Vilallonga, *El Rey*, pp.221–2; Pozuelo, *Los últimos 476 días*, pp.224–5; López Rodó, *Claves*, pp.151–2; Figuero & Herrero, *La muerte de Franco*, pp.35–6; Herrero, *El ocaso*, pp.237–42.

26 Fernández-Miranda, *Lo que el Rey*, p.93.

27 Armada had been promoted to General in July 1975. Author's interview with Alfonso Armada; Pozuelo, *Los últimos 476 días*, pp.226–7; López Rodó, *Claves*, pp.153–7; Figuero & Herrero, *La muerte de Franco*, pp.50–1; Herrero, *El ocaso*, pp.249–50.

28 López Rodó, *Claves*, p.169.

29 Fernández-Miranda, *Lo que el Rey*, pp.94–8.
30 Pozuelo, *Los últimos 476 días*, p.230; Figuero & Herrero, *La muerte de Franco*, pp.63–6; López Rodó, *La larga marcha*, p.491.
31 *ABC*, 2, 7 November; *Ya*, 29, 30 October, 9, 14, 18 November 1975.
32 Armada, *Al servicio*, pp.189–90.
33 Preston, *The Politics of Revenge*, pp.184–8.
34 Figuero & Herrero, *La muerte de Franco*, p.67; Vilallonga, *El Rey*, p.224.
35 Armada, *Al servicio*, pp.191–2; Vilallonga, *El Rey*, p.225; López Rodó, *Claves*, pp.163–4; Prego, *Así se hizo*, pp.290–2; Cernuda, *30 días*, pp.45–7, 54–64, 89–90; Herrero, *El ocaso*, pp.258–60.
36 Manuel Hidalgo Huerta, *Cómo y porqué operé a Franco* (Madrid, 1976), pp.18–35, 42–55; Pozuelo, *Los últimos 476 días*, pp.231–6.
37 'As Juan Carlos Sees It', *Newsweek*, 3 November 1975.
38 *Arriba*, 14, 18 November 1975; Figuero & Herrero, *La muerte de Franco*, pp.35–6, 51; López Rodó, *Claves*, pp.163, 170–1; Vilallonga, *El Rey*, p.226; Cernuda, *30 días*, p.117.
39 Fernández-Miranda, *Lo que el Rey*, pp.100–1; Morán, *Suárez*, pp.18–19.
40 Toquero, *Don Juan*, pp.367–8; Palacios, *Los papeles secretos*, pp.562–4; Víctor Salmador, *Don Juan. Los secretos*, pp.94–5; Sainz Rodríguez, *Un reinado*, pp.319–20.
41 Joaquín Bardavío, *El dilema: un pequeño caudillo o un gran Rey* (Madrid, 1979), pp.20–4; López

Rodó, *Claves*, pp.169–70 (where the date is erroneously given as 13 October); Fernández-Miranda, *Lo que el Rey*, pp.102–4; José Oneto, *Anatomía de un cambio de régimen* (Barcelona, 1985), p.190; Figuero & Herrero, *La muerte de Franco*, pp.84–8; Herrero, *El ocaso*, pp.271–4.
42 Hidalgo Huerta, *Cómo y porqué operé*, pp.59–69; Pozuelo, *Los últimos 476 días*, pp.238–41; Herrero, *El ocaso*, pp.274–8.
43 Figuero & Herrero, *La muerte de Franco*, p.96.
44 *Arriba*, 20 November 1975; *Ya*, 20 November 1975; Pozuelo, *Los últimos 476 días*, p.243; Figuero & Herrero, *La muerte de Franco*, pp.102–12; Herrero, *El ocaso*, pp.279–80; Cernuda, *30 días*, pp.133–41.
45 Herrero, *El ocaso*, p.281.
46 Franco, *Pensamiento político de Franco*, I, p.xix; Prego, *Así se hizo*, pp.324–6.
47 López Rodó, *La larga marcha*, p.490.
48 Jaime Peñafiel, *El General*, pp.132–6.
49 Cernuda, *30 días*, pp.149, 165.
50 Carrillo, *Memorias*, pp.587–9; Cernuda, *30 días*, pp.30–5; Fernández-Miranda, *Lo que el Rey*, pp.105–9.
51 Figuero & Herrero, *La muerte de Franco*, pp.125–6, 130.
52 *El País*, 20 November 1985.
53 López Rodó, *La larga marcha*, p.493–5.
54 Tusell, *Juan Carlos*, pp.644–5; Figuero & Herrero, *La muerte de Franco*, p.147.
55 *Guardian*, 21, 26, 28 November; *Daily Telegraph*, 21 November; *Times*, 28 November; *Newsweek*, 1 December 1975; Figuero &

Herrero, *La muerte de Franco*, pp.135–7; Prego, *Así se hizo*, pp.332–6; Cernuda, *30 días*, pp.165–9.

56 *ABC*, 26 November 1975; Carlos Fernández, *Los militares en la transición política* (Barcelona, 1982), pp.51–4.

57 José Luis Morales y Juan Celada, *La alternativa militar: el golpismo después de Franco* (Madrid, 1981), p.29.

58 On Prado's visit to Paris, see Prego, *Así se hizo*, pp.343–6; Cernuda, *30 días*, pp.155–63.

59 Author's interview with Joe Haines.

60 Philip Ziegler, *Wilson. The Authorised Life of Lord Wilson of Rievaulx* (London, 1993), p.464.

61 Rafael Díaz Salazar, *Iglesia, dictadura y democracia: Catolicismo y sociedad en España (1953–1979)* (Madrid, 1981), p.315; *Financial Times*, 28 November 1975; Prego, *Así se hizo*, pp.348–53.

62 *Times*, 27 November; *Guardian*, 1 December; *Daily Telegraph*, 8 December 1975.

63 Figuero & Herrero, *La muerte de Franco*, pp.141–2; Cernuda, *30 días*, pp.189–90.

64 López Rodó, *Claves*, p.118.

65 Vilallonga, *The King*, pp.162–3. This is missing from the equivalent passage in Vilallonga, *El Rey*, p.212.

66 Bardavío, *El dilema*, pp.42–9, 56–61; Fernández-Miranda, *Lo que el Rey*, pp.109–12; Morán, *Suárez*, pp.15–16; Figuero & Herrero, *La muerte de Franco*, pp.147–63; Prego, *Así se hizo*, pp.357–63; Cernuda, *30 días*, pp.189–91, 195–200, 209–11.

67 Fernández-Miranda, *Lo que el Rey*, pp.125–8; Prego, *Así se hizo*, pp.365–9.

68 Silva Muñoz, *Memorias*, pp.228–9; Cernuda, *30 días*, pp.12–13, 221.

69 Pedro J. Ramírez, *Así se ganaron las elecciones* (Barcelona, 1977), p.52.

70 *Mundo Obrero*, 25 November; *Servir al Pueblo*, no.45, November; *Correo del Pueblo*, 18 November, 6 December; *Frente Libertario*, no.57, December 1975.

71 Fernández-Miranda, *Lo que el Rey*, pp.115–19, 175; Bardavío, *El dilema*, pp.75–7; Figuero & Herrero, *La muerte de Franco*, pp.164–73.

72 Gutiérrez Mellado, *Un soldado*, pp.40–3, 47, 132–4; José María de Areilza, *Diario de un ministro de la monarquía* (Barcelona, 1977), pp.76–7; Fernando Puell de la Villa, *Gutiérrez Mellado. Un militar del siglo XX (1912–1995)* (Madrid, 1997), pp.175–6.

73 Víctor Salmador, *Don Juan. Los secretos*, p.71.

74 Garrigues, *Diálogos*, p.163; Areilza, diary entries for 9, 10, 30 December 1975, *Diario*, pp.13–16, 38; Manuel Fraga Iribarne, *En busca del tiempo servido* (Barcelona, 1987), pp.20–2.

75 Alfonso Osorio, *Trayectoria*, pp.46–50.

76 Fernández-Miranda, *Lo que el Rey*, pp.119–21; Morán, *Suárez*, pp.15–20; Samuel Eaton, *The Forces of Freedom in Spain 1974–1979: A Personal Account* (Stanford, 1981), pp.32–3; *Guardian*, 12 December 1975; Bardavío, *El dilema*, pp.79–84.

77 Fernández de la Mora, *Río arriba*, p.255; López Rodó, *Claves*, pp.196–8.

78 Fernández-Miranda, *Lo que el Rey*, p.121; Osorio, *Trayectoria*, pp.54–5.

79 *Arriba*, 29 January 1976; Osorio, *Trayectoria*, pp.56–62; Areilza, diary entry for 28 January, *Diario*, pp.73–6; Fernández-Miranda, *Lo que el Rey*, pp.147–51; Prego, *Así se hizo*, pp.391–4.

80 Areilza, diary entry for 11 February 1976, *Diario*, p.84; *Observer*, 1 February 1976; Osorio, *Trayectoria*, pp.65–7; Fernández-Miranda, *Lo que el Rey*, pp.151–4; Eaton, *The Forces of Freedom*, pp.36–7; Bardavío, *El dilema*, p.105.

81 Rodolfo Martín Villa, *Al servicio del Estado* (Barcelona, 1984), p.16; Victor Díaz Cardiel et al., *Madrid en huelga: enero 1976* (Madrid, 1976), pp.91–150; *Cambio 16*, 19–25 January; *Guardian*, 5, 7, 8, 9, 14, 15, 20 January; *Sunday Times*, 11, 18 January; *Mundo Obrero*, 20, 27 January 1976; Martín Villa, *Al servicio*, p.17; Areilza, diary entry for 12 January 1976, *Diario*, p.51. For a leftist critique of the strike, see *Cuadernos de Ruedo Iberico*, Nos 51–53, May-October 1976, pp.127–78.

82 Areilza, diary entry for 17 January 1976, *Diario*, p.54.

83 'Spain: Out on a Limb', *Newsweek*, 19 April 1976.

84 Eaton, *The Forces of Freedom*, p.38.

85 *Mundo Obrero*, 4, 11 February; *Cambio 16*, 9–15 February; 1–7 March 1976.

86 Salvador Sánchez-Terán, *De Franco a la Generalitat* (Barcelona, 1988), pp.47–55; *Mundo Obrero*, 25 February 1976; López Rodó, *Claves*, pp.225–6; *La Vanguardia*, 21 February; *El País*, 28 May 1976.

87 Carrillo, *Memorias*, p.613.

88 Bardavío, *Los silencios*, pp.147–60; Prego, *Así se hizo*, pp.374–81; Carrillo, *Memorias*, p.617; Santiago Carrillo, *El año de la peluca* (Barcelona, 1987), pp.37–8; author's conversations with Santiago Carrillo; *Mundo Obrero*, 28 April, 5 May 1976.

89 Mario Onaindia, *La lucha de clases en Euskadi (1939–1980)* (San Sebastián, 1980), pp.121–6; José María Portell, *Euskadi: amnistia arrancada* (Barcelona, 1977), pp.37–42, 61–98.

90 'Gasteiz', *Vitoria, de la huelga a la matanza* (Paris, 1976), pp.117–32, 185–202; Martín Villa, *Al servicio*, pp.26–8; Prego, *Así se hizo*, p.409.

91 Fraga, *En busca*, pp.39–40, 52.

92 Fernández-Miranda, *Lo que el Rey*, pp.128–47; Osorio, *Trayectoria*, pp.75–85.

93 Fernández-Miranda, *Lo que el Rey*, pp.170–2; Prego, *Así se hizo*, pp.415–20; Bardavío, *Los silencios*, pp.172–3.

94 Areilza, diary entry for 29 March 1976, *Diario*, p.122.

95 *Mundo Obrero*, 27 January, 4, 11 February 1976; *Newsweek*, 19 April 1976; Fernando Claudín, *Santiago Carrillo: crónica de un secretario general* (Barcelona, 1983), pp.231–4; Areilza, diary entries for 29 March, 5, 8 April 1976, *Diario*, pp.122, 127, 133.

96 *Mundo Obrero*, 9 April 1976; Osorio, *Trayectoria*, pp.91–4;

Areilza, diary entry for
29 March 1976, *Diario*, p.122.

97 Areilza, diary entries for 2, 3,
15 April 1976, *Diario*, pp.124–6,
146; Suárez, FOG/Toledo.

98 Areilza, diary entries for 27,
29 March, 9, 10, 15, 23 April
1976, *Diario*, pp.119–20, 122,
136–8, 146, 153; Emilio Attard,
Vida y muerte de UCD
(Barcelona, 1983), p.49; Felipe
González, FOG/Toledo. Fraga
himself denies this, *En busca*,
pp.44–6.

99 *Cambio 16*, 15–21 March 1976;
Morán, *Suárez*, pp.31–2;
Osorio, *Trayectoria*, pp.86–91;
'Gasteiz', *Vitoria*, pp.117–32;
Martín Villa, *Al servicio*,
pp.28–9; Prego, *Así se hizo*,
pp.411–14.

100 Figuero, *UCD*, pp.23–6; Areilza,
diary entry for 30 April 1976,
Diario, p.165; Antonio
Izquierdo, *Yo, testigo de cargo*
(Barcelona, 1981), p.41.

101 Suárez, FOG/Toledo.

102 Suárez, FOG/Toledo.

103 Minutes of *Coordinación
Democrática* meeting held on
9 April 1976, Oposición
Española, *Documentos secretos*
(Madrid, 1976), pp.108–12.

104 Suárez, FOG/Toledo.

105 Sainz Rodríguez, *Un reinado*,
p.318; Areilza, diary entries for
8, 24 March 1976, *Diario*,
pp.105, 118.

106 Fernández-Miranda, *Lo que el
Rey*, pp.176–80.

107 Areilza, diary entry for 8 April
1976, *Diario*, p.133; 'Juan
Carlos Looks Ahead',
Newsweek, 26 April 1976;
Ricardo de la Cierva, *La lucha
por el poder. Así cayó Arias
Navarro* (Madrid, 1996), p.158.

108 Areilza, diary entries for 15, 27,
28, 29 April, 3 May 1976,
Diario, pp.146–8, 161–8;
Fernández-Miranda, *Lo que el
Rey*, pp.159–61; Raymond Carr
& Juan Pablo Fusi, *Spain.
Dictatorship to Democracy*
(London, 1979), p.215.

109 Osorio, *Trayectoria*, p.123.

110 Fernández-Miranda, *Lo que el
Rey*, p.181.

111 *El País*, 20, 21, 22 May; *La
Vanguardia*, 21 May 1976.

112 Eaton, *The Forces of Freedom*,
pp.38–9; Prego, *Así se hizo*,
pp.443–4.

113 Areilza, diary entry for 12 May
1976, *Diario*, p.178.

114 Eaton, *The Forces of Freedom*,
p.40; Areilza, diary entries for 2,
3, 4, 5, 6 June 1976, *Diario*,
pp.188–99; Prego, *Así se hizo*,
pp.466–71.

115 Author's interview with the
journalist, Herbert Spencer.

116 Suárez, FOG/Toledo; Prego, *Así
se hizo*, pp.474–83.

117 Areilza, diary entries for 1, 2,
3 July 1976, *Diario*, pp.214–17;
Fraga, *En busca*, pp.52–3;
Osorio, *Trayectoria*, pp.126–7;
Arias Navarro interview in
Bayod, *Franco visto por sus
ministros*, p.313; Fernández de
la Mora, *Río arriba*, pp.257–8;
Javier Tusell, *Juan Carlos I*
(Madrid, 2002), p.138; Patricia
Sverlo, *Un Rey golpe a golpe.
Biografía no autorizada de Juan
Carlos de Borbón* (Pamplona,
2000), p.144.

118 Fernández-Miranda, *Lo que el
Rey*, pp.23–4; Prego, *Así se
hizo*, pp.491–3.

119 Areilza, diary entries for 14 &
15 July 1976, Areilza,
Cuadernos de la transición

(Barcelona, 1983), pp.23–6; *Guardian*, 3 July 1976.

120 Fernández de la Mora, *Río arriba*, p.255.

121 Silva Muñoz, *Memorias*, pp.334–5, 340.

EIGHT: *The Gamble*

1 López Rodó, *Claves*, p.201; Federico Ysart, *Quien hizo el cambio* (Barcelona, 1984), p.57.

2 Fernández-Miranda, *Lo que el Rey*, pp.191–202.

3 López Rodó, *Claves*, p.260; Osorio, *Trayectoria*, p.90.

4 *Cambio 16*, 12–18, 19–25 July; *Mundo Obrero*, 14 July 1976; Carlos Iniesta Cano, *Memorias y recuerdos* (Barcelona, 1984), pp.240–1; remarks made by Adolfo Suárez, FOG/Toledo.

5 Suárez, FOG/Toledo; Oneto, *Anatomía*, pp.155–9; Charles Powell, *El piloto del cambio. El Rey, la Monarquía y la transición a la democracia* (Barcelona, 1991), pp.177–80.

6 *Mundo Obrero*, 7 July 1976.

7 Fraga, *En busca*, p.53.

8 Osorio, *Trayectoria*, pp.127–36; Álvarez de Miranda, *Del "contubernio"*, pp.107–9.

9 *El País*, 6, 21 July; *Cambio 16*, 12–18 July 1976; Areilza, diary entries for 4 & 5 July 1976, *Cuadernos*, pp.15–16; Suárez, FOG/Toledo; Osorio, *Trayectoria*, p.136; Bardavío, *El dilema*, pp.173–4; Javier Fernández López, *El Rey y otros militares. Los militares en el cambio de régimen político en España (1969–1982)* (Madrid, 1998), pp.87–8; Cardona, *Franco y sus generales*, p.270.

10 Suárez, FOG/Toledo; Prego, *Así se hizo*, pp.507–8.

11 López Rodó, *Claves*, p.268.

12 *ABC*, 24 July; *El País*, 25, 27, 28, 29, 30 July 1976.

13 Fernández López, *El Rey y otros militares*, pp.88–9.

14 *Cambio 16*, 9–15, 23–29 August; *Mundo Obrero*, 26 July– 2 August, 1 September 1976; Joaquín Bardavío, *Sábado santo rojo* (Madrid, 1980), pp.42–4, 52; Morán, *Suárez*, p.337; López Rodó, *Claves*, p.266.

15 José María Maravall, *The Transition to Democracy in Spain* (London, 1982), p.13; J.A. Sagardoy & David Leon Blanco, *El poder sindical en España* (Barcelona, 1982), p.161.

16 *El País*, 7 August 1976.

17 *El País*, 14 August 1976.

18 *El País*, 10 August 1976.

19 *Cambio 16*, 26 July–1 August, 16–22 August 1976; remarks of Felipe González at FOG/Toledo and to the author; Ysart, *Quien*, pp.83–4.

20 Bardavío, *Sábado santo*, pp.51–8; Morán, *Suárez*, pp.331–2; Osorio, *Trayectoria*, pp.162–4; Suárez, FOG/Toledo.

21 Remarks of Santiago Carrillo at FOG/Toledo and to the author.

22 Fernández-Miranda, *Lo que el Rey*, pp.222–34; pp.80–91; Martín Villa, *Al servicio*, pp.52–3; Osorio, *Trayectoria*, pp.176–7; Prego, *Así se hizo*, pp.529–33.

23 López Rodó, *Claves*, p.226.

24 Vilallonga, *El Rey*, p.125.

25 *El Alcázar*, 27 October 1976; Fernández, *Los militares*, p.63.

26 Figuero, *UCD*, p.40; Suárez, FOG/Toledo.

27 Vilallonga, *El Rey*, p.124; Suárez,

FOG/Toledo; Fernández de la Mora, *Río arriba*, pp.261–2; Sabino Fernández Campo, 'Prólogo', in Fernández López, *El Rey y otros militares*, pp.16–18; Puell de la Villa, *Gutiérrez Mellado*, pp.185–6; Prego, *Así se hizo*, pp.536–8; Miguel Platón, *Hablan los militares. Testimonios para la historia (1939–1996)* (Barcelona, 2001), pp.398–400.

28 *El País*, 23, 24 September 1976; Osorio, *Trayectoria*, pp.183–6; Fernández, *Los militares*, pp.109–11; Colectivo Democracia, *Los Ejércitos . . . más allá del golpe* (Barcelona, 1981), p.63.

29 López Rodó, *Claves*, p.276; Fernández de la Mora, *Río arriba*, pp.272–3.

30 *El País*, 3 October 1976; Osorio, *Trayectoria*, pp.188–9; Fernández, *Los militares*, pp.111–13; Iniesta Cano, *Memorias*, pp.242–50; Bardavío, *El dilema*, pp.184–92; Cardona, *Franco y sus generales*, pp. 271–3.

31 *El Alcázar*, 23, 27 September; *Cambio 16*, 4–10, 11–17 October 1976.

32 *Mundo Obrero*, 15 September 1976.

33 Osorio, *Trayectoria*, p.206.

34 Areilza, diary entries for 22 September, 28 November, 6 December 1976, *Cuadernos*, pp.47–8, 71, 78.

35 Morán, *Suárez*, p.334; Claudín, *Santiago Carrillo*, pp.238–40; Eduardo Chamorro, *Felipe González: un hombre a la espera* (Barcelona, 1980), pp.133–6.

36 *El País*, 30 October 1976.

37 *Mundo Obrero*, 1–7 November 1976.

38 Ana Romero, *Historia de Carmen. Memorias de Carmen Díez de Rivera* (Barcelona, 2002), pp.120–1.

39 *Mundo Obrero*, 1–7, 15–21, 22 November; *Cambio 16*, 22–28 November, 5 December 1976; Osorio, *Trayectoria*, pp.208–9; Manuel P. Izquierdo, *De la huelga general a las elecciones generales* (Madrid, 1977), pp.29–30; Martín Villa, *Al servicio*, pp.54–7.

40 *El País*, 11 November 1976; Suárez, FOG/Toledo; Gonzalo Fernández de la Mora, *Los errores del cambio* (Barcelona, 1986), p.162; Prego, *Así se hizo*, pp.555–6.

41 Fernández-Miranda, *Lo que el Rey*, pp.234–42, 269–81; Miguel Primo de Rivera y Urquijo, *No a las dos Españas. Memorias políticas* (Barcelona, 2002), pp.177–94; Cardona, *Franco y sus generales*, p.273.

42 *El País*, 18, 19 November; *Cambio 16*, 22–28 November 1976; Emilio Attard, *La Constitución por dentro* (Barcelona, 1983), p.76; Suárez, FOG/Toledo.

43 Osorio, *Trayectoria*, pp.230–46; Areilza, diary entry for 25 November 1976, *Cuadernos*, p.67; Carr & Fusi, *Spain*, p.222; Morán, *Suárez*, pp.312–16.

44 *El País*, 17, 23 November 1976; Cardona, *Franco y sus generales*, p.273.

45 *El País*, 28 November; *Mundo Obrero*, 6–12 December 1976; López Rodó, *Claves*, pp.286–7; Prego, *Así se hizo*, pp.570–1.

46 *El País*, 7 December 1976; Pilar Ortuño, *European Socialists and Spain. The Transition to*

Democracy, 1959–77 (London, 2002), pp.180–1.

47 Mundo Obrero, 20–26 December 1976.

48 Fernández-Miranda, Lo que el Rey, p.200; Powell, El piloto, pp.212–13; Jaime Peñafiel, ¡Dios salve . . . también al Rey! (Madrid, 1995), p.138.

49 El País, 14, 15, 16, 17 December 1976; Cambio 16, 26 December 1976, 2 January 1977; Osorio, Trayectoria, pp.252–3; Felipe González, FOG/Toledo; Prego, Así se hizo, pp.600–1.

50 El País, 24 December; El Alcázar, 28 December 1976; Cambio 16, 3–9 January 1977; Martín Villa, Al servicio, p.60; Fernández, Los militares, pp.151–3; Cardona, Franco y sus generales, pp.273–4; Fernández López, El Rey y otros militares, pp.98–9; Santiago Segura & Julio Merino, Las vísperas del 23-F (Barcelona, 1984), pp.192–4. On the authorship of the speech, author's interview with General Armada.

51 Armada, Al servicio, p.150.

52 Powell, El piloto, pp.219–20; Suárez, FOG/Toledo.

53 Manuel Durán, Martín Villa (San Sebastián, 1979), passim.

54 Mundo Obrero, 20–26 December 1976; Bardavío, Sábado santo, pp.88–111; Osorio, Trayectoria, pp.254–8; Claudín, Santiago Carrillo, pp.2–9, 239–41; Romero, Historia de Carmen, pp.127–9.

55 El País, 12 December 1976; Cambio 16, 31 January– 6 February 1977; Pío Moa Rodríguez, De un tiempo y de un país (Madrid, 1982), pp.217–33; Alejandro Muñoz Alonso, El terrorismo en España (Barcelona,

1982), pp.76–85; Durán, Martín Villa, p.79; Osorio, Trayectoria, pp.246–9.

56 Mundo Obrero, 31 January– 6 February 1977; Bardavío, Sábado santo, pp.142–7; Xavier Casals i Meseguer, La tentación neofascista en España (Barcelona, 1998), p.217; Romero, Historia de Carmen, pp.144–8.

57 Morán, Suárez, pp.43–4, 324–8; Osorio, Trayectoria, pp.97–108, 190–7, 291–9.

58 Cambio 16, 27 September– 3 October, 18–24 October 1976; Areilza, diary entries for 13, 23 September, 22 October 1976, Cuadernos, pp.43–4, 50, 56; Osorio, Trayectoria, pp.200–5; Ramírez, Así se ganaron las elecciones, pp.92–108.

59 Suárez, FOG/Toledo.

60 Powell, Juan Carlos, pp.134–5.

61 Attard, Vida y muerte, pp.34–50; Osorio, Trayectoria, pp.190–7; Álvarez de Miranda, Del "contubernio", pp.112–20.

62 El País, 25 March; Cambio 16, 4–10 April 1977; Areilza, diary entries for 6 February, 19, 20, 21, 22, 24 March 1977, Cuadernos, pp.92–4, 108–23; Osorio, Trayectoria, pp.300–2; Attard, Vida y muerte, pp.39–40; Pedro J. Ramírez, Así se ganaron las elecciones, pp.29–31.

63 Attard, Vida y muerte, pp.50–3; Figuero, UCD, pp.57–61; Fernando Jaúregui & Manuel Soriano, La otra historia de UCD (Madrid, 1980), pp.61–4.

64 Cambio 16, 16–22 May; El País, 6, 7, 8 May 1977; Diario 16, 28 January 1978; Figuero, UCD, pp.232–4; Attard, Vida y muerte, p.57; Ramírez, Así se ganaron las elecciones, pp.116–21, 139–49,

158–9; Álvarez de Miranda, *Del "contubernio"*, pp.127–9.

65 *El País*, 1 February; *Cambio 16*, 7–13 February 1977; Colectivo Democracia, *Los Ejércitos*, pp.75–6; Fernández López, *El Rey y otros militares*, pp.101–2.

66 Suárez, FOG/Toledo; Morán, *Suárez*, pp.320–1; José Oneto, *Los últimos días de un presidente: de la dimisión al golpe de Estado* (Barcelona, 1981), p.86.

67 *Mundo Obrero*, 7–13 March 1977; Romero, *Historia de Carmen*, pp.134–42, 150–2; Bardavío, *Sábado santo*, pp.158–71.

68 *Mundo Obrero*, 21–27 March, 4–10, 11–17 April; *Cambio 16*, 18–24 April 1977; Claudín, *Santiago Carrillo*, pp.245–8; Morán, *Suárez*, p.338; Osorio, *Trayectoria*, pp.286–7; Prego, *Así se hizo*, pp.643–58; Romero, *Historia de Carmen*, pp.160, 168, 201.

69 Author's interview with Sabino Fernández Campo, and his 'Prólogo' to Fernández López, *El Rey y otros militares*, pp.18–19. See also Javier Fernández López, *Sabino Fernández Campo. Un hombre de Estado* (Barcelona, 2000), p.100.

70 Manuel Soriano, *Sabino Fernández Campo. La sombra del Rey* (Madrid, 1995), pp.157–9.

71 *Cambio 16*, 25 April–1 May 1977; Suárez, FOG/Toledo; Pilar Urbano, *Con la venia: yo indagué el 23 F* (Barcelona, 1982), pp.14–15; Bardavío, *Sábado santo*, pp.196–200; Colectivo Democracia, *Los Ejércitos*, pp.64–8.

72 *El País*, 15, 16 April; *ABC*, 14 April; *Cambio 16*, 2–8 May

1977; Osorio, *Trayectoria*, pp.287–91; Martín Villa, *Al servicio*, p.66; Armada, *Al servicio*, p.151; Platón, *Hablan los militares*, pp.432–3; Fernández López, *El Rey y otros militares*, pp.104–8; Prego, *Así se hizo*, pp.658–65.

73 Colectivo Democracia, *Los Ejércitos*, pp.68–70; Urbano, *Con la venia*, p.16.

74 López Rodó, *Claves*, p.327.

75 *Cambio 16*, 14–20, 21–27 March, 23–29 May; 30 May–5 June 1977; Portell, *Euskadi: amnistia*, pp.9–18, 168–239; Onaindia, *La lucha de clases en Euskadi*, pp.131–4.

76 *El País*, 15 May 1977.

77 Platón, *Hablan los militares*, pp.443–4; Cardona, *Franco y sus generales*, p.279.

78 Sainz Rodríguez, *Un reinado*, pp.266–7.

79 Primo de Rivera, *No a las dos Españas*, pp.211–12, 223–5; Powell, *El piloto*, pp.228–31; Powell, *Juan Carlos*, pp.131–2.

80 *ABC*, 15 May; *El País*, 15 May; *El Alcázar*, 18 May 1977.

81 Bardavío, *Sábado santo*, pp.149–50.

82 *El País*, 1 June 1977; Alcocer, *Fernández-Miranda*, pp.120–6; Primo de Rivera, *No a las dos Españas*, pp.222–3; Powell, *El piloto*, pp.233–4; Fernández de la Mora, *Río arriba*, pp.270–1.

83 Cardona, *Franco y sus generales*, pp.279–80.

84 *Cambio 16*, 6–12 June 1977. The author was able to attend numerous political meetings in the course of the campaign.

85 Ramírez, *Así se ganaron las elecciones*, pp.52, 127–32, 228–44, 304–6.

86 *Cambio 16*, 13–19 June 1977;
author's personal observation.
87 *Cambio 16*, 20–26 June,
27 June–3 July; *El País*, 15, 22,
29 May 1977; Ramírez, *Así se
ganaron las elecciones*,
pp.208–11, 248–9, 284–90;
Monica Threlfall, 'Women and
Political Participation' in
Christopher Abel & Nissa
Torrents, editors, *Spain:
Conditional Democracy* (London,
1984).
88 *El País*, 21 February 1982;
Armada, *Al servicio*, pp.210–14;
Javier Fernández López, *Diecisiete
horas y media. El enigma del
23-F* (Madrid, 2000), p.33;
Fernández López, *Sabino
Fernández Campo*, pp.109–11;
Soriano, *Sabino Fernández
Campo*, pp.151–67.
89 *El País*, 26 June 1977.

NINE: *More Responsibility, Less
Power: the Crown and* Golpismo

1 Osorio, *Trayectoria*, pp.327–36;
Jaúregui & Soriano, *UCD*,
pp.86–7.
2 *El País*, 23 July 1977; Julia
Navarro, *Nosotros, la transición*
(Madrid, 1995), pp.162, 238.
3 *El País*, 17, 18, 21 August 1977,
17 September 1979.
4 *El País*, 9 June 1977.
5 *El País*, 28 February 1978.
6 Fernández López, *El Rey y otros
militares*, pp.113–14; Ricardo
Pardo Zancada, *23-F. La pieza
que falta. Testimonio de un
protagonista* (Barcelona, 1998),
p.49.
7 *El País*, 29 July 1977.
8 *Cambio 16*, 4–10 July 1977;
Natxo Arregi, *Memorias del KAS:
1975/78* (San Sebastián, 1981),
pp.285–98; Luciano Rincón, *ETA
(1974–1984)* (Barcelona, 1985),
pp.14, 46, 57, 66.
9 *Cambio 16*, 18–24 July, 8–14,
15–21, 22–28 August,
5–11 September; *El País*,
11 September 1977; Miguel
Castells Arteche, *El mejor
defensor el pueblo* (San Sebastián,
1978), pp.78–88, 141–53.
10 *Cambio 16*, 24–30 October
1977.
11 *El País*, 29 November 1977.
12 Author's interview with General
Sabino Fernández Campo; Julio
Busquets, *Militares y demócratas.
Memorias de un fundador de la
UMD y diputado socialista*
(Barcelona, 1999), pp.277–9.
13 *El País*, 20 September; *Cambio
16*, 3–9 October 1977;
Fernández, *Los militares*,
pp.181–3; Colectivo Democracia,
Los Ejércitos, pp.70–1; Amadeo
Martínez Inglés, *La transición
vigilada. Del Sábado Santo 'rojo'
al 23-F* (Madrid, 1994), pp.98–9;
Cardona, *Franco y sus generales*,
pp.281–2; Pardo Zancada, *23-F*,
pp.53–4.
14 *El Alcázar*, 20 September 1977;
Juan Pla, *La trama civil del golpe*
(Barcelona, 1982), p.85; Urbano,
Con la venia, p.16; Muñoz
Alonso, *El terrorismo*, pp.245–6;
Colectivo Democracia, *Los
Ejércitos*, p.96; Cardona, *Franco
y sus generales*, p.266.
15 *El País*, 1 November; *Cambio 16*,
24–30 October,
14–20 November 1977; interview
held by the author in Madrid
with General Prieto in February
1983; Armada, *Al servicio*,
pp.209–14; Soriano, *Sabino
Fernández Campo*, pp.164–7;
Fernández López, *El Rey y otros*

militares, pp.117–19; Fernández, *Los militares*, pp.209–13.

16 Josép Tarradellas, *"Ja soc aquí"*. *Recuerdo de un retorno* (Barcelona, 1990), pp.34–9.

17 Osorio, *Trayectoria*, pp.319–24; Salvador Sánchez-Terán, *De Franco a la Generalitat*, pp.282–3; Miguel Herrero de Miñón, *Memorias de estío* (Madrid, 1993), p.98; Martín Villa, *Al servicio*, p.176.

18 Tarradellas,*"Ja soc aquí"*, pp.90–105.

19 *El País*, 30 June 1977; Sánchez-Terán, *De Franco a la Generalitat*, pp.284–9; Tarradellas, *"Ja soc aquí"*, pp.112–59, 223–9; López Rodó, *Claves*, pp.328–9. For a brilliant portrait of Coloma Gallegos, see Cardona, *Franco y sus generales*, p.254.

20 *Cambio 16*, 11–17 July, 10–16 October 1977; Suarez, FOG/Toledo.

21 *El País*, 7 December 1977; Navarro, *Nosotros*, p.74.

22 *Cambio 16*, 17–23 October; *El País*, 4, 11 October 1977; Gutiérrez Mellado, *Un soldado*, pp.135–6; Cardona, *Franco y sus generales*, p.282.

23 Information provided by Gabriel Cardona; Busquets, *Militares y demócratas*, pp.105–8, 174, 190; Fernando Reinlein, *Capitanes rebeldes. Los militares españoles durante la Transición: De la UMD al 23-F* (Madrid, 2002), pp.58–60, 117–18, 127–9, 145.

24 José María de Areilza, *Diario*, p.20.

25 José Ignacio Domínguez, *Cuando yo era un exiliado* (Madrid, 1977), pp.182–92; José Fortes & Luis Otero, *Proceso a nueve militares demócratas: las Fuerzas Armadas y la UMD* (Barcelona, 1983), pp.155–79; Colectivo Democracia, *Los Ejércitos*, pp.60–2; Fernández, *Los militares*, pp.70–9; Reinlein, *Capitanes rebeldes*, pp.426–8.

26 *El País*, 7 January 1978; Cardona, *Franco y sus generales*, p.285; Fernández López, *El Rey y otros militares*, pp.119–20; Francisco Franco Bahamonde, 'Discurso de despedida en el cierre de la Academia General Militar', *Revista de Historia Militar*, Año XX, No.40, 1976, pp.335–7.

27 *El País*, 27 April 1978; interview with General Sabino Fernández Campo.

28 *Cambio 16*, 12–18 December 1977, 26 December 1977–1 January 1978, 9–15 January 1978; Txiki Benegas, *Euskadi: sin la paz nada es posible* (Barcelona, 1984), pp.80–2; Manuel Clavero Arevalo, *España, desde el centralismo a las autonomias* (Barcelona, 1983), pp.46–50.

29 Herrero de Miñón, *Memorias*, pp.127–9; José Oneto, *Anatomía*, pp.188–9; Fraga, *En busca*, pp.112–13; López Rodó, *Claves*, pp.366–9.

30 *Cambio 16*, 21–27 November 1977; Attard, *La Constitución*, p.111.

31 Silva Muñoz, *Memorias*, p.396.

32 Attard, *La Constitución*, pp.23–31, 77–90, 119–23, 223; Soledad Gallego-Díaz & Bonifacio de la Cuadra, *Crónica secreta de la Constitución* (Madrid, 1989), pp.27, 50, 90–3; Fernández López, *El Rey y otros militares*, pp.137–8.

33 Gallego-Díaz & Cuadra, *Crónica secreta*, pp.97–101; pp.63–73; *El País*, 10 May 1978; Carrillo, *Memorias*, pp.674–6.

34 Herrero de Miñón, *Memorias*, p.138; *El País*, 24 January 1978.

35 Soriano, *Sabino Fernández Campo*, pp.395–6; Fernández López, *Sabino Fernández Campo*, pp.119–21, 127–8; Sverlo, *Un Rey*, pp.160–1.

36 *El País*, 30 May 1978; Sverlo, *Un Rey*, pp.162–4; Gallego-Díaz & Cuadra, *Crónica secreta*, pp.91–2; Powell, *Juan Carlos*, pp.147, 153–4. See also Fernando Gracia, *Elena. Crónica de noviazgo real* (Madrid, 1995), pp.115–18.

37 Attard, *La Constitución*, pp.92–107; Martín Villa, *Al servicio*, p.86.

38 Fernández López, *El Rey y otros militares*, pp.123–4; Cardona, *Franco y sus generales*, p.288.

39 *Cambio 16*, 28 May, 30 July 1978; Gutiérrez Mellado, *Un soldado*, pp.77–82, 98–9; Morales & Celada, *La alternativa militar*, pp.39–41; Fernández, *Los militares*, pp.218–20, 227–8; author's interview with General Prieto.

40 Fernández López, *El Rey y otros militares*, pp.124–5; Fernández López, *Sabino Fernández Campo*, p.125; Cardona, *Franco y sus generales*, pp.288–9.

41 *El País*, 10 June 1978.

42 *El Alcázar*, 22 June 1978.

43 *El País*, 30 July 1978.

44 *Tribuna*, 10 February 1992; *Informaciones*, 16 August 1978; José María Zavala, *Matar al Rey. La Casa Real en el punto de mira de ETA* (Madrid, 1998). pp.61–6.

45 *El País*, 30 June, 29 July; *Cambio 16*, 30 July; *El Imparcial*, 31 August 1978.

46 *Cambio 16*, 29 October 1978.

47 *El País*, 1 November; *Cambio 16*, 12, 19 November 1978; Luciano Rincón, *ETA (1974–1984)*, pp.21–2; Benegas, *Euskadi*, pp.88–9.

48 *Fuerza Nueva*, 2 November 1978.

49 *El País*, 7 November 1978.

50 *El País*, 17, 19, 21 November; *Cambio 16*, 3 December 1978; Colectivo Democracia, *Los Ejércitos*, pp.78–85; Morales & Celada, *La alternativa*, pp.43–7; Cardona, *Franco y sus generales*, pp.292–4; Martín Villa, *Al servicio*, pp.148–50; Urbano, *Con la venia*, p.19; Reinlein, *Capitanes rebeldes*, pp.220–5; Pardo Zancada, *23-F*, pp.68–70. On Tejero, see José Oneto, *La noche de Tejero* (Barcelona, 1981), pp.27–34; Antonio Izquierdo, *Claves para un día de febrero* (Barcelona, 1982), pp.28–9; Pilar Urbano, *Yo entré en el CESID* (Barcelona, 1997), pp.341–2.

51 Vilallonga, *El Rey*, p.258.

52 *El País*, 26 August, 28, 29 November; *Cuadernos para el Diálogo*, 26 August 1978; Powell, *Juan Carlos*, p.155.

53 *El País*, 28 December 1978; Primo de Rivera, *No a las dos Españas*, p.242.

54 *El Alcázar*, 4, 11 January; *El País*, 3, 4, 5 January; *Cambio 16*, 14 January 1979; José Luis Rodríguez Jiménez, *Reaccionarios y golpistas. La extrema derecha en España: del tardofranquismo a la consolidación de la democracia (1967–1982)* (Madrid, 1994), pp.278–9; Cardona, *Franco y sus generales*, pp.295–6; Urbano,

Con la venia, p.20; Fernández López, *El Rey y otros militares*, pp.140–1.

55 *Cambio 16*, 18 March 1979; Josép Meliá, *Así cayó Adolfo Suárez* (Barcelona, 1981), p.29; Pedro J. Ramírez, *Así se ganaron las elecciones 1979* (Madrid, 1979), pp.179–263.

56 *Cambio 16*, 15 April 1979; Cardona, *Franco y sus generales*, pp.297–8.

57 *El País*, 4, 5, 6 April; *Cambio 16*, 15 April 1979; Suárez, FOG/ Toledo.

58 *Cambio 16*, 22 April, 27 May, 10 June 1979.

59 Anson, *Don Juan*, p.415.

60 Silva Muñoz, *Memorias*, p.375.

61 Oneto, *Anatomía*, pp.194–5.

62 El País, 8, 12, 13 December 1978; Julio Feo, *Aquellos años* (Barcelona, 1993), pp.83–4.

63 *El País*, 12 May 1979; Cardona, *Franco y sus generales*, pp.298–9; Armada, *Al servicio*, pp.215–16; Morales & Celada, *La alternativa*, pp.51–3; Fernández López, *El Rey y otros militares*, pp.145–7. On the King's reaction, author's interview with General Sabino Fernández Campo.

64 *El País*, 26 May 1979.

65 *El País*, 27, 29 May; *El Alcázar*, 27, 20 May; *Cambio 16*, 10 June 1979.

66 Urbano, *Con la venia*, p.26.

67 *El País*, 6, 10 June; *Cambio 16*, 10 June 1979; Morales & Celada, *La alternativa*, pp.43–9.

68 *Cambio 16*, 24 June, 1, 15, 22, 29 July, 5 August 1979; Attard, *Vida y muerte*, pp.70–2; Jaúregui & Soriano, *UCD*, pp.129–30.

69 Urbano, *Con la venia*, pp.21–2; Pardo Zancada, *23-F*, pp.77–8.

70 *El Alcázar*, 21 September; *Cambio 16*, 7 October 1979.

71 Author's interview with General Sabino Fernández Campo.

72 Morales & Celada, *La alternativa*, pp.74–7; Armada, *Al servicio*, pp.216–17; Urbano, *Con la venia*, pp.20–1; Reinlein, *Capitanes rebeldes*, pp.225–8, 233–5; Pardo Zancada, *23-F*, pp.75–7.

73 Urbano, *Con la venia*, pp.20–3; Fernández López, *El Rey y otros militares*, pp.150–2; Pardo Zancada, *23-F*, pp.78–9, 392–3.

74 *El País*, 8 January 1980; Fernández López, *El Rey y otros militares*, pp.149–50.

75 *El Alcázar*, 20 October 1979; *El País*, 27 January; *Diario 16*, 25 January; *Cambio 16*, 10 February 1980; Colectivo Democracia, *Los Ejércitos*, pp.85–91; Morales & Celada, *La alternativa*, pp.57–61; Busquets, *Militares y demócratas*, pp.272–5; Reinlein, *Capitanes rebeldes*, pp.225–8, 233–8.

76 *Cambio 16*, 25 November 1979; *El Alcázar*, 7 May, 29 June, 3, 9 July; *El País*, 13 September 1980; Colectivo Democracia, *Los Ejércitos*, pp.91–3; Fernández López, *Diecisiete horas y media*, pp.43–5.

77 *El Alcázar*, 11, 15, 18, 23, 26 April 1980; author's interview with General Prieto; Urbano, *Con la venia*, p.29; Pla, *La trama civil*, p.164; Reinlein, *Capitanes rebeldes*, pp.244–5.

78 *Cambio 16*, 20 January, 3, 17, 24 February, 16, 23, 30 March; *El País*, 18 February, 2, 3, 22 March 1980; Martín Villa, *Al servicio*, p.90.

79 *El País*, 25 April 1980.

80 *Cambio 16*, 2 March, 6, 13 April, 18, 25 May, 21 September 1980; Josép Meliá, *Así cayó*, p.39; Jaúregui & Soriano, *UCD*, pp.31–3.

81 *El País*, 29 April 1980; Fraga, *En busca*, pp.201–2.

82 Author's interview with Suárez's then press chief, Alberto Aza Arias.

83 *El País*, 3, 4 May; *Cambio 16*, 18 May, 3 August 1980.

84 *El País*, 21, 22, 23, 29, 30 May; *Cambio 16*, 16 March, 1, 8 June 1980; Martín Villa, *Al servicio*, p.94.

85 *Cambio 16*, 13 July, 17 August 1980; Meliá, *Así cayó*, p.42; Jaúregui & Soriano, *UCD*, pp.15–20, 34–5.

86 *Cambio 16*, 17, 31 August 1980; Urbano, *Con la venia*, pp.31–2.

TEN: *Fighting for Democracy*

1 *El País*, 22 June; *Cambio 16*, 13, 20 July, 24 August, 7 September 1980; Rincón, *ETA (1974–1984)*, p.63.

2 *Cambio 16*, 17 August 1980.

3 *El País*, 10 September; *Cambio 16*, 21 September 1980; Meliá, *Así cayó*, pp.51–9.

4 *Cambio 16*, 5, 12 October 1980; Oneto, *Los últimos días*, pp.67–8.

5 *Cambio 16*, 12, 19 October; *El País*, 2, 13 October 1980; Muñoz Alonso, *El terrorismo*, p.227.

6 Segura & Merino, *Las vísperas del 23-F*, pp.297–301.

7 *El Alcázar*, 16, 21 September, 2 December 1980; conversations of the author with Felipe González; *Cambio 16*, 9 March 1981; Armada, *Al servicio*, pp.216, 223–7; Morales &

Celada, *La alternativa*, pp.122–5; Urbano, *Con la venia*, pp.232–5. In 1996, Leopoldo Calvo Sotelo alleged that Reventós had suggested to Armada that he assume the presidency of the government – *Diario 16*, 24 February 1996 and in Santos Juliá, Javier Pradera & Joaquín Prieto, coordinadores, *Memoria de la Transición* (Madrid, 1996), p.522. See also Pilar Cernuda, Fernando Jaúregui & Manuel Ángel Menéndez, *23-F. La conjura de los necios* (Madrid, 2001), pp.8–10.

8 Fraga, *En busca,* p.226; Pardo Zancada, *23-F*, pp.105–6; Josép Benet, *El President Tarradellas en els seus textos (1954–1988)* (Barcelona, 1992), pp.480–3.

9 Alfonso Osorio, *De orilla a orilla* (Barcelona, 2000), pp.384–5; Emilio Romero, *Tragicomedia de España*, p.275; Fernández López, *Sabino Fernández Campo*, pp.131–2.

10 *El País*, 24, 25, 26 October; *Cambio 16*, 3 November 1980.

11 Vilallonga, *El Rey*, pp.166–7; Jorge Semprún, *Federico Sánchez se despide de ustedes* (Barcelona, 1993), p.194; author's interview with Semprún.

12 *Cambio 16*, 10, 17, 24 November; *El País*, 11 November 1980; Benegas, *Euskadi*, pp.110–11; Muñoz Alonso, *El terrorismo*, pp.229–31.

13 Morales & Celada, *La alternativa*, pp.89–91, 122–5; *Cambio 16*, 17 November 1980; Urbano, *Con la venia*, pp.24–5.

14 Cernuda et al., *La conjura*, pp.29–36; Reinlein, *Capitanes rebeldes*, pp.239–42; interview

with Suárez in Juliá, Pradera & Prieto, *Memoria*, pp.455–6.

15 The ingenious claim of a 'designer coup' is made by Jesús Palacios, *23-F: El golpe del CESID* (Barcelona, 2001), pp.25–30. For more plausible reflections on Cortina's role, see Urbano, *Con la venia*, pp.85–112; Pilar Urbano, *Yo entré en el CESID*, pp.40–1, 340–54; Reinlein, *Capitanes rebeldes*, pp.250–62; Joaquín Bardavío, Pilar Cernuda & Fernando Jaúregui, *Servicios secretos* (Barcelona, 2000), pp.98–9, 211, 225–31; Fernández López, *El Rey y otros militares*, pp.166–7.

16 Fraga, *En busca*, pp.223–4; Urbano, *Con la venia*, pp.42–3.

17 *El País*, 27 September 1980; Osorio, *De orilla*, pp.385–7; Urbano, *Con la venia*, pp.29–31, 49; Attard, *Vida y muerte*, pp.182–4.

18 Álvarez de Miranda, *Del "contubernio"*, p.145; Antxón Sarasqueta, *De Franco a Felipe* (Barcelona, 1984), pp.28–9.

19 Santiago Segura & Julio Merino, *Jaque al Rey: las "enigmas" y las "incongruencias" del 23-F* (Barcelona, 1983), pp.53–6; Pardo Zancada, *23-F*, pp.174–5.

20 Armada, *Al servicio*, p.225; Diego Carcedo, *23-F. Los cabos sueltos* (Madrid, 2001), pp.173–6, 178–83; Reinlein, *Capitanes rebeldes*, pp.271–2.

21 *El País*, 7 January 1981; Morales & Celada, *La alternativa*, pp.125–6; Urbano, *Con la venia*, pp.52–5; Sergio Vilar, *La década sorprendente 1976–1986* (Barcelona, 1986), pp.98–9.

22 Segura & Merino, *Jaque al Rey*, pp.57–9, 77–8; Urbano, *Con la*

venia, pp.58–61; Pardo Zancada, *23-F*, p.175; Reinlein, *Capitanes rebeldes*, pp.272–3.

23 Pardo Zancada, *23-F*, pp.177–81; Urbano, *Con la venia*, pp.61–8; Fernández López, *Diecisiete horas y media*, pp.77–9; Reinlein, *Capitanes rebeldes*, pp.262–3.

24 Author's interview with General Sabino Fernández Campo; Suárez, FOG/Toledo; Armada, *Al servicio*, p.228. See also interview with Armada in Juliá, Pradera & Prieto, *Memoria*, pp.493–4.

25 Meliá, *Así cayó*, pp.59–63; Oneto, *Los últimos días*, pp.69–70; *Diario 16*, 12 January; *Cambio 16*, 26 January 1981.

26 Attard, *Vida y muerte*, p.189.

27 *El Alcázar*, 24 January; *Cambio 16*, 2 February 1981; Meliá, *Así cayó*, pp.13–19, 68–74.

28 Attard, *Vida y muerte*, pp.190–1; Fernández López, *El Rey y otros militares*, p.160.

29 *El País*, 30 January; *El Alcázar*, 30 January; *Diario 16*, 30 January 1981; Oneto, *Los últimos días*, pp.113, 119, 152; Meliá, *Así cayó*, pp.74–5; Leopoldo Calvo Sotelo, *Memoria viva de la transición* (Barcelona, 1990), pp.24–32; Navarro, *Nosotros*, pp.366–9; Victoria Prego, *Presidentes. Veinticinco años de historia narrada por los cuatro jefes de Gobierno de la democracia* (Barcelona, 2000), pp.105–10.

30 This has been persuasively argued by Fernández López, *Diecisiete horas y media*, pp.82–6.

31 Silvia Alonso-Castrillo, *La apuesta del centro. Historia de la UCD* (Madrid, 1996), pp.444–5.

32 *El País*, 31 January 1981.

33 *El País*, 2, 3 February 1981.

34 'Las tertulias de Madrid', *ABC*, 31 January 1981.

35 Joaquín Prieto & José Luis Barbería, *El enigma del "Elefante". La conspiración del 23-F* (Madrid, 1991), p.123; Reinlein, *Capitanes rebeldes*, p.292; Martín Prieto, *Técnica de un golpe de Estado: el juicio del 23-F* (Barcelona, 1982), p.93.

36 Reinlein, *Capitanes rebeldes*, p.292.

37 Suplemento Especial Fuerzas Armadas, *Diario 16*, 6 January 1981, pp.12–13; Reinlein, *Capitanes rebeldes*, pp.247–9; Cernuda et al., *La conjura*, pp.90–1.

38 'Análisis político del momento militar', *El Alcázar*, 17 December 1980.

39 'La hora de las otras instituciones', *El Alcázar*, 22 January 1981.

40 'La decisión del Mando Supremo', *El Alcázar*, 1 February 1981.

41 Morales & Celada, *La alternativa*, pp.127–30; Urbano, *Con la venia*, pp.47–8; *Cambio 16*, 22 June 1981; Pla, *La trama civil*, pp.59–69; Pardo Zancada, *23-F*, pp.151–5; Fernández López, *Diecisiete horas y media*, pp.238–43; Cernuda et al., *La conjura*, pp.54–6; Palacios, *23-F*, pp.266–72.

42 *El País*, 5, 6, 7 February; *Cambio 16*, 16 February 1981; Benegas, *Euskadi*, pp.132–4; Urbano, *Con la venia*, pp.73–5; Fernández López, *El Rey y otros militares*, pp.162–3.

43 *El País*, 17 April; *Cambio 16*, 16, 23 February, 27 April 1981; Rincón, *ETA (1974–1984)*, pp.123–4, 172–6.

44 Fernández López, *Diecisiete horas y media*, pp.92–3; Soriano, *Sabino Fernández Campo*, pp.367–8.

45 *El Alcázar*, 8 February 1981.

46 Herrero de Miñón, *Memorias*, pp.232–6; Calvo Sotelo, *Memoria viva de la transición*, pp.59–65.

47 José Antich, *El Virrey ¿Es Jordi Pujo un fiel aliado de la Corona o un caballo de Troya dentro de la Zarzuela?* (Barcelona, 1994), p.82; José Oneto, *La verdad sobre el caso Tejero* (Barcelona, 1982), p.xiv.

48 Author's conversations with Sabino Fernández Campo, Felipe González and Santiago Carrillo.

49 Armada, *Al servicio*, p.210; Oneto, *La verdad*, p.xv; Urbano, *Con la venia*, p.37; Fernández López, *Diecisiete horas y media*, pp.98–100; Soriano, *Sabino Fernández Campo*, pp.369–70.

50 Cernuda et al., *La conjura*, pp.190–2.

51 Pardo Zancada, *23-F*, pp.193–201; Fernández López, *Diecisiete horas y media*, pp.100–3; Reinlein, *Capitanes rebeldes*, pp.297–8.

52 *El País*, 21, 22 February; *Cambio 16*, 23 February 1981; Pla, *La trama civil*, pp.46–50; Urbano, *Con la venia*, pp.76–7.

53 *El País*, 2 May 1981.

54 Pardo Zancada, *23-F*, pp.204–9, 215–26; Urbano, *Con la venia*, pp.94–120; Reinlein, *Capitanes rebeldes*, pp.298–9; Fernández López, *Diecisiete horas y media*, pp.103–11.

55 Urbano, *Con la venia*, pp.120–1, 130–2, 143–6; Oneto, *La verdad*, pp.158–70; Martín Prieto, *Técnica de un golpe de Estado*, pp.104–11; Fernández López,

Diecisiete horas y media, pp.113–28; Cernuda et al., *La conjura*, pp.121–6.

56 Urbano, *Con la venia*, pp.158–65, 174–9. For an excellent survey of the speculation, see Fernández López, *Diecisiete horas y media*, pp.218–23.

57 Urbano, *Con la venia*, pp.143, 365–7; Fernández López, *Diecisiete horas y media*, pp.127–33, 140–3; Cernuda et al., *La conjura*, pp.126–30.

58 Author's interview with Sabino Fernández Campo; Urbano, *Con la venia*, pp.146–51; Fernández López, *Diecisiete horas y media*, pp.136–7; Cardona, *Franco y sus generales*, pp.317–19; Carcedo, *Los cabos sueltos*, pp.262, 292.

59 Author's interview with Anna Balletbó; Andreu Farràs & Pere Cullell, *El 23-F a Catalunya* (Barcelona, 1998), pp.36–8; Joaquín Bardavío, *Las claves del Rey. El laberinto de la transición* (Madrid, 1995), p.193.

60 Urbano, *La Reina*, pp.291–3; Cernuda et al., *La conjura*, pp.195–8.

61 Author's interview with Sabino Fernández Campo; Reinlein, *Capitanes rebeldes*, pp.319–20; Cernuda et al., *La conjura*, pp.135–6, 142–5.

62 Urbano, *Con la venia*, pp.167–74; Fernández López, *Diecisiete horas y media*, pp.133–5, 138–9; Cernuda et al., *La conjura*, pp.145–8.

63 Notes of General Quintana Lacaci, *El País*, 17 February 1991; Antich, *El Virrey*, p.86; Farràs & Cullell, *El 23-F a Catalunya*, pp.79–85.

64 Notes of General Quintana Lacaci, *El País*, 17 February 1991; José Luis de Vilallonga, *Le Roi. Entretiens* (Paris, 1993), p.186. Juan Carlos's comments on González del Yerro were removed from the Spanish version.

65 Notes of General Quintana Lacaci, *El País*, 17 February 1991; Fernández López, *Diecisiete horas y media*, pp.147–54; Reinlein, *Capitanes rebeldes*, pp.320–33; Prieto & Barbería, *El enigma del "Elefante"*, pp.172–5; Martínez Inglés, *La transición vigilada*, pp.99–111.

66 Author's interview with Sabino Fernández Campo; Vilallonga, *El Rey*, pp.169–70; Armada, *Al servicio*, pp.240–1; Fernández López, *El Rey y otros militares*, pp.174–5; Cernuda et al., *La conjura*, pp.150–2.

67 Cernuda et al., *La conjura*, pp.200–2.

68 Author's interview with Sabino Fernández Campo; Fernández López, *Diecisiete horas y media*, pp.147–54.

69 Author's interview with Eduardo Sotillos; Fernández López, *Diecisiete horas y media*, pp.154–7, 165–6.

70 Amadeo Martínez Inglés, *23-F. El golpe que nunca existió* (Madrid, 2001), pp.191–7.

71 Soriano, *Sabino Fernández Campo*, p.351; Carcedo, *Los cabos sueltos*, pp.345–6; Prieto & Barbería, *El enigma del "Elefante"*, pp.300–1.

72 Armada, *Al servicio*, pp.241–3; Reinlein, *Capitanes rebeldes*, pp.337–8; Fernández López, *Diecisiete horas y media*, 159–65; Fernández López, *El Rey y otros militares*, pp.167, 175–7;

Cernuda et al., *La conjura*, pp.153–8; Carcedo, *Los cabos sueltos*, pp.349–51, 356–9.

73 Pedro de Silva, *Las fuerzas del cambio. Cuando el Rey dudó el 23-F* (Barcelona, 1996), pp.204–5.

74 Author's interview with Sabino Fernández Campo; Reinlein, *Capitanes rebeldes*, p.319; .

75 Segura & Merino, *Jaque al Rey*, p.132; Pardo Zancada, *23-F*, pp.328–30; Fernández López, *El Rey y otros militares*, p.193.

76 Pardo Zancada, *23-F*, pp.330–2; Soriano, *Sabino Fernández Campo*, pp.353–7; Cernuda et al., *La conjura*, pp.210, 216; Carcedo, *Los cabos sueltos*, pp.371–2, 375–6.

77 Informe de Alberto Oliart al Congreso, *El País*, 18 March 1981; Pardo Zancada, *23-F*, pp.340–65; Eduardo Fuentes Gómez de Salazar, *El pacto del capó. El testimonio clave de un militar sobre el 23-F* (Madrid, 1994), pp.105–36; Armada, *Al servicio*, pp.246–7; Cernuda et al., *La conjura*, pp.159–61.

78 Author's interview with Sabino Fernández Campo.

79 Pardo Zancada, *23-F*, pp.368–70; Martínez Inglés, *El golpe que nunca existió*, pp.191–7; Sverlo, *Un Rey*, pp.181–208.

80 Informe de Alberto Oliart al Congreso, *El País*, 18 March 1981.

81 Vilallonga, *Le Roi*, p.195. This sentence was removed from the Spanish edition (and also the English).

82 Alonso-Castrillo, *La apuesta*, p.437.

83 *El País*, 10 November 1981.

84 Author's interview with Santiago Carrillo; *El País*, 25 February 1981; Fraga, *En busca*, p.235; Reinlein, *Capitanes rebeldes*, p.344; Fernández López, *Diecisiete horas y media*, pp.183–4.

85 *El País*, 26 February 1981.

86 *El País*, 28 February 1981.

87 *El País*, 1 March 1981; Fernández López, *El Rey y otros militares*, pp.197–9.

88 *El País*, 8 March 1981.

89 Vilallonga, *El Rey*, p.193.

ELEVEN: *Living in the Long Shadow of Success*

1 Martín Villa, *Al servicio*, p.96.

2 *ABC*, 12 April; *Cambio 16*, 20 April 1981; Morales & Celada, *La alternativa*, pp.166–8.

3 *Cambio 16*, 23 March; *El País*, 6, 7, 20, 21, 22 March 1981.

4 *Cambio 16*, 30 March 1981.

5 *El País*, 5, 6, 8, 9 May; *Cambio 16*, 11, 18 May 1981.

6 *El País*, 25 June; *Cambio 16*, 25 May, 29 June, 6 July 1981.

7 *El País*, 23 July 1981.

8 PSOE, *El PSOE ante la situación política* (Madrid, 1981); *Cambio 16*, 21, 28 September 1981.

9 *El País*, 14, 16 October 1981.

10 Attard, *Vida y muerte*, p.270.

11 *El País*, 19 November 1981.

12 *Cambio 16*, 7 December; *El País*, 7, 8 December 1981; Martín Villa, *Al servicio*, pp.100, 117.

13 *Cambio 16*, 3, 31 August 1981; Reinlein, *Capitanes rebeldes*, p.178.

14 *El País*, 11, 12 December; *Cambio 16*, 14, 21 December 1981, 11 October 1982; Cernuda et al., *La conjura*, pp.252–5.

15 *El País*, 12, 14 December 1981.

16 *El País*, 14, 15 January; *Times*, 15 January 1982.
17 *El País*, 7 January 1982.
18 *El País*, 2 May 1981.
19 *El País*, 29 September 1981.
20 *El País*, 26 August, 24 October; *La Vanguardia*, 27 August 1981, 10 March 1982; Fernández López, *Diecisiete horas y media*, p.99.
21 *El País*, 29, 31 May 1982.
22 *Cambio 16*, 17, 24, 31 May 1982; Martín Villa, *Al servicio*, p.100.
23 *El País*, 4, 5 June; *Cambio 16*, 31 May, 7, 14 June 1982; Cernuda et al., *La conjura*, pp.245–6; Segura & Merino, *Jaque al Rey*, pp.214–40; Fernández López, *Diecisiete horas y media*, pp.195–8.
24 *El País*, 24 December 1988.
25 *El País*, 31 July; *Cambio 16*, 26 July, 2 August 1982.
26 *El País*, 1, 26, 27, 28 August; *Cambio 16*, 9, 23, 30 August 1982.
27 *El País*, 3, 4, 5, 6, 7, 8 October; *Cambio 16*, 11, 18 October 1982; Cernuda et al., *La conjura*, pp.255–61.
28 *El País*, 14 October; *El Alcázar*, 6, 7 October; *Cambio 16*, 22 October 1982.
29 *El País*, 14 October 1982.
30 *El País*, 29, 30 October; *Cambio 16*, 1 November 1982. The best account of the campaign and the results can be found in Alejandro Muñoz Alonso et al., *Las elecciones del cambio* (Barcelona, 1984).
31 *El País*, 23, 26 November 1982.
32 Feo, *Aquellos años*, pp. 287–8; Cernuda et al., *La conjura*, pp.261–2.
33 *El País*, 20 December 1984.
34 *El País*, 28 December 1995.
35 *Egín*, 12 January 1996.
36 Cernuda et al., *La conjura*, pp.262–3.
37 *El País*, 30 January 1984.
38 *El País*, 9 February 1988.
39 *El País*, 3 June 1989.
40 Powell, *Juan Carlos*, pp.185–6.
41 *El País*, 7 January 1994; Powell, *Juan Carlos*, p.190.
42 *El País*, 7, 8, 9, 11 January 1994.
43 *Interviú*, 21 August 1995; *Tiempo*, 30 July 1996; *El País*, 22 July 1995, 4 August 1996.
44 *Tiempo*, 4 August 1986, 24 April 1989; Fernando Gracia, *Objetivo matar al Rey* (Madrid, 1996), pp.133–62; Zavala, *Matar al Rey*, pp.66–7.
45 *El País*, 15, 19 October 1997.
46 *El País*, 12 March, 3, 4 June 1996.
47 *El País*, 1, 3, 4, 5 April, 3, 5, 6 October 1997.
48 *El País*, 5, 16, 17, 18 May 1985.
49 *El País*, 7 January 1984, 7 January 1985.
50 'The Consolidation of Democracy in Spain: Military Reform', lecture delivered at the London School of Economics, 26 January 1999; conversations of the author with Narcís Serra.
51 *El País*, 17 February 1991, 9 December 1997.
52 Powell, *Juan Carlos*, pp.191–205.
53 *El País*, 15, 19 April 1985.
54 *El País*, 28 January 1989.
55 *El País*, 7, 19 November 1993.
56 Peñafiel, *¡Dios salve . . . también al Rey!*, pp.200–1; Sverlo, *Un Rey*, p.278.
57 *El País*, 21 January 1990, 25 January 1991; Soriano, *Sabino Fernández Campo*, pp.413–21; López Fernández, *Sabino Fernández Campo*, pp.204–8.

58 *El País*, 20, 21 June; *Época*, 6 July 1992; Soriano, *Sabino Fernández Campo*, pp.433–58; Peñafiel, *¡Dios salve . . . también al Rey!*, pp.203–9.

59 *El País*, 26 July 1992; Powell, *Juan Carlos*, pp.188–9.

60 *Diario 16*, 20 August; *El País*, 21 August 1992.

61 Ernesto Ekaizer, *Banqueros de rapiña. Crónica secreta de Mario Conde* (Barcelona, 1994), pp.330–6; Jesús Cacho, *M.C. Un intruso en el laberinto de los elegidos* (Madrid, 1994), pp.208–43, 358–61, 380–7, 474–7; Soriano, *Sabino Fernández Campo*, pp.462–80, 485–98; Sverlo, *Un Rey*, pp.280–90.

62 *El País*, 7, 8 January; *El Mundo*, 10 January 1993; Soriano, *Sabino Fernández Campo*, pp.491–516; Fernández López, *Sabino Fernández Campo*, pp.224–9, 239–44, and, on Vilallonga's biography, pp.234–5. Peñafiel, *¡Dios salve . . . también al Rey!*, pp.109–11; Jesús Cacho, *El negocio de la libertad* (Madrid, 1999), pp.413–16, 430–4; Sverlo, *Un Rey*, pp.267–8.

63 *El País*, 19 January 1993.

64 *El País*, 4, 8 April 1993; Borràs, *El Rey de los Rojos*, pp.284–92.

65 *El País*, 10, 14, 17 November 1995; Cacho, *El negocio*, pp.387–406, 434–8; Soriano, *Sabino Fernández Campo*, pp.480–5; Díaz Herrera & Durán, *El saqueo de España*, pp.19–87; Sverlo, *Un Rey*, pp.291–321.

INDEX

ILLUSTRATIONS

19. Princess Sofía in the presidential box at the annual Victory Parade in 1974. (*Agencia Europa Press*)
20. Juan Carlos at a cabinet meeting held at the Caudillo's summer residence, 1974. (*Agencia EFE*)
21. Franco and Juan Carlos, 1975. (*Agence France Press*)
22. The King and Queen after a requiem mass for Franco, 1975. (*Agencia EFE*)
23. Juan Carlos addressing troops in the Spanish Sahara, 1975. (*Agencia Europa Press*)
24. Juan Carlos with the first government of his reign, 1975. (*Agencia Europa Press*)
25. Cabinet meeting, 1976. (*Agencia Europa Press*)
26. General Jaime Milans del Bosch and Juan Carlos, 1977. (*Agencia EFE*)
27. Don Juan formally renounces his dynastic rights and recognises Juan Carlos as King, 1977. (*Agencia EFE*)
28. Juan Carlos greets Santiago Carrillo, 1977. (*Archivo fotográfico de Plaza & Janés*)
29. Juan Carlos with Josep Tarradellas, 1978. (*Agencia EFE*)
30. Juan Carlos shaking hands with Felipe González, 1978. (*Agencia EFE*)
31. Juan Carlos with Prince Felipe, 1979. (*Bettmann/Corbis*)
32. Appearing on television during the failed military coup, 1981. (*Agencia Europa Press*)
33. Juan Carlos with political leaders, 1981. (*Agencia Europa Press*)
34. The King sailing. (*Foto Dalda*)
35. At the 1992 Olympic Games in Barcelona. (*Agencia EFE*)
36. Juan Carlos and Queen Sofía at a requiem mass for the King's mother, 2000. (*Agencia EFE*)
37. Juan Carlos giving away his daughter Elena at her marriage, 1995. (*Corbis Sygma*)
38. Juan Carlos and his heir, Prince Felipe. (*Cover*)